ESSENTIAL PROGRAMMING FOR THE TECHNICAL ARTIST

This book is based on a successful curriculum designed to elevate technical artists, with no programming experience, up to essential programming competency as quickly as possible. Instead of abstract, theoretical problems, the curriculum employs familiar applications encountered in real production environments to demonstrate each lesson.

Written with artists in mind, this book introduces novice programmers to the advantageous world of Python programming with relevant and familiar examples. Any digital artists (not just technical artists), will find this book helpful in assisting with day-to-day production activities.

Concentrating upon subjects relevant to the creation of computer graphic assets, this book introduces Python basics, functions, data types, object-oriented programming, exception handling, file processing, graphical user interface creation, PEP 8 standards, and regular expressions. Programming within the SideFX Houdini 3D animation software provides a familiar environment for artists to create and experiment with the covered Python topics.

ESSENTIAL PROGRAMMING FOR THE TECHNICAL ARTIST

Chris Roda

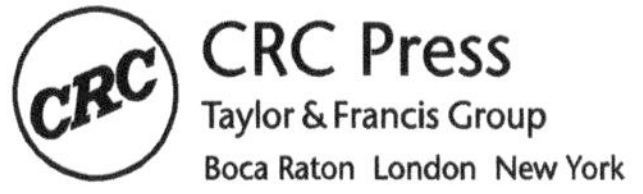

CRC Press is an imprint of the
Taylor & Francis Group, an **informa** business

Designed cover image: Chris Roda

First edition published 2024
by CRC Press
2385 NW Executive Center Drive, Suite 320, Boca Raton, FL 33431

and by CRC Press
4 Park Square, Milton Park, Abingdon, Oxon, OX14 4RN

CRC Press is an imprint of Taylor & Francis Group, LLC

ISBN: 978-0-367-86009-7 (hbk)
ISBN: 978-0-367-82040-4 (pbk)
ISBN: 978-1-003-01642-7 (ebk)

DOI: 10.1201/9781003016427

Typeset in Futura
by codeMantra

Dedication

To my best friend, Ha. From day one, you are the most important thing in my life.

Contents

Acknowledgments

This book would not have come into existence if it were not for two remarkable technical artists: Pat Corwin and Chris Lesage. These are two artists whom I have never met in person. They are the brave individuals who answered my reviewer requests posted on https://tech-artists.org. To say that their contributions to the project were significant would be an understatement.

Their patience and steadfast persistence when reviewing arduous chapters (especially dealing with object-oriented programming) were remarkable. Through the most challenging of criticisms, they remained professional, respectful, and encouraging. They are true technical art paragons: they do whatever it takes to deliver outstanding content through creative pipelines and make artists feel wonderful about the process.

Pat's technical understanding of the Python language knows no bounds. Yet he also understands how to use correct verbiage required to communicate core messages. His personal experiences and suggestions were invaluable when evaluating lesson effectiveness.

Chris' mastery of technical language is unparalleled. He identified language inconsistencies and provided valuable, alternative suggestions for incoherent content. He streamlined information flow by pruning irrelevant material and calling out missing details.

Thank you, Pat and Chris! Working with you gentlemen enlightened me to many new concepts and perspectives. I feel I am the student. I did my best to accommodate to all of your suggestions. Your contributions made this a far more effective text. I am lucky to have you on my team!

Finally, I would like to acknowledge SideFX, the creators of Houdini. I suppose it is obvious I am more than just a bit biased about this software. I have had the honor of collaborating with some of the brightest minds in 3D computer graphics. Houdini and SideFX were my most consistent teammates throughout my career of almost three decades. I could not have asked for more cooperative partners. Kim Davidson and SideFX team has always been there to assist in any way possible. Thank you for your consistent support.

About the Author

Chris Roda is a Technical Art instructor at the *Florida Interactive Entertainment Academy* (FIEA), a graduate degree program in interactive, real-time application development at the University of Central Florida. Early in his career, Chris was a visual effects artist in the film and television industries where he contributed visual effects for films such as *Spiderman*, *Titanic*, and *Fifth Element*. Before coming to FIEA, Chris was a CG Supervisor at Electronic Arts, where he worked on video game titles such as *NCAA Football* and *Madden NFL Football*. In addition to teaching, Chris works on generating tools and pipelines for the creation of *digital immersive experiences*, the amalgamation of the narrative of films, the interactivity of video games, and the immersion of theme parks.

INTRODUCTION

Programming is an essential component to becoming a world-class digital artist. This applies to technical artists and any artists with the ambition of leading practitioners of their fields. They all need to learn some kind of programming. Mastery is not essential but familiarity is. The world's greatest painters need to be familiar with some chemistry to master their pigments. Likewise, digital artists need to be familiar with programming: communicating with computers.

Computers are powerful tools. They can accomplish anything they are instructed to do. The challenge is instructing them in their proper language. Digital artists do not need to like talking with computers. They just need to be comfortable with them. This book does not substitute traditional, computer science texts which provide full topic coverage. The information covered in this book is adequate to introduce all technical and digital artists with essential programming skills necessary to tell computers what to do.

WHY THIS BOOK?

While working in the real-time game industry, I encountered a wide variety of technical artists with a wide variety of programming skills. Many were familiar with scripts which they had had copied from web-based tutorials. They were familiar with the desired end results and a little about input. However, they possessed only vague understandings of how the scripts started with input and produced output. These fragile script relationships were problematic when errors inevitably arose, or they required customization to satisfy specific situational needs.

As a computer graphics supervisor, I was aware that many technical artists could fly under the radar of programming accountability by scouring the web for relevant information. This strategy possessed small value when extrapolation or lateral thinking was required. To remedy this situation, I created a base curriculum providing technical artists with fundamental programming understanding which would aide them to understand any scripting situation. They would still be able to copy scripts from the web, but now they could understand how they were accomplishing their results and could easily modify the existing code to satisfy their needs.

This book is the result of that curriculum. Coming from a traditional programming background, I realize that this book's contents are a subset of what a full computer science course would cover. I also recognize core topics necessary for a technical artist programming toolkit. This text covers only those topics essential for production of computer graphics. It is folly to believe that one text covers all technical artist programming demands. However, I believe this book provides fundamentals required for entry-level technical artists to begin learning and understanding how to instruct computers to assist in creating digital art.

INTENDED AUDIENCE

As the name of this book implies, this text was originally created as a technical artist programming resource. The term "technical artist" is redefined by each development company. Technical artists tend to fall within four principle responsibility domains: pipelines, rigging and animation, lighting and rendering, and visual effects. There are a plethora of sub-domains and discipline fusions, enough to fill other books with their variations. The contents of this book should be adequate assisting with the primary four domains and their unlimited variations.

Pipeline artists utilize programming every day. Custom scripts are essential for the shepherding and conditioning of the billions of art assets required to fuel the real-time industry every day. Scripting provides oxygen for rigging

DOI: 10.1201/9781003016427-1

and animation technical artists. What requires weeks to accomplish by hand is now expected to be achieved in hours by competent riggers. While lighting and rendering appear to be pure artistic expression, they quickly become the most complicated and demanding coding environments. Familiarity with rendering, shading, and material principles is required for even the most artistic of art directors. (See *Lighting and Rendering for the Technical Artist.*) Many visual effects artists believe they can get by without programming. It does not take long for clients to demand visual output outside of what default interfaces provide and the need for custom code becomes essential.

All real-time artists and designers benefit with some programming foundation. Character, prop, and environmental 3D artists use scripting for creating, conditioning, and moving their assets to facilitate faster, in-engine verification. Animators are dependent on code to not only create their character rigs and controls but also to wrangle and manipulate billions of animated channels stemming from motion capture and key-frame animation. Designers make their living wielding procedurality: a discipline leveraging the power of programming to create infinitely more than achievable by hand. The days of designing scenes and levels are over. Modern real-time applications demand creation of entire worlds.

HOW THIS BOOK IS ORGANIZED

This book is broken into 20 chapters. Anxious readers desiring to get right into Python programming should jump directly to Chapter 6. Chapters 6–14 cover using Python within the Houdini context and focus on specific Python-related topics. Chapters 15–20 explain topics through the Python perspective but are applicable to any programming language. The first five chapters address the philosophical aspects of this book: relationships of technical artists with programming, why Python is the prime focus of this book, and a history of how this book came into being.

- **Chapter 1: Introduction** provides a quick explanation of how and why this book came into being, and how it is organized.
- **Chapter 2: The Role of Programming in Technical Artist Life** discusses technical artist roles and their relationships with programming.
- **Chapter 3: Programming Strategies** offers fundamental technical artist programming philosophies.
- **Chapter 4: Computer Languages** surveys modern programming languages and explains why technical artists should learn Python.
- **Chapter 5: Programming Inspiration** describes the six-week curriculum this book is based upon. Justification for using Houdini as the Python programming environment is provided.
- **Chapter 6: Python Setup and Orientation** provides instructions for Houdini installation, accessing Python, and orienting readers with Python functionality.
- **Chapter 7: Python Basics** explains how Python handles string manipulation, commenting, and expressions. Example scripts get programmers creating technical artist-like tasks.
- **Chapter 8: Python Logic** covers Python script data flow. Explanation of code blocks, conditional statements, and looping is provided.
- **Chapter 9: Python Functions** explains Python function integration. Instructions for handling external functions and defining custom functions are provided.
- **Chapter 10: Python Data Types** covers the different types of data intrinsically included in all Python installations.
- **Chapter 11: Python Object-Oriented Programming: Foundation** introduces working with and authoring Python object-oriented programming classes.

- **Chapter 12: Python Object-Oriented Programming: Inheritance** describes how Python classes can take advantage of class derivation and composition.
- **Chapter 13: Python Exceptions** explains how Python deals with special situations, including errors and warnings. The Python *try-except* protocol prevents special situations from interrupting program flow.
- **Chapter 14: Python File Processing** demonstrates how Python reads and writes to external files. Instructions and examples of *JSON* and *XML*, and pickling file formats are provided.
- **Chapter 15: Command Line** introduces readers to the concept of interacting with Python outside of graphical user interfaces. This style of interfacing is useful when managing day-to-day pipeline operations.
- **Chapter 16: Python Graphic User Interface** describes graphical interface tools available to Python. In-depth instructions are provided for getting users familiar with the *Pyside 2* interface toolkit.
- **Chapter 17: QtDesigner** provides instructions how to use *QtDesigner* to design PySide and PyQt interfaces.
- **Chapter 18: Python PEP8 Standards** describes the PEP8 standards; conventions encouraging efficient, effective, and readable Python code.
- **Chapter 19: Regular Expressions** introduces readers to *regular expressions*; formalized, textual pattern recognition strings used for identifying patterns within input strings.
- **Chapter 20: Conclusion** concludes this book and provides a few words of encouragement.

CONVENTIONS

This text presumes that the majority of readers do not come from technical backgrounds nor necessarily have affinity for the technical field. Regardless of background, this book treats all readers as technical artists, folks who create art using technology. Hopefully, this definition encourages the greatest number of people.

There may exist some confusion between *technical artist* and *technical director* roles. In the broadest perspective, *technical artists* and *technical directors* share almost identical responsibilities. Their skillsets are similar. The big difference between the two is that technical artists deal with real-time art pipelines and technical directors deal with off-line renderers. Real-time applications include video games, simulations, and immersive experiences. In general, technical directors who operate off-line renderers are more concerned with quality and less concerned about performance. This differentiation becomes fuzzier every day as teams use real-time engines for creating off-line, film-quality cinematics, and traditional off-line companies use the same real-time engines for virtual productions.

Confusion may occur when labeling *real-time technical directors*. *Technical directors* within real-time environments are experienced programmers responsible for implementing all technologies required for a successful project. The role should not be confused as an artist appointment.

SOFTWARE DISCLAIMER

Houdini, from SideFX, is used as the demonstrational Python environment. There are two motivations behind this decision. This first is simply the author is most familiar and created the curriculum within the Houdini environment. The second reason is that Houdini Python is very object-oriented and there is clear separation between the Python code and the Houdini graphics *application programming environment* (API). Motivated readers are highly encouraged to replace Houdini portions with APIs from their favorite software. This exercise reinforces the Python lessons and bolsters understanding of the Houdini and other software graphics APIs. The author is happy to assist with any questions dealing with future conversions.

PREREQUISITES

The only real prerequisite for this text is the open mindedness to learn. While not apparent, any attempts to absorb this material will have exponential results. The examples in this text were taken directly from a curriculum dedicated to teaching basic programming to novice technical artists. Even simply transcribing the examples establishes muscle memory that cannot be unlearned. Playing with and ultimately breaking the examples accelerate the learning process. Continuous diligence to this discipline provides consistent returns. Like going to the gym, results are gained while there is work. All students who follow this curriculum achieve some sort of programming comfort as long as they are willing to try. While some take faster to the material than others, all are able to apply this book's contents to their daily activities. The author is confident that you will too. Enjoy the process.

INTRODUCTION

The foremost responsibilities of technical artists are to do *whatever* is required to assist artists' delivery to real-time experiences such that the art's integrity is not challenged or the stability of the experience is not jeopardized. *Whatever*, often translates to performing tasks that are unpleasant and potentially confusing. Examples include updating file paths from one version of an iterative project to the next, retargeting all animation clips from one character to another, or building tools for generating inverse and forward kinematic rigging for arbitrary characters of various sizes and proportions. Sometimes these responsibilities include achieving rapid results devoid of creativity such as copying and renaming thousands of files to satisfy spontaneous marketing requests. Often technical artists get by with brute force or performing each task step by hand. However, the time demands of most situations typically dictate the need for programming or scripting solutions.

The context of the situation has significant impact on the technical artist's decision to program or not. Once the programming decision has been made, the technical artist must decide what tasks the tool must achieve, its stability and how interactive it is. Figuring out the tool's root demands are essential for understanding clear tool solutions and requirements. Many of these decisions are dependent on the artist's role within her organization. Other times, these decisions are made by her disciplinary context. For example, a quick script traversing a character rig to search for misspelled joints is dramatically different from a tool for reliably relocating project files within version control. A technical artist's programming life is made significantly easier when the programming expectations are understood in advance.

TECHNICAL ARTIST PROGRAMMING RULE #1

The first rule of technical artist programming is, "When a task is to be repeated more than twice, a script should be written". Of course, there are exceptions to this rule and they are dependent on "return of invested time" required to create the tool. For example, if five animation clips require keyframes at frame -10, then a script probably would not be worth the invested time. When the investment of time required to create the script is significantly greater than the time the tool will save, the script is not worth creating. However, as in the previous example, the same keyframe needs to be created for hundreds of characters and thousands of animation clips; a script should probably be created. Tools that satisfy a need only once are called *one-offs*. One-offs should generally be avoided unless they perform prohibitive tasks such as populating a unique stadium with thousands of fans.

EXPECTATIONS OF A TECHNICAL ARTIST PROGRAMMER

When working within the context of a professional development environment, technical artist programmers will take on one of two roles, a guerilla problem solver or tools programmer. Their programming expectations are dependent on their role.

Guerilla Problem Solver

When functioning as a guerilla problem solver, technical artists must first consider practicality and then make sure that the code is clean, safe, and functional. The code does not necessarily need to be efficient or robust. The code only needs to achieve the requirements of the task and be written and employed within the shortest time period. Standard questions of interface design should be considered: *what*, *who*, *where*, and *when*.

DOI: 10.1201/9781003016427-2

"What does the tool do?" is an important consideration for keeping the code in scope. Within the context of this question, the code should perform only one task which its name implies. When the tool does more than the one task, the opportunity for miss-use and redundancy escalate.

"Who is using the code?" is a question which has a strong impact on the expectations of the code. When the code is written only for the coder to use, the code may be a bit rougher than when written for other users. The coder has an intimate relationship with the tool and understands its eccentricities. When written for other users, the code needs to be logical, the names need to make sense, and there should be robust documentation. When written in this fashion, others examining the code should be able to quickly and easily understand what the code is doing and how it is doing it. Even when the code is written by technical artists for personal use, they do forget things and it is good practice to write code to enhance future understanding and prevent confusion.

"Where the code is going to be used?" is also an important question. Does the code function as a stand-alone tool? Does it work within the context of a *Digital Content Creation Tool* (DCC)? Does it complement the asset conditioning pipeline? Stand-alone tools tend to be less demanding while DCC and pipeline scripts need to be written with understandability, re-use, and maintainability in mind.

Lastly, "When does the tool need to be done?" has a direct impact on code quality. Code created to put out today's raging fire is going to be rougher than code scheduled with ample planning time.

The *Minimum Viable Product, MVP,* of a script is the minimal number of tasks the code is expected to accomplish. Guerilla programmers must only provide the minimal amount work required to achieve the MVP. Focusing on the MVP maximizes technical artists' time and minimizes the time to get into the hands of the end-user. Focusing on code to contribute to the MVP reduces the amount of superfluous work and minimizes time spent on duplicate or redundant code. The need for the code to achieve its MVP is higher than the need for the code to be efficient and clean.

Suppose a game team suddenly pivots to create a crowd scene environment in order to take advantage of recently acquired *Motion Capture,*(MOCAP), data. A cache of 50, pre-modeled characters is available but none have skeletons compatible with the data. The marketing team needs footage of the scene to meet an important deadline. The team rigger decides to create a tool to semi-automate the skeleton creation process for the characters which reduces the rigging time from weeks to a day. Since the characters are to be animated using specific MOCAP data, there is no need to include other typical rigging functions such as IK/FK switching, spline spines, or reverse foot IK. Since this tool is a *one-off* and will only be used to rig these specific characters for the MOCAP data, the script writer focuses less on efficiency, readability, and re-use and more on rapidly completing the task to meet the marketing deadline.

In the prior example, the lack of a robust, efficient, and re-usable functionality is no permission for the code to be intentionally unpolished. However, technical artists should devote no more time than is essential for accomplishing the MVP and then move on.

Tools Team Member

When technical artists shift from being guerilla problem solvers to being a members of tools teams, their programming expectations make a radical shift. As guerilla problem solvers, technical artists create minimal amounts of code accomplishing only immediately needed tasks. As members of a tools team, technical artists produce tool experiences which not only satisfy necessary needs and requirements but also generate positive feelings of accomplishment. Creative focused tools must generate "the warm fuzzies" when used. Most often, creative artists are the users of technical artist tools. Artists respond more favorably to tools which empower them to feel creative over tools which behave logically. As artists, technical artists are equipped with the creative ability to code positive emotional experiences. Team member coding expectations must not only satisfy the best software engineering traditions but also appeal to the artist experience.

One of the most fascinating models of technical artists creating tools for artists is Deep Silver Volition studios. At Volition, the programming team develops and maintains the core real-time engine and exposes functionality in a python API. Technical artists take the API and develop tools for the artists and designers. With this model, technical artists focus on creating tools and interfaces dedicated to the artists, keeping them happy while freeing programmers to generate effective and efficient engine code.

When working for a tools team, technical artists must create tools which are "artist-proof". In other words, interfaces must persist so that no artist input, intentional, or unintentional, can prevent the tools from functioning as expected. Tool makers should think and behave like artists to create interfaces generating warm fuzzies and anticipating workflow barriers which hinder artistic experience. As a general rule of thumb, any time a tool crashes or interrupts creative workflow, regardless of programming error or un-anticipated artist input, it is the tool maker's responsibility to make sure the situation cannot repeat.

A tool must be stable while satisfying its MVP while being robust enough to provide artists with enough freedom to easily customize output and satisfy creative intention. Because a tool is created within the context of the programming team, the tool must solve a unique problem which has not already been solved by another tool. Its code must be well documented for explaining algorithmic intention, future maintenance, and re-use. The code itself must be efficient and stable while structured for future expansion and integration. Unpolished and unprofessional code is unacceptable.

DISCIPLINE-BASED EXPECTATIONS

The programming expectations imposed on guerilla problem solvers and tools team members are different and so too are the needs of the various technical art disciplines. The following sub-section describes of the fundamental responsibilities for each of the technical art types: pipeline, procedural world building, rigging, animation, technical animation, rendering and lighting, and visual effects.

Pipeline

Programming skills are essential for pipeline technical artists. Almost every activity involves digital asset processing: conditioning, transportation, version control, and troubleshooting.

Conditioning

Translating digital art assets into formats which real-time engines understand is a programming art form. Commercial real-time engines such as Unreal, Unity, and Lumberyard are amazing. Remarkable attention has been devoted to making the experience of translating digital art assets into engine compatible formats as easy and painless. No two real-time engines are the same. Larger production companies mostly employ in-house engines or customized commercial engines. Unique engines impose conditions upon art assets so they may be imported successfully. The requirements increase in proportion to the uniqueness of the real-time engine. Many engines venture outside the familiar *FBX digital intermediate* format when importing content. (Thorough details on this topic are covered in *Technical Artist Pipelines and Workflows.*)

When digital assets fail to meet these requirements, the import process fails and often causes engine failure. Sophisticated tools condition art assets for successful engine import. It is the pipeline technical artist's responsibility to build, maintain, and expand these conditioners to meet each team's production needs. This is a full-time production job and technical artists devote significant portions of their day simply addressing production emergencies. When asset conditioning pipelines work efficiently, they are transparent. However, when broken they represent huge losses of expensive time.

Transportation

Data wrangling is a crucial component for maintaining stable asset pipelines. Clean and orderly data flow contribute to a project's profitability. Technical artists must collaborate with the programming and production staff early in project pre-production to establish standards which the entire team needs to follow. It is often the role of the technical artist to set up these standards as well as enforce them.

Data file organizational structure is essential for maintaining team communication. Lost assets are a common occurrence. Valuable production time is lost in the search for these assets. Establishing and enforcing directory structure dramatically reduce the number of misplaced assets. Successful structure also ensures future file communication. Assets fall into logical slots without the need for explanation or redirection. When assets reside where they are expected and are found without additional clarification, digital asset pipelines run smoothly. Listing 2.1 is a hypothetical example of a typical art asset file structure.

- ***Art Assets***
  - ***Characters***
    - Character A
      - Mesh
      - Skeleton
      - Animation Clips
      - Materials
        - Textures
    - Character B
    - ⋮
  - ***Environments***
    - Environment A
      - Mesh
      - Materials
        - Textures
    - Environment B
    - ⋮
  - ***VFX***
    - Mesh
    - Skeleton
    - Sim Data
    - Materials
      - Textures
  - ***Materials***
    - Textures

Listing 2.1 Typical Art Asset Structure

Every production company has its own custom structure designed to satisfy its unique needs. One structure is not necessarily better than another as long as consistency is maintained. When the structure is maintained and defended, it behaves as intended.

Digital asset naming conventions are similar to file structures. Naming conventions provide the essential information required to organize, classify, and identify any assets exclusively through the structure of their name. Naming conventions identify individual file categories, types and unique descriptions. Adherence to naming conventions is crucial for smooth production workflow. At any time, teams may wish to alter their convention to better suit their needs. However, changes made later into the project are more challenging to implement. Initial time invested at the beginning of a project from the lead technical artist, designer, and programmer will pay off in the long run.

The following example is a naming convention template for generic digital assets:

⟨*Category*⟩_⟨*Asset*⟩_⟨*Item*⟩_⟨*Detail*⟩_⟨*Type*⟩

Listing 2.2 contains example names conforming to this convention.

```
Mesh_Bink_Torso_Hi
Texture_Painesville_Firehydrant_1K_Diffuse
Simulation_BridgeCollapse_VersionA_Long
Material_Firehydrant_Worn
```

Listing 2.2 Typical Asset Names

All abbreviations, nicknames, and codes should be established in the naming conventions. Their effectiveness is dependent directly to their adherence.

Version Control

Most organizations and production teams employ some sort of *version control software* (VCS). VCS systems manage all changes to computer programs, data sets, digital assets, and any documents which may be needed for future reference. The software systems make historical digital backups of its documents and allow retrieval at any point along the document's history. Digital production teams rely heavily on RCS systems to prevent catastrophic information loss and minimize the amount of overlapping work.

While VCS systems are essential production tools, their cumbersome interfaces make them unpopular with artists. It is the technical artist's responsibility to guarantee artist participation within the system. This task often includes creating easy-to-use tools to register assets with the system, modify the assets, rename, move, and delete the assets from the system.

Registering

Registering a digital asset with a VCS system makes the system aware of the asset's location and assigns system control over the asset. This is the first and most important operation for the artist to comply with the system. It is the technical artist's responsibility to implement workflows and tools for easy and painless asset registration. Assets which do not get registered with VCS tend to be lost or forgotten.

Updating

When digital assets need to be edited, modified, or otherwise updated they must first request control from the VCS system. The system will not allow modification to an asset until control has been formally granted. The artist is free to edit the asset once control of it has been granted. The artist also exercises exclusive control over the asset at this time. After modification, the artist pushes the changes to the server and relinquishes control back to the VCS system. Initially, this process appears cumbersome. Technical artists provide tools to facilitate this process and minimize the opportunity for artist error. Technical artists must collaborate with the artists when creating tools which are not only easy and inviting but also empower the artists to register frequent changes with the VCS system.

Renaming, Moving and Deleting

During typical production, assets need to be renamed, moved, and deleted. These are precarious updates to the VCS system that must be handled sensitively as not all systems handle such manipulations uniformly and may require necessary operations to be executed predictably and safely. Most VCS tangled messes occur from improper handling of these operations. Technical artists significantly improve production workflow by providing interfaces and workflows which guarantee successful file renaming, moving, and deleting, and minimize operational mistakes.

Troubleshooting

Pipeline technical artists devote most of their time troubleshooting. Problems have the tendency of appearing in the most unusual places and circumstances. While these situations slow production, they do not clearly indicate where future tools and scripts are needed. Quite often, tools need to be created to help identify troublesome situations. For example, consider a situation of thousands of animation clips registered with VCS with incorrect naming which blocks all character creation and animation. Days of artist time are necessary to correct this situation by hand. However, a technical artist could create a script and resolve the situation within an hour. The technical artist is praised as a hero for the next few minutes or until the next troubling issue rears its ugly head.

Procedural World Building

Production teams are often presented with tasks of creating digital assets which are impossible or cost prohibitive to create by hand. Technical artists provide procedural world building tools to assist artists with the creation of these assets. Examples are cities, forests, world terrain, crowds, swarms and herds, very large objects such as galaxies and the very small such as sub-cellular viral infestations.

Technical artists employ proceduralism in their world building tools. Proceduralism is the creation of computer tools and systems which leverage the talents of artists to assist with creating digital assets which could not be achieved by talent alone. The concept of proceduralism is often misunderstood with automation. While automation requires no artist input, proceduralism is dependent on artist input which provides soul and life to the resulting assets. Outside of visual effects, procedural world building is the most creative endeavor for technical artists. The pursuit of proceduralism is often the gate through which artists enter into the realm of programming. More than randomness, proceduralism applies artist inspired filters to create intentional assets instead of hoping to find a few valuable pieces found in a sea of chaos.

While procedural world building tools are essential for creating assets too complex to be generated by hand, they are limited. Proceduralism is excellent for creating assets which provide volume to theme worlds yet are not the targets of participant attention. These are the assets which make the world feel genuine and complete. Hero, or attention drawing assets, should be generated by hand whenever possible. The intention of proceduralism is to reduce the costs associated with the creation of very large and precise data sets. When the costs of creating procedural systems to achieve specialized results exceed the costs of creating the assets manually, the later should be chosen. Artists are always capable of adding minute attention and detail where the cost of creating procedural systems cannot be justified. For example, consider a professional sports stadium. Procedural tools are outstanding for generating the facility structure. However, proceduralism cannot duplicate the unique statues decorating the environment. Proceduralism generates assets to fill the world and frees time for artists to create attention driving assets.

Rigging

Rigging is an essential component of bringing animated digital characters to life. Once a character model has been created and before an animator can start animating it, a technical artist, (called a rigger), must convert the model into a digital puppet. The core principles of rigging include creation of a skeleton, skinning the model to the skeleton, and creation of a control structure to manipulate the skeleton. Skeletons are the bio-mechanical structures, composed of bones or a sequence of joints, used for moving the character. Skinning is the process of mapping the character model to its relative bones and joints. For example, the character's left arm must be mapped to the corresponding bones comprising the skeleton's left arm. The control structure provides easy and accessible handles for the animator to quickly animate the character's bones. Technically, the control structure is not essential. However, most animators find animation of the character's skeleton difficult and challenging without the assistance of the controls.

The rigging process is an art unto itself and numerous books are devoted to the skills of the craft (see *Rigging for the Technical Artist*). While the fundamental primitive strategies are easily explained, the puzzles and challenges surrounding the implementation of unique character rigs are endless. An artist could devote an entire career focused to the task. The process at times can be tedious, frustrating, and prone to human error. When problems arrive, the debugging process may be more resource expensive than recreating the rig. This cumbersome task is remedied through the process of procedural rigging; the creation of tools and scripts which leverage the artistic skills of the rigger. This process requires creative input from the rigger to generate bio-mechanically correct movement. The skinning, joints and control structure for the character in Figure 2.1 were procedurally generated.

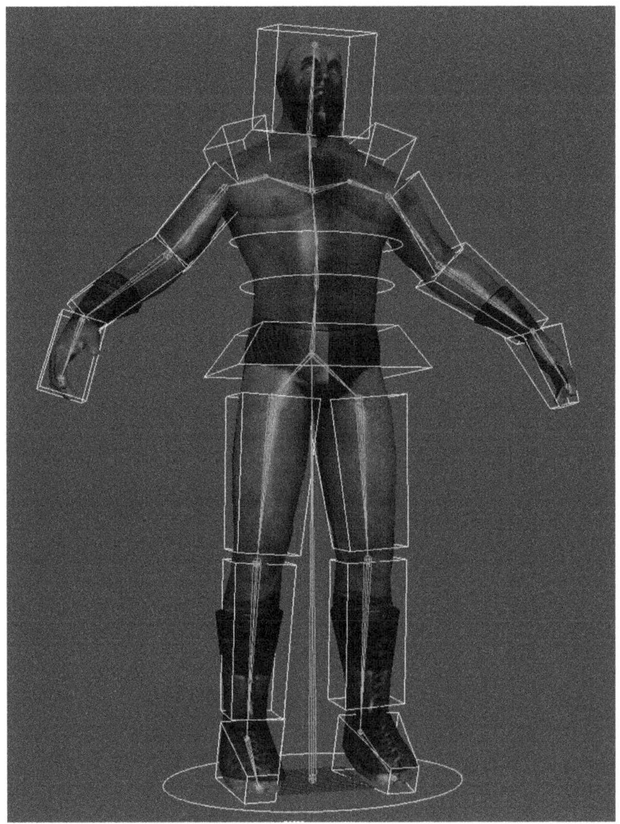

FIGURE 2.1 Character skin, joints, and control structure.

There is no standard set of tools used for rigging. Each technical artist must create her own set of tools and scripts which complement her individual style, wants, and needs. The process of creating procedural rigging tools feels intimidating at first. However, once completed, the tools make the fundamental process of rigging fast, reliable, and most importantly, predictable. Analysis of rigging code makes the process of debugging problems easier and faster than when done by hand. Rigging modifications are implemented by altering rigging code and regenerating rigs. Without the assistance of scripts, regenerating rigging can be an exhausting process. Over the course of production development, a single character rig may need to be regenerated hundreds of times. When the bulk of the rigging process is handled with tools and scripts, technical artists are allotted time for solving more complex problems which define the art form.

Lighting, Rendering, and Look Development

Most modern, three-dimensional, real-time rendering engines are equipped with node-based material editors. Material editors are front-end interfaces for sophisticated shaders which are often thousands of lines long. Written in dedicated shading languages such Open GL (GLSL), DirectX High-Level (HLSL), or Metal, shaders program the GPU's rendering pipeline. The rendering pipeline is the engine infrastructure that executes the shader's commands and produces visual output. Material editors are intended to be artist friendly and expose as many shader input controls as possible. However, when the desired visual output exceeds the material editor's exposed controls, programming solutions must be employed. There are two methods for interfacing with the rendering pipeline: manipulation of the pipeline code and modification of the shaders. Technical artists collaborate with the rendering pipeline through one or both of these techniques, depending on the artists' programming ability.

Pipeline Manipulation

Any modifications to the rendering pipeline's structure, algorithms, or the introduction of any new features require fabrications to be made in the pipeline's native language. In most situations, the language is C++. When programming within the rendering pipeline, a technical artist must take on the persona of a tools team member and be sensitive to the coding standards established by the pipeline rendering team. Effective communication with the team's Technical Director must be established to explain the technical artist's intentions. The technical artist must conform to the reviewing, testing, vetting, and documenting standards established by the team. Even when debugging engine rendering problems, special attention to communication with the programming team must be maintained.

Shader Programming

Instructions to the GPU's pipeline are implemented within the pipeline's programmable shaders. Modifications to the shader beyond exposed material editor input require programming in dedicated shading languages such Open GL (GLSL), DirectX High-Level (HLSL), or Metal. Real-time rendering pipeline shaders have seven stages: Figure 2.2 show the relationship between pipelines, shaders and materials. the input assembler, the vertex shader,

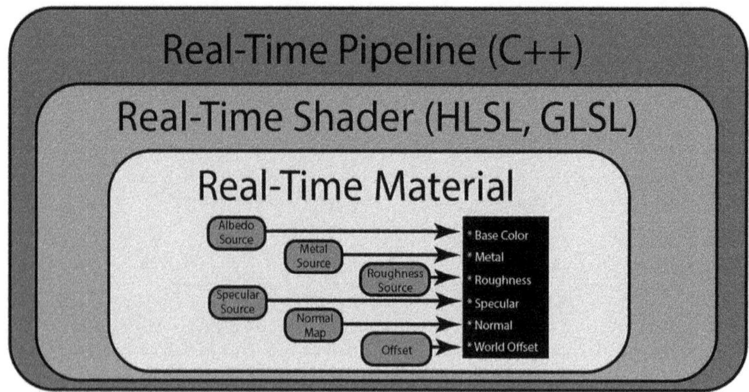

FIGURE 2.2 Real-time rendering pipeline hierarchy.

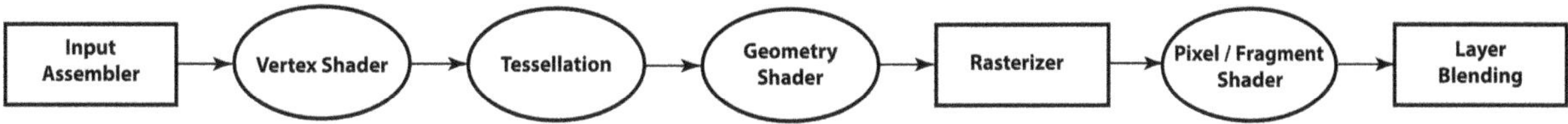

FIGURE 2.3 Real-time rendering pipeline stages.

the tessellation stage, the geometry shader, rasterization, the pixel shader, and the layer blending stage. Figure 2.3 shows the sequential order of the real-time rendering pipeline.

The input assembler collects the scene data from the CPU and organizes the data to be inputted to the pipeline. While not programable, this stage is configurable within the shader code. The vertex shader is programmable and configures all vertex attributes. Aside from manipulating all vertex data, the vertex shader's primary role is to transform vertices from object space to the appropriate camera projection space. The optional tessellation stage is programmable and instructs the pipeline how to subdivide the input geometry. The geometry shader, also optional, programs the pipeline to add or remove geometry. The configurable rasterization stage converts the three-dimensional geometry into a two-dimensional pixel bitstream. The programmable pixel shader provides instructions required to calculate color information for every pixel. A significant proportion of programming time is devoted to pixel shader programming. The configurable layer blending stage blends the recently rendered bitstream with prior processed layers. A thorough introduction to programming real-time shaders is given in the book *Lighting and Rendering for the Technical Artist.*

Visual Effects

Visual effects are specialized manipulations to the real-time engine and pipeline which manifest narrative enhancing phenomena to the real-time experience. Infinite in variety and approaches, visual effects are broken into four primary categories: in-camera effects, in-material effects, simulations, and particle effects. In-camera effects, such as camera flares, are performed exclusively within the last two stages of the rendering pipeline. While simple manipulations can be implemented within the material editor, more sophisticated strategies need to be programmed directly into the pipeline shader. In-material effects, as the name implies, manipulate all stages of the rendering pipeline and can be implemented within the material editor. However, extreme visual effect complexity must be handled in the pipeline shader. Elaborate editor materials maybe more computationally expensive compared to those implemented in the shader. Simulations attempt to duplicate natural physical phenomena. Any alterations to the physical simulation algorithms need to be programmed in the engine code. Technical artists programming in this context need to be aware of the conventions established by the engine programming team. Sophisticated modifications to the simulations' materials need to be programmed into the shader while simpler adjustments can be handled by the material editor. Particle effects are the combination of the three prior effect types: in-camera, in-material and simulations. Depending on the context, modifications to particle effects are made in the particle physical editor or in the material editor. More complex adjustments to particle simulation behavior need to be made in engine. Sophisticated adjustments to the particle's visual display may be programmed into the engine or into the pipeline shader. In-depth coverage of these visual effects categories is covered in the book *Real-Time Visual Effects for the Technical Artist.*

Technical Animation

Depending on their structure, certain production companies employ the talents of technical animators. Technical animators support keyframe animators by providing technical assistance beyond the capabilities of the DCCs at hand. Technical animators provide tools and scripts for assisting with the keyframe animation processes such as channel and keyframe editing as well as time manipulation. Tools may be required to assist with the MOCAP pipeline where the data require massaging, filtering, and cleaning. Custom tools assisting animation retargeting from one character to another are common. Most animation DCCs provide fundamental tools for supporting the animation and MOCAP processes. However, many tasks prove to be too laborious and time consuming to be performed without the assistance of additional technical animator tools.

Technical animators often aid with non-keyframe or procedural animation. They assist with real-time engine animation state machines and other procedural constructs which assist with the organizational blending of animation clips. Instead of being covered by a visual effects team, technical animators provide character related simulations. Secondary animations such hair and clothing animation, fat and muscle jiggle, and dangling accessory motion are generated with the aid of technical animator tools. As with other visual effects, DCCs are effective for generating basic behavior but anything beyond must be assisted with technical animator programming.

CONCLUSION

Too numerous to list, the types of tasks requiring technical artist programming skills are limited only by artists' imaginations. As a good rule of thumb, stick with the first rule of technical artist programming, "Any task that is performed more than twice should be replaced by a script or tool". The robustness of the tool should be determined by the context at which the tool is to be used. When the tool solves a quick and temporary problem, it can be rough and unrefined. When the tool is to be used by multiple individuals in a production setting, extra consideration must be made to make the tool user friendly, easy to understand, and easy to maintain.

There are six discipline-based topic areas where most technical artists need to program scripts or create tools for: pipeline, procedural world building, rigging, lighting, visual effects, and technical animation. Pipeline is the discipline where the largest proportion of scripts are created. The process of conditioning, shepherding, and troubleshooting game assets requires endless programming and tool creation. Procedural world creation relies heavily on dedicated DCCs but is enhanced significantly with additional programming. Character rigging is a demanding discipline requiring complex problem solving and is prone to human error. Procedural rig creation, driven by scripts, maintains repeatable techniques and reduces human error. The DCC user interface unintentionally limits user opportunity. Lighting, rendering, and look development require additional programming to reach beyond these limits. Many visual effects may be achieved through tools exposed through interface alone. However, as most clients desire original visual effects, programming and scripting are required to achieve unique results. Blending pipeline, animation, and visual effects, technical animators use programming to wrangle animation and MOCAP data and procedurally generate animated motion.

INTRODUCTION

Many technical artists do not have formal programming education. Many come from traditional fields like computer graphics, robotics, or artificial intelligence. Many are self-taught. They don't necessarily have knowledge about traditional software engineering. In the heat of production, these principles, while valuable, can feel distracting and time-consuming. This chapter covers strategies technical artists can employ immediately. Task identification effectively defines the scope and expectation of scripts and tools. Testing code as it is written is most often faster than debugging gobs of untested code. The dangers of blindly relying on resources and scripts found on the internet are also presented.

TASK IDENTIFICATION

Understanding exactly what a script or tool needs to do is the first step for creating effective code. When requested, technical artists must be careful to listen for what clients or teammates need and not necessarily what they are asking for. Often, requests call for specific techniques or strategies which sound essential but originate from insufficient technological understanding or lack of appreciation of applicable context. Effective communication is necessary for understanding vital tasks and strategies. Technical artist programmers must provide only what is needed: not too much and certainly not too little.

When at all possible, technical artists should initially perform requested tasks by-hand before implementing code. Working in this order has multiple benefits. Performing operations by-hand identifies repetitious patterns and sequences. Delegation of these patterns with code allocates more time for artists to focus on creative expression instead of repetitious procedures. This strategy educates technical artists how to successfully apply techniques. Often, they do not understand how necessary operations are performed, let alone implement relevant scripts. Executing by-hand provides ground truth evidence that solutions are achievable and endows them with knowledge of having successfully accomplished tasks at least once. Once there is understanding of how tasks are accomplished with respect to repeatable patterns, technical artists can start writing code.

ONE LINE AT A TIME

When writing code, an important strategy to adopt, especially by novice coders, is to write only one line at a time, followed by testing. This approach may seem counter-intuitive and slow. In the long run, it proves to be a faster and more stable strategy. Testing code after every written line has multiple benefits. The first is the code's correctness is verified. This functions as a granular type of unit testing. Establishing code effectiveness provides technical artist feedback and removes doubt of uncertain behavior. Identifying correctness also exposes bugs. Observing functioning code informs programmers where and when events happen so that they may be referenced in the future with minimal amounts of searching. The last benefit of this strategy establishes programming momentum. Often, coding feels alien and uncomfortable. Observing small amounts of success builds enthusiasm and whittles away doubt that hinders novice programmers.

Contrary to popular belief, programming is not magic. It is not something that simply flows through fingertips. Of course, there are a rare few for whom this is true. However, if you were one of them, you would not be reading this book. Novice programmers need to resist the temptation to write all of their code in one attempt and expect it to be functional upon first execution. That is magic! When coders know exactly what needs to be done and tasks are broken into many smaller objectives, each is implemented and corroborated without slowing forward momentum. Many novice programmers write all their code and then start the lengthy process of debugging. This painful process is often drawn-out when logic and alien behaviors arise. This approach often takes considerably

DOI: 10.1201/9781003016427-3

longer than when writing one line at a time. When the coder is not blessed with magical fingers from which perfect code flows like a river, the tried and true method of writing one line of working code at a time often delivers the fastest results.

ONLINE INSTRUCTION

The internet is an outstanding informational resource. Almost anything the technical artist needs to know can be found on the web. This is a blessing and this is a curse. While any single piece of guidance can be found, there is often too much information, some of which is relevant and some less than credible. Some information is created with different target audiences in mind. Some is simply out of date. How is a novice technical artist programmer supposed to navigate through this endless sea of information?

The credibility of anything found on the web is dubious. There are many fine instructors as there are many videos created by individuals who have no idea what they are demonstrating. The only way for beginning programmers to understand the value of online instruction is attempting to follow the instructions, examining the quality of the results, and answering the following questions. Did the resource solve the problem? It is rare to find a web-based instruction that addresses the technical artists' immediate needs. Was the instructor able to communicate the solution effectively? Did she explain each step along the way or did she expect each step to be mimicked? Was the technique delivered in such a manner as to be understood and implementable? Understanding how to push buttons and pull sliders may solve immediate problems but does the information transfer to other situations?

Unless the online information is created by a technical artist for technical artists, the information may be challenging to understand. Many solutions are provided by traditionally trained programmers who provide solutions for other trained programmers. Their language as well as their foundation of understanding may be beyond the technical artist's experience level. While attempting to understand the context of the solution, technical artists can lose focus and never solve their original problem. How do novice programmers know when the presented solution is worth the time and energy to understand and implement?

Time is technical artists' most valuable resource. When presented with unknown problems or situations, she must find solutions in the shortest time possible. Understanding resource credibility requires time and patience. Technical artists must employ trials and errors to implement and test the results of new online resources. Is the solution's thought process transferred effectively? Can the technique be extrapolated for solving other problems? Does the resource present information in an understandable language? The time required to vet solution plausibility is often greater than the time required to generate an original solution. Is the solution a black box? Black boxes are dangerous chunks of blindly pre-generated code, modules, or plugins with no functional or implementational understanding. (Nightmares of generating fractal harmonics or edge detection come to mind.) Do not alter the structure of original scene files to conform to the needs of black boxes. Running untested processes without thorough understanding is dangerous. Unless necessary, and carefully tested, black-box solutions should be avoided.

EXTERNAL CODE REFERENCES

External code references are found everywhere. Websites, online tutorials, and books offer unlimited, pre-written examples. Code may even be borrowed or taken from other writers. With enough dedication and resourcefulness, technical artist programmers should be able to find pre-created code to do whatever is needed to accomplish their tasks. Found code has potential to solve relevant problems quickly without re-invention. They provide working demonstrations how techniques and algorithms are intended to be implemented. They even expose new perspectives by approaching problems and implementing solutions from different and unexpected angles.

As beneficial as the results may seem, as a good rule of thumb, technical artist programmers should never use externally generated code unless it is thoroughly understood. Running code without understanding is another type of black box. While externally generated references have their benefits, they also have their disadvantages. They may force coders into a direction with disadvantageous directions from which there are undesirable or disastrous consequences. Ironically, implementing unfamiliar code often consumes more time than the promised savings. The time required to hunt down the sources of unfamiliar errors and unanticipated results often takes longer than when implemented by-hand. The code itself may be challenging to understand. It may be written poorly, use math beyond the understanding of the programmer, or use an exotic or unfamiliar language structure. Understanding these factors before implementation saves time and effort in the long run.

Technical artist programmers should do their best to reverse engineer every line of pre-generated code. However, when time is of the essence, this may not be a possibility. Who has the luxury of vetting all python library code? Hopefully, there is robust and easy to understand supporting documentation. When that is unavailable, the only recourse is thorough experimentation. Understanding output and how input impacts its behavior should eliminate most unexpected results. Regardless of documentation and experimentation, it is the technical artist's responsibility to understand any external code before implementation.

CONCLUSION

Most technical artists do not come from traditional software engineering backgrounds. This limitation should not prevent them from generating clean, safe, and functional code. Clearly understanding required tasks and solutions is essential for generating effective results. Before writing any code, automated solutions should be executed by-hand first, ensuring thorough understanding of essential steps. Coding is not magic, and the chance of getting it right in your first attempt is small. Exercise patience. Writing, testing, and understanding one line of code at a time result in fewer mistakes and faster solutions. Instructions, tutorials, and other guides found online need to be treated with care and diligence. They may be fantastic places to start when solving challenging situations. However, without thorough investigation and verification, these resources may create more trouble than they solve. The same diligence must be employed when implementing externally generated code. When possible, every line of code should be reverse engineered to verify understanding and correct results.

INTRODUCTION

Computer languages provide interfaces between technical artists and their CPUs and GPUs. While there are dozens of different programming languages, this chapter only deals with the languages which technical artists deal with on regular bases. Some languages, such as Lisp, are becoming less common, while others such as Rust are up and coming. This chapter only deals with the languages technical artists are likely to encounter at the time of writing.

Technical artists utilize whatever available tools are needed to deliver digital art. The languages listed in this chapter are ordered in terms of their absolute effectiveness and potential with respect to technical artist responsibilities. Avoiding political discussion on which languages are best, (an emotionally charged topic), the author wishes to declare that all the listed languages are excellent and very effective. Each has its best use cases and should be employed when the circumstances call for them.

Of the listed languages, some are compiled, some are interpreted, and others are hybrid. This chapter is written from the perspective technical artists work on Microsoft Windows or Apple macOS operating systems. The use of UNIX-based operating systems in the real-time community, at the time of writing, is scarce yet common in the off-line community. Since this book's primary focus is on real-time applications, its primary attention is on readily available, real-time languages.

C/C++

C and its extension C++ were developed in the early 70s and 80s and are two of the most influential languages. Most modern languages such as C#, Java, Java Script, and Python are C derivatives. C is the instrumental backbone of modern operating systems such as early versions of Unix and Linux. C++ was released in 1983 and has since become the primary language for most primary high-performance software such as Microsoft Office, Adobe products, and modern real-time engines such as Unreal and Unity. Within the computer graphics industry, most major digital content creation tools (DCCs), applications, and operating systems are written in C or C++.

C and C++ are sensitive and responsive languages. Like high-end sports cars, they trust that programmers know what they are doing. With understanding of what needs to be done combined with accomplishment strategies, a programmer can do just about anything. They are compiled languages and are translated to machine code which processors execute. This makes them fast and efficient and gives potential to deal directly with the CPU, access sensitive memory information, and control external devices. When necessary, programmers may extend the language to meet specific needs. Translating to machine code ultimately means that any kind of program can be created, from low level systems programming to high-level graphics user interfaces (GUIs).

On the opposite side of the spectrum, C and C++ can be hostile, unforgiving languages. C is a crude and primitive language with no safety mechanisms. Memory pointers are powerful tools and are essential components to both languages. Their utility demands much responsibility and could potentially crash programs and even machines, when used improperly. Neither language provides convenience functionality for memory management, and force programmers to do most of the work themselves. C++ is large, complex, and complicated and is a cognitive load for most programmers. Learning either requires learning language mechanics at the same time as problem solving, slowing the learning pace and requiring rigorous practice.

DOI: 10.1201/9781003016427-4

While C and C++ represent the most powerful and prominent languages for technical artists, most will rarely have the opportunity of using them. Artists who are members of high-end tools teams will program in C++. Because their explorations often go beyond the reach of commercially available DCCs, high-level research and development artists will most probably program in C++ as well. Other than these high-level tasks, technical artists rarely have opportunity for programming in these languages.

If C and C++ are hard to learn, challenging, and are rarely used, should technical artists learn these languages? The answer is a resonating, "Yes!" C and C++ are the language choices of the most experienced and competent technical artists. Most other languages at technical artists' disposal are derivatives. Once mastered, all new languages can literally be learned over night. Of course, thorough comprehension takes longer but functional competence is achieved in short time. Unbound by interface or DCC functionality, technical artists can create their own tools and applications. They can explore topic areas where no commercially available products have ventured. Most DCCs and applications provide C or C++ SDKs empowering technical artists to build onto and extend existing packages. Within the context of production environments, technical artists with C or C++ understanding provide valuable assistance debugging frustrating real-time engine issues. Technical artists are not necessarily better programmers than the engineers. But as artists, they have different perspectives on how art data structures are used and manipulated, and anticipate "creative" ways artists may use the data. Except for the time required to learn these languages, technical artists have everything to gain and nothing to lose through their mastery.

PYTHON

While not as fast or as capable as C and C++, all technical artists should have a working, functional understanding of Python. This book is devoted to the development of technical artist Python skills. Almost all DCCs and real-time engines now have Python interfaces. It is supported on Microsoft Windows, Linux/Unix, Apple macOS, and other operating systems as well. It is available as a permissive software license which is compatible with the GNU General Public License. Being permissive allows programmers to customize Python's libraries and distribute their alterations. It is readily available and easily accessible. Python is the primary scripting language for the computer graphics industry.

As a tribute to the British comedy group, Monty Python, Python was created to be easy and fun. Its design philosophy promotes code readability and empowers programmers to write a clear, logical code for small- and large-scale projects. Python is readable and well-structured which makes it easy to learn and is often used as an introductory language. It is dynamically-typed and garbage-collected, freeing programmers from memory management and the responsibility of declaring variable types before usage. Like C and C++, Python is object-oriented and functional which makes it as productive as the prior languages but requires less code to accomplish the same tasks. It is an interpreted language which stops execution when bugs are encountered and reports their locations and logical traceback which helps with debugging. Almost all major DCCs and real-time engines support Python or can be easily extended to support it. Python is also the language of choice for artificial intelligence (AI) and Machine Learning. While these fields have not yet integrated with real-time rendering, Python's availability will facilitate the combination. AI is already becoming a familiar component in animation, motion capture, and rigging.

While Python is a good alternative for C and C++, it does have its drawbacks. Because it is interpreted, it tends to be computationally "slower". The interpretation and dynamically-typed variables are computationally expensive and require extra memory. Some find Python to be too simple as it is harder to achieve fine machine control afforded by C and C++. With extra effort, it can be extended to these languages. While Python is interpreted and good for identifying syntax errors, it also tends to generate more run-time errors.

Python is the essential language for technical artists to learn. Since most of the major-packages and real-time engines support it, it is an excellent language for duplicating and automating artist workflows. Almost all pipeline work and project management tasks are performed in Python.

HLSL/GLSL

High-Level Shading Language (HLSL) and OpenGL Shading Language (GLSL) are the two primary languages used for programming real-time graphics pipelines. HLSL is a proprietary language developed by Microsoft for the Direct 3D 9 *Application Programming Interface* (*API*) and has a syntax based in the C programming language. GLSL is also a high-level shading language developed by the OpenGL Architecture Review Board (ARB) and shares the same C based syntax. The two languages are analogous. Apple created its own shading language called Metal Shading Language (MSL). MSL is used for Apple devices and is rare to see outside of these contexts.

Almost all commercial real-time rendering engines speak either HLSL, GLSL, or both. All real-time graphics editors and visual effects packages utilize either language. Traditionally, HLSL has been directed exclusively toward Microsoft devices and GLSL for everything else. HLSL should run faster on Microsoft products, while OpenGL should run faster on everything else. Up and coming platform, Vulcan, can take either language because of its SPIR-V intermediate language ecosystem.

It should be every technical artists' goal to attain at least a working familiarity with either of these languages. (A fundamental introduction to HLSL is included in *Lighting and Rendering for the Technical Artist.*) Most real-time rendering engines and packages support either or both. While not essential for entrance into the industry, careers are significantly embellished by their understanding. HLSL and GLSL are very similar to each other and the exercise of translating shaders between them not only increases language familiarity with their subtle nuances but also reinforces effective shader programming skills. Neither is necessarily better than the other and should be chosen based on the resulting end devices: HLSL for Microsoft and GLSL for everything else.

C#

C# was developed by Microsoft as part of the .NET framework, designed for the Common Language Infrastructure (CLI). It is a statically-typed compiled language which means that it should outperform other interpreted languages such as Python; yet its development time is slow due to the compiling overhead. Like Python, it is an object-oriented language making it ideal for generating procedural workflows. In 2017, Microsoft made C# open-source and available free of charge.

Within the context of real-time rendering, C# is the go-to language for Unity Engine development. Unity supports two scripting languages, C# and UnityScript (also known as Javascript for Unity). While the two languages are effective, all of the Unity libraries are built using C#. Unity engine considers C# to be the true canonical language for its development. C# is also used in the development for projects and applications for the Microsoft Hololens augmented reality device.

C# is a popular developer's language because of its design and object-oriented paradigm. Programmers familiar with Java are able to learn it quickly. However, the language has more constructions than Python such as assemblies, namespaces, classes, and methods which are essential to begin programming. Novice programmers may be more intimidated by C#'s structure compared to Python. While Python shares similar constructions, understanding is not required to begin programming.

C# is an outstanding language for supporting Unity and Microsoft integration which rely on standard syntax and libraries. It is essential for tools development within studios built upon the .NET framework. However, outside of the context of these specific situations, C# is not as popular or widely used as Python. These reasons should not discourage the technical artist from learning C#. However, unless working in an environment where the language is essential, other languages such as Python should be considered first.

JAVA

Java is arguably one of the most popular of all computer languages and is used everywhere especially in client-server web applications. It is both a compiled and interpreted language because its source code is first compiled into a binary byte-code and then is usually run on software-based interpreters known as Java Virtual Machines. Released in 1995 by Sun Microsystems, Java was designed to have as few implementation dependencies as possible. It is the primary programming language for Android mobile game development and, when combined with Flash, used for other web-based games.

Java is simple, object-oriented, and platform independent. While memory is easier to manage than C and C++, it does require management. Because it is both a compiled and interpreted language, Java will run slower than compiled C and C++. Its "write once, use anywhere philosophy" is good for generating predictable behavior on multiple platforms but also lacks the specific device control C and C++ afford. While simple real-time rendering engines and games have been created using Java, creations of such applications are rare and usually performed as exercises or experiments.

OTHER SCRIPTING LANGUAGES

During the daily course of real-time development, technical artists will need to be familiar with a plethora of situational dependent languages. These languages are typically devoted to special use cases and local environments. While most of the included languages do not have common acceptance, technical artists should be familiar with them and be prepared to learn or re-learn them in little to no time.

JavaScript

After substantial understanding of one of the languages mentioned prior in this chapter, all technical artists should have cursory understanding of JavaScript. Commonly used for dynamic behavior and visual effects to web pages, JavaScript has many real-time applications. It is one of the three scripting languages used with Adobe Creative Suite. It, however, is the only language which can work on Microsoft Windows and Apple macOS operating systems.

Bourne Shell/C Shell

Bourne Shell and C Shell are popular command-line shell interpreters used for interfacing with Unix-like operating systems. Each is a command language, used for providing operating system commands, and a scripting language providing procedural system control through *shell scripts*. Bourne Shell, and its modern incarnation Bourne-Again Shell (bash) can be found on most Linux implementation. Bash is still available on Apple macOS systems while its default is now *Z Shell*(ZSH). C Shell and its improved version, *tcsh,* can be found on most traditional Unix implementations.

As combinations of command languages and scripting languages, shell interpreters are superior pipeline workflow tools. Novice users may be discouraged by the lack of graphics user interface (GUI). However, after an acclimation period, users will become aware that when used effectively, shell interpreters are faster and more powerful than any GUI. The ability to swiftly and easily customize the interfaces to technical artists' own styles make shells unparalleled production management tools. Not all production environments are built upon Unix-like operations systems. For those environments that are, technical artists must attain shell mastery in order to perform their responsibilities effectively.

DOS

Windows Batch Scripting and Windows *Powershell* are Microsoft Windows-based shell interfaces built on older *DOS* (Disk Operating System), commands, and logic. Like Unix-like shells, these interfaces are command languages and scripting languages. Based on archaic DOS, Batch Scripting is more limited and awkward than other shell languages. Powershell is Microsoft's suggested way of interfacing with the operating system. Created with enhanced logic control, it provides significantly improved control over traditional Batch Scripting. However, due to the condition of adding an extra module to the environment, Powershell may not be a viable alternative for many production environments. Due to DOS-based awkwardness, limitations to Powershell implementation, and the removal of the requirement to run Windows with DOS, most Windows users stick with the base GUI. While certain technical art tasks demand Batch Scripting or Powershell usage, most technical artists in Windows-based environments can perform their daily responsibilities without the mastery of these tools. (In fact, there are many practicing technical artists who are unaware of the Windows command-line or Powershell.)

HScript/VEX

HScript and VEX are the embedded languages inside Side FX Houdini. HScript is the legacy scripting language present since the first version of the software. A bit more like C Shell, the language is more than robust enough to replace the interface and expose full control to the user. It is common Houdini usage to operate the software without the graphical interface through pure command-line HScript usage. While the Python API is the suggested scripting language, HScript is still present to ensure backward compatibility. Users also find HScript's brevity more convenient and less verbose than the Python equivalent.

VEX is a small, efficient, and general-purpose language used for writing in-software shaders and custom nodes. Roughly based on the C language, VEX is inspired by the Renderman Shading Language to be a fast language for modifying digital assets. Due to its SIMD (Single Instruction Multiple Data) architecture, all points of data are processed in parallel, making VEX faster than HScript or Python and almost as fast as compiled C++. However, this structure requires concurrent data access and more elaborate algorithms, preventing it from being an all-purpose language.

MEL

MEL, (Maya Embedded Language), is Autodesk Maya's metaprogramming language which instructs its node architecture to perform tasks and solve problems. In the software's early versions, Maya and MEL were the same. Any performed operation originated from a MEL command. The language is outstanding for speeding up complicated or repetitive tasks. Written to feel a bit like the PERL and TCL languages, MEL can be somewhat limited as it lacks associative arrays and object-orientation. However, as an interface processing language, it performs its purpose very well. These days, Maya has a Python API with a Python interface to both MEL and to the C++ API, and MEL is mostly supported as a legacy language.

MAXScript

MAXScript is the built-in, Autodesk 3ds Max scripting language. 3ds Max is a very popular three-dimensional modeling and animation software and is considered to be easier than Autodesk Maya. It is limited only to Microsoft Windows. MAXScript can be used to automate repetitive tasks, combine existing functionality, and create new tools and interfaces to speed up existing workflows. The language has a loyal support base. While 3ds Max may also support Python and C# APIs, MAXScript is the go-to language with the widest functionality.

Lua

While not as prevalent as the prior mentioned languages, *Lua* is a popular development scripting language technical artists will encounter. It is a lightweight language used in game programming or as an embedded scripting tool. It has a similar structure to Python but is simpler to learn and smaller to embed.

CONCLUSION

There are many computer languages available to technical artists but only a handful will be practical on an everyday basis. If there could only be one language to learn, all technical artists should have a fundamental understanding of Python. Nearly every digital content creation (DCC) software and real-time engine support a Python interface. Python is the language of real-time, three-dimensional computer graphics, as well as artificial intelligence, machine learning and many other disciplines. It often behaves as the glue between different applications. It was designed to be easy to read and easy to learn. As a modular, object-oriented language, it grants users considerable capability with only a small amount of code. It is a slower language than many others. However, its functionality outweighs its handicaps.

When presented with the opportunity, all technical artists should learn C or C++. Nearly all DCCs and real-time engines are written in C++, or have C++ APIs for writing high-performance tools and plugins. They are the Latin of modern computer languages. Mastery will make the learning of other languages a simple task. Regretfully, students must devote months of study and practice to master the languages.

Other languages are excellent when dealing with specific technical artist tasks. C# is an excellent, all-around language and is essential for working within the Unity real-time engine. HLSL and GLSL are crucial languages for interfacing and editing real-time rendering pipelines. Most DCCs have built-in languages which maximize tool control. HScript and VEX are used in SideFX Houdini. MEL is found in Autodesk Maya. MAXScript is used in Autodesk 3dsMax. There are multiple shell scripting languages which are very helpful for operating system level pipeline management. Bourne Shell and C Shell are used in Unix-like systems. DOS is used in Microsoft Windows.

INTRODUCTION

Inspiring artists to program can be challenging. Overcoming traditional social biases through the inception of greater creative freedom is difficult to impart. Becoming a great programmer is a life-long pursuit. However, fundamental and relevant Python can be taught to artists in a six-week curriculum. The class is by no means thorough or encompassing. However, it introduces the students to the programming world in a manner that is relevant to them using familiar 3D tools. Fledgling technical artist programmers do not need to be experts. They need to create code that is clean, safe, and functional which helps encourage creative workflow. Working with familiar tools and solving familiar problems provide opportunity for artists to start their programming journey. This book utilizes the SideFX Houdini DCC as the Python integrated development environment, (IDE). Not all students will be familiar with Houdini but will be familiar with traditional shapes, objects, and materials regardless of their background. Some may argue the effectiveness of using a commercial interface as a Python IDE instead of using the command-line. While it is true the command-line approach is more powerful, the goal at this stage is to encourage artist potential which is easily achieved through friendly, familiar environments.

CHALLENGE OF TECHNOLOGY

Ironically, technological development may not encourage artist programming but may unintentionally hinder it. Due to interface limitations, software developers bloat their products with greater amounts of functionality. The internet provides instruction and guidance for employing this functionality. However, there is too much information on the internet and navigation through these informational mazes is challenging. As toolsets increase in functionality, artists are expected to produce more content in less time. The ever-increasing churn for content does not promote time for developing career enhancing skills.

TRADITIONAL TRAINING

Python taught in traditional, structured environments will be effective and thorough. However, this thoroughness and lack of relevant applications fail to inspire artist interest. Traditional courses need to provide the greatest amount of material for serving the greatest number of potential applications. For technical artists, there is need for concise instruction which quickly instructs only relevant skills in the most rapid timeframe.

PYTHON IN SIX WEEKS

In the university program where the author instructs, students have only 12 months to learn everything they need for embarking on careers in the game, film, or simulation industries. Removing vacations, breaks, time in-between semesters, and other required classes, technical art students have only six weeks to prepare to support their 20-plus person capstone project teams. Once their collaborative team projects start, the students' ability to focus on intensive, essential skills for supporting their teams is diminished. The six-week period is all they have to cement strong Python programming foundations until they decide to dedicate future effort once attaining employment in the industry. This period must not only instill a solid programming base but must also demonstrate, through example, how they can immediately put their skills to work supporting their teams. The instructional curriculum must cover only the essentials and demonstrate using only familiar, pragmatic situations found in everyday real-time development.

DOI: 10.1201/9781003016427-5

The details of this curriculum are described in this book. The course topics include the following:

1. Python setup within a familiar commercial DCC, (Houdini)
2. Python basics including printing, comments, and simple expressions
3. Python logic structure
4. Python functions
5. Intrinsic Python data types
6. Object-Oriented Programming, including inheritance
7. Python exceptions
8. Python file processing
9. Python graphical user interfaces (GUI)
10. Standard Python coding standards

Is this curriculum thorough? No. The covered topics barely give students enough resources for reverse engineering some external code and writing their own simple scripts. To obtain more thorough programming mastery, students may need to spend considerable time studying additional resources or even re-take a more formal course. When presented a second time, the information will be absorbed more efficiently and cleanly.

Is the curriculum adequate? Yes. In the short-term, students will have the fundamental tools for performing guerilla-like programming support for pipelines, rigging, and artist support. Technical art students will be able to immediately support their teams to whatever capacity they are willing to try. By consistent application of their learned topics, they will be able to cement solid programming skills which will further reinforce and expand with continual use. Students will have only enough Python understanding to accomplish basic technical artist responsibilities yet have enough room for continuous learning.

Is the curriculum effective? The answer to this question is dependent on the students and their willingness to apply what they have learned to their daily operations. Regardless of their skill, the students who proactively apply themselves will advance more rapidly than those who program only when requested or are required.

FAMILIAR ENVIRONMENT

Working on familiar and relevant real-time development responsibilities is the primary benefit for learning Python in a 3D environment, such as Houdini. Beyond file organization and manipulation, technical artist programming focuses on three other items: scene objects, polygons, and colors. Scene objects may be environments, characters, props, visual effects, sounds, lights, cameras, or other supporting constructs such as regional volumes. Polygons are the object composing components. Polygonal data may include points, vertices, lines, polygons, and adjacencies. Colors are the primary properties defining the visual appearance of these objects in real-time rendering engines.

The examples in this Python course focus on tasks such as scene object creation, position, orientation, the manipulation, manipulation of colors, and pure polygonal generation. Introducing Python concepts to address these tasks encourages artists to apply Python scripting to everyday and future situations.

Real-time application APIs can be challenging to learn. Conveniently, technical artists are already familiar with their results. Additional API functionality instruction is not required. All relevant API code is provided with minimal explanation to encourage the focus on Python language basics, not on the DCC and its API.

HOUDINI IDE

SideFX Houdini provides the Python environment used in this text. A free learning version, *Apprentice* , is downloadable from the SideFX website, https://www.sidefx.com. Installation instructions are provided in Chapter 6 of this book. This free learning version of Houdini is limited and not adequate for full CGI production but fully supports Python and is functional enough to provide an ideal Python learning environment.

There are many reasons why Houdini is selected as the Python development environment. Houdini is supported on Microsoft Windows, Mac OS, and Linux. The Python language exposes the object-oriented nature of the API and lends itself for what can be described as "Pythonic" code writing. The package provides multiple Python user interfaces ranging from the trivial to the complex. The easiest is demonstrated in this book. The language implementation is stable. The evolution from Python 2 to Python 3 has had only a minimal impact on the language implementation. Any attribute alterable through the graphical interface is easily adjusted through the object-oriented Python API. Houdini is an extensive, package and instruction on the full Python API would be exhausting. This course focuses only on teaching fundamental, technical artist Python and exposes only enough Houdini to provide support.

This Python course instructs fundamental Python 3. While Houdini has supported Python 3 for many beta versions, the first production version using Python 3 is Houdini 18.5.

Could this Python course be structured with other DCCs such as Autodesk Maya, Blender or Autodesk 3DS Max? Yes! These other packages are professional staples and the course could easily be adjusted to collaborate with any of them. As of the time of this book's writing, the author is most familiar with Houdini and its Python implementation. Please contact the author for assistance in integrating the course with any of these packages.

The author does not suggest attempting to integrate the course with modern real-time engines such as Epic Games Unreal, Unity, or Nvidea Omniverse. While these engines do support Python integration, their implementation is simply too recent to be understood or too complicated to introduce Python basics. This book addresses the basics of the language first. Once understood, later integration into these environments will be easier.

COMMAND-LINE VERSUS IDE

Students may consider working on the old-school style of programming in the command-line instead of within a DCC IDE. Working in the command-line means using external editors to write and edit code and use systems' command-line interfaces to execute scripts. PowerShell and the cmd.exe command prompt are the operating system tools for Microsoft Windows. The *Shell* Prompt is the tool for Linux and Mac systems.

There are many reasons why working from the command-line is an advantageous way of learning. Zed Shaw from the *Learning to Program the Hard Way* series believes very strongly in this approach and the author of this book agrees. The command-line is the primitive computer interface and programming this way teaches direct interaction. Once students understand how computers function, programming tasks become less intimidating. Assembling sequences of instructions generating specific behavior becomes obvious and less mysterious. Working from the command-line is more effective than from graphical user interfaces, especially when supporting production pipelines.

While this book aims to instruct technical art students with only the essential Python required to launch careers in the game, film, and simulation industries, it also appreciates students who are less enthusiastic about learning program. Using DCCs exclusively is less intimidating than working from the command-line. Most modern DCCs have command-line access to their Python APIs. This book attempts to expose programming as simplistically as possible to beginning technical art students. Command-line access and functionality are available to more proactive students.

CONCLUSION

This chapter attempts to illustrate many of the mental issues facing beginning programming students. It exposes some of the insecurities and educational demands modern students deal with when learning new skills. Most traditional programming instruction is effective providing students with robust language understanding and covering any potential application. However, these courses are lengthy and provide extra material not needed for technical art students.

This book proposes to resolve this situation with a six-week introduction to Python programming directly focused on skills required by beginning technical artists. The course starts with a simplistic introduction to using Python within the context of a commercial DCC, basic print statements and simple expressions. The course then covers the Python logic structure, Python functions, and intrinsic Python data types. Considerable time is devoted to the introduction of object-oriented programming. Cleaner programming is reinforced with Python exception handling and file handling. The course concludes with the introduction of basic Python graphical user interfaces.

Introducing Python material within familiar production environments is effective with artists. They are familiar with scene objects, polygons, colors and their creation, modifications, positions, and orientations. SideFX Houdini is the DCC employed in this text. Houdini has built-in Python interfaces and its object-oriented structure integrates naturally with the software's API. Effort is made to focus on the basic Python structure instead of explaining more complicated Houdini Python integration. This book provides a Python course using the Houdini interface but could be adjusted to work with other DCCs such as Autodesk Maya, Blender, and Autodesk 3D Studio Max.

Instead of learning Python in the context of a commercial DCC, it is possible to learn through the basic command-line interface. There are many advantages of learning how to program this way as it teaches the students to think more like the computer does. However, this course provides artists with the easiest, most direct method for instructing the language as rapidly as possible. The command-line interface is left for more proactive students.

INTRODUCTION

This Python course begins with downloading and installing SideFX Houdini software. Depending on environment, this may have already been done for the students.

Once the software is installed and operating, students are given a quick introduction to the Houdini interface. The Python shell is introduced. This tool provides students their first exposure to Python by executing simple commands and performing simple mathematical operations. The concept of the programming variable is introduced. This chapter concludes with transitioning from the Python shell to Python script creation.

SOFTWARE INSTALLATION

Students who already have access to Houdini may ignore this installation section and progress to the *Python Shell* section of the chapter. The SideFX Houdini software package can be downloaded from the SideFX website, https://www.sidefx.com/.

The first production version of Houdini to support Python 3 by default is version Houdini 18.5. When downloading, please download version Houdini 18.5 or more recent.

SideFX requires an account to download the software. The account creation is accessed through the *Login* button in the upper right corner of the SideFX website. Figure 6.1 shows the *Login* button location.

The *Login* process requires a username and password. Since there is no account yet, the process is started by pressing the *Please Register* text. Figure 6.2 shows the *Please Register* location.

All the fields of the registration form designated with an asterisk, *, are required to be filled out. The *Terms of use* and *Privacy Policy* opt-ins are required but the subscription and profile visibility choices are optional. Finish registration by pressing the *Register* button. Figure 6.3 shows a completed registration form.

The software is downloaded from the *Get* tab at the top of the site. Choose the *Download* option. Figure 6.4 shows the *Download* option location.

Press the *Download Launcher* button to initiate the download process. Figure 6.5 displays the SideFX launcher window.

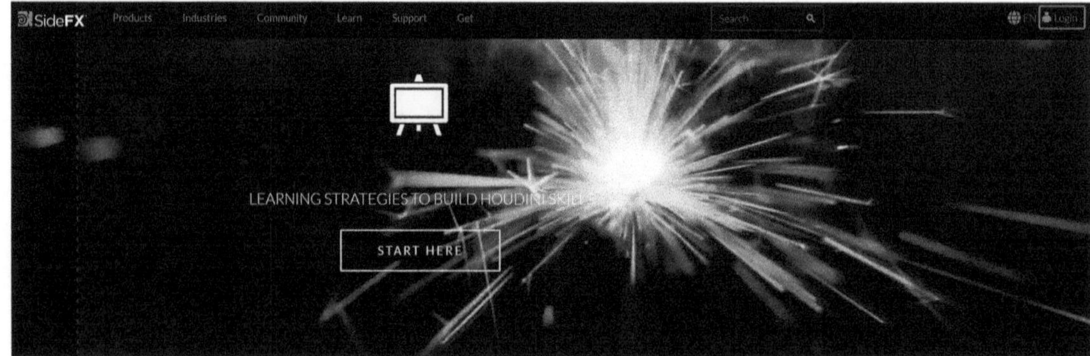

FIGURE 6.1 SideFX Houdini website.

DOI: 10.1201/9781003016427-6

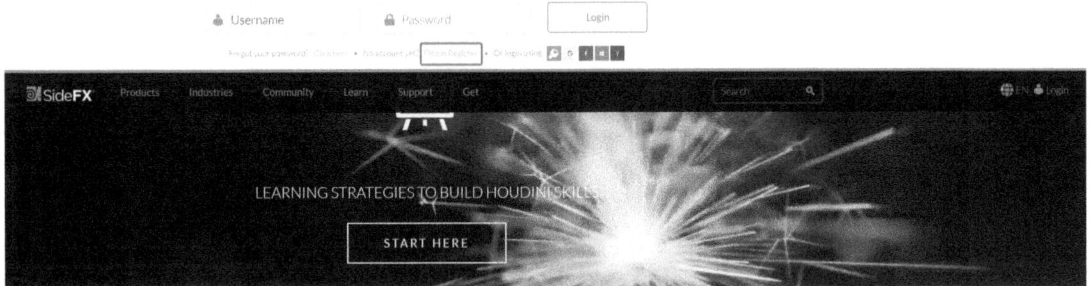

FIGURE 6.2 SideFX account login.

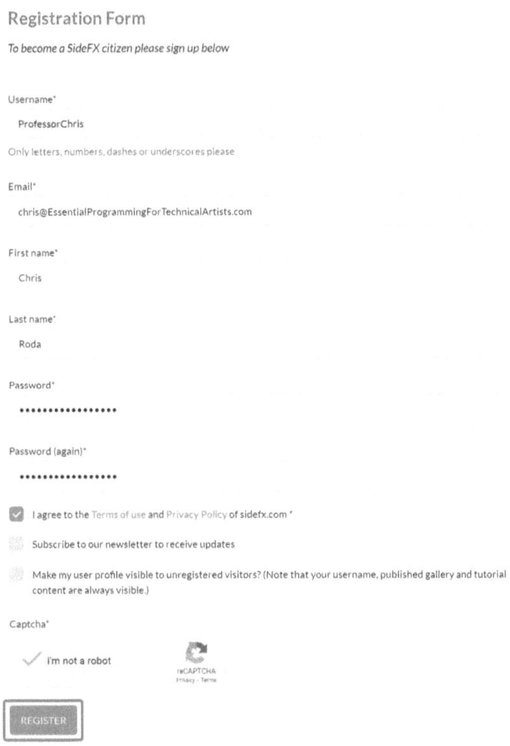

Registration Form

To become a SideFX citizen please sign up below

Username*

ProfessorChris

Only letters, numbers, dashes or underscores please

Email*

chris@EssentialProgrammingForTechnicalArtists.com

First name*

Chris

Last name*

Roda

Password*

••••••••••••••••

Password (again)*

••••••••••••••••

I agree to the Terms of use and Privacy Policy of sidefx.com *

Subscribe to our newsletter to receive updates

Make my user profile visible to unregistered visitors? (Note that your username, published gallery and tutorial content are always visible.)

Captcha*

I'm not a robot

reCAPTCHA

REGISTER

FIGURE 6.3 SideFX registration form.

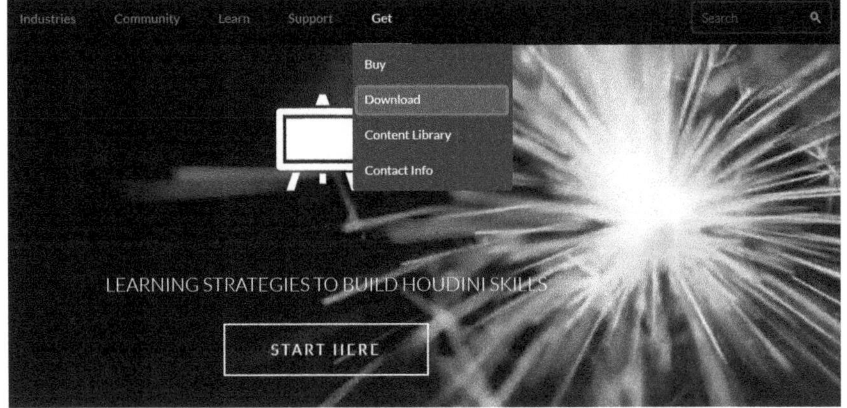

FIGURE 6.4 SideFX download selection.

FIGURE 6.5 SideFX launcher option.

The *install-houdini-launcher.exe* should begin downloading immediately and will be stored in your *Downloads* folder.

Double clicking the downloaded file initiates the installation process. A setup window introduces users to the installation window. Press the *Next* button to continue. Figure 6.6 displays the Houdini setup window and *Next* button location.

The launcher will query for an install location. Unless there is a different desired install location, leave the default destination folder and press the *Install* button. Figure 6.7 shows the *Install* button.

The Houdini Installer should download and install. Upon completion, users are queried if the *Start Menu* and *Desktop* shortcuts are desired. Unless unwanted, leave the default settings and press the *Finish* button. Figure 6.8 shows the shortcut options.

FIGURE 6.6 Houdini setup window.

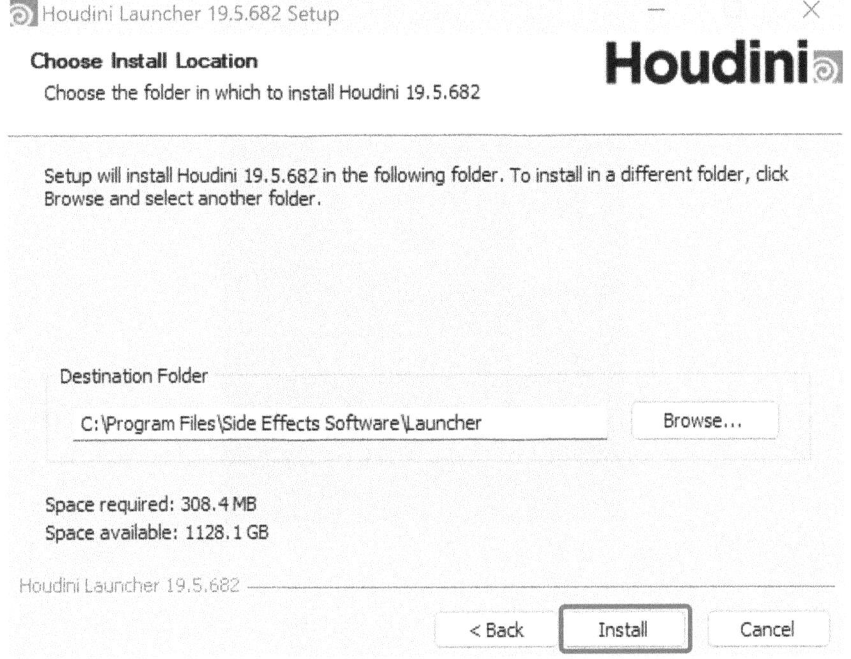

FIGURE 6.7 Houdini installer location folder.

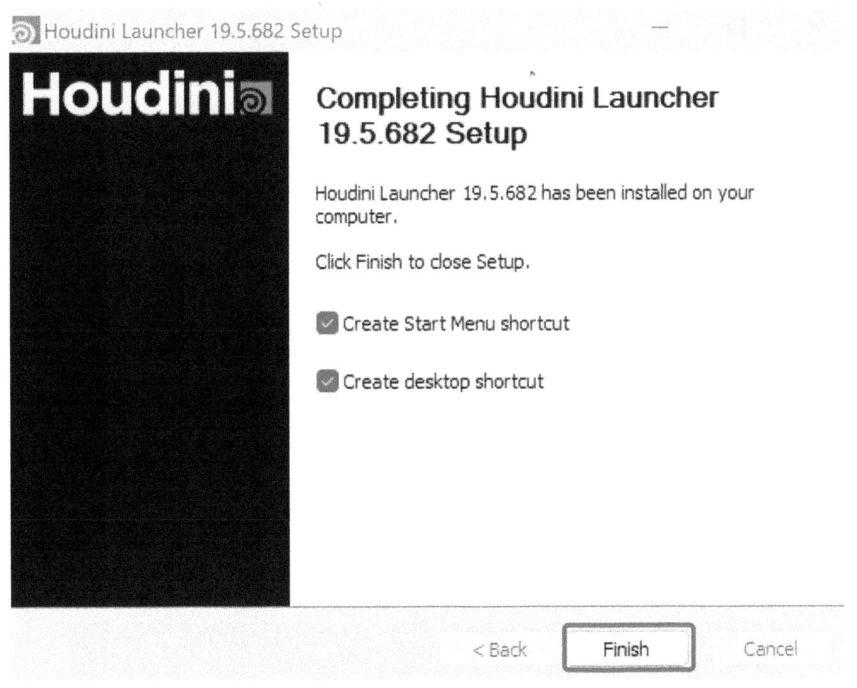

FIGURE 6.8 Houdini shortcuts menu.

FIGURE 6.9 Houdini launcher icon.

The *Houdini Launcher* icon should be installed on your desktop display.

Launch the *Houdini Launcher* (double mouse click). Figure 6.9 displays the *Houdini Launcher* application icon.

Prior Houdini Installation

If readers have never installed Houdini before, skip this section and go to the *Initial Houdini Installation* section. When readers already have a prior version of Houdini installed, they are queried if they want to import the Houdini Installations. Press the *Yes* button. Figure 6.10 chooses to import Houdini installations.

Select the *OK* button once all of the prior installations have been accounted for. Readers may now skip to the *Houdini Environment Setup* section.

Initial Houdini Installation

When installing Houdini for the first time, The *Houdini Launcher* window will appear. Press the *Log in* button to login to the Launcher. Figure 6.11 shows the *Houdini Launcher Login* button.

The user will be directed to the *Houdini Launcher* website. Enter the name and password used to register and hit the *Login* button to complete the process. Figure 6.12 displays the login process.

The user may now return back to the *Houdini Launcher* app window. Press the *Install Houdini+* button to select the Houdini version. Figure 6.13 displays the installation command button.

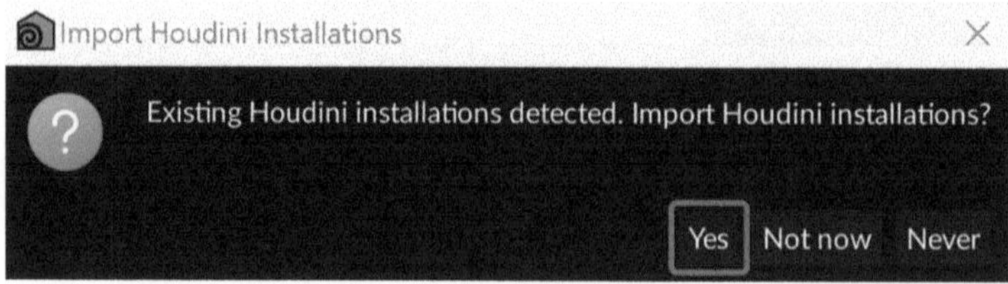

FIGURE 6.10 Houdini prior installation.

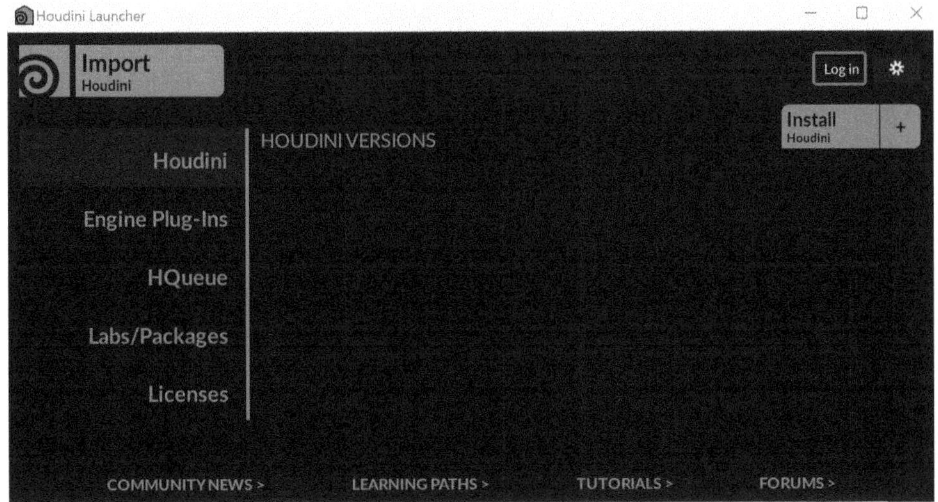

FIGURE 6.11 Houdini launcher.

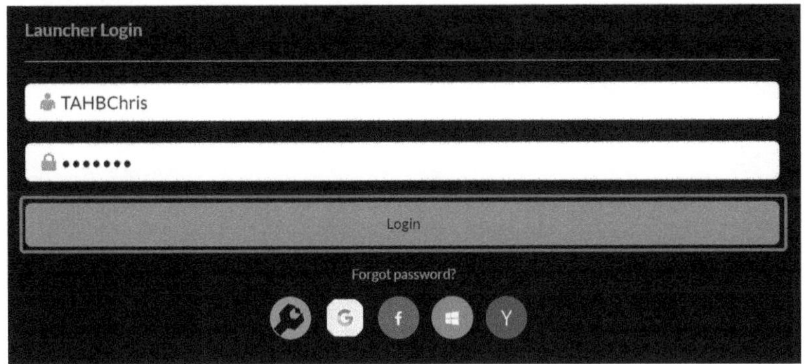

FIGURE 6.12 Houdini launcher login.

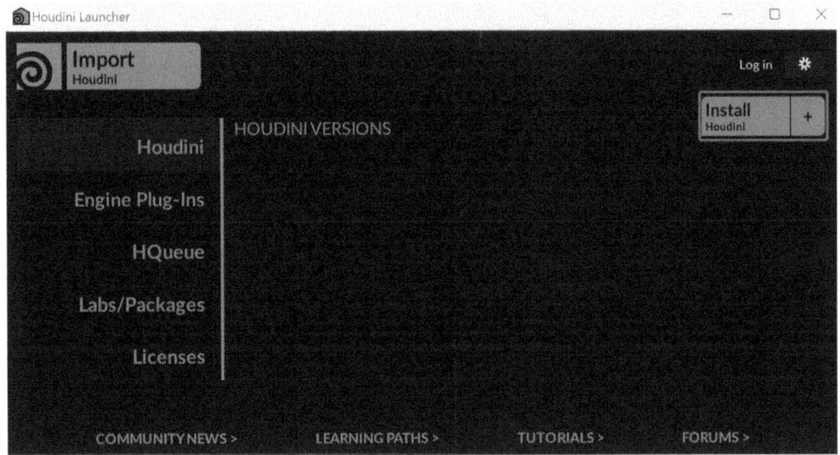

FIGURE 6.13 Houdini install +.

Select the highest number Production Build available in the *Version Selection* window. Unless essential, always select *Production Builds*, as in Figure 6.14.

In the *Houdini Preferences* window, the *Automatically Install License Server, Start Menu Shortcut, and File Associations* option should be selected. The *Create Desktop Shortcut* choice is optional. Press the *Install* button to continue. Figure 6.15 displays typical, default preferences.

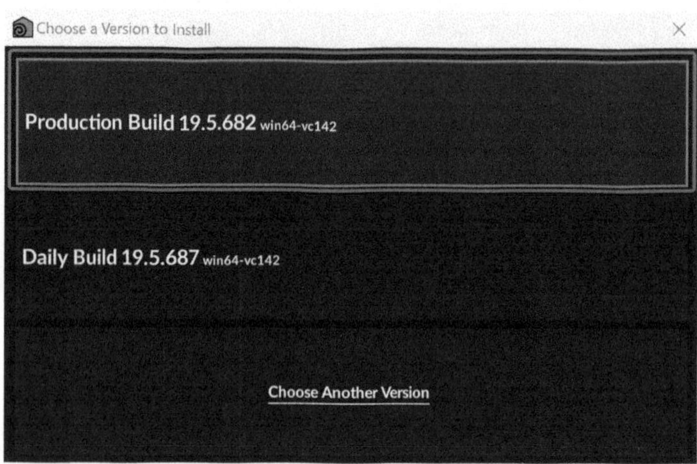

FIGURE 6.14 Houdini version selection window.

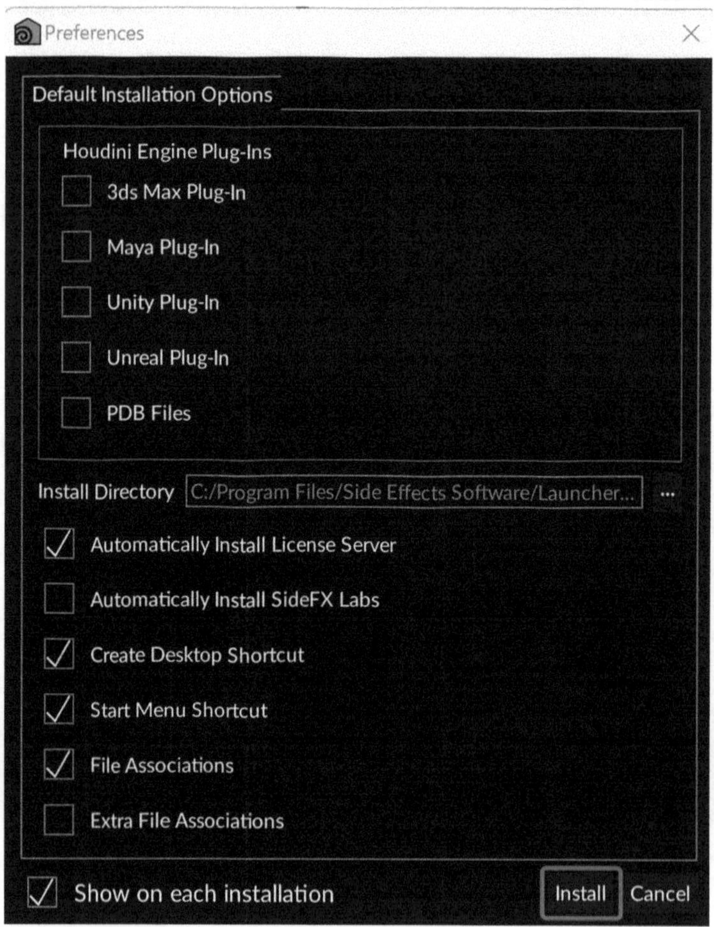

FIGURE 6.15 Houdini installation preferences.

Look through the license agreement and select the *I agree* button. Figure 6.16 shows the *I Agree* button at the end of the license agreement.

Houdini software will now install on your computer.

Once Houdini has completed installation, use the *Houdini Launcher* to start it. Press the big orange *Launch* button in the upper left corner of the window or the *Launch* button adjacent to the gear icon on the same line as the build version. Figure 6.17 shows which version to launch.

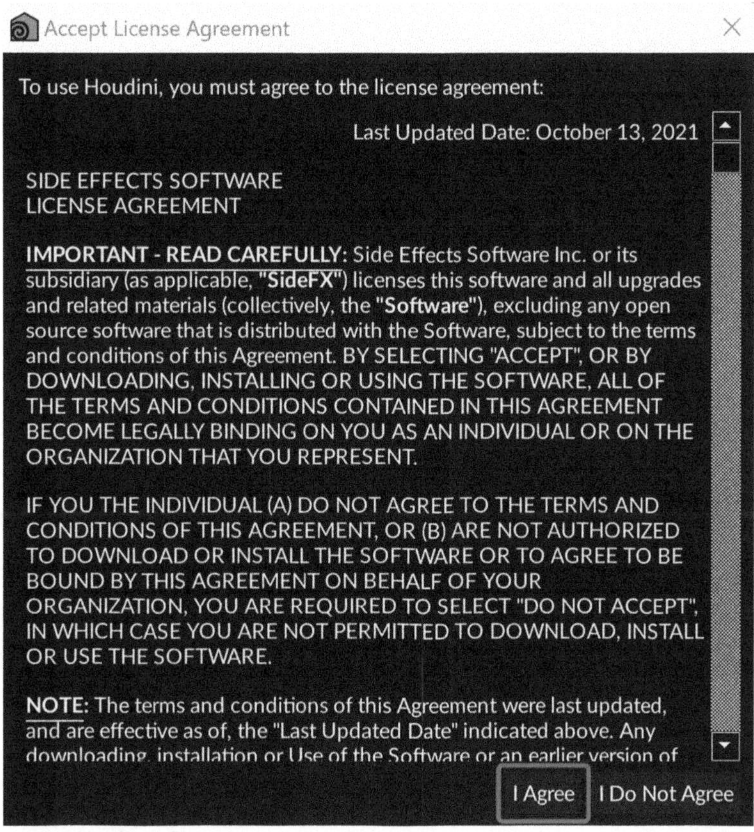

FIGURE 6.16 Houdini license agreement.

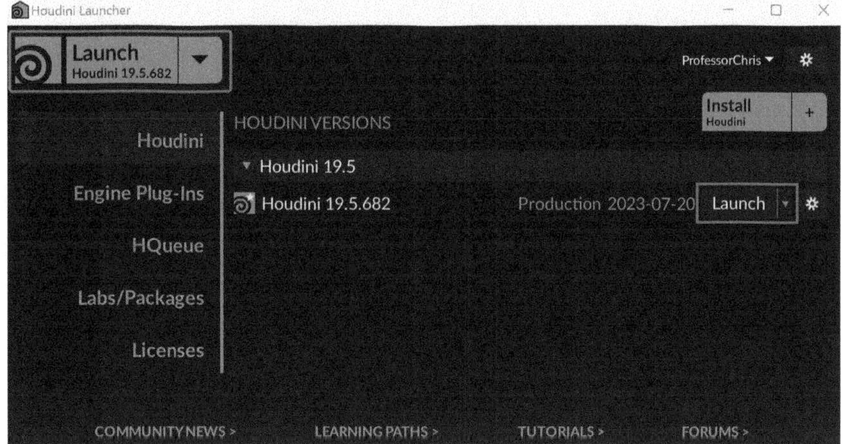

FIGURE 6.17 Start Houdini from launcher.

Assuming that the user is accessing the free *Apprentice* version of Houdini, an error will occur when the software is invoked for the first time. Press the *OK* button to clear it. Figure 6.18 acknowledges the need for *Apprentice* version.

When starting Houdini for the first time, the *Houdini License Administrator* presents the user with multiple options. Select the *Install (or reinstall) my free Houdini Apprentice License*. Press *Next* to continue. Figure 6.19 displays the *Apprentice* license choice.

The user is prompted to accept the SideFX *End User License Agreement*. Select *Accept* to continue. Figure 6.20 accepts the *End User License Agreement*.

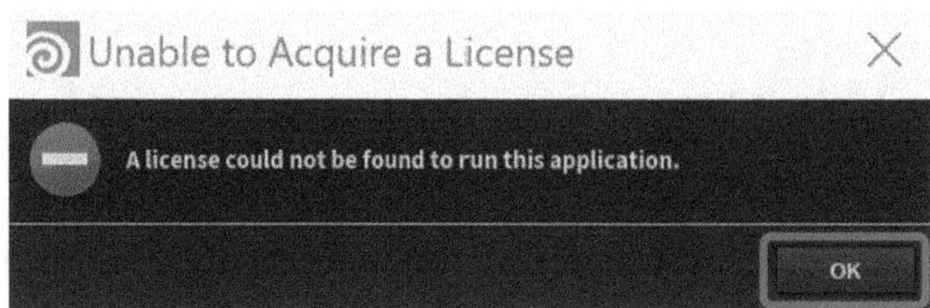

FIGURE 6.18 Houdini launch error.

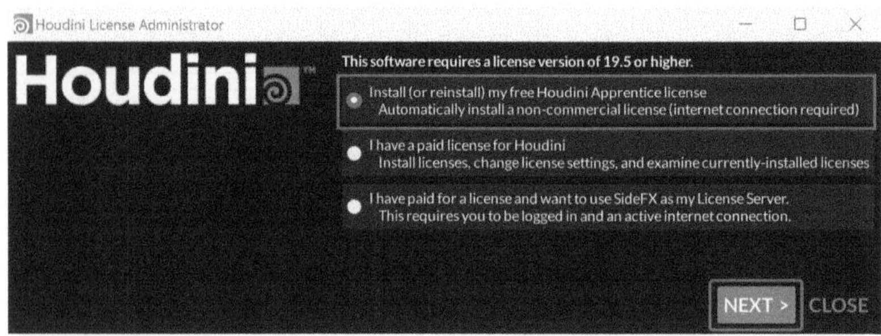

FIGURE 6.19 Apprentice license selection.

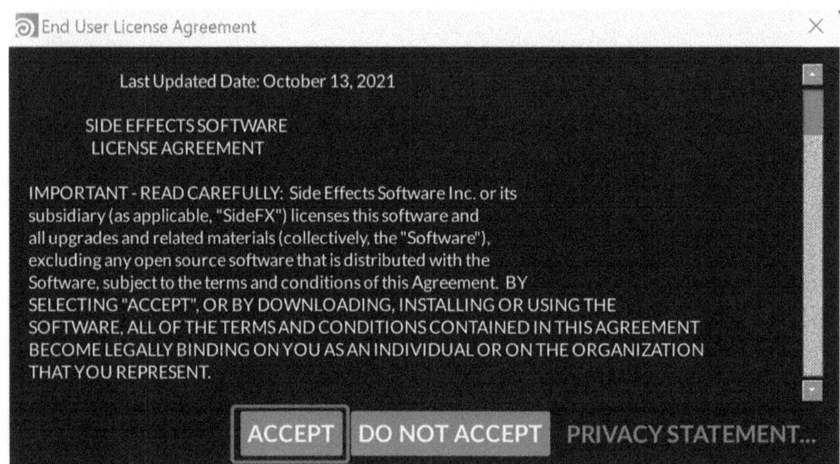

FIGURE 6.20 SideFX end user license agreement.

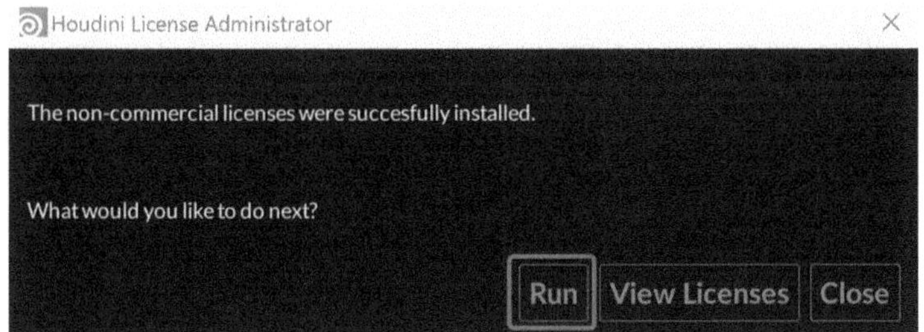

FIGURE 6.21 Houdini installation confirmation.

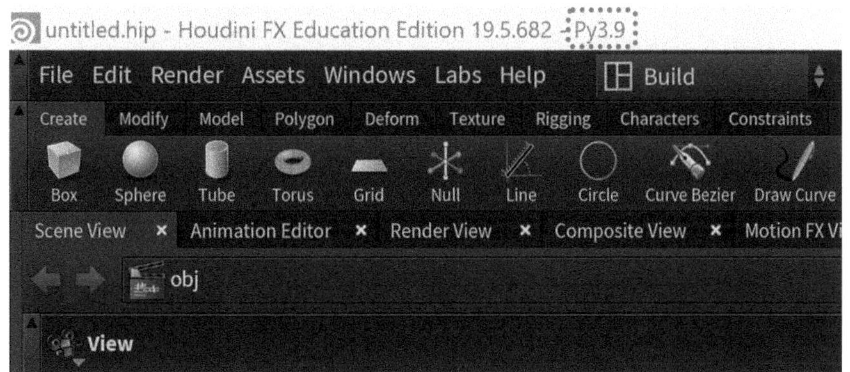

FIGURE 6.22 Houdini Python version.

The user should receive an announcement that the non-commercial license was successfully installed. Finally, press the *Run* button to launch the software. Figure 6.21 launches Houdini.

Once the *Apprentice* license has been designated, the Houdini interface should execute. Confirmation of the correct Python version is verified by the indication in the upper left corner of the window indicating the installed Python version. Figure 6.22 displays the Python version location.

HOUDINI ENVIRONMENT SETUP

Houdini is a dynamic, sophisticated tool. It is easy for novice users to become distracted by the number of buttons, tabs, and icons displayed in the software window. To help remedy this situation, users may choose to create a *custom desktop environment* with a reduced interface to prevent accidental button pushing. If the user is already familiar with Houdini or does not wish to take advantage of the reduced desktop, please skip this section and go to the *Python Shell* section.

To create a new desktop, Select the *Build* tab in the upper left portion of the main window and select the *New Desktop* option. Figure 6.23 shows the *New Desktop* location.

This operation generates a clean new desktop with a reduced interface. Figure 6.24 displays a fresh, clean, new desktop.

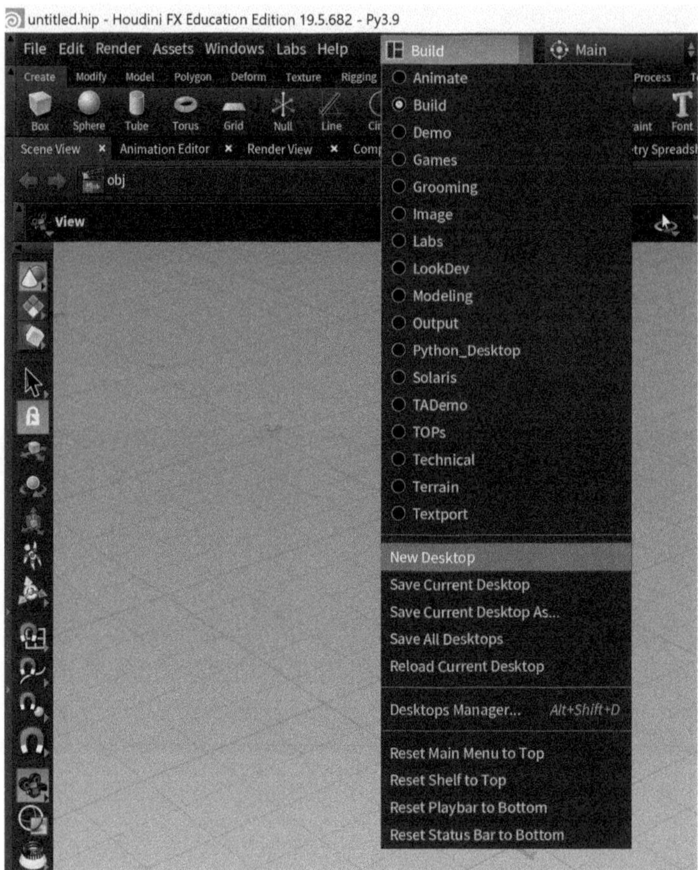

FIGURE 6.23 New desktop option.

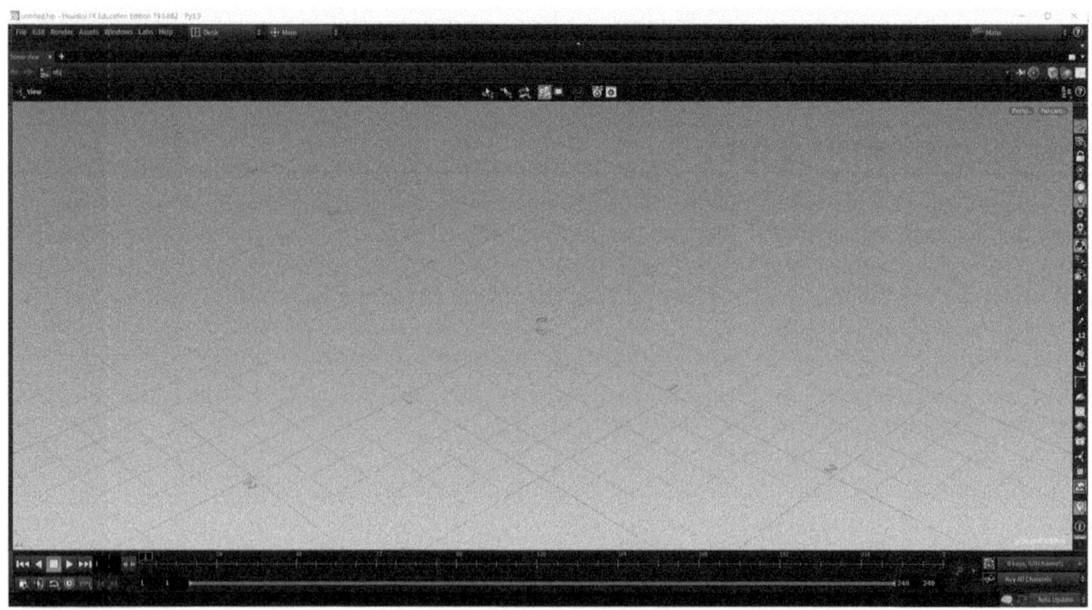

FIGURE 6.24 New desktop.

The desktop pane must be split vertically into two horizontal windows. Press the *Pane Tab Operations* icon in the upper right corner of the window and select *Split Pane Left/Right*. (The users may also type *Alt+[* .) Figure 6.25 shows the location for the horizontal split.

The split pane into two windows is shown in Figure 6.26.

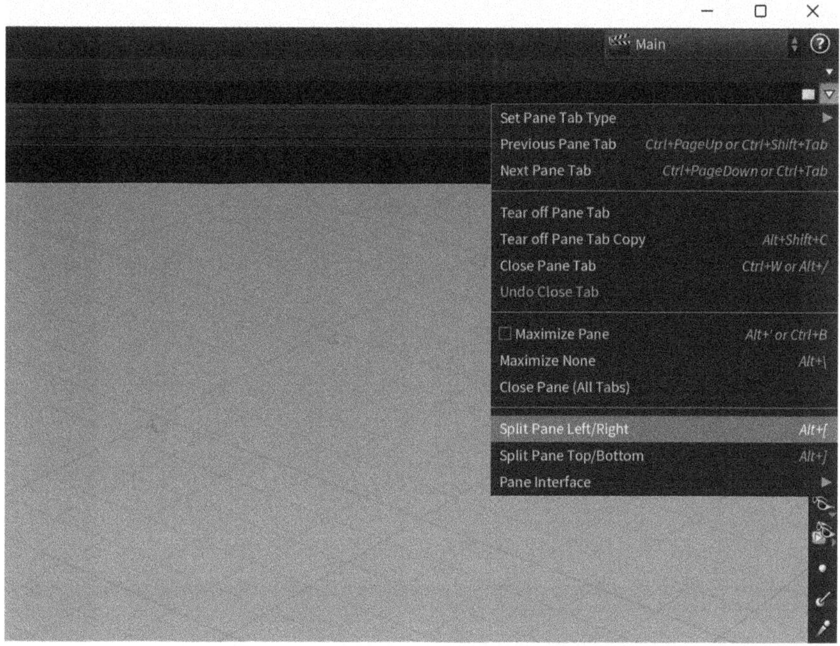

FIGURE 6.25 Split right and left panes.

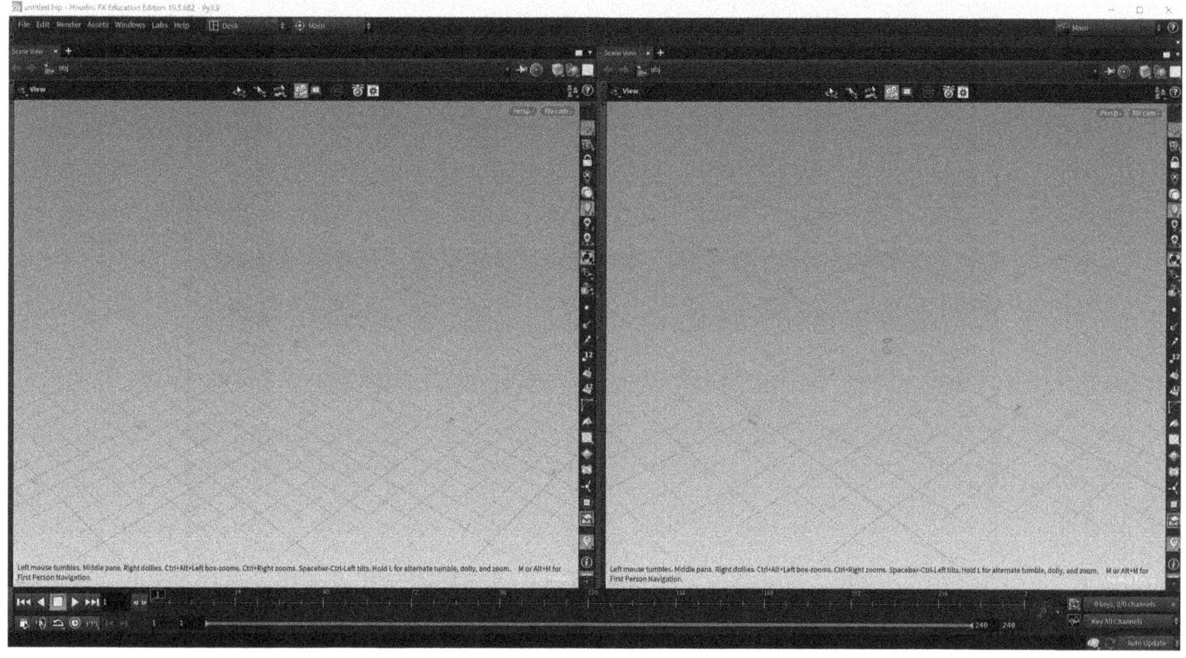

FIGURE 6.26 Two vertical windows.

The left pane is devoted to the three-dimensional display and the Python shell. The right pane is devoted to the network and its parameter windows.

The left pane must be split into upper and lower panes. On the left pane, select the *Pane Tab Operations* and select *Split Pane Top/Bottom*. (Users may also type *Alt+[* .) Figure 6.27 displays the location of this command.

Figure 6.28 displays the resulting upper and lower panes of the split left pane.

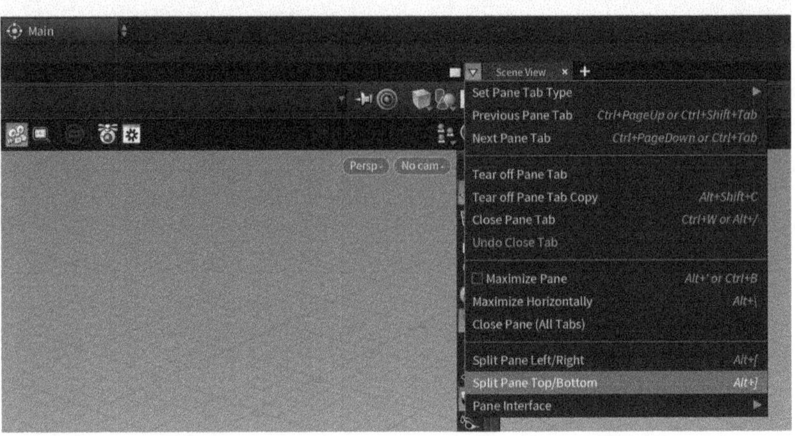

FIGURE 6.27 Split top and bottom panes.

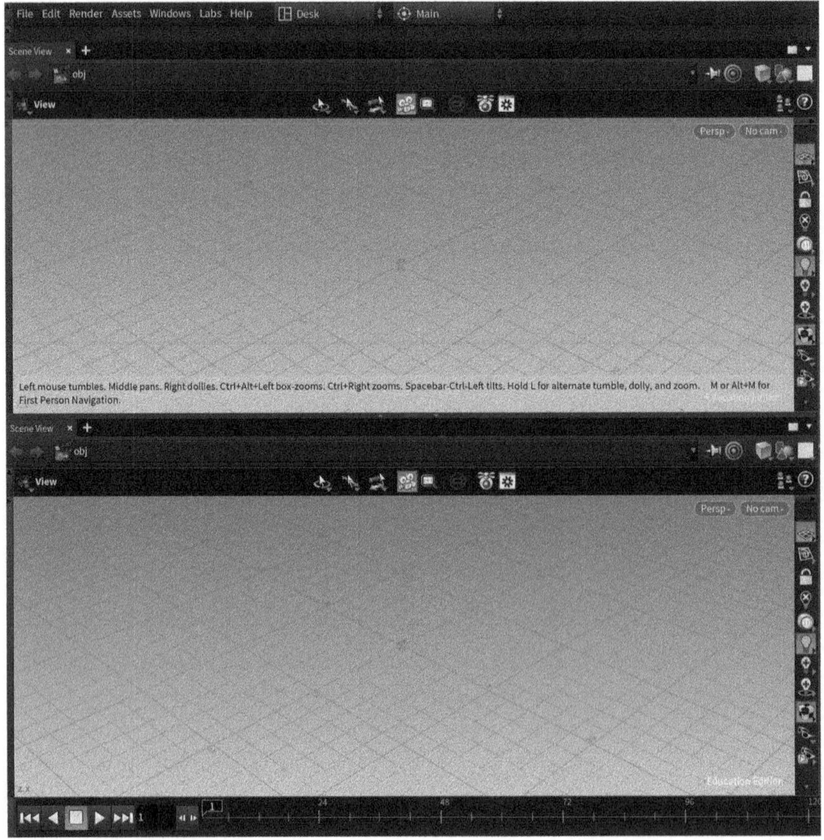

FIGURE 6.28 Upper and lower left panes.

Press the "+" icon in the upper left corner of the lower pane and select *New Pane Tab Type* and then select *Python Shell*, as shown in Figure 6.29. This operation places a Python shell in the lower pane.

If there is no text in the Python shell, hit the *Enter* key to initiate a prompt. Press the little *X* button next to the word *Scene View*, as displayed in Figure 6.30, to remove the Scene View tab from the lower pane.

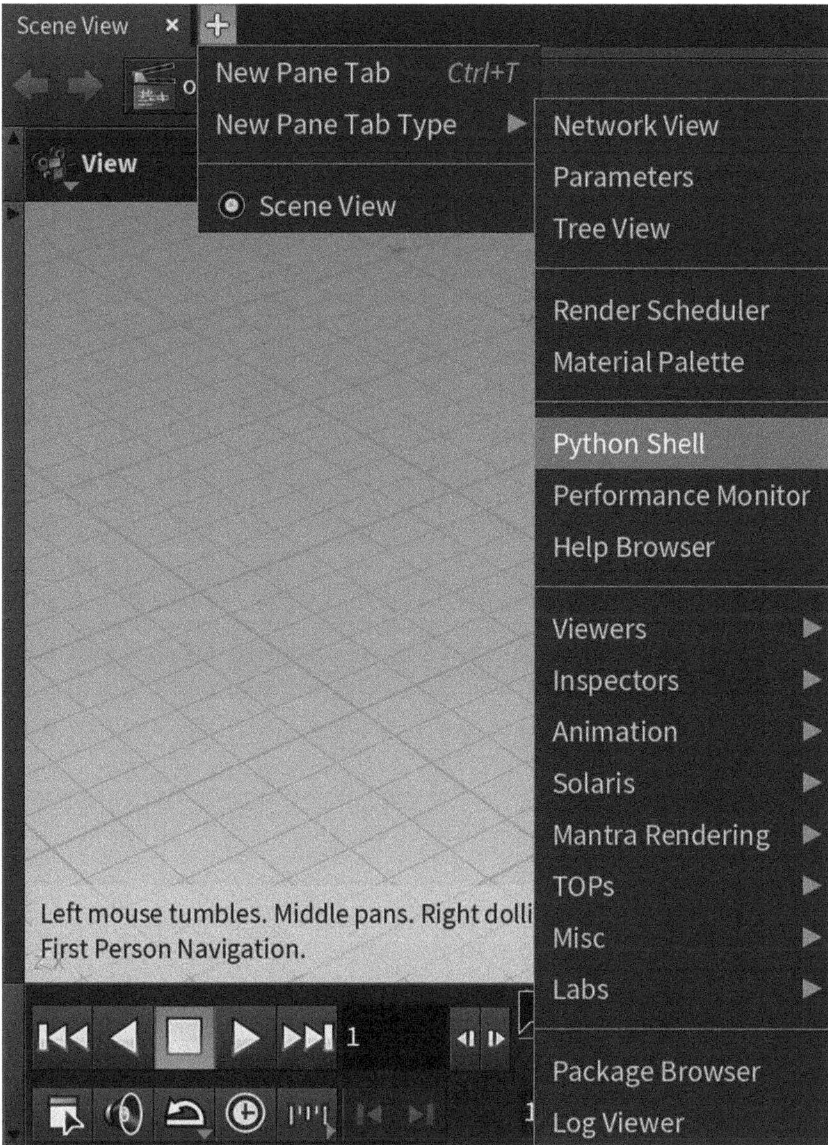

FIGURE 6.29 Add python shell.

```
Scene View  ×  Python Shell  ×  +
Python 3.9.10 (main, Jan 26 2023, 21:56:03) [MSC v.1929 64 bit (AMD64)] on win32
Houdini 19.5.682 hou module imported.
Type "help", "copyright", "credits" or "license" for more information.
>>>
```

FIGURE 6.30 Remove scene view tab.

Return to the right pane, select the *Pane Tab Operations*, and select *Split Pane Top/Bottom*. (Users may also type *Alt+[* .) The result of this split is shown in Figure 6.31.

Press the "+" icon in the upper left corner of the upper pane and select *New Pane Tab Type*, and then select *Network View* as displayed in Figure 6.32. This operation adds a Network View tab to the pane.

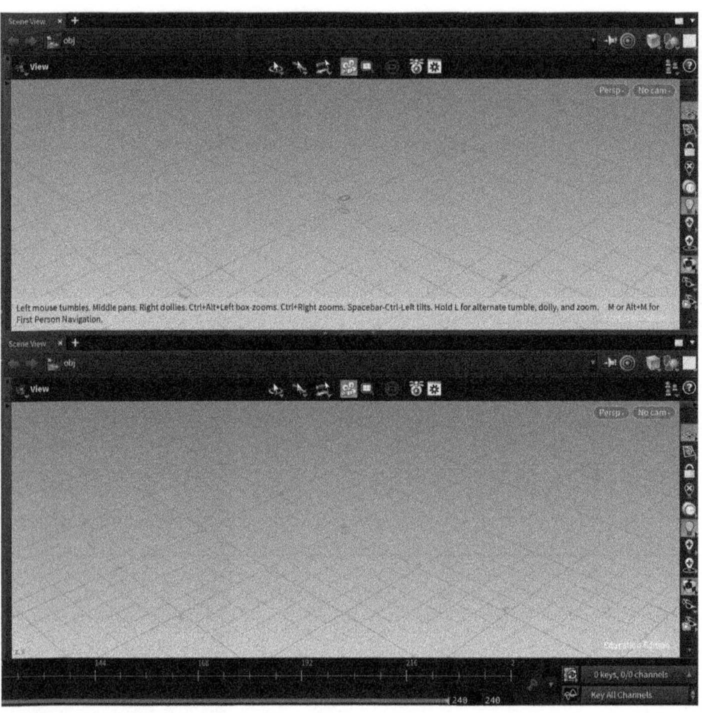

FIGURE 6.31 Split right view pane.

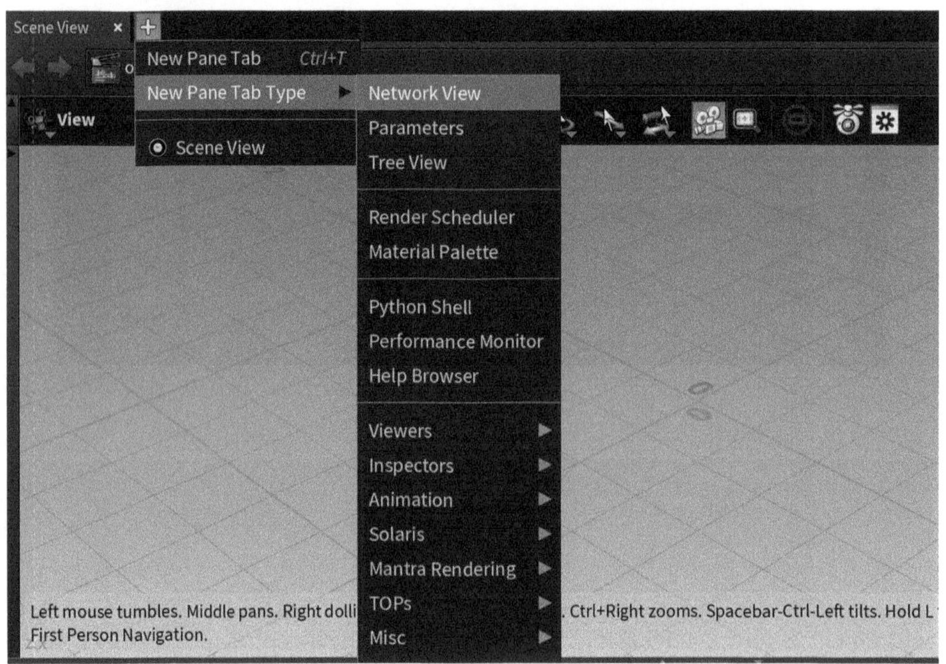

FIGURE 6.32 Add network view.

Press the little *X* button next to the word *Scene View*, shown in Figure 6.33. This operation removes the Scene View tab from the upper pane.

Press the "+" icon in the upper left corner of the lower pane and select *New Pane Tab Type*, as displayed in Figure 6.34, and then select *Parameters*. This operation adds a Parameters tab to the pane.

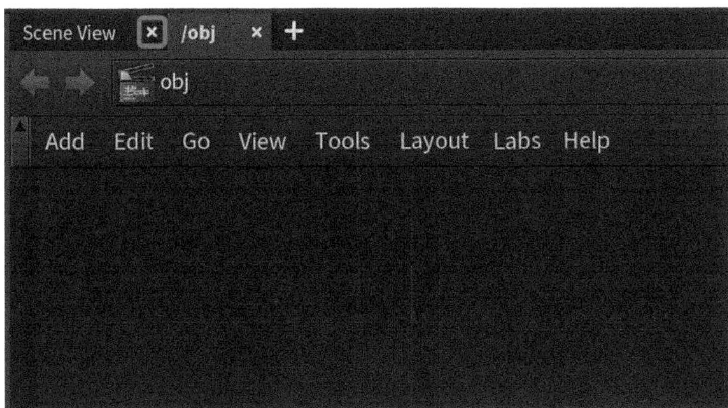

FIGURE 6.33 Remove scene view tab.

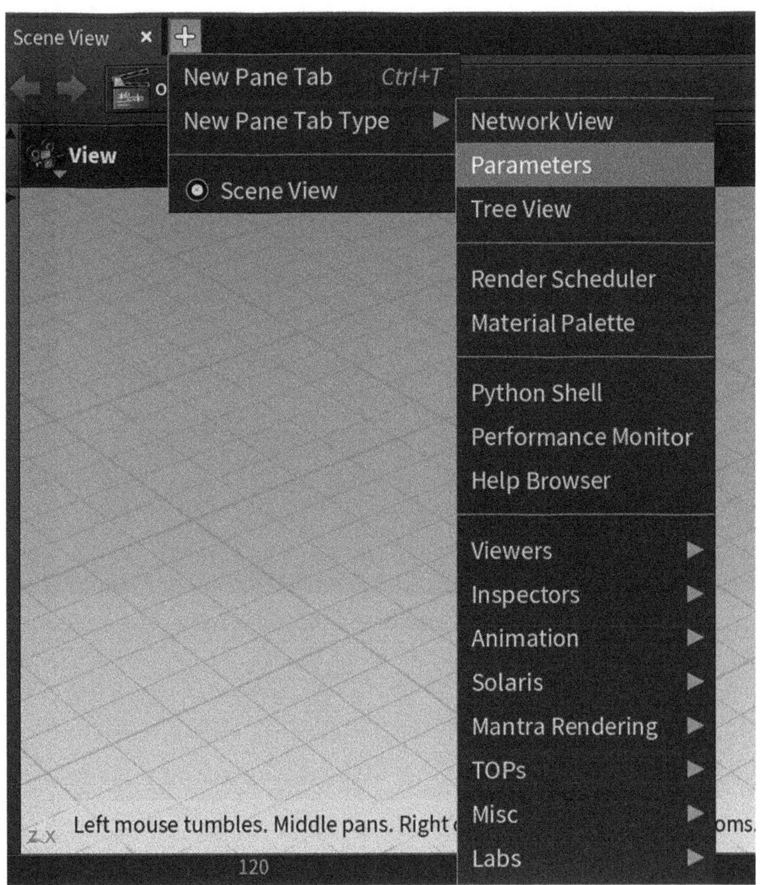

FIGURE 6.34 Add parameters tab.

Press the little *X* button next to the word *Scene View*, as shown in Figure 6.35. This operation removes the Scene View tab from the lower pane.

The custom Python environment configuration is complete. Figure 6.36 demonstrates how the desktop is broken into four principle windows.

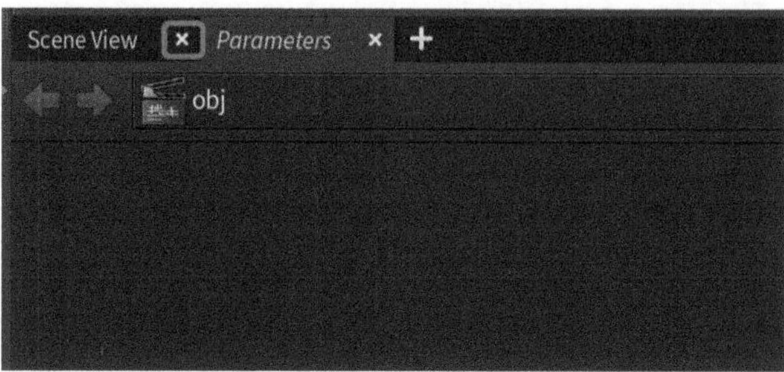

FIGURE 6.35 Remove scene view tab.

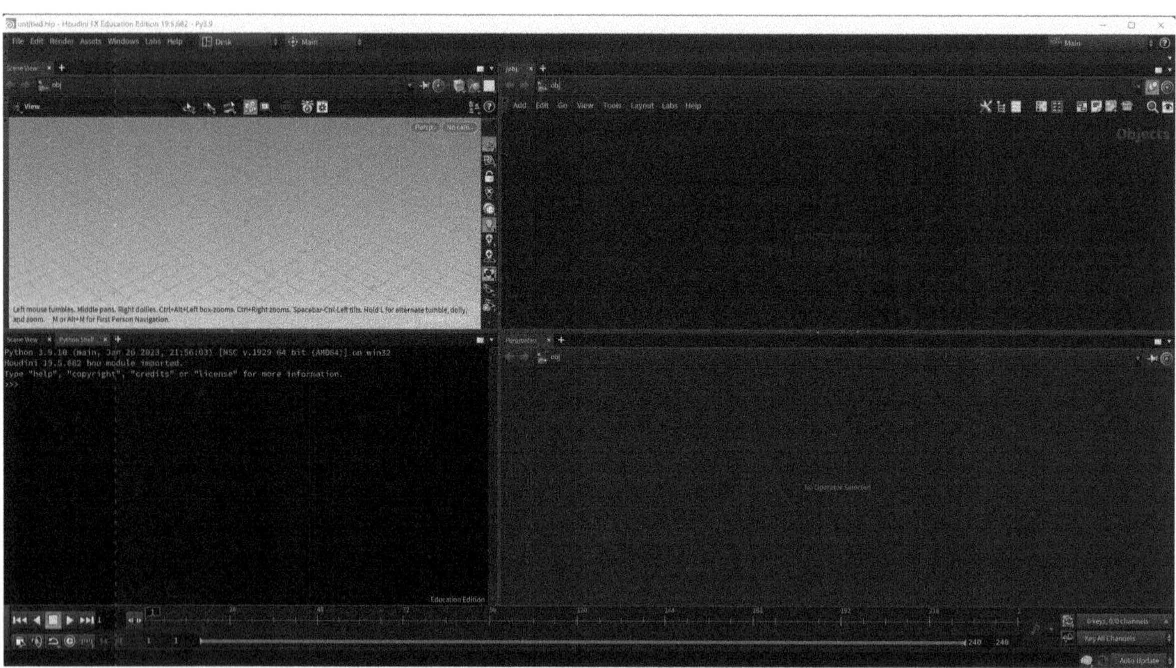

FIGURE 6.36 Custom Python environment.

Press the *Desk* button in the upper left portion of the Houdini window, as shown in Figure 6.37, and select *Save Current Desktop As ...* .

A small *Save As* prompt appears. Type in *Python Desktop* in the *Desk Name* slot and press the *Save* button. Press the *OK* button, Figure 6.38, when queried.

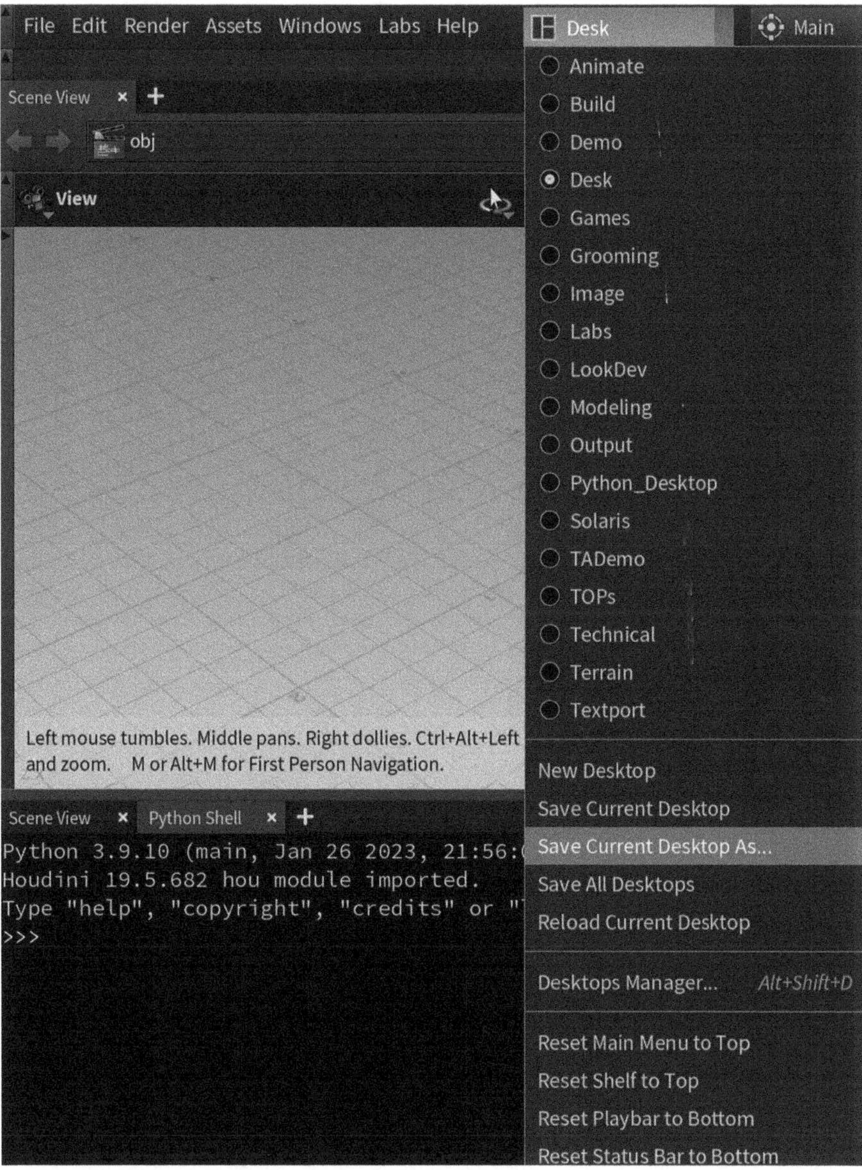

FIGURE 6.37 Save current desktop.

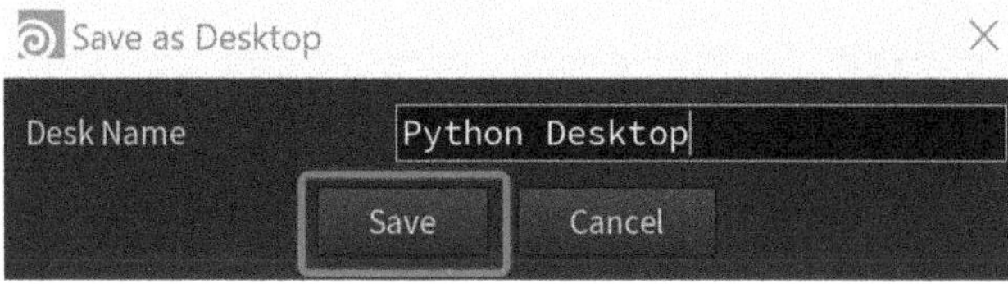

FIGURE 6.38 Save Python desktop.

Because we are only using Houdini as a Python IDE, we want our custom environment to always appear when starting Houdini by configuring the user interface preferences. In the upper left Houdini menu, as shown in Figure 6.39, select *Edit* → *Preferences* → *General User Interface*. (The user may also type *Ctrl*+,.)

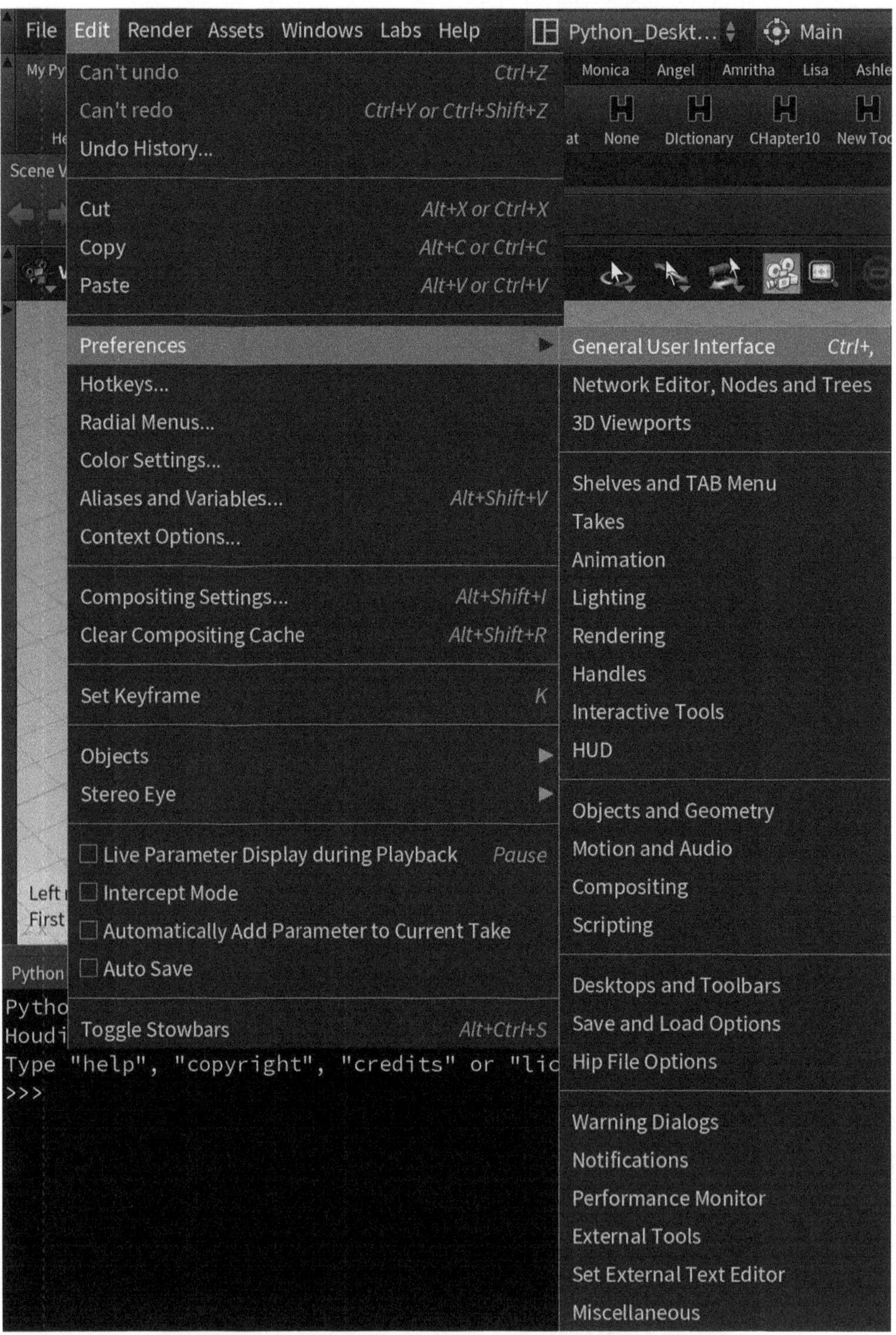

FIGURE 6.39 Access general user interface.

A menu is displayed. Select the *Startup in Desktop* pulldown, Figure 6.40, and select the *Python_Desktop* environment. Finish the selection by pressing the *Accept* button.

Houdini now always starts in our custom Python environment.

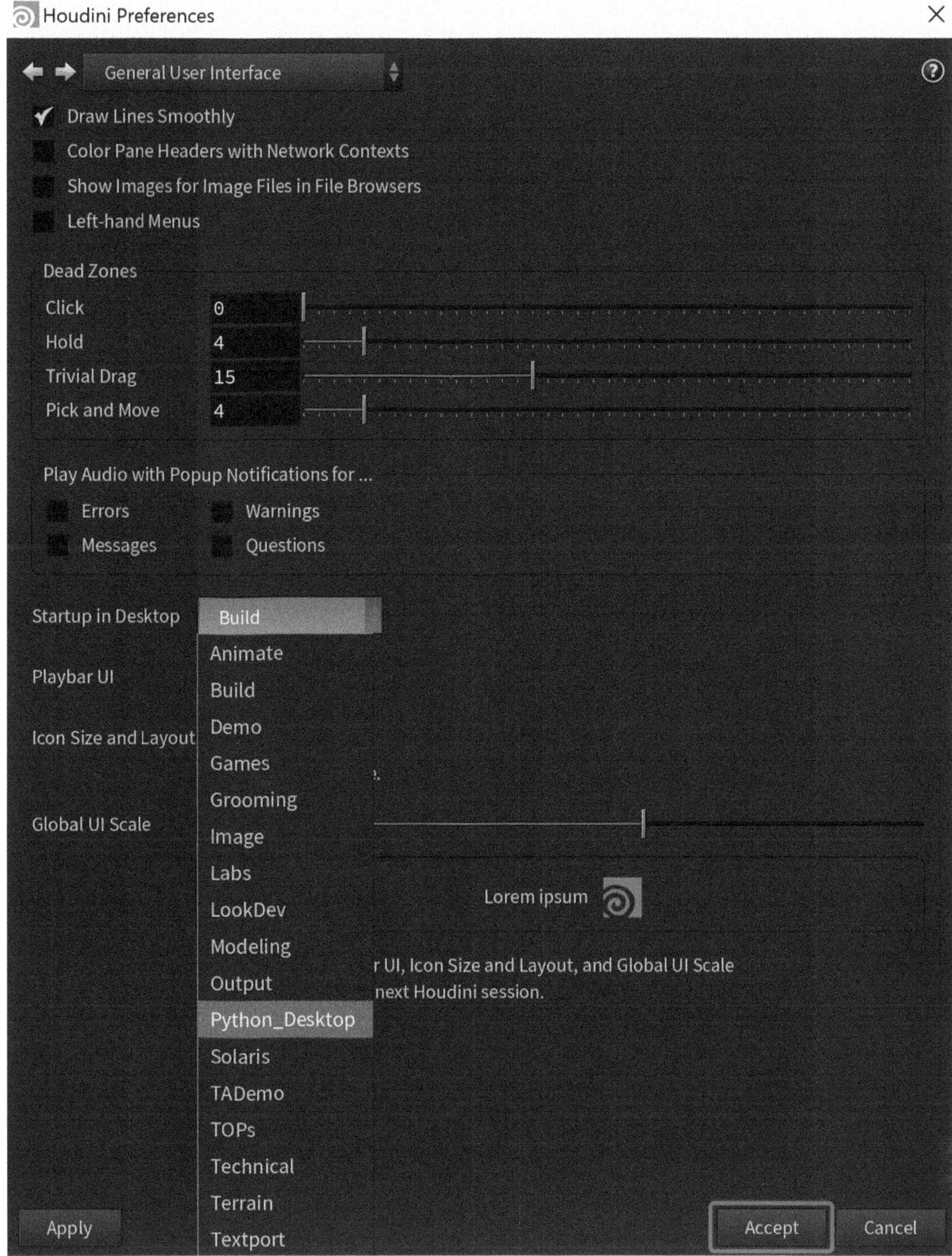

FIGURE 6.40 Identify python_desktop on startup.

PYTHON SHELL

Once the custom Python environment has been created, the Python Shell always appears in the lower left Houdini window. When the custom environment is unavailable, the Python Shell is invoked through the *Windows* tab, *Python Shell* option, Figure 6.41. (Users may also type *Alt+Shift+P.*)

Houdini's Python shell is the interface between the software and the Python interpreter. From this window, as shown in Figure 6.42, the user types in Python commands and instructs Houdini to perform operations through the Python language.

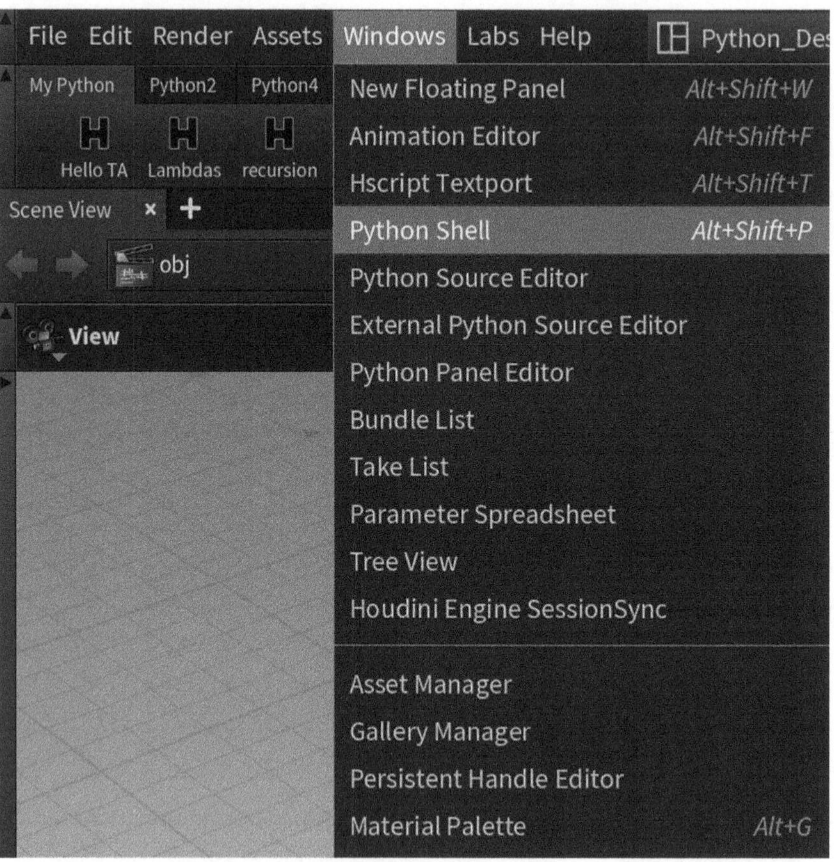

FIGURE 6.41 Invoking python shell.

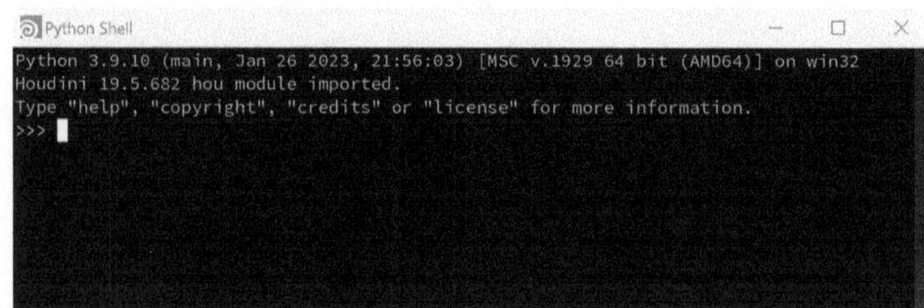

FIGURE 6.42 Python shell.

PYTHON CALCULATOR

In its most primitive behavior, the Python shell behaves as a calculator. Type the number *8* in the shell and press the *enter* key. The Python shell should return with the number *8* (Shell Example 6.1).

```
>>> 8
8
```

Shell Example 6.1 Number 8

The Python shell echoes the last given command. Try again but with the number *10* (Shell Example 6.2).

```
>>> 10
10
```

Shell Example 6.2 Number 10

The results are different but predictable.

Now, type in *8 * 10* and enter (Shell Example 6.3).

```
>>> 8 * 10
80
```

Shell Example 6.3 8 * 10

The Python shell reads the typed values and evaluates the expression.

Try again with other numbers and other operators (Shell Example 6.4).

```
>>> -9 + 12
3
>>> 27 / -6.7
-4.029850746268656
>>> 20.7 - 8.1
12.6
>>> 5 * 11.5 - 13 + 7.2
51.7
```

Shell Example 6.4 Math Calculations

PRINT COMMAND

Behaving as a calculator is nice but the Python shell can do much more such as displaying messages to the window. Try the following command (Shell Example 6.5):

```
>>> print("Welcome to programming for technical artists")
Welcome to programming for technical artists
```

Shell Example 6.5 First Print Command

The Python shell takes the message bound by quotes and parentheses and displays the contents to the window. The messages displayed to the shell window may be very simple or be spiced with a bit of formatting, (*\n\t\t*) (Shell Example 6.6).

```
>>> print("Displaying messages is nice \n\t but we could do much \n\t\t more!")
Displaying messages is nice
     but we could do much
          more!
```

Shell Example 6.6 Print Statement with Simple Formatting

We will cover message string formatting in more detail in the next chapter. This example demonstrates that Python language can do more than display messages verbatim.

VARIABLES

Variables are programming language memory cells. Each memory cell has its own identification, or name, and stores a single piece of information. This single piece of information may be as simple as an individual number or as complicated as an entire video game. We will stick with the simple numbers at first and spend the rest of the course explaining how to create more sophisticated variables.

Variables are created by entering a unique identification, or name, and assigning it using the equal sign character, =, to some value (Shell Example 6.7).

```
>>> first = 36
>>>
```

Shell Example 6.7 Assigning 36 to Variable "`first`"

Nothing visually happens once the *enter* key is pressed. However, Python does much with the information. It creates a memory location, called *first*, and it stores the value of *36* inside that memory location. Nothing visually happens because we did not tell Python to do anything else other than to create the variable named *first*. To verify Python did understand and process the command, we can instruct it to display *first's* content (Shell Example 6.8).

```
>>> print(first)
36
```

Shell Example 6.8 Display `first's` Content

We can tell Python to create as many variables as we want. Create two more variables called *second* and `sillyValue` (Shell Example 6.9).

```
>>> second = 76
>>> sillyValue = -84.76
```

Shell Example 6.9 Assigning "`second`" and "`sillyValue`" Variables

Always provide Python with unique variable names otherwise it will simply over-write the old variable value with new information. This common situation is called *information clobbering*.

Just as math operations are performed on numbers, they can also be performed on variables (Shell Example 6.10).

```
>>> sum = first + second
>>> sum
112
>>> print(f"The sum of {first} and {second} is {sum}")
The sum of 36 and 76 is 112
```

Shell Example 6.10 Math Operations on Variables

The first command creates a new variable, called *sum*, and assigns its value to the result of the sum of the *first* and *second* variables. The second command instructs Python to display *sum*'s value. The third command displays a formatted message containing all variable values.

Remember, variable content can be overwritten and changed, but its functionality still remains the same (Shell Example 6.11).

```
>>> second = 69
>>> sum = first + second
>>> print(f"The sum of {first} and {second} is {sum}")
The sum of 36 and 69 is 105
```

Shell Example 6.11 Overwriting Variables

In the prior example, a new value is given to the *second* variable. Notice the only code difference is a redeclaration of the *second* variable. The *sum* variable needs to be recalculated, and the message needs to be re-displayed in order to observe the new contents.

HELP()

A useful tool available to novice and experienced programmers is the *help()* command which invokes the interactive, built-in, Python help system. The system provides valuable usage information for all Python commands and objects.

The command has two input modes: from the command-line and interactive 'Help' window. Assistance concerning specific Python objects is directly available from the command-line by entering Python objects between the parentheses of the *help()* command. Note object names should be surrounded by quotations for proper interpretation (Shell Example 6.12).

```
>>> help('print')
Help on built-in function print in module builtins:

print(...)
  print(value, ..., sep=' ', end='\n', file=sys.stdout, flush=False)

  Prints the values to a stream, or to sys.stdout by default.
  Optional keyword arguments:
  file:  a file-like object (stream); defaults to the current sys.stdout.
  sep:   string inserted between values, default a space.
  end:   string appended after the last value, default a newline.
  flush: whether to forcibly flush the stream.
```

Shell Example 6.12 `help()` With a Python Object

Information can also be invoked interactively through the *help()* system (Shell Example 6.13).

```
>>> help()

Welcome to Python 3.9's help utility!

If this is your first time using Python, you should definitely check out
the tutorial on the Internet at https://docs.python.org/3.9/tutorial/.

Enter the name of any module, keyword, or topic to get help on writing
Python programs and using Python modules.  To quit this help utility and
return to the interpreter, just type "quit".

To get a list of available modules, keywords, symbols, or topics, type
"modules", "keywords", "symbols", or "topics".  Each module also comes
with a one-line summary of what it does; to list the modules whose name
or summary contain a given string such as "spam", type "modules spam".

help> print
Help on built-in function print in module builtins:

print(...)
  print(value, ..., sep=' ', end='\n', file=sys.stdout, flush=False)

  Prints the values to a stream, or to sys.stdout by default.
  Optional keyword arguments:
  file:  a file-like object (stream); defaults to the current sys.stdout.
  sep:   string inserted between values, default a space.
  end:   string appended after the last value, default a newline.
  flush: whether to forcibly flush the stream.
```

Shell Example 6.13 Interactive help() **Usage**

FIRST PYTHON SCRIPT

Entering one line of code at a time is good for doing quick calculations but is not very efficient for creating a more robust Python structure. The shell may execute one Python command at a time. Instead of entering single lines of Python code, most programmers create collections of code in single sources, called *scripts*, which execute multiple lines of code in succession. Scripts are very convenient for performing many Python operations at the same time.

While most scripts are stored as single computer files, we will be creating our first scripts within the context of the Houdini Python scripting environment. To prepare the environment for our scripts, a *script shelf* must first be created. A *script* shelf is a row of buttons at the top of the Houdini window. Press the "*triangle*" icon in the upper right corner of the Houdini window, as shown in Figure 6.43, and select *New Shelf Set*.

A new shelf, labeled *New Shelf*, appears in the left portion of the Houdini window, as displayed in Figure 6.44.

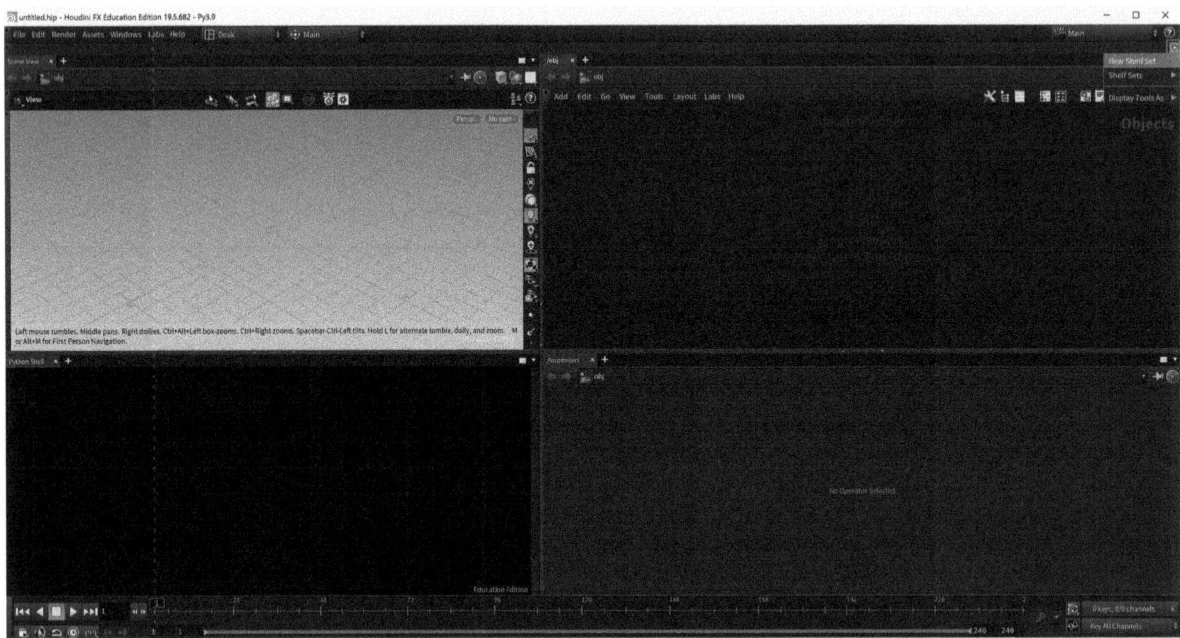

FIGURE 6.43 Create new shelf.

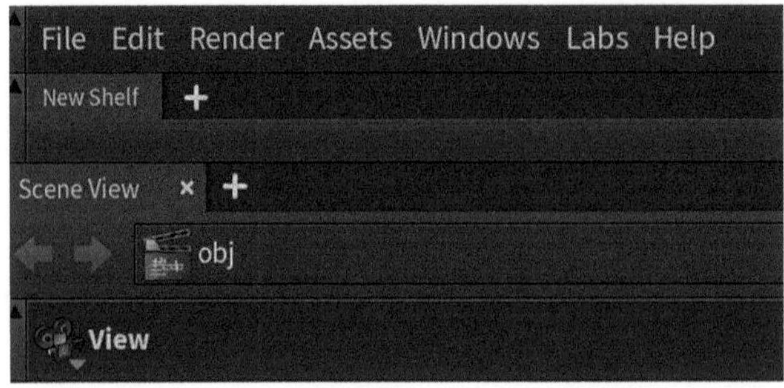

FIGURE 6.44 New shelf tab.

Give the shelf a more descript name by clicking the right mouse button (RMB) in the *New Shelf* tab and selecting *Edit Shelf Tab*, as shown in Figure 6.45.

An *Edit Shelf* tool appears, Figure 6.46. Type in *myPython* in the *Name* slot and *My Python* in the *Label* slot. Finish by selecting the *Accept* button.

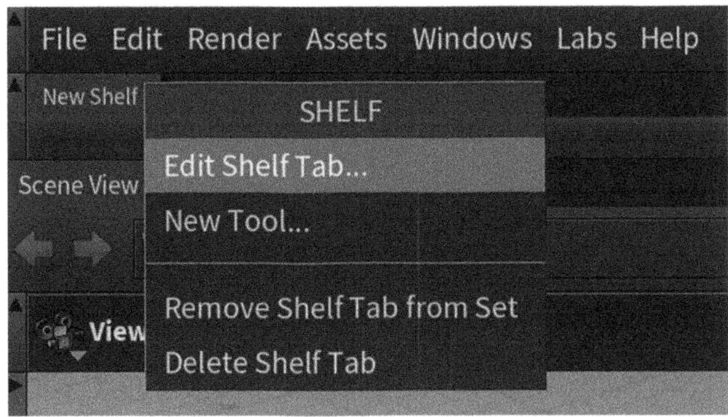

FIGURE 6.45 Edit shelf tab.

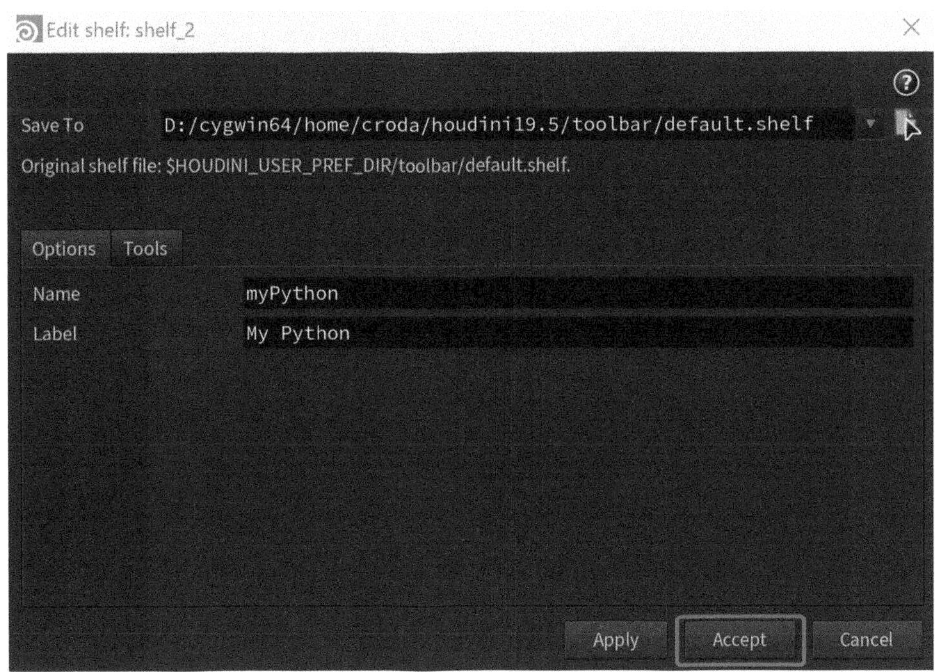

FIGURE 6.46 Edit shelf tool.

Figure 6.47 displays a customized tool shelf devoted for our Python scripts. We will not need to perform this operation again.

To create our first script, click right mouse button (RMB) in our *My Python* shelf and select *New Tool*, Figure 6.48.

Figure 6.49 displays the Script Tool editing window. Most of our scripts will be authored using this tool. In the script tool editing window, press the *Options* tab. Enter *helloTA* in the *Name slot* and *Hello TA* in the *Label* slot.

FIGURE 6.47 My Python shelf.

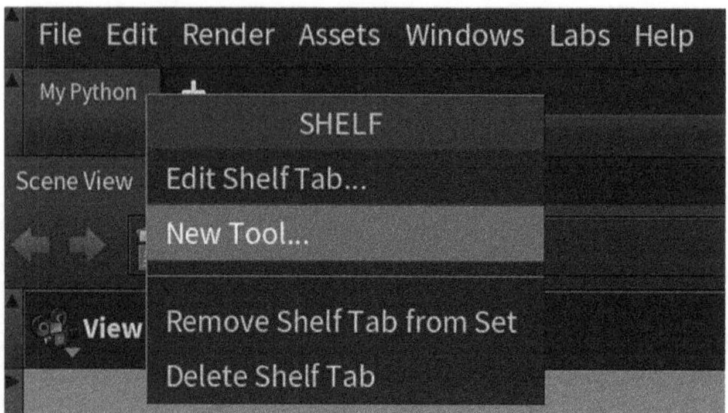

FIGURE 6.48 Create new shelf tool.

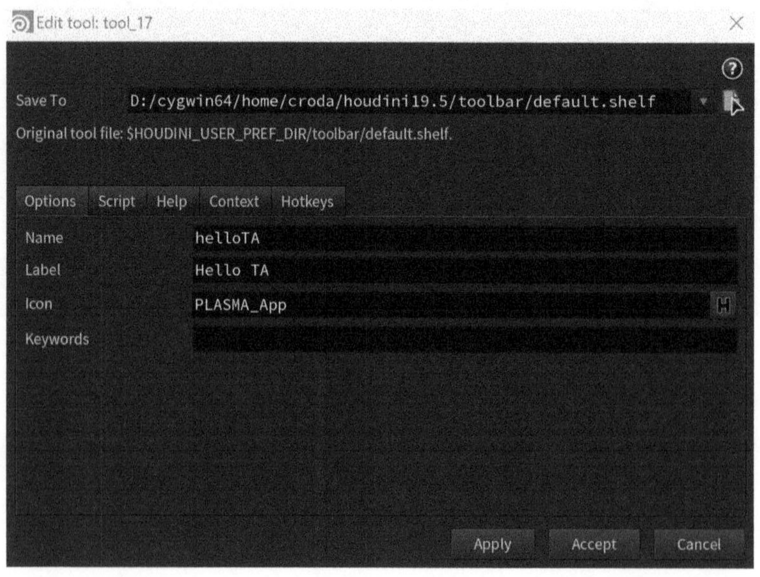

FIGURE 6.49 Script editing tool.

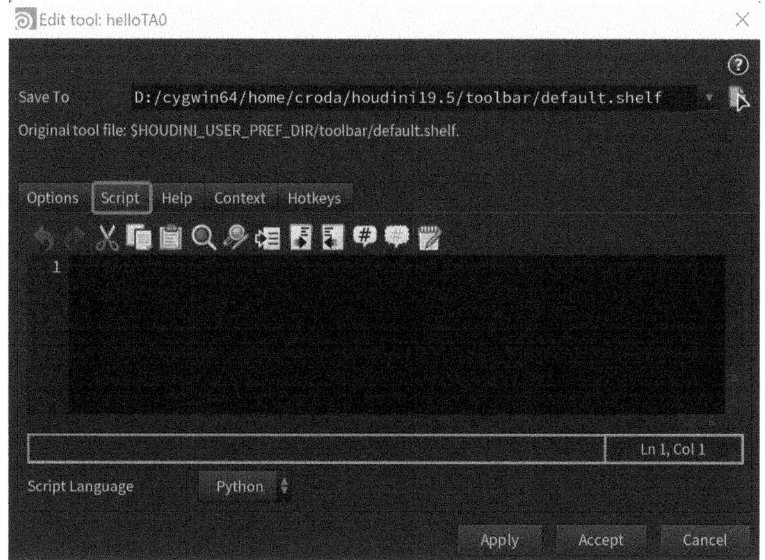

FIGURE 6.50 Hello TA script.

Select the *Script* tab, Figure 6.50, to enter the script editor.

Type in your first script, Code Sample 6.1, into the script editor.

```
myMessage = "Hello Technical Artists!"
print(myMessage)
```

Code Sample 6.1 Hello TA Code

In Figure 6.51, the first line of the code defines a new variable, named *myMessage*, with a simple text string message, "Hello Technical Artists"! The second line of the code displays the contents of *myMessage* variable to the Python Shell.

Press the *Accept* button to accept the code.

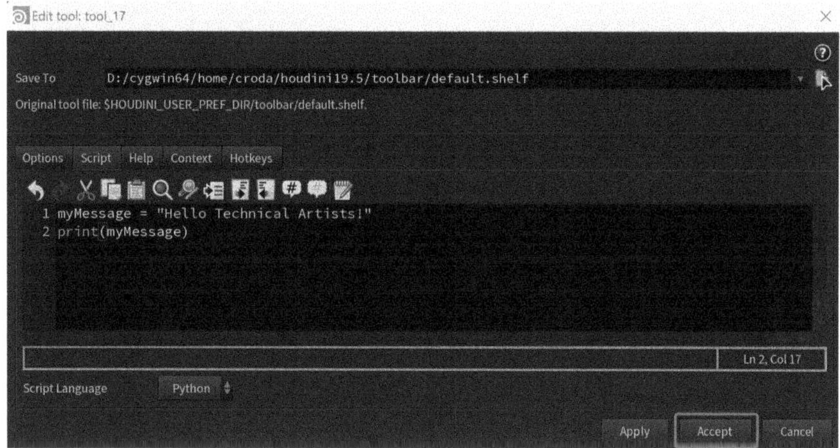

FIGURE 6.51 Hello TA script icon.

Figure 6.52 demonstrates that in our *My Python* tool shelf, there is now a little button which says *Hello TA*.

After a script is placed on our *My Python* tool shelf, it may be invoked any time. Press the *Hello TA* icon. Our epic greetings to all technical artists are displayed to the Python shell.

The reader will most probably want the tool shelf to always appear whenever Houdini is opened to the custom desktop. To fix the tool shelf to the desktop, press the layout selection button in the upper left corner of the Houdini window, Figure 6.53, and pull down to the *Save Current Desktop option.*

Press the *OK* when prompted to continue. The Python tool shelf will now always appear with the Python_Desktop whenever upon opening

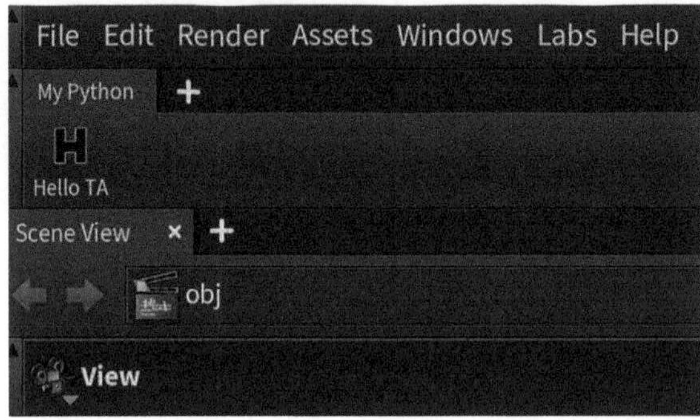

FIGURE 6.52 Hello TA tool.

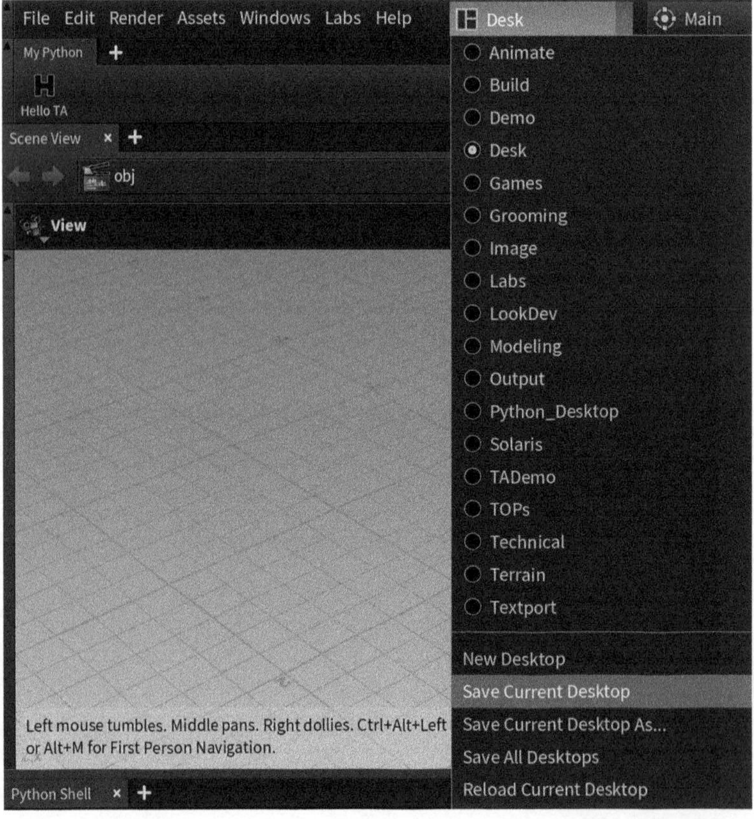

FIGURE 6.53 Update desktop with tool shelf.

CONCLUSION

Quite often, the initial steps in learning a new skillset are the most challenging. If users have no prior Houdini experience, then this process may seem taxing. However, the goal of this chapter is to ensure proper installation of the Houdini Python IDE and introduce a few of the most basic Python programming concepts.

We first access the SideFX website, https://www.sidefx.com/, and download the software. After downloading, the software is installed. Instructions are provided to assist the user creating a custom Python environment which reduces the visual complexity of the Houdini environment and provides the user with an easy access interface to their Python tools.

The Python shell is introduced as a primitive interface for Houdini Python. Basic calculator functions and displaying simple messages are simple operations which can be administered through the Python shell. Commands are administered through the Python shell one command at a time.

The concept of variables is introduced. Variables are the fundamental building blocks for all programming. They are memory containers with unique identification that may hold anything from simple numbers to entire applications.

Creating variables and entering simple commands in the Python shell are a good way to get started. However, since the shell can only execute one command at a time, programmers use *scripting* to execute multiple commands with one Python call. We create our first Python script which defines a simple variable which holds a message and then displays the message to the Python shell.

INTRODUCTION

In the prior chapter, beyond covering the downloading and installation of SideFX Houdini and the configuration of a customized Python environment, a few key concepts were introduced that can be found in any modern programming language. Using Python as a calculator was demonstrated. This simplistic use is handy for doing math but is not unique to the Python language. Almost any *interpretive* language, such as Python, exhibits similar functionality. The concept of variables was also introduced. All computer languages employ variables. They are the fundamental building blocks for all programming languages. The ability to display messages to a text port or window was also demonstrated. All computer languages have some functionality to display messages to whatever display device is available to the computer.

Python, like all other modern programming languages, exhibits other types of fundamental behaviors. These behaviors are executed uniquely in the Python context. This chapter is devoted to introducing these fundamental yet uniquely Python basics.

This chapter starts with a second simple script demonstrating how information can be queried and inputted into Python. The script reviews some of the concepts introduced in the prior chapter and introduces some new concepts.

Text messages are essential for providing valuable user feedback and debugging information. Quotation marks designate text messages. The rules for proper structuring and mixing of quotations are introduced along with the inclusion of several special text characters which configure the visual appearance of text messages.

Early versions of Python displayed simplistic text messages to display ports. As the language evolved, so did the methods for formatting text messages. Multiple strategies for formatting Python messages are introduced including formatted string literals, *f-strings*, str.format() method, manual formatting, and the old school formatting method.

There are occasions when programmers need to leave messages within the Python code itself. These messages are called comments. Comments are not executed but they communicate to other code-readers what the programmer is thinking and explains potentially confusing logic. Comments are essential components in any programming language where labeling and explaining code significantly enhances code readability.

Expressions are also essential language components which provide a fundamental Python structure. Simply explained, expressions are small snippets of code evaluated within a Python command before the command is executed. Evaluation of expressions may deliver Boolean values, yielding true or false, or numerical or text values. Expression operators control how expressions are evaluated. The Python language supports multiple operators used when evaluating expression. Many are beyond the scope of this book. The three types of operators most valuable to technical artists include mathematical, comparison, and Boolean operators.

So far, all of the code explained in this book is of non-graphical nature. A simple script is provided at the end of the chapter to demonstrate how three-dimensional objects can be created and manipulated through Python code and quickly introduce object-oriented programming.

DOI: 10.1201/9781003016427-7

SECOND SCRIPT

The prior chapter covered topics familiar with all programming languages such as variables. This new script is a reminder of what was covered in the prior chapter and introduces some new concepts, such as comments and formatted output strings.

If, for some reason, your Houdini session is not displaying the custom Python desktop, press the desktop selection in the upper left corner of the window and select *Python_Desktop*, as displayed in Figure 7.1.

Open the script editor by clicking the right mouse button inside of the *My Python* shelf and selecting *New Tool*, as shown in Figure 7.2.

Inside of the script editor, Figure 7.3, enter *simpleInput* into the *Name* slot and *Simple Input* into the *Label* slot. Select the *Script* tab to open the code editor.

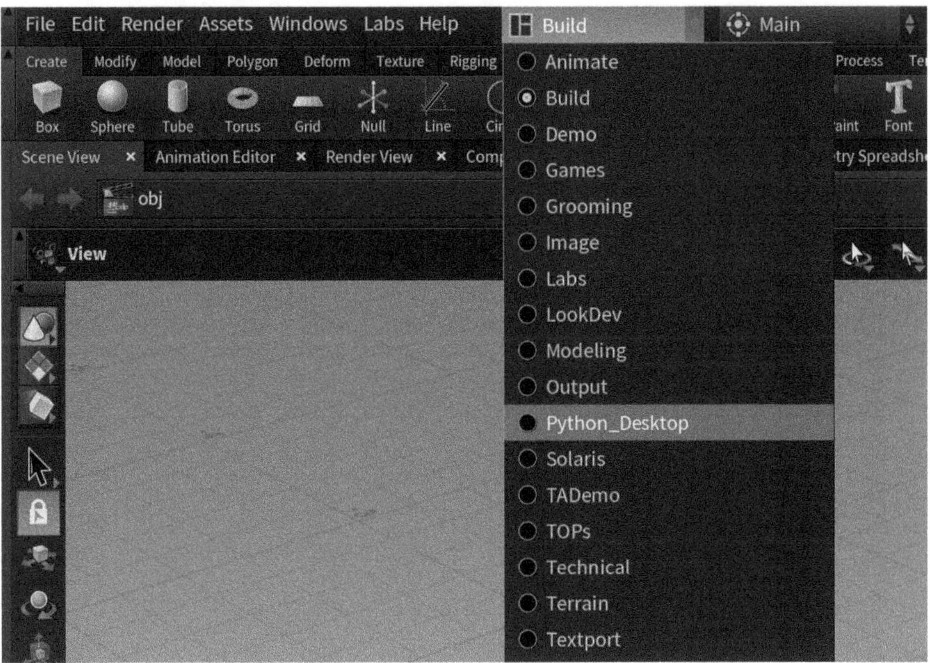

FIGURE 7.1 Put Houdini into Python_Desktop.

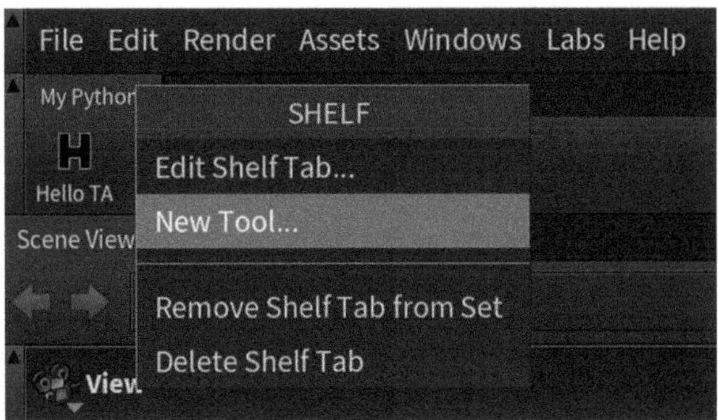

FIGURE 7.2 Create new tool.

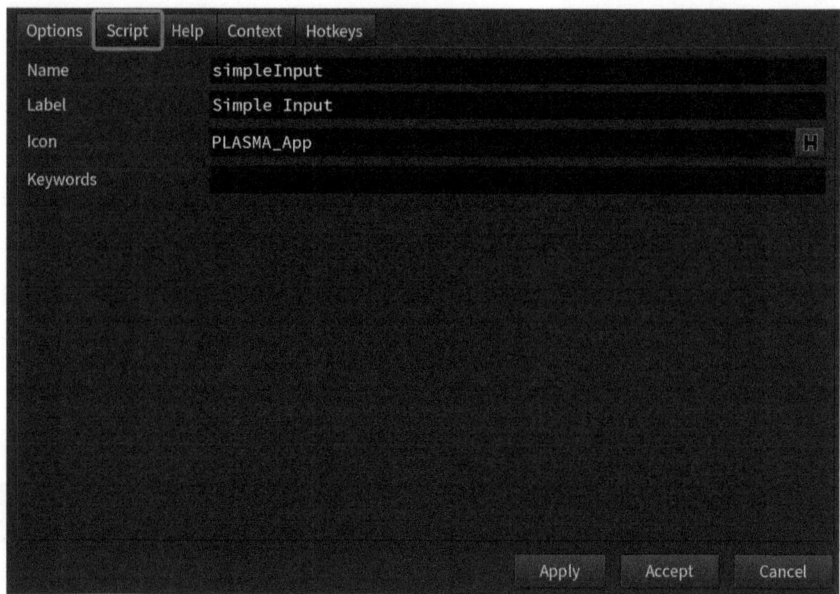

FIGURE 7.3 Simple input script.

Enter Code Sample 7.1 into the script editing window:

```
# Get user input
input = input("Enter the first and second values: ")

# Split input into first and second values
first, second = input.split()

# Convert values to integers
first = int(first)
second = int(second)

# Add the two values
sum = first + second

# display the sum result
print(f"Sum of {first} and {second}  = {sum}")
```

Code Sample 7.1 User Input Query

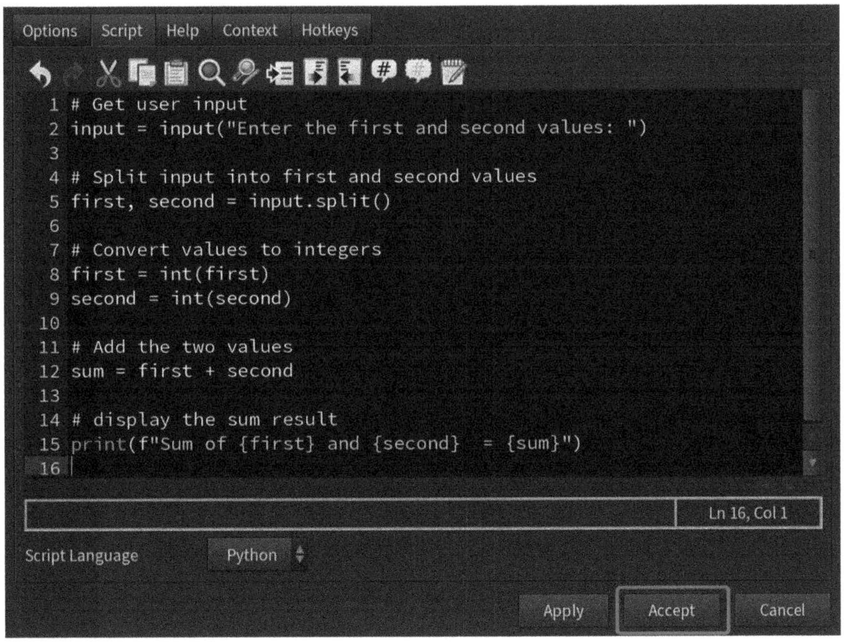

```
1 # Get user input
2 input = input("Enter the first and second values: ")
3
4 # Split input into first and second values
5 first, second = input.split()
6
7 # Convert values to integers
8 first = int(first)
9 second = int(second)
10
11 # Add the two values
12 sum = first + second
13
14 # display the sum result
15 print(f"Sum of {first} and {second} = {sum}")
16
```

FIGURE 7.4 Save new script.

Press the *Accept* button to save the code, Figure 7.4.

Press the *Simple Input* Icon on the toolbar. The message, "Enter the first and second values" appears in the Python Shell. Enter two numbers, for example, "76 84", and hit the *Enter* key. Python Shell Example 7.1 returns a message displaying the sum of the two values.

```
>>> Enter the first and second values: 76 84
Sum = 160
```

Shell Example 7.1 Simple Input Shell Interactions

The first line is called a *Comment*. It starts with the pound character, '#', and has no impact on code behavior. Its purpose is to communicate the intentions of the programmer. The second line tells Python to display a message and then wait for the user to type in some information, and hit the *Enter* key. Once entered, the content typed into the shell is assigned to the variable named *input*.

When Python receives user input it is received as a text message called a *string*. Strings are composed of letters, numbers, and punctuation characters. (Technically, these characters are called *Unicode* characters and are explained further in Chapter 10.) Strings are convenient Python data containers which can be easily split into smaller messages. The next code line (line 5) splits the *input* into two new variables, *first* and *second*. By default, split uses whitespaces as the separation positions when breaking into multiple variables.

Even though the *first* and *second* variables were created from the *input* variable, they are still strings and not numbers and there is not much Python can do other than display them as text. To make the *first* and *second* usable, the next two lines of code convert them into integer numbers.

As integer numbers, the *first* and *second* are added together and the sum is assigned to the variable named, *sum*. The last line tells Python to display a message containing the first and second values and the result of their sum.

STRING FORMATTING

Strings are verbal text messages displayed wherever words may be seen. They are displayed in the Python shell requesting information or reporting status on an operation. Strings are the building blocks for reading and writing information to external files. They are the labels observed inside buttons and all other graphical user interfaces. Whenever Python needs to deal with words that are not variables or Python commands, it organizes those words in strings. Strings may be assigned to variables, provide input to functions, or be typed directly to Python shells.

Quotations

Text strings are essential components used for generating readable feedback informing users of script progression and interactive information. Strings are also used for providing valuable debugging information. Python is a robust language and its treatment of text strings is far from simplistic. Quotations. delimit text strings. They mark the beginning and end of a string.

Quote Types

There are three different types of quotations or quotes: single quotes, double quotes, and triple quotes.

The most simplest types of quotes are single quotes. A pair of single quotes, ' ', identify the beginning and end of a string. Single quotes are demonstrated in Shell Example 7.2.

```
>>> 'This is a simple string with single quotes'
'This is a simple string with single quotes'
```

Shell Example 7.2 Single Quotes String

Shell Exmaple 7.3 demonstrate how double quotes, " ", provide the same functionality.

```
>>> "This is a simple string with double quotes"
'This is a simple string with double quotes'
```

Shell Example 7.3 Double Quotes String

Note that even though when original strings are delimited by double quotes, Python echoes them with single quotes. Python identifies all of its strings with single quotes.

While not as common, Python supports a third type of quotes: triple quotes. Triple quotes may be triple-single quotes, ''' ''', or triple double quotes, """ """. Triple quotes are demonstrated in Shell Example 7.4.

```
>>> '''This is a simple string with triple-single quotes'''
'This is a simple string with triple-single quotes'
>>> """This is a simple string with triple-double quotes"""
'This is a simple string with triple-double quotes'
```

Shell Example 7.4 Triple Single and Triple Double Quotations

While possible to use as standard string identification, Python traditionally reserves triple quotes for commenting messages. Comments are covered later in this chapter.

With three different types of quotations, the important rule to remember is that Python expects the beginning and end of all strings to be delimited by the same type of quotes. There can be no mixing of quotation types when marking the beginning and end of strings. Shell Example 7.5 demonstrates the resulting syntax error of incorrect quotes.

```
>>> 'This string is bound by incorrect quotes"
  File "<console>", line 1
    'This string is bound by incorrect quotes"
                                              ^
SyntaxError: EOL while scanning string literal
```

Shell Example 7.5 Incorrect Quotation Beginnings and Endings

Python responds with error messages when identifying strings bound with different quotation types.

Mixing Quotation Types

Things get a little confusing when quotation types are mixed within the same string. Shell Example 7.6 shows how mixing quotation types is valid when bound by the original quote type.

```
>>> 'This is a mixed string with "inside double quotes", bound by single
quotes'
'This is a mixed string with "inside double quotes", bound by single quotes'
```

Shell Example 7.6 Mixing Quotation Types

When mixing quote types, almost any combination is valid as long as the same types of delimiting quotes are not used in the interior of the string. This situation confuses Python as it identifies the end of string when encountering the same type of quote that started it. Shell Example 7.7 correctly mixes quote types.

```
>>> "This is a 'valid text message with a '''mish-mash''' of quotes"
"This is a 'valid text message with a '''mish-mash''' of quotes"
>>> '''Almost any "type" of quote is valid'''
'Almost any "type" of quote is valid'
```

Shell Example 7.7 Valid Quotation Mixing

Shell Example 7.8 is an illegal combination.

```
>>> "This is an "Invalid" text"
  File "<console>", line 1
    "This is an "Invalid" text"
                      ^
SyntaxError: invalid syntax
```

Shell Example 7.8 Illegal Quotation Mixing

In this last example, Python identifies two strings, "This is an", and "Text", and stumbles on the word, "Invalid", which it unsuccessfully attempts to interpret as a Python command.

Escape Characters

When a string character follows a backslash character, \, the character is said to be *escaped* or an *escape character.* The backslash tells that Python has a different meaning than expected. Quotes normally terminate a string but when a backslash precedes a quotation, the quotation character is displayed instead. Quotations following backslashes are used when the same type of quote needs to be referenced in a string delimited by the same type. Shell Example 7.9 correctly escapes single quote characters.

```
>>> 'This string has a single \' quote and is bound by \'single\' quotes'
"This string has a single ' quote and is bound by 'single' quotes"
```

Shell Example 7.9 Escaped Single Quote Characters

There are multiple types of special escape characters; characters when following a backslash, \, take on special string formatting functionality. The most common escape character types are *\t*, the tab character, *\f*, the formfeed character, and *\n*, the newline or linefeed character. Shel Example 7.10 demonstrates escaped tabs and linefeeds.

```
>>> print('This is an example of a \t tab character')
This is an example of a          tab character
>>> print('This is an example of a \n linefeed character')
This is an example of a
 linefeed character
```

Shell Example 7.10 Escaped Tab and Linefeed

Raw Strings

Raw strings are used when backslashes and other special characters, such as \, -, *]*, *^*, *$*, *, . are required but without the use of the escaping backslash character, \. A preceding *r* or *R* character in front of a string is required to construct a raw string. Shell Example 7.11 Creates a raw string.

```
>>> print(r'Here are unescaped \, -, ], ^, $, *, . special characters')
Here are unescaped \, -, ], ^, $, *, . special characters
```

Shell Example 7.11 Raw String Creation

Be aware that an unescaped backslash, \, at the end of a raw string will generate an error. Shell Example 7.12 shows how not to terminate a string with a backslash.

```
>>> print(r'This is an illegal raw string \')
  File "<console>", line 1
    print(r'This is an illegal raw string \')
                                            ^
SyntaxError: EOL while scanning string literal
```

Shell Example 7.12 Incorrect String Terminating Backslash

Formatted Output

Strings have many uses such as in expressions which echo messages to display devices, input for functions, (such as input for *print()* functions), and content for reading and writing external file data. Rarely are string values taken literally from between quotes. Programmers often need to create dynamic messages which change with respect to script behavior. Shell Example 7.13 creates a static, non-dynamic string.

```
>>> print('This is a literal string that cannot be altered')
This is a literal string that cannot be altered
```

Shell Example 7.13 Non-Dynamic String

Python provides four methods for generating dynamic string content: formatted string literals, the str.format() method, manual formatting, and old school formatting.

Formatted String Literals

Formatted string literals are considered as the most modern and official way of formatting strings in Python. String literals are a Python 3 feature and may not be covered in older Python references. They are created by preceding a string bound by quotes with an *f* or an *F* character. Shell Example 7.14 creates a formatted string literal.

```
>>> f'This is a formatted string literal'
'This is a formatted string literal'
>>> F'This is another formatted string literal'
'This is another formatted string literal'
```

Shell Example 7.14 String Literal Creation

Inside the string, any expression bound by curly braces, *{}*, is evaluated and the result inserted between. Shell Example 7.15 inserts variable values in the curly braces.

```
>>> first = 32
>>> second = -27
>>> f'the sum of {first} and {second} is {first+second}'
'the sum of 32 and -27 is 5'
```

Shell Example 7.15 String Literal Expression Evaluation

The format of the evaluated expression is configured using the colon character, *:*. When an integer follows the color, Python ensures that the string will be minimally as wide the integer specified, even when white spaces are required. In Shell Example 7.16, white spaces are set in string curly braces, after the colons.

```
>>> a = 'Tech'
>>> b = 'Artists'
>>> c = 'Program'
>>> f'{a:10}{b:10}{c:10}real-time'
'Tech      Artists   Program   real-time'
```

Shell Example 7.16 Colon Integer In String Literal

When the colon is followed by a decimal float, the evaluated output is rounded to the float's number places. (A float is a number containing decimals. For example, `30.0` is a float, while `30` is an integer.) In Shell Example 7.17, decimals after colons set float value precision.

```
>>> pi = 3.1415926
>>> print(f'pi = {pi:.3f}')
pi = 3.142
```

Shell Example 7.17 Colon Decimal Float in String Literal

Str.format() Method

The str.format() technique formats text like formatted string literals except that the contents of the curly braces are configured by the content of the trailing *.format()* method. This function evaluates expressions before inserting them between the curly braces. Shell Example 7.18 demonstrates the str.format() method.

```
>>> first = -13.39
>>> second = 36.76
>>> print('The sum of {} and {} is {}'.format(first, second, first+second))
The sum of -13.39 and 36.76 is 23.37
```

Shell Example 7.18 Str.format Technique

Inserting integers between the curly braces allows users to change their order. Shell Example 7.19 shows how the order of the string values can be altered.

```
>>> print('{0}, {1}, {2}, {3}, {4}'.format('Mark', 'Jerry', 'Bob1',
'Bob2', 'Allen'))
Mark, Jerry, Bob1, Bob2, Allen
>>> print('{3}, {0}, {4}, {1}, {2}'.format('Mark', 'Jerry', 'Bob1',
'Bob2', 'Allen'))
Bob2, Mark, Allen, Jerry, Bob1
```

Shell Example 7.19 Integers in Curly Braces

Evaluated expressions are also configured using colons. An integer following a colon configures the total number of spaces the number will occupy. When the total number of spaces is followed by a period and a single float value, the result is rounded to that number of places. When the total number of spaces is preceded by a *0*, the result is padded with *0s*. Shell Example 7.20 changes decimal precision and zero padding.

```
>>> pi = 3.1415926
>>> nat = 2.7182818
>>> print('{0} {1}'.format(pi, nat))
3.1415926 2.7182818
>>> print('{0:10} {1:10}'.format(pi, nat))
 3.1415926  2.7182818
>>> print('{0:10.3f} {1:10.3f}'.format(pi, nat))
     3.142      2.718
>>> print('{0:10.2f} {1:10.2f}'.format(pi, nat))
      3.14       2.72
>>> print('{0:010.2f} {1:010.2f}'.format(pi, nat))
0000003.14 0000002.72
```

Shell Example 7.20 Formatting with Colons, Periods, Floats, and Zeros

Manual Formatting

Manual formatting allows programmers to display result strings from left to right. Shell Example 7.21 demonstrates manual formatting.

```
>>> pi = 3.1415926
>>> nat = 2.7182818
>>> print(pi, nat)
3.1415926 2.7182818
```

Shell Example 7.21 Manual String Formatting

Addition symbol characters, +, are used to combine strings. Shell Example 7.22 uses the addition symbol to combine strings.

```
>>> print('foo'+'bar')
foobar
>>> 'foo'+'bar'
'foobar'
```

Shell Example 7.22 Formatting with Addition Symbol Characters

When used within other functions, such as *print()*, a comma also combines strings and inserts a single white space between each string. Shell Example 7.23 uses commas to organize strings.

```
>>> a = 'foo'
>>> b = 'bar'
>>> print(a, b, 'snafu')
foo bar snafu
```

Shell Example 7.23 Formatting Using Commas

This technique may seem the most intuitive to novice programmers. However, it is also the most cumbersome and restrictive. White spaces and line feeds must be combined as additional strings. Shell Example 7.24 demonstrates how line feeds and white spaces are inserted into strings.

```
>>> print(pi, '\n       ', nat)
3.1415926
        2.7182818
```

Shell Example 7.24 Additional White Spaces and Line Feeds

Alternative string functions may be required for generating fancier formatted strings.

Old School Formatting

The old school formatting technique is very thorough and should handle any formatted text requirement. It is also complicated. To avoid unnecessary confusion, the description provided in this section only introduces the most common applications.

Based loosely on the C language function *sprintf()*, old school formatting requires a percent character, %, as a specifier and the known type of variable being displayed. The structure of old school formatting is: Language Template 7.1 contains the old school formatting technique.

```
'string' % (values)
```

Language Template 7.1 Old School Formatting structure

Any percent character instance within strings is replaced with zero or more elements from the values, represented as tuples. Shell Example 7.25 shows how variable string variables are substituted.

```
>>> pi = 3.1415926
>>> nat = 2.7182818
>>> print('%f %f' % (pi, nat))
3.141593 2.718282
```

Shell Example 7.25 Old School Formatting

Each percent character instance must be accompanied by the variable type it represents. As of this book's writing, there are 16 types that may be converted in the string. Three of these types are used more than all others: 'd' for integers, 'f' for floats, and 's' for strings. Shell Example 7.26 demonstrates integers, floats and strings.

```
>>> myInt = 76
>>> myFloat = -28.84
>>> myString = 'Tech Art'
>>> print('print an integer %d, a float %f, and a string %s' %
(myInt, myFloat, myString))
print an integer 76, a float -28.840000, and a string Tech Art
```

Shell Example 7.26 Variable Types and Their Corresponding Values

Similar to the str.format() technique, numbers preceding types indicate the number of spaces the converted string will occupy. Shell Example 7.27 demonstrates how display spaces are controlled.

```
>>> print('print an integer %10d, a float %10f, and a string %10s' %
(myInt, myFloat, myString))
print an integer         76, a float -28.840000, and a string   Tech Art
```

Shell Example 7.27 Controlled Display Spaces

When displaying a float type, an integer decimal following the space number will configure the float precision. Shell Example 7.28 demonstrates display of float precision.

```
>>> myFloat = -28.8493
>>> print('display a rounded float: %10.2f' % (myFloat))
display a rounded float:     -28.85
```

Shell Example 7.28 Displayed Float Precision

COMMENTING

Comments are non-executing, python code statements. They can be used to explain code, describe an algorithm, or clarify a thought process, as in Code Sample 7.2.

```
pi = 3.141592
nat = 2.7182818
# Print Pi and natural log to 5 characters
print(f'Pi={pi:.5} Nat={nat:.5}')
```

Code Sample 7.2 Inserted Comment

They can be used to make code more readable by establishing visual boundaries or landmarks. (To avoid visual clutter, attempts should be made to minimize boundary usage.) This is demonstrated in Code Sample 7.3.

```
########################
# Define my variables
########################
pi = 3.141592
nat = 2.7182818

########################
# print my values
########################
print(f'Pi={pi:.5} Nat={nat:.5}')
```

Code Sample 7.3 Comments Enhancing Readability

Comments are also used to prevent execution of code when testing. They are not executed and effectively toggle code while debugging, as demonstrated in Code Sample 7.4.

```
print('This code is executed')
#print('This code is not executed')
```

Code Sample 7.4 Debugging Comment

There are two commenting structures in Python: the pound character, #, and the triple quote. Python ignores all code on a line after a pound character. Pound characters, #, may appear at the start or anywhere else on a line.

The results of Code Sample 7.5 are shown in Shell Example 7.29.

```
#This is a comment in script
print("Tech Art") # at the end of a line
#print("Rocks!")
```

Code Sample 7.5 Comments Posted Anywhere

```
>>> Tech Art
```

Shell Example 7.29 Script Output

The third line of Code Sample 7.5 starts with a #. Notice that the legitimate code after, (*print("Rocks!")*), is not executed.

Code Sample 7.6 demonstrates how triple quote comments empower programmers to create multi-line comments. Triple quotes may be ''' or """, as long as they consistently mark comment start and end.

```
''' This is an example
    of a multi-line comment
    and may be extended to as many lines as needed
'''
```

Code Sample 7.6 Multi-line Comment

The results of Code Sample 7.7 are shown in Shell Example 7.30.

```
print("this is an example of ")
"""
This is an example of
print("multi-line editing")
No code within the Triple quotes
print('is executed')
"""
```

Code Sample 7.7 Multi-line Comments to Turn Off Code

Produces the following output:

```
>>> this is an example of
```

Shell Example 7.30 Script Output

Be aware that mixing quote types within the comments will produce syntax errors. Like single and double quote strings, triple quotes are regular Python strings that allow new lines.

EXPRESSIONS

Expressions are sophisticated computer science components that define the Python language structure. Mastering the nuances of expressions provides users with the greatest amount of power to utilize Python to its potential. However, full coverage of expressions requires a dedicated chapter. Most beginning technical artist programmers only need to be familiar with the most primitive expression aspect: expressions are snippets of code evaluated before execution of the entire command line.

While Python is structured by multiple expression types, this chapter covers three technical artists need to be aware of: mathematical, comparison, and Boolean operations. Other types of expressions, such as *lambda*, are introduced later in book.

Mathematical Operations

Any mathematical operator, (+, -, *, /), constructs a mathematical expression operation. Expression are evaluated before the entire Python code line is executed. Python follows a strict order when evaluating mathematical expressions. The precedence of mathematical operators is covered in Table 7.1.

TABLE 7.1 Python Mathematical Operator Precedence

Operators	*Operations*	*Order of Evaluation*
()	Parenthesis	Evaluated first. Nested Parentheses have precedence. Left to Right.
**	Exponentiation	Evaluated second. Right to Left.
* / // %	Multiplication, Division, Floor Division, Modulus	Evaluated third. Left to Right.
+ -	Addition, Subtraction	Evaluated fourth. Left to Right.

Evaluating complex mathematical expressions, as in demonstrated in Code Sample 7.8, effectively demonstrates operator precedence.

```
a = 2
x = 5
b = 3
c = 7
y = a * x **2 + b * x + c
print(f'y = {y}')
z = a * x % a + b / (x - a)
print(f'z = {z}')
```

Code Sample 7.8 Math Expression Operator Order

Code Sample 7.8 produces the output in Shell Example 7.31.

```
y = 72
z = 1.0
```

Shell Example 7.31 Code Output

The variable *y* is evaluated in the following order. The exponent is the highest order of evaluation:

$$y = a * x * * 2 + b * x + c$$

$$y = a * 5 * * 2 + b * x + c$$

$$y = a * 25 + b * x + c$$

Multiplication is the next highest in priority:

$$y = 2 * 25 + 3 * 5 + c$$

$$y = 50 + 15 + c$$

Addition and subtraction are the lowest in priority:

$$y = 50 + 15 + 7$$

$$y = 72$$

When evaluating the variable z, there is no exponent but there is a parenthesis which is evaluated first:

$$z = a * x \% a + b / (x - a)$$

$$z = a * x \% a + b / (5 - 2)$$

$$z = a * x \% a + b / 3$$

The next order of evaluation is *multiplication*, then *division*, and then *modulus*.

$$z = 2 * 5 \% a + b / 3$$

$$z = 10 \% 2 + 3 / 3$$

$$z = 10 \% 2 + 1$$

$$z = 0 + 1$$

The final operation in precedence is addition:

$$z = 1$$

Understanding the order of operations is crucial for accurate mathematical computations.

Comparison Operations

Comparison operations evaluate to either *Boolean True* or *False*. These tests validate the integrity of an expression which compare the numerical quantity of two values, test if one value is contained in another set, or identify if two values are equivalent.

Table 7.2 lists comparison operators and their verbal meaning:

TABLE 7.2 Python Comparison Operators

Operator	*Usage*	*Meaning*
in	`x in y`	x is contained in set y
not in	`x not in y`	x is not contained in set y
is	`x is y`	x is the same object as y
is not	`x is not y`	x and y are different value
<	`x < y`	x is less than y
<=	`x <= y`	x is less than or equal to y
>	`x > y`	x is greater than y
>=	`x >= y`	x is greater than or equal to y
!=	`x != y`	x is not equal to y
==	`x == y`	x is equal to y

The *in* and *not in* operators are reserved for testing for the inclusion in sequences. Sequences, such as tuples, lists and dictionaries, are covered in Chapter 10. Strings are also sequences: as demonstrated in Shell Example 7.32.

```
>>> 'a' in 'apple'
True
>>> 'x' in 'apple'
False
>>> 'x' not in 'apple'
True
```

Shell Example 7.32 `in` and `not in` Operators

Shell Example 7.33 demonstrates how numerical comparison operators, (<, <=, >, >=), test the numerical value of one number against another.

```
>>> 5 < 9
True
>>> 10 <= 9
False
>>> 5 > 7
False
>>> 5 >= 5
True
```

Shell Example 7.33 Numerical Comparison Operators

Equivalency operators, (*is, is not,* !=, ==), are functionally similar but are not the same. Operators != and == test the equivalency of two values. Operators *is* and *is not* test if the two are the same Python object type. Python object types are covered in Chapter 10. Code Sample 7.9 demonstrates equivalency operators versus *is* and *is not.*

```
a = 'apples'
b = 'oranges'
print(f'Are a and b the same Python Object? {a is b}')
print(f'Do a and b have the same value? {a == b}')

x = 100.0
y = 100
print(f'Are x and y the same Python Object? {x is y}')
print(f'Do x and y have the same value? {x == y}')

>>> Are a and b the same Python Object? False
Do a and b have the same value? False
Are x and y the same Python Object? False
Do x and y have the same value? True
```

Code Sample 7.9 Equivalency Operators

Note that value equivalency operators behave the same way regardless of the type of value. 100 == 100.0 returns *True* even though one is an integer and one is a float. Numerical values can be compared to sequences and strings. For readability purposes, convention requests that numerical values use traditionally numerical operators, (!=, ==), and non-numerical values, including strings and sequences, and use the verbal equivalency operators, (*is, is not*).

Boolean Operations

There are three Boolean operators available for combining multiple expression values when logic is required: *and*, *or*, and *not*.

The *and* operator returns *True* when both sides of the operator are also *True*. Shell Example 7.34 demonstrates the Python *and* operator.

```
False
>>> (4 < 5) and (9 < 10)
True
>>> 'apples' is 'oranges' and (4 < 5)
False
```

Shell Example 7.34 Python `'and'` Operator

The or operator returns True when at least one of the two sides is True. Shell Example 7.35 demonstrates the Python *or* operator.

```
>>> 'apples' is not 'oranges' or (4 > 5)
True
```

Shell Example 7.35 Python 'or' Operator

The *not* operator returns *True* only when the right side of the operator is *False*. Shell Example 7.36 demonstrates the Python *not* operator.

```
>>> not 'apples' is 'oranges'
True
>>> not 4 < 5
False
```

Shell Example 7.36 Python `'not'` Operator

Convention requests both sides of Boolean operators to be Boolean values. Using numerical values, string and sequences will work but their use in this context may be frowned upon in some programming circles.

CREATE A SPHERE

Many Python basics are introduced in this chapter but there is no reference yet how to use Python to interact with Houdini. This section covers the basic commands required to create objects in Houdini. The code provides instructions for creating basic spheres and is easily altered to create other geometric objects.

A new script is required to demonstrate this example. On the *My Python* tool shelf, as seen in Figure 7.5, press right mouse button and select *New Tool*.

After the script editor pops up, enter *MakeSphere*, into the *Name* slot and *Make Sphere* into the *Label* slot. Select the *Script* tab, shown in Figure 7.6, to enter the script editor.

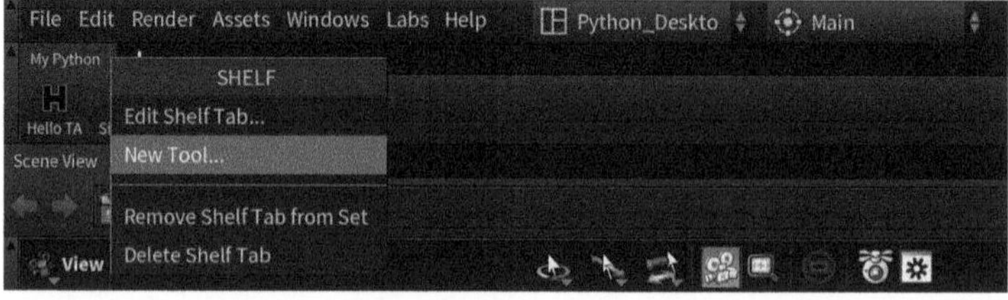

FIGURE 7.5 Create a new tool.

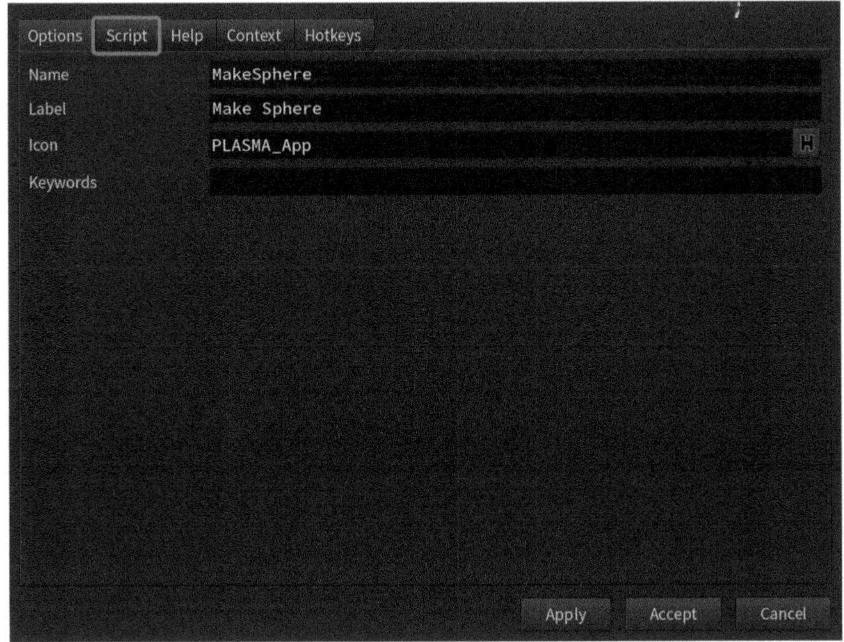

FIGURE 7.6 Name and label the script.

Enter Code Sample 7.10 in the editor and select the *Accept* button, as shown in Figure 7.7, to save the script and hide the editor:

```
# Grab the top level object
objNode = hou.node("/obj")

# Create the sphere's container
container = objNode.createNode("geo", "sphereGeo")

# Create a sphere SOP
sphere = container.createNode("sphere", "mySphere")
```

Code Sample 7.10 Create A sphere

Press the *MakeSphere* button on the tool shelf, shown in Figure 7.8, and a simple sphere appears in the Houdini display.

The first line of code creates a Python anchor variable, named *objNode*. The path in the Houdini node command, '*/obj*', identifies where to set the anchor. In this situation, '*/obj*', references the location where all of the Houdini scene objects are created. This is called the Houdini *Object Level*.

```
# Grab the top level object
objNode = hou.node("/obj")

# Create the sphere's container
container = objNode.createNode("geo", "sphereGeo")

# Create a sphere SOP
sphere = container.createNode("sphere", "mySphere")
```

FIGURE 7.7 Make sphere code.

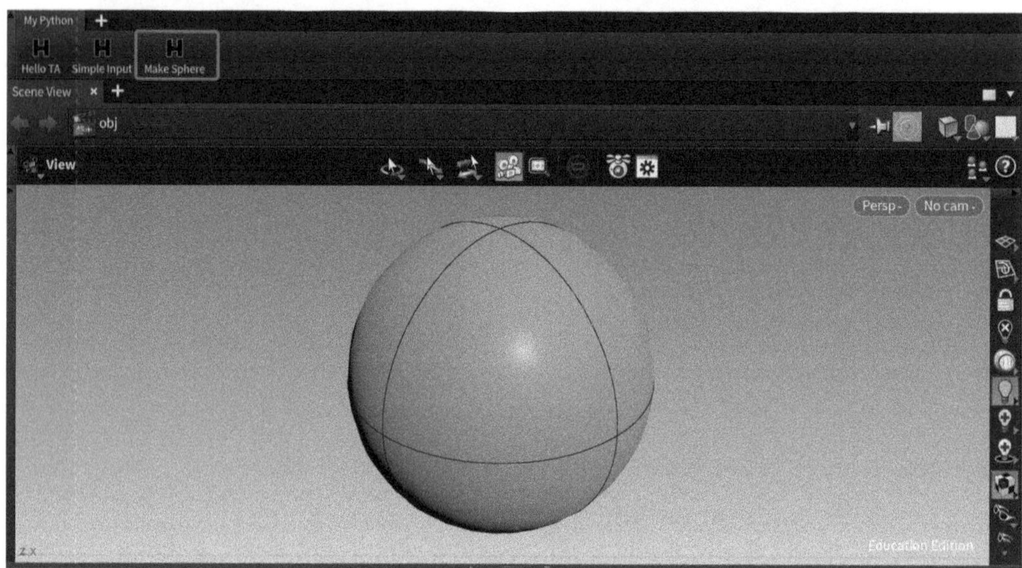

FIGURE 7.8 Make sphere results.

In this first command to create the anchor, *hou.node*, is preceded by the word, *hou*. This word tells Python that the following command is not a built-in command in the standard Python library and is provided by Houdini as a tool set. More information on non-Python tool libraries is discussed in Chapter 9.

The next line of code creates an object in the Houdini scene and stores it in a variable named *container*. Python is an object-oriented language and the anchor variable, *objNode*, has certain capabilities. The command, *objNode.createNode*, taps into the *objNode* functionality to create a new Houdini scene object and assigns it to the *container* variable. The string *'geo'* tells *objNode* what type of object to create. In this situation, *'geo'* means create an empty geometry container. (Other objects to create in the *Object Level* include cameras, ('cam'), and lights, ('light').) The string, *'sphereGeo'*, provides the name of the container as it is displayed in the Houdini scene.

The last line of code creates a sphere inside the object container, *container*, and assigns it to a variable named *sphere*. The variable *container* is a child of *objNode* and inherits all of its capabilities, including creating a new node. The variable *container* uses the same command, *createNode*, to create its own child, and assigns it to the variable *sphere*. The string, *'sphere'*, identifies what type of primitive to create. (There are many primitive objects including boxes, 'box', tubes, 'tube', doughnuts, 'torus', and rubber toys, 'testgeometry_rubbertoy'). The string, *'mySphere'*, provides a Houdini display label for the sphere object.

Three commands may seem like a lot of work for generating a sphere. The object-oriented nature of Python empowers programmers to do many things with single commands. A graphics display needs to perform many operations to generate a single sphere. Object-oriented commands provide artist-programmers with the power to have nearly infinite power over their creations. Object-oriented programming is covered in Chapters 11 and 12.

CONCLUSION

Before covering more complicated functionality, there are a few essential fundamentals for understanding Python. Some of these fundamentals include string formatting, commenting, and the concept of expressions.

A simple script is provided and explains how to query the user for two numbers, add them, and display the results. This script re-enforces the concepts introduced in the prior chapter and re-introduces the process for creating scripts in Houdini.

Understanding the methods for formatting text strings is essential for creating readable feedback which informs users on script progression and provides valuable debugging information. Python is a robust language and its treatment of text strings is far from simplistic. Quotations, (quotes), are used to delimit text strings. There are three types of Python quotations: single, double, and triple quotes. Instructions for proper quote usage and mixing are provided along with coverage of escape characters which structure how text messages are displayed. There are four methods for assembling dynamic strings: formatted string literals, the str.format() method, manual formatting, and the old school formatting techniques.

Comments are another essential Python structure that identifies non-executing text information. Text which does not impact script behavior is useful for communicating intention for code readers and provides valuable instruction for script maintenance. Comments are essential debugging tools. They non-destructively isolate code and manipulate flow that would otherwise be undesirable during script execution. Comments also help provide visual barriers and structures which enhance code readability. There are two commenting techniques: the # and triple quote methods.

Expressions define an essential Python language structure. While thorough coverage of expressions is beyond the scope of this chapter and book, essential mathematical, comparison, and Boolean operations are introduced. Mathematical operation precedence is crucial for structuring consistent mathematical formulas. Much of the Python structure is guided by *True* and *False* logic values. Comparison operations structure proper logical evaluations. Boolean operations glue multiple mathematical and comparison operations into more sophisticated expressions.

A script at the end of the chapter provides instructions for generating a single sphere in the Houdini display window. This example demonstrates simple usage of strings for naming objects and introduces the concept of object-oriented programming.

INTRODUCTION

Expressions were introduced in Chapter 7 as important language components that give Python its structure. *Conditional* statements and *looping* statements play significant roles in controlling logic flow. There is one Python conditional statement: the *if* statement. There are two looping statements: the *while* and *for* statements.

This chapter starts with a quick review project to reiterate how Houdini uses Python to create objects. Conditional statements are covered using *if* statements to provide a logic branching structure. Looping statements are used to repeat logic flow. *While* loops execute tasks multiple times. *For* loops are like *while* loops in that they empower programmers to repeat tasks multiple times but controlled with items called *iterators*. A larger project concludes the chapter by covering all Python topics up until that point.

REVIEW PROJECT

The last script in Chapter 7 simply demonstrates how Python is used to create objects in the Houdini editor. The following script accomplishes similar results except instead of a sphere, Roberto will be displayed. Who is Roberto? Follow this new script and find out.

Open Houdini and make sure the *Python Desktop* is the active desktop as shown in Figure 8.1.

Right mouse click on the *My Python* tool shelf and select *New Tool*. When the script editor appears, change the name to *roberto* and the label to *Roberto*. Select the *Script* tab to enter the script editor as shown in Figure 8.2.

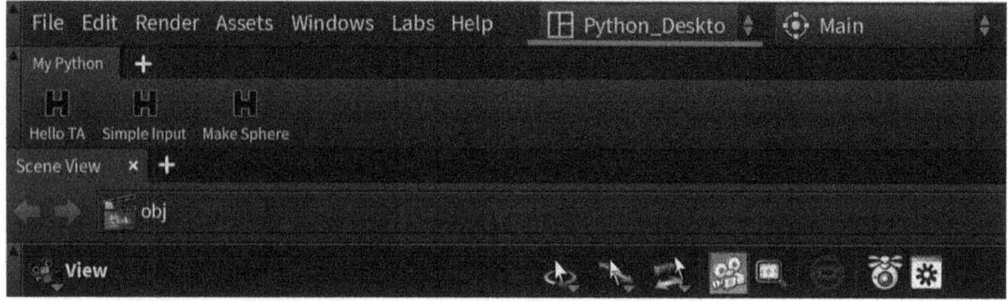

FIGURE 8.1 Python desktop is the active desktop.

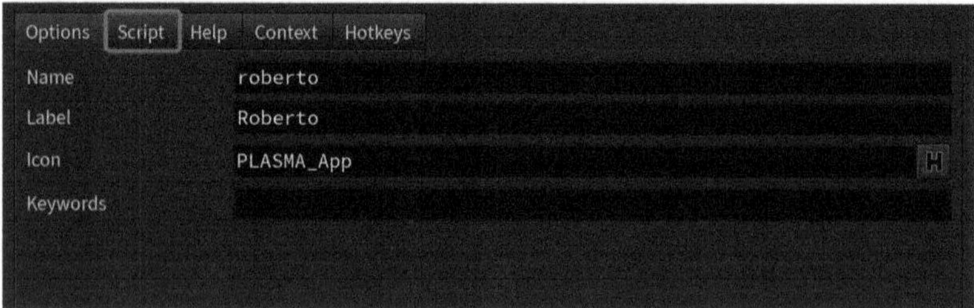

FIGURE 8.2 Create Roberto script.

DOI: 10.1201/9781003016427-8

Enter Code Sample 8.1 into the editor.

```
#grab the top-level object anchor
objNode = hou.node("/obj")

#Create the Roberto's container
container = objNode.createNode("geo", "RobertoGeo")

#create a Roberto SOP
container.createNode("testgeometry_rubbertoy", "Roberto")
```

Code Sample 8.1 Review Project

The first command line grabs the top-level object anchor and assigns it to the *objNode* variable. In the next command line, the *objNode* variable creates a geometry container, named "RobertoGeo", and assigns it to the *container* object variable. In the last line of code, the *container* object creates a rubber toy, `('testgeometry_rubbertoy')`, within itself and labels it *Roberto*.

Select the *Accept* button to save the script and close the editor as shown in Figure 8.3.

Press the *Roberto* icon on the *My Python* tool shelf. Roberto, like Figure 8.4, appears!

The key takeaway from this exercise is that while Roberto is radically different from the sphere from the prior chapter, the scripts are almost identical. The significant difference is in the first parameter of the `container.createNode` command. In the first script the value is "sphere", and in the second it is `'testgeometry_rubbertoy'`. This parameter establishes the type of object created within a Houdini object node. All Houdini objects are similar. The reader is encouraged to edit the script. Other object types may be entered into the parameter including "box", "torus", "testgeometry_pighead", and "testgeometry_squab". Note that the *Apply* button may be pressed to save the script without closing the editor window. This allows the user to rapidly change a script's parameter without opening and closing the editor interface. (Warning: the geometry containers need to be *deleted* after every invocation less they stack on top of each other every time the *Roberto* icon is pressed.)

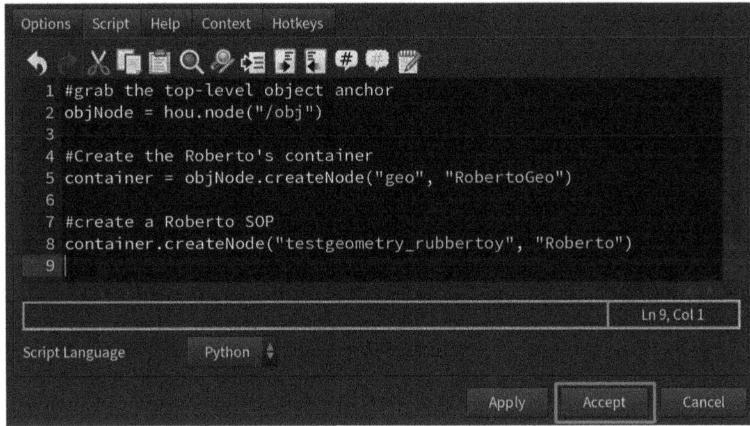

FIGURE 8.3 Accept the Roberto script and close the interface.

FIGURE 8.4 Roberto.

CODE BLOCKS

Python, like other programming languages, identifies groups of programming commands, called *code blocks*, that are executed as units and behave effectively as single commands. Many languages use special characters, such as curly braces, *{}*, to delimit or enclose code blocks. Python is a visually oriented language and avoids clutter with a rigorous indenting structure to maintain structured appearance.

Starting with zero indentation, an indented line of Python code initiates a code block. By standard, indentation must be four spaces, "   ". Technically, the number of spaces may vary but Python is very sensitive against inconsistent spacing. Code text editors may be configured to translate the *tab* key into four spaces.

Code blocks may be embedded into other code blocks. They are identified with additional indentation. The indentation number groups blocks of code.

```
Code block 1 begins
Code block 1 continues
    Code block 2 begins
    Code block 2 continues
        Code block 3 begins
    Code block 2 continues
        Code block 4 begins
Code block 1 continues
```

Language Template 8.1 Code Block Examples

In Language Template 8.1, code block 1 is identified with zero indentation. Block 2 is identified by single indentation and blocks 3 and 4 are identified by two indents. Technically, there are no limits to the amount of indentation. Blocks become challenging to track when there are more than a few per page or when one block occupies more than a single page.

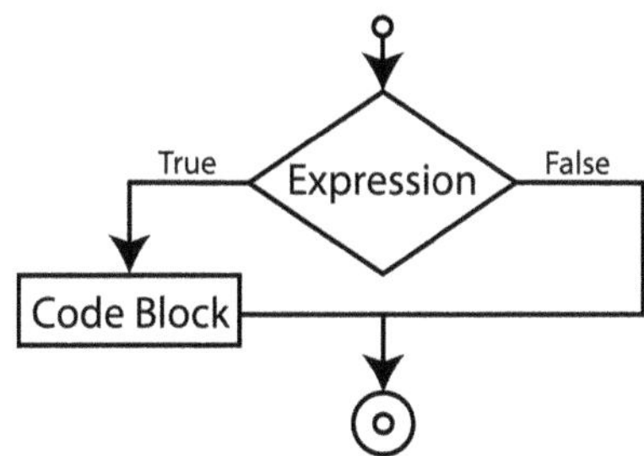

FIGURE 8.5 Python logical if flow.

CONDITIONAL STATEMENTS

The *if* conditional statement branches Python logic flow depending on the results of an expression evaluation. When the expression evaluates to positive or True, flow branches to an alternative code block. When the expression evaluates negative or false, the code block is ignored. Figure 8.5 displays how flow returns to the original block after false expression evaluation or after branched block execution.

Python conditionals are structured with the *if* statement followed by the expression and terminated with a colon. The following indented code block of Language Template 8.2 executes when the expression evaluates to *True*. Code Sample 8.2 demonstrates Python *if* statement utilization.

```
if expression == True:
    True Code Block
```

Language Template 8.2 If Statement Structure Code Sample 8.2

```
# First code block
a = 69
b = 76
c = 0

# If statements are followed by an expression and a ':'
if a < b :
    # Second code block
    c = a + b

# Flow returns to the First code block
print(f'a = {a}, b= {b}, c = {c}')

>>> a = 84, b= 76, c = 145
```

Code Sample 8.2 Python If Statement

The first three lines in Code Sample 8.2 assign values to the *a*, *b*, and *c* variables. The *if* statement evaluates the truth of the expression, "is *a* less than *b*". The code block after the *if* statement re-assigns the *c* variable. Flow returns back to the original block and prints the variable values.

Suppose the programmer wishes to execute a different code block when the expression evaluates to *False*. An alternative code block is introduced by an *else* statement which is also followed by a colon. Code Sample 8.3 demonstrates when the expression evaluates to *False*, the flow skips the first code block and continues with the block after the *else* statement.

```
# First code block
a = 84
b = 76
c = 0

# If statements are followed by the expression and a ':'
if a < b :
    # This statement is in the second code block
    c = a + b

# This block executed when expression evaluates to False
else:
    # Alternative code block
    c = a - b

# Flow returns to the original code block
print(f'a = {a}, b= {b}, c = {c}')

>>> a = 84, b= 76, c = 8
```

Code Sample 8.3 If-Else Statement

The indentation of the *else* code block is the same as the if code block. Flow skips the first indented code block and executes the block after the *else* before returning the original flow.

Additional flow alternatives are achieved with *elif* statements. (*elif* is a Python contraction of *else if*.) When the prior expression evaluates *False*, an *elif* statement introduces a new expression and an alternative code block is executed when it evaluates *True*. Like an *if* statement an expression follows the *elif* declaration and is terminated by a colon. Code Sample 8.4 demonstrates the *if-elif-else* sequence.

```
# First code block
a = 84
b = 76
c = 0

# If statements are followed by the expression and a ':'
if a < b :
    # This statement is in the second code block
    c = a + b

# This code block is evaluated when the first expression
# Evaluates to False
elif a > b:
    # Alternative code blockw
    c = a - b

# Flow returns to the original code block
print(f'a = {a}, b= {b}, c = {c}')

>>> a = 84, b= 76, c = 8
```

Code Sample 8.4 If-Elif-Else Statement

Code Sample 8.5 demonstrates how *else* statements, when combined with *if* and *elif* statements, provide default code alternatives when all other prior expressions evaluate *False* Code Sample 8.5.

```
a = 76
b = 76
c = 0

# If statements are followed by the expression and a ':'
if a < b :
    # This statement is in the second code block
    c = a + b
```

```
# This code block is evaluated when the first expression
# Evaluates to False
elif a > b:
    # Alternative code block
    c = a - b

# default code block
else:
    c = a * b

# Flow returns to the original code block
print(f'a = {a}, b= {b}, c = {c}')

>>> a = 76, b= 76, c = 5776
```

Code Sample 8.5 Else Used as Default

Code Sample 8.6 demonstrates how *if* statements may be embedded, or *nested*, inside code blocks.

```
score = 84

if score > 60:
    if score > 70:
        if score > 80:
            if score > 90:
                grade = 'A'
            else:
                grade = 'B'
        else:
            grade = 'C'
    else:
        grade = 'D'
else:
```

```
    grade = 'F'

print(f'Score of {score} is letter grade {grade}')

>>> Score of 84 is letter grade B
```

Code Sample 8.6 Nested If Statements

While technically correct, utilizing embedded *if* statements introduces code that is visually cluttered and difficult to follow. Code Sample 8.7 appears cleaner and is easier to follow when equivalent *elif* statements are used.

```
score = 93

if score < 60:
    grade = 'F'
elif score < 70:
    grade = 'D'
elif score < 80:
    grade = 'C'
elif score < 90:
    grade = 'B'
else:
    grade = 'A'

print(f'Score of {score} is letter grade {grade}')

>>> Score of 93 is letter grade A
```

Code Sample 8.7 Nested Elif Statements

LOOPING STATEMENTS

One of the most important reasons why technical artists are so dependent on scripting and coding is because of code's ability to repeat tasks, or *loop*. When a process can be performed once, it can be duplicated an unlimited number of times. Sometimes the process is needed to repeat indefinitely until it is told to stop. In other situations, a specific number of repetitions are required. Python offers two structures for generating loops: the *while* statement and the *for* statement. Both structures equivalently do the same thing but their control methods change to suit the requirements of the task.

While Loops

While loops empower programmers to perform blocks of code indefinitely until told to stop. Attention must be provided to prevent the code from repeating indefinitely. A *while* statement is followed by an expression, a colon, and a block of code, as demonstrated in Language Template 8.3.

```
while expression:
    code block
```

Language Template 8.3 While Statement

Figure 8.6 displays *while* loop behavior. The block of code is repeated as long as the expression evaluates to *True* or positive value. Once the expression evaluates to *False*, zero or negative, the flow returns to the original code block. Code Sample 8.8 demonstrates basic *while* loops.

```
# Provide initial expression state
myExpression = True
# Test the expression
while myExpression:
    # While loop code block
    print('Technical Art Rocks!')
    # Adjust the value of the expression
    myExpression = False

print('Flow returns to the original block')

>>> Technical Art Rocks!
Flow returns to the original block
```

Code Sample 8.8 While Loop

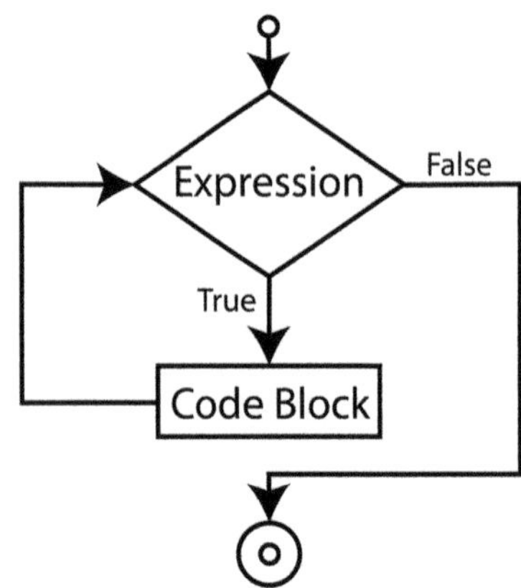

FIGURE 8.6 Python while loop logic flow.

In Code Sample 8.8, the code block is only executed once. Because the expression may evaluate to *False* at any time, the code block may execute no times, one time, or continue indefinitely. A *counter* variable typically prevents the loop from repeating forever. A counter variable is given an initial state before the loop declaration and is adjusted every time the block is executed. Typical usage of a counter variable allows the code block to loop a specific number of times. This concept is demonstrated in Code Sample 8.9 and visualized in Figure 8.7.

```
# Establish Houdini anchor
objNode = hou.node("/obj")
# Initial counter variable state
counter = 0
# Start loop
while counter < 5:
  # While Loop code block
  # Create new name
  name = f'Roberto{counter}'
  # Create geometry container
  geoContainer = objNode.createNode('geo', name)
  # Generate Roberto
  toy = geoContainer.createNode('testgeometry_rubbertoy', 'Roberto')
  # Translate Roberto in X
  toy.parm('tx').set(2*counter)

  # Increment counter
  counter += 1
```

Code Sample 8.9 Roberto While Loop Figure 8.7

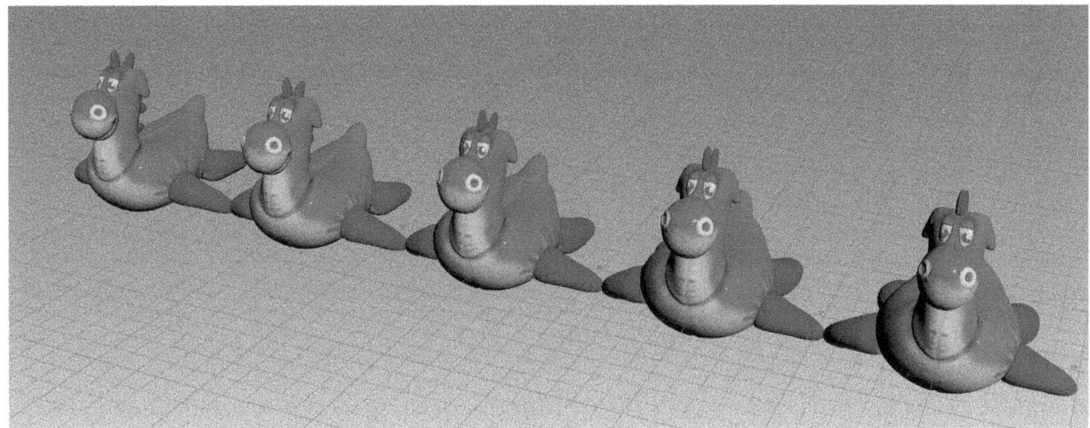

FIGURE 8.7 While loop output.

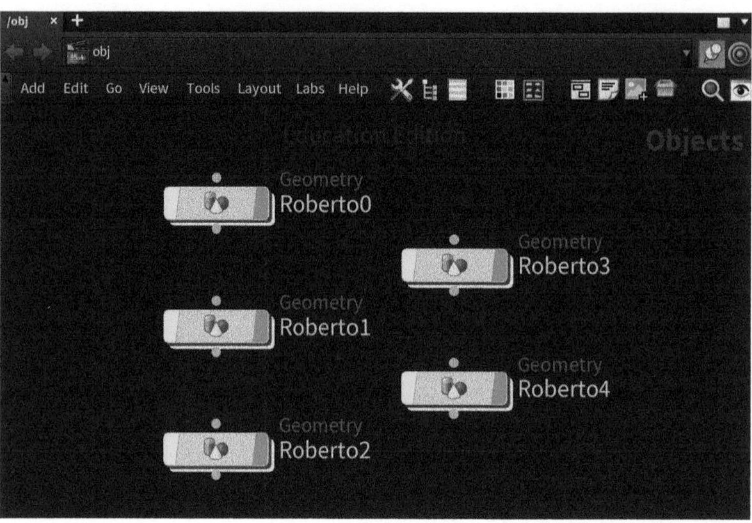

FIGURE 8.8 Houdini network after execution.

In Code Sample 8.9, the counter variable, called "counter", is given a value of `0`. The *while* statement tests if the counter value is less than `5`. As long as the counter value is less than five, the expression evaluates *True* and the loop continues. Every time the loop executes, a geometry container is created with a Roberto. In the first line of the code block, a new name variable, called *name*, is created based on the current value of the counter variable. When each container is created, it is assigned the name stored in the *name* variable. The "toy. parm("tx").set(2*counter)" statement moves each Roberto instance two times the counter value in the X-axis. This line of code takes advantage of Python object-oriented programming, introduced in Chapter 11. The last line of code increments the counter value by `1`. This code is a Python abbreviation for "counter=counter+1".

Incrementing the counter variable value pushes the counter value closer to evaluating *False* after every iteration.

When the "L" key is pressed in the Houdini network window, the containers holding each of the Roberto models are arranged in an orderly fashion. Figure 8.8 displays the results of this operation.

Note that each geometry container displays the value of the counter variable when the container is created. The variable named *counter* is not only used as the test variable in the *while* expression but is also used to label the geometry containers and control the amount of movement of each Roberto along the X-axis.

Unless performed with awareness, *while* loops are potentially dangerous as they may put a computer into an *infinite loop* state. These situations require the program or script to be forcibly interrupted or crashed and sometimes to reset the computer. When using *while* loops, always utilize some types of counter variables unless indefinite looping is desired.

Here is one extra word of warning when playing with this little script. Make sure to delete all of the Robertos before executing the script multiple times. Every time the script runs, new Robertos join in the scene. Just because they are laying on top of each other does not mean that they are not there. Before executing the script again, left mouse select all of the Robertos and hit the *delete* key to remove them all. The scene is easier to manage without hundreds of Robertos running around!

For Loops

Another Python looping structure is the *for* loop. The *for* loop is similar to a *while* statement except that it loops a code block a specific number of times by iterating over a list of objects, called a sequence. They are called "*for*" loops because they loop once for every member of the list. Special components, called i*terators*, control the number of times code block loops repeat.

Structure

Language Template 8.4 contains *for* loop structure, which is dependent on *iterators* and *sequences*. The iterator variable follows the *for* statement, followed by the word, *in*, and then the iterating sequence. It is terminated with a colon. Figure 8.9 displays the for loop structure. Code Sample 8.10 contains a simple example.

```
for iterator in sequence:
    code block
```

Language Template 8.4 For Loops

Sequences are pre-defined sets of objects called *iterables*. Abstractly, the contents of sequences may be as simple as counting numbers, words on a page, letters in a word, files in a folder, or as entire levels of games. Chapter 10 is devoted to sequences. The code block is executed once for every element, or *iterable*, in the sequence. After the code block executes for every iterable, flow returns to the prior block.

```
for counter in (1, 2, 3, 4):
    print(counter)


>>> 1
2
3
4
```

Code Sample 8.10 For Loop

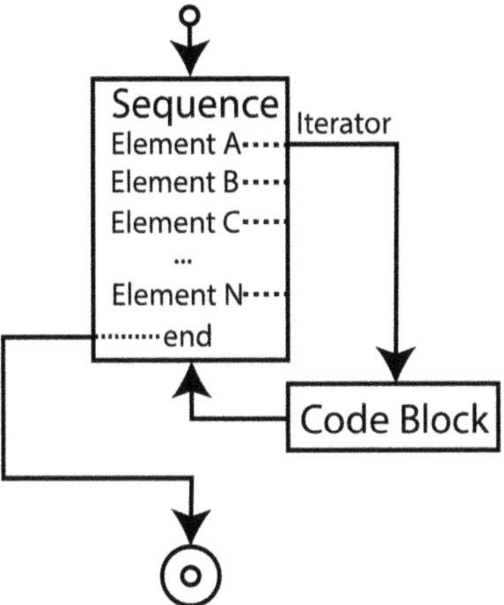

FIGURE 8.9 Python for loop structure.

In the prior code sample, the *counter* iterator represents each element of the sequence inside the code block when printing its value.

Code Sample 8.11 demonstrates how a sequence may be defined in the *for* loop command line:

```
for letter in 'Tech Art':
    print(letter)

>>> T
e
c
h

A
r
t
```

Code Sample 8.11 For Loop with Constant Iteration

Code Sample 8.12 demonstrates how a sequence may be represented by a variable.

```
Ramones = ['Johnny', 'Joey', 'Dee Dee', 'Tommy']
for musician in Ramones:
    print(musician)

>>> Johnny
Joey
Dee Dee
Tommy
```

Code Sample 8.12 For Loop with Variable Iteration

It is possible to replace, add, or remove sequence elements from within the code block while the for loop is running. While possible to do, unpredictable results may occur and are highly discouraged.

Ranges

Range sequences are commonly used in conjunction with for loops. A *range* is an unchangeable sequence type composed of numbers used for looping specific numbers of times in *for* loops, as demonstrated by Shell Example 8.1.

```
>>> list(range(10))
[0, 1, 2, 3, 4, 5, 6, 7, 8, 9]
```

Shell Example 8.1 Range Sequence

Language Template 8.5 provides *range* sequence format.

```
range(start, stop[, step])
```

Language Template 8.5 Range Sequence

The values of start, stop, and step must be integers. The values of a *range* begin with the *start* parameter and count sequentially to one less than the *stop* parameter. Because the default value of start is `0`, a *range* statement may simply ignore the start. Default and typical range sequences are demonstrated in Shell Example 8.2.

```
>>> list(range(5))
[0, 1, 2, 3, 4]

>>> list(range(6,12))
[6, 7, 8, 9, 10, 11]
```

Shell Example 8.2 Default and Standard Range Sequences

The *step* parameter controls the count increase with every iteration. The parameter defaults to `1` and may be any integer. Shell Example 8.3 provides various step range sequences.

```
>>> list(range(-3, 7, 1))
[-3, -2, -1, 0, 1, 2, 3, 4, 5, 6]

>>> list(range(2, 20, 2))
[2, 4, 6, 8, 10, 12, 14, 16, 18]

>>> list(range(0, 50, 5))
[0, 5, 10, 15, 20, 25, 30, 35, 40, 45]
```

Shell Example 8.3 Variable Step Range Sequences

Negative *step* parameters are legal. To work properly, the *start* parameters must be larger than the *end* parameter; otherwise, the range value returns nothing. Correct usage is demonstrated in Shell Example 8.4.

```
>> list(range(10, 0, -1))
[10, 9, 8, 7, 6, 5, 4, 3, 2, 1]

>>> list(range(20, -10, -4))
[20, 16, 12, 8, 4, 0, -4, -8]

>>> list(range(1, 5, -1))
[]
```

Shell Example 8.4 Negative Step Range Sequences

Language Template 8.6 integrates *range* sequences with *for* loops:

```
for iterator in range(start, stop[, step]):
    code block
```

Language Template 8.6 Range Sequences and For Loops

The range sequence replaces the list sequence. The iterator takes on each element of the *range* sequence when executing in the code block.

```
# Establish Houdini anchor
objNode = hou.node("/obj")

# Start loop
for xpos in range(5, -5, -2):
    # For Loop code block
    # Create geometry container
    geoContainer = objNode.createNode('geo', 'RobertoContainer')
    # Generate Roberto
    toy = geoContainer.createNode('testgeometry_rubbertoy', 'Roberto')
    # Translate Roberto in x-axis current xpos value
    toy.parm('tx').set(xpos)
```

Code Sample 8.13 For Loop with Range Sequence

The results for Code Sample 8.13 are similar to the *while* loop code sample. Instead of creating Robertos from position `0 to 10` by increments of 2, the *for* loop creates them from .5 to –5 in increments of –2. Instead of implementing a counter variable to control the flow and provide a position for each Roberto, the *for* loop uses the *xpos* variable to iterate over the *range* elements.

Escapes

There are times when script flow is required to eject from loops or skip portions of code blocks. These are the functions of the Python *break* and *continue* statements.

Break Statements

The *break* statement ejects script flow from the current loop. When a script executes a *break*, the flow immediately stops the current loop structure and continues with the next code block. It behaves the same in *while* and *for* loops.

```
count=0
# Prints 0 through 4
while 1:
    print(f'while ->{count}')
    count += 1

    if count >= 5:
        break

# Prints 0
for foo in range(10):
    print(f'for ->{foo}')
    break

>>> while ->0
while ->1
while ->2
while ->3
while ->4
for ->0
```

Code Sample 8.14 Break Statements in While and For Loops

The first *while* statement in Code Sample 8.14 plays with fire. The *while* loop is instructed to repeat indefinitely. The *count* variable stores the index of the executed loop.

The "count += 1" statement increments the *count* variable by *1*.

The *if* statement tests if the *count* variable is greater than or equal to `5`. When it is, the *break* command is executed and the flow ejects from the current *while* loop and continues to the *for* loop portion of the script.

The *for* loop simply iterates over the *range sequence,* [0, ..., 9]. After printing the value of the *foo* iterator only once, the *break* statement is encountered and flow exits the script.

Continue Statements

The *continue* statement skips the remainder of the code block loop and continues with the next iteration. The following statement to be executed after a *continue* in a *while loop* is the test expression. In *for* loops, flow immediately returns to the iterators. Flow exits the loop after iterating over the last sequence element and continues with the next code block.

```
for num in range(10):
  if num%2 == 0:
     print(f"found an even number:{num}")
  else:
     # Skip loop remainder and move to next loop step in the loop
     continue
     print(f"found an odd number:{num}")

>>> found an even number:0
found an even number:2
found an even number:4
found an even number:6
found an even number:8
```

Code Sample 8.15 For Loop Continue Statement

Code Sample 8.15 simply counts between `0` and `9`. When the result of the number modulus 2 is 0, an even number is announced. When the result is 1, *continue is* called and flow returns to the *for loop*. The code after the *continue* is skipped and the "Found an odd number" statement is never executed.

```
# Establish Houdini anchor
objNode = hou.node("/obj")
count = 0

# Loop to a count of 5
while count < 5:
   # Increment value of count by 1
   count += 1
   # create no more than two piggies
   if count > 2:
```

```
        continue

    # Create geometry container
    geoContainer = objNode.createNode('geo', 'PiggyContainer')
    # Generate Piggy
    piggy = geoContainer.createNode('testgeometry_pighead', 'Piggy')
    piggy.parm('tx').set(2 * count)
```

Code Sample 8.16 While Loop Continue Statement

Code Sample 8.16 demonstrates and example where only two pig heads are generated while the *while* variable, *count*, is less than 5. Before pig head generation, the counter variable, *count*, is incremented and evaluated. When the evaluation is greater than the value 2, flow skips the rest of the loop and returns to the *while* statement.

Notice the location of the *count* incrementation. Placing it anywhere else creates an infinite loop. When placed after the *if* statement, the *count* value never increases large enough to satisfy the evaluation. When placed before or after creating the pig head, *count* never increments since the portion of the loop is skipped after the prior *if* statement. Care must always be taken when implementing *while* loops.

PROJECT: VARIABLE CIRCLE

Code Sample 8.17 is longer than prior scripts. It is the combination of all the Python concepts covered to this point. The script queries the user to provide an object type, the number of desired objects, and a scale at which the objects are to be displayed, as in Figure 8.10. The number of desired objects is generated in a circle and displayed in the Houdini window. Most of the concepts in the script are covered in this and the prior two chapters.

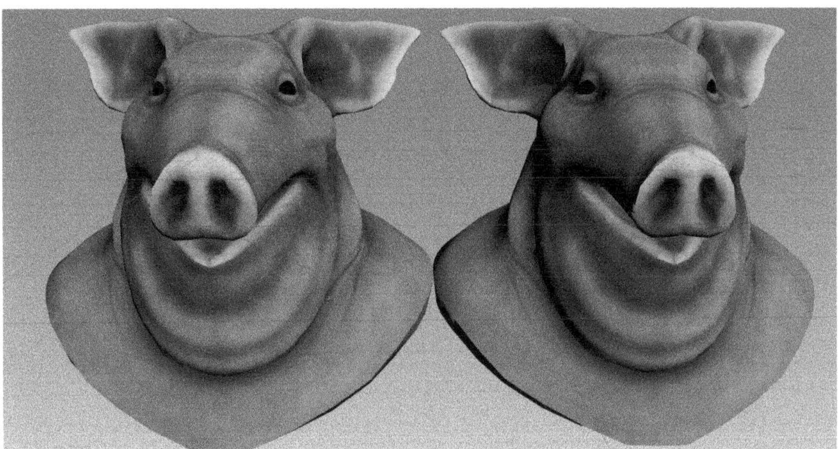

FIGURE 8.10 While loop with continue.

```
# Needed for the trig functions
import math

# Collect all of your input values
userinput = input('Enter object type(box, sphere, torus, tube) and number
of objects:')
objectType, objectNumber = userinput.split()
# convert objectNumber to an integer
objectNumber = int(objectNumber)
# create procedural scale based on number
objectScale = float(4.0/objectNumber)

# Create a top node anchor
objNode = hou.node('/obj')

# Creat constants for radius and rotational increments
# Tau is 2 * Pi
rotationIncrement = math.tau/objectNumber
pivotIncrement = 360.0 / objectNumber
pivot = 90
radius = 1.0

# Create all of your objects and position them in a circle
for counter in range(objectNumber):
    geoName = f'{objectType}{counter}'
    geoNode = objNode.createNode('geo', geoName)
# Set the scale for good measure
    geoNode.parm('scale').set(objectScale)

    #If the user types in something incorrect, this will catch the error
    if objectType == 'box':
        geotype = 'box'
    elif objectType == 'sphere':
        geotype = 'sphere'
```

```
    elif objectType == 'torus':
        geotype = 'torus'
    elif objectType == 'tube':
        geotype = 'tube'
    elif objectType == 'roberto':
        geotype = 'testgeometry_rubbertoy'
    elif objectType == 'piggy':
        geotype = 'testgeometry_pighead'
    elif objectType == 'squidward':
       geotype = 'testgeometry_squab'
    else:
        geotype = 'sphere'

    # Create the child primitive node
    child = geoNode.createNode(geotype,'child')

    # Position the objects along a circle of radius 1
    xpos = radius * math.cos(counter*rotationIncrement)
    zpos = radius * math.sin(counter*rotationIncrement)
    geoNode.parm('tx').set(xpos)
       geoNode.parm('tz').set(zpos)

    # Rotate the container such that the object always points to the outside
    geoNode.parm('ry').set(pivot)
    pivot -= pivotIncrement

    # Optional color sop to get fancy
    # Create the colorNode, set its input and turn on its display flag
    colorNode = geoNode.createNode('color', 'color')
    colorNode.setInput(0, child)
    colorNode.setDisplayFlag(True)

    # Calculate the hue value of the color node and get the Red, Green
and Blue equivalents
```

```
    # Create new Houdini Color
    myColor = hou.Color((0.0, 0.0, 0.0))
    hVal = float(counter)/objectNumber * 360.0
    sVal = 1.0
    vVal = 1.0
    myColor.setHSV((hVal,sVal, vVal))
    colorNode.parmTuple('color').set(myColor.rgb())

>> Enter object type(box, sphere, torus, tube) and number of
objects:squidward 20
```

Code Sample 8.17 Variable Circle Project

When executed with 'squidward 20' as input, the script produces the following results shown in Figure 8.11.

The first line tells Python we wish to use the advanced *math* library. The library is required to evaluate trigonometry functions. More information on Python libraries is covered in Chapter 9.

The first block of code queries the user to provide an object type and the number of desired objects. The user input string, *userinput'*, is split into two sub-string variables: *objectType* and *objectNumber*. *ObjectNumber* is converted from a string to an integer. The *objectScale* variable is a rough procedural attempt to scale the objects to fit within a circle of `radius = 1.0`. It is calculated by dividing the intended number of objects, *objectNumber*, into constant value, *4.0*.

The script then creates an anchor variable, *objNode*, which represents the parent container for all of the objects in the scene.

Two variables, *rotationIncrement* and *pivotIncrement*, are created to store the amount of rotation each object must be transformed to fit within the circle. Because the *rotationIncrement* variable is used with the *sine* function to calculate each object's position, the value must be in radians and not degrees. There are **2π** radians in a circle and thus each object is rotated `math.tau`{ XE "math.tau"}`/objectNumber` radians to complete an entire circle. *Math.tau* is a constant in the *math* library for `2*π`. The *pivotIncrement* variable is similar except each

FIGURE 8.11 Variable circle output.

object orients around its own pivot point to align in the circle. This rotation must be calculated in degrees. There are `360°` in a circle thus each object must pivot in increments of `360.0/objectNumber`. Because the first created object is the rightmost object, an initial *pivot* angle variable is provided at `90°`. We are working with a unit circle, and thus the *radius* variable must have a value of `1.0`.

A *for loop* generates the object instances. A *while* loop could have been implemented, but a *for loop* is safer. *For Loops* are good for iterating over a specific number and *while loops* repeat until a condition is met. The variable *counter* iterates precisely over the *range(objectNumber)* and removes possibility of infinite looping

The upper portion of the *for loop* block prepares and creates a container to store each new object. The string *geoName* concatenates the *objectType* and the current value of *counter*. Each newly created container is stored as a *geoNode* variable. The scale of the *geoNode* is set to the pre-computed value, *scaleObject*.

Input object validity is tested against a series of expected type names with *if* and subsequent *elif* statements. When a match is found, the string variable *geotype* is set with the appropriate geometry type. When the user enters an incorrect or unexpected name string, the type defaults to "sphere". Testing the name types enables users to enter expected type names, such as "box", incorrect names, which default to "sphere", and some unexpected names such as "squidward".

The *child* variable stores the geometry object container. When created, the object is located at the world origin. The X and Z-axis coordinates are calculated and stored in the *xpos* and *zpos* variables, using a little bit of trigonometry on a unit circle using *sine* and *cosine* functions. The angles for the *sine* and *cosine* functions start at *0.0* and increase with the *rotationIncrement* amount with each new object. The *xpos* and *zpos* values are then set into the "tx" and "tz" parameters of the *child* container.

The current value of the *pivot* variable aligns the container along the circle radius by assigning the Y-axis rotation, "*ry*". Note that the *pivot* variable is decremented each iteration of the loop by subtracting the *pivotIncrement* amount: *pivot -= pivotIncrement*. (This particular style is Python shorthand for *pivot=* pivot – *pivotIncrement*. Python operators are replaceable using this convention.)

The last two chunks of the *for loop* code block are optional and a bit advanced. They add a fancy touch by slightly changing the color of the object with each iteration of the loop. It does this in two steps. In the first step, a *color* node is created in the container along with the existing object node; *colorNode=geoNode.createNode("color", "color")*. The input to the *colorNode* is set to the object node, *child*. Within a Houdini container there may be unlimited nodes but only one is displayed. The command, *colorNode.setDisplayFlag(True)*, turns on *colorNode*'s display flag. The network in each container looks like Figure 8.12.

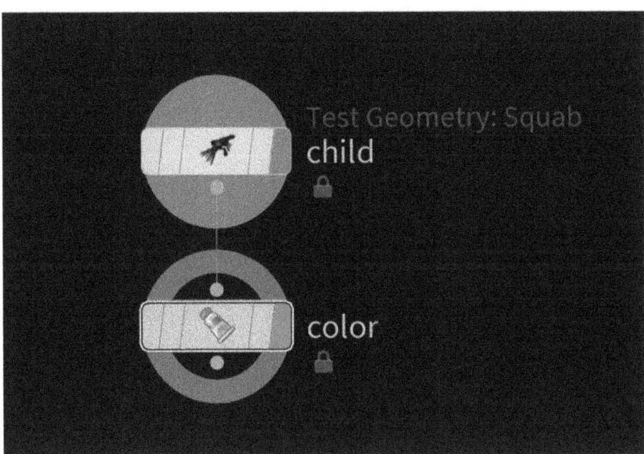

FIGURE 8.12 Container node contents.

Once the *colorNode's* display flag is turned on, its color parameter needs to be set. Normally, this is done by setting the node's parameters: *colorr, colorg,* and *colorb.* To make each color unique and bold, instead of using the *RGB* representation of color, the script borrows from the *HSV* representation; hue, saturation, and value. To access this representation, a new Houdini Color object is created and assigned to the *myColor* variable. The hue parameter ranges between `0` and `360`. A unique hue value, *hval,* is created by dividing the current *counter* value by the total number of objects, *objectNumber,* and multiplying by *360.0.* To ensure saturated and bright colors, *sVal* and vVal are set to *1.0.* The *myColor* object's HSV values are set with the *hval, sVal,* and *vVal* variables: *myColor.setHSV((hVal, sVal, vVal)).* Notice there is an extra set of parentheses, *(),* in the command. The expression *(hVal, sVal, vVal)* generates a Python sequence called a *Tuple.* Tuples allow programmers to group sets of values and access them as single units. Tuples are covered in Chapter 10. When the *colorNode's colorr, colorg,* and *colorb* parameters are set, another tuple is required as input. The *myColor* function, *myColor.rgb(),* outputs a tuple containing the red, green, and blue values converted from the equivalent hues, saturation, and value amounts. All of these tuple assignments are performed in one Python statement: `colorNode.parmTuple('color').set(myColor.rgb())`. Note that when accessing the tuple parameter, the name truncates from *"colorr", "colorg",* and *"colorb"* to simply *"color".* Each individual Houdini object now has its own unique color. The *for* loop block is complete.

CONCLUSION

Logic flow is an essential component for making any computer language functional. Not only does Python logic flow need to be easy to use but also needs to be easy to read. It does this arranging code into *code blocks.* Code blocks are groups of Python commands. Code blocks are identified with uniform indentation. (Standards preach four spaces; '   '.) Code blocks may be nested within each other and are identified with additional indention units. Organizing code in this manner removes extra characters such as curly braces, *{},* and contributes to a visually organized structure.

Python provides logical branching between two directions with the conditional *if* statement. When the result of an *if* statement expression evaluation is *True* or non-zero, the subsequent code block is executed. When the expression evaluates to *False, 0,* or negative, the code block is ignored and flow continues to the next code block. An *else* statement identifies an alternative code block. Additional alternative branches are identified with *elif* statements. *Elif* statements combine *else* and nested *if* statements to create code that is clean to read and easy to follow. When used with *elif* statements, *else* statements identify default branch directions: Language Template 8.7.

```
if expression 1:
    code block A
elif expression 2:
    code block B
else:
    code block C
```

Language Template 8.7 Conditional If Structure

Looping repeats logic flow multiple times. Python provides two loop structures: *while* and *for* loops. *While* loops are used to be repeat code blocks indefinitely. Like an *if* statement, expression evaluations control *while* loops. When expressions evaluate to *True* or non-zero, subsequent code blocks are executed and return back to the evaluations. Flow repeats until the evaluations fail. Responsibility is necessary when using *while* loops because they could loop indefinitely. Counter variables are used in the expression and modified in the code block to guarantee eventual loop termination: Language Template 8.8.

```
while expression:
    code block
```

Language Template 8.8 While Loop Structure

Python *for loops* are used to loop over groups of things, or when the number of loops needs to be a specific number. *For loops* are composed of sequences (collections of numbers), and variables which iterate through each element in the sequence, once for every pass through the subsequent code block. The iterating variable is called an *iterator*: Language Template 8.9.

```
for iterator in sequence:
    code block
```

Language Template 8.9 For Loop Structure

Python includes a special sequence type for *for loops* called a *range*. A *range* is a sequence which counts sequentially from a *start* value to one less than a *stop* value. When the increment requires to be something other than *1*, a *step* value provides an alternative increment amount: Language Template 8.10.

```
for iterator in range(start, stop[, step]):
    code block
```

Language Template 8.10 For Loop with Range

INTRODUCTION

Python logic provides two techniques for looping through blocks of code: *while* loops and *for* loops. Loops are useful in that they allow programmers to execute specific code once, multiple times or not at all. Loops have their limitations. Loops with different inputs require more loops. Tracking flow through loops within loops (*nested loops*) becomes quickly confusing. Loop output can be vague. Loops are not reusable. When their code needs to be repeated in other code locations, they must be copied and pasted. Duplicated loops must be modified to support their new locations; an error prone process.

Python *functions* address the previous concerns. They are self-contained objects. Functional input is organized and is easily tracked within the function context. Output is also easy to understand. Every function must have only one output, even when output defaults to *None*. Functions are also mobile. They are defined once and can be referenced and reused as often as needed throughout the body of the script.

This chapter provides formats for defining local functions intended to be run within the scripts they were written. Special functional behavior is available with lambdas and recursion. Lambdas are stealthy functions which may receive unlimited input but evaluate only one expression. Recursion is a powerful functional feature allowing functions to call themselves.

Functions can even be referenced externally, from other scripts. This chapter introduces and explains the hierarchal relationship with externally defined *modules* and *packages*. Mobility is an essential function characteristic. The Python functional library is extensive. Of the thousands of externally available modules and packages, there are two that technical artists must be familiar with: the *math* and *random number* libraries.

This chapter finishes with a Houdini project employing functions to create procedural fractals.

FUNCTION ORGANIZATION HIERARCHY

In the workplace, the military, a family, or any social organization, hierarchy establishes who is responsible for getting what work needs to be done. The boss delivers abstract requests. Without diving into management theory, the boss' best use of time comes from providing non-specific instruction to her underlying managers. The boss may make very specific and precise requests to anyone within the organization. However, with all that needs to be accomplished, she would spend most of her energy breaking down tasks and delegating them to individuals. Figure 9.1 shows how this is carried out. Managers assume most of that responsibility, allowing the boss to return to larger problems and strategies. Managers receive abstract requests from the boss, break them down into specific tasks, and delegate them to individuals underneath them. The process continues until the most defined tasks are accomplished by the lowest members of the hierarchy.

When the organization functions effectively, the boss does not need to understand the minute details managers perform as long as the tasks are completed. (Like bosses, upper level managers do not need to understand the task details of lower level managers.) Managers are responsible for distributing tasks to their teams and monitoring their progress.

Python functions perform similarly as how managers contribute to large organizations. They receive abstract requests with whatever information is given to them. They identify the necessary tasks, delegate them to other

 DOI: 10.1201/9781003016427-9

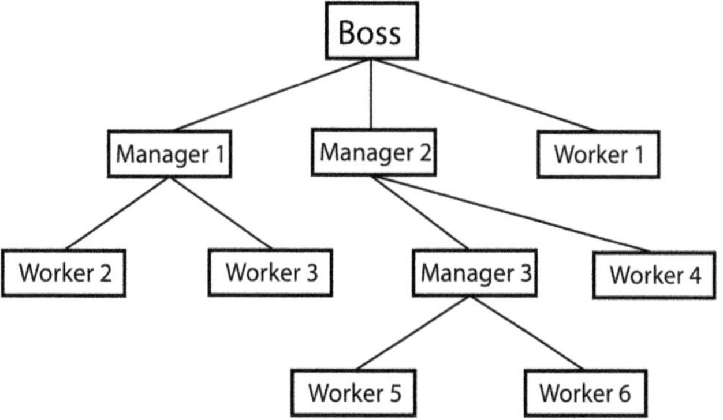

FIGURE 9.1 Functional organization hierarchy.

functions or specific lines of code, and return the accumulated results. Invoking structures are not concerned with how functions generate their results. They are only concerned with returned output from supplied input.

Just as organizational bosses are resourceful, so too are functions. When bosses realize that their organizations do not have the resources to accomplish their desired goals, they employ external collaborators and contractors. Python scripts do not need to generate all new code for their tasks. From artificial intelligence to physics simulations, they have access to externally generated content to assist with any situation. There are three tiers of external functionality: local functions, modules, and packages.

Local Functions

No amount of external code will address every possible functional need. Local functions address context specific requests. They provide specific solutions for specific tasks by conditioning data for input to be used with other functions, digesting returned output, and returning their results to their invoking entities.

Language Template 9.1 defines how local Python functions are invoked.

```
functionName(argument 1, argument 2, ..., argument N)
```

Language Template 9.1 Python Function Invocation

Arguments define the desired functional input. The order and content of the input are crucial for the function to behave properly. Prior understanding how input is formatted to meet the requirements of specific functions is required. The number of arguments is dependent on the function structure. Some functions may require no input, while, others require libraries of data.

All functions must return some type of result. Often functional results are assigned to variables. Language Template 9.2 defines how function values are returned to variables.

```
variableX = functionName(argument1, argument2, ..., argumentN)
```

Language Template 9.2 Assigning Function Results to Variable

Functions may return any single objects other than keywords. By default, when functions return nothing, the value *None* is received. While *None* contains no direct value, it is a special value and could be implemented to indicate function failure. Code Sample 9.1 demonstrates how different functions return different objects.

```
foo = range(5)
fooContent = list(foo)
print(fooContent)

>>> [0, 1, 2, 3, 4]
```

Code Sample 9.1 Functions in Use

While *range* is a Python sequence, the command *range()* is still a function and returns the requested range sequence. The results of the *range()* function are assigned to the *foo* variable. The *list()* function converts its input to a displayable list sequence. (List sequences are covered in Chapter 10.) The *list()* results are assigned to *fooContent*. Finally, the *print()* function converts *fooContent* into a string and pushes it to the display.

Code Sample 9.1 contains a lot of code for simple output. Functions may provide input for other functions. It can be converted into a single line of code, as demonstrated with Code Sample 9.2.

```
print( list( range(5)))
>>> [0, 1, 2, 3, 4]
```

Code Sample 9.2 Collapsed Functions

There are no output differences between the two scripts. They both produce the same results from the same input. The second example is simply more concise than the prior. The *range()* function is an input argument for the *list()* function which provides input for the *print()* function. The ability to collapse functional output to other functions may seem challenging to read at first. With practice and always starting from the inside and working outwards, collapsing functions produces clean and efficient code.

Modules

Modules are external files containing collections of functions. The functions are typically encompassed by a central theme. For example, the functions within the *math* module provide mathematical functionality beyond what is provided within core Python.

Because modules are not contained with local scripts, they must be brought in using the *import* statement. Language Template 9.3 defines how the *import* command tells Python to read in all of the functions contained within an external module and make them available as if they were defined locally.

```
# Loads external module for local availability
import moduleName
```

Language Template 9.3 Importing Modules

Language Template 9.4 defines how module functions are invoked by prefixing them with the module name followed by a period ('.'), the function name identifier and its arguments. Code Sample 9.3 uses the Python *math* module.

```
moduleName.identifier(functionArguments)
```

Language Template 9.4 Function Invocation

```
import math

numberWedges = 10
angleIncrement = 360.0 / numberWedges

angle = 0
for wedge in range(numberWedges):
    print(f'{math.sin(math.radians(angle)):.5f}')

    angle += angleIncrement

>>> 0.00000
0.58779
0.95106
0.95106
0.58779
0.00000
-0.58779
-0.95106
-0.95106
-0.58779
```

Code Sample 9.3 Math Module Usage

The first line of code in Code Sample 9.3 imports the *math* module. The number of desired wedges is stored in the *numberWedges* variable and is used to calculate the angular increase for every wedge, *angleIncrement*. An angle register is initialized with the *angle* variable. Within the *for* loop, the *wedge* variable iterates through the range created by *numberWedges*. The print statement makes extensive usage of the *math* module. The *angle* variable starts at *0.0* and increases by *angleincrement* with every iteration of the loop. Trigonometry in the *math* module requires its angles to be in radians and not degrees. The *math.radians(angle)* call converts the number of degrees stored in *angle* into radians. The returned value, stored in radians, inputs to the sin function, *math.sin ()*.

The remainder of the print function formats the output to five decimal places. The loop finishes by incrementing the angle amount by *angleIncrement.*

When importing modules, module functions are placed inside *namespaces.* In the *math.radians*() example, math is the namespace which identifies radians to be from the math module. Module namespaces prevent Python from being confused when multiple imported modules share the same function names. Namespaces also behave as excellent references for programmers tracking function origination.

Programmers may wish to create pseudonyms for their imported libraries to shorten their names for brevity. These are known as *aliases.* Language Template 9.5 defines how aliases are created by following the import statement and module name with an *as* command followed by the new namespace. Code Sample 9.4 creates an alias, *rand*, for the *random* library.

```
import moduleName as newNamespace
```

Language Template 9.5 Alias Namespace Assigned to Imported Module

```
import random as rand

print(rand.randint(69, 91))

>>> 74
```

Code Sample 9.4 Alias Module Name Space

In Code Sample 9.4, the *import* statement reads in the *random number* library and gives it the local alias of *rand*. The next line accesses the *random number* module function, *randint()*, to return a random integer between the values of *69* and *91*. The return value is inputted to the *print()* function.

For clarity and conciseness, programmers may wish to import only a subset of functions instead of the entire module library. In these situations, Language Template 9.6 defines how the *from* command imports a list of desired function identifiers from the module.

```
from moduleName import identifierA(, identifierB, identifierC, …)
```

Language Template 9.6 Importing Identifiers from Modules

Importing individual function on unique lines is valid. However, convention encourages all function from the same module to be imported on the same line.

There are situations when programmers not only wish to import entire modules but also remove their namespaces. Language Template 9.7 defines how namespaces are removed when the list of function identifiers is replaced with the wildcard symbol, *. Code Sample 9.5 removes the module namespace.

```
from moduleName import *
```

Language Template 9.7 Removing Module Namespace

```
from math import *

angle = 90

print(f'sine of {angle} = {sin(radians(angle)):.3}')
print(f'cosine of {angle} = {cos(radians(angle)):.3}')

>>> sine of 90 = 1.0
cosine of 90 = 6.12e-17
```

Code Sample 9.5 Removing Math Module Namespace

The import statement in Code Sample 9.5 imports the entire *math* module and removes the namespace. No namespace is required when the print statement invokes the *sin()*, *cos()*, and *radians()* functions.

Attention must be provided when importing using wildcards without namespaces. While feasible, this is generally discouraged. Imported functions contain names which clash with local functions, resulting in confusing bugs. Programmers cannot use namespaces once they have been removed. Python throw errors and complains of undefined names. Namespaces provide clarity and are highly encouraged.

Programmers may wish to change the name of a function identifier. Language Template 9.8 defines how this is done using the *from* statement followed by the module name, the *import* command, the identifier, the *as* command, and finally the new function identifier name. Code Sample 9.6 creates a new name, *sn*, for the sine function.

```
from moduleName import identifier as newName
```

Language Template 9.8 Renaming Function Identifier

```
from math import sin as sn

angle = 0

print(f'sine of {angle} = {sn(angle):.3}')
>>> sine of 0 = 0.0
```

Code Sample 9.6 Converting Identifier Name

The first line Code Sample 9.6 imports the *sin()* function from the *math* module and changes its local name to *sn*. The function call to *print()* uses the new function name, *sn*. Note, the namespace was not required to call the function after rename.

Packages

Packages are collections of modules arranged into folders. Package sub-folders are called *sub-packages*. While modules are collections of functions related with a common purpose, packages are assemblages of modules related to a common theme. Take for example, a fictional tool package of modules related to real-time world development as shown in Figure 9.2.

Note that for Python to consider a folder to be a package, there needs to be a *__init__.py* file located in the folder. This file contains instructions telling Python what to do when the package is included. In the simplest situation, the file is empty. The *__init__.py* file prevents folders with common names from hiding other modules and functions that may interfere with each other.

To import package modules, Language Template 9.9 is used. Code Sample 9.7 demonstrates how sub-packages are imported.

```
import package.sub-package(.sub-package. ...).module
```

Language Template 9.9 Importing Package Modules

```
import rtworld.character.skeleton

corneliusSkeleton = rtworld.character.skeleton.initBiped(name='Cornelius')
```

Code Sample 9.7 Importing Sub-package Modules

The *initBiped()* function is found deep within the *skeleton.py* module in the *character* sub-package in the *rtworld* package. Notice how the nested namespaces, *rtworld.character.skeleton*, show the structure of where things are imported from. When accessing functions within package modules, full package names must be referenced.

```
rtworld/                                        # Top Level Package
        __init__.py                             # Initialize the rtworld package
        character/                              # Sub-packages related to characters
                __init__.py                     # Initialize the character sub-package
                anim.py
                mocap.py
                skeleton.py
                rig.py
        env/                                    # Sub-package related to environments
                __init__.py
                hardSurface.py
                organics.py
                props.py
        common/                                 # Sub-package related to common tools
                __init__.py
                mesh.py
                textures.py
```

FIGURE 9.2 Fictional package layout.

Note the parentheses after *initBiped* in the previous example. The keyword *name='Cornelius'* argument is declared in the *initBiped()* argument list. The technique of labeling function arguments is covered later in this chapter.

As an alternative to typing the full sub-package name when referencing a function, Language Template 9.10 defines how the entire submodule may be loaded.

```
from package.sub-package(.subpackage...) import module
```

Language Template 9.10 Importing Entire Submodules

Code Sample 9.8 demonstrates how this techniques removes the need for package prefix inclusion.

```
from rtworld.common import mesh
loRezMesh = mesh.polyreduce(mesh=RudeyMesh, reductionLevel=2)
```

Code Sample 9.8 Referencing Submodule Functions

Language Template 9.11 defines how indicvidual functions may be imported.

```
from package.sub-package(.subpackage...).module import function
```

Language Template 9.11 Importing Submodule Functions

Code Sample 9.9 is an example of how the full package prefix name is ignored when imported with this strategy.

```
from rtworld.environment.hardSurfaces import roundEdges
smoothSword = roundEdges(object=roughSword, cuspAngle=60)
```

Code Sample 9.9 Submodule Function without Package Prefix

When authoring code from within a package or among multiple other modules, sibling packages may be accessed using relative imports. Instead of providing full paths of desired modules, they are imported using only their relative locations to current code. Language Template 9.12 defines how other modules within concurrent packages may be accessed using a period, '.', for the path.

```
from . import module
```

Language Template 9.12 Importing Sibling Modules within Packages

Suppose, for example, when programming in the *character* submodule, the *anim.py* module is required. Code Sample 9.10 demonstrates this technique.

```
from . import anim
baseClip = anim.createEmptyClip()
```

Code Sample 9.10 Functions from Sibling Modules

Language Tempolate 9.13 defines how different sub-packages are accessed using double periods, '..', as the sub-package path.

```
from .. import sub-package
```

Language Template 9.13 Importing Alternative Sub-packages

When programming in the *character* sub-package, the *common* sub-package is imported using relative pathing. Code Sample 9.11 demonstrates how relative pathing can be used to import sub-packages.

```
from .. import common
clampTexture = common.texture.setWrapMode(myTexture, 'clamp')
```

Code Sample 9.11 Accessing Alternative Sub-packages

Language Template 9.14 defines how modules are imported for other sub-packages.

```
from ../sub-package import module
```

Language Template 9.14 Importing Sub-package Modules Code Sample 9.12

```
from ../common import texture
clampTexture = texture.setWrapMode(myTexture, 'clamp')
```

Code Sample 9.12 Importing Sub-package Modules

TECHNICAL ART LIBRARIES

There are thousands of pre-written modules and packages available for inclusion into any Python script. Aside from location specific and custom created modules, there are two primary modules technical artists need to be familiar with: *math* and *random*.

Math

The math module includes all of the mathematical functions defined by the C standard library. All of these functions return floats unless otherwise noted. From the library, there are only a dozen or so functions which technical artists use on a regular basis. Before access, all math module functions must be imported from the *math* module as explained in Language Template 9.15.

The most common technical artist math functions are listed in Table 9.1.

Code Sample 9.13 demonstrates usage of these functions.

```
import math
```

Language Template 9.15 Importing Math Module

TABLE 9.1 Common Technical Art Math Functions

`math.sin (x)`	Returns sine of x in radians
`math.cos (x)`	Returns cosine of x in radians
`math.tan (x)`	Returns tangent of x in radians
`math.asin (x)`	Returns arc sine of x in radians, between $\frac{-\pi}{2}$ *and* $\frac{\pi}{2}$
`math.acos (x)`	Returns arc cosine of x in radians, between 0 and π
`math.atan (x)`	Returns arc tangent of x in radians, between $\frac{-\pi}{2}$ *and* $\frac{\pi}{2}$
`math.degrees (x)`	Converts x radians to degrees
`math.radians (x)`	Converts x degrees to radians
`math.sqrt (x)`	Returns the square root of x
`math.pow (x, y)`	Returns x raised to the power of y
`math.ceil (x)`	Returns the nearest integer greater than or equal to x
`math.floor (x)`	Returns the nearest integer less than or equal to x
`math.fmod (x, y)`	Returns the float modulus equivalent to $x - n * y$ for some n
`math.pi`	A constant variable representing π
`math.tau`	A constant variable representing 2π

```
import math

print(f'sine of 90 degrees = {math.sin(math.radians(90))}')
print(f'{math.pi} is {math.degrees(math.pi)} degrees')
print(f'5 raised to the 2.76 power = {math.pow(5, 2.76)}')
print(f'Floor of 3.26 is {math.floor(3.26)}')
print(f'Fmod of 10.6 % 3.1 is {math.fmod(10.6, 3.1)}')


>>> sine of 90 degrees = 1.0
3.141592653589793 is 180.0 degrees
5 raised to the 2.76 power = 84.94879288608136
floor of 3.26 is 3
fmod of 10.6 % 3.1 is 1.2999999999999994
```

Code Sample 9.13 Math Module Examples

Random

The random module yields pseudo-random numbers for various distributions. Note these return values are not true random numbers but are reproducible through use of the *seed()* function. The value configured by *seed()* behaves as a key to a reproducible sequence of numbers. The module is extensive and capable of generating statistical results. Technical artists typically employ a subset of these functions. As defined by Language Template 9.16, all random number functions must be imported from the *random* module Table 9.2 contains the most common technical art random functions. Many of these functions are demonstrated in Sample Code 9.14.

```
import random
```

Language Template 9.16 Importing Random Module

TABLE 9.2 Common Technical Art Random Functions

`random.seed(a)`	Initializes random number generator based the value of a
`random.random()`	Returns random float *N* between 0 ≤ *N* < 1.0
`random.uniform(a,b)`	Returns random float *N* between *a* ≤ *N* < *b*
`random.randint(a,b)`	Returns random integer *a* between *a* ≤ *N* ≤ *b*
`random.randrange(start,stop[,step])`	Returns random integer *a* between *a* ≤ *N* < *b*
`random.choice(sequence)`	Returns random element from non-empty *sequence*

```
import random

start = 1
stop = 10
myString = 'Tech Art Rocks!'

print('seed(84)')
random.seed(84)
print(f'random()-> {random.random()}')
print(f'uniform({start}, {stop})-> {random.uniform(start, stop)}')
print(f'randint({start}, {stop})-> {random.randint(start, stop)}')
print(f'randrange({start}, {stop})-> {random.randrange(start, stop)}')
print(f'choice({myString})-> {random.choice(myString)}')
print('seed(84)')
random.seed(84)
print(f'random()-> {random.random()}')
```

```
print(f'uniform({start}, {stop})-> {random.uniform(start, stop)}')
print(f'randint({start}, {stop})-> {random.randint(start, stop)}')

>>> seed(84)
random()-> 0.731531130400211
uniform(1, 10)-> 9.226556114659717
randint(1, 10)-> 1
randrange(1, 10)-> 8
choice(Tech Art Rocks!)-> T
seed(84)
random()-> 0.731531130400211
uniform(1, 10)-> 9.226556114659717
randint(1, 10)-> 1
```

Code Sample 9.14 Random Module Examples

FUNCTION AUTHORING

Using pre-authored functions is empowering and provides access to a virtually unlimited catalog of pre-written, topic driven code. Creating custom functions enables programmers to adjust the results of other functions and tailor the behavior of functions to fit scripts' contextual needs. When creating custom functions, scope rules must be followed to avoid clashing similar named variables within the main script. When variables and functions have the name, they overwrite each other. Default parameters provide programmers freedom to rearrange function arguments and omit them during invocation. Lamdas are convenient, anonymous functions which receive unlimited input but evaluate only one expression.

Format

Python function declaration, as defined in Language Template 9.17, initialized using the *def* command followed by the function's name, parameter list, and a colon. The declaration line must be followed by a code block of at least one line. The block may be as simple as the *pass* statement which does nothing, a simple math expression, or as complex as a rendering engine. Functions must return some value. The *return* statement sends flow back to the original invoking statement with the value. When no *return* statement is provided, functions return the value of *None*. While functions may have multiple *return* statements, one is typically found in the last line of the code block. Code Sample 9.15 declares and invokes a simple function.

```
def functionName(ParameterList):
    codeBlock
    return value
```

Language Template 9.17 Function Declaration

```
def square(y):
  return y*y

number = 15
print(f'{number} squared = {square(number)}')

>>> 15 squared = 225
```

Code Sample 9.15 Simple Function Declaration and Invocation

Python is a strongly, dynamically typed language which means that variables, including parameters, have relevant type which impacts how they are evaluated and are defined only during runtime. Functions may be vague on their input parameters types, and yet behave similarly regardless of input. Code Sample 9.16 exploits this ambiguity.

```
def clamp(value, min, max):
  result = value

  if result < min:
      result = min
  if result > max:
      result = max

  return result

print(f'2.75 clamped by 2.0 and 2.5 is {clamp(2.75, 2.0, 2.5)}')
print(f'"fallLine" clamped by "fineCode" and "fubar" is {clamp("fallLine",
"fineCode", "fubar")}')

>>> 2.75 clamped by 2.0 and 2.5 is 2.5
"fallLine" clamped by "fineCode" and "fubar" is fineCode
```

Code Sample 9.16 Function Parameters with No Type

The *clamp()* function in Code Sample 9.16 receives three inputs: a value, a minimum, and a maximum. The types of these inputs are not specified. The code body takes the input value, binds it by the *minimum* and *maximum* values, and returns the result. The function is tested twice: once with floats and once with strings. Once translated to ascii, strings have numerical value and can be compared against each other. Python performs the translations for us when it evaluates the expressions. The function clamps the float value 2.75 by 2.5 since 2.75 ≥ 2.5. Similarly, string "fallLine" is clamped by string "fineCode" since it precedes the later alphabetically.

Scope

The variables introduced inside unique functions belong to those functions. This means that a variable defined within the context of a function can only be used within that function. Code Sample 9.17 demonstrates Python variable *scope*.

```
def yummy():
  treat = 'biscuits'
  print(f'treat={treat}')


treat='chocolate'
yummy()
print(f'treat={treat}')


>>> treat=biscuits
treat=chocolate
```

Code Sample 9.17 Python Function Scope

The variable *treat* is defined in the *yummy* function as *'biscuits'*. The variable *treat* is also re-defined in the main code block as *'chocolate'*. Within the context of the function, *treat* has one value and within the context of the main block, it has another. Within a function, any variable is free to take on any value, regardless of how the variable is used outside the function.

When functions wish to access variables defined outside their contexts and ultimately alter their values, their variables must be declared within the functions with the *global* command. The *global* command instructs Python to use the external value of the variable instead of creating its own version. Code Sample 9.18 uses *global* and local variables.

```
# global variable
foo = 1
def a():
    foo = 25
    print(f"Function 'a' local variable 'foo' is {foo}")
    foo += 1
    print(f"Leaving 'a', local variable 'foo'  is {foo}")

def b():
    global foo
    print(f"Function 'b' local variable 'foo'  is {foo}")
    foo *= 10
    print(f"Leaving 'b', local variable 'foo'  is {foo}")

foo=7
print(f'Global foo = {foo}')

a()
b()
a()
b()

print(f'Global foo = {foo}')

>>> Global foo = 7
Function 'a' local variable 'foo' is 25
Leaving 'a', local variable 'foo'  is 26
Function 'b' local variable 'foo'  is 7
Leaving 'b', local variable 'foo'  is 70
Function 'a' local variable 'foo' is 25
Leaving 'a', local variable 'foo'  is 26
Function 'b', local variable 'foo'  is 70
Leaving 'b', local variable 'foo'  is 700
Global foo = 70
```

Code Sample 9.18 Global Command Affecting Function Behavior

The first line of the script defines the global value of *foo*. Ultimately, this code is used for reference as this line contributes nothing to the final results. Function *a()* creates a local variable named *foo* and performs operations on it. The function *b()* performs very similar operations. However, it declares foo as *global* instead of defining it locally. The changes that the *b()* function makes to the variable impact it globally.

In the main code block, the value of *foo* is set once again. Functions *a()* and *b()*are called twice, in that order. Function *a()* has no impact on the global value of *foo* while the function *b()* does. The final value of *foo* is displayed once again and has the same value as when leaving *b()*.

Default Arguments

One of the easiest topics in Python to misunderstand is using default parameters in function declarations and configuring them properly in function calls. (*Parameters* are variables inside function definition parentheses. *Arguments* are values sent to called functions.) There are two types of function parameters: positional and default. Functions are called utilizing three types of arguments: default, positional, and keyword. (Technically there are five types of arguments. The other two, arbitrary positional, and arbitrary keyword are beyond the scope of this text.)

Parameter Types

Functions are structured with the *def* command, the function name, followed by a list of input parameters and a colon. Code Sample 9.19 demonstrates positional function parameters.

```
def boxVolume(length, width, depth):
    return length*width*depth


l = 2
w = 4
d = 6
print(f'the volume of my {l}x{w}x{d} box is {boxVolume(l,w,d)}')

>>> the volume of my 2x4x6 box is 48
```

Code Sample 9.19 Positional Function Parameters

Function behavior depends on parameter positional arrangement and arrangement of arguments in the function call. The arrangement of the function definition parameters is described as positional.

The ability to use default parameters when defining functions affords programmers great freedom. Default parameters are defined by setting parameters with initial, or default values. Default values provide the option to call functions without values for all arguments. Missing arguments are covered by default parameters. Code Sample 9.20 demonstrates how functions may be defined by default parameters.

```
def boxVolume(length=1, width=1, depth=1):
  return length*width*depth
```

```
l = 2
w = 4
d = 6
print(f'the volume of my box is {boxVolume()}')
print(f'the volume of my {l} box is {boxVolume(l)}')
print(f'the volume of my {l}x{w} box is {boxVolume(l,w)}')
print(f'the volume of my {l}x{w}x{d} box is {boxVolume(l,w,d)}')


>>> the volume of my box is 1
the volume of my 2 box is 2
the volume of my 2x4 box is 8
the volume of my 2x4x6 box is 48
```

Code Sample 9.20 Function Defined with Default Parameters

When the *box()* function is called, instead of Python throwing errors with missing arguments, it substitutes default values defined by the default parameters.

Function parameter types may be mixed as long as all of the positional parameters are defined before the default. Python complains when default arguments are defined before positional. Code Sample 9.21 mixes-up parameter order.

```
def boxVolume(length, width, depth=1):
  return length*width*depth

l = 2
w = 4
d = 6
print(f'the volume of my {l}x{w} box is {boxVolume(l,w)}')
print(f'the volume of my {l}x{w}x{d} box is {boxVolume(l,w,d)}')

>>> the volume of my 2x4 box is 8
the volume of my 2x4x6 box is 48
```

Code Sample 9.21 Mixed Function Parameter Types

Even with the presence of default parameters, positional arguments must be provided in their proper order for functions to behave correctly.

Argument Types

As demonstrated in the previous examples, functions may be called with positional arguments (Code Sample 9.19) or default arguments (Code Sample 9.20). Keyword arguments are the third type of argument. Keyword arguments are declared with the parameter name, the equals character, =, and the argument value. In Code Sample 9.22, the *boxVolume* function is called using keyword arguments.

```
def boxVolume(length, width, depth):
  return length*width*depth

l = 2
w = 4
d = 6
print(f'the volume of my {l}x{w}x{d} box is
       {boxVolume(length=l,width=w,depth=d)}')

>>> the volume of my 2x4x6 box is 48
```

Code Sample 9.22 Calling Functions with Keyword Arguments

Using keyword arguments allows shuffling of the function call arguments. In Code Sample 9.23, the same function call shuffles argument order.

```
def boxVolume(length, width, depth):
    return length*width*depth

l = 2
w = 4
d = 6
print(f'the volume of my {l}x{w}x{d} box is
       {boxVolume(depth=d,length=l,width=w)}')

>>> the volume of my 2x4x6 box is 48
```

Code Sample 9.23 Shuffled Function Keyword Arguments

Special attention must be provided when mixing different argument types. As a rule-of-thumb, the following guidelines should be followed when mixing arguments:

1. Default arguments are optional and must follow all other types
2. Keyword arguments must follow positional arguments
3. While order is not important, keyword arguments must match only one of the defined function parameters
4. One argument must correspond to one and only one function parameter

Python is sensitive of the order of function arguments and will throw errors when the preceding guidelines are not followed. Code Sample 9.24 demonstrates correct argument type order.

```
def boxVolume(length=1, width=1, depth=1):
    return length*width*depth


l = 2
w = 4
d = 6
print(f'the volume of my {l}x{w} box is {boxVolume(l, width=w)}')

>>> the volume of my 2x4 box is 8
```

Code Sample 9.24 Correct Argument Type Order

Strategies

The number of variations of functional parameters and argument types provides programmers freedom and maneuverability. However, they also contribute to programmer confusion and Python errors. To minimize chaos, all programmers should invent strategies when employing variable types of parameters and arguments. Any strategy is good as long as it does not generate errors and is used consistently.

"Keep it simple!" is a great strategy. Eliminate argument and parameter type mixing. All parameters must either be positional or default, but not both. All arguments must be keyword or default. While this strategy requires extra typing, it removes the need for conforming to the exact order defined by the function parameters. This is especially helpful when formal parameter list definitions are unavailable.

Lambda

A *lambda* function in Python is a simple, anonymous function that has no name. They are "one-time" use functions and can only be used where they are defined. This means they can be used in places where function names are not relevant. They are often used as variable arguments for *higher-order* functions: functions that take other functions as arguments.

Language Template 9.18 defines how Python *lambdas* are formed.

```
lambda argument(s): expression
```

Language Template 9.18 Python Lambda Function

Lambda functions may have any number of arguments but only one expression. When called, their expressions are evaluated and returned just like other functions.

Lambdas are useful for creating fast and short variable argument functions. They side-step the additional clutter traditional functions require. Code Sample 9.25 demonstrates what a non-lambda function looks like.

```
def square(x):
  return x*x


print(square(7))


>>> 49
```

Code Sample 9.25 Short Function

Code Sample 9.26 replaces the entire function with a lambda function.

```
square = lambda x: x*x
print(square(8))


>>> 64
```

Code Sample 9.26 Function Replaced with a Lambda

In the prior example, the lambda function receives *x* as an input argument and returns the product *x*x*. The lambda is assigned to the identifier named *square* and reused.

Lambda functions are useful for generating multiple variations of abstract variable functions, as demonstrated by Code Sample 9.27.

```
def x(value):
    return lambda y: y*value


x4 = x(4)
print(f'x4(2) = {x4(2)}')
print(f'x4(3.54) = {x4(3.854)}')
```

```
x8_4 = x(8.4)
print(f'x8_4(2) = {x8_4(2)}')
print(f'x8_4(3.3) = {x8_4(3.3)}')

>>> x4(2) = 8
x4(3.54) = 15.416
x8_4(2) = 16.8
x8_4(3.3) = 27.72
```

Code Sample 9.27 Abstract Function Using Lambda

In Code Sample 9.27, two functions are generated from the one abstract function. The first function multiplies the input by *4*. The second multiplies the input by *8.4*.

Technical artists use lambdas to reduce the need to create highly repetitious yet subtly variable functions. In the early portion of Chapter 7, Code Sample 9.28 was introduced to generate a Houdini Roberto.

```
# Grab the top-level object anchor
objNode = hou.node("/obj")

# Create the Roberto's container
container = objNode.createNode("geo", "RobertoGeo")

# Create a Roberto SOP
container.createNode("testgeometry_rubbertoy", "Roberto")
```

Code Sample 9.28 Roberto Generating Script

A different script is needed to produce a squab or a pig head.

Code Sample 9.29 uses a lambda statement to generate a variable object with any name in just a single line.

```
obj = lambda name, type: hou.node('/obj').createNode(
      'geo', f'{name}Geo').createNode(
      f'testgeometry_{type}', name)


obj('boy', 'tommy')
obj('Roberto', 'rubbertoy')
```

Code Sample 9.29 Abstract Generating Lambda

In Code Sample 9.29 the lambda is assigned to the identifier variable called *obj*, and takes the Houdini/*obj* node, creates a geometry container based on the *name* argument, and inside the container, creates new geometry from the input *name* and *types* arguments. The output is Figure 9.3.

ARGS AND KWARGS

Python has two special symbols for passing in a variable number of arguments to functions: **args* (non-keyword arguments) and ***kwargs* (keyword arguments).

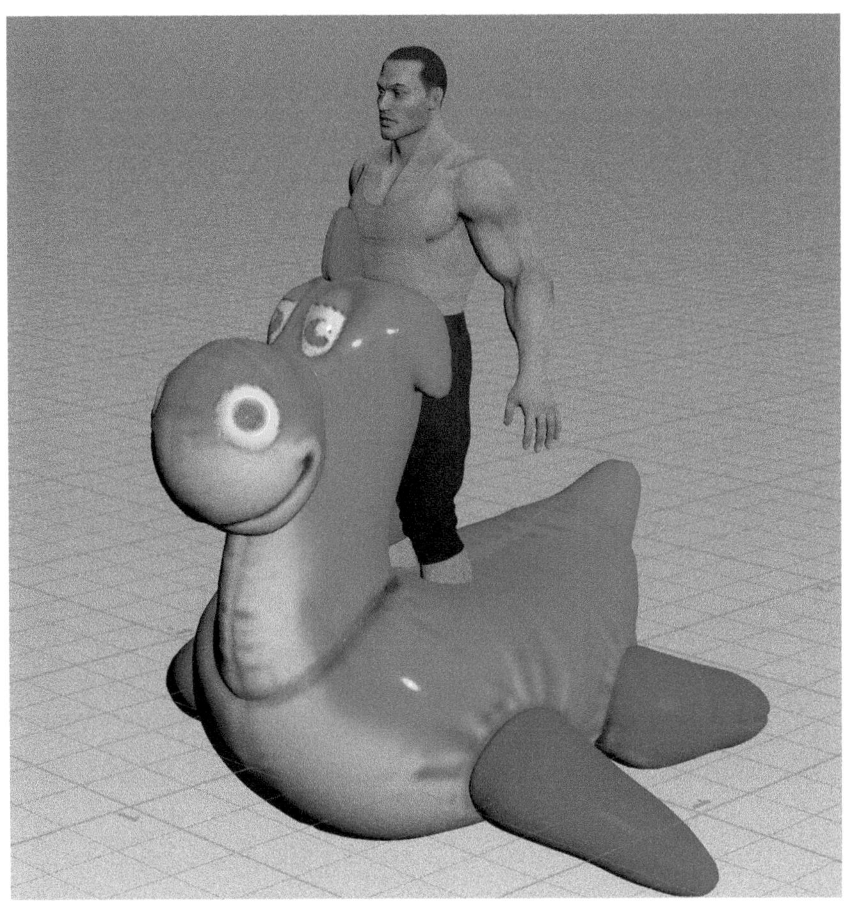

FIGURE 9.3 Lambda script visual output.

The **args* symbol enables a variable number of arguments to be passed to functions. Any number of arguments may be used, including no arguments. (Any function parameter associated with an asterisk, *, makes that parameter iterable.) Code Sample 9.30 takes advantage of a variable number of arguments.

```
# The * symbol enables a variable number of arguments
def soundOff(*args):
# iterate through all of the variable arguments
  for name in args:
    print(f'{name}')

soundOff('Jerry', 'Mark', 'Bob1', 'Bob2', 'Allen')


>>> Jerry
Mark
Bob1
Bob2
Allen
```

Code Sample 9.30 Variable Number of Arguments

The **kwargs symbol enables a variable number of keyword arguments to be passed to functions. The arguments are treated like a dictionary where the keys and values are independent of sequence and order. Dictionaries are data types covered in Chapter 10. (Any function parameter associated with a double asterisk, **, enables a variable number of keyword arguments.) Code Sample 9.31 takes advantage of a variable number of keyword arguments.

```
def character(**kwargs):
  container = hou.node('/obj').createNode('geo', kwargs['name'])
  return container.createNode(
         f'testgeometry_{kwargs["type"]}', kwargs["name])

# First Character
char1 = character(type='rubbertoy', name='Roberto')
char1.parm('tx').set(-2.0)

# Second Character
char2 = character(name='Squidward', type='squab')
```

Code Sample 9.31 Variable Number of Keyword Documents

When combining **args* with ***kwargs*, it is important to define the **args* before the ***kwargs* since the **args* are order dependent.

RECURSION

In all previous examples, function definitions call other, different functions. But when a function calls itself, it is called *recursion*. Recursion is a classic computer science technique that creates functions that perform an incredible amount of work with very little coding. They are especially good for traversing node-based graphs and tree-based hierarchies. All technical artist riggers and users of node-based programming environments, such as Houdini and Unreal Engine, should be familiar with recursion basics.

A recursive function needs two components: a *base case* to resolve and a *call to self*. The base case is a condition within the function that prevents the function from calling itself indefinitely. Without the base case, or *brake*, the function will continue calling itself until the computer runs out of memory and crashes. Most languages, including Python, have restrictions on the number of times a function can call itself. The second component in a recursive function is a call to self. This is typically located after the base case. Code Sample 9.32 Introduces a simple recursive factorial function.

```
# Takes integers as input and returns factorials
# example: 4! = 4 * 3 * 2 * 1 = 24
def factorial( number ):
  #base case
  if number < 1:
      return 1
  else:
      #recursive call to self
      return number * factorial(number -1)

print(factorial(int(input("Enter an integer: "))))

>>> Enter an integer: 5
120
```

Code Sample 9.32 Recursive Factorial Function

The most complicated element in the previous example is the function call itself. The *input* requests the user to enter an integer. The *int()* function converts the input into an integer and passes it to the *factorial()* function. The factorial result is printed to the display.

The *factorial()* function starts with a base case which considers if the input number is smaller than one. If so, the function halts its recursion. If not, the product of the *factorial()* function of *number* – 1 and the input *number* is returned. The *factorial()* function calls itself until the *number* value reduces to zero and the function is allowed to unwind itself, multiplying each of the *factorial()* results while returning to the original call.

While Recursion is not effective in all situations, traversing node-based networks and character rigging hierarchies are natural applications. A quick rig traversing script is provided below. To generate the sample rig, in a fresh Houdini scene, right mouse click in the Houdini network window and select Characters->Simple Female, as displayed in Figure 9.4. A female character similar to the character shown in Figure 9.5 is created.

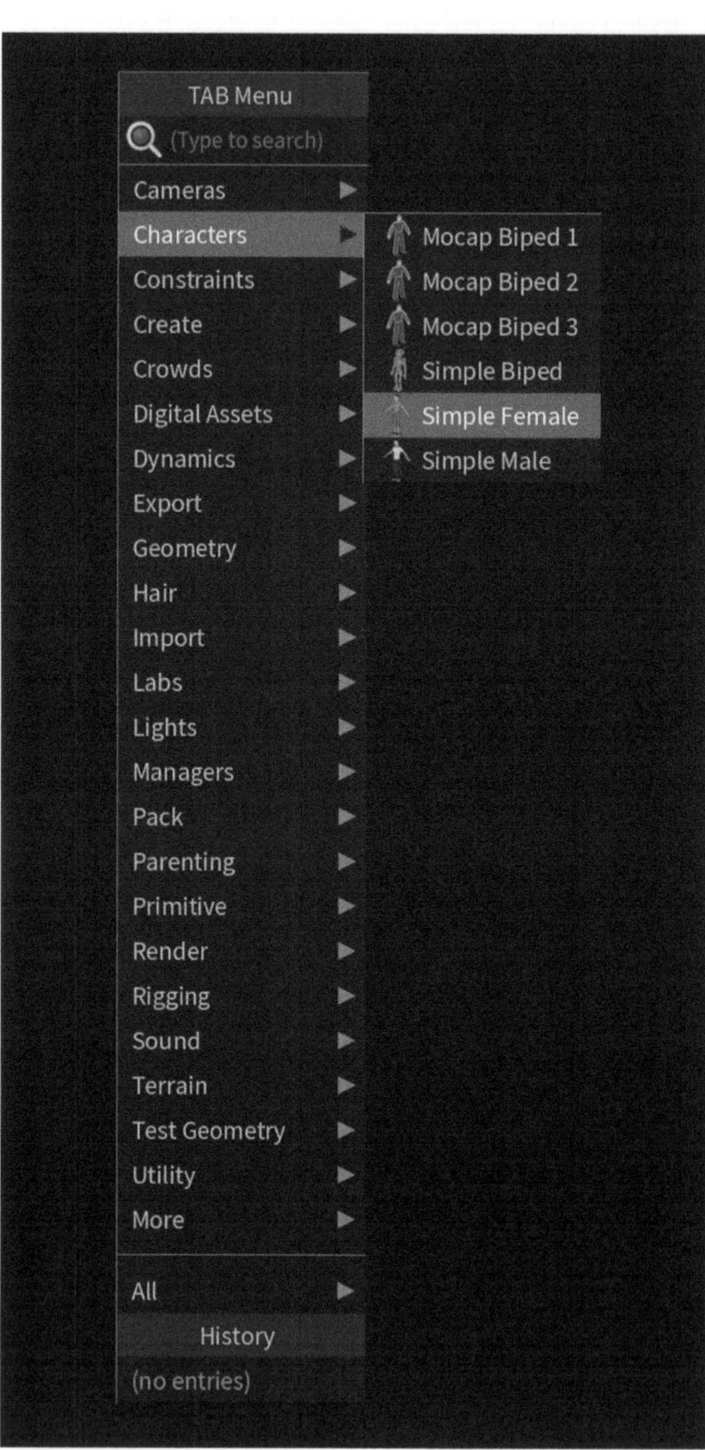

FIGURE 9.4 Houdini simple female.

Double-clicking the *SimpleFemale* node drops the user into the object level. Figure 9.6 demonstrates the node network is anything but simple.

Traversing this node network to identify the bone names is a daunting task. The job becomes simpler when using a recursive script, such as Code Sample 9.33, instead of verifying each node one at a time.

```
def boneFinder(level, node):
  # Base Case
  if node.type().name() == 'bone':
     print(f"{level*' '}{node.name()}")

  # Get all children
  children = node.outputs()
  # for each child
  for child in children:
    newLevel = level + 1
    # Recurse to each child
    boneFinder(newLevel, child)

# Initial call
boneFinder(0, hou.node('/obj/simplefemale1/ctrl_cog'))
>>>          ctrl_rig_bone_hand_right
        rig_bone_little_1_right
         rig_bone_little_2_right
          rig_bone_little_3_right
        rig_bone_ring_1_right
         rig_bone_ring_2_right
          rig_bone_ring_3_right
        rig_bone_index_1_right
         rig_bone_index_2_right
          rig_bone_index_3_right
        rig_bone_middle_1_right
          rig_bone_middle_2_right
           rig_bone_middle_3_right
```

Python Functions

```
        rig_bone_thumb_1_right
          rig_bone_thumb_2_right
            rig_bone_thumb_3_right
  rig_bone_thigh_right
    rig_bone_calf_right
      rig_bone_foot_right
        rig_bone_toe_right
```

Code Sample 9.33 BoneFinder Traverse Script and Output

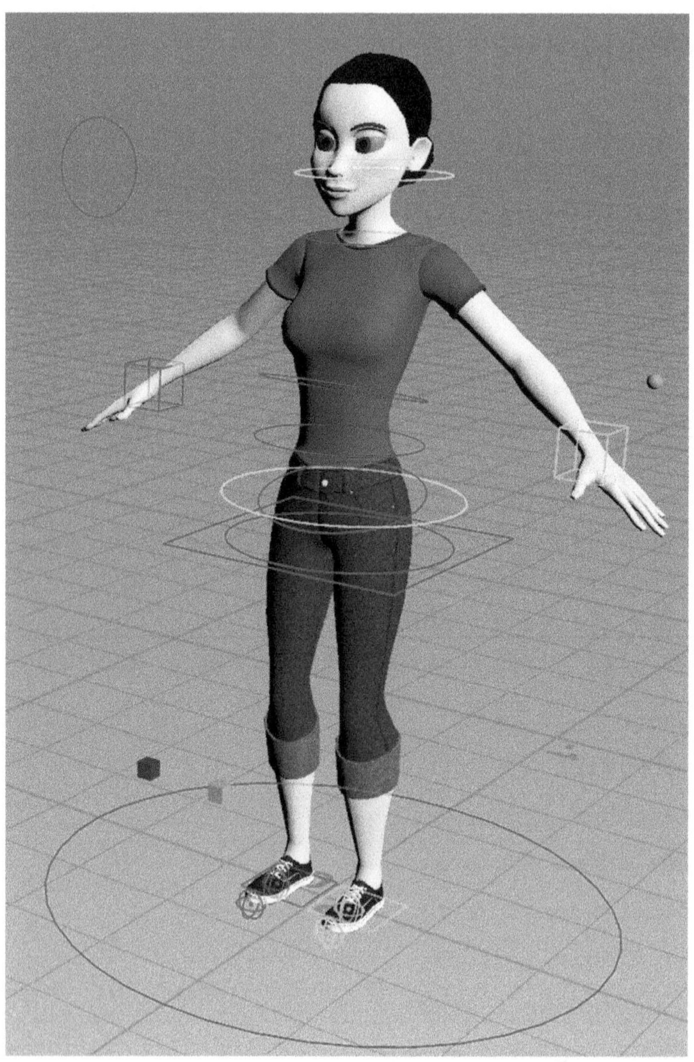

FIGURE 9.5 Houdini simple female.

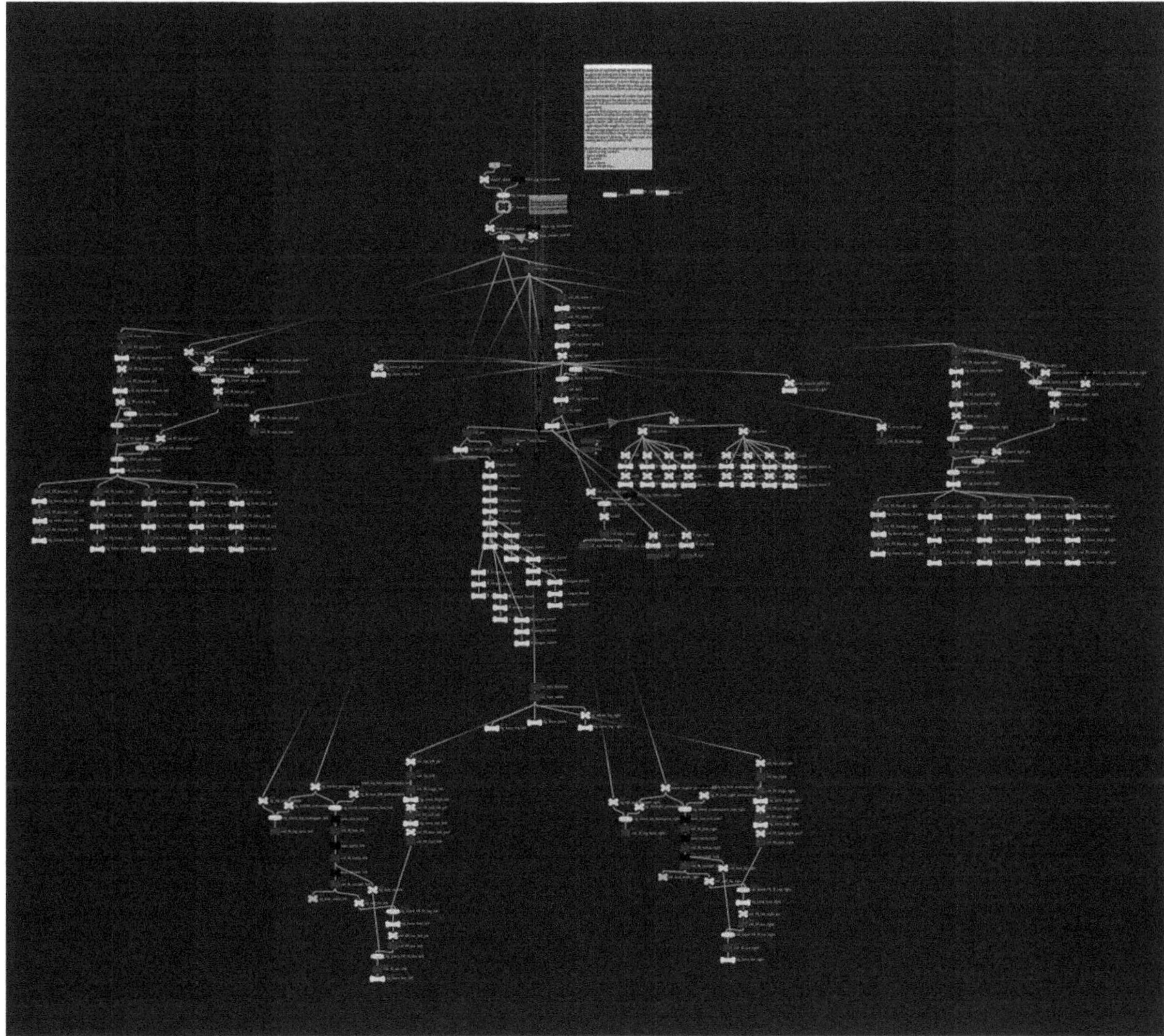

FIGURE 9.6 Simple female node network.

The output for this Code Sample 9.33 extends further than what is displayed. The *boneFinder()* function takes a node reference and an indentation level as input. The base case is tested first. When the node type is a *bone*, the name is displayed with the *level* amount of indentation. After considering the base case, the child nodes are acquired and the *boneFinder()* function is called again for each.

Recursion not only simplifies complex tasks but makes code look cleaner and more elegant. Recursive functions do have their drawbacks. They are hard to debug since their logic is challenging to follow. They can also be slow and inefficient and consume vast amounts of memory.

FRACTAL EXAMPLE

Little demonstrates the visual potential of functions more than fractals. Dramatic results are achieved with very little code. The Mandelbrot set is a classic fractal function that takes a complex number as input and returns how rapidly the input value converges to a solution or spins off to infinity. No knowledge of complex numbers is required

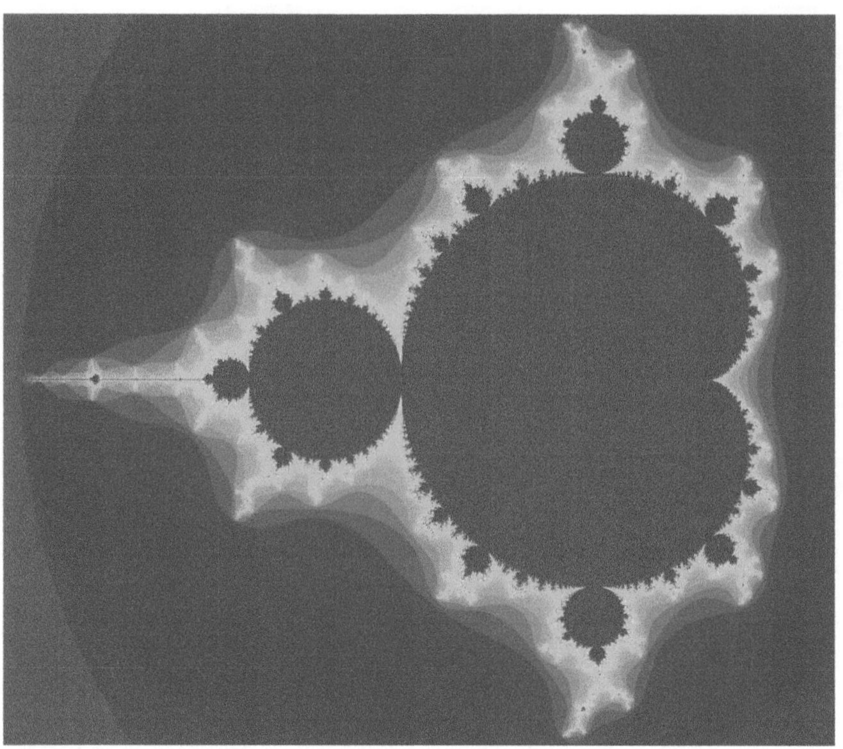

FIGURE 9.7 Mandelbrot set.

other than they are composed of two numbers: a real and an imaginary number. Code Sample 9.34 produces the classical Mandelbrot set, like the one shown in Figure 9.7, which requires very little programming.

Before programming the Mandelbrot set, some preparation is needed. A new Houdini scene is required. Create a new scene by selecting *File ->New Scene*, shown in Figure 9.8.

As shown in Figure 9.9, create a new *geometry* container object by hitting the *tab* key and selecting *Geometry ->Geometry*. Rename the new object, "MandelbrotGrid".

Double left mouse click the "MandelbrotGrid" geometry object and drop into its contents. A grid is needed to hold the points we will be painting. Hit the *Tab* key and select *Create ->Grid*, as shown in Figure 9.10.

Adjust the grid parameters to ensure it is 130 units wide and 110 units high and has 130 rows and 110 columns as shown in Figure 9.11. This is a suitable number of available points to develop the Python script. The row and column numbers will be increased once the Python script is finished.

The grid will need a base color to work from. Like displayed in Figure 9.12, left mouse drag from the *grid1* output node, hit the *tab* key, and select *Material ->Color*. This appends a *color* node to the *grid1* node and provides the grid with initial color information.

Select the rightmost chicklet on the *color1* node to identify it as the network display node to look like Figure 9.13.

Left mouse drag from under the *color1* node, hit the *tab* key, and select *Utility ->Python*. This appends a *Python* node and provides a location to create a Python script to paint the grid points and generate the Mandelbrot set.

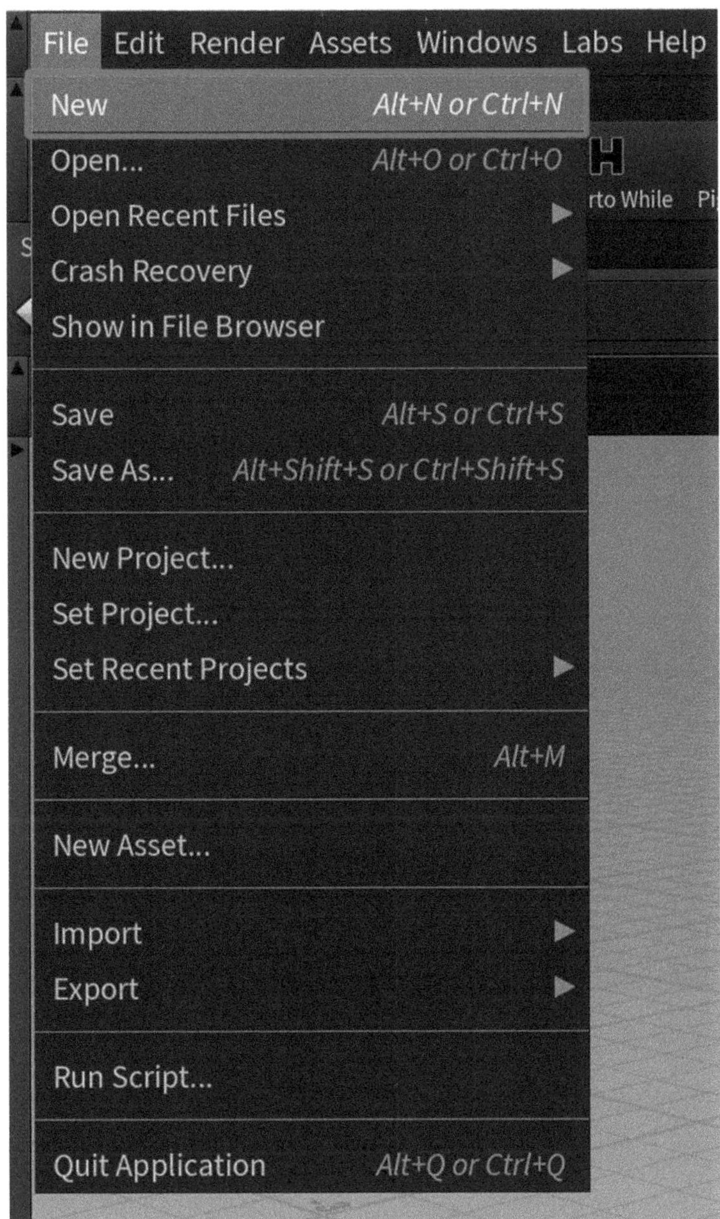

FIGURE 9.8 Create new Houdini scene.

Rename the Python node to "Mandelbrot". Click the rightmost chicklet on the Mandelbrot node to set it as the network display. The default Python node should look like Figure 9.14.

Remove the existing Python code and replace it with Code Sample 9.34.

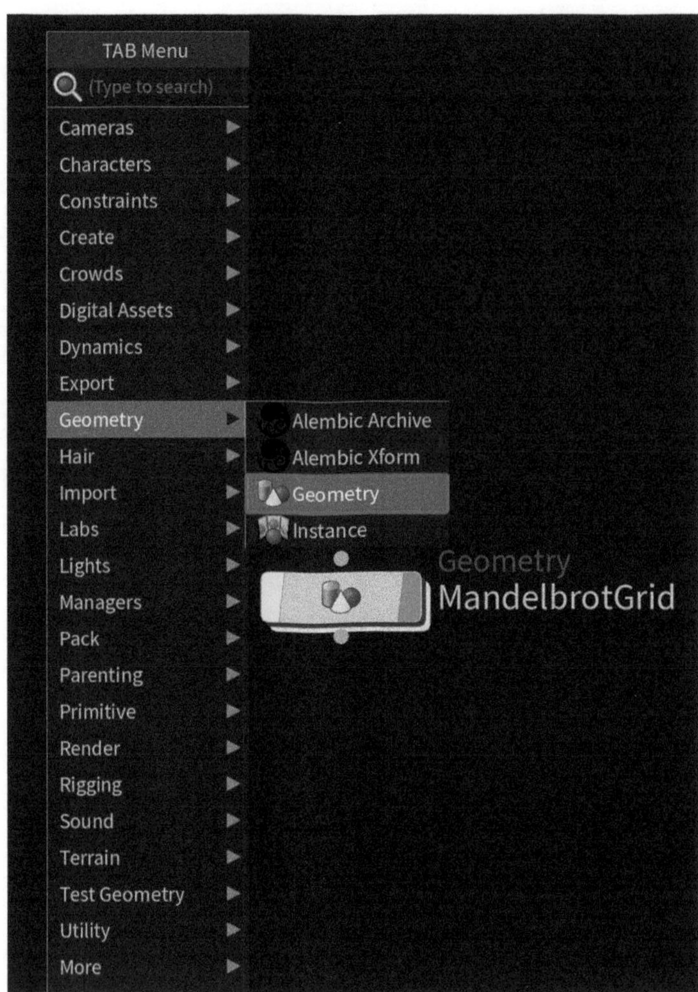

FIGURE 9.9 Create new geometry container object.

Working with Python nodes is a different pipeline than working with shelf scripts introduced in earlier chapters. The workflow injects Python code into the data flow. Whenever there is a change in the data, change focus from the code editor, or hit *Cntrl + Enter*, the Python code executes automatically. Script invocation is not required. The resulting grid should like Figure 9.15.

Figure 9.15 does not appear as finely detailed as *Figure 9.6* because the number of rows and columns in the *grid1* node are set to relatively small number `s(130 x 110)`. Working with small numbers is advantageous for script debugging and adjusting which executes and iterates quickly. When the number of rows and columns are set to higher numbers, the processing time takes longer and is difficult to experiment and make changes. When the results are comparable to *Figure 9.14*, change the number of rows and columns in the *grid1* node from *130* and *110* to *1,300* and *1,100*. The script will take longer to process but the final image should look like *Figure 9.6*.

The first line of code imports the *pow()* function from the *math* library. The next three lines of code grab data from the Houdini geometry data flow. Only the grid points are desired. The *geo.points()* function returns all the points in a single list labeled *points*. Chapter 10 covers the concept of lists. The *MAX_ITER* provides the maximum

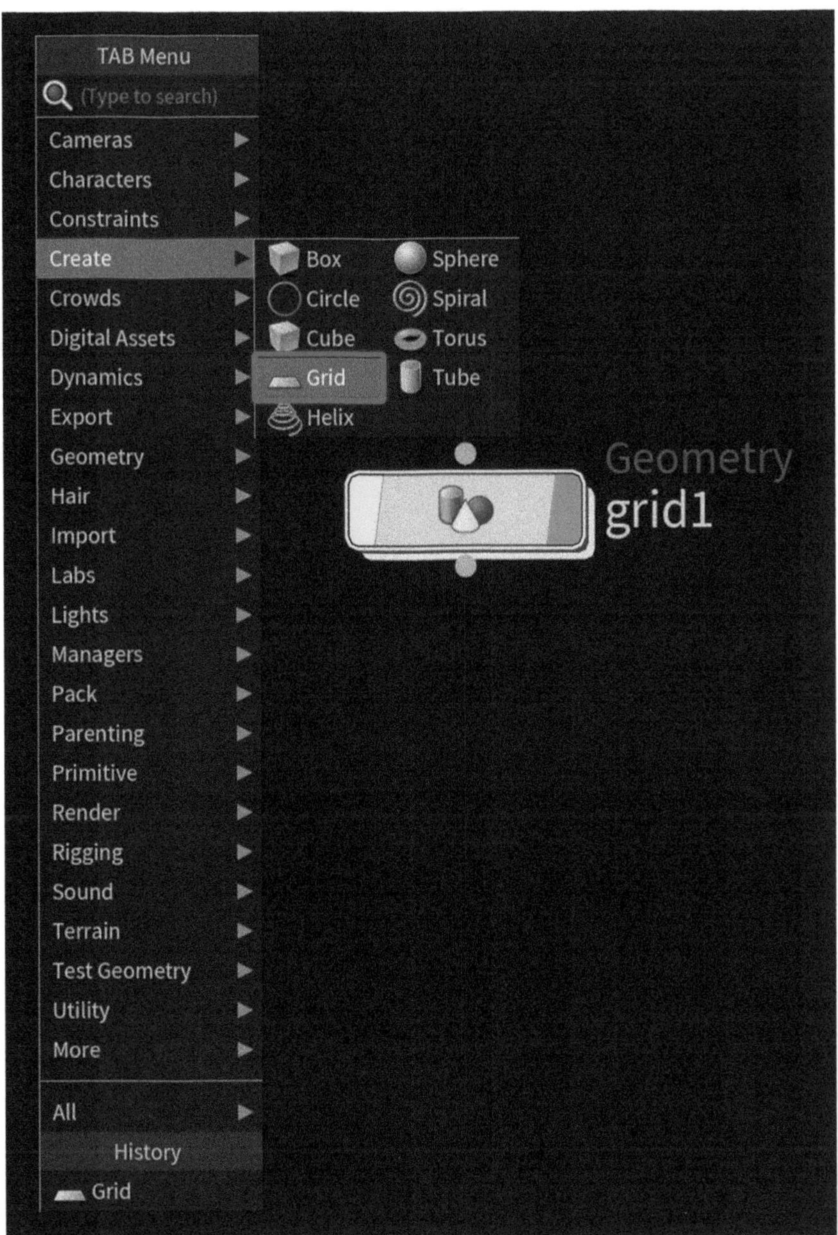

FIGURE 9.10 Create a grid.

number of attempts the *mandelbrot()* function will attempt to find a solution before giving up. Note the use of capitals in *MAX_ITER*. This naming convention informs programmers that the value is constant and should not be changed.

The *mandelbrot()* function is defined next. Its input is a tuple named *sp* which represents a complex number. A complex number is defined by two numbers: a real and an imaginary number. A tuple is a collection of items which behave as just one object. Tuples are covered in Chapter 10.

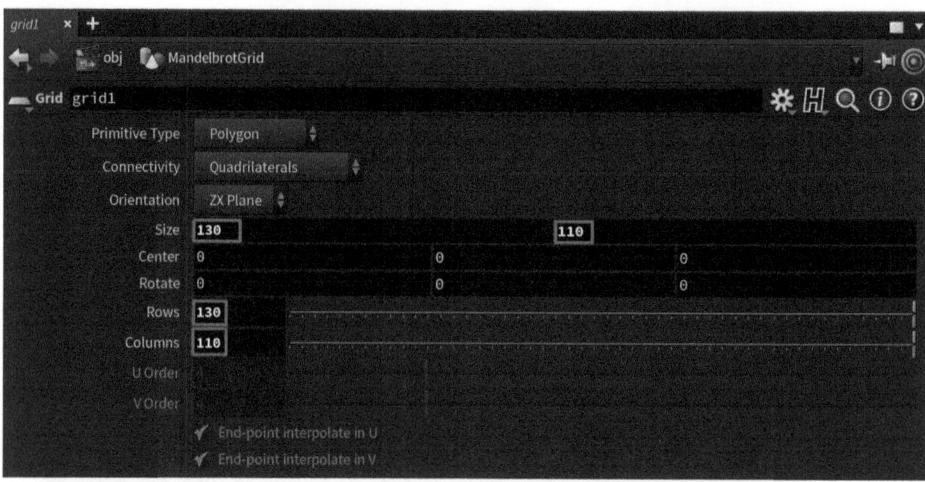

FIGURE 9.11 Grid parameters.

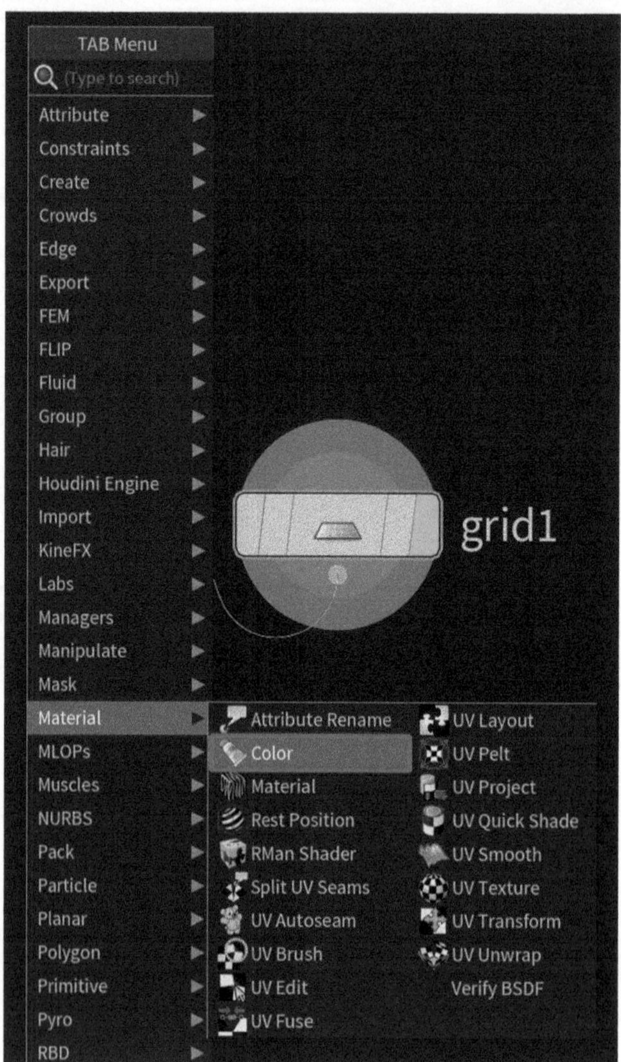

FIGURE 9.12 Append a color node to the grid node.

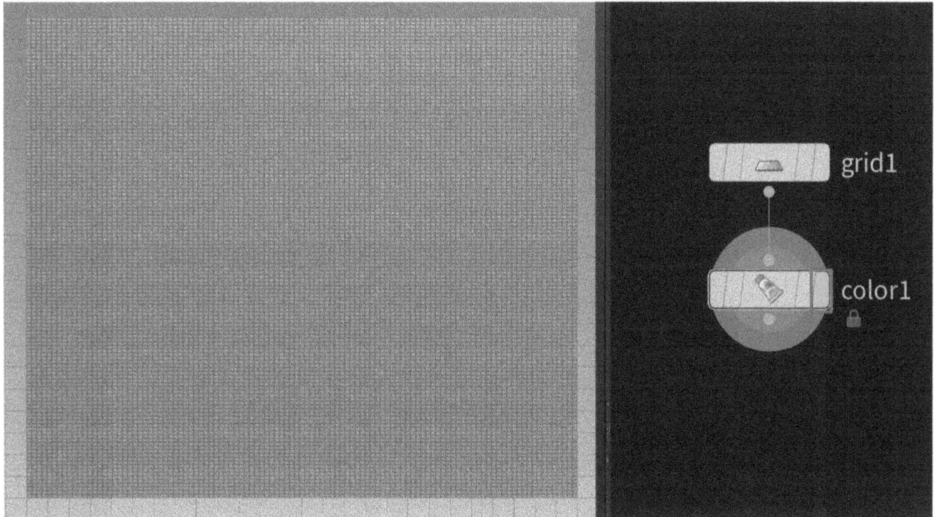

FIGURE 9.13 Grid and object network.

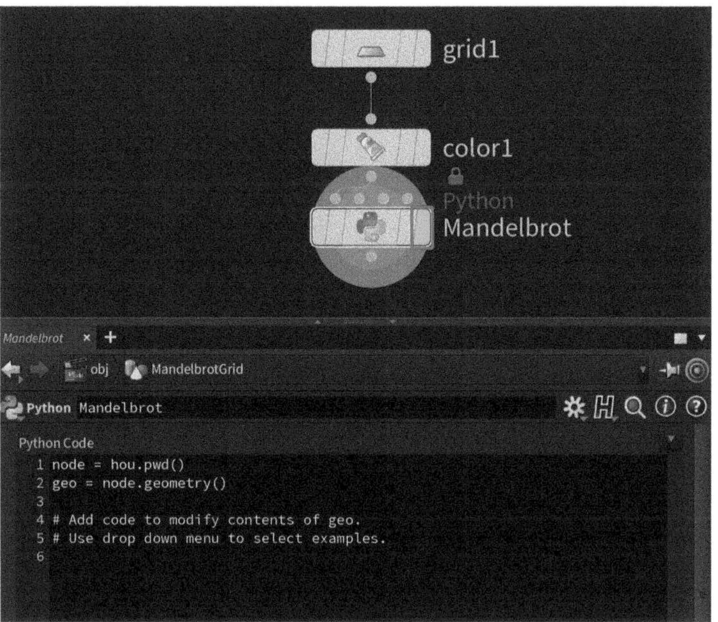

FIGURE 9.14 Mandelbrot Python node.

The *mandelbrot()* function initializes complex number, *z*, and iteration counter, *its*, to zero. The function then enters a loop which repeats a maximum of *MAX_ITER* times. The loop iterator is stored in *i*. The dot product of *z* and itself is calculated. While not broken, the complex number *z* is recalculated with Equation 9.1.

$$z = \left(z.x^2 - z.y^2,\ 2 * z.x * z.y\right) + sp$$

Equation 9.1 Iterative Mandelbrot Equation

```
from math import pow

# Anchor to the Python node
node = hou.pwd()
# Get node's geometry
geo = node.geometry()
# Get geometry points
points = geo.points()

MAX_ITER = 80

# Calculate the Mandelbrot() function on a given input
# Input is a complex number, Output is number of calculated iterations
# Output is divided by MAX_ITER to produce a value between
# 0.0 and 1.0
def mandelbrot(sp=(0.0, 0.0)):
  # Seed
  z = (0, 0)
  # Number of iterations
  its = 0

  # Repeat this loop until the dot product of Z is greater than or equal to
  # 4 or the number of iterations exceeds MAX_ITER
  for i in range(MAX_ITER):
    # Compute dot product of Z
    dot = z[0]*z[0] + z[1]*z[1]
    # Break the loop when dot product exceeds 4.0
    if dot > 4.0: ]
       break

    # Recalculate Z = (z.x^2 - z.y^2, 2*z.x*z.y) + sp
    z = (z[0]*z[0]-z[1]*z[1] + sp[0], 2.0 * z[0] * z[1] + sp[1])
```

```
    # Increment the number of iterations.
    its += 1

    # Divide the number of iterations by MAX_ITER for a result between
    # 0.0 and 1.0
    return float(its) / MAX_ITER

# Number of rows from grid
numRows = hou.node('../grid1').parm('rows').eval()
# Number of columns from grid
numCols = hou.node('../grid1').parm('cols').eval()
# Adjustment aspect ratio for non-square grid
ratio = float(numRows)/float(numCols)
# Zoom factor for increased visibility
zoom = 2.3
# Center shift for improved visibility
offset = (0.7, 0.0)

pt = 0
for row in range(numRows):
    for col in range(numCols):
        # Our imaginary axis goes between -0.5 and 0.5
        v = float(row)/float(numRows) - 0.5
        # Adjust the real number axis to account for non-square grid
        u = (float(col)/float(numCols) - 0.5)*ratio
        # Zoom and offset for better visibility
        sp = (u * zoom - offset[0], v * zoom - offset[1])

        # Send complex number to Mandelbrot function
        m = mandelbrot(sp)
        # Math trick to make result more colorful
        m = pow(m, 0.4)
```

```
# Create a Houdini Color
color = hou.Color((0,0,0))
# Use the Mandelbrot result as color hue.
# Saturation and Value are maxed at 1.0
color.setHSV(((1-m)*360, 1, 1))
# Color point with RGB equivalent to HSV
points[pt].setAttribValue('Cd', color.rgb())

# Process the next point
pt += 1
```

Code Sample 9.34 Python Mandelbrot Generator

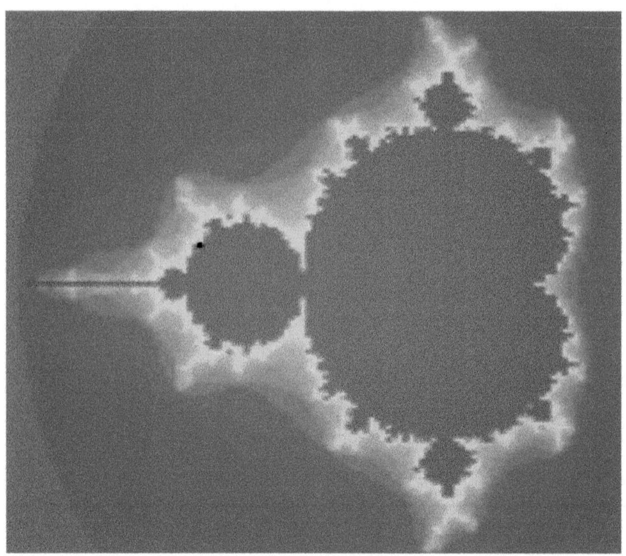

FIGURE 9.15 Initial Mandelbrot set.

When the dot product of *z* is 4.0 or greater, it no longer converges to a solution and no further iterations are required

After *z* is recalculated, the value of *its* is increased by one and the loop repeats. Once the loop finishes, the counter, *its*, is divided by *MAX_ITER* and returns as the *Mandelbrot()* function result. The result is a value between *0.0* and *1.0*.

The rest of the script is defined after the *mandelbrot()* function. The number of rows and columns defined in the *grid* node are stored in *numRows* and *numCols*. Because the number of rows and columns may not be the same, each sub-grid may not be square. The aspect ratio of columns to rows is calculated to compensate for this non-squareness and stored in the *ratio* variable. The *zoom* and *offset* variables are defined to make the image look nicer. Zoom controls the scale of the fractal and offset controls how it is centered.

A point counter, *pt*, is initialized to zero. The script enters a nested *for loop*, iterating over every point in the grid. For each point an imaginary number is created. The real portion, *u*, is calculated by subtracting *0.5* from the ratio of the current column number divided by the total number of columns. This results in a number between `-0.5 and 0.5`. This is then multiplied against the non-square *ratio* variable. The imaginary portion, *v*, is calculated by subtracting *0.5* from the ratio of the current row divided by the total number of rows. This results in a number between `-0.5 and 0.5`. A complex number, *sp*, is assembled by creating a tuple of *u* and *v*. Each component in *sp* is multiplied by the *zoom* variable and subtracts the equivalent *offset* value.

The *mandelbrot()* function is called with *sp* and the result is stored in *m*. The value of *m* is recalculated, Equation 9.2, by taking it to the *0.4 power*.

$$m = m^{0.4}$$

Equation 9.2 M taken to the 0.4 Power

The power operation is an old-fashioned math trick which gives the *m* value a smoother distribution between *0.0* and *1.0* and makes the resulting image appear brighter.

A Houdini color object, *color*, is initialized. The *color* object is transformed into an HSV color by subtracting the *m* value from *1.0*, multiplying by *360* and assigning the result to the *hue* component, Equation 9.3.

$$hue = (1.0 - m) * 360$$

Equation 9.3 Hue Component Generation

Subtracting the *m* value from *1.0* shifts the color palette from yellow-greens to blue-reds. (The author subjectively chose the color palette.) The *hue* component needs to be between *0.0* and *360*, and is scaled by *360*.

The point color is set using the *setAttribValue()* function. The "Cd" attribute is a reference to the points' diffuse color value and *color.rgb()* converts the color from HSV to RGB. The point counter, *pt*, is increased by 1 and the nested *for loop* is continued.

CONCLUSION

Functions are programming language structures that help languages be repeatable and portable. They are repeatable in that they can be written once and referenced infinitely within the script body without re-creation. Within Python, functions are portable, not only because they can be referenced multiple times within the same script, but they can also be imported into different scripts and referenced as if written locally.

All functions receive some kind of input and return some kind of output. The input may be as complex as the health statistics of all warriors on a field of battle or as simple as *no input*. Similarly, functional output may be as complex as the weather forecast for a mountain region or as simple as completion confirmation. Once written, input configures functional behavior. It not only provides data for the function to consume but also instructs how to process information.

Within Python, functions may be written to external files called modules. Modules must be imported to Python scripts for their functions to be accessed. Two module libraries all technical artists need to be familiar with are the *math* and *random* number modules. These libraries afford artists more mathematical opportunity than those found in native operations. Multiple modules, bound by themes, are collected into packages. Module and package names must be included when referencing functions to avoid confusion from similarly named functions in different packages. Similarly, variables defined within functions are exclusive to those functions unless declared as *global* variables.

Functional input may be assigned default values. Default values provide the minimal data for successful function completion and empowers users to change order and possibly ignore certain input. *Lambdas* are simple anonymous functions that have no name. They are useful when using functions as input to other functions. Recursion is a powerful technique for functions to reference themselves within their code. This strategy solves complex problems easily with clean code but can also be expensive and create unrecoverable infinite loops.

INTRODUCTION

Python data types are also referred to as Python objects. A Python object is any type of information that can be assigned to a variable. Up to this point in this book, all demonstrated variables have been simple strings, integers, or floats, assigned to one variable at a time. However, Python was structured so that its data could be as robust as needed. The objects described in this chapter are the fundamental building blocks (built into the language), from which other sophisticated data types (called *classes*) are constructed. Python classes are stored in Chapters 11 and 12.

The topic of Python data types can be extensive and complicated, requiring entire books to provide thorough analysis. However, this chapter focuses on providing basic coverage required for all technical artists to get started in the industry. The mutability of data is an important topic to consider when evaluating data types, as some can be changed after creation while others cannot. When evaluating numerical data, there are only three objects: integers, floats, and sometimes complex numbers. Prior book examples have only paired single values with single variables. Python's ability to store multiple values in a single object is done with *sequences, dictionaries*, and *sets*. Python has four sequence strategies: *strings*, *tuples*, *lists*, and *ranges*. *Dictionaries* and *sets* are more context sensitive than sequences. *Boolean* objects are simple in value but are crucial for programming logic flow. Other specialty purpose data types include *None*, *File*, and *Unicode*. The chapter concludes with an example using Python data types for procedural world generation.

MUTABLE VERSUS IMMUTABLE DATA

Many of Python's responsibilities, such as memory management, are hidden from users. Memory management is important to consider when dealing with Python's two primary types of data: *mutable* and *immutable*. Mutable objects can be altered after their creation while immutable objects cannot.

Data may be considered like boxes of memory. Variables are labels for those boxes. Boxes may have multiple labels. When data are mutable, the box contents are changeable: they may be rewritten, added to, or made smaller. The box changes in size to address the needs of the data. Immutable data cannot be changed. When immutable data need to be altered, new boxes are created with the new data.

Consider strings which are immutable. Two variable labels may apply to the same memory box. However, if one of the label boxes is altered, Python generates a new box to hold the changed data and applies the label to the new memory box. The other label is left to still point to the old box. This memory box storage is demonstrated in Code Sample 10.1 and Figure 10.1.

```
# Strings are immutable, they cannot be changed
# Variable label 'a' addresses a memory box containing string 'Hello World'
a = 'Hello world! '
#The same memory box now has a new label, 'b'
b = a
print(f'a: {a}, b: {b}')
```

DOI: 10.1201/9781003016427-10

```
# 'a' now addresses a new box has been created to store the new changes
a += 'Tech art rocks!'
# Variable 'b' still addresses the old memory box
print(f'a: {a}, b: {b}')

>>> a: Hello world!, b: Hello world!
a: Hello world! Tech art rocks!, b: Hello world!
```

Code Sample 10.1 Immutable Strings

Immutable objects are less computationally demanding than mutable. Requiring little overhead, immutable objects are ideal for representing static data. Mutable objects are dynamic. This capability requires additional overhead and memory management. Luckily, Python maintains the data invisibly and makes mutable objects easy to alter. Changing immutable objects is "expensive" requiring data duplication and integration. As a convenient rule thumb, use mutable objects when the data have the potential to change and use immutable objects when representing information that does not change. The mutability of Python types is reflected in Table 10.1.

NUMERIC

There are three types of Python built-in numeric data: integers, floating point ("*floats*"), and complex. Unadorned numbers (numbers containing no other characters other than numbers) are interpreted as integers. Numbers with decimal points yield floats. Numbers with appended "j" or "J" yield complex numbers.

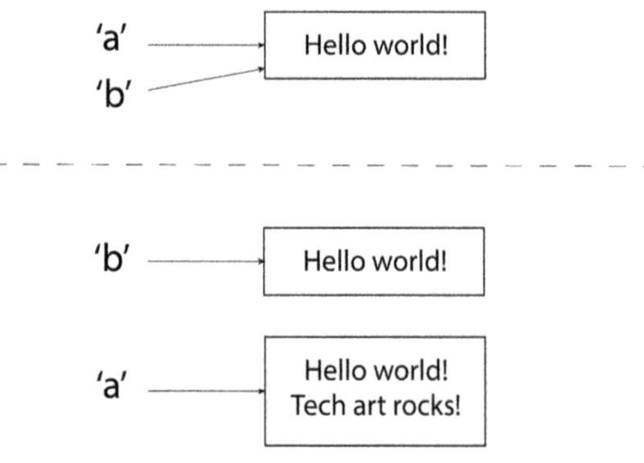

FIGURE 10.1 Immutable strings.

TABLE 10.1 Mutability of Python Data Types

Immutable	*Mutable*
Boolean	List
Integer	Dictionary
Floating Point	Set
Complex	
String	
Tuple	
Frozen Set	

TABLE 10.2 Numerical Operations

Operation	*Result*
x+y	Addition: Sum of x and y
x−y	Subtraction: Difference of x and y
x * y	Multiplication: Product of x and y
x/y	Division: Quotient of x and y
x//y	Integer Division: Floored Quotient of x and y
x%y	Modulus: Remainder of x/y
−x	Negative: x Negated
+x	Positive: x Unchanged
abs(x)	Absolute Value: Magnitude of x

Python numerical types support the operations listed in Table 10.2.

Python allows different numeric types to be mixed with each other. When doing so, the *narrower* number is converted to match the other and the operation is performed. Integers are narrower than floating point numbers which are narrower than complex. For example, when integer 3 is added to the floating point number 4.5, 3 is converted to a float, 3.0, and added to 4.5, resulting in a new floating point number, 7.5.

Integers

Integers are counting numbers including zero and negative numbers. They have no fractional component. Examples of integers are `101, -2, 0, 9, and 204`.

The *int()* function converts floating point numbers to integers. When doing so, Python simply cuts off all value after the decimal point, effectively rounding down. Shell Example 10.1 demonstrates this conversion.

```
>>> foo = -34.84
>>> int(foo)
-34
>>> bar = 24.78
>>> int(bar)
24
```

Shell Example 10.1 Integer Conversions

Warning: In Python 2.7 and earlier versions, when dividing two integers, the result returns an integer. When the result is not an integer, the value after the decimal is removed and returned as an integer. This behavior is demonstrated in Shell Example 10.2.

```
>>> 3 / 4
0
```

Shell Example 10.2 Python 2.7 Integer Division

In Python 3.0 and later, the division of two integers returns a floating point number. More recent integer division is demonstrated in Shell Example 10.3.

```
>>> 3 / 4
0.75
>>> 4 / 2
2.0
```

Shell Example 10.3 Python 3 Integer Division

When the older style of integer division result is desired, the double forward slash, //, operator is used. Shell Example 10.4 demonstrates this older, floored quotient division.

```
>>> -5 // 6
-1
>>> 8 // 10
0
>>> 6 // 3
2
```

Shell Example 10.4 Python 3 Floored Quotient

Floating Point

Floating point numbers (also called "*floats*") are rational numbers or numbers with fractions. Floating point numbers are represented with a whole number, followed by a decimal point, ., and then the fractional portion. Floating point number examples are `-51.995, -1.1, 0.0, 4.0, and 19.19`. They are implemented with the *double* type in the *C* language.

The *float()* function converts integers to floating point numbers. The process takes the integer, appends a decimal point, and assigns zero as the fractional portion. This conversion is demonstrated in Shell Example 10.5.

```
>>> float(-67)
-67.0
>>> float(47)
47.0
```

Shell Example 10.5 Float Conversion

The division of a floating point number and an integer always results in a float. Mixed type division is demonstrated in Shell Example 10.6.

```
>>> 3.0 / 4
0.75
```

Shell Example 10.6 Floating Point and Integer Division

Complex

Complex numbers are the mathematical equivalent of numbers that do not exist, such as $\sqrt{1}$. Unless dealing with sophisticated calculus, differential equations, or quaternion math, technical artists rarely deal with complex numbers in their daily programming. This section provides quick coverage for reference purposes.

Python complex numbers have two parts (both represented with floats): a real and an imaginary part. The imaginary portion is appended with a "*j*" or a "*J*". Python complex numbers are demonstrated in Shell Example 10.7.

```
>>> foo = 2+3j
>>> foo
(2+3j)
>>> bar = 4-5J
>>> bar
(4-5j)
>>> snafu = 6j
>>> snafu
6j
```

Shell Example 10.7 Complex Number Construction

The real and imaginary components of a complex number *z* are stored in the *z.real* and *z.imag* attributes. Shell Example 10.8 demonstrates these components.

```
>>> foo = 2+3j
>>> print(f'{foo.real} and {foo.imag} make complex number {foo}')
2.0 and 3.0 make complex number (2+3j)
```

Shell Example 10.8 Complex Number Attributes

Integers and floating point numbers are converted to complex using the *complex()* function. All integers and floats are converted to complex by appending `0j`. Shell Example 10.9 demonstrates this default conversion.

```
>>> foo = complex(3)
>>> foo
(3+0j)
>>> bar = complex(-7)
>>> bar
(-7+0j)
```

Shell Example 10.9 Complex Number Conversion

More robust mathematical functions for complex numbers are provided in the *cmath* library module.

SEQUENCES

Sequences are groups of values stored in singular objects. They are typically data structures which store related data items. They are often called *arrays* in other programming languages. All Python sequences store data in relative proximity so that each element is accessible through a specific index address. There are three types of immutable sequences: strings, tuples, and ranges. There is only one type of mutable sequence: list.

Operations

A common set of operations may be performed on all sequence types. Sequence size is accessed through the *len()* function. Content is accessed through indexing and unpacking. All sequences have minimum and maximum values and may test for value containment.

Length

Sequences may contain many, one, or possibly no objects. Defined in Language Template 10.1, Python provides the *len()* function to return the length, or number of objects, currently present within a sequence. Understanding the length of a sequence is important when indexing or accessing specific sequence objects, as demonstrated in Shell Example 10.10.

```
sequenceLength = len(SequenceObject)
```

Language Template 10.1 Sequence len() Function

```
>>> foo = 'abcdefghi'
>>> len(foo)
9
>>> bar = ['Johnny', 'Joey', 'Deedee', 'Tommy']
>>> len(bar)
4
```

Shell Example 10.10 Sequence len() Function

Indexing

All data in Python sequences are stored in relative order to each other so they may be indexed sequentially. In other words, sequence data can be counted and predictably accessed according to sequential order. Take for example the string "abcdefghi". The character *a* is in the first position, *b* is in the second, and so on until *i* is in the ninth position. Starting at `0`, each element has an address, or *index*, which indicates its position in the sequence. A sequence index is identified by square brackets, "*[]*" Code Sample 10.2 displays how to access sequence information with square bracket indexing.

```
foo = 'abcdefghi'
index = 0
print(f'String foo = {foo}')
while index < 9:
```

```
    print(f'foo[{index}]={foo[index]}')
    index +=1

>>> String foo = abcdefghi
foo[0]=a
foo[1]=b
foo[2]=c
foo[3]=d
foo[4]=e
foo[5]=f
foo[6]=g
foo[7]=h
foo[8]=i
```

Code Sample 10.2 Indices of a String

In the Code Sample 10.2 statement, *foo[index]* accesses the string value of foo at the *index* position.

Python indices start at `0` for the first element and increase sequentially to `n-1` for the last position, where `n` represents the total number of elements in a sequence. Indices may also count in reverse to access the sequence in reverse order. Index reversal is demonstrated in Code Sample 10.3.

```
foo = 'abcdefghi'
index = -1
print(f'String foo = {foo}')
while index > -10:
    print(f'foo[{index}]={foo[index]}')
    index -=1
>>> String foo = abcdefghi
foo[-1]=i
foo[-2]=h
foo[-3]=g
foo[-4]=f
foo[-5]=e
```

```
foo[-6]=d
foo[-7]=c
foo[-8]=b
foo[-9]=a
```

Code Sample 10.3 Indices of a String in Reverse Order

In the prior example, the element in the `-1` position is the last position while the first is in the `-9` position. When indexing in reverse, index ranges start at the negative of the length, `(length)`, and increase to `-1`.

By default, Python assumes that sequence indices start at zero and continue through to the `sequence length-1` position. Shell Example 10.11 displays the sequence contents of the last index.

```
>>> foo = 'abcdefghi'
>>> foo[8]
'i'
```

Shell Example 10.11 Indexing by Position

When a start and end position are supplied, separated with a colon, :, the elements from the start position through to the *`end-1`* position are returned. This is called a *slice*. Shell Example 10.12 demonstrates a simple *slice*.

```
>>> foo = 'abcdefghi'
>>> foo[1:7]
'bcdefg'
```

Shell Example 10.12 Indexing with Start and End

The start through *`end-1`* positions are returned by stepped increment values, followed by a colon, such as every 2nd value, instead of default 1 when given start and end positions (Shell Example 10.13).

```
>>> foo = 'abcdefghi'
>>> foo[1:9:2]
'bdfh'
```

Shell Example 10.13 Indexing with Start, End, and Increment

When a slice is provided with only a start position, Python returns the specified start through to the end positions: Shell Example 10.14.

```
>>> foo = 'abcdefghi'
>>> foo[4:]
'efghi'
```

Shell Example 10.14 Indexing with Default End

Similarly, when no start position is identified, the first through to the specified `end-1`values are returned: Shell Example 10.15.

```
>>> foo = 'abcdefghi'
>>> foo[:5]
'abcde'
```

Shell Example 10.15 Indexing with Default Start

Finally, when no start or end position are identified, the entire contents of the sequence are delivered: Shell Example 10.16.

```
>>> foo = 'abcdefghi'
>>> foo[:]
'abcdefghi'
```

Shell Example 10.16 Indexing with Default Start and End

Python sequence indexing rules are listed in Table 10.3.

TABLE 10.3 Sequence Indices

Sequence Index (sequence[n])	*Return Value*
Sequence[0→(*length* – 1)]	Content of the *n* – 1 position
Sequence[–*length* → –1]	Content of the *length* – *n* + 1 position
Sequence[*start*:*end*]	Items *start* through (*end* – 1)
Sequence[*start*:*end*:*increment*]	Items *start* through (*end* – 1) by increment
Sequence[*start*:]	Items *start* through to the end
Sequence[*end*]	Items at beginning through (*end* – 1)
Sequence[:]	All items

Unpacking

Unpacking is a strategy for accessing the contents of a sequence by directly assigning variables for each component of the sequence. Language Template 10.2 defines how unpacking is achieved by providing a group of variables, separated by commas, and assigning the sequence components to the group members.

```
>>> variable1, variable2, variable3(, ...) = sequence
```

Language Template 10.2 Sequence Unpacking

Shell Example 10.17 demonstrates how there must be exactly one variable for every component in the sequence for the unpacking to work successfully.

```
>>> # Unpacking a string
>>> a, b, c = 'XYZ'
>>> print(f'a = {a}, b = {b}, c = {c}')
a = X, b = Y, c = Z
>>> # Unpacking a tuple
>>> a, b, c = 69, 76, 84
>>> print(f'a = {a}, b = {b}, c = {c}')
a = 69, b = 76, c = 84
>>> # Unpacking a list
>>> a, b, c, d = ['Johnny', 'Joey', 'Deedee', 'Tommy']
>>> print(f'a = {a}, b = {b}, c = {c}, d = {d}')
a = Johnny, b = Joey, c = Deedee, d = Tommy
>>> # Unpacking a range
>>> a, b, c = range(3)
>>> print(f'a = {a}, b = {b}, c = {c}')
a = 0, b = 1, c = 2
```

Shell Example 10.17 Unpacking Sequences

Python 3 introduces a new unpacking feature. When an unpacking variable is preceded with an asterisk, *, Python treats that variable as a wildcard list with zero or more elements. (Lists are explained later in the chapter). The wildcard matches zero or more elements to align the sequence with the unpacking variables. Wildcard unpacking is demonstrated in Shell Example 10.18.

```
# 1-1 Unpacking
>>> a, b, *c, d = ['Johnny', 'Joey', 'Deedee', 'Tommy']
>>> print(f'a={a}, b={b}, c={c}, d={d}')
```

```
a=Johnny, b=Joey, c=['Deedee'], d=Tommy

# Wildcard multiple unpacking
>>> a, b, *c, d = ['Jerry', 'Mark', 'Bob1', 'Bob2', 'Allen']
>>> print(f'a={a}, b={b}, c={c}, d={d}')
a=Jerry, b=Mark, c=['Bob1', 'Bob2'], d=Allen

# Empty Wildcard Unpacking
>>> a, b, *c, d = ['Gordon', 'Stuart', 'Andy']
>>> print(f'a={a}, b={b}, c={c}, d={d}')
a=Gordon, b=Stuart, c=[], d=Andy
```

Shell Example 10.18 Wildcard Unpacking

Minimum/Maximum

All sequences have minimum and maximum values. The *min()* function returns the smallest item. The *max()* function returns the largest item. The *min()* and *max()* functions are demonstrated in Shell Example 10.19.

```
>>> foo = 'XYZ'
>>> min(foo)
'X'
>>> max(foo)
'Z'
>>> foo = (69, 76, 84, 99)
>>> min(foo)
69
>>> max(foo)
99
>>> foo = ['Johnny', 'Joey', 'Deedee', 'Tommy']
>>> min(foo)
'Deedee'
>>> max(foo)
'Tommy'
```

Shell Example 10.19 Minimum and Maximum Sequence Values

Containment

All sequences may test if a value is contained within it. The *in* operation tests if a value is equal to any component within a sequence. The *not in* operation tests if no component is equal to any value. Shell Example 10.20 tests sequence containment.

```
>>> foo = (69, 76, 84, 99)
>>> 76 in foo
True
>>> 84 not in foo
False
```

Shell Example 10.20 Sequence Containment Tests

Strings

Python strings are immutable sequences of Unicode objects. A Unicode object represents an alpha-numeric or text-based character. Unicode objects are explained later in this chapter.

Construction

Defined in Language Template 10.3, string sequences are constructed by surrounding text data with single, double, or triple quotes.

```
>>> singleQuoteString = 'single quote string'
>>> singleQuoteString = 'single quote string'
>>> doubleQuoteString = "double quote string"
>>> tripleSingleQuoteString = '''Single triple quotes string '''
>>> tripleDoubleQuoteString = """ Double triple quotes string """
```

Language Template 10.3 String Formation Techniques

More information on constructing strings is supplied in Chapter 7.

Strings are either displayed or they are stored as variables to be re-used or combined with other strings. They are displayed by either simply entering their variable names into the Python shell or using the *print()* function, as demonstarted in Shell Example 10.21.

```
>>> myString = "Essential Programming for the Technical Artist"
>>> myString
'Essential Programming for the Technical Artist'
>>> print(myString)
Essential Programming for the Technical Artist
```

Shell Example 10.21 String Display

Note when string variables are displayed directly the shell, Python wraps them in single quotes, '', to designate them as strings. When displayed as function parameters, strings are presented as pure sequences of characters. As variables, strings may be re-used in a plethora of different directions from database entries to labels placed on buttons and sliders.

Formatting

There are four methods for formatting strings: Python formatting, *format()* function, manual formatting, and old school % format. These methods are explained in Chapter 7.

Immutable

Strings are immutable sequences. Once they are defined, they cannot be altered. Shell Example 10.22 demonstrates the results of attempting to alter and immutable sequence (string).

```
>>> myString = 'Technical Arf Python'
>>> myString[12] = 't'
Traceback (most recent call last):
  File "<console>", line 1, in <module>
TypeError: 'str' object does not support item assignment
```

Shell Example 10.22 Attempting String Alteration

While strings may be immutable, they can be easily recreated or replaced. Shell Example 10.23 re-creates a string.

```
>>> myString = 'Technical Arf Python'
>>> myString = 'Technical Art Python'
>>> myString
'Technical Art Python'
```

Shell Example 10.23 String Re-creation

String Methods

Python 3 includes many methods for performing operations on strings. The methods most often employed by technical artists are described below. They assist with reading file paths, parsing names, and regenerating new labels.

str

The *str(data)* method translates Python data into strings. Shell Example 10.24 demonstrates translation to strings.

```
>>> myList = [ 22, 33, 44]
>>> myTuple = 23.5, 17, False
>>> myRange = range(1, 11, 2)
>>> str(myList)
```

```
'[22, 33, 44]'
>>> str(myTuple)
'(23.5, 17, False)'
>>> str(myRange)
'range(1, 11, 2)'
```

Shell Example 10.24 Python str()

find

The *.find(sub)* operation returns the first index in a string where the substring *sub* is found. The method returns `-1` when *sub* is not found: Shell Example 10.25.

```
>>> foo = "Technical Artists program in Python"
>>> foo.find('Art')
10
```

Shell Example 10.25 String .find() Method

rfind

The *.rfind(sub)* operation looks backward from the right and returns the last index in the string where the substring sub is found. The method returns `-1` when sub is not found: Shell Example 10.26.

```
>>> foo = "Technical Artists program in Python to make Technical Art"
>>> foo.rfind('Art')
54
```

Shell Example 10.26 String rfind() Method

join

The *.join(sequence)* function returns a new string where the source string is inserted between every pair of elements contained within the given *sequence*: Shell Example 10.27.

```
>>> foo = "Technical Artists program in Python"
>>> foo.join(['All ', ' daily'])
'All Technical Artists program in Python daily'
>>> '.'.join('FUBAR')
'F.U.B.A.R'
```

Shell Example 10.27 String .join() Method

lstrip
The *.lstrip([chars])* method returns a copy of the source string where the leading characters have been removed. Removal halts as soon as a character not contained in the input is encountered. Input order is not considered: Shell Example 10.28.

```
>>> foo = "Technical Artists program in Python"
>>> foo.lstrip('cTeh')
'nical Artists program in Python'
```

Shell Example 10.28 String .lstrip() Method

rstrip
The *.rstrip([chars])* method returns a copy of the source string where the trailing characters have been removed. Removal halts as soon as a character not contained in the input is encountered. Input order is not considered: Shell Example 10.29.

```
>>> foo = "Technical Artists program in Python"
>>> foo.rstrip('otnh')
'Technical Artists program in Py'
```

Shell Example 10.29 String rstrip() Method

strip
The *.strip([chars])* method returns a copy of the source string where the leading and trailing characters have been removed. Removal halts as soon as characters not contained in the input *chars* are encountered. Input order is not considered: Shell Example 10.30.

```
>>> foo = "technical Artists program in Python"
>>> foo.strip('notech')
'ical Artists program in Py'
```

Shell Example 10.30 String strip() Method

Replace
The *.replace(old, new)* function returns a copy of the source string with all occurrences of the *old* string replaced with the *new* string: Shell Example 10.31.

```
>>> foo = "Technical Artists program in Python"
>>> foo.replace(' ', '.')
'Technical.Artists.program.in.Python'
```

Shell Example 10.31 String replace() Method

split

The *.split(separator)* function returns a list of words in the source string, using the separator as the delimiter. When no *separator* is present, Python uses a whitespace as the delimiter: Shell Example 10.32.

```
>>> foo = "Technical Artists program in Python"
>>> foo.split()
['Technical', 'Artists', 'program', 'in', 'Python']
>>> foo.split('Artists')
['Technical ', ' program in Python']
```

Shell Example 10.32 String split() Method

Tuples

Tuples are immutable collections of data. Tuple elements do not need to be the same data type. As shown in Shell Example 10.33, they can be different.

```
>>> aTuple = 69, 76, 84
>>> anotherTuple = "Technical Artists", 24, 24.66
>>> tupleOfTuples=((1, 2, 3), (11.2, 36.9))
```

Shell Example 10.33 Sample Tuples

Tuples are useful for storing unlike, *heterogeneous*, types of data, where accessing the information is done using indexing or unpacking. Tuples are also useful for returning multiple function values as one object. Code Sample 10.4 returns multiple values as one tuple.

```
def circleData(radius = 1):
    pi = 3.1415
    circumference = 2.0 * pi * radius
    volume = pi * radius * radius

    return (circumference, volume)

print(circleData(12))
>>> (75.396, 452.376)
```

Code Sample 10.4 Function Tuple Return

Language Template 10.4 defines two strategies for building tuples. Tuples are composed of values separated by commas. The composition may be surrounded by parentheses but is only necessary when generating nested tuples.

```
>>> aTuple = value1, value2(, ..., valueN)
>>> aTuple = (value1, value2(, ..., valueN))
```

Language Template 10.4 Generating Tuples

Language Template 10.5 generates empty and single tuples with and without parentheses. Empty tuples are generated with a pair of parentheses. Single value tuples must be followed with a comma, even when surrounded with parentheses.

```
>>> emptyTuple = ()
>>> singleValueTuple = value,
>>> singleValueTuple = (value,)
```

Language Template 10.5 Empty and Single Value Tuples

Shell Example 10.34 demonstrates how tuples are always displayed with bounding parentheses.

```
>>> animals = 'dragons', 'tigers', 'bears'
>>> animals
('dragons', 'tigers', 'bears')
```

Shell Example 10.34 Tuple Display

Other than common sequence operations, there is only one tuple method, *tuple()*. The *tuple(data)* constructor converts Python lists and ranges into tuples, as demonstrated with Shell Example 10.35.

```
>>> myList = [ 22, 33, 44]
>>> myRange = range(10)
>>> tuple(myList)
(22, 33, 44)
>>> tuple(myRange)
(0, 1, 2, 3, 4, 5, 6, 7, 8, 9)
```

Shell Example 10.35 Python tuple()

Tuples are immutable and may not be altered after definition. They may be redefined but any attempt to change their contents results in error. Shell Example 10.36 demonstrates the consequences.

```
>>> a = ('dog names', ['Bandit', 'Fido'])

# Unsuccessful attempt to change tuple data
>>> a[0] = 'Cat Names'
Traceback (most recent call last):
  File "<console>", line 1, in <module>
TypeError: 'tuple' object does not support item assignment

# Unsuccessful attempt to change tuple data
>>> a += 'Cat Names'
Traceback (most recent call last):
  File "<console>", line 1, in <module>
TypeError: can only concatenate tuple (not "str") to tuple

# Successful attempt to re-define tuple data
>>> a = ('Cat Names', ['Sheeba', 'Felix'])
```

Shell Example 10.36 Attempting to Alter Tuple Content

Lists

Lists are mutable collections of data. Like tuples, lists may be composed of different types of data. Shell Example 10.37 demonstrates these differences.

```
>>> aList = [ 36, 48, 69, 76, 84, 99]
>>> anotherList = [23, '3D', 'Technical Art', 67.45]
>>> nestedList = [[1, 0, 0], [0, 1, 0], [0, 0, 1]]
```

Shell Example 10.37 Example Lists

Lists are great for storing data that may be iterated over, indexed, or unpacked. Like tuples, lists are useful for returning multiple function values in one object. Unlike tuples, lists are mutable and their contents are alterable after definition.

Construction

Language Template 10.6 establishes lists designated as multiple values bound by square brackets, *[]*. Empty lists are generated with only a pair of square brackets. Single values have no punctuation and multiple values are separated by commas.

```
>>> aList = [ value1, value2[, ..., valueN]]
>>> emptyList = []
>>> singleList = [ value ]
```

Language Template 10.6 List, Empty List and Single Value List

Language Template 10.7 explains lists may also be constructed using list comprehension. This is a fancy term for generating a list by bounding a *for loop* with square brackets. Shell Example 10.38 demonstrates list comprehension in action.

```
>>> aList = [ x for x in iterable]
```

Language Template 10.7 List Comprehension Construction

```
>>> names = 'Johnny', 'Joey', 'Deedee', 'Tommy'
>>> aList = [ name for name in names]
>>> aList
['Johnny', 'Joey', 'Deedee', 'Tommy']
```

Shell Example 10.38 List Comprehension Construction

Mutable Operations

Lists are mutable which means they can be changed after their creation. The following operations may be performed on pre-existing lists.

Replacement

Existing list items are replaceable with new items. When new items are iterables, the existing slice lengths must match the length of the new iterables (Shell Example 10.39).

```
>>> aList = [ 1, 2, 3, 4, 5, 6, 7, 8, 9]
>>> aList[3] = 44
>>> aList
[1, 2, 3, 44, 5, 6, 7, 8, 9]
>>> aList[7:9] = [77, 88, 99]
>>> aList
[1, 2, 3, 44, 5, 6, 7, 77, 88, 99]
>>> aList[0:9:2] = [22, 42, 66, 98, 100]
>>> aList
[22, 2, 42, 44, 66, 6, 98, 77, 100, 99]
```

Shell Example 10.39 List Replacement

Deletion
The *del (index)* operation removes list items identified by the index slice. Shell Example 10.40 demonstrates multiple list deletions.

```
>>> aList = [1, 2, 3, 4, 5, 6, 7, 8, 9]
>>> del aList[0:9:2]
>>> aList
[2, 4, 6, 8]
>>> del aList[2:4]
>>> aList
[2, 4]
>>> del aList[1]
>>> aList
[2]
```

Shell Example 10.40 List Deletion

Append
The *append(item)* operation appends a new item to the end of a list: Shell Example 10.41.

```
>>> aList = [11, 22, 33]
>>> aList.append(44)
>>> aList
[11, 22, 33, 44]
```

Shell Example 10.41 List append()

Clear
The *clear()* operation removes all content from lists: Shell Example 10.42.

```
>>> aList = [2, 4, 6, 8]
>>> aList.clear()
>>> aList
[]
```

Shell Example 10.42 List clear() Operation

Copy
The *copy()* operation returns copies of lists: Shell Example 10.43.

```
>>> aList = [5, 10, 15, 20]
>>> copyList = aList.copy()
>>> copyList
[5, 10, 15, 20]
```

Shell Example 10.43 List copy()

Lists copied using this function are not new labels addressing existing predefined data blocks. They are entirely new: Shell Example 10.44.

```
>>> foo = [1,2,3,4]
>>> bar = foo.copy()
>>> foo.append(5)
>>> print(foo, bar)
[1, 2, 3, 4, 5] [1, 2, 3, 4]
```

Shell Example 10.44 Copy() Creates New Data

Extension
The *extend(t)* , or *lists* += *t*, operation extends a list by *t*: Shell Example 10.45.

```
>>> aList = [5, 10, 15, 20]
>>> foo = [25, 30, 35, 40]
>>> aList += foo
>>> aList
[5, 10, 15, 20, 25, 30, 35, 40]
```

Shell Example 10.45 List extend()

Insert
The *insert(index, item)* operation inserts an *item* into a list at the *index* position. The item may be any data component: Shell Example 10.46.

```
>>> aList = [12.8, 25.6, 51.2]
>>> aList.insert(1, 19.2)
>>> aList
[12.8, 19.2, 25.6, 51.2]
```

Shell Example 10.46 List insert()

Pop

The *pop(index)* operation removes the list item from the index position and returns its value. By default, the index value is `-1` and the last list item is removed and returned: Shell Example 10.47.

```
>>> aList = [2, 4, 6, 8]
>>> foo = aList.pop(2)
>>> print(f'foo = {foo}, aList = {aList}')
foo = 6, aList = [2, 4, 8]
```

Shell Example 10.47 List pop()

Remove

The *remove(item)* operation removes the first instance of an item from a list: Shell Example 10.48.

```
>>> aList = ['dragons', 'tigers', 'bears']
>>> aList.remove('tigers')
>>> aList
['dragons', 'bears']
```

Shell Example 10.48 List remove()

Reverse

The *reverse()* operation reverses list contents: Shell Example 10.49.

```
>>> aList = [0, 2, 4, 6, 8, 10]
>>> aList.reverse()
>>> aList
[10, 8, 6, 4, 2, 0]
```

Shell Example 10.49 List reverse()

Methods

Lists have other methods exclusive from other data types including *count(), index(), list(), and sort()*.

Count

The *count(item)* operation returns the number of times an item appears in a list: Shell Example 10.50.

```
>>> aList = [0, 2, 4, 6, 8, 2, 4, 8, 16, 2, 12, 22]
>>> aList.count(2)
3
```

Shell Example 10.50 List count()

Index

The *index(item[, start[, end]])* operation returns the index of the first instance of an item between the start and end locations. The *start* and *end* arguments are optional: Shell Example 10.51.

```
>>> aList = [0, 2, 4, 6, 8, 2, 4, 8, 16, 2, 12, 22]
>>> aList.index(2, 4)
5
```

Shell Example 10.51 List index()

List

The list(item) constructor converts a non-list sequence to a list: Shell Example 10.52.

```
>>> list(('dragons', 'lions', 'tigers', 'bears'))
['dragons', 'lions', 'tigers', 'bears']
>>> list('FUBAR')
['F', 'U', 'B', 'A', 'R']
>>> list(range(4))
[0, 1, 2, 3]
```

Shell Example 10.52 List list()

Sort

The *sort()* operation re-organizes list contents alpha-numerically: Shell Example 10.53.

```
>>> aList = [76.98, 61, 89.67, 33.15]
>>> aList.sort()
>>> aList
[33.15, 61, 76.98, 89.67]
```

Shell Example 10.53 List sort()

Lists versus Tuples

Lists and tuples are similar data types in that both store collections of data and both are afforded operational methods. They are both good for assembling multiple items and returning them as single objects. List and tuples both can store nested data which makes them ideal for representing data structures such as matrices (see below for matrix coverage).

Lists are mutable which means that they can grow, shrink, and change content value. This makes them ideal for performing basic database functionality. Their dynamic structure also makes them consume more memory.

Tuples are immutable and cannot change once they have been created. This makes them less versatile than lists. They do, however, consume less memory.

Ranges

Ranges are immutable data types storing sequential integers used for looping specific numbers of iterations in *for* loops.

Ranges are constructed using the *range()* constructor. Its usage is demonstrated in Language Template 10.8. The function takes *start*, *stop*, and *increment* integer input arguments. The function returns an integer sequence starting with the *start* argument and increases the input increment amount until one less than the *end* argument. The input *increment* argument is optional and defaults to `+1`. When the end value is less than the start value, the sequence reduces until one greater than the *end* argument. The *start* argument is also optional and defaults to zero when omitted.

```
>>> myRange = range([start,] end[, increment])
```

Language Template 10.8 Range Construction

Ranges are displayed within the context of the *range()* constructor. To display their contents, they need to be converted to lists or tuples using the *list()* or *tuple()* constructors. Shell Example 10.54 demonstrates how *ranges* may be displayed.

```
>>> range(10)
range(0, 10)
>>> range(10)
range(0, 10)
>>> foo = range(10)
>>> list(foo)
[0, 1, 2, 3, 4, 5, 6, 7, 8, 9]
>>> tuple(foo)
(0, 1, 2, 3, 4, 5, 6, 7, 8, 9)
>>> myRange = range(1, 11)
>>> list(myRange)
[1, 2, 3, 4, 5, 6, 7, 8, 9, 10]
>>> myRange = range(1, 11, 2)
>>> list(myRange)
[1, 3, 5, 7, 9]
>>> list(range(5, -5, -1))
[5, 4, 3, 2, 1, 0, -1, -2, -3, -4]
```

```
>>> list(range(0))
[]
>>> list(range(10,-1))
[]
```

Shell Example 10.54 Python range()

Matrices

Tuples and lists may contain any type of Python object in any order, including other tuples and lists. Lists and tuples which contain other lists and tuples are referred to as being *nested*. Nested lists and tuples make ideal matrices.

Language Template 10.9 demonstrates how matrices are defined using nested lists and tuples.

```
>>> listMatrix = [ [listA], [listB], ... ]
>>> tupleMatrix = ( (TupleA), (TupleB), ...)
```

Language Template 10.9 List and Tuple Matrices

Matrix values are accessed using single sequence indexing for every dimension in the matrix. Shell Example 10.55 manipulates a matrix of three rows and three columns. Code Sample 10.5 demonstrates how the matrix can be printed.

```
>>> listMatrix = [[1, 2, 3], [4, 5, 6], [7, 8, 9]]
>>> listMatrix[2][2]
9
>>> listMatrix[1][0]
4
```

Shell Example 10.55 Defining and Accessing Matrices

```
def printMat(matrix):
    buff = '\n'
    for i in range(len(matrix)):
        for j in range(len(matrix[i])):
            buff += f'{str(matrix[i][j])} '
        buff += '\n'

    print(buff)
```

```
listMatrix = [[1, 2, 3], [4, 5, 6], [7, 8, 9]]
printMat(listMatrix)


>>>
1 2 3
4 5 6
7 8 9
```

Code Sample 10.5 Displaying Matrix Contents

Matrices are not a built-in Python data type. Displaying and performing operations in the manner described above can be awkward and taxing. A convenient Python library supporting matrices and other linear algebra structures is the *numpy* library. Numpy is an open source library created to facilitate Python numerical computing. Numpy provides data classes and operations making matrix usage fast and painless. Shell Example 10.56 explains how the same previous matrix is manipulated using the *numpy* library.

```
>>> import numpy as np
>>> myMat = np.matrix([[1, 2, 3], [4, 5, 6], [7, 8, 9]])
>>> print(myMat)
[[1 2 3]
 [4 5 6]
 [7 8 9]]
```

Shell Example 10.56 Numpy Usage

DICTIONARIES

A Python *dictionary* is a collection of *key-value* pairs. Dictionary *keys* are objects mapped to hashable values. A hashable value is any object which is immutable or does not change. Dictionary *values*, on the other hand, may be any Python object including immutable data types. Dictionary values are accessed via their associated keys.

Construction

Language Template 10.10 visualizes how key-value pairs are constructed with an immutable key and any object, separated with a colon.

```
>>> keyValuePair = key : object
```

Language Template 10.10 Key-Value Pair

In Python context, Language Template 10.11 displays how dictionaries are comma-separated lists of key-value pairs, surrounded with curly braces, *{}*. An empty pair of braces constitutes an empty dictionary. Shell Example 10.57 demonstrates dictionary generation.

```
>>> dictionary = { keyValuePairA, keyValuePairB[, ...keyValuePairN]}
```

Language Template 10.11 Python Dictionaries

```
>>> dict = {}
>>> dict = {'one':1, 'two':2, 'three':3}
>>> dict = {69.1:'Technical', 76.2:'Artist', 84.3:'Programmers'}
>>> dict = {1:83.22, 2:71.99, 3:66.81}
>>> dict = {(1, 2, 3):'tupleKey', 23.1:'floatKey', 86:'integerKey'}
```

Shell Example 10.57 Python Dictionaries

Dictionary can also be created using dictionary comprehension: Shell Example 10.58.

```
>>> dict = {x:x*10 for x in range(5)}
>>> dict
{0: 0, 1: 10, 2: 20, 3: 30, 4: 40}
```

Shell Example 10.58 Dictionary Comprehension

Access Methods

There are multiple ways of accessing dictionary data. Some return dictionary *views* which provide snapshots of a dictionary's contents. Dictionary views are iterable.

Key Index

The value of a dictionary entry is accessed with the key in square brackets,*[]*: Shell Example 10.59.

```
>>> myDict = {'a':'Jerry', 'b':'Mark', 1:'Bob1', 2:'Bob2', 'c':'Allen'}
>>> myDict[2]
'Bob2'
```

Shell Example 10.59 Dictionary Key Access

Get

The *get(key)* operation returns the value for a *key* if the *key* exists in a dictionary. Otherwise, it returns *None*: Shell Example 10.60.

```
>>> myDict = {'a':'Jerry', 'b':'Mark', 1:'Bob1', 2:'Bob2', 'c':'Allen'}
>>> myDict.get('b')
'Mark'
```

Shell Example 10.60 Dictionary get()

The *get()* method is useful for its *default* and *None* return values. For example, the *get()* method will not return an error when an improper key is provided, as demonstrated by Shell Example 10.61.

```
>>> myDict = {'a':'Jerry', 'b':'Mark', 1:'Bob1', 2:'Bob2', 'c':'Allen'}
>>> print(myDict.get('Josh'))
None
>>> print(myDict['Josh'])
Traceback (most recent call last):
  File "<console>", line 1, in <module>
KeyError: 'Josh'
```

Shell Example 10.61 Get() versus Index Accessing

Items

The *items()* operation returns a view of a dictionary's keys and values: Shell Example 10.62.

```
>>> myDict = {'a':'Jerry', 'b':'Mark', 1:'Bob1', 2:'Bob2', 'c':'Allen'}
>>> myDict.items()
dict_items([('a', 'Jerry'), ('b', 'Mark'), (1, 'Bob1'), (2, 'Bob2'),
('c', 'Allen')])
```

Shell Example 10.62 Dictionary items()

Iter

The *iter(dictionary)* method returns an iterator over the keys of a dictionary: Shell Example 10.63.

```
>>> myDict = {'a':'Jerry', 'b':'Mark', 1:'Bob1', 2:'Bob2', 'c':'Allen'}
>>> list(iter(myDict))
['a', 'b', 1, 2, 'c']
```

Shell Example 10.63 Dictionary iter()

Keys

The *keys()* operation returns a view of a dictionary's keys: Shell Example 10.64.

```
>>> myDict = {'a':'Jerry', 'b':'Mark', 1:'Bob1', 2:'Bob2', 'c':'Allen'}
>>> myDict.keys()
dict_keys(['a', 'b', 1, 2, 'c'])
```

Shell Example 10.64 Dictionary keys()

List

The *list(dictionary)* constructor returns a list of a dictionary's keys: Shell Example 10.65.

```
>>> myDict = {'a':'Jerry', 'b':'Mark', 1:'Bob1', 2:'Bob2', 'c':'Allen'}
>>> list(myDict)
['a', 'b', 1, 2, 'c']
```

Shell Example 10.65 Dictionary list()

Values

The *values()* operation returns a view of a dictionary's values: Shell Example 10.66.

```
>>> myDict = {'a':'Jerry', 'b':'Mark', 1:'Bob1', 2:'Bob2', 'c':'Allen'}
>>> myDict.values()
dict_values(['Jerry', 'Mark', 'Bob1', 'Bob2', 'Allen'])
```

Shell Example 10.66 Dictionary values()

Containment

There are two methods for testing a dictionary's containment of a key: *in* and *not in*: Shell Example 10.67.

```
>>> myDict = {'a':'Jerry', 'b':'Mark', 1:'Bob1', 2:'Bob2', 'c':'Allen'}
>>> 'c' in myDict
True
>>> 'Elvis' not in myDict
True
```

Shell Example 10.67 Dictionary In and Not In

Mutable Operations

Dictionaries are mutable which means that their vale content may be changed and items may be removed or added. They preserve their insertion order. New keys are always appended to the end of a dictionary, even after a deletion.

Key Set

Every object within a dictionary is modifiable by assigning a new value to a dictionary indexed with the intended key: Shell Example 10.68.

```
>>> myDict = {'a':'Jerry', 'b':'Mark', 1:'Bob1', 2:'Bob2', 'c':'Allen'}
>>> myDict['c'] = 'Josh'
>>> myDict
{'a': 'Jerry', 'b': 'Mark', 1: 'Bob1', 2: 'Bob2', 'c': 'Josh'}
```

Shell Example 10.68 Dictionary Key Set

Delete

The *del* Python function removes an object from a dictionary indexed by its key: Shell Example 10.69.

```
>>> myDict = {'a':'Jerry', 'b':'Mark', 1:'Bob1', 2:'Bob2', 'c':'Josh'}
>>> del myDict[2]
>>> myDict
{'a': 'Jerry', 'b': 'Mark', 1: 'Bob1', 'c': 'Josh'}
```

Shell Example 10.69 Dictionary del Command

Clear

The *clear()* function removes all objects from a dictionary: Shell Example 10.70.

```
>>> myDict = {'a':'Joe', 'b':'Mick', 'c':'Paul', 'd':'Terry'}
>>> myDict.clear()
>>> myDict
{}
```

Shell Example 10.70 Dictionary clear()

Copy

The *copy()* function returns a copy of a dictionary: Shell Example 10.71.

```
>>> myDict = {'a':'Jerry', 'b':'Roddy', 'c':'Neville', 'd':'John',
    'e':'Dick', 'f':'Rico'}
>>> myDictB = myDict.copy()
>>> myDictB
{'a': 'Jerry', 'b': 'Roddy', 'c': 'Neville', 'd': 'John', 'e': 'Dick',
'f': 'Rico'}
```

Shell Example 10.71 Dictionary copy()

Pop

The *pop(key)* function removes a key from a dictionary and returns its value: Shell Example 10.72.

```
>>> myDict = {'a':'Jerry', 'b':'Roddy', 'c':'Neville', 'd':'John',
    'e':'Dick', 'f':'Rico'}
>>> objectA = myDict.pop('a')
>>> print(f'objectA={objectA}, myDict={myDict}')
objectA=Jerry, myDict={'b': 'Roddy', 'c': 'Neville', 'd': 'John', 'e':
'Dick', 'f': 'Rico'}
```

Shell Example 10.72 DIctionary pop()

Popitem

The *popitem()* removes the last item in a dictionary and returns its key and value: Shell Example 10.73.

```
>>> myDict = {'a':'Jerry', 'b':'Roddy', 'c':'Neville', 'd':'John',
    'e':'Dick', 'f':'Rico'}
>>> key, value = myDict.popitem()
>>> print(f'key={key}, value={value}, myDict={myDict}')
key=f, value=Rico, myDict={'a': 'Jerry', 'b': 'Roddy', 'c': 'Neville',
'd': 'John', 'e': 'Dick'}
```

Shell Example 10.73 Dictionary popitem()

Update

The *update([other])* function replaces a dictionary with key-value pairs from *other*, overwriting existing keys: Shell Example 10.74.

```
>>> myDict = {'a':'Debbie', 'b':'Chris', 'c':'Clem', 'd':'Jimmy',
'e':'Frank'}
>>> myDict.update({'d':'Leigh', 'e':'Matt'})
>>> myDict
{'a': 'Debbie', 'b': 'Chris', 'c': 'Clem', 'd': 'Leigh', 'e': 'Matt'}
```

Shell Example 10.74 Dictionary update()

SETS

Sets are un-ordered collections of *distinct* objects. In other words, their order is uncertain, and they cannot contain object duplicates. The objects must be hashable which means that they must be immutable. Sets are used for membership testing, pruning duplicate objects, and performing Boolean set operations such as union, intersection, difference, and symmetric difference.

There are two types of Python sets: sets and frozensets. Sets are mutable and frozensets are immutable.

Language Template 10.12 displays how sets are created by surrounding curly braces, *{}* around a comma-separated list of elements or by using the *set(list)* constructor. Shell Example 10.75 displays simple sets in action.

```
>>> mySet = { elementA, elementB[, ..., ElementN]}
>>> mySet = set(list)
```

Language Template 10.12 Python Sets

```
>>> mySet = {'Jerry', 'Mark', 'Bob1', 'Bob2', 'Allen'}
>>> mySet
{'Allen', 'Bob1', 'Bob2', 'Jerry', 'Mark'}
>>> set([ 1, 3, 5, 7, 9])
{1, 3, 5, 7, 9}
>>> set('FUBAR')
{'R', 'B', 'U', 'A', 'F'}
```

Shell Example 10.75 Python Sets

Sets are also created using *set comprehension*: Shell Example 10.76.

```
>>> {letter for letter in 'Mississippi' if letter not in 'si'}
{'p', 'M'}
```

Shell Example 10.76 Python Set Comprehension

Language Template 10.13 introduces how *frozensets* are created using the *frozenset(list)* constructor. Shell Example 10.77 displays *frozensets* in context.

```
>>> myFrozenset = frozenset(list)
```

Language Template 10.13 Python Frozensets

```
>> frozenset('SNAFU')
frozenset({'N', 'S', 'U', 'A', 'F'})
>>> frozenset(['Joe', 'Mick', 'Paul', 'Terry'])
frozenset({'Joe', 'Paul', 'Terry', 'Mick'})
```

Shell Example 10.77 Python frozenset()

Operations

The following operations can be performed on sets or frozensets.

Len

The *len(set/frozenset)* operation returns the number of elements in the set or frozenset: Shell Example 10.78.

```
>>> len({'Jerry', 'Mark', 'Bob1', 'Bob2', 'Allen'})
5
>>> len(frozenset(['Joe', 'Mick', 'Paul', 'Terry']))
4
```

Shell Example 10.78 Set len()

Copy

The *copy()* operation returns a copy of the set or frozenset: Shell Example 10.79.

```
>>> mySet = {'Joe', 'Mick', 'Paul', 'Terry'}
>>> mySet2 = mySet.copy()
>>> mySet2
{'Joe', 'Paul', 'Terry', 'Mick'}
```

Shell Example 10.79 Set copy()

Membership

The *in* and *not in* key words are used to test for set membership: Shell Example 10.80.

```
>>> mySet = {'Johnny', 'Joey', 'Deedee', 'Tommy'}
>>> myFrozen = frozenset(['Jerry', 'Mark', 'Bob1', 'Bob2', 'Allen'])
>>> 'Deedee' in mySet
True
>>> 'Debbie' not in myFrozen
True
```

Shell Example 10.80 Set Membership

Disjoint

The *.isdisjoint(other)* operation returns True when no elements in the set or in the other set are the same: Shell Example 10.81.

```
>>> mySet = {'Johnny', 'Joey', 'Deedee', 'Tommy'}
>>> myFrozen = frozenset(['Jerry', 'Mark', 'Bob1', 'Bob2', 'Allen'])
>>> mySet.isdisjoint(myFrozen)
True
```

Shell Example 10.81 Set isdisjoint()

Subsets

Sets use the *.issubset(other)* as well as comparison operators to test if the set elements are contained within *other*: Shell Example 10.82.

```
>> myFrozen = frozenset(['Jerry', 'Mark', 'Bob1', 'Bob2', 'Allen'])
>>> other = frozenset(['Allen', 'Bob1', 'Bob2'])
>>> other.issubset(myFrozen)
True
```

```
>>> other == myFrozen
False
>>> other <= myFrozen
True
```

Shell Example 10.82 Set Subsets

Supersets

Sets use the *.issuperset(other)* as well as comparison operators to test if the *other* elements are contained within the set: Shell Example 10.83.

```
>>> mySet = {'Debbie', 'Chris', 'Clem', 'Jimmy', 'Frank'}
>>> other = {'Chris', 'Clem'}
>>> mySet.issuperset(other)
True
>>> mySet >= other
True
>>> other > mySet
False
```

Shell Example 10.83 Set Supersets

Union

Sets use the *union(other)* operation or a vertical bar character, |, to combine a set with the *other*: Shell Example 10.84.

```
>>> mySet = {'Debbie', 'Chris', 'Clem', 'Jimmy', 'Frank'}
>>> other = {'Johnny', 'Joey', 'Deedee', 'Tommy'}
>>> mySet.union(other)
{'Johnny', 'Joey', 'Frank', 'Tommy', 'Debbie', 'Chris', 'Clem', 'Deedee',
'Jimmy'}
>>> mySet | other
{'Johnny', 'Joey', 'Frank', 'Tommy', 'Debbie', 'Chris', 'Clem', 'Deedee',
'Jimmy'}
```

Shell Example 10.84 Set Union

Intersection

Sets use the *intersection(other)* operation or an ampersand, *&*, to combine common elements found in a set and the *other*: Shell Example 10.85.

```
>>> myFrozen = frozenset(['Jerry', 'Mark', 'Bob1', 'Bob2', 'Allen'])
>>> mySet = {'Jerry', 'Bob2'}
>>> myFrozen.intersection(mySet)
frozenset({'Bob2', 'Jerry'})
>>> myFrozen & mySet
frozenset({'Bob2', 'Jerry'})
```

Shell Example 10.85 Set Intersection

Difference

Sets use the *difference(other)* operation or the minus character, -, to identify set elements not in *other*: Shell Example 10.86.

```
>>> mySet = {'Joe', 'Mick', 'Paul', 'Terry'}
>>> other = {'Joe', 'Paul'}
>>> mySet.difference(other)
{'Terry', 'Mick'}
>>> mySet - other
{'Terry', 'Mick'}
```

Shell Example 10.86 Set Difference

Symmetric Difference

Sets use the symmetric_*difference(other)* operation or the caret character, ^, to identify elements in either the set or the *other* but not both: Shell Example 10.87.

```
>>> mySet = {'Mark', 'Bob1', 'Allen'}
>>> other = {'Jerry', 'Bob2', 'Allen'}
>>> mySet.symmetric_difference(other)
{'Bob1', 'Bob2', 'Jerry', 'Mark'}
>>> mySet ^ other
{'Bob1', 'Bob2', 'Jerry', 'Mark'}
```

Shell Example 10.87 Set Symmetric Difference

Set Operations

The following operations are applicable only to *sets* since they are mutable and frozensets are immutable.

Update

Sets use the update(others) and the |= characters to combine the elements from all of the others: Shell Example 10.88.

```
>>> mySet = {'Johnny', 'Joey', 'Deedee', 'Tommy'}
>>> otherA = {'Joe', 'Mick', 'Paul', 'Terry'}
>>> otherB = {'Pete', 'Howard', 'Steve', 'John'}
>>> mySet.update(otherA, otherB)
>>> mySet
{'Howard', 'Johnny', 'Joey', 'Terry', 'Tommy', 'Joe', 'Paul', 'Mick',
'John', 'Deedee', 'Steve', 'Pete'}
```

Shell Example 10.88 Set update()

Add

Sets use the *add(element)* operation to add *element* to the set: Shell Example 10.89.

```
>>> mySet = {'Jerry', 'Mark', 'Bob1', 'Bob2', 'Allen'}
>>> mySet.add('Debbie')
>>> mySet
{'Allen', 'Debbie', 'Bob1', 'Bob2', 'Jerry', 'Mark'}
```

Shell Example 10.89 Set add()

Remove

Sets use the *remove(element)* operation to remove *element* from the set. The method throws an error when the element does not exist within the set: Shell Example 10.90.

```
>>> mySet = {'Jerry', 'Mark', 'Bob1', 'Bob2', 'Allen'}
>>> mySet.remove('Allen')
>>> mySet
{'Bob1', 'Mark', 'Jerry', 'Bob2'}
>>> mySet.remove('Josh')
Traceback (most recent call last):
  File "<console>", line 1, in <module>
KeyError: 'Josh'
```

Shell Example 10.90 Set remove()

Discard

Sets use the *discard(element)* to remove the *element* when present. Errors are not thrown when elements are not found within the set: Shell Example 10.91.

```
mySet = {'Johnny', 'Joey', 'Deedee', 'Tommy'}
>>> mySet.discard('Tommy')
>>> mySet
{'Joey', 'Johnny', 'Deedee'}
>>> mySet.discard('Marky')
>>>
```

Shell Example 10.91 Set discard()

Pop

The *.pop()* operation removes and returns an arbitrary element from the set: Shell Example 10.92.

```
>>> mySet = {'Pete', 'Howard', 'Steve', 'John'}
>>> element = mySet.pop()
>>> print(f'element={element} mySet={mySet}')
element=Pete mySet={'Steve', 'John', 'Howard'}
```

Shell Example 10.92 Set pop()

Clear

The *.clear()* operation removes all elements from the set: Shell Example 10.93.

```
>>> mySet = {'Joe', 'Mick', 'Paul', 'Terry'}
>>> mySet.clear()
>>> mySet
set()
```

Shell Example 10.93 Set clear()

Intersection Update

Sets use the *.intersection_update(other)* operation, or ampersand equals characters, *&=*, to identify only the common elements found in a set and the *other*, and returns the results as the set's elements: Shell Example 10.94.

```
>>> mySet = {'Mark', 'Bob1', 'Allen'}
>>> mySetB = {'Jerry', 'Bob2', 'Allen'}
>>> mySet &= mySetB
>>> mySet
{'Allen'}
```

Shell Example 10.94 Set Intersection Update

Difference Update

Sets use the *.difference_update(other)* operation, or minus equals characters, -=, to remove only the common elements found in a set and the other: Shell Example 10.95.

```
>>> mySet = {'Mark', 'Bob1', 'Allen'}
>>> mySetB = {'Jerry', 'Bob2', 'Allen'}
>>> mySet -= mySetB
>>> mySet
{'Mark', 'Bob1'}
```

Shell Example 10.95 Set Difference Update

Symmetric Difference

Sets use the *.symmetric_difference_update(other)* operation, or caret equals characters, ^=, to remove only the common elements found in a set and the other and keep the rest: Shell Example 10.96.

```
>>> mySet = {'Mark', 'Bob1', 'Allen'}
>>> mySetB = {'Jerry', 'Bob2', 'Allen'}
>>> mySet ^= mySetB
>>> mySet
{'Mark', 'Bob2', 'Jerry', 'Bob1'}
```

Shell Example 10.96 Set Symmetric Difference Update

BOOLEAN

Boolean data are the foundation of Python logic. A Boolean behaves like a one-bit integer and may be *True* or *False*. Their values are 1 and 0, respectively. There is only one Boolean related function, *bool*, and three operations which can be performed on Booleans: *or*, *and*, and *not*.

bool

The *bool(object)* function translates any value to a Boolean. When performed on numerical objects, non-zero values always return *True*. For all other data types, any non-empty objects return *True*: Shell Example 10.97.

```
>>> bool(0.0)
False
>>> bool(0.1)
True
>>> bool(0)
False
>>> bool(0.0)
False
>>> bool(7)
True
>>> bool('')
False
>>> bool(['Python', 'data', 'types'])
True
```

Shell Example 10.97 Python bool()

Or

The *X or Y* operation returns *True* if either *X* or *Y* is *True*: Shell Example 10.98.

```
>>> X = True
>>> Y = False
>>> X or Y
True
```

Shell Example 10.98 Boolean Or

And

The *X and Y* operation returns *True* only when *X* and *Y* are True: Shell Example 10.99.

```
>>> X = True
>>> Y = False
>>> X and Y
False
```

Shell Example 10.99 Boolean And

Not

The *Not X* operation returns *True* only when *X* is *False*. This may also be thought of inverting the *X* clause: Shell Example 10.100.

```
>>> X = True
>>> not X
False
```

Shell Example 10.100 Boolean Not

Python is impartial to where the *not* appears in an expression: Shell Example 10.101.

```
>>> myList = [1, 2, 3]
# Expression reflecting speech
>>> 4 not in myList
True

# Expression reflecting computer language
>>> not 4 in myList
True
```

Shell Example 10.101 Boolean Not Order

OTHER PYTHON DATA TYPES

There are multiple other Python data types not covered in this chapter. However, there are only three others technical artists will encounter: unicode, None, and file.

Unicode

Unicode is a lengthy topic that could demand its own chapter for thorough explanation. Technical artists, however, rarely deal with Unicode. Unless dealing with non-english alphabets or international websites, the topic of Unicode rarely pops up.

Python strings are composed of individual characters. Unicode was developed to handle situations when more characters are needed than the venerable English alphabet encoding, ASCII, can provide. Unicode is an abstract data template that is configured to structure character definitions called codepoints. There are many standards used for configuring Unicode codepoints. The most common standard is *UTF-8*.

Python 3 uses two types of string data: *str* and *bytes*. *Str* are sequences of Unicode codepoints created using the quotation methods described in Chapter 7, prepending the quoted string with a *u*, or using the *str()* function. *Bytes* are sequences of 8-bit integers used for storing data on file systems or sending data on the internet. Language Template 10.14 explains to define a byte variable, a *b character* is placed before the quoted string.

```
>>> bytesVariable = b'Text String'
```

Language Template 10.14 Bytes String Formation

There are two methods, introduced in Language Template 10.15, for translating between unicode and bytes: *encode()* and *decode()*. Shell Example 10.102 demonstrates unicode encoding to bytes and Shell Example 10.103 displays bytes decoding to unicode.

```
>>> bytesString = unicodeString(unicodeStandard)
>>> unicodeString = bytesString(unicodeStandard)
```

Language Template 10.15 Translating Between Unicode and Bytes

```
>>> unicodeString = "\u0411"
>>> unicodeString.encode('utf-8')
b'\xd0\x91'
```

Shell Example 10.102 Unicode Encoding to Bytes

```
>>> data = b"\xbc cup of flour"
>>> data.decode("latin-1")
'¼ cup of flour'
```

Shell Example 10.103 Bytes Decoding to Unicode

The most common error types when programming in Python 3 are *UnicodeEncodeError* and *UnicodeDecodeError*. UnicodeEncodeErrors occur when attempting to encode a Unicode string into a standard that can't accept it. Shell Example 10.104 demonstrate the *UnicodeEncodeError*.

```
>>> unicodeString = "\u0411"
>>> unicodeString.encode("iso-8859-15")
Traceback (most recent call last):
  File "<console>", line 1, in <module>
  File "C:/PROGRA~1/SIDEEF~1/HOUDIN~1.455/python37\lib\encodings\
iso8859_15.py", line 12, in encode
```

```
    return codecs.charmap_encode(input,errors,encoding_table)
UnicodeEncodeError: 'charmap' codec can't encode character '\u0411' in
position 0: character maps to <undefined>
>>> data.encode('utf-8')
b'\xd0\x91'
```

Shell Example 10.104 Python 3 UnicodeEncodeError

UnicodeDecodeErrors occur when attempting to decode a string that does not fit properly into the standard ASCII character set. Shell Example 10.105 demonstrate the *UnicodeDecodeError*.

```
>>> bytesString = b"\xbc"
>>> bytesString.decode("utf-8")
Traceback (most recent call last):
  File "<console>", line 1, in <module>
UnicodeDecodeError: 'utf-8' codec can't decode byte 0xbc in position 0:
invalid start byte
>>> bytesString.decode("latin-1")
'¼'
```

Shell Example 10.105 Python3 UnicodeDecodeError

Most of these encoding and decoding issues can be avoided following these basic principles.

- Do not mix unicode and bytes: stick with one or the other.
- Do not mix Python 2 and Python 3 encodings. Python 2 handles Unicode, bytes, and strings differently from Python 3.
- Always know your encoding standard. When in doubt, use *UTF-8*.

None

None is a Python keyword defining a null variable or object. The *None* object is assignable to any variable but cannot be created. All variables and objects with *None* value reference the same *None* object, as demonstrated in Shell Example 10.106.

```
>>> myNone = None
>>> print(myNone)
None
```

Shell Example 10.106 Python None

Because *None* supports both *is* and == operators, they are useful for error checking and debugging. When functions and other operations fail to execute as anticipated, they often return *None*, indicating something went incorrectly. Assigning a return value in a function is a helpful strategy indicating successful function execution. Code Sample 10.6 demonstrates *None* functional usage.

```
def myFunction(param):
    returnValue = None

    if param:
        return "Successful Function"

    return returnValue

funcVal = myFunction(True)
if funcVal == None:
    print('myFunction did not execute correctly')
else:
    print(f'my funcVal = {funcVal}')

>>> my funcVal = Successful Function
```

Code Sample 10.6 None within Functions

None is its own data type. It is not the same as *False*, 0, or the empty string, "". Comparing *none* with any other object than *None* will always return *False*. Shell Example 10.107 displays how None is neither 0 nor empty string.

```
>>> myNone = None
>>> if myNone is True or myNone != 0 or myNon != '':
...     print("None is something else")
...
None is something else
```

Shell Example 10.107 Comparing None with Other Types

File

File objects are references to external files. They are used for reading, writing, and otherwise interacting with data found within references. Language Template 10.16 defines how file objects are created. File objects are created using the *open(filename, mode)* function. The *filename* is a text string containing the file system path to the external file. The *mode* indicates if the file will read, be written to or be appended to.

```
>>> myFileObject = open(filename, mode)
```

Language Template 10.16 File Object Creation

Reading and writing of external files, as well as all methods associated with file objects, are covered in Chapter 14.

FUNCTIONAL ARGUMENTS

All Python functions return only one data object. However, that data object may be of any Python data type. Sequences, Dictionaries, and Sets are Python containers which store multiple objects as just one. These container types make the returning of complex objects from Python functions possible. Code Sample 10.7 demonstrates functional returning of complex data.

```
def genComplex():
  myDict = {'a':'Johnny', 'b':'Joey', 'c':'Deedee', 'd':'Tommy'}
  mySet = {'Jerry', 'Mark', 'Bob1', 'Bob2', 'Allen'}

  # Return a tuple composed of a dictionary and a set
  return (myDict, mySet)

# Unpacking the function's return values
aDict, aSet = genComplex()
print(f'aDict={aDict},\naSet={aSet}')

>>> aDict={'a': 'Johnny', 'b': 'Joey', 'c': 'Deedee', 'd': 'Tommy'},
aSet={'Mark', 'Jerry', 'Bob1', 'Bob2', 'Allen'}
```

Code Sample 10.7 Complex Functional Arguments

In the prior code sample, the first two lines of the *genComplex()* function generate a Python dictionary and set. The last line returns a single tuple containing a dictionary and set objects. The first line of the script's body unpacks the results of the called *genComplex()* to *aDict* and *aSet* variables. The last line displays their contents.

HOUDINI EXAMPLE

Code Sample 10.8 attempts to take advantage of many different types of Python data including sets, Booleans, integers, and floats. The script also builds on the prior chapters and strives to be modular. In other words, when a process is repeated more than twice, a function is created to facilitate and replicate the utility.

World building is a hot topic in real-time production and proceduralism is an essential component. Although it is a challenging concept to understand, proceduralism enables small teams of artists to leverage the power of programming to complement their creativity to generate worlds instead of single stages or simple environments.

This script queries the user to enter a number. Given a valid number, the script generates a simple environment and populates it with the inputted number of objects distributed evenly over multiple geometry types. No two objects can share the same center point nor the same color. No objects may interpenetrate the ground plane.

Once generated, the procedurally generated world appears like Figure 10.2.

FIGURE 10.2 World building script result

```
import random

# Create a generic container with a designated position
def newContainer(parent, name = "default", xpos = 0, ypos = 0):
  # Create the geometry node
  container = parent.createNode("geo", name)

  # Position the node based on its input
  container.parm("tx").set(xpos)
  container.parm("tz").set(ypos)

  # Return the new container
  return container

# Add a color node to the current sub-network
def addColor(parent, color=(1.0, 1.0, 1.0)):
   # Create the new color Node
    colorNode = parent.createNode("color", "newColor")
```

```
  # Assign the new color values
  colorNode.parmTuple("color").set(color)

  return colorNode

# Create a new sphere with random radius
# The radius can be controlled by a min and max term
# Add random color to the sphere
def newSphere(parent, name = "sphere", minRadius = .1,
          maxRadius = 3.0, color=(1.0, 1.0, 1.0)):
  # Create the Sphere node
  mySphere = parent.createNode("sphere", name)

  # Provide a random radius
  radius = random.uniform(minRadius, maxRadius)
  mySphere.parmTuple("rad").set((radius, radius, radius))

  # bonus: No Penetration
  mySphere.parm("ty").set(radius)

  # Create a color node to the sphere network
  colorNode = addColor(parent, color)
  colorNode.setInput(0,mySphere)
  # Set it's display to be true
  colorNode.setDisplayFlag(True)

# Create a new cone with random height and radius
# Add random color to the Cone
def newCone(parent, name = "Tube", height = 3.0,
          maxRadius=3.0, color=(1.0, 1.0, 1.0)):
  # Create the Tube node
  myCone = parent.createNode("tube", name)
```

```
    innerRadius = 0
    # Give the outer ring a random radius
    outterRadius = random.uniform(0.25, maxRadius)
    myCone.parmTuple("rad").set((innerRadius, outterRadius))

    # Give the cone a random height
    height = random.uniform(0.25, height)
    myCone.parm("height").set(height)

    #Bonus: No Penetration
    myCone.parm("ty").set(height * .5)

    # Create a color node to the sphere network
    colorNode = addColor(parent, color)
    colorNode.setInput(0,myCone)
    # Set it's display to be true
    colorNode.setDisplayFlag(True)

# Create a new cone with random height and radius
# Add random color to the Donut
def newDonut(parent, name = "Torus",
          maxRadius=3.0, color=(1.0, 1.0, 1.0)):
    # Create the torus node
    myDonut = parent.createNode("torus", name)

    # Give the base radius a random value
    radx = random.uniform(.1, maxRadius)
    rady = radx
    #Keep searching until inner radius is smaller
    while rady >= radx:
        rady = random.uniform(.1, maxRadius)
    myDonut.parmTuple("rad").set((radx, rady))
```

```
  # Bonus: No Penetration
  myDonut.parm("ty").set(rady)

  # Create a color node to the donut network
  colorNode = addColor(parent, color)
  colorNode.setInput(0,myDonut)
  # Set it's display to be true
  colorNode.setDisplayFlag(True)


# Create a new Crag Character with a unique color
def newCrag(parent, name = "Crag",
            maxScale=10, color=(1.0, 1.0, 1.0)):
  # Drop a Crag Node
  myCrag = parent.createNode("testgeometry_crag", name)

  randScale = random.uniform(.1, maxScale)
  myCrag.parm("scale").set(randScale)

  randRot = random.uniform(0, 360)
  myCrag.parm('ry').set(randRot)

  # Create a color node to the Crag Character
  colorNode = addColor(parent, color)
  colorNode.setInput(0,myCrag)
  # Set it's display to be true
  colorNode.setDisplayFlag(True)


# Create a ground grid with input width and depth
# Add a predefined color to the ground
def newGround(parent, name = "Ground",
            width = 100.0, depth = 100.0):
  # Create the grid node
  myGround = parent.createNode("grid", name)
```

```
    myGround.parmTuple("size").set((width, depth))

    # Create a predefined color Node
    colorNode = addColor(parent, (.126, 0.060, .028))
    colorNode.setInput(0,myGround)
    # Set it's display to be true
    colorNode.setDisplayFlag(True)


# Create an empty Set
objectPos = {()}
# Create an empty list
objectColor = []
obj = hou.node("/obj")
# Create boundaries for the floor
xmin = -50
xmax = 50
ymin = -50
ymax = 50

# Querry the user for the number of world objects
# until a valid number is entered validNumber = 0
while validNumber == 0:
    # Get the number objects, prompt for value
    numObjs = int(input("Enter number of Objects:\n"))

    #Check for valid value
    if numObjs > 0:
        validNumber = 1
    else:
        print(f"\tValue of {numObjs} not valid, Try another value:\n")
```

```
# Create the desired number of objects to fill our world
for geo in range(numObjs):
  # Find a unique position for the object
  # Create a random XY pair and keep generating pairs
  # untill the pair is not contained in objectPos
  # When a unique pair is encountered, add it to objectPos
  xpos = random.randint(xmin, xmax)
  ypos = random.randint(ymin, ymax)
  # Iterate until an xpos, ypos pair is unique
  while (xpos, ypos) in objectPos:
      xpos = random.randint(xmin, xmax)
      ypos = random.randint(ymin, ymax)
  # Append the new position to the Set
  objectPos.add((xpos,ypos))

  # Find a unique hue for the object
  # Generate a random number between 0 and 360 and
  # Keep generating until a unique hue value is generated.
  # When found, append the hue to the objectHue list
  red = random.random()
  green = random.random()
   blue = random.random()
   while (red, green, blue) in objectColor:
       red = random.random()
       green = random.random()
       blue = random.random()
  objectColor.append((red, green, blue))

  # Create a container object
  parent = newContainer(obj, "envObject", xpos, ypos)

  # One quarter distribution of ...
    if geo >= 3*numObjs/4:
```

```
            # ... Donuts
            child = newDonut(parent, color=(red, green, blue))
        elif geo >= 2*numObjs/4:
            # ... Cones
            child = newCone(parent, color=(red, green, blue))
        elif geo >= numObjs/4:
            # ... Crags
            child = newCrag(parent, color=(red, green, blue))
        else:
            # ... Spheres
            child = newSphere(parent, color=(red, green, blue))

# Create the ground object
parent = newContainer(obj, "Ground", 0, 0)
ground = newGround(parent, "ground",
                   (xmax-xmin)+10, (ymax-ymin)+10)
```

Code Sample 10.8 World Building Script

The procedural decomposition of this script makes it easy to digest. After the first line of script imports the *random* module, it is broken into two sections: the upper functional and lower instructional. The upper functions provide utility for the lower instructions to construct the world.

The lower, instructional portion of the script, marks where script execution begins. Two empty containers are created: *objectPos* and *objectColor. objectPos* is an empty set and *objectColor* is an empty list. These containers keep track of objects' position and color information to prevent repetition. The use of a set and a list is arbitrary and is chosen for demonstrational purposes only. In this context, both data types are interchangeable. The next four variables, *xmin, xmax, ymin,* and *ymax,* define the boundaries for the world ground geometry.

The following section is a while loop that queries the user for the number of desired objects until a valid number is provided. The script finishes by creating new ground geometry beneath the other objects.

The upper, functional portion of the script, contains all of the re-usable functions used by the lower portion. The first function, *new_container(),* is used for the creating the same foundational structure for every created object. It receives parent, name, and positional parameters. It creates a new *geometry* container node from the parent and name parameters and sets its world space position with the supplied coordinates. The resulting geometry container is returned.

The next six functions are very similar in that they create new Houdini nodes which generate geometric objects. They adjust their unique geometric parameters and append color nodes to provide unique object color.

Resulting geometry networks are finally returned. The first of these functions, *addColor()*, is a utility used by the other five to provide respective color information. It receives a red, green, and blue tuple which transfers to the node's color attributes. The following five functions, *newSphere()*, *newCone()*, *newDonut()*, *newCrag()*, and *newGround()* are near duplicates. Color nodes are appended to their networks and their *display flags* are toggled.

CONCLUSION

This chapter is the longest in the book. Python attempts to keep the language easy and fun to use requires additions of new datatypes with each sequential version. As of the time of this book's writing, version 3.10 is the current standard with 3.11 close behind. The evolving nature of the language means that this chapter on Python data types will always be playing catch-up.

The most significant distinction of Python data types is that some are alterable after they have been created (mutable), while others are not (immutable). Mutable data are dynamic and code quickly. It also performs slower and consumes more memory. Immutable data are static and require additional intention to implement effectively. It also executes quickly and uses less memory. Situational context helps programmers decide which data types are best for situations.

Python data types are broken into five major categories: *numeric*, *sequences*, *dictionaries*, *sets*, and *Booleans*. The numeric data types (*integers*, *floating point*, and *complex*) are static and provide numerical value. Sequences are containers storing collections of other Python objects. *Strings*, *tuples*, and *ranges* are immutable, while *lists* are mutable. They share similar functionality identifying size and accessing content information. *Strings* and *lists* have special functions which complement their utility. Dictionaries are mutable containers that use hashable values, called keys, to index and access their information. Sets are also containers which have no order and are used for identifying inclusion. There are two types of sets, mutable *sets*, and immutable *frozensets*. Both share common functionality while *sets* have additional functions which address their mutable nature. *Booleans* are perhaps the simplest of data types as they may only assume one of two states, *True* or *False*. While simplistic they constitute core Python functionality.

Three other data types technical artists will encounter are *Unicode*, *None*, and *Files*. Unicodes are fundamental string building blocks that enable multiple characters and languages beyond basic English to be displayed. *None* is a data type representing nothing. It is useful for logic flow, debugging and initializing containers. *Files* represent access to external data content. All external data reading and writing are done using *file* variables.

This chapter concludes with a Houdini world building script which employs previously introduced concepts. While longer than previous scripts, it is conveniently broken into two sections: the instructional section which applies instructions to build the world and a functional section which provides the tools used by the prior.

INTRODUCTION

Object-oriented programming is one of the most important aspects of modern programming languages. The ability to create "smart-objects" leverages programmers' ability to accomplish tasks logically and thematically. The object-oriented aspect of Python is no exception. While many artists insist they do not program or take advantage of object-oriented constructs, they do not realize they probably already use these tools. Unreal Blueprints, Unity Prefabs, and Houdini Digital Assets are node-based examples of object-oriented constructs. They provide support for core data elements and essential methods for manipulating and supporting data. Object-oriented character is not only in programming languages but in almost all real-time applications.

Object-oriented programming in Python is implemented within object *classes*. To avoid overwhelming novice programmers with Python class details, this concept is broken into two chapters. The first chapter explains the structure and format of classes and provides simple and practical examples how they may be used. The second chapter explains how Python classes take advantage of inheritance, leveraging pre-created Python objects to create even more focused and powerful tools.

The goal of this first chapter is to lay down the rules for constructing classes in Python. Basic class structure is provided with implementation examples. Special attention addresses class attributes, methods, and operator overloading, a powerful strategy for object-oriented interfacing. The chapter contains two robust Houdini examples: an *Arrow* class and a *ColorSwatch* class.

This two-chapter coverage of Python classes is spartan at best. Full coverage of the topic requires a separate book devoted to the subject. This chapter covers the essential components artists need to be familiar with when entering the real-time industry.

STRUCTURE

Python object-oriented structures are called *classes*. Classes are self-contained collections of Python object variables and functions. The object variables, called *attributes*, store and provide data required for class creation and operation. Dedicated functions used for accessing, managing, and manipulating class attribute data are called *methods*. *Methods* and *functions* are synonymous. The *method* term implies inclusion and devotion, and can only be called through their respective class. Realized classes operating as active Python objects are called *instances*.

Classes

Python classes are declared with the *class* keyword followed by the class name and a colon, as explained in Language Template 11.1. Technical artists should follow with comments, bookended by triple quotes.
While optional, the comments work with the interpreter to provide an avenue for accessing vital class information without reviewing code. Attention should be provided to this documentation to provide relevant class intention, purpose, and caveats. Merely repeating the class' name does little to explain class behavior and history, essential for perpetuating understanding and maintenance.

DOI: 10.1201/9781003016427-11

```
class ClassName:
    """ Auto-Documenting Comment"""
```

Language Template 11.1 Python Class Declaration

Beyond the declaration, the first item within the class is the *constructor method*. The constructor method is a function that is called immediately upon class instantiation, as shown in Language Template 11.2. It is declared as an indented block with the *def* keyword followed by the name, "*__init__*", its input arguments and a colon. The indented code block defines the method's behavior. The constructor's name is always "*__init__*". The first member of the argument list, *self*, points to specific class instances and provides access to instance attributes and methods. The name, "*self*", is optional but convention encourages its usage. Additional arguments are optional and provide essential configuration required to initialize class instances. Comments bound by triple quotes, auto-documenting comments, contribute to class documentation, automatically. Constructor comments are valuable and should be provided to ensure class construction, operation, and maintenance.

```
class ClassName:
    ''' Auto-documenting class comment '''

    def __init__(self[, constructor_arguments]):
        ''' Auto-documenting constructor comment '''
        CodeBlock
```

Language Template 11.2 Python Class with Constructor Method

Additional methods compose the remainder of the class definition. Language Template 11.3 demonstrates every method after the constructor follows the same structure: the keyword *def* followed by the method name, its argument list, and a colon followed by the indented code block. *Self* must be the first argument in the method's argument list. Optional triple-quote comments automatically contribute to class documentation.

```
class ClassName:
    ''' Auto-documenting Comment '''

    def __init__(self[, constructor_arguments]):
        ''' Auto-documenting constructor comment '''
        CodeBlock

    def methodA(self[, method_arguments]):
        '''Auto-documenting method comment '''
        CodeBlock
```

```
    def methodB(self[, method_arguments]):
        '''Auto-documenting method comment '''
        CodeBlock

  ...
```

Language Template 11.3 Python Full Class Declaration

Self

The *self* variable represents the instance of a class, so the class can communicate with itself and call its own methods and properties. It binds all class attributes and methods within a self-contained Python object. In C and C++ terms, *self* is a pointer addressing the current object. Not only does it provide a mechanism for objects within a class to access each other but also provides external object access to instanced class content. *Self* is the first parameter for all class methods that are intended to be used by other methods within the same class. The *self* variable is explicitly required in parameter lists when defining class methods. It is implicit when the method is invoked.

Attributes

An attribute is a single Python data object contained within a class. Attributes, as demonstrated in Language Template 11.4, may be created or modified at any location within. They may even be created or modified independently of class methods. (This ability is not suggested due to debugging challenges.) Within the class definition, all class attributes must be created, modified and accessed using the *self.* prefix.

```
class myClass:
    def classMethod(self):
        # Class Attribute creation or modification
        self.attributeName = <Object Value>

        # accessing Class Attribute content
        localVariable = self.attributeName
```

Language Template 11.4 Class Attribute Creation, Modification and Access

Without the *self.* designation, the variable is treated locally and maintains no persistence outside of its initial context.

Creating and modifying class attributes are liberating but also complicate debugging. Understanding where and when class attributes are created can be challenging. Technical artists are encouraged to create and provide default values for all class attributes within the class constructor. This habit facilitates easier class maintenance and helps future developers understand attribute intention. Code Sample 11.1 demonstrates constructor attribute creation.

```
class myClass:
    ''' A quick class created to demonstrate out-of-context attributes '''
    def __init__(self):
        ''' Define all attributes belongiong to class'''
        self.attribute1 = 'This attribute belongs to the class!'

    def displayContents(self):
        ''' Display the attributes found in the class and those that are
          out-of-context'''
        attribute1 = 'I want to be part of the class'
        # Print local variable
        print(f'local variable: {attribute1}')
        # Print attribute from class
        print(f'attribute: {self.attribute1}')

foo = myClass()
# Calling class method
foo.displayContents()
# Accessing class' attribute
print(f'Outside of class: {foo.attribute1}')

>>> local variable: I want to be part of the class
attribute: This attribute belongs to the class!
Outside of class: This attribute belongs to the class!
```

Code Sample 11.1 Defining Attributes in Constructor

Instantiation

Classes are abstract definitions. They do nothing until they are *instantiated* into a local Python variable, now called an *object*. Class objects are stored for further use by invoking class names and arguments and assigning to local Python variables, as explained in Language Template 11.5.

```
localVariable = className([argument list])
```

Language Template 11.5 Class Instancing with Optional Argument List

When classes are instantiated, their *__init__* constructors are executed. Argument lists are used to pass information into each instance as they are constructed.

Language Template 11.6 shows an object's attributes are accessed via the instance name followed by a period and the attribute name. Attributes are created and modified similarly.

```
# Accessing an instance attribute
myValue = objectName.Attribute


# Modifying an instance attribute
objectName.Attribute = newValue
```

Language Template 11.6 Accessing, Creating, and Modifying Instance Attributes

Much like functions, instantiated class methods are invoked by means of the object name followed by a period, the method's name, and its argument list within parenthesis. Invoking instance methods is explained in Language Template 11.7. The *self* variable is not included in the argument list.

```
# Calling an instanced method
myValue = objectName.methodName([argument list])
```

Language Template 11.7 Calling an Instance's Method

Example: MyTime

The *MyTime* class, generated in Code Sample 11.2, is a simple demonstration. Class attributes store hours, minutes, and seconds. There are two hour modes: standard and military. Standard time hours are represented by integers 0 through 11 followed by *AM* or *PM* which designate day and night cycles, respectively. Military is represented by integers from 0–to23. The class handles this duality with two display functions: one for standard and one for military. For simplicity, all time is stored in military format. Standard time is only considered during display.

```
# Python MyTime Class Definition
class MyTime:
    ''' MyTime abstract data class. Data is stored as hours, minutes
       and seconds '''

    def __init__(self, hours=0, minutes=0, seconds=0):
        ''' By default, time is stored in Military mode '''
        self.hour = hours
        self.minute = minutes
        self.second = seconds

    # Print Militarey Method. No input required
    def printMilitary(self):
        ''' Print the class value in military mode '''
        print(f"{self.hour:02}:{self.minute:02}:{self.second:02}")

    # Print Standard Method. No input required
    def printStandard(self):
        ''' Print the class value in standard time mode.
            Note: special consideration must be made to differentiate
            day and night cycles and when AM Or OPM is to be displayed '''
        # Provide a default starting value
        standardTime = ""
        # When midnight or noon, display hour as 12 instead of 0
        if self.hour == 0 or self.hour == 12:
            standardTime +="12"
        else:
            # Otherwise, display the hour modulus 12
            standardTime += f"{self.hour%12:02}"

        standardTime += f":{self.minute:02}:{self.second:02}"

        # When in the morning cycle, display AM
        if self.hour < 12:
            standardTime += " AM"
```

```
        # Otherwise display PM
        else:
            standardTime += " PM"
        print(standardTime)

# Class instantiation and object execution
localTime = MyTime()
localTime.printMilitary()
newTime = MyTime(10, 32, 27)
newTime.printStandard()

>>> 00:00:00
10:32:27 AM
```

Code Sample 11.2 Python MyTime Class

The example script is broken into two sections: the upper, class definition, and the lower, object instantiation and execution.

Within the *MyTime* class definition, notice the use of triple quotes immediately after any class or method declaration. The triple quotes are optional. However, they exercise the auto-documentation feature within Python. These comments explain class functionality and describe method intention and strategy.

__init__ Is the class constructor. *Self* is the first parameter. *Hours*, *minutes*, and *seconds* follow and are defaulted to `0`. The constructor assigns the input parameters to their equivalent class attributes: *self.hour*, *self.minute*, and *self.second*.

The first class method, *PrintMilitary*, displays *MyTime* class contents in military format. It requires no parameters other than *self*. Component values are padded with zeros to two decimal places.

Like the first class method, the second, *printStandard*, takes no additional parameter other than *self*. It buffers an empty string, *standardTime*, to receive the standard time components. Technically, *standardTime* is redefined when new values are appended. The empty string initialization informs variable intention to future programmers. *Self.hour* is the first attribute appended to the buffer. The modulus `12` of the value, padded with zeros, is displayed unless the hour is midnight or noon in which `"12"` is displayed. The minute and second attributes are appended and padded with zeros. When the hour attribute is less than `12`, *AM* is appended to the buffer. Otherwise *PM* is appended. The method finishes with printing the *standardTime* string buffer.

The lower portion of the script instantiates and assigns a new *MyTime* class to the *localTime* object. The instance's attributes are printed using the *printMilitary()* method. Because no arguments are given during *localTime* class instantiation, the class attributes default to `0`.

A second instantiation is assigned to the *newTime* object. Initial values are provided as class arguments. The instance is displayed using the *standardTime()* method.

Note that none of the instance method calls included *self*. The first argument of an argument is implied to be *self* and does not need to be included.

EXAMPLE: ARROW

The Houdini object structure naturally lends itself to Python logic. Individual graphical objects make ideal class instances. The following example declares the *Arrow* class. The *Arrow* class receives an object name along with X, Y, and Z coordinates. The class draws a three-dimensional arrow at the origin and points to the input coordinates. The following demonstration generates a simple bouquet of arrows, drawn with random colors and positions.

Code Sample 11.3 is broken into two portions: The upper containing the class definition and the lower containing a simple test script. Figure 11.1 displays the result of Code Sample 11.3.

```
import random
import math
from time import time

# Arrow class definition
class Arrow:
    ''' This class generates a Houdini arrow of random,
        given the arrows X, Y and Z vector coordinates '''
    def __init__(self, name='arrow', x=0.0, y=0.0, z = 0.0):
        ''' Absorb the arrow vector input then display the results
            of the vector using random colors '''
        self.name = name
        self.x = x
        self.y = y
        self.z = z

        #Draw the visual Representation of the arrow
        self.drawArrow()


    def length(self):
        ''' Convenience class function to quickly generate arrow length '''
```

```
        # compute the Pythagorean length of the tube
        length = math.sqrt(self.x*self.x +
                           self.y*self.y +
                           self.z*self.z)
        return length


    def generateColor(self):
        ''' Generate a random color based on system time '''
        # Use position as color seed
        random.seed(time())
        # Create new Houdini Color
        color = hou.Color()
        # Assign color a random Hue
        color.setHSV((360*random.random(), 1, 1))
        # Return randomized color object
        return color


    def createContainer(self):
        ''' Method gets the Houdini OBJ node reference,
            the container which holds the geometry and
            temporary look at object to be used to rotate the
            arrow into place '''
        # Get the OBJ Node
        objNode  = hou.node('/obj')

        # Create the class container
        self.container = objNode.createNode('geo', self.name)

        # Create a temporary lookat Object
        self.lookAt = objNode.createNode('geo', 'lookat')
        # Position lookAt object to where arrow will point to
```

```
        self.lookAt.parmTuple('t').set((self.x, self.y, self.z))


    def drawShaft(self):
        ''' draw the arrow the length to the lookat object '''
        # Create the tube node
        self.shaft = self.container.createNode('tube', 'shaft')
        # Assign the tubes length
        self.shaft.parm('height').set(self.length())
        # Make sure the tube lays flat
        self.shaft.parm('orient').set(0)
        # Shift tubes position to start at origin
        self.shaft.parm('tx').set(0.5*self.length())
        # Make sure tube is skinny
        self.shaft.parm('radscale').set(.1)
        # Cap the ends of the tube
        self.shaft.parm('cap').set(True)


    def drawHead(self):
        ''' Draw a cone and place it at the tip of the shaft '''
        # Create the tube node
        self.head = self.container.createNode('tube', 'head')
        # Assign the tubes length
        self.head.parm('height').set(1.0)
        # Pinch cone end
        self.head.parm('rad1').set(0.0)
        # Make sure the tube lays flat
        self.head.parm('orient').set(0)
        # Shift tubes position to start at origin
        self.head.parm('tx').set(self.length()-0.3)
        # Make cone a bit more narrow
        self.head.parm('radscale').set(.5)
```

```
        # Cap the ends of the cone
        self.head.parm('cap').set(True)


    def finishArrow(self):
        ''' perform the final operations to the container network to
           make it presentable '''
        # Create a merge node to collect objects
        merge = self.container.createNode('merge')
        # Connect Shaft and Head to the merge node
        merge.setInput(0, self.shaft)
        merge.setInput(1, self.head)

        # Create a color node for the combined object
        colorNode = self.container.createNode('color')
        colorNode.setInput(0, merge)
        randColor = self.generateColor()
        # Assign color node RGB value of HSV color
        colorNode.parmTuple('color').set(randColor.rgb())

        # Append a transform sop to rotate the object
        xform = self.container.createNode('xform')
        # 90 degrees in Y to make the 'lookat' function work properly
        xform.setInput(0, colorNode)
        xform.parm('ry').set(90)

        # Append an output node to be the final display
        output = self.container.createNode('output')
        output.setInput(0, xform)
        # set the display flag to be true
        output.setDisplayFlag(True)
```

```
        # Clean up the node in the container to be visually pleasing
        self.container.layoutChildren()

    def pointArrow(self):
        '''Point the arrow to look at the lookat object.
          Remove the lookat object after it is no longer needed '''
        # Rotate the shaft so that it points to the lookAt Object
        self.container.setWorldTransform(
            self.container.buildLookatRotation(self.lookAt))

        # Remove the LookAt node as it is no longer needed
        self.lookAt.destroy()

    def drawArrow(self):
        ''' Draw the arrow using the input vector coordinates
           using a random color '''
        self.createContainer()
        self.drawShaft()
        self.drawHead()
        self.finishArrow()
        self.pointArrow()


# Demonstration loop to generate a bouquet of 36 arrows
for i in range(36):
    # Calculate rotation amount
    rot = math.radians(i*10)
    # Compute X, Y and Z coordinates
    x = 5 * math.sin(rot)
    z = 5 * math.cos(rot)
    y = 10*random.random()
    # Generate each arrow
    arrow = Arrow(f'arrow{i}', x, y, z)
```

Code Sample 11.3 Arrow Class with Demonstration

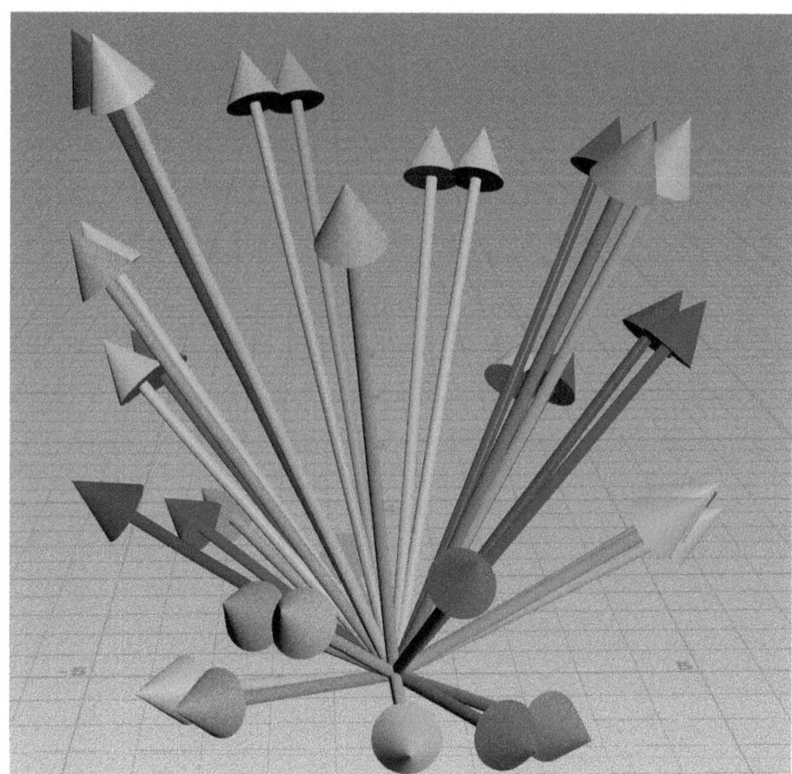

FIGURE 11.1 Arrow class script results.

Graphically, the *Arrow* class creates a tubular shaft equivalent to the distance from the input coordinates to the origin. An arrow head, (a cone), is placed at the far end of the shaft. The arrow object is assigned a random color and rotated to point to the input coordinates.

The *Arrow* class takes advantage of the *math, random,* and *time* modules. The class constructor, *__init__*, takes in a name and three floats: x, y, and z. Their default values are float `0.0`. The input parameters are assigned to class attributes, (*self.name, self.x, self.y,* and *self.z*), and the arrow is visually generated by calling the *drawArrow* method.

The *drawArrow* method calls five other methods: *createContainer(), drawShaft(), drawHead(), finishArrow(),* and *pointArrow()*. The success of each of these methods is dependent on the results of their prior methods. To generate the proper output, these methods must execute in sequential order.

The *createContainer()* method generates a reference to the Houdini */obj* node and from that creates a geometry container, *self.container.* The container is visually labeled with the self.*name* attribute. The method also generates a second container variable called *self.lookAt.* This new container is positioned at the coordinates defined by the *self.x, self.y,* and *self.z* attributes. This second container remains invisible and is used as the look at target for the last step of the *pointArrow()* method.

The *drawShaft()* method generates a slender tube object which starts at the origin and lays flat along the X-axis. Calls to the *length()* class method are used to calculate the length of the tube based on the distance from the input coordinates and the origin.

The *drawHead()* method generates a new tube, wider and shorter than the shaft. The tip of the tube is pinched to create the cone shape. Using the *length()* class method, the head is translated to the end of the shaft.

The *finishArrow()* method completes the arrow geometry and prepares it for its final rotation. An appended *merge* node combines the shaft and head into one object. An appended *color* node assigns color to the merged geometry. The *generateColor()* class method is used to generate a random color placed in the color node. Instead of randomly generating red, green, and blue color channels, *HSV* color is used. The only random component is *hue*. *Saturation* and *value* are set to constant `1.0`. Assigning color with this method guarantees vibrant colors.

The arrow object must point down the *Z-axis* for the rotation function to work properly. A *transform* node is appended to the color node and rotates the arrow object `90`° in the *Y-axis* to achieve *Z-axis* alignment. For visual clarity, an *output* node is appended to the chain and its display flag is turned on. The final command, *self.container.layoutChildren()*, organizes the container nodes in a clean and organized hierarchy.

The *pointArrow()* method finishes the *drawArrow()* sequence by rotating *self.container* to point at the *self.lookAt* object. Built-in Houdini functionality addresses the complicated mathematics required to calculate these rotations. After the final rotations, the command, *self.lookAt.destroy()*, deletes the *self.lookAt* object.

The demonstration portion of the script generates 36 arrows in a *for* loop. The arrows are each spaced `10`° from each other as they complete one circle around the origin. Inside each arrow iteration, the rotation amount is calculated by multiplying the iterator, *i*, by `10`. The *x and z* coordinates are calculated using the *sine* and *cosine* values of the rotation amount and multiplied by a radius of `5`. The y coordinate is simply a random number between `0.0 and 10.0`. The arrow's name and its x, y, and z coordinates are used to generate each new *Arrow* class instance.

SPECIAL ATTRIBUTES

Python classes and their objects have a number of special built-in attributes. While these attributes are not accessed regularly, they do provide valuable information about the class and the state of each instanced object.

The following technical artist friendly attributes are found in all class definitions and instanced objects.

(The following examples assumes the *MyTime* class has been predefined or has been imported as an external module. More information is found in Chapter 12.)

Class Attributes

__bases__

When taking advantage of class hierarchy (see Chapter 12), this attribute contains which classes the current class is derived from. By default, all classes are of type "object". Shell Example 11.1 demonstrates this attribute.

```
>>> print(Time.__bases__)
(<class 'object'>,)
```

Shell Example 11.1 __bases__ Class Attribute

__dict__

This attribute contains the entire class definition within one dictionary object: Shell Example 11.2.

```
>>> print(Time.__dict__)
{'__module__': 'Time', '__doc__': ' Time abstract data class. Data is
stored as hours, minutes and seconds ', '__init__'
: <function Time.__init__ at 0x00000000A1282160>, 'printMilitary': <func-
tion Time.printMilitary at 0x00000000A12820D0>,
'printStandard': <function Time.printStandard at 0x00000000A1282040>,
'__dict__': <attribute '__dict__' of 'Time' object
s>, '__weakref__': <attribute '__weakref__' of 'Time' objects>}
```

Shell Example 11.2 __dict__ Class Attribute

__doc__

This attribute accesses the automated document string in the class' definition: Shell Example 11.3.

```
>>> print(Time.__doc__)
 Time abstract data class. Data is stored as hours, minutes and seconds
```

Shell Example 11.3 __doc__ Class Attribute

A more convenient strategy for accessing special class attributes is the *help()* command. The *help()* command displays a classes document strings in a convenient, formatted structure. Shell Example 11.4 shows the help() command.

```
>>>help(MyTime)
>>> Help on class MyTime in module builtins:

class myTime(object)
 |  myTime(hours=0, minutes=0, seconds=0)
 |
 |  myTime abstract data class. Data is stored as hours, minutes and seconds
 |
 |  Methods defined here:
 |
```

```
 |  __init__(self, hours=0, minutes=0, seconds=0)
 |      By default, time is stored in Military mode
 |
 |  printMilitary(self)
 |      Print the class value in military time mode
 |
 |  printStandard(self)
 |      Print the class value in standard time mode.
 |      Note: special consideration must be made to differentiate
 |      day and night cycles and when AM Or OPM is to be displayed
 |
 |  ----------------------------------------------------------------------
 |  Data descriptors defined here:
 |
 |  __dict__
 |      dictionary for instance variables (if defined)
 |
 |  __weakref__
 |      list of weak references to the object (if defined)
```

Shell Example 11.4 Python help() Command

__module__

This attribute contains the current module containing the class. By default, this attribute contains the name of the class: Shell Example 11.5.

```
>>> print(MyTime.__module__)
MyTime
```

Shell Example 11.5 __module__ Class Attribute

__name__

This attribute contains the namespace which identifies the class: Shell Example 11.6.

```
>>> print(MyTime.__name__)
MyTime
```

Shell Example 11.6 __name__ Class Attribute

Object Attributes

The following attributes are found in all object instances.

__class__

The attribute contains a pointer to the class definition from which this object was instanced: Shell Example 11.7.

```
>>> MyTime = MyTime(8, 16, 24)
>>> print(MyTime.__class__)
<class 'Time.Time'>
```

Shell Example 11.7 __class__ Instance Attribute

(Note: The extra name, *MyTime.MyTime*, comes from the module namespace from which this class was defined.)

__dict__

This attribute provides a dictionary snapshot of all object attributes and their current values: Shell Example 11.8.

```
>>> MyTime = MyTime(8, 16, 24)
>>> print(MyTime.__dict__)
{'hour': 8, 'minute': 16, 'second': 24}
```

Shell Example 11.8 __dict__ Instance Attribute

CLASS VARIABLES

Class variables are variables defined in classes and are shared by all instances. They are declared within classes but outside instance methods and constructors. Class attributes, declared within class constructors and other class methods, are not shared. Each instance has its own attribute copy. Class variables are declared upon script execution. All instances share the same class variable values, and when changes are made, they are reflected in all instances.

Class variables are declared inside the class but outside all constructors and methods. They can be accessed within class constructors and methods prefixing the variable name with *self* or the class name. Convention encourages using class name. Class variables are accessible outside of the class using either the object reference or class name. Code Sample 11.4 demonstrates class variable usage.

```
class Biscuit:
    ''' This is a simple class demonstrating Class Variables '''
    # Class variable shared by all instances
    numBiscuits = 0

    def __init__(self, consumer='me'):
        ''' Constructor for the Biscuit class '''
        self.consumer = consumer
        # Increment the class variable with every instance
        Biscuit.numBiscuits += 1

# Class name must be used when referencing outside class
print(f'The number of Biscuit instances is {Biscuit.numBiscuits}')
breakfast = Biscuit('Rolando')
print(f'The number of Biscuit instances is {breakfast.numBiscuits}')
lunch = Biscuit('Jeri')
print(f'The number of Biscuit instances is {lunch.numBiscuits}')
print(f'Total number of Biscuits:{Biscuit.numBiscuits}')

>>> The number of Biscuit instances is 0
The number of Biscuit instances is 1
The number of Biscuit instances is 2
Total number of Biscuits:2
```

Code Sample 11.4 Python Class Variable

In the prior example, *numBiscuits* is defined as a class variable. Its value is updated in the constructor using the class name, *Biscuit*, instead of *self*. It is accessed with the instance name or the class name.

OVERLOADING

Overloading allows programmers to customize existing language functionality. When accessed within the context of Python classes, their function definition is used instead of the default language implementation. While overloaded class methods are manually callable, they are invoked automatically within the context of their classes. Of all the affordances object-oriented programming provides to programmers, overloading is one of the most powerful because it enables programmers to redefine how their objects interact with their environments without the need for extra code.

Language Template 11.8 defines how all overloaded class methods are invokable through the object name followed by two underscores, __, the function name, and two more underscores. The argument list changes with the nature of the method.

```
object.__methodName__(argumentList)
```

Language Template 11.8 Overloaded Class Method Invocation

Much of language functionality is customizable through overloading. Technical artists are problem solvers and require access to as much functionality as possible. The overloading methods covered in this text include core overloading, data interface overloading, binary, unary and extended operator overloading. For the most thorough coverage of all overloading techniques, please consult with `https://docs.python.org/3/reference/datamodel.html`.

Core Overloading

Core overloading techniques are essential for class creation, initializing, and deletion. Certain techniques such as *__init__* have already been introduced. Other techniques such as *__new__* and *__del__* are useful when creating very sophisticated, memory intensive classes. However, they are almost never utilized in every-day, real-time production.

Data Interface Overloading

Data interface overloading is used when creating, accessing, or deleting object data. While very useful when generating more complicated scripts, there are few opportunities for technical artists to take advantage of these tools.

Binary Operator Overloading

Binary operator overloading allows programmers to customize existing Python language binary operations such as +, -, *, /, <, and >, within class context. In other words, standard Python understands how to add two integers, `2 + 2`, or two strings, 'foo' + 'bar'. When adding two complex classes, vectorA + vectorB, more instruction is required to instruct Python how to execute the operation. Programmers use binary operator overloading to replace existing binary operations with class specific instructions. As defined in Language Template 11.9, overload methods receive two parameters: *self* and *other. Self* references the current class instance and *other* references a second instance.

```
object.__BinaryOperator__(self, other)
```

Language Template 11.9 Python Binary Operator Overload Method

There are two ways to access an overloaded method. The first is to use the intended binary operation in its typical context with two instances of the same class. The second is to invoke the method from the first instance using the second instance as input. Code Sample 11.5 demonstrates both techniques.

```
class AVal:
    ''' A simple one attribute class '''
    def __init__(self, value):
        ''' Initialize the class with value input '''
        self.val = value

    def __add__(self, other):
        ''' overload the add, (+), opererator '''
        return AVal(self.val + other.val)

valA = AVal(23)
valB = AVal(76)

# Overloading binary operator
valC = valA + valB
print(f'valC val = {valC.val}')

valD = AVal(88.3)
valE = AVal(11.7)

# Accessing overloaded method
valF = valD.__add__(valE)
print(f'valF val = {valF.val}')

>>> valC val = 99
valF val = 100.0
```

Code Sample 11.5 Addition Operator Overloading

The add operator is overloaded in the above example. Within the method, a new instance, *valC*, is created from the sum of the first instance value, *valA*, and the second instance value, *valB*, and then returned. Two techniques are employed for accessing this method. The first technique overloads the add operator, +. The second technique accesses the first instance's method with the second instance as an input argument.

The ability for the class to behave correctly with both integers and floats is an example of a *polymorphism*, which is explained in Chapter 12.

Binary operator overloading works for all binary mathematical operators, Table 11.1, extended assignments, Table 11.2, and comparison operators, Table 11.3.

TABLE 11.1 Mathematical Binary Operator Overloading

<table>
<tr><th>Operator</th><th>Method</th></tr>
<tr><td>+</td><td>object.__add__(self, other)</td></tr>
<tr><td>-</td><td>object.__sub__(self, other)</td></tr>
<tr><td>*</td><td>object.__mul__(self, other)</td></tr>
<tr><td>//</td><td>object.__floordiv__(self, other)</td></tr>
<tr><td>/</td><td>object.__truediv__(self, other)</td></tr>
<tr><td>%</td><td>object.__mod__(self, other)</td></tr>
<tr><td>**</td><td>object.__pow__(self, other)</td></tr>
<tr><td><<</td><td>object.__lshift__(self, other)</td></tr>
<tr><td>>></td><td>object.__rshift__(self, other)</td></tr>
<tr><td>&</td><td>object.__and__(self, other)</td></tr>
<tr><td>^</td><td>object.__xor__(self, other)</td></tr>
<tr><td>|</td><td>object.__or__(self, other)</td></tr>
</table>

TABLE 11.2 Extended Assignment Binary Operator Overloading

<table>
<tr><th>Operator</th><th>Method</th></tr>
<tr><td>+=</td><td>object.__iadd__(self, other)</td></tr>
<tr><td>-=</td><td>object.__isub__(self, other)</td></tr>
<tr><td>*=</td><td>object.__imul__(self, other)</td></tr>
<tr><td>//=</td><td>object.__ifloordiv__(self, other)</td></tr>
<tr><td>/=</td><td>object.__idiv__(self, other)</td></tr>
<tr><td>%=</td><td>object.__imod__(self, other)</td></tr>
<tr><td>**=</td><td>object.__ipow__(self, other)</td></tr>
<tr><td><<=</td><td>object.__ilshift__(self, other)</td></tr>
<tr><td>>>=</td><td>object.__irshift__(self, other)</td></tr>
<tr><td>&=</td><td>object.__iand__(self, other)</td></tr>
<tr><td>^=</td><td>object.__ixor__(self, other)</td></tr>
<tr><td>|=</td><td>object.__ior__(self, other)</td></tr>
</table>

TABLE 11.3 Comparison Operator Overloading

Operator	*Method*
<	object.__lt__(self, other)
<=	object.__le__(self, other)
==	object.__eq__(self, other)
!=	object.__ne__(self, other)
>=	object.__ge__(self, other)
>	object.__gt__(self, other)

TABLE 11.4 Unary Operator Overloading

Operator	*Method*
-	object.__neg__(self)
+	object.__pos__(self)
abs()	object.__abs__(self)
~	object.__invert__(self)
complex()	object.__complex__(self)
int()	object.__int__(self)
long()	object.__long__(self)
float()	object.__float__(self)
oct()	object.__oct__(self)
hex()	object.__hex__(self)

Unary Operator Overloading

Unary operator overloading, Language Template 11.10, requires just one instance of the class to execute. All unary overload methods receive one parameter, *self* which references a class instance: Table 11.4.

```
object.__UnaryOperator__(self)
```

Language Template 11.10 Python Unary Operator Overload Method

There are two ways to access a unary overloaded method. The first is to use the intended unary operation in its typical context with a class instance. The second is to invoke the method from the first instance. No input argument is necessary.

String and Repr() Overload Methods

The string and *repr()* overload methods produce similar output but with different intentions. They can be very useful when debugging. Both function definitions receive only *self* parameter input, and must return only string objects. The *repr()* function is a built-in Python function used for displaying objects' "official" string representations. Ideally, output is a Python expression which could be used for object re-creation. Overloading the *__repr__()* method defines *repr()* output. Returned strings should be information rich and unambiguous. The *__str__()* method defines how classes are represented as strings when using the *print()*, *format()*, and *str()* functions. Ideally, the method should format all class content to be easy to read when displayed. Code Sample 11.6 demonstrates the the differences between __repr__() and __str__().

```
class Character:
    ''' This is a example class to demonstrate the __str__ Overload '''
    def __init__(self, name, age, race, occupation):
        ''' Character class constructor -> absorb input data '''
        self.name = name
        self.age = age
```

```
        self.race = race
        self.occupation = occupation

    # Repr overload method
    def __repr__(self):
        buff = f'Character(\'{self.name}\', {self.age}, '
        buff += f'\'{self.race}\', \'{self.occupation}\')'
        # Returns a string
        return buff

    # String overload method
    def __str__(self):
        ''' String overload to display class content '''
        buff = f'{self.name}, {self.age} years old, '
        buff += f'is a {self.race} {self.occupation}'
        # Returns a string
        return buff

myCharacter = Character('Stosh', 24, 'Half-Orc', 'Barbarian')
print(f'repr() overload: {repr(myCharacter)}')
print(f'str overload: {myCharacter}')

>>> repr() overload: Character('Stosh', 24, 'Half-Orc', 'Barbarian')
str overload: Stosh, 24 years old, is a Half-Orc Barbarian
```

Code Sample 11.6 Python String and str() Overload Methods

VECTORS

Vectors are essential technical artist data structures. The *Arrow* class already provides an excellent strategy for displaying what a vector could look like. The *Arrow* is expanded upon to create the *vizVector* class, by incorporating essential vector functionality such as inverse, addition, subtraction, and cross product. These methods are overloadable with their functional equivalents: ~, +, -, *. Other necessary vector methods include *dot product* and *unitize*. (Technically the official term is *normalize* and not *unitize*. *Unitize* sounds more functionally accurate.) There are two a vector product strategies for overloading the multiply, *, operator: cross product and dot product. The dot product generates a float value and the cross product generates a new vector. Because the other overloaded operators return new class instances, the cross product is chosen over the dot product. The *__str__()* method is overloaded and provides a convenient strategy for displaying the vector's attributes.

Code Sample 11.7 is broken into two portions: the upper containing the class definition and the lower containing a simple test script. Figure 11.2 displays the result of the test script.

```
import random
import math
from time import time

# vizVector class definition
class vizVector:
    ''' The vizVector class generates visual, three-dimensional vectors
       and provides functionality to easily perform operations on them
       as if they were single-value objects. '''
    def __init__(self, name = "vector", x = 0.0, y=0.0, z = 0.0):
        """ myVector3 Constructor initializes all the values, otherwise
             use defaults"""
        self.name = name
        self.x = x
        self.y = y
        self.z = z

        self.drawArrow()

    def __str__(self):
        ''' String overload for easy to read content display '''
        return(f'{self.name}:({self.x:.2f}, {self.y:.2f}, {self.z:.2f})\
        ||{self.length():.3}|| ')

    # Method computes the inversion of the vector and returns a new vector
    def __invert__(self):
        ''' return a vector going in the opposite direction '''
        newName = f'inv_{self.name}'
        return vizVector(newName, -1*self.x, -1*self.y, -1*self.z)

    #Operator override for '+', returns a new vector
    def __add__(self, other):
        """Add the components of the two instances and return a new vector"""
        newName = f'{self.name}Plus{other.name}'
```

```
        return vizVector(newName, self.x+other.x, self.y+other.y, self.
z+other.z)

    #Operator override for '-', returns a new vector
    def __sub__(self, other):
        """Add the components of the two instances and return a new vector"""
        newName = f'{self.name}Minus{other.name}'
        return vizVector(newName, self.x-other.x, self.y-other.y,
self.z-other.z)

    ''' There are two potential multiplication operations performed
       on vectors: a dot product and a cross product. Since the rest
       of the overloaded techniques return new vectors, this
       operation returns the cross product.  Either technique could
       be overloaded '''
    def __mul__(self, other):
        '''Cross Source vector to destination vector and return result'''
        newName = f'{self.name}Cross{other.name}'
        # Return the cross product of the input vectors
        return vizVector(newName, (self.y*other.z)-(self.z*other.y),
                                  (self.z*other.x)-(self.x*other.z),
                                  (self.x*other.z)-(self.z*other.x))

    ''' There are two potential multiplication operations performed
       on vectors: a dot product and a cross product. The
       cross product is already overloaded so the dot product is
       its own method  Either technique could be overloaded '''
    def dot(self, other):
        '''Multiply corresponding components, add their product
          and return the sum'''
        '''Returns a float. Do not return a new vizVector '''
        return self.x*other.x + self.y*other.y + self.z*other.z

    def length(self):
```

```
        ''' Convenience class function to quickly generate arrow length '''
        # Compute the Pythagorean length of vector
        length = math.sqrt(self.x*self.x +
                           self.y*self.y +
                           self.z*self.z)
        return length

    # Unitize the current vector
    # Since there is no unary operators left that make sense
    # in this context, this is a non-overloaded operator
    def unitize(self):
        ''' Compute the vector length then use that length to divide
           into each component and return a new vizVector '''
        vlength = self.length()
        # Look out for division by zero!
        if vlength == 0.0:
            raise ZeroDivisionError("Vector Length is Zero!")

        # Label unitized vector with u
        newName = "u{}".format(self.name)
        return vizVector(newName, self.x/vlength,
                         self.y/vlength, self.z/vlength)

    def generateColor(self):
        ''' Generate a random color based on system time '''
        random.seed(time())# Use position as color seed
        color = hou.Color()# Create new Houdini Color
        color.setHSV((360*random.random(), 1, 1)) # Assign color a random Hue
        return color# Assign local color to class color

    def createContainer(self):
        ''' Method gets the Houdini OBJ node reference,
            the container which holds the geometry and
            temporary look at object to be used to rotate the
```

```
            arrow into place '''
        # Get the OBJ Node
        objNode  = hou.node('/obj')
        # Create the class container
        self.container = objNode.createNode('geo', self.name)

        # Create a temporary Lookat Object
        self.lookAt = objNode.createNode('geo', 'lookat')
        # Position lookAt object to where arrow will point to
        self.lookAt.parmTuple('t').set((self.x, self.y, self.z))

    def drawShaft(self):
        ''' Draw the arrow the length to the lookat object '''
        # Create the tube node
        self.shaft = self.container.createNode('tube', 'shaft')
        # Assign the tubes length
        self.shaft.parm('height').set(self.length())
        # Make sure the tube lays flat
        self.shaft.parm('orient').set(0)
        # Shift tubes position to start at origin
        self.shaft.parm('tx').set(0.5*self.length())
        # Make sure tube is skinny
        self.shaft.parm('radscale').set(.1)
        # Cap the ends of the tube
        self.shaft.parm('cap').set(True)

    def drawHead(self):
        ''' Draw a cone and place it at the tip of the shaft '''
        # Create the tube node
        self.head = self.container.createNode('tube', 'head')
        # Assign the tubes length
        self.head.parm('height').set(1.0)
        # Pinch cone end
```

```
        self.head.parm('rad1').set(0.0)
        # Make sure the tube lays flat
        self.head.parm('orient').set(0)
        # Shift tubes position to start at origin
        self.head.parm('tx').set(self.length()-0.3)
        # Make cone a bit more narrow
        self.head.parm('radscale').set(.5)
        # Cap the ends of the cone
        self.head.parm('cap').set(True)

    def finishArrow(self):
        ''' Perform the final operations to the container
           network to make it presentable '''
        # Create a merge node to collect objects
        merge = self.container.createNode('merge')
        # Connect Shaft and Head to the merge node
        merge.setInput(0, self.shaft)
        merge.setInput(1, self.head)

        # create a color node for the combined object
        colorNode = self.container.createNode('color')
        colorNode.setInput(0, merge)
        randColor = self.generateColor()
        # Assign color node RGB value of HSV color
        colorNode.parmTuple('color').set(randColor.rgb())

        # Append a transform sop to rotate the object
        # 90 degrees in Y to make the 'lookat' function
        # Work properly
        xform = self.container.createNode('xform')
        xform.setInput(0, colorNode)
        xform.parm('ry').set(90)
```

```
        # Append an output node to be the final display
        output = self.container.createNode('output')
        output.setInput(0, xform)
        # Set the display flag to be true
        output.setDisplayFlag(True)

        # Organize the container
        self.container.layoutChildren()

    def pointArrow(self):
        ''' Point the arrow to look at the lookat object.
           Remove the lookat object as it is no longer needed '''
        (# Rotate the shaft so that it points to the lookAt Object
        self.container.setWorldTransform(
            self.container.buildLookatRotation(self.lookAt))

        # Remove the LookAt node as it is no longer needed
        self.lookAt.destroy()

    def drawArrow(self):
        ''' Draw the arrow using the input vector coordinates using
           a random color '''
        self.createContainer()
        self.drawShaft()
        self.drawHead()
        self.finishArrow()
        self.pointArrow()

# vizVector test script
# Declare vec1
vec1 = vizVector('vec1', 1, 2, 3)
# Display its contents
print(vec1)
```

```
# Create the inverse of vec1
inversevec1 = ~vec1
# Declare vec2
vec2 = vizVector('vec2', 3, 2, -1)
# Add vec1 and vec2
myAdd = vec1+vec2
# Subtract vec2 from vec1
mySub = vec1-vec2
# Cross vec1 to vec2
myCross = vec1*vec2
# Take dot product of vec1 and vec2
print(f'The dot product of {vec1} and {vec2} is {vec1.dot(vec2)}')
# Return unitized version of cross product
myUnit = myCross.unitize()

>>> vec1:(1.00, 2.00, 3.00)
The dot product of vec1:(1.00, 2.00, 3.00) and vec2:(3.00, 2.00, -1.00) is 4
```

Code Sample 11.7 VizVector Class with Examples

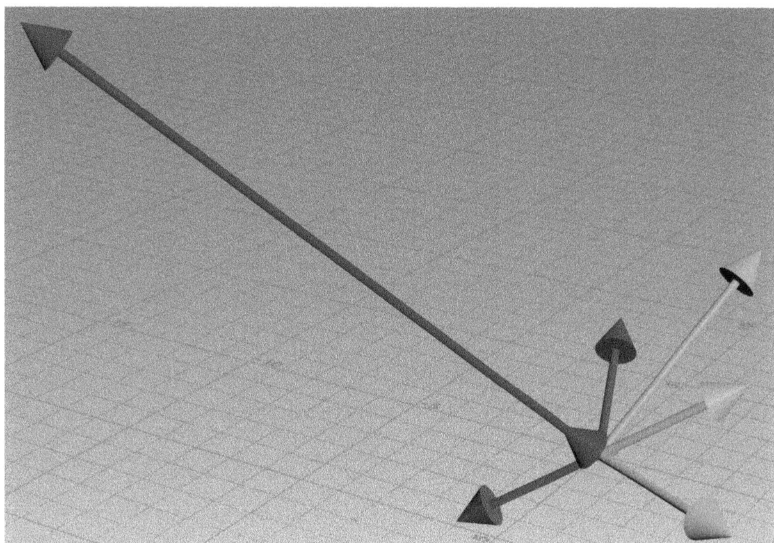

FIGURE 11.2 vizVector test results.

The *vizVector* class is almost a duplicate of the *Arrow* class except it uses operator overloading to perform vector related operations on the *Arrow* components. Operator overloading enhances the instance interaction capability of the *Arrow* class. The *__str__()* overload method provides a clean way for displaying current instance state.

The only overloaded unary operator is the ~, or the *__invert__()*, method. After receiving the *self* input parameter, the *__invert__()* method generates a new name based on the old. A new *vizVector* instance is generated from the new name and opposite coordinates.

The binary overloaded methods *__add__()*, *__sub__()*, and *__mul__()* are invoked with a second instance parameter: *other*. In each of these methods, a new name is generated based on the names of the input instances. A new instance is generated using the new name and combination of the input coordinates. The *__add__()* method sums corresponding coordinate components. The *__sub__()* method returns the difference between the *self* and *other* coordinates. The *__mul__()* method returns the cross product of the two instances.

The *dot* and *unitize* methods are new, non-overloaded methods. The *dot* method performs the dot product of the *self* with the *other* instance. Since the dot product returns only a float, no new name or new class instance is required. The *unitize* method returns a normalized vector of unit length, `(length = 1.0)`. The method could have been overloaded, but since the *invert* operation already uses the tilde, ~ operator, there are no other logical, available unary operators. The length of the vector is calculated. Division by zero situation is avoided by only allowing the method to continue when the length is greater than `0.0`. A new name is derived and a new instance is returned using the new name and the individual coordinates, each divided by the length, as input.

COLOR CALCULATOR

A color calculator is a tool that allows users to create and perform operations on color swatches. Color swatches are Python class instances containing simple colored rectangles. Colors are represented as tuples of red, green, and blue values. After creating the color swatches, users may perform operations on the swatches such as addition, subtraction, and multiplication. Like vectors described in the chapter's *Overloading* section, color swatch operations are overloadable.

The Color Calculator script, Code Sample 11.8, is broken into two portions: The upper containing the class definition and the lower containing a simple test script. Figure 11.3 displays the result of the test script.

```
# Class Definition
class ColorSwatch:
    ''' Class contains a container into which multiple class instances
        are placed. A class instance consists of a three-tuple defining
        a color and a rectangle represent it.The class organizes and
        places the instances in a rectangular grid. '''

    numSwatches = 0# Class attribute

    def __init__(self, name='color', red=1.0, green=1.0, blue=1.0):
        ''' Initialize each color swatch and display it on the screen.
            If the swatch is the first instance then the class
            infrastructure is created. '''
        self.name = name
        self.color = (self.clamp(red), self.clamp(green), self.clamp(blue))
```

```
        self.drawSwatch()

    def clamp(self, colorVal):
        # When colorVal is greater than 1.0, clamp to 1.0
        color = colorVal if colorVal < 1.0 else 1.0

        # When color is less than 0.0, clamp to 0.0
        color = color if color > 0.0 else 0.0
        return color

    def __str__(self):
        ''' String overload displays swatch name and color values '''
        return(f'{self.name}:({self.color[0]:.2f},\
        {self.color[1]:.2f}, {self.color[2]:.2f})')

    def __invert__(self):
        ''' Invert the color, return a new ColorSwatch '''
        name = f'{self.name}'
        red = 1.0 - self.color[0]
        green = 1.0 - self.color[1]
        blue = 1.0 - self.color[2]
        return ColorSwatch(name, red, green, blue)

    def __add__(self, other):
        ''' Add the two Colors together, return a new ColorSwatch '''
        name = f'{self.name}+{other.name}'
        red = self.color[0] + other.color[0]
        green = self.color[1] + other.color[1]
        blue = self.color[2] + other.color[2]
        return ColorSwatch(name, red, green, blue)

    def __sub__(self, other):
        ''' Subtract the other color from self, return a new ColorSwatch '''
```

```
        name = f'{self.name}-{other.name}'
        red = self.color[0] - other.color[0]
        green = self.color[1] - other.color[1]
        blue = self.color[2] - other.color[2]
        return ColorSwatch(name, red, green, blue)

    def __mul__(self, other):
        ''' Subtract the other color from self, return a new ColorSwatch '''
        name = f'{self.name}*{other.name}'
        red = self.color[0] - other.color[0]
        green = self.color[1] - other.color[1]
        blue = self.color[2] - other.color[2]
        return ColorSwatch(name, red, green, blue)

    def initClassNetwork(self):
        ''' Initialize the class Network. The container is where all
           the geometry is placed. The mergeSOP is the final node
           in the network with the engaged display flag. '''
        # Isolate Top node
        top = hou.node('/obj')
        # Create the class container attribute
        ColorSwatch.container =
             top.createNode('geo', 'ColorCalculator')
        # Create the class merge SOP attribute
        ColorSwatch.mergeSOP =
             ColorSwatch.container.createNode('merge',
            'CalculatorDisplay')

    def makeSwatch(self):
        '''generate the swatch grid node'''
        swatch = ColorSwatch.container.createNode("grid",
                                            "swatch")
        swatch.parmTuple("size").set((1, 1))
        swatch.parm("rows").set(2)
        swatch.parm("cols").set(2)
```

```
        swatch.parm("orient").set(0)
        return swatch

    def makeSwatchColor(self, swatch):
        """ give the grid the swatch color"""
        swatchColor = ColorSwatch.container.createNode("color",
                                                       "SwatchColor")
        swatchColor.parmTuple("color").set((self.color))
        swatchColor.setInput(0, swatch)
        return swatchColor

    def repoSwatch(self, colorNode):
        """ Reposition the combined object to some place more
            visually pleasing"""
        colorXform = ColorSwatch.container.createNode("xform",
                                                      "ColorXform")
        colorXform.setInput(0, colorNode)
        # X position is modulus numSwatch over 5 times offset
        xOffset = 1.12 * (ColorSwatch.numSwatches%5)
        # y Position is numSwatch divided by 5 times offset
        yOffset = -1.12 * (ColorSwatch.numSwatches//5)
        colorXform.parmTuple("t").set((xOffset, yOffset, 0))
        return colorXform

    def drawSwatch(self):
        ''' create new geometry for the colorSwatch then append it
           to the display network '''
        if ColorSwatch.numSwatches == 0:
            # Initialize Class network first instance
            self.initClassNetwork()

        # create a swatch grid
        swatchNode = self.makeSwatch()
        # Append a color node
```

```
        colorNode = self.makeSwatchColor(swatchNode)
        # Append a transform node and position it in place
        xformNode = self.repoSwatch(colorNode)

        # Connect new swatch to merge node
        ColorSwatch.mergeSOP.setInput(ColorSwatch.numSwatches, xformNode)
        # Layout the node to look pretty
        ColorSwatch.container.layoutChildren()

        # Increment Class numSwatches count upon successful creation
        ColorSwatch.numSwatches += 1


# Test Script
color1 = ColorSwatch("A", .23, .45, 0.88)
color2 = ~color1
color3 = color1 + color2
color4 = color1-color2
color5 = color1*color2
color6 = ColorSwatch("b", .69, .76, .84)
print(color2 * ~color6)


>>> ~A*~b:(0.46, 0.31, 0.00)
```

Code Sample 11.8 Color Calculator

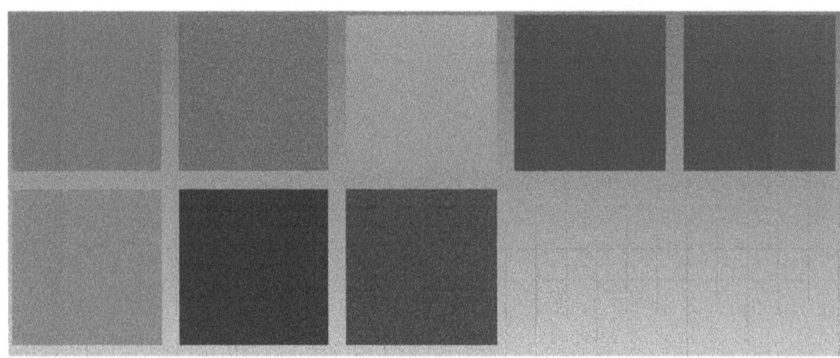

FIGURE 11.3 Color calculator results.

The ColorSwatch class is similar to the vizVector class defined earlier in this chapter. The major difference is instead of drawing arrows, it draws color swatches. Another significant difference, with respect to Houdini, is that instead of each instance being its own Houdini object, all instances are child objects of just one object container node, *container*, which is defined as a class attribute. The advantage of storing *container* as a class attribute is that all instances are child objects of the one container instead of existing as unique objects. There are two other class attributes, *numSwatches* which count the number of ColorSwatch instances and *mergeSOP*, a child node of the container, which merges all the ColorSwatch objects into one displayable object.

The class constructor receives the name of the ColorSwatch along with red, green, and blue color values. The class stores the color values into one, three-tuple attribute. The utility function, *clamp()*, is used to force each of the color channels to be bound between `0.0 and 1.0`. The *drawSwatch()* method is called to visually display each swatch as it is created.

The *drawSwatch()* method is the heart of *ColorSwatch* class and is responsible for generating and displaying the class geometry. It tests if the current instance is the first. If it is, the *initClassNetwork()* `method is called`. The *initClassNetwork()* creates the *container*, (a Houdini geometry node), and *mergeSOP* (a Houdini *Merge SOP)*, as class attributes. All future instance nodes are created from the one *container* node. The *mergeSOP* is a child of the container. This node merges each instanced geometry into one displayable node. After the preparations are made for the first instance, *drawSwatch()* creates the geometry for each instance. It does this by calling three other methods, each returning new Houdini SOP nodes: *makeSwatch()*, *makeSwatchColor()*, and *repoSwatch()*. The result of the *repoSwatch()* method, *xformNode*, is appended to the *mergeSOP* input and is displayed with all other ColorSwatch instances. The *layoutChildren()* operation is performed on the *container* to organize its contents into a visually clean format. The method finishes by incrementing the *numSwatches* class attribute by one.

The *makeSwatch()* method returns a simple Houdini rectangle. The *makeColorSwatch()* method generates a color node using the instance's *color* attribute. The method appends the new color node under the *makeSwatch()* rectangle. The *repoSwatch()* method appends a transform node to the color node and moves the swatch to a procedural location. The *X* and *Y* channel offsets are calculated using the *numSwatches* class attribute. The *xoffset* variable is generated by taking the modulus of *numSwatches* over `5.0`. Modulus returns the remainder which is then multiplied by arbitrary constant `1.12`. The *yoffest* is generated similarly using floor division. The *yoffset* is adjusted after every fifth new ColorSwatch instance.

The remainder of the ColorSwatch methods overloads traditional operations.

The *__str__* method overloads all class string activity. It displays the state of instance attributes in a simple, easy to read format. The string formatting breaks the *color* attribute into its individual components, each limited to two decimal places.

The *__invert__* method is the only overloaded unary operation in the ColorSwatch class. Unlike vectors, colors are not invertible by multiplying each component by `-1.0`. Instead, each component is subtracted from `1.0`. The method returns a new ColorSwatch instance containing a new name and the inverted color.

The *__add__, __sub__, and __mul__* methods are overloaded binary operations. They all receive the *self* instance reference and another, *other*, instance reference. A new name is generated by the combination of both instance names and the operation symbol each overloads. The corresponding components of both instances are combined based on the overloaded operation: addition for *__add__*, subtraction for *__sub__*, and multiplication for *__mul__*. All three methods return new ColorSwatch instances containing new names and combined color values.

CONCLUSION

Object-oriented programming is possibly one of the most important capabilities of Python. It empowers programmers to create class objects which not only contain data but also provide the necessary operations required to effectively access and manipulate class content without employing external code.

Fundamental behavior of Python classes is provided. Class structure is introduced. Instructions for their instantiation are constituted. Instance attributes are created. Methods for their access and manipulation are defined. A simple time-based class, *MyTime*, demonstrates these principles. A more sophisticated, Houdini graphical object class, the *Arrow* class, exhibits how abstract, graphical procedural objects are created using object-oriented principles.

The process of creating class objects and assigning them to variables is called instantiation. Data attributes are stored and maintained within the class before, during and after instantiation. Included with each class instance are methods, class functions devoted to manipulating class attributes. Within the class structure are special attributes: __basses__, __dict__, __doc__, __module__, and __name__. These attributes contain the origin from where the class originated, a mapping of the entire class definition, the class' embedded documentation, the current module containing the class, and the class' namespace, respectively. There are also special attributes associated with each class instance: __class__ and __dict__. These attributes contain pointers to the class from which the instance originated and snapshots of the current state of the class instance attributes. *Class Variables* are accessible externally and to all class instances.

Overloading allows Python programmers to customize language functionality within class context. Overloaded class methods may be *core*, *data interface*, *binary operator*, *unary operator*, and *string overload* methods. Core methods manipulate how class instances are created, initialized, and deleted. Data interface methods customize how class attributes are created, accessed, and deleted. Unary and binary operator methods override how all default language operators behave. The string overload methods define formatted output when classes are converted to strings. The *visVector* class is provided as a demonstration how a basic Python class, *Arrow*, can be extended using overloading.

The chapter finished with the color calculator example. Similar to the *Arrow* class, the *ColorSwatch* class stores name and color information within class attributes and displays color swatches representing the color they define. The *ColorSwatch* class extends the class definition by overloading multiple methods which enable addition, subtraction, and multiplication of class instances and provide formatted text output when translated to a string.

INTRODUCTION

In Chapter 11, the concept of object-oriented programming is introduced through Python classes. Classes are collections of attributes and methods perform operations on them. Class methods may be made more powerful by replacing the existing language structure through overloading. This chapter focuses on class *inheritance* and *composition*. Inheritance and composition expand the capability of object-oriented programming by modeling the relationships between multiple classes.

Inheritance allows the reuse of class code, the ability to expand and repurpose generations of classes. Composition enables creation of complex types through combining pre-existing types. These two strategies empower programmers to expand their functionality without having to rewrite the existing code.

This chapter is broken into four sections. The first section, focusing on module and path creation, is an extension of Chapter 9, Python Functions within the context of classes. The second, the inheritance section, is the heart of the chapter. It explores the implementation of Python class inheritance and the relationships between base and child classes. Multiple examples are provided to reinforce concepts. The third section, focusing on composition, demonstrates how new classes are created by combining existing class types. Consideration of when composition should be employed instead of inheritance is explored. The last section demonstrates how built-in language types can be customized and expanded through these strategies.

MODULE/PACKAGE CREATION

Until now, the modules used in this text have been standard, default Python libraries. Python does a good job understanding where its external modules and libraries are stored and knows where to find them. There are literally thousands of external libraries which can be downloaded and integrated with any Python installation. The default folder where these packages are stored is in the "site-packages" folder, ("../Python3/Lib/site-packages"). Python installation protocols, such as *pip*, should be used for installing and removing packages. Novice programmers are advised to not append libraries to the "site-packages" folder by hand unless they understand the process and have the blessings from their system administrators. For modules that are still in development and not quite ready for installation there are two alternative avenues: the PYTHONPATH system variable and the Houdini *pythonlibs* folder.

PYTHONPATH

The system *PYTHONPATH* variable is a convenient alternative for programmers to append specific folders to their Python search path without having to tamper with delicate installations in "site-packages". When modules are imported into scripts, Python for them remains in the same folders where the scripts are launched from. It will then search in the locations identified in the system *PYTHONPATH* variable. After exhausting the prior options, Python searches its default installation directories in *site-packages*.

All operating systems support system variables. PYTHONPATH is a variable string listing all of the custom-based locations where Python should search for included modules. The tricky part of the PYTHONPATH variable is setting it correctly considering the machine's operating system and your Python installation interface. Readers are encouraged to seek documentation for their Python installation for setting their PYTHONPATH correctly.

DOI: 10.1201/9781003016427-12

Houdini Path

Houdini provides a convenient folder location, *pythonlibs*, for users to integrate custom modules with current Python sessions. This folder is found in the current Houdini version folder in the user's *Home* or *Documents* folder. Note the Python version is inserted between *python* and *libs*: *python<Python Version>libs*. For example, the *pythonlibs* folder on Windows machines is *C:\Users\<user name> \Documents\<Houdini version>\python3.7libs*. The folder is found on Linux machines in */home/<user name>/<Houdini version>/python3.7libs*. The folder will need to be created by hand the first time it is utilized. It is available after Houdini is restarted.

Module Creation

The most important rule to consider when creating Houdini Python modules is importing the *hou* module into a script. As a convenience, the *hou* library is automatically imported to Houdini's Python shell and to scripts stored in the tool shelf. When accessed as an external module, any reference to the *hou* namespace requires the *hou* module to be imported. Code Sample 12.1 is a simple, external file.

```
# Example external Houdini Python Module
# Generate a quick Roberto upon inclusion
# Import the hou module
import hou

# Create the object anchor
topnode = hou.node("/obj")
# Create the container node
container = topnode.createNode("geo", "InstantRoberto")
# Insert Roberto in the container
Roberto = container.createNode("testgeometry_rubbertoy",
                               "Roberto")

# This script needs to be saved as InstantRoberto.py in the users'
# pythonlibs folder
```

Code Sample 12.1 InstantRoberto.py External Module

To be externally accessible, the previous code needs to be saved into the user's Houdini *pythonlibs* folder. Once saved to the folder, Houdini will need to be restarted. After restarting, the saved module is accessible through the *import* command. As an imported module, Roberto is immediately created in the session. Shell Example 12.1 shows how the script is called and Figure 12.1 displays the results.

```
Python 3.7.4 (1 file(s) copied., Apr 14 2021, 13:51:28) [MSC v.1928 64
bit (AMD64)] on win32
Houdini 19.0.455 hou module imported.
Type "help", "copyright", "credits" or "license" for more information.
>>> import InstantRoberto
```

Shell Example 12.1 Importing Custom InstantRoberto Module

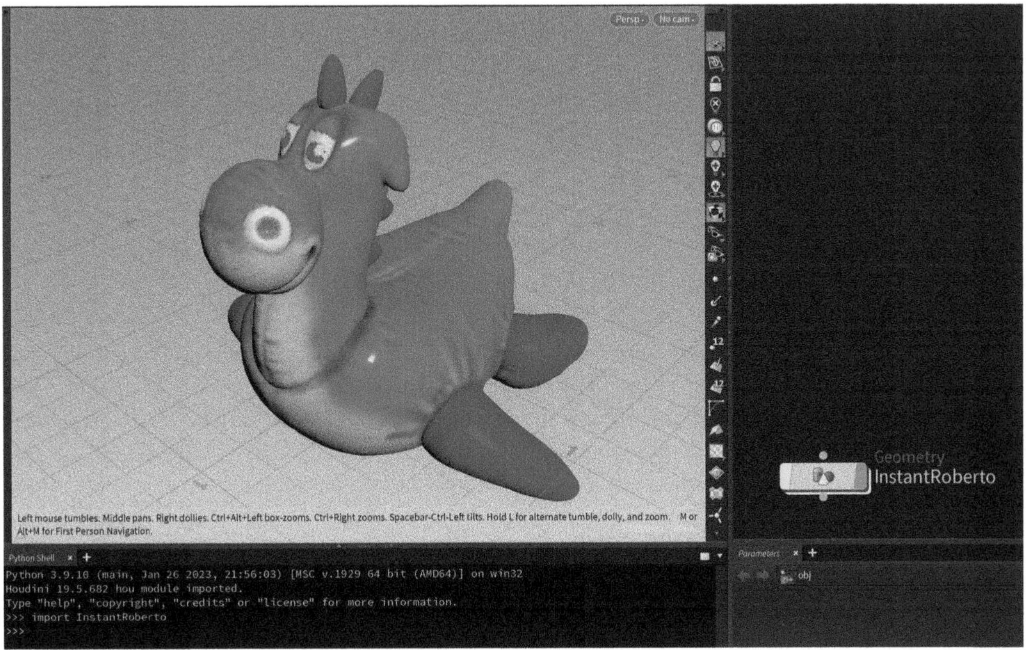

FIGURE 12.1 Importing InstantRoberto.py module.

An important factor to remember when importing custom modules is to **not** include ".py" when importing external modules. When importing modules containing periods, ".", Python attempts to import sub-modules or packages. Python throws an error when a "py" sub-module or package is not found. Shell Example 12.2 demonstrates the incorrect way for importing an external file.

```
>>> import InstantRoberto.py
Traceback (most recent call last):
  File "<console>", line 1, in <module>
  File "C:\PROGRA~1\SIDEEF~1\HOUDIN~1.455\python37\lib\site-packages-forced\shiboken2\files.dir\shibokensupport\__featur
e__.py", line 142, in _import
    return original_import(name, *args, **kwargs)
ModuleNotFoundError: No module named 'InstantRoberto.py'; 'InstantRoberto' is not a package
```

Shell Example 12.2 Improper Custom Module Importing

INHERITANCE

Re-using code is an essential object-oriented language feature. Python inheritance models the relationships between two related classes. It enables classes to be *derived* from *base* classes and become extended class versions. Derived classes create deviations, special cases, and functional subclasses. Inheritance allows programmers to start from general and abstract base classes and extend them toward specific, purpose-driven tools.

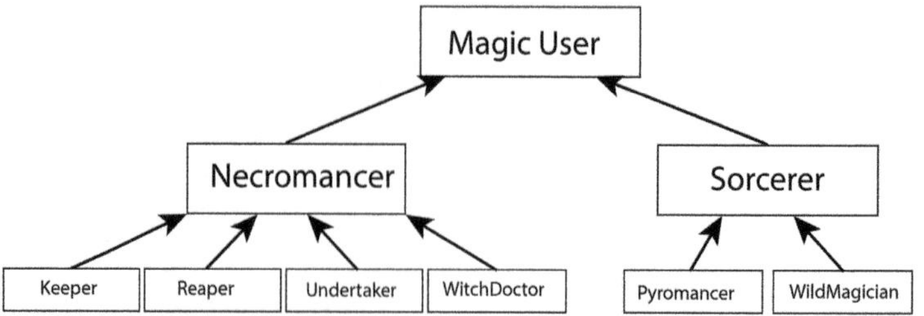

FIGURE 12.2 "Is A" relationship with A base and derived classes.

Inheritance depicts a *"is a"* relationship between two classes. When a subclass derives from a base class, it *"is a"* version of the base class. It inherits all of the attributes and methods from the base class. Take for example Figure 12.2. Suppose *MagicUser* is a base class and *Necromancer* is its derived class. A Necromancer *"is a"* MagicUser and extends the *MagicUser* class. The Necromancer can do anything a MagicUser can do and more. Suppose a *Sorcerer* class is also derived. It also *"is a" Magic User* but extends functionality in a different direction from the *Necromancer.*

Suppose *Keeper, Reaper, Undertaker,* and *WitchDoctor* are derived from *Necromancer* and *Pyromancer* and *WildMagician* are derived from *Sorcerer.* A *Keeper* is not a *Witch Doctor* but both are Necromancers. Similarly, an *Undertaker* is not the same as a *WildMagician*, yet both are still *Magic Users*. Subclasses may extend in very specific directions. Hierarchy keeps them related to each other.

Base Class

A *base class* is the source class from which future classes are derived. All classes implicitly inherit from the built-in Python *"object"* class. Defining a base class requires no additional or special syntax. Optionally, programmers may intentionally designate the base class to inherit from no class. Language Template 12.1 displays how this is achieved by following the class name with empty parenthesis. The parentheses are not mandatory but convention encourages their usage.

```
Class BaseClassName():
        pass
```

Language Template 12.1 Optional Base Class Designation

Base classes are also called *superclasses* or *parent classes*. Code Sample 12.2 establishes a more thorough, *MagicUser* base class.

```
# Establishing MagicUser Base Class
class MagicUser():
    ''' Defining Base Class from which all other Magic Users will extend '''
    def __init__(self, name="magic user", occupation="Magic User"):
        ''' Magic User Constructor '''
        self.name = name
        self.occupation = occupation
```

```
        # Start character at 1st level, by default
        self.level = 1
        # Character knows no spells, by defaul
        self.knownSpells = []


    def __str__(self):
        ''' Overload the class string functionality '''
        # Return a string reporting name and race
        buff = f'{self.name}({self.level}) -> {self.occupation}'
        buff += f'\nSpells Known:'

        if len(self.knownSpells) == 0:
            buff += '\n\t<none>'
        else:
            for spell in self.knownSpells:
                buff += f'\n\t{spell}'

        return buff


    def learnSpell(self, spellName):
        ''' Append new spell to the list of known spells'''
        # Append the new spell to knownSpells
        self.knownSpells.append(spellName)

milo = MagicUser("Milo")
milo.learnSpell("Magic Missle")
print(milo)

>>> Milo(1) -> Magic User
Spells Known:
        Magic Missile
```

Code Sample 12.2 MagicUser Base Class

Derived Class

A *derived class* inherits or receives all of the attributes and methods from its base class. Language Template 12.2 demonstrates to define a derived class, the name of the base class must be enclosed in parenthesis after the derived class name.

```
Class DerivedClassName(BaseClassName):
    pass
```

Language Template 12.2 Defining a Derived Class

Derived classes are also called *subclasses, subtypes,* or *child classes* and are said to *derive, inherit,* or *extend* a base class.

Outside the context of class definitions, Language Template 12.3 exposes derived class instances have access to all base class methods and attributes when prefixed with the derived class instance namespace.

```
variable = derivedClassInstance.baseClassAttribute
methodResults = derivedClassInstance.baseClassMethod()
```

Language Template 12.3 Accessing Base Class Attributes and Methods

Base class attributes require initialization before they can be accessed. Unless scripters desire to re-initialize them, they will need to be initialized via base class methods. There are two strategies for accessing base class methods in derived class code: the *super()* function and directly invoking the base class methods using base class namespaces.

The first and preferred technique is the use of the *super()* function. The *super()* function provides in-class access to base class methods from within the subclass. Language Template 12.4 defines the essential structure. When called within the derived class code, the *super()* function command is followed by the desired method and its arguments in parentheses. The *self* keyword is not included.

```
super().baseClassMethod(<arguments>)
```

Language Template 12.4 Using super() to invoke Base Class Methods

Language Template 12.5 displays how the *super()* function is used for invoking base class constructors, substituting *__init__*as the base class method.

```
super().__init__(<arguments>)
```

Language Template 12.5 Using super() to invoke Base Class Constructor

The second alternative to access base class methods is via the base class namespace, as introduced in Language Template 12.6. Access to any base class method is available through this technique. Because this is technically an external reference to a base class method, the *self* keyword is required.

```
BaseClassName.BaseClassMethod(self, <arguments>)
```

Language Template 12.6 Alternative Access to Base Class Methods

Language Template 12.7 displays how base class contructors are invoked by substituting *__init__* as the base class method.

```
BaseClassName.__init__(self, <arguments>)
```

Language Template 12.7 Alternative Access to Base Class Constructor

Code Sample 12.3 assumes that the *MagicUser* base class, Code Sample 12.2, has already been defined.

```
# Assuming prior MagicUser class definition
class Necromancer(MagicUser):
    ''' Necromancer is is a derived class from the MagicUser class '''
    def __init__(self, name):
        ''' Call MagicUser class constructor to initialize attributes '''
        # Call super class' constructor
        super().__init__(name, 'Necromancer')
        # Alternative technique for invoking base constructor
        #MagicUser.__init__(self, name, 'Necromancer')

randi = Necromancer("Randi")
print(randi)
randi.learnSpell('Grant Enlightenment')
print(randi)

>>> Randi(1) -> Necromancer
Spells Known:
        <none>
Randi(1) -> Necromancer
Spells Known:
        Grant Enlightenment
```

Code Sample 12.3 Necromancer Derived Class Definition

The *Necromancer* class is a simple derivation of the *MagicUser* class. The *super()* Python function is used to access the base class constructor to initialize the instance. The new constructor does not take in a parameter for *occupation*. That information is supplied by default in the constructor. An alternative strategy for invoking the base class constructor is accessing the base class directly with its namespace followed by its constructor, *(MagicUser.__init__(self, <Arguments>))*. The syntax is commented out in the example.

Derived classes extend their base classes by rewriting and supplementing what their base classes provide. New attributes are introduced without challenging base class integrity. Derived classes are free to rewrite methods to service specialized functionality.

In Code Sample 12.4, the *Necromancer* class extends the *MagicUser* base class. Within the derived class constructor, the base class constructor is invoked and new attributes, *specialSkills* and *specialization*, are appended to the class. The string overload method, *__str__*, calls the base class string overload method and appends additional information to the returned string. The *learnSpells* method replaces the base class method. It verifies the new input spell integrity by testing its validity within the *availalableSpells* set.

```
class Necromancer(MagicUser):
    def __init__(self, name):
        ''' Call base class constructor to initilize attributes '''
        # Call super class' constructor
        super().__init__(name, 'Necromancer')

        # Necromancer special skills
        self.specialSkills = ['Chill Touch', 'Decompose',
                              'Sapping Sting', 'Spare the Dying',
                              'Toll the Dead']
        # Place holder for declared specification
        self.specialization = '<Not Declared>'

    def __str__(self):
        ''' Take advantage of the parent method and extend it '''
        buff = super().__str__()

        buff += '\nSpecial Skills:'
        # List all of the necromancer special skills
        for skill in self.specialSkills:
            buff += f'\n\t{skill}'
```

```
        buff += '\nSpecialization:\n\t'
        # Append specialization to the instance printout
        buff += self.specialization

        return buff

    def declareSpecialization(self, specialization):
        ''' Upon third level or greater, character may declare
           a specialization '''
        availableSpecializations = {'Keeper', 'Reaper',
                                    'Undertaker',
                                    'Witch Doctor'}
        if self.level > 1:
            # Specialize when level 2 or greater and valid specialization
            if specialization in availableSpecializations:
                self.specialization = specialization
            # Report invalid or unavailable specializations
            else:
                print(f'Necromantic specialization: \
                     {specialization} unavailable')
        else:
            print(f'{self.name} may not specialize yet')

    def learnSpell(self, spellname):
        ''' Rewrite base class method '''
        availableSpells = {'Cause Fear', 'False Life',
                         ='Inflict Wounds', 'Ray of Sickness'}
        :# Check for valid spell
         if spellname in availableSpells
            self.knownSpells.append(spellname)
        else:
            # Report invalid spell name
            print(f'{spellname} not a learnable spell')
```

```
randi = Necromancer("Randi")
randi.learnSpell('Inflict Wounds')
randi.declareSpecialization('Keeper')
print(randi)

Randi may not specialize yet
Randi(1) -> Necromancer
Spells Known:
        Inflict Wounds
Special Skills:
        Chill Touch
        Decompose
        Sapping Sting
        Spare the Dying
        Toll the Dead
Specialization:
        <Not Declared>
```

Code Sample 12.4 Derived Class Extending Base Class

New subclasses, *Keeper*, *Reaper*, *Undertaker*, and *WitchDoctor*, are identified as future derived classes from the *Necromancer* parent class. These new subclasses will inherit everything declared in the *Necromancer* and *MagicUser* base classes and customize attributes and methods to augment their unique functionalities.

To avoid redundancy, Code Sample 12.5 only demonstrates the *Keeper* sub-class. Depending on their specific needs, the *Reaper*, *Undertaker*, and *WitchDoctor* classes could mirror the *Keeper* class with subtle alterations. These similarities demonstrate *polymorphisms* where same-named methods, used in different contexts, produce different results. Detailed *polymorphism* information is included later in this section.

```
class Keeper(Necromancer):
    ''' Keeper is derived from Necromancer class and is a
       MagicUser sub-sub class '''
    def __init__(self, name):
        ''' Inherit the Necromancer and MagicUser constructors '''
        super().__init__(name)
        self.level = 2
        self.declareSpecialization('Keeper')
```

```
        # Create default specialAbilities
        self.specializedAbilities = []
        # Configure specializations
        self.configureSpecialization()

    def __str__(self):
        ''' Inherit the Necromancer and MagicUser string overloads
           and append specialized abilities '''
        # Start with the supers overload
        buff = super().__str__()

        # List the specialized abilities
        buff += '\nSpecialized Abilities:\n'
        for ability in self.specializedAbilities:
            buff += f'\t{ability}'

        return buff


    def configureSpecialization(self):
        ''' Depending on the Necromancers level ,
           reconfigure her abilities'''
        abilities = {2:'Life on Demand', 5:'Expanded Intellect',
                9:'Aura of Wellbeing', 14:'Refusal'}
        # Go through all of the abilities and test if they match
        for level, ability in abilities.items():
            # If the character level matches, append specialization
            if self.level >= level:
                self.specializedAbilities.append(ability)


randi = Keeper("Randi")
randi.learnSpell('Inflict Wounds')
randi.learnSpell('Cause Fear')
```

```
randi.learnSpell('Ray of Sickness')
print(randi)




>>> Randi(2) -> Necromancer
Spells Known:
        Inflict Wounds
        Cause Fear
        Ray of Sickness
Special Skills:
        Chill Touch
        Decompose
        Sapping Sting
        Spare the Dying
        Toll the Dead
Specialization:
        Keeper
Specialized Abilities:
        Life on Demand
```

Code Sample 12.5 Keeper Sub-class

Arrows and Vectors

The *Arrow* and *vizVector* classes introduced in Chapter 11 work adequately as unique classes. The *vizVector* class is managed more robustly when re-written as a derivation from the *Arrow* class. The translation integrating inheritance is direct and straight forward.

Suppose the *Arrow* class remains nearly the same as introduced in Chapter 11 and is written as an external module, *ArrowModule.py*, to the Houdini *pythonlibs* folder. The inclusion of a string overload method provides robust functionality helpful for derived classes. Because this module is external form Houdini, the *hou* module must be imported. Code Sample 12.6 demonstrates how the *Arrow* class can be written as an external module.

```
import random
import math
# Include Houdini Python Object Library
import hou
```

```
from time import time

class Arrow:
    ''' This class generates a houdini arrow of random,
        given the arrows X, Y and Z vector coordiantes '''
    def __init__(self, name='arrow', x=0.0, y=0.0, z = 0.0):
        ''' absorb the arrow vector input then display the results
            of the vector using random colors '''
        self.name = name
        self.X = x
        self.Y = y
        self.Z = z

        # Draw the visual Representation of the arrow
        self.drawArrow()


    def __str__(self):
        ''' String overload for easy to read content display '''
        return(f'{self.name}({self.X:.2f}, {self.Y:.2f}, {self.Z:.2f})')


    def length(self):
        ''' Convenience class function to quickly generate
           arrow length '''
        # compute the Pythagorean length of the tube
        length = math.sqrt(self.X*self.X +
                           self.Y*self.Y +
                           self.Z*self.Z)
        return length


    def generateColor(self):
        ''' Generate a random color based on system time '''
```

```
        # Use position as color seed
        random.seed(time())
        # Create new Houdini Color
        color = hou.Color()
        # Assign color a random Hue
        color.setHSV((360*random.random(), 1, 1))
        # Return randomized color object
        return color


    def createContainer(self):
        ''' Method gets the Houdini OBJ node reference,
            the container which holds the geometry and
            temporary look at object to be used to rotate the
            arrow into place '''
        # Get the OBJ Node
        objNode  = hou.node('/obj')

        # Create the class container
        self.container = objNode.createNode('geo', self.name)

        # Create a temporary Lookat Object
        self.lookAt = objNode.createNode('geo', 'lookat')
        # Position lookAt object to where arrow will point to
        self.lookAt.parmTuple('t').set((self.X, self.Y, self.Z))
        return


    def drawShaft(self):
        ''' draw the arrow the length to the lookat object '''

        # Create the tube node
        self.shaft = self.container.createNode('tube', 'shaft')
```

```
        # Assign the tubes length
        self.shaft.parm('height').set(self.length())
        # make sure the tube lays flat
        self.shaft.parm('orient').set(0)
        # Shift tubes position to start at origin
        self.shaft.parm('tx').set(0.5*self.length())
        # Make sure tube is skinny
        self.shaft.parm('radscale').set(.1)
        # Cap the ends of the tube
        self.shaft.parm('cap').set(True)


    def drawHead(self):
        ''' Draw a cone and place it at the tip of the shaft '''
        # Create the tube node
        self.head = self.container.createNode('tube', 'head')
        # Assign the tubes length
        self.head.parm('height').set(1.0)
        # Pinch cone end
        self.head.parm('rad1').set(0.0)
        # Make sure the tube lays flat
        self.head.parm('orient').set(0)
        # Shift tubes position to start at origin
        self.head.parm('tx').set(self.length()-0.3)
        # Make cone a bit more narrow
        self.head.parm('radscale').set(.5)
        # Cap the ends of the cone
        self.head.parm('cap').set(True)


    def finishArrow(self):
        ''' perform the final operations to the container network
            to make it presentable '''
```

```
        # Create a merge node to collect objects
        merge = self.container.createNode('merge')
        # Connect Shaft and Head to the merge node
        merge.setInput(0, self.shaft)
        merge.setInput(1, self.head)

        # create a color node for the combined object
        colorNode = self.container.createNode('color')
        colorNode.setInput(0, merge)
        randColor = self.generateColor()
        # Assign color node RGB value of HSV color
        colorNode.parmTuple('color').set(randColor.rgb())

        # Append a transform sop to rotate the object
        xform = self.container.createNode('xform')
        # 90 degrees in Y to make the 'lookat' function work
        xform.setInput(0, colorNode)
        xform.parm('ry').set(90)

        # Append an output node to be the final display
        output = self.container.createNode('output')
        output.setInput(0, xform)
        # set the display flag to be true
        output.setDisplayFlag(True)

        # Clean up the node in the container to be visually pleasing
        self.container.layoutChildren()


    def pointArrow(self):
        ''' point the arrow to look at the lookat object.
            Remove the lookat object as it is no longer needed '''
```

```
        # Rotate the shaft so that it points to the lookAt Object
        self.container.setWorldTransform(
            self.container.buildLookatRotation(self.lookAt))

        # Remove the LookAt node as it is no longer needed
        self.lookAt.destroy()


    def drawArrow(self):
        ''' Draw the arrow using the input vector coordinates using a
random color '''
        self.createContainer()
        self.drawShaft()
        self.drawHead()
        self.finishArrow()
        self.pointArrow()
```

Code Sample 12.6 ArrowModule.py

In Code Sample 12.7, the *Vector2* class is derived from the *Arrow* class. The *Arrow* class manages the majority of the Houdini display and allows *Vector2* to focus almost exclusively on vector mathematics. The string overload and *drawArrow()* methods are significant modifications. The string overload method augments the base class method by appending the vector length information to the output string. The *drawArrow()* modification uses the *super()* method to draw the arrow and appends text information with a new *font* node.

```
import random
import math
from time import time
from ArrowModule import *

class Vector2(Arrow):
    ''' The Vector2 class extends the Arrow class. No attributes are
        added but the functionality increases with the mathematical
        overloading and the addition of vector information to
        the arrow geometry'''
```

```
def __init__(self, name = "vector", x = 0.0, y=0.0, z = 0.0):
    """ Vector2 Constructor initializes all the values, otherwise
        use defaults"""
    self.name = name# Every attribute assignment invokes __setAttr__
    self.X = x
    self.Y = y
    self.Z = z

    self.drawArrow()

#Sets the dictionary values of all the attributes
def __setattr__(self, attrName, value):
    ''' Override of SetAttr, Sets value to an attribute, The only
       allowed attributes are in classAttrs'''
    classAttrs = {'X', 'Y', 'Z', 'name', 'container', 'lookAt',
            'shaft', 'head'}
    # test if attrName is the valid attributes
    if attrName in classAttrs:
        object.__setattr__(self, attrName, value)
    else:
        raise ValueError(
        f'SetAttr: Invalid vizVector Attribute: {attrName}')

def __str__(self):
    ''' Use the parent method and append the vector
       length information '''
    return(f'{super().__str__()} ||{self.length():.2f}||')

''' Method computes the inversion of the vector and returns
   a new vector '''
def __invert__(self):
    ''' Return a vector going in the opposite direction '''
    newName = f'inv_{self.name}'
```

```
        return Vector2(newName, -self.X, -self.Y, -self.Z)

    #Operator override for '+', returns a new vector
    def __add__(self, other):
        """Add the components of the two instances and return
            a new vector"""
        newName = f'{self.name}Plus{other.name}'
        return Vector2(newName, self.X+other.X, self.Y+other.Y,
                    self.Z+other.Z)

    #Operator override for '-', returns a new vector
    def __sub__(self, other):
        """Subtract the components of the two instances and return
            a new vector"""
        newName = f'{self.name}Minus{other.name}'
        return Vector2(newName, self.X-other.X, self.Y-other.Y,
                    self.Z-other.Z)
    ''' There are two potential multiplication operations performed
        on vectors: a dot product and a cross product. Since the
        rest of the overloaded techniques return new vectors, this
        operation returns the cross product. Either technique could
        be overloaded '''
    def __mul__(self, other):
        '''Cross Source vector to destination vector and return result'''
        newName = f'{self.name}Cross{other.name}'
        return Vector2(newName, (self.Y*other.Z)-(self.Z*other.Y),
                      (self.Z*other.X)-(self.X*other.Z),
                      (self.X*other.Z)-(self.Z*other.X))

    ''' There are two potential multiplication operations performed
        on vectors: a dot product and a cross product. The cross
        product is already overloaded so the dot product is its own
        method. Either technique could be overloaded '''
```

```
def dot(self, other):
    '''Multiply corresponding components, add their products
      and return the sum'''
    '''Returns a float. Does not return a new Vector2'''
    return self.X*other.X + self.Y*other.Y + self.Z*other.Z

''' Unitize the current vector. Since there are no unary operators
   left that make sense in this context, this will need to be a
   non-overloaded operator. '''
def unit(self):
    ''' compute the vector length then use that length to divide
        into each component and return a new Vector2 '''
    vlength = self.length()
    # Look out for division by zero!
    if vlength == 0.0:
        raise ZeroDivisionError("Vector Length is Zero!")
        return

    # tag the name with u to know it is the unitized version
    newName = "u{}".format(self.name)
    return Vector2(newName, self.X/vlength, self.Y/vlength,
                self.Z/vlength)

def drawArrow(self):
    ''' Use the supers method and display the vector
        information on the arrow'''
    # Call the super Method to generate Arrow
    super().drawArrow()

    # Create a new font node
    fontNode = self.container.createNode('font','Info')
    # Reduce the size of the text
    fontNode.parm('fontsize').set(.15)
```

```
        fontLocation = 0.75 * fontNode.node('../shaft').parm('tx').
eval()# Identify text position
        fontNode.parmTuple('t').set((fontLocation, 0.2, 0))
        # Generate text string from string Overload
        fontNode.parm('text').set(f'{self.__str__()}')

        # Identify the merge node
        mergeNode = hou.node(f'{self.container.path()}/merge1')
        # Merge the font with the arrow
        mergeNode.setInput(2, fontNode)
        # Clean up network
        self.container.layoutChildren()

vec1 = Vector2('vec1', 1, 2, 3)
print(vec1)
inversevec1 = ~vec1
vec2 = Vector2('vec2', 3, 2, -1)
myAdd = vec1+vec2
mySub = vec1-vec2
myCross = vec1*vec2
print(f'The dot product of {vec1} and {vec2} is {vec1.dot(vec2)}')
myUnit = myCross.unit()
```

Code Sample 12.7 Vector2 Derived Class from Arrow

The last nine lines of code test the *Vector2* class. After instancing the first vector, *vec1*, the object is converted to string format to test the string overload. The inverse of *vec1* is referenced to a new object, *inversevec1*. A new vector is referenced to the *vec2* object. The *myAdd*, *mySub*, and *myCross* variables test the addition, subtraction, and cross-product operations. The dot-product operation is tested. The test code finishes by generating an instance of the unitized cross-product representation.

Polymorphism

The concept of *Polymorphism* in object-oriented programming is important and is one of the key reasons why it is so powerful. Inherited polymorphism is the ability of different objects of different classes to respond uniquely to the same method calls. In other words, the same method calls may have radically different effects depending on the contexts of their object classes. Base classes are extensible and may be enhanced to yet unknown classes, performing yet unknown purposes. Newly derived methods append to base class methods or overwrite them entirely. Classes derived in different directions from their base classes may share the same-named methods and attributes but treat them differently.

Code Sample 12.8 demonstrates inherited polymorphism in the *MagicUser* class string overload method. When called, the base class method displays the name, occupation, and currently known spells.

```
class MagicUser():
    def __init__(self, name="magic user", occupation="Magic User"):
        ...

    def __str__(self):
        ''' Overload the class string functionality '''
        # Return a string reporting name and race
        buff = f'{self.name}({self.level}) -> {self.occupation}'
        buff += f'\nSpells Known:'

        if len(self.knownSpells) == 0:
            buff += '\n\t<none>'
        else:
            for spell in self.knownSpells:
                buff += f'\n\t{spell}'

        return buff

milo = MagicUser("Milo")
milo.learnSpell("Magic Missile")
print(milo)

>>> Milo(1) -> Magic User
Spells Known:
        Magic Missile
```

Code Sample 12.8 MagicUser String Overload Method

The *Necromancer* string overload method, as demonstrated in Code Sample 12.9, builds upon the base class method. It takes advantage of the data structure inherited by the base class and uses the *super()* function and extends the method to concatenate special skills and specialization information to the output string.

```
class Necromancer(MagicUser):
    def __init__(self, name):
        …

    def __str__(self):
        ''' Take advantage of the parent method and extend it '''
        buff = super().__str__()

        buff += '\nSpecial Skills:'
        # List all of the necromancer special skills
        for skill in self.specialSkills:
            buff += f'\n\t{skill}'

        buff += '\nSpecialization:\n\t'
        # Append specialization to the instance printout
        buff += self.specialization

        return buff
…

randi = Necromancer("Randi")
randi.learnSpell('Inflict Wounds')
print(randi)

>>> Randi(1) -> Necromancer
Spells Known:
        Inflict Wounds
Special Skills:
        Chill Touch
        Decompose
        Sapping Sting
        Spare the Dying
        Toll the Dead
Specialization:
        <Not Declared>
```

Code Sample 12.9 Necromancer Extended String Overload Method

The *Keeper* and *WitchDoctor* classes from Code Sample 12.10, extend the string overload method further by taking advantage of the data structure inherited from the *Necromancer* class and supplement additional information based on information found only within their unique specializations: the *Keeper's specializedAbilities* and the *WitchDoctor's originationClan* attributes.

```
class Keeper(Necromancer):
    ''' Keeper is derived from Necromancer class and
       is a MagicUser sub-sub class '''
    def __init__(self, name):
        ...

    def __str__(self):
        ''' Inherit the Necromancer and MagicUser string
           overloads and append specialized abilities '''
        # Start with the super overload
        buff = super().__str__()

        buff += '\nSpecialized Abilities:\n'
        # Display the specialized abilities
        for ability in self.specializedAbilities:
            buff += f'\t{ability}'

        return buff
        ...


class WitchDoctor(Necromancer):
    ''' WitchDoctor is derived from Necromancer class and
        is a MagicUser sub-sub class '''
    def __init__(self, name):
        ...

    def __str__(self):
        ''' Inherit the Necromancer and MagicUser string overloads
           and append specialized abilities '''
```

```
        # Start with the super overload
        buff = super().__str__()

        # Display the origination clan
        buff += '\nOrigination Clan:\n'
        buff += f'\t{self.originationClan}'

        return buff
        …


herbert = Keeper('Herbert')
stosh = WitchDoctor('Stosh')
print(herbert)
print(stosh)

>>> Herbert(2) -> Necromancer
Spells Known:
        <none>
Special Skills:
        Chill Touch
        Decompose
        Sapping Sting
        Spare the Dying
        Toll the Dead
Specialization:
        Keeper
Specialized Abilities:
        Life on Demand

Stosh(2) -> Necromancer
Spells Known:
        <none>
```

```
Special Skills:
        Chill Touch
        Decompose
        Sapping Sting
        Spare the Dying
        Toll the Dead
Specialization:
        Witch Doctor
Origination Clan:
        Zlichane
```

Code Sample 12.10 Keeper and WitchDoctor Extended String Overload Methods

Within this example, the string overload method takes on four different behaviors depending on the object context. Each derived class method takes advantage of its base class methods and augments them.

Derived classes may elect to rewrite base class methods. Even though derived class methods share the same name as the base class, they are not required to reuse the same code. Code Example 12.11 demonstrates the freedom afforded to derived classes. Each of the derived classes rewrites the base class method, *drawMe()*, to suit the needs of the new class. The results of this example are displayed in Figure 12.3.

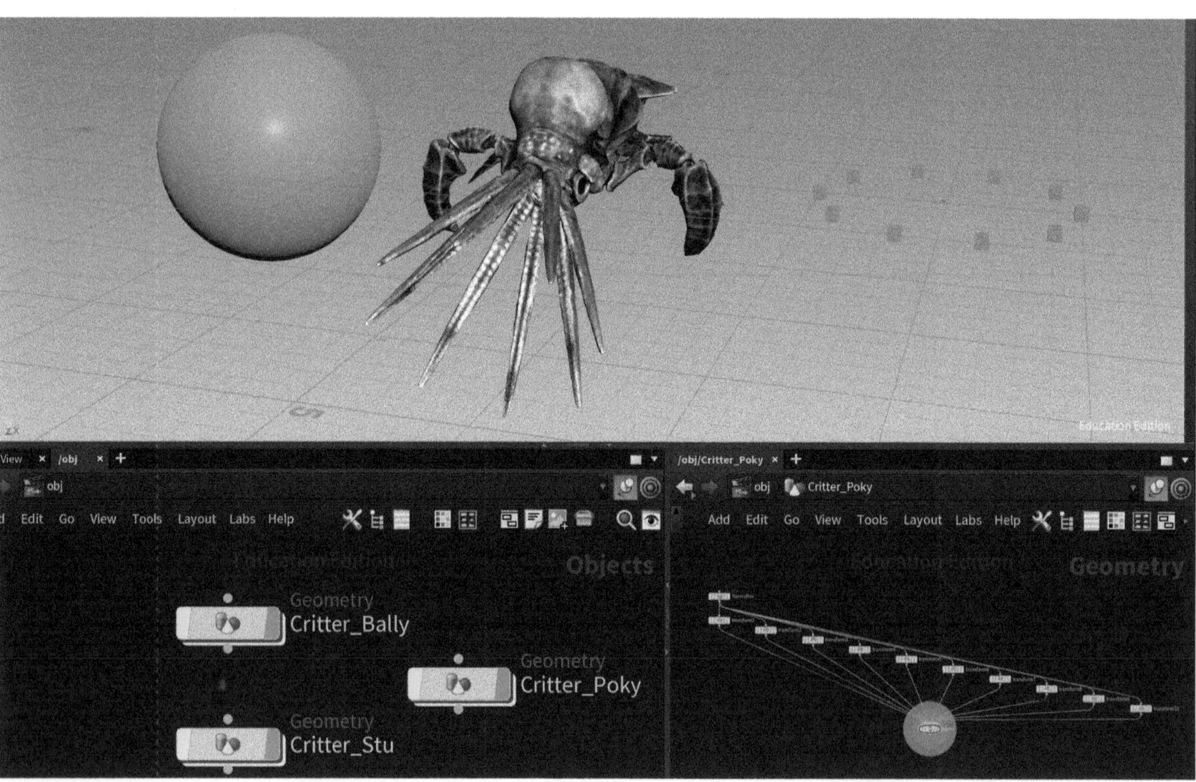

FIGURE 12.3 Derived `drawMe()` methods.

```
import math

class Critter:
    ''' Define the base class which draws a simple sphere '''
    # input is name and position
    def __init__(self, name='name', pos=(0.0, 0.0, 0.0))
        self.name = name
        top = hou.node('/obj')
        # Create the object container
        self.container = top.createNode('geo', f'Critter_{name}')
        # position the container
        self.container.parmTuple('t').set(pos)
        # clean up the node arrangement
        top.layoutChildren()

    def drawMe(self):
        ''' default base class method for displaying a
           Critter's geometry '''
        # Display a default sphere
        self.critter = self.container.createNode('sphere', self.name)


class Squidward(Critter):
    ''' Define a derived class which draws a squab instead of
       a sphere '''
    # Call Base class constructor
    def __init__(self, name, pos):
        super().__init__(name, pos)

    def drawMe(self):
        ''' Derived Method is similar to base but different '''
```

```
        # Generate Squab Geometry
        self.critter = self.container.createNode('testgeometry_squab',
self.name)


class Boxes(Critter):
    ''' Define a derived class which draws a ring of boxes instead
       of a sphere '''
    # Derived class takes in an additional argument, (number)
    def __init__(self, name, pos, number=5):
        super().__init__(name, pos)
        # make number a class attribute
        self.number = number

    def drawMe(self):
        ''' Derived method is radically different for base class method.
           Draw a ring of boxes instead of a single sphere '''
        # Create an anchor merge node
        self.merge = self.container.createNode('merge', 'boxes')
        # Create a master box geometry
        self.box = self.container.createNode('box', 'SourceBox')
        # Set the source box scale
        self.box.parm('scale').set(.1)

        # Draw the number of boxes
        for i in range(self.number):
            # Define the angle and calculate the X and Z coordinates
            angle = math.radians(i * 360.0/self.number)
            xpos = math.cos(angle)
            zpos = math.sin(angle)
            # Transform duplicates and translates the master box
            transform = self.container.createNode('xform')
            transform.parmTuple('t').set((xpos, 0.0, zpos))
```

```
            # Connect the transform to the source box
            transform.setInput(0, self.box)
            # Connect the transform the merge node
            self.merge.setInput(i, transform)

        # Clean up the node arrangement
        self.container.layoutChildren()


# Create Base Class default geometry
bally = Critter('Bally', (-3, 0, 0))
bally.drawMe()

# Create derived Squidward geometry
stu = Squidward("Stu", (0, 0, 0))
stu.drawMe()

# Create derived ring of boxes
poky = Boxes("Poky", (3, 0, 0), 10)
poky.drawMe()
```

Code Sample 12.11 Critter Base and Squidward and Boxes Derived Classes

In the above example, the *Critter* classes define how to draw a sphere to the Houdini scene. The *Squidward drawMe()* method deviates from *Critter* class and draws a Squidward character instead of a sphere. The *Boxes* subclass entirely rewrites the *drawMe()* method. Instead of displaying just one test geometry character, it generates a ring of boxes. All three classes depend heavily on the *drawMe()* method yet each utilizes it uniquely.

Multiple Inheritance

Object-oriented classes may be derived from multiple base classes. Derived classes inherit from multiple parents but working with them may be a logistical nightmare. Unless the programmer is extremely comfortable with inheritance, deriving from multiple classes is discouraged.

Big problems result when multiple base classes share the same-named attributes and methods. Juggling attribute and method inheritance from multiple base classes require understanding of Python *MRO, Method Resolution Order*. MRO is used by the *super()* function to determine which base class current methods and attributes derive from. Thorough explanation of MRO is beyond the scope of this text. Direct access to base classes may be necessary to manipulate attributes and methods instead of reliance on the *super()* function.

An alternative strategy from deriving from multiple base classes is to ignore inheritance altogether and practice class *composition*. Composition strategy is explained in depth, later in this chapter. Instead of inheriting, composition classes instance component class attributes and methods. There are no hierarchies between base and derived classes. While multiple component classes may share same-named attributes and methods, they are never confused as they are component references, identified by their reference namespace. Working with composites of multiple component classes is often easier to manage than working with hierarchical relationships.

Inheritance Functions

As base classes and subsequent derived classes evolve, users may become confused understanding the lineage of their object instances. To provide clear navigation through hierarchical class trees, Python provides two utility functions for piloting inheritance: *isinstance()* and *issubclass()*.

Isinstance()

Python function *isinstance()*, as defined in Language Template 12.8, tests if the current object is an instance of any class in the hierarchal branch of the input class. When the object is an instance of the class branch, *True* is returned.

```
result = isinstance( CurrentObject, TestClass)
```

Language Template 12.8 isinstance() Usage

Issubclass()

Python function *issubclass()*, as defined in Language Template 12.9, tests if the current class is contained in the hierarchical branch of the input class. When the current class is found in the input class branch, *True* is returned.

```
result = issubclass( CurrentClass, TestClass)
```

Language Template 12.9 issubclass() Usage

Code Sample 12.12 assumes that all of the classes from Code Sample 12.10 have already been defined.

```
herbert = Keeper('Herbert')

# Test if Herbert is a MagicUser
print(f'Herbert is a MagicUser:{isinstance(herbert, MagicUser)}')

# Test if Herbert is a Keeper
print(f'Herbert is a Keeper:{isinstance(herbert, Keeper)}')
```

```
# Test if Herbert is a WitchDoctor
print(f'Herbert is a WitchDoctor:{isinstance(herbert, WitchDoctor)}')

# Test if WitchDoctor is a Necromancer sub-class
print(f'WitchDoctor is a Necromancer subclass:\
        {issubclass(WitchDoctor, Necromancer)}')

>>> Herbert is a MagicUser:True
Herbert is a Keeper:True
Herbert is a WitchDoctor:False
WitchDoctor is a Necromancer subclass:True
```

Code Sample 12.12 issubclass() Function

COMPOSITION

An alternative strategy of expanding class functionality is with *Composition*. Instead of extending functionality through derivation, composition combines complementary classes which contribute to more dynamic functionality than to their original classes. In other words, *composite* classes take advantage of the functionality afforded by each of its *component* classes to expand its purpose. Compositions are created with *"has a"* relationships. A composite class *"has a"* component instance of another class.

A composition's *"has a"* relationship is said to be loosely coupled. When composite classes change, they have no impact on their component classes. Depending on the context, when component classes change, they may or may not have an impact on their composite class.

Consider the following hierarchal classes in Figure 12.4.

GeoContainer creates an empty Houdini Geometry object. *MergeContainer* extends it by adding merge node functionality. *Character* is the base class and supplies almost all character functionality. *Roberto, Squidward,* and *Rocky* are derived from *Character* and provide specific instructions for generating specific characters. These component classes can be composited into a more dynamic composition class, *CompSphere* (shown in Figure 12.5), which takes advantage of all of their functionalities.

The *CompSphere* class is a composite of only *MergeContainer, Roberto, Squidward,* and *Rocky* class instances. Through inheritance and *"is a"* relationships, the functionalities of *GeoContainer* and *Character* are included by default. The *MergeContainer* instance creates a Houdini Geometry container and the *Roberto, Squidward,* and *Rocky* classes generate individual characters.

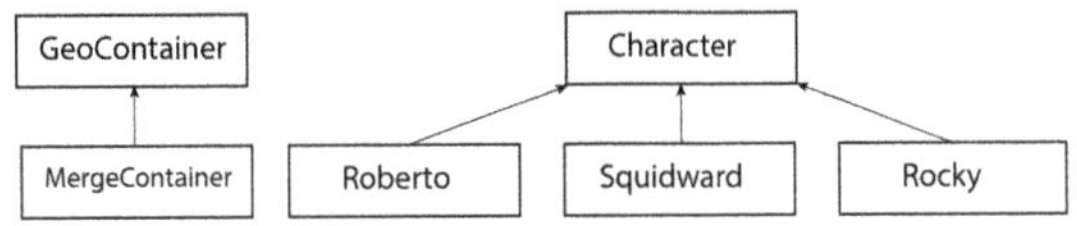

FIGURE 12.4 Pre-existing classes.

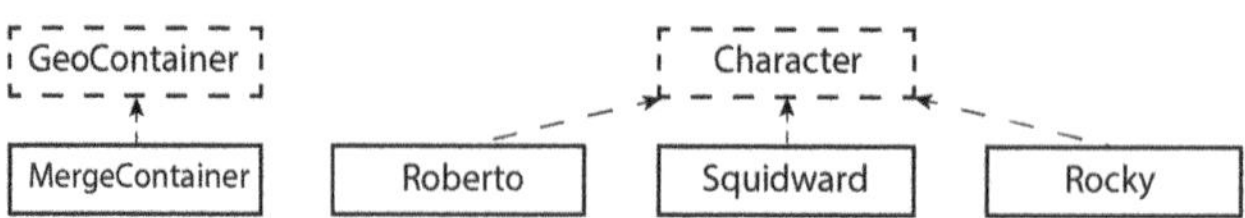

FIGURE 12.5 CompSphere composition.

Houdini Example

To illustrate the *composition* strategy, consider Code Sample 12.13. The example defines seven classes: *CompSphere, GeoContainer, MergeContainer, Character, Roberto, Squidward,* and *Rocky*. The *CompSphere* class instances *GeoContainer* and *Character* subclass objects, (*MergeContainer, Roberto, Squidward,* and *Rocky*), to populate a sphere of randomly placed characters. The results look something like Figure 12.6.

The *Character* base class performs all of the heavy lifting for the derived *Roberto, Squidward,* and *Rocky* classes. The *MergeContainer* subclass supplements the *GeoContainer* base class and generates a Houdini Geometry container with merge node functionality. The *CompSphere* class takes advantage of all of these objects and invokes almost no Houdini commands itself.

The *GeoContainer* base and derived *MergeContainer* classes manage Houdini preparations for new geometry containers with anchoring merge nodes. The merge nodes combine all future geometry content into one node.

The *Character* base class handles all of Houdini operations for creating and manipulating new geometry subnetworks. Each subnetwork contains three chained geometry nodes: a transform node which sets the object's

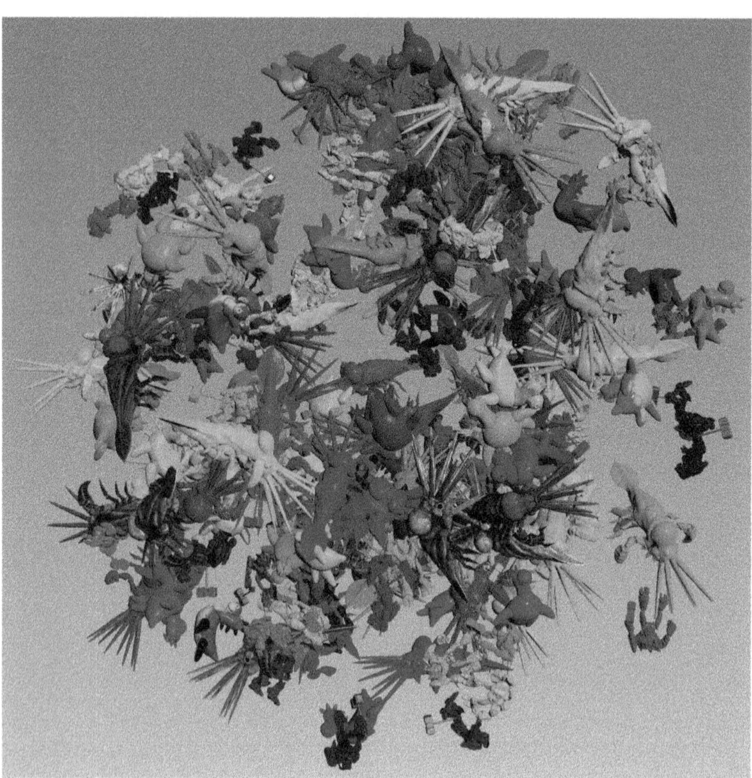

FIGURE 12.6 CompSphere script results.

position and orientation, a color node to give each character a unique look, and an output node. The *createCharacterNode()* method generates an abstract character node and attaches it to the front of the chain. Other utility methods, such as *setPos()* and *setRot()*, adjust character position and orientation. The *Roberto*, *Squidward*, and *Rocky* subclasses extend the *Character* base class and provide custom character information.

The *CompSphere* class is a composition of all previously mentioned component classes. It generates a *MergeContainer* instance and populates it with *Roberto*, *Squidward*, and *Rocky* instances. The new class organizes the characters into a sphere-like structure. The *CompSphere* class instances *MegeContainer*, *Roberto*, *Squidward*, and *Rocky* classes but never alters their code.

Code Sample 12.13 finishes with a single *CompSphere* instance.

```
import random
import math

# A simple class for a geometry container
class GeoContainer():
    ''' Define the GeoContainer class which generates a Houdini
      geometry container'''
    def __init__(self, name='Geometry'):
        ''' GeoContainer constructor'''
        top = hou.node('/obj')
        # Create the geometry container
        self.containerNode = top.createNode('geo', name)


class MergeContainer(GeoContainer):
    ''' Define a derived GeoContainer that provides all of the
      functionality of a merge network '''
    def __init__(self, name):
        super().__init__(name)
        # Create the merge node
        self.mergeNode = self.containerNode.createNode('merge',
                                  f'{name}_merge')

    def appendMerge(self, inputNode):
        ''' Utility method for connecting geometry to the
          merge node '''
```

```
        self.mergeNode.setNextInput(inputNode)

    def layoutChildren(self):
        ''' Utility method for cleaning up the container network '''
        self.containerNode.layoutChildren()



# A base class for all specific character types
class Character():
    ''' Define the Character Base class for all future character
       classes. Constructor creates the subnetwork and all nodes
       except the character node. This class only creates
       Geometry nodes. All object nodes are handled by
       different classes '''
    # Input is a geometry container node
    def __init__(self, container=None):
        # Create a Subnet node
        self.subnetNode = container.createNode('subnet')
        # Transform node is anchor
        self.anchorNode = self.subnetNode.createNode('xform',
                                 'anchor')
        # Append a Color Node
        self.colorNode = self.createRandomColorNode()
        self.colorNode.setInput(0, self.anchorNode)
        # Output node to terminates the geometry chain
        self.outNode = self.subnetNode.createNode('output',
                                   'output')
        self.outNode.setInput(0, self.colorNode)
        self.outNode.setDisplayFlag(True)
        self.outNode.setRenderFlag(True)
        # Clean network
        self.layoutChildren()
```

```
def createRandomColorNode(self):
    ''' Utility function for generating a random color. Technique
       uses HSV color to get fulkl saturation and value '''
    # Generate the initial color node
    node = self.subnetNode.createNode('color', 'color')
    # Create new Houdini Color
    myColor = hou.Color((0.0, 0.0, 0.0))
    # Generate a random hue value
    hVal = random.random() * 360.0
    myColor.setHSV((hVal,1.0, 1.0))
    # Set the Color node parameter
    node.parmTuple('color').set(myColor.rgb())
    return node

def createCharacterNode(self, type='null', name='name'):
    ''' Utility node generating the character geometry node
       and sticking it at the top of the chain. This utility is
       intended to be used by derived classes '''
    )# Create the Character geometry node
    self.characterNode = self.subnetNode.createNode(
                         type , name)
    # Change all the names
    self.renameCharacter(name)
    # Stick the new node at the front of the chain
    self.attach(self.characterNode)
    # Clean network
    self.layoutChildren()

def layoutChildren(self):
    ''' Utility node for placing all the network nodes in a
       readable fashion '''
    self.subnetNode.layoutChildren()
```

```
    def renameCharacter(self, newName='newName'):
        ''' Utility Node renameing all nodes of a subnetwork '''
        self.subnetNode.setName(newName, unique_name=True)
        self.outNode.setName(f'{newName}_out')

    def attach(self, newNode):
        ''' Utility node for attaching any geometry node to the front
           of the network chain '''
        self.anchorNode.setInput(0, newNode)

    def setPos(self, pos):
        ''' Utiltiy node for positioning the geometry using the
           transformation node. Input is a translation 3-tuple '''
        self.anchorNode.parmTuple('t').set(pos)

    def setRot(self, rot):
        ''' Utiltiy node for rotating the geometry using the
           transformation node. Input is a rotation 3-tuple '''
        self.anchorNode.parmTuple('r').set(rot)



class Roberto(Character):
    ''' Define the derived Roberto class which generates a
       Roberto character'''
    def __init__(self, container=None):
        ''' Roberto constructor '''
        # Call the base class constructor
        super().__init__(container)
        # Generate a Roberto character
        self.characterNode = self.createCharacterNode(
                              'testgeometry_rubbertoy',
                              'Roberto')
```

```
class Squidward(Character):
    ''' Define the derived Squidward class which generates a
       Squidward character'''
    def __init__(self, container=None):
        ''' Squidward constructor '''
        # Call the base class constructor
        super().__init__(container)
        # Generate a Squidward character
        self.characterNode = self.createCharacterNode(
                             'testgeometry_squab',
                             'Squidward')


class Rocky(Character):
    ''' Define the derived Rocky class which generates a
       Rocky character'''
    def __init__(self, container=None):
        ''' Rocky constructor '''
        # Call the base class constructor
        super().__init__(container)
        # Generate a Rocky character
        self.characterNode = self.createCharacterNode('
                             testgeometry_crag',
                             'Rocky')


class CompSphere():
    ''' Composite class that takes advantage of the pre-existing
        structure of its component classes.
        This class spawns characters and places them in unique
        locations and orientations to populate a sphere. The
        GeoContainer class provides the main structure. The sphere
        is populated with instances from the Roberto, Squidward and
```

```
        Rocky characters, all derived from the Character class. The
        CompSphere class allows components to do the Houdini work
        so it can focus on organizing the sphere. '''
    def __init__(self, radius=10, name='CompositeSphere'):
        ''' CompSphere Constructor. Its only input is the radius '''
        self.radius = radius
        # Create the geometry container
        self.container = MergeContainer(name)
        # Initialize a list to hold all of the characters
        self.characters = []
        # Populate the sphere
        self.populateSphere()
        # Clean the container network
        self.container.layoutChildren()

    def populateSphere(self):
        ''' Core engine to populate the characters into a sphere.
           The concept is simple. For every character, keep generating
           3-D locations until it is within distance of the radius. '''
        # Number characters based on the input radius
        count = 2*(self.radius*self.radius)
        for i in range(count):
            ''' Each character is assigned an index. Take the
               modulus 3 of that index to decide if a Roberto, Squidward
               or Rocky is instanced '''
            id = i%3
            if id == 0:
                character = Roberto(self.container.containerNode)
            elif id == 1:
                character = Squidward(self.container.containerNode)
            else:
                character = Rocky(self.container.containerNode)
```

```
        # Find a random placement for character
        self.randomSpherePlacement(character)
        # Append the character into the class list
        self.characters.append(character)
        # Merge character to container merge node
        self.container.appendMerge(character.subnetNode)

def randomSpherePlacement(self, character):
    ''' Keep generating random positions until a unique position
       is found within the class radius '''
    inSphere = False
    while not inSphere:
        # Random position between [-radius, radius)
        tx = 2*((random.random() * self.radius)-(0.5*self.radius))
        ty = 2*((random.random() * self.radius)-(0.5*self.radius))
        tz = 2*((random.random() * self.radius)-(0.5*self.radius))

        # Calculate the distance of the new position
        distance = math.sqrt(tx*tx + ty*ty + tz*tz)
        # Reject when distance is greater than radius
        if distance < self.radius:
            # Check for unique position
            if not self.inCharacter((tx,ty,tz)):
                # When unique, kick out of the loop
                inSphere = True

    # Set the Character position
    character.setPos((tx, ty, tz))
    # Random axis rotation between [-360, 360)
    rx = 2*((random.random() * 360.0)-(180.0))
    ry = 2*((random.random() * 360.0)-(180.0))
    rz = 2*((random.random() * 360.0)-(180.0))
```

```
        # Set the character rotational orientation
        character.setRot((rx, ry, rz))


    def inCharacter(self, pos):
        ''' Utility function to check if the input tuple duplicates the
           position of an existing character '''
        # Examine all of the existing characters
        for character in self.characters:
            characterPos = character.anchorNode.parmTuple('t').eval()
            # Return True When character position matches input
            if pos[0] == characterPos[0] and pos[1] == characterPos[1]
                                and pos[2] == characterPos[2]:
                return True

        return False


# Demonstration portion of the script
# Generate one instance
funball = CompSphere(10, 'myFunball')
```

Code Sample 12.13 CompSphere Composite Class

Inheritance versus Composition

Understanding of when to use inheritance versus composition is subjective. Although not discussed in this text, there is an underlying rule which states, "Whenever possible, avoid duplicating code". The process squanders time and indicates lack of preparation and planning. Both inheritance and composition are outstanding strategies for creating *re-usable* code without duplicating prior effort.

Python inheritance allows derived classes to take advantage of and extend their base classes. This creates a somewhat rigid relationship between the two as changes to the base class may have a dramatic impact on its subclasses. Care must be taken when altering base classes once subclasses have been derived.

Inheritance establishes an *"is a"* relationship between multiple classes. Derived classes customize base classes while leveraging the interface and functionality afforded by base classes. When there is confusion of the direction of this leverage, the *switch test* should be employed: swapping the roles in the *"is a"* relationship. When this relation still works when the roles are switched, inheritance should not be used. Inheritance is best used when the two classes are very similar, change slightly, and still maintain a common theme or intention.

Composition exhibits *"has a"* relationships. Composite classes join the interfaces and functionalities of multiple component classes. This strategy is ideal when programmers wish to create classes reused by multiple other classes. Composition leverages different components into new packages which may or may not be radically diverse from the intentions of the original components. The relationships between composite and component classes are *loosely coupled*. Compositions may change radically while never challenging the integrity of component classes.

Conventional programming also suggests favoring composition over inheritance whenever possible. Without getting into language theory, this guideline works. It enables programmers to mix and match diverse and powerful classes without concern of maintaining fragile relationships between base and derived classes. Novice programmers wanting the best of everything while creating diverse functionality are suggested to explore this direction. Technical artists, on the other hand, require repeatability, specialization, and familiarity. The rigid relationship inheritance provides encourage long-term maintenance of tools and functionalities which can be easily backtracked without hunting down multiple sources of documentation.

The choice between using inheritance or composition is context sensitive. Understanding class strengths and weaknesses given situational contexts is critical for long-term success. With proper preparation and planning, technical artists aware of long-term needs of end products are empowered to make the correct choices required for creating effective tools.

INHERITING FROM BUILT-IN TYPES

Technical artists are over-achievers and are always trying to customize their production tools to achieve their exact needs and requirements. The author is confident many readers will want to rewrite or derive subclasses based on pre-existing Python data types. While this is an available strategy, it is highly discouraged. Subclassing built-in data types is good, bad, and ugly. Hopefully the bad and ugly aspects outweigh the good.

The good aspect is that it is possible to create customized classes based on predefined existing Python objects. The bad news is building these subclasses is not easy and requires extreme object-oriented confidence. Explaining the thought process is beyond the scope of this book. However, for informational purposes, this section includes a brief explanation of how this can be done, a simple example and a practical alternative for descending down this path.

The ugly aspect is Python built-in class customization starts with *abstract base classes* and *collections abstract base classes: abc* and *collections.abc* modules, respectively. The *abc* module provides the rawest access to object-oriented functionality. The *collections.abc* module provides Python data types available for customization. Either module requires inclusion for access: *import ABC, import collections.abc*. When deriving from collections.abc, certain abstract methods must be implemented to function properly. Please consult with official Python documentation under *abc* and *collections.abc* when deriving from abstract base classes. Code Sample 12.14 demonstrates how classes are derived from the Python Set Abstract base class.

```
# Import the Python Abstract Base Classes
import collections.abc


# MySet is derived from collections.abc.Set
class MySet(collections.abc.Set):
    ''' Simple derived class from Python Set abstract base class '''
```

```
def __init__(self, iterable):
    ''' Constructor for MySet class. Transfer the iterable
       contents to the built in Set data storage '''
    # initialize the storage
    self.elements = []
    # Move the iterable content to storage
    for value in iterable:
        # Append only when not already present
        if value not in self.elements:
            self.elements.append(value)

def __iter__(self):
    ''' Essential Method. Iterable overload Method '''
    # Return an iterators for set content
    return iter(self.elements)

def __contains__(self, value):
    ''' Essential Method. Overload returns True when value
       is in contents '''
    return value in self.elements

def __len__(self):
    ''' Essential Method. Length overload: Return the length
       of the contents '''
    return len(self.elements)

def __str__(self):
    ''' Non-Essential Method. Convert class to a string
       displaying content '''
    # Initialize a default string
    buff = ''
```

```
        # Append string with space delimited content
        for i in self.elements:
            buff += f' {i}'
        # Resulting string
        return buff


# Define two new custom sets
group1 = MySet(('Mark', 'Jerry', 'Bob1', 'Bob2', 'Allen'))
group2 = MySet(('Mark', 'Jerry', 'Bob1', 'Josh'))
# Display intersection
print(f'Inside both ={group1 & group2}')
print(f'MySet is a Set: {issubclass(
            MySet, collections.abc.Set)}')
print(f'group1 is a Set instance: {isinstance(
            group1, collections.abc.Set)}')

>>> Inside both = Mark Jerry Bob1
MySet is a Set: True
group1 is a Set instance: True
```

Code Sample 12.14 Derived Class from Python Set Abstract Base Class

In the prior example, the *MySet* class is derived from the Python *collections.abc.Set* class. The class inherits all of the functionality afforded to a Python Set object type. However, in order to behave properly, the *__iter__*, *__contains__*, and *__len__* methods must be implemented. The additional *__str__* method is overloaded to make the class displayable. To test the new class, two instances are created and their intersection is displayed. The results of the *subclass* and *Instance* verifications are displayed.

Deriving from built-in types can be done but is awkward, requires object-oriented familiarity and requires substantial base-level programming. It is advisable for the fledgling programmers to skip this capability and practice class composition. Unless the task requires extreme, base-level customization, composition is robust enough for combining object type functionalities into single cohesive classes.

As an instructional exercise, ambitious programmers may wish to *scratch refactor* build-in data types: making copies and experimenting with the existing code. During most scratch refactors programmers quickly discover "a few minor changes" snowball into an avalanche of reprogramming. The necessity of overhauling existing data types is usually sufficient to dissuade programmers from subclassing built-in data types.

CONCLUSION

This chapter introduces two object-oriented philosophies which encourages the economic reuse of code: inheritance and composition. Inheritance provides *"is a"* relationship between classes: Is class B a variation of class A? Composition provides *"has a"* relationship: does class B have an instance of class A? Both strategies empower programmers to reuse pre-created code and provide customization which either expands, alters, or rewrites the functionality from original classes.

Inheritance allows for *subclasses* to be derived from base classes. Derived classes initially inherit all base class attributes and methods. Derived classes may alter, expand, and rewrite existing, inherited functionality. A tightly coupled relationship is established between base classes and their derived classes. Changes to base classes may have a dramatic impact on derived classes. Attention must be made to the changes made to base classes after derivation. The *super()* function is the preferred technique for invoking base class functionality from within derived classes. The *super()* function takes advantage of Python *method resolution order* to organize attributes and methods and ensures derived class access to proper base class functionality. Derivation from multiple base classes is possible but is discouraged. As a functional example, the *Arrow* class from Chapter 11 is introduced as a base class for the new *Vector*-derived class. The derived class accesses, rewrites, and expands upon the original base class methods.

When multiple classes have same-named attributes and methods which perform different functionalities, they exhibit what is called *polymorphism*. Polymorphism enables different classes to behave predictively yet exhibit context sensitive behavior.

Instead of extending functionality through derivation, composition combines complementary classes which contribute to more dynamic functionality than to their original classes. *Compositions* are *composites* of *component* class instances. The relationship between composite classes and components is loosely coupled. Changes to component classes may impact composite class behavior but composite class changes have no impact on component classes. Loosely coupled relationships often foster composite classes which are easier to maintain and update compared to their derived counterparts. A Houdini class for generating a sphere composed of multiple random characters is provided to demonstrate class composition.

Python provides the capability for programmers to derive from core Python data types, called abstract base classes. Readers are discouraged from exploring this avenue unless comfortable with base-level, object-oriented programming. Composition is strongly suggested as a strategy alternative.

The choice between inheritance and composition is subjective and is dependent on the context of desired class utility. While there are many opportunities for both strategies to be interchangeable, thorough planning and understanding are required for effectively implementing, facilitating ease of use, and future maintenance.

INTRODUCTION

Technical artists are some of the hardest working people in the real-time computer-graphics industry. They struggle for hours identifying hints, clues and signposts pointing to solutions for their most taxing production headaches. Once glimmers of opportunity are found, they jump on them. They master them and make them their own. They spend days understanding the problems, squeezing out solutions and wrangling the parameters influencing the myriad of outcomes. They spend days to weeks fleshing out scripts creating the world's greatest production tools. They deliver them to artists expecting to revolutionize the art community. Five minutes into users' experiences, artists enter name-based typos and the scripts freeze or crash. Without understanding the circumstances, they tell their supervisor that the tools (built on blood sweat and tears) are broken, or even worse, don't work. (They suck!) Hard working technical artists are forbidden from spending more tool time and return to fighting production fires. Stories like these are common for technical artists and are avoidable with exception handling implementation.

Guerilla Programming

Previously in this book, technical artists are described as being guerilla programmers. They jump into dangerous and unfamiliar territories and program tools that are clean, safe, and functional. Upon saving the day with their amazing tools, they descend quietly into the brush, searching for the next production quandaries to overcome. Technical artists don't have time to handle user errors or deal with obscure abnormalities to their ingenious solutions. Implementing such precautions takes time, interrupts creative flow, and slows the hero process.

Handling exceptions often seems to be an unnecessary process. If artists only understood the sins they are committing, there would be no need for them. If designers would only stick to their areas of expertise, the world would be perfect. However, the production realm is chaotic and certain necessary precautions (necessary evils!) must be implemented.

User Experience

Technical artists are expected to create tools fostering positive user experiences. User experiences are positive emotional feeling artists and designers achieve from using technical artist tools. When artists and designers use new tools and are able to successfully navigate them to accessible states, user experiences are good. The more positive the user experiences, the more artists will fancy the technical artists' tools which ultimately translates into bolstering technical artist careers.

There are two principal components required for establishing positive user experiences beyond effective tool design: graphic user interface construction and exception handling. Graphics user interface (GUI) construction is handled in Chapter 16. This chapter focuses on the essentials of Python exception handling.

What to Expect

Exception handling can be a dry topic. However, with the inclusion of creative computer graphics, it becomes a palatable subject. This chapter begins with explaining what special events are and how Python translates those special events into exceptions. An explanation of how exceptions are created, or raised, is introduced followed by exposition of how Python deals, or handles, those exceptions. Instructions on how to create customized exceptions are provided followed by optimizations how dealing with exceptions can actually speed up and make programming more efficient.

DOI: 10.1201/9781003016427-13

SPECIAL EVENTS

Special events are flagged when interesting occurrences happen during code execution. Not all are errors. Most occurrences are ignored. However, those tagged as special events raise flags and demand attention. Examples may include characters entering specific regions within their worlds, grabbing specific objects or prop objects colliding with one another.

Special technical artist events may include wrangling *graphic user interfaces* (*GUIs*) (covered in Chapter 16). Artists selecting items, pressing buttons, and dialing in values trigger special events. Technical artists also deal with errors and problems such as dividing by zero, handling incorrect path names, and organizing operations performed out of sequence. It is in technical artists' best interest to deal with error special events without drawing attention to them.

A simple example of a technical artist, non-error, special event is scene file saving. Whenever an artist saves her scene file, a list contents may be written to an external file. The following code reports this information. Type *Code Sample 13.1* in an external editor and save the contents to (on a windows machine) *C:\Users\<user name>\Documents\<Houdini Version>\scripts\afterscenesave.py*. On a Linux machine, save the file to *home/<user name> /<Houdini Version>/scripts/afterscenesave.py*.

```
# Setting the top Python anchor
top = hou.node('/obj')

print("Houdini attempted to save the following items:")
# Iterating through all the houdini objects
for child in top.children():
    # Display path of each object
    print(f'\t{child.path()}')
```

Code Sample 13.1 Scene Saving Event Script

The action of saving a Houdini file is a special event. The script name and location tell Houdini what to do when a *save scene* special event is triggered. Upon invocation, the script creates a top node anchor variable. One by one the script displays the path of each of the node's sub-nodes (children).

EVENT HANDLING

Without event handling knowledge, beginning programmers attempt to deal with code events with *if* statements. *If* statements multiply and make logic difficult to trace. Multiple *if* statements create branching code trees which are challenging to differentiate between proactive code and event processing code.

The most important reason why special events should not be handled with *if* statements is that they may navigate code to *inaccessible states*. In other words, applications may still freeze, crash, or become unresponsive. For example, when scripts read from external files, those files are locked and don't allow other applications to access them. If the scripts were to freeze or crash, the external files stay locked and can't be accessed. Often the only resolution is machine reboot. *Non-if*-related approaches are necessary to avoid file lock-out after script failure.

RAISING EXCEPTIONS

When errors happen during Python execution, they are called *exceptions*. Not all exceptions are fatal. Their impact, however, is dictated by the context of the situation they occur. Python has an extensive hierarchy of built-in exception classes. (The full listing of Python built-in exception is found at https://docs.python.org/3/library/

exceptions.html.) All exception classes derive from the original *BaseException* class. The hierarchy is extensive and addresses most common situations. Custom exceptions are derivable and are discussed later in this chapter.

In order for an exception to be referenced and come into being, the system or the programmer must *raise* the exception. Raising exceptions is the system process of declaring and identifying error occurrences. The *raise* command, as defined by Language Template 13.1, initiates the reference process followed by its exception class and arguments. The arguments are typically the desired messages to be displayed upon exception raising.

```
raise ExceptionClass(Arguments)
```

Language Template 13.1 Raising an Exception

When an exception is raised in the Python command line, it is followed by a *traceback* identifying its location and type and delivering its message, as demonstrated in Shell Example 13.1.

```
>>> raise ZeroDivisionError("Raising an Exception!")
Traceback (most recent call last):
  File "<console>", line 1, in <module>
ZeroDivisionError: Raising an Exception!
```

Shell Example 13.1 Raising an Arbitrary Exception

When raised within a Houdini script, an *Exception Tool* interface pops up identifying that an exception has occurred and delivers an exception message similar to Figure 13.1.

When the *Show Details* option is selected when the *OK* button is pressed, the tool brings up a text window displaying the traceback information, the exception class and the exception message. The *OK* button, Figure 13.2, dismisses the Exception Tool.

In Code Sample 13.2, a simple Roberto is generated. Its *uniformscale* attribute is tested and when larger than `0.5`, it raises a *ValueError* declaring, "Roberto scale too large". By default, the value is 1.0 and an exception must be raised, resulting with an exception messages like Figure 13.3.

```
# Create Roberto!
top = hou.node('obj')
roberto = top.createNode('geo').createNode('testgeometry_rubbertoy')


# Roberto Scale
if roberto.parm('uniformscale').eval() > 0.5:
    # Raise a Value Error when too large
    raise ValueError('Roberto scale too large!')
```

Code Sample 13.2 Roberto ValueError Exception

FIGURE 13.1 Houdini exception tool.

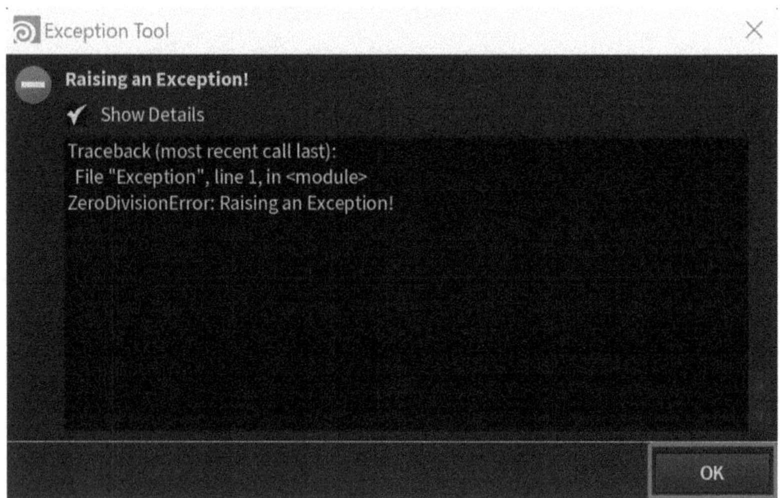

FIGURE 13.2 Full exception tool message.

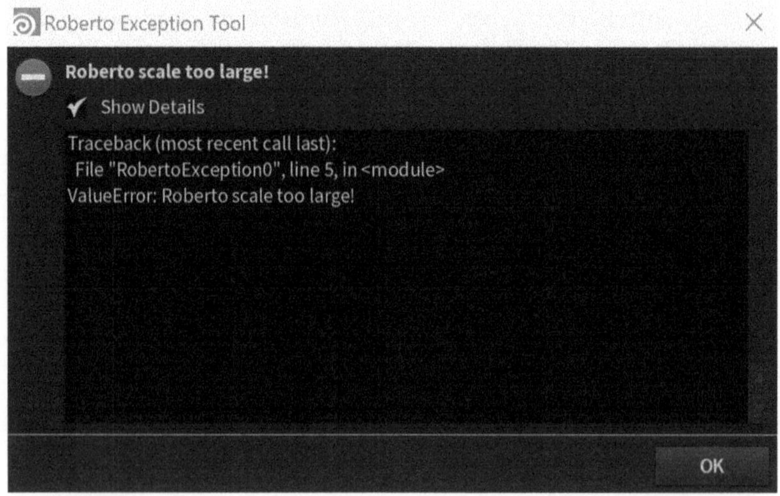

FIGURE 13.3 Roberto scale exception.

Note that there is a timing discrepancy. Although the exception raises after Roberto is generated, the exception event prevents the Roberto model from displaying.

HANDLING EXCEPTIONS

Raising exceptions is an effective way for identifying special events. Handling those special events is the strategy for catching those situations (especially errors!) and dealing with them without breaking script flow. Python provides a protocol for handling exceptions (sometimes called catching exceptions).

Try-Except

The *try* command causes Python to enter exception awareness mode and react proactively when exceptions are encountered. *Exception clauses* tell Python what actions are performed when specific exceptions are triggered. Their format is defined in Language Template 13.2. The *try* statement and *exception clauses* are followed by blocks of code.

```
try:
    Code Block
except <Exception Type>
    Code Block
```

Language Template 13.2 Try and Except

The protocol is initiated when the code block following the *try* is executed. If an exception raises during the attempt, Python finds the code block associated with the triggered exception type and executes it. Code Sample 13.3 demonstrates this behavior while catching a *ZeroDivisionError*.

```
# Import math Library
import math
# Anchor the top node
top = hou.node('/obj')

# Enter Python into exception mode
try:
    # Query user for pig number
    num = int(input('Enter number of pigs: '))
    # Calculate iterative angle
    angle = math.radians(360 / num)

    # Create pig circle
    for i in range(num):
```

```
        # Create geometry container
        container = top.createNode('geo', f'piggy{i}')
        # Create each pig
        piggy = container.createNode('testgeometry_pighead')

        # Arrange each pig into a circle
        container.parmTuple('t').set((2*math.sin(i*angle), 0, 2*math.
cos(i*angle)))

# Catch all division by zero errors
except ZeroDivisionError:
    # Explain situation
    print('Cannot enter zero pigs
```

Code Sample 13.3 Handling ZeroDivisionError

In Code Sample 13.3, the code creates a top anchor and enters into a *try* state. It queries the user for the number of desired pigs, calculates the iterative angle, and then generates the desired number of pigs assembled into a circle which looks like Figure 13.4.

Figure 13.5 shows the results when a value of `0` is entered for the number of pigs, the code displays simple instructions stating zero is not a valid number of pigs.

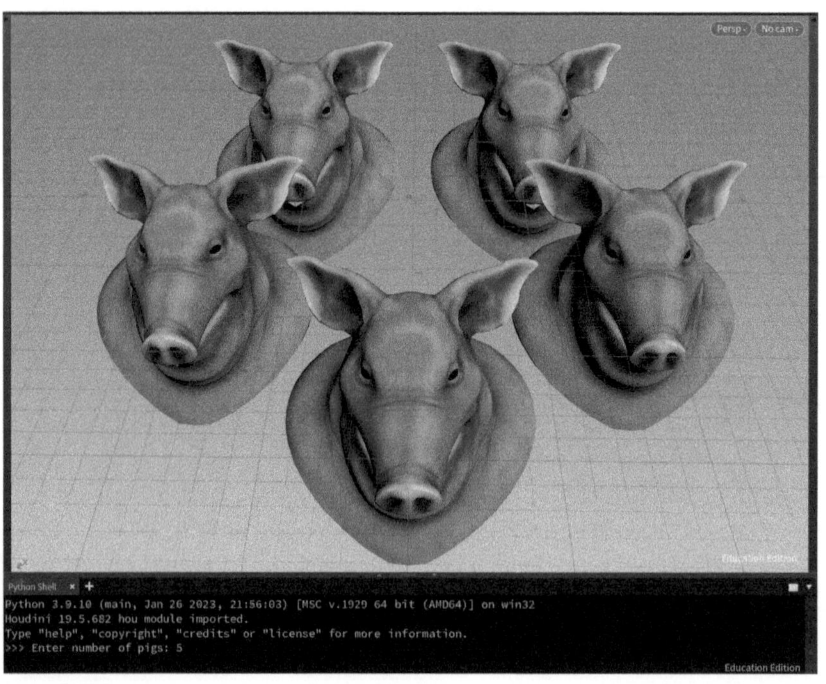

FIGURE 13.4 Successful pig circle.

```
Python Shell
Python 3.9.10 (main, Jan 26 2023, 21:56:03) [MSC v.1929 64 bit (AMD64)] on win32
Houdini 19.5.682 hou module imported.
Type "help", "copyright", "credits" or "license" for more information.
>>> Enter number of pigs: 0
Cannot enter zero pigs!
```

FIGURE 13.5 Attempt to generate zero pigs.

```
Python Shell
Python 3.9.10 (main, Jan 26 2023, 21:56:03) [MSC v.1929 64 bit (AMD64)] on win32
Houdini 19.5.682 hou module imported.
Type "help", "copyright", "credits" or "license" for more information.
>>> Enter number of pigs: Pigs!
Number of Pigs must be a valid integer!
```

FIGURE 13.6 Correctly catching a ValueError.

When the code enters the *try* block, the code fails after an input of `0` when attempting to divide `360` by `0`. Instead of crashing the script and displaying an ugly, "Division by Zero" message, the code immediately drops into the exception block identified by *ZeroDivisionError*, and displays an explanation why the user input did not work.

Any *try* statement can be followed by an unlimited number of *exception clauses*, each identifying a different exception type. When an exception is caught, Python checks its type against the first clause. When there is no match, the next clause type is attempted. This continues until the exception type is encountered. Code Sample 13.4 catches the *ZeroDivisionError* and the non-integer *ValueError*.

```
# Import math Library
import math
# Anchor the top node
top = hou.node('/obj')

# Enter Python into exception mode
try:
    # Query user for pig number
    num = int(input('Enter number of pigs: '))
    # Calculate iterative angle
    angle = math.radians(360 / num)

    # Create pig circle
    for i in range(num):
        # Create geometry container
        container = top.createNode('geo', f'piggy{i}')
        # Create each pig
        piggy = container.createNode('testgeometry_pighead')
```

```
        # Arrange each pig into a circle
        container.parmTuple('t').set((2*math.sin(i*angle), 0, 2*math.
cos(i*angle)))

# Catch all division by zero errors
except ZeroDivisionError:
    print('Cannot enter zero pigs!')

# Catch all non-integers
except ValueError:
    print('Number of Pigs must be a valid integer!')
```

Code Sample 13.4 Handling ValueError

Code Sample 13.3 has been extended with an exception clause which catches non-integer number errors, *ValueErrors*. When the exception is encountered, it is vetted as a *ZeroDivisionError*. When that is not found, the exception is verified as a *ValueError*. That condition is satisfied. Figure 13.6 displays the caught error.

When an exception occurs within the context of a *try* statement, Python attempts to match the triggered exception with one of *exceptions*. After exhausting all possibilities, Python throws up its hands and raises an *UnhandledException*. This situation is as bad as having no *try-except* structure in the first place.

Placing a final *Exception* statement will handle any unaccounted-for errors, avoiding all possibility of *UnhandledExceptions*. *Exception* is the base class from which all other exceptions are derived. All exceptions *are an Exception*! Because this is the broadest of all conditions and catches all exceptions, it is best practice to place this as the last of the conditions in the *exception* chain. It is not mandatory to provide this final exception. However, when encountering unaccounted-for errors that cannot be traced, extending the exception chain with this one final condition prevents the end-user from dealing with un-warranted situations. Code Sample 13.5 catches any unaccounted for *Exception*.

```
# Import math Library
import math
# Anchor the top node
top = hou.node('/obj')

# Enter Python into exception mode
try:
    # Query user for pig number
    num = int(input('Enter number of pigs: '))
```

```
    # Calculate iterative angle
    angle = math.radians(360 / num)

    # Create pig circle
    for i in range(num):
        # Create geometry container
        container = top.createNode('geo', f'piggy{i}')
        # Create each pig
        piggy = container.createNode('testgeometry_pighead')

        # Arrange each pig into a circle
        container.parmTuple('t').set((2*math.sin(i*angle), 0, 2*math.
cos(i*angle)))

# Catch all division by zero errors
except ZeroDivisionError:
    print('Cannot enter zero pigs!')

# Catch all non-integers
except ValueError:
    print('Number of Pigs must be a valid integer!')

# Exception to handle unhandled exception
except Exception:
    print('Something went wrong - the sky must be falling')
```

Code Sample 13.5 Try-Except with Final Exception

Else

The *try* statement is a little like the *if* statement introduced in Chapter 8: the following activities are performed when specific conditions are met. An *else* statement provides instructions when the exception conditions are unmet. Within the *try* protocol, defined in Language Template 13.3, the *else* statement provides instructions what to do when exceptions do not occur. The *try* code block is attempted and when exceptions do not occur, the *else* code block is performed.

```
try:
    Code Block
except <Exception Type>
    Code Block
else:
    Code Block
```

Language Template 13.3 Try-Except-Else

When Code Sample 13.5 is extended with an *else* statement, its code block is executed only when no exception is triggered. The *else code*, in Code Sample 13.6, *block* creates a Roberto in the circle of pigs only when exceptions have not been encountered. Figure 13.7 displays when the *Else* exception is handled.

```
# Import math Library
import math
# Anchor the top node
top = hou.node('/obj')

# Enter Python into exception mode
try:
    # Query user for pig number
    num = int(input('Enter number of pigs: '))
    # Calculate iterative angle
    angle = math.radians(360 / num)

    # Create pig circle
    for i in range(num):
        # Create geometry container
        container = top.createNode('geo', f'piggy{i}')
        # Create each pig
        piggy = container.createNode('testgeometry_pighead')

        # Arrange each pig into a circle
        container.parmTuple('t').set((2*math.sin(i*angle), 0, 2*math.
cos(i*angle)))
```

```
# Catch all division by zero errors
except ZeroDivisionError:
    print('Cannot enter zero pigs!')

# Catch all non-integers
except ValueError:
    print('Number of Pigs must be a valid integer!')

# Exception to handle unhandled exception
except Exception:
    print('Something went wrong - the sky must be falling')

# When no exceptions happen
else:  ...
    container = top.createNode('geo', 'Roberto')
    # ... Create a Roberto
    roberto = container.createNode('testgeometry_rubbertoy')
```

Code Sample 13.6 If-Except-Else with Pigs and Roberto

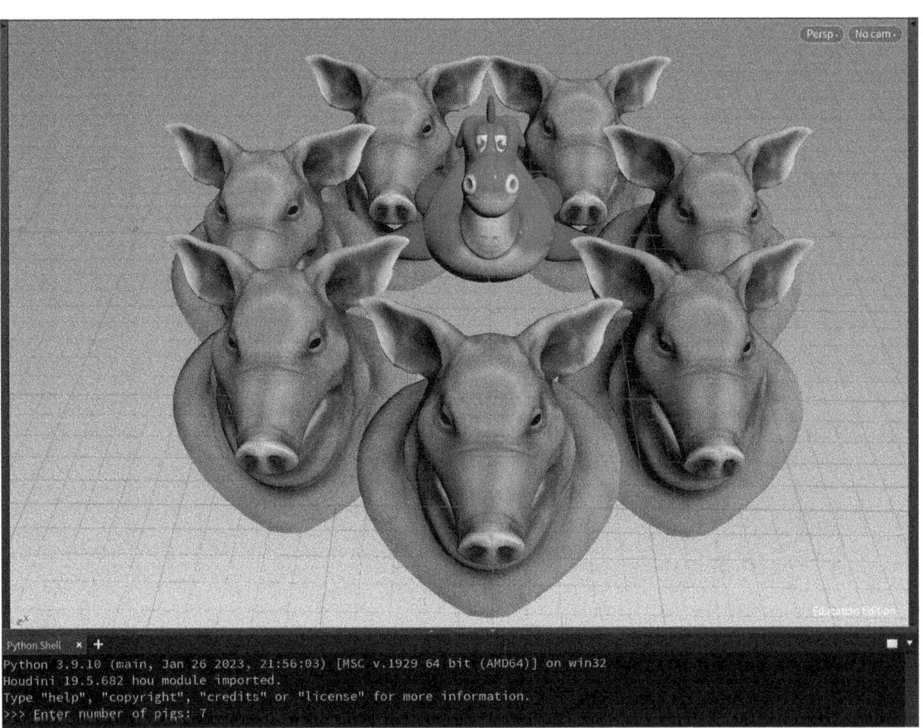

FIGURE 13.7 Try-except-else with Roberto.

Finally

"Clutter" often accompanies *try-except* sequences. Resources and other essential system components are acquired and may be left "in limbo" when exceptions occur. For example, files may be left open upon exceptions and depending how they handled, they may be perpetually locked, preventing all future processes from accessing their contents. This situation is explained further in Chapter 14.

Python provides one additional construct to the *try-except* protocol: the *finally* statement. The *finally* statement and its subsequent code block must be executed, regardless of exception occurrence. This code is crucial for cleaning up the clutter that may have been acquired, locked-off, or otherwise left incomplete upon exception. The *finally* statement is not mandatory and may not be applicable in all situations. However, it provides a method for returning a script environment to a stable and clean state suitable for further functionality. The finally protocol is shown in Language Template 13.4.

```
try:
    Code Block
except <Exception Type>
    Code Block
else:
    Code Block
finally:
    Code Block
```

Language Template 13.4 Try-Except-Else-Finally

The pig example is concluded in Code Sample 13.7 with a *finally* statement that constructs a podium platform for the pigs regardless of exceptions occurring during their creation. The *finally* platform is shown in Figure 13.8.

```
# Import math Library
import math
# Anchor the top node
top = hou.node('/obj')

# Enter Python into exception mode
try:
    # Query user for pig number
    num = int(input('Enter number of pigs: '))
    # Calculate iterative angle
    angle = math.radians(360 / num)
```

```
    # Create pig circle
    for i in range(num):
        # Create geometry container
        container = top.createNode('geo', f'piggy{i}')
        # Create each pig
        piggy = container.createNode('testgeometry_pighead')

        # Arrange each pig into a circle
        container.parmTuple('t').set((2*math.sin(i*angle), 0, 2*math.
cos(i*angle)))

# Catch all division by zero errors
except ZeroDivisionError:
    print('Cannot enter zero pigs!')

# Catch all non-integers
except ValueError:
    print('Number of Pigs must be a valid integer!')

# Exception to handle unhandled exception
except Exception:
    print('Something went wrong - the sky must be falling')

# When no exceptions happen
else:  ...
    container = top.createNode('geo', 'Roberto')
    # ... Create a Roberto
    roberto = container.createNode('testgeometry_rubbertoy')
# Finally code block must execute
finally:
    container = top.createNode('geo', 'platform')
    platform = container.createNode('tube')
    # Convert tube to polygons
    platform.parm('type').set(1)
```

```
# Give the platform a surface
platform.parm('cap').set(True)
# Place platform under the pigs
platform.parm('ty').set(-1.8)
# Widen the platform to support the pigs
platform.parm('radscale').set(3)
# Make platform smoother
platform.parm('cols').set(40)

# Append a color node
color = container.createNode('color')
# Send platform output to color node
color.setInput(0, platform)
# Set platform color light-orange
color.parmTuple('color').set((1.0, 0.7, 0.5))
# Display the colored platform
color.setDisplayFlag(True)
```

Code Sample 13.7 Try-Except-Else-Finally with Platform

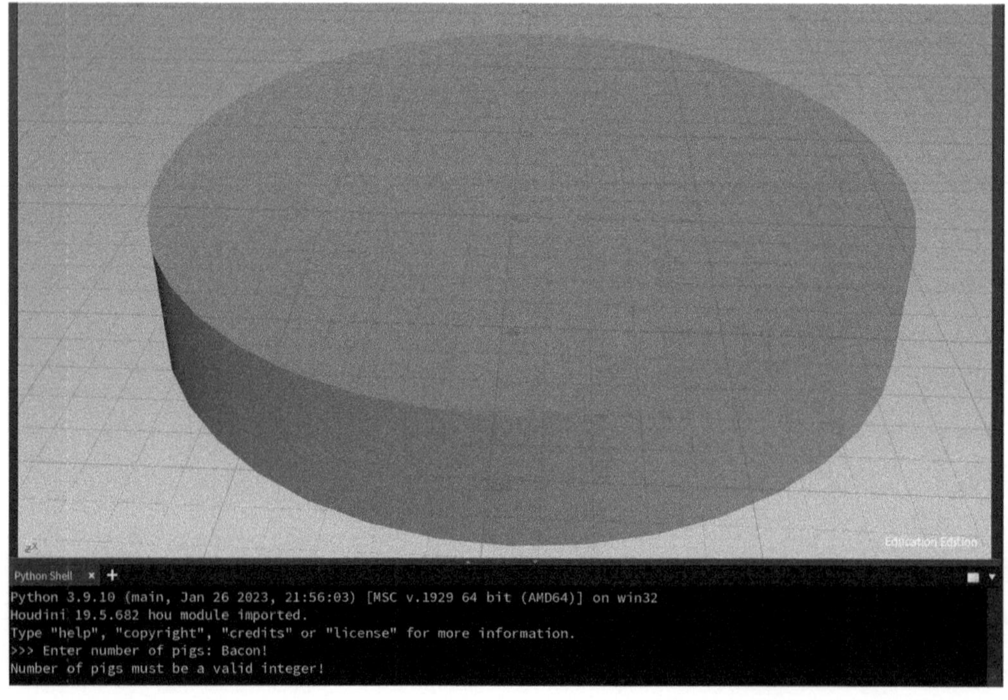

FIGURE 13.8 Try-except-else-finally with platform.

CUSTOM EXCEPTIONS

All exceptions are classes derived from the *BaseException* class., as demonstrated in Shell Example 13.2. Non-system-exiting exceptions are derived from the *Exception* subclass. Each derived subclass handles more precisely defined malfunctions than the errors caught by the parent class and specializes in the error it identifies.

```
>>> print(Exception.__doc__)

Common base class for all non-exit exceptions.

>>> print(Exception.__dict__)

{'__init__': <slot wrapper '__init__' of 'Exception' objects>, '__new__':
<built-in method __new__ of type object at 0x0

0007FF84630E2E0>, '__doc__': 'Common base class for all non-exit
exceptions.'}
```

Shell Example 13.2 Exception Class Doc and Dict Strings

The Python exception derived hierarchy is extensive and handles any typical situation a programmer may encounter. The full listing of Python built-in exception is found at https://docs.python.org/3/library/exceptions.html.

Exception Customization

There may come a time in programmers' careers when they need to further extend the precision of one of the exceptions listed above. However, rewriting existing classes is not advised without thorough experience in coding exception handling.

Many exception types are vague and difficult to interpret. Programmers may re-associate types of malfunctions with appropriately named sub-classes in order to improve readability. This highly encouraged practice facilitates greater functional communication and easier maintenance.

When maintaining base class integrity, the declaration of the derived class needs to only include the *pass* command in the derivation body. Language Template 13.5 demonstrates *pass* usage.

```
class CustomClassName(PreExistingBaseClass):

    ''' This class is a renaming of the parent base class '''

# The pass-through does nothing

    pass
```

Language Template 13.5 Derivation of Custom Exception Class

The new derived subclass inherits all of the functionality afforded by its base class. It can be raised and handled as if it was a built-in exception.

In the prior examples, exceptions are provided to handle when zero pigs and when non-integers are inputed. There is no exception to handle when the entered pig number is a valid integer but less than zero. To resolve this, Code Sample 13.8 generates a new exception class, *SubzeroPigsError*, as derived from *ValueError*.

There is nothing this new class needs to perform so its contents are only the *pass* command. After the number of pigs is entered it is checked if less than zero. When true, a *SubzeroPigsError* is raised and the consequence of entering fewer than zero pigs is executed. The results are displayed in Figure 13.9.

```
# import math Library
import math

# Create a special type of ValueError exception
# ... that doesn't do much
class SubzeroPigsError(ValueError):
    pass

# Anchor the top node
top = hou.node('/obj')

# Enter Python into exception mode
try:
    # Query user for pig number
    num = int(input('Enter number of pigs: '))
    # Calculate iterative angle
    angle = math.radians(360 / num)

    # Create pig circle
    for i in range(num):
        # Create geometry container
        container = top.createNode('geo', f'piggy{i}')
        # Create each pig
        piggy = container.createNode('testgeometry_pighead')

        # Arrange each pig into a circle
        container.parmTuple('t').set((2*math.sin(i*angle), 0, 2*math.
cos(i*angle)))

# Catch all division by zero errors
except ZeroDivisionError:
    print('Cannot enter zero pigs!')
```

```
# Catch a SubzeroPigsError
except SubzeroPigsError:
    # Execute the ramifications of providing subzero pigs
    container = top.createNode('geo', 'Squidward')
    squidward = container.createNode('testgeometry_squab')
    squidward.parmTuple('t').set((0, -0.7, 0))

# Catch all non-integers
except ValueError:
    print('Number of pigs must be a valid integer!')

# Exception to handle unhandled exception
except Exception:
    print('Something went wrong - the sky must be falling')

# When no exceptions happen ...
else:
    container = top.createNode('geo', 'Roberto')
# Create a Roberto
    roberto = container.createNode('testgeometry_rubbertoy')

# Finally code block must execute
finally:
    container = top.createNode('geo', 'platform')
    platform = container.createNode('tube')
# Convert tube to polygons
    platform.parm('type').set(1)
# Give the platform a surface
    platform.parm('cap').set(True)
# place platform under the pigs
    platform.parm('ty').set(-1.8)
# Widen the platform to support the pigs
    platform.parm('radscale').set(3)
```

```
# Make platform smoother
    platform.parm('cols').set(40)

# Append a color node
    color = container.createNode('color')
# Send platform output to color node
    color.setInput(0, platform)
# Set platform color light-orange
    color.parmTuple('color').set((1.0, 0.7, 0.5))
# Display the colored platform
    color.setDisplayFlag(True)
```

Code Sample 13.8 Handling Subzero Pigs Exception

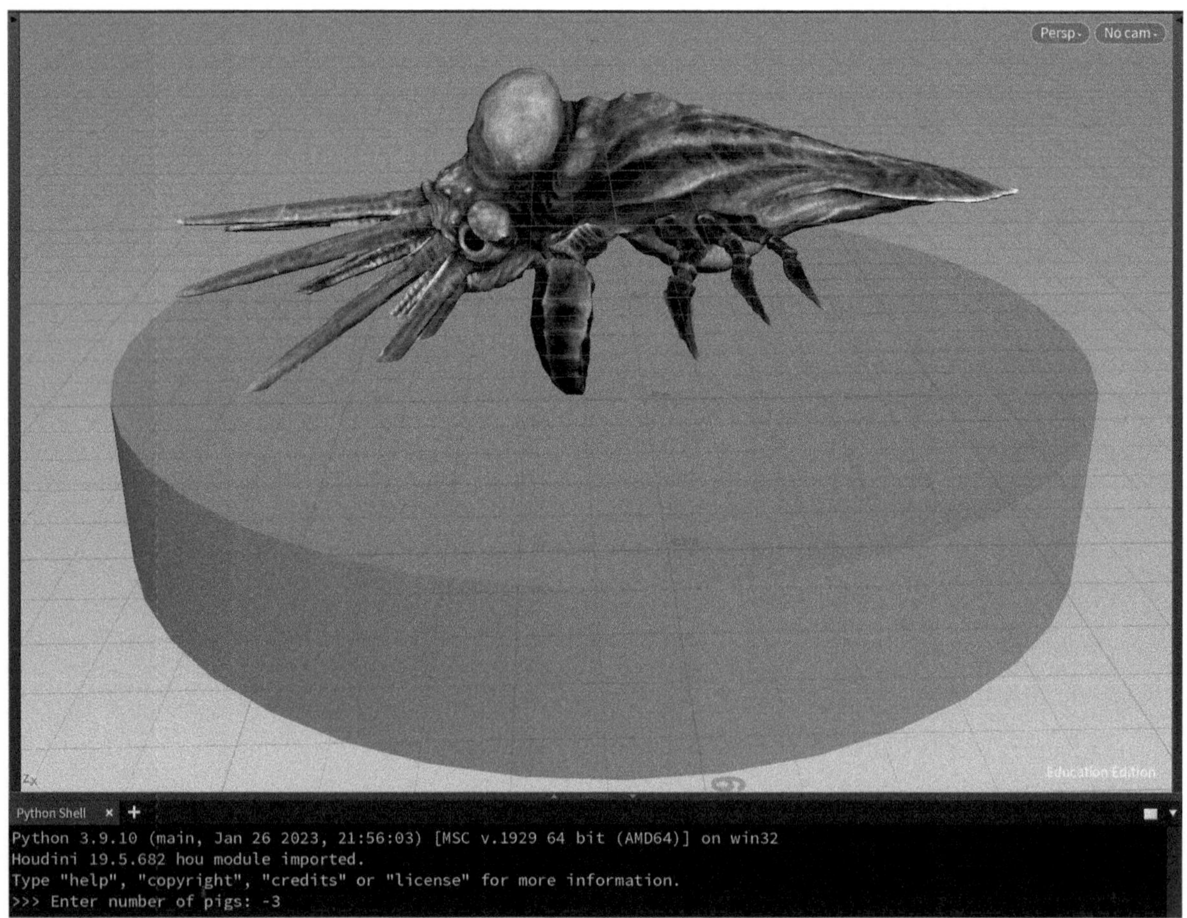

FIGURE 13.9 Handling subzero pigs exception.

In this new example, note that the *SubzeroPigsError* is handled before the *ValueError*. *SubzeroPigsError* is a special case of a *ValueError* and must be addressed before the broader base case. When their positions are swapped, the *SubzeroPigsError* is never caught since the broader *ValueError* always catches them first. The less than zero number of pigs situation could have been handled with a complicated series of *if* statements. However, when handled as an exception, the flow is clean, predictable, and easy to debug.

Guidelines for Customization

When handling exceptions and creating custom derivations, there are a few guidelines that should be followed. First, not all exceptions are created equal so when there is an understanding of the exception class being handled, the exception must be handled specifically. In the prior example, because *SubzeroPigsError* is a special case of *ValueError*, it is handled before the *ValueError* case. Exception blocks must be handled in specificity order.

Do not catch *exceptions* that cannot be dealt with. For example, when a script performs no division operations, it makes no sense to create a subclass of a *ZeroDivisionError*. It could never be triggered!

When subclassing multiple custom exception names (such as SubzeroPigsError), it is best to define them all in one location, to make code easier to read and maintain. Wrap the smallest amount possible to avoid catching other errors of the same type and dealing with them incorrectly.

As a rule of thumb, do not create new exception classes when the built-in ones already have the necessary functionality. Most probably, programmers reading this book do not need to create new exception functionality.

'WITH' AND CONTEXT MANAGERS

The finally component of the try-except protocol was created to assist with the management of important resources. Regardless of events occurring while executing the try code block, the finally code block ensures responsible handling and releasing of those resources. Python 3 attempts to factor out standard use cases of try ...except... finally with context managers. Among other uses, context managers are useful for allocating resources and responsibly releasing them without creating havoc.

The *with* construct is a popular Python *context manager* for accessing structured classes. Context managers allow for blocks of code to be used under control of just a single object. While not uncommon to use context managers, beginning programmers rarely need to author or edit them. Examples of using context managers for managing resources during externa file access are provided in Chapter 14.

TRACEBACKS

The process of user proofing scripts against all potential exceptions takes time. When time is of the essence and scripts are written to execute only once, this process is superfluous. However, when creating user tools, it is essential and pays dividends in the long run. (Your users will be very happy you did!)

When starting the exception writing process, all potential exceptions may not be known. When throwing an exception, Houdini, does an effective job displaying where the exception happened, the chain of function calls that lead to the exception, and the exception type. However, script execution should never stop to throw up an exception, even when they are pleasantly displayed. They should be handled elegantly and when necessary, the exception information stored for later usage. The Python *traceback* module is helpful for this.

The *traceback* module extracts, formats, and prints all the functional steps a program performs. It creates a roadmap of all functional behavior leading to an exception. The *print_exception()* (or shortcut *print_exc()*) records the type of exception, where it occurred and the functional path leading to the exception in one convenient string. Language Template 13.6 defines this string may be displayed or stored for future access.

```
# Import the traceback module
import traceback
# Output exception information to a string
traceback.print_exc()
```

Language Template 13.6 Traceback Exception Usage

Suppose the programmer is just starting to debug the pig script above and identifies no exceptions other than the *catch-all Exception*. Instead of simply executing the script and dealing with exceptions as they occur, the programmer keeps a list recording of all exceptions, *myExceptions*, and at the termination of script, displays the recorded list (Code Sample 13.9).

```
# Import math Library
import math
# Import the traceback module
import traceback

# Create a buffer to store all of the exception tracebacks
myExceptions=[]

# Anchor the top node
top = hou.node('/obj')
# Enter Python into exception mode
try:
    # Query user for pig number
    num = int(input('Enter number of pigs: '))

    # Calculate iterative angle
    angle = math.radians(360 / num)

    # Create pig circle
    for i in range(num):
        # Create geometry container
        container = top.createNode('geo', f'piggy{i}')
```

```
        # Create each pig
        piggy = container.createNode('testgeometry_pighead')

        # Arrange each pig into a circle
        container.parmTuple('t').set((2*math.sin(i*angle), 0, 2*math.
cos(i*angle)))

# Exception to handle all exceptions
except Exception:
    # Append the exception to the myExceptions list
    myExceptions.append(traceback.print_exc())
# When no exceptions happen
else:
    container = top.createNode('geo', 'Roberto')
    # Create a Roberto
    roberto = container.createNode('testgeometry_rubbertoy')

# This portion of code is to be used by programmer to understand the
nature of exceptions
# Display all of the collected exceptions
for myExcept in myExceptions:
    print('-'*10)
    # Print each traceback
    print(myExcept)
```

Code Sample 13.9 Pig Ring Exception Report

The traceback module needs to be imported to access this functionality. An empty list, *myExceptions*, is created to store all triggered exceptions. There is no *exception* handling in the script other than the *except Exception* code block. This block must handle all exceptions and appends their *traceback.print_exc()* contents to the *myExceptions* list. Upon the termination of the script, the contents of the list are displayed. The script is run three times delivering the results in Figure 13.10.

During the first execution of the script, a *division by zero* exception is encountered but does not halt the script progression. The second execution triggers an *invalid literal* error which is a special type of *ValueError*. The programmer is now aware that the script needs to handle *ZeroDivisionError* and *ValueError* exceptions. In the final execution, no *exception* is thrown when the value is a negative number. No pigs are drawn and no *exception* is caught. Because there is technically nothing *wrong* with this situation, a customized derivation of a *Value Error* must be created and raised to prevent that situation from happening.

```
Python 3.9.10 (main, Jan 26 2023, 21:56:03) [MSC v.1929 64 bit (AMD64)] on win32
Houdini 19.5.682 hou module imported.
Type "help", "copyright", "credits" or "license" for more information.
>>> Enter number of pigs: 0
Traceback (most recent call last):
  File "exceptionReport", line 10, in <module>
ZeroDivisionError: division by zero
----------
None

>>> Enter number of pigs: FUBAR
Traceback (most recent call last):
  File "exceptionReport", line 8, in <module>
ValueError: invalid literal for int() with base 10: 'FUBAR'
----------
None
```

FIGURE 13.10 Pig ring exception results.

CONCLUSION

When creating emergency scripts to quench raging production fires, technical artists handling program errors is unnecessary and potentially costly. However, when creating production tools, users must never be forced to deal with interruptions and crashes. These are examples of *special events*. *Special events* are program occurrences that require attention. Sometimes these events are benign, such as characters accidently walking on water. Others interrupt execution, such as when a value is divided by zero. This chapter focuses on handling *special events* which cause interrupts and crashing.

Special events are *raised* when attention to them needs to be drawn. The act of *raising* an event is done with the *raise* command. Raised events are handled through the *try-except* protocol. The *try* command provides a block of code to be executed under tight scrutiny. When a special event is triggered during execution of that block, an exception is raised and Python attempts to identify the type of exception. For each type of potential exception, the programmer provides a block of code based on its name. When the matching exception code block is found it is executed, resolving the error without alerting users. Programmers provide code blocks identified by with *else* statements to handle situations when no exceptions are encountered. *Finally* code blocks may also be provided to execute regardless of exception occurrence.

All exception classes are derivations of the *BaseException* and *Exception* classes. The built-in hierarchy of exception classes is extensive and sufficient enough to handle most situations. (The full list of the built-it Python exception hierarchy is provided in https://docs.python.org/3/library/exceptions.html.) Sometimes, customized exceptions are required. In these situations, base classes closest to addressing similar circumstances are derived to create new exception types. Python does not know when to instinctively raise these new exceptions. However, programmers identify them in code and the *raise* them instead. When raised the new exceptions are handled the same as built-in types.

Python provides the *traceback* module to create a path record of all executed commands of a Python script. The module is equipped with an exception focused method, *print_exception()*, which displays all functions preceding exceptions, their exact locations, and types. Recording of these *traceback* messages is effective for debugging and fine-tuning exception handling.

INTRODUCTION

Beyond creating geometry and arranging them in interesting patterns and shapes, *file processing* is arguably the most important purpose of Python or any programming language. Readers of this book are either immersed in or curiously interested in computer graphics production. Computers are used to crunch and process enormous quantities of data. All computer graphics applications and creative pipelines use enormous amounts of file processing: opening external communication media, writing image data to or reading data from the media, processing that data, and transmitting it between departments, computers, and servers.

The bare basics of computer graphics production revolve around the input and output of data. The data may be in the format of models, scene information, textures, images, animation clips, or similar data streams, configuration data defining materials and rendering parameters, project management reports, and subscripted data containing embedded commands for further processing. File processing is the foundational component of the computer graphics pipelines. Without this vital component, there simply is no sustainable production.

File processing is also essential for tracking tool behavior without being part of the integral application code. Information on tool configuration must be stored externally from its code base to maintain program stability regardless of state. In other words, applications must not be dependent on configuration data in order to function successfully. For example, many applications open the first time in generic states. As users interact with them, they externally store vital data such as history, user preferences, and custom configurations. Subsequent application sessions recall these data to create more comfortable, intuitive, and ultimately more enjoyable user experiences.

Numerous books and courses have been developed around the topic of file processing. This chapter is broken into two sections applying directly to daily, technical artists' responsibilities: core file access strategy and data serialization. The core file strategy covers file opening, reading and writing of data, and file closing. Essential considerations of exception handling while file processing are discussed. The data serialization section covers formats technical artists are most likely to encounter: JSON, XML, and pickling.

An essential warning must be included when discussing anything related to file processing. Files from untrusted sources should never be opened or read. The techniques discussed in this book are not secure and cannot prevent against malicious intent. File processing may be computer graphics production life blood but is also the conduit for unscrupulous behavior. Stick to this simple rule, "When data sources are in doubt, leave the files out!"

FILE PROCESSING BASICS

Technical artists deal with hundreds of files every day. Wrangling models, textures, animation clips, DCC scenes, and experience (game) data is more than a full-time job, it is a lifestyle. As applications evolve their database dependencies and inter-process communication streaming protocols require even higher levels of data comprehension. Keeping communication data secure is more important than ever as understanding of encryption and blockchain technologies is essential for competitive survival. It is easy to understand why file management is an overwhelming topic for beginning programmers.

From the technical artists' perspective, the topic does not need to be complicated but downright simple. That is the purpose of this chapter section: to introduce the barest components of Python file managements. As with all topics introduced in this text, readers are encouraged to explore this topic in greater depth once familiarity is

DOI: 10.1201/9781003016427-14

achieved and need is present. In addition to file management fundamentals, understanding the dependency of special events and exceptions is required

Essential Strategy

The core essence of technical artist file management is boiled down to a simple four-step process:

1. Open a file.
2. Read and/or …
3. … Write a data string to that file.
4. Close the file.

There is not much else technical artists need to know to accomplish their daily responsibilities. Of course, topics how to prepare, parse, and interpret data strings require tomes of additional information. The most common data formats are described later in this chapter and the most important tool for data parsing, regular expressions, is introduced in Chapter 18.

Exceptions

There are a myriad of typical, everyday maladies plaguing production file processing: incorrect file names and paths, obsolete formats, versions and protocols, data corruption, and other unanticipated data interruptions. Any of these issues cause scripts to crash and burn, instantaneously. The only protection against these common situations is to integrate the *try-except* protocol explained in Chapter 13. When used properly, crashing or freezing scripts is avoided. Exceptions are triggered and the situations are handled without interrupting the end user.

Integrating the *try-except* protocol when file processing is optional! Technical artists always have the choice of utilizing these safety features. There are situations when there is simply not enough time to employ them. However, since this is an instructional text and pushes for best practices, inclusion of exception handling is always demonstrated with file management examples.

Opening Files

Opening external files in Python is accomplished with the *open()* command. As outlines in Language Template 14.1, the *open()* command allocates system resources to external files and returns file pointers.

```
fileName = 'SystemPathToFile'
filePointer = open( fileName, mode)
```

Language Template 14.1 Python File Open

The mode attribute informs the system of the intention of how the resources are going to be used: for reading, writing, appending, or all of these. Table 14.1 introduces the basic file accessing modes with descriptions of their behavior.

TABLE 14.1 Python Open Modes

Mode	*Description*
'r'	Opens a file for reading. Raises an *IOError* when file does not exist.
'w'	Opens a file for writing. Truncates when file already exists. Creates when file does not exist.
'r+'	Opens a file for reading or writing. Raises an *IOError* when file does not exist.
'w+'	Opens a file for writing or reading. Truncates when file exists. Creates if does not exist.
'a'	Appends to the end of file. Creates when file does not exist.
'x'	Creates a new file and opens it for writing.

Closing Files

Closing an external file in Python is accomplished with the *close()* method. As explained by Language Template 14.2, the *close()* method terminates connections to the external file and returns the resource back to the system.

```
filePointer.close()
```

Language Template 14.2 Python File Close() Method

The *close()* method is possibly more important than *open* command. When a system resource is allocated to the file, the system will not allow another process to alter the file contents until the file is closed and the resource is released to the system. This is the reason why it is important to close the accessed file once it is no longer needed. When scripts crash or terminate while files are open, re-opening them with other processes becomes extraordinarily challenging. Depending on situation severity, users may need to log-out and log back in to release access. Often machine reboot is required.

The *try-except* protocol helps mitigate this risk significantly. The *finally* component of the protocol specifically targets releasing any claimed resources during handled exceptions. To complement these systems, it is best practice to release these resources as soon as they are longer necessary. *Context managers*, covered later in the chapter, are more powerful and safer methods for opening and closing file resources responsibly.

Reading and Writing

Reading and parsing of external data may appear to be a daunting task. Similarly, writing of data back to files may be equally as complicated. Most technical artists, however, should not focus on these sophisticated systems. Figure 14.1 show Technical artists only need to open external files, input their data to strings, and immediately close them. Similarly, they should pre-author all data to local strings, open the external files, write out the string contents, and immediately close them.

In the early days of computer graphics, computer RAM was a rare and expensive resource. Today's systems have enough available space to store thousands of lines of information. It is easier for technical artists to assemble output strings before file access and parse input strings after than to deal with the hassles of reading and writing individual lines of data. Of course, sophisticated applications will require more subtle approaches to file access. However, for most guerilla coding requirements, this strategy is adequate.

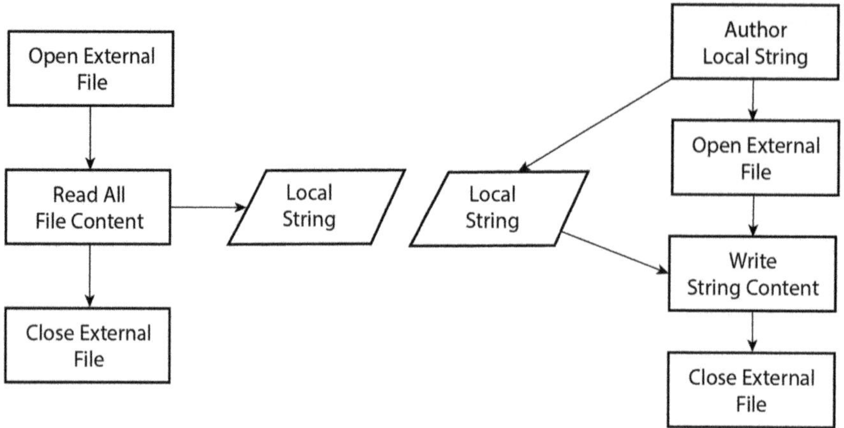

FIGURE 14.1 Reading and writing to external files.

Language Template 14.3 defines how the *read()* method is used to input a file's contents to a single string.

```
localString = filepointer.read()
```

Language Template 14.3 Reading Input File Content to Local String

Language Template 14.4 introduces the *write()* method is used to write a local string to an external output file.

```
filePointer.write(localString)
```

Language Template 14.4 Writing a Local String to External Output File

There are many situations requiring reading data from files, processing them, and immediately writing the results back. While it appears convenient to leave file pointers connected to external files during processing, it is safer to close them after reading and re-open them before writing.

Example

Code Sample 14.1 writes Python code to an external file, reads the file content, stores it to a string variable, *robertoString*, and then displays the variable's contents.

```
# Create Top Anchor
top = hou.node('/obj')
# Create the Roberto Geometry container
roberto = top.createNode('geo', 'Roberto')
# Create a Roberto Model
robertoGeo = roberto.createNode('testgeometry_rubbertoy')

# Initialize the Roberto String
robertoString = ''
```

```
# Initiate open file for writing protocol
try:
    # Attempt to open a file for writing
    robertoFile = open('RobertoFile.py', mode='w')
    # Write the Roberto string to the file

robertoFile.write(roberto.asCode(recurse=True))
    # Close the file
    robertoFile.close()

# Handle a file IO Error
except IOError as outputError:
    # Display IO Error message
    print(f'!!! Could not open output file !!! {outputError}')

# Delete the Roberto container and model
roberto.destroy()

# Initiate open file for reading protocol
try:
    # Attempt to open filr for reading
    newRobertoFile = open('RobertoFile.py', mode='r')
    # Read file contents to robertoString
    robertoString = newRobertoFile.read()
    # Close the file
    newRobertoFile.close()

# Handle IO
except IOError as inputError:
    # Display IO Error message
    print(f' !!! Could not open file for exporting !!! {inputError}')

# Display file content in string form
print(robertoString)
```

Code Sample 14.1 File Reading and Writing

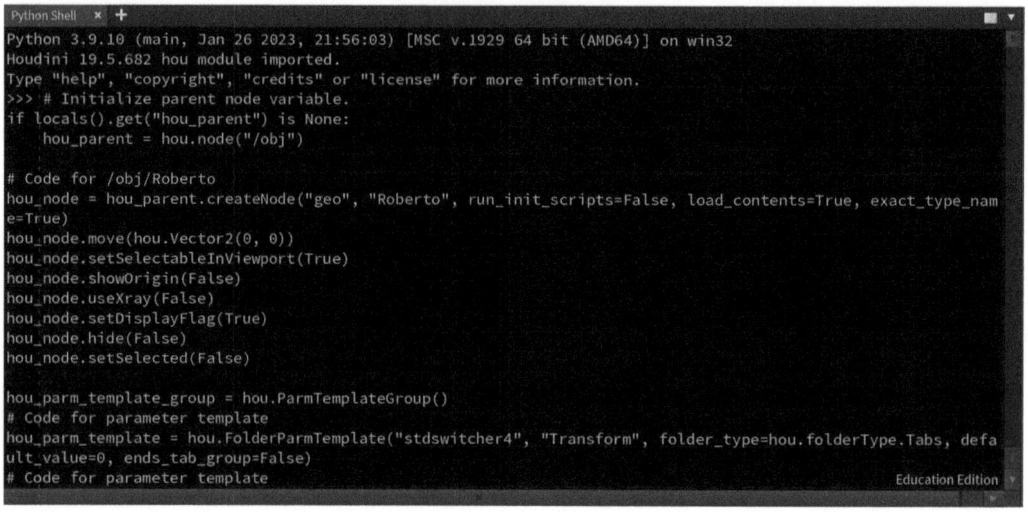

```
Python Shell  ×  +
Python 3.9.10 (main, Jan 26 2023, 21:56:03) [MSC v.1929 64 bit (AMD64)] on win32
Houdini 19.5.682 hou module imported.
Type "help", "copyright", "credits" or "license" for more information.
>>> # Initialize parent node variable.
if locals().get("hou_parent") is None:
    hou_parent = hou.node("/obj")

# Code for /obj/Roberto
hou_node = hou_parent.createNode("geo", "Roberto", run_init_scripts=False, load_contents=True, exact_type_nam
e=True)
hou_node.move(hou.Vector2(0, 0))
hou_node.setSelectableInViewport(True)
hou_node.showOrigin(False)
hou_node.useXray(False)
hou_node.setDisplayFlag(True)
hou_node.hide(False)
hou_node.setSelected(False)

hou_parm_template_group = hou.ParmTemplateGroup()
# Code for parameter template
hou_parm_template = hou.FolderParmTemplate("stdswitcher4", "Transform", folder_type=hou.folderType.Tabs, defa
ult_value=0, ends_tab_group=False)
# Code for parameter template
Education Edition
```

FIGURE 14.2 Display robertoString contents.

Figure 14.2 displays the size of the *robertoString* contents.

The top three lines of the script create a Houdini top anchor, generate a geometry container named 'Roberto', and produce Roberto geometry. The following line initializes an empty *robertoString* variable. The subsequent section initiates a *try-except* protocol opening a file for export. The first line of the *try* block opens a file pointer to the new file, 'RobertoFile.py', and assigns it to the *robertoFile* variable. The file mode, *'w'*, requests the opening of a new file for writing or rewriting of an existing file. The variable contents are written to the output file pointer. The *asCode(recurse=True)* statement displays, as a single string, all of the Python commands Houdini performs when creating Roberto geometry. The *recurse=True* argument tells Houdini to not only include the *Roberto* node to the string but also its children's content as well. As soon as the string is written, the file is closed.

Upon conclusion of exporting the *Roberto* Python code sequence to 'RobertoFile.py', the *Roberto* geometry object is deleted. A new *try-except* protocol for reading an external file is initiated. The first line in the *try* block attempts to open the 'RobertoFile.py' for reading and assigns the file pointer to the *newRobertoFile* variable. The *'r'* file mode informs Python that the external file is being opened for reading purposes only. The *read()* method absorbs the contents of the file and assigns them to the *robertoString* string variable. The file pointer is immediately closed. After input, the data stored in the *robertoString* variable are displayed to the console window.

RESOURCE MANAGEMENT

When Python opens an external file for reading or writing, it communicates with the system which allocates a file pointer to that resource. The resource is now locked for editing until the file pointer is removed and the resource released. During that time, no other application may alter the file contents. Certain applications, such as image editing and word processing software, may unable to open files being used by other programs.

When applications with allocated resources freeze or crash, the system still believes that the file pointers are valid and continues safeguarding the resources from editing. This challenging state may require the user to log-out and log back in or even reboot the machine to release the resources. Programmers take advantage of the *try-except* protocol to prevent the situation from occurring. This strategy is made easier using the *with context manager.*

Try – Finally

Occasionally, some applications must allocate file resources for extended periods, prolonging the time in which they are not accessible. The *try-finally* protocol removes the possibility of file lock-up from occurring. As outlined by Language Template 14.5, the *finally* block of code **must** execute regardless of exception state. The *close()*

method is placed in the *finally* code block to responsibly release the resource. The *finally* code block does not handle exceptions but does guarantee execution.

```
myFilePointer = open(myFile, mode)
try:
        performOperations(myFilePointer)
finally:
        myFilePointer.close()
```

Language Template 14.5 Try-Finally File Access Protocol

Before entering *try* states, users open external files and allocate resources. Within the *try* code block, the user performs operations with the file. Regardless of what happens to the program while executing the *try* code clock, the *finally* block must execute, closing, and releasing the resource. Exceptions still occur and must be handled appropriately. When employed, this preventative action prevents resources from ever being locked up.

With Context Manager

Context managers allow groups of statements to be run under the control of a single object. Their fundamental structure is defined in Language Template 14.6. In other words, pre-created context managers sandwich blocks of code between two distinct pieces of logic: the *enter()* method and the *exit()*. method. Authoring context managers is beyond the scope of this text. However, the *open()* command returns context managers which automatically close themselves when their code blocks complete. The *with* command activates *open()* returned context managers. Programmers combining *open()* commands with *with* statements do not need to *close()* their resources since the context managers handle those tasks for them. The embedded functionality of this combination makes it possible to factor out the *try-finally* protocol.

```
with contextManager.Expression as targetVariable:
  doSomething(targetVariable)
```

Language Template 14.6 Context Manager and 'with' Statement

When employing context managers, Language Template 14.7 and Language Template 14.8 demonstrate how the '*open for reading*', '*open for writing*', and *try-finally* protocols can be written as two line sequences. These are the preferred, recommended ways for dealing with files in Python.

```
with open(fileName, mode='r') as fileVariable:
  inputString = fileVariable.read()
```

Language Template 14.7 File Reading 'with' Sequence

```
with open(fileName, mode='w') as fileVariable:
  fileVariable.write(outputString)
```

Language Template 14.8 File Writing 'with' Sequence

These sequences allow programmers to open and access file content without requiring code to responsibly handle all file closing. The *file.close()* and *finally* statements are embedded in the context manager code.

Code Sample 14.2 demonstrates how Code Sample 14.1 is simplified using context managers.

```
# Create Top Anchor
top = hou.node('/obj')
# Create the Roberto Geometry container
roberto = top.createNode('geo', 'Roberto')
# Create a Roberto Model
robertoGeo = roberto.createNode('testgeometry_rubbertoy')

# Initialize the Roberto String
robertoString = ''

# Open context manage with statement
with open('NewRobertoFile.py', mode='w') as file:
    # Write the string contents to the file pointer
    file.write(roberto.asCode(recurse=True))

# Delete the Roberto container and model
roberto.destroy()

# Open context manage with statement
with open('NewRobertoFile.py', mode='r') as file:
    # Write the string contents to the file pointer
    robertoString = file.read()

# Display file content in string form
print(robertoString)
```

Code Sample 14.2 Code Rewritten with Context Managers

Rewriting the code cleans the visual appearance and facilitates easier reading. However, exceptions such as *IOErrror*, *AttributeError*, and *NameError* may still happen and should be mitigated accordingly.

DATA FORMATS

From the technical artist perspective, the challenging responsibility of file processing does not come from opening, reading and writing, and closing external files, but from parsing and interpreting the data. Technical artists read entire file contents to single strings. Similarly, they pre-author entire file contents to single strings so they may be written to files with one command. How are technical artists supposed to know what data are stored on those files and how should they author them so others may successfully access the written data? Data formats help remove much of the guesswork. There is a plethora of data formats accessible to technical artists, complete with their own tools and libraries. When absolutely necessary, they may also choose to invent their own. *JSON* and *XML* are two data formats technical artists will most likely encounter. Most other data formats are derivatives. Occasionally, technical artists encounter data which have been *pickled*.

JSON Data

Python *dictionaries* are convenient data objects which store unlimited amounts of organizable data. *JSON, (Java Script Object Notation)*, data files are dictionaries stored to files. Many data formats are built upon JSON structure. Understanding them is not challenging once programmers understand the data are laid out in dictionary format.

Format

The JSON structure is based on two primary constructs:

1. A collection of *name/value* pairs called objects.
2. An ordered list of *values* called an array.

Figure 14.3 displays how JSON objects may have zero, one or multiple name/value pairs. Name/value pairs are equivalent to Python dictionary key/value pairs except the keys are restricted to strings.

Figure 14.4 demonstrates how JSON arrays are very similar to Python lists containing zero, one, or multiple values.

Figure 14.5 displays how a JSON *value* may be any single *object, array*, number, string, 'true', 'false', or 'null'. Code Sample 14.3 is a JSON file example.

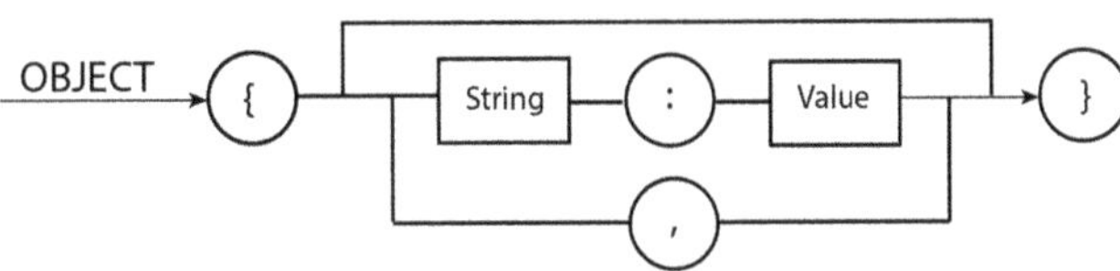

FIGURE 14.3 JSON object.

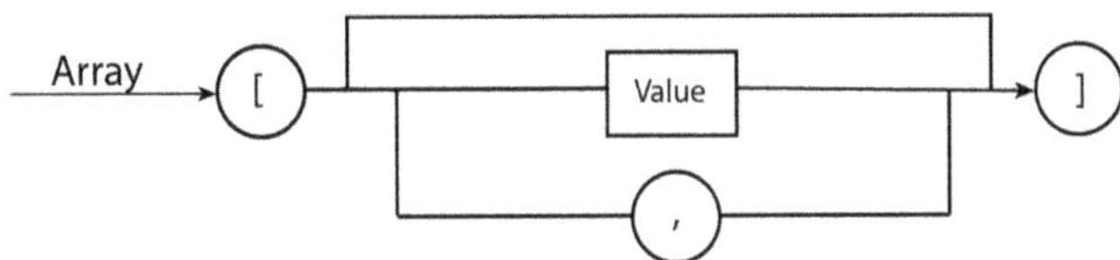

FIGURE 14.4 JSON array.

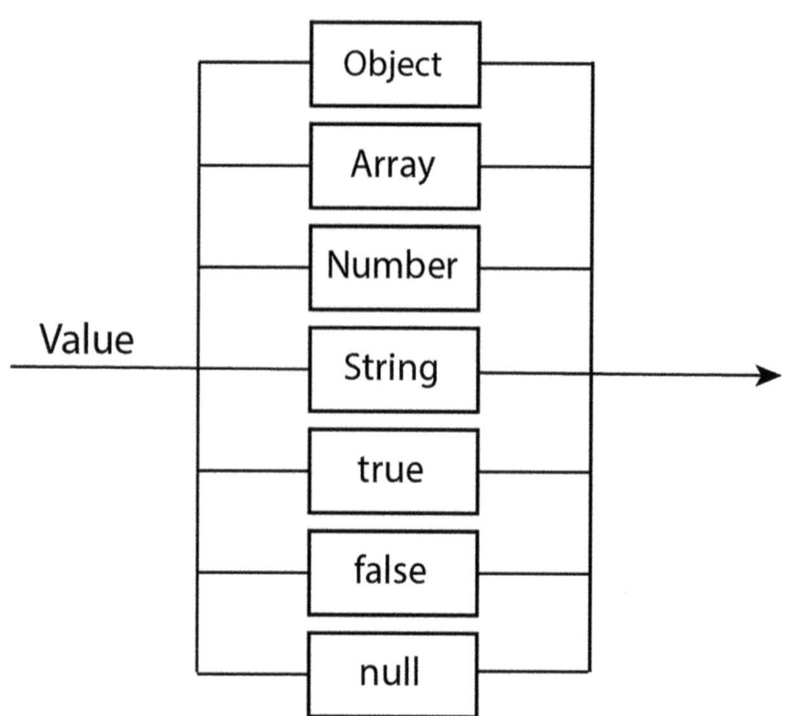

FIGURE 14.5 JSON Value.

```
{
    "MyCharacters" :
    [
        {
            "Name": "Cornelius Fluffwhistle",
            "Race": "Halfling",
            "Occupation": "Cleric",
            "Skills":
            [
                "Cure Wounds",
                "Detect Magic"
            ]
        },
        {
            "Name": "Felix Bombershmidt",
```

```
            "Race": "Gnome",
            "Occupation": "Rogue",
            "Skills":
            [
                "Sneak Attack",
                "Cunning Action"
            ]
        }
    ]
}
```

Code Sample 14.3 MyCharacters.json File

This file can be manually created using a simple, non-formatted, and text editor such as *Notepad, Sublime,* or *TextEdit* . When manually creating this *JSON* file on a Windows PC, save the file in the *C:\Users\<User Name>* folder. On Macintosh the path is /Users/<user Name>. These locations are Houdini's default file locations and it will look for and save files in these folders before searching elsewhere.

In the above example, *MyCharacters.json,* the name or primary entry of the file has an object name of *"MyCharacters"* and its value is an array of *character* objects. Each character object is composed of character attributes defined by an attribute name and value. Some attribute values, such as *"Skills"*, have multiple components and are contained in lists of strings instead of single strings.

Implementation

Reading and writing of JSON files are facilitated by the *JSON* Python module. The module translates JSON imported file strings to Python objects and exports Python objects to JSON strings to be written out to file.

json.loads()
Language Template 14.9 outlines how JSON strings are translated to Python objects using the *json.loads()* method.

```
import json
newPythonObject = json.loads(JSONFileString)
```

Language Template 14.9 JSON loads method

Code Sample 14.4 displays how a JSON file's contents are open and inputed into a script. After the file string has been read from file, the string is parsed to a Python object using the json.loads() method (Code Sample 14.4).

```
# Import JSON Module
import json

# Open external file using  with context manger
with open('MyCharacters.json', 'r') as file:
    # Read the file contents to fileString
    fileString = file.read()

myJSONObject = json.loads(fileString)

# Access 'MyCharacters' from Python Object
myCharacters = myJSONObject['MyCharacters']
# For every Character
for character in myCharacters:
    # Create an empty display String
    buff = ''
    buff += f'Name: {character["Name"]}\n'
    buff += f'\tRace: {character["Race"]}\n'
    buff += f'\tOccupation: {character["Occupation"]}\n'
    buff += '\tSkills:\n'
    for skill in character['Skills']:
        buff += f'\t\t{skill}\n'

    # Display the output string
    print(buff)

>>> Name: Cornelius Fluffwhistle
        Race: Halfling
        Occupation: Cleric
        Skills:
                Cure Wounds
                Detect Magic
```

```
Name: Felix Bombershmidt
        Race: Gnome
        Occupation: Rogue
        Skills:
                Sneak Attack
                Cunning Action
```

Code Sample 14.4 JSON.loads() Method

Before attempting to execute the above code, make sure to enter the *MyCharacters*.json file to the *C:\User\<User name>* folder on a Windows machine or to /Users/<user Name> on a Mac Device. In the above code sample, the first line imports the *json* module. The script utilizes the *with* context manager protocol to open the external file and access its contents. Using the *json.loads()* method *fileString* is converted to a Python object, *myCharacters*. As a dictionary-like Python object, *myCharacters* is easily parsed into its individual components and displayed.

json.dumps()

Language Template 14.10 outlines how Python objects are translated back into JSON file strings using the *json.dumps()* method.

```
import json
newJSONString = json.dumps(myPythonObject)
```

Language Template 14.10 json.dumps() Method

The method takes a Python object and translates it into a *JSON* string suitable for file export.

Code Sample 14.5 extends Code Sample 14.4 by creating new character attributes stored in the *characterAttributes* dictionary. Note that the dictionary is composed of multiple key/value pairs. The *characterAttributes* list automatically appends to the existing Python dictionary object, *myCharacters*. The dictionary is translated back to a new JSON string, *newJSONString*, using the *json.dumps()* method. The new JSON string is written to a new file, *MyNewCharacters.json*.

```
# import JSON Module
import json

# JSON Import
# Open external file using  with context manger
with open('MyCharacters.json', 'r') as file:
```

```
    # Read the file contents to fileString
    fileString = file.read()

myJSONObject = json.loads(fileString)

# Access 'MyCharacters' from Python Object
myCharacters = myJSONObject['MyCharacters']
# For every Character
for character in myCharacters:
    # Create an empty display String
    buff = ''
    buff += f'Name: {character["Name"]}\n'
    buff += f'\tRace: {character["Race"]}\n'
    buff += f'\tOccupation: {character["Occupation"]}\n'
    buff += '\tSkills:\n'
    for skill in character['Skills']:
        buff += f'\t\t{skill}\n'
    # Display the output string
    print(buff)

# JSON Export
characterAttributes = { 'Name': 'Phineas Rushfyr',
            'Race' : 'Half-Elf',
                              'Occupation': 'Ranger',
            'Skills': ['Charm Person',
                        'Hunter's Mark']}
# Append the attributes list to the MyCharcters list
myCharacters.append(characterAttributes)

newJSONString = json.dumps(
            myJSONObject, indent=4,
            separators=(',', ':'))
```

```
# Open output file using with context manager
with open('MyNewCharacters.json', 'w') as file:
    # Write new file contents
    file.write(newJSONString)
```

Code Sample 14.5 JSON dumps() method

When the reader views the results of the *MyNewCharacters.json* file, she will notice the file contents are written to only one line. By default, unless the input object string has been formatted for text display, the *json.dumps()* method only writes to one continuous line.

To remedy this situation, *json.dumps()* has parameters for formatting text output. Replacing Code Sample 14.6 in Code Sample 14.5 should remedy the situation.

```
newJSONString = json.dumps(myJSONObject, indent=4,
                           separators=(',', ':'))
```

Code Sample 14.6 Updated JSON.dumps() Method

The *indent* parameter indicates the number of spaces to insert with every new line. The *separators* parameter identifies the *item separator* and *key separator* characters. Use these parameters to generate the readable JSON content in Code Sample 14.7.

```
{
    "MyCharacters":[
        {
            "Name":"Cornelius Fluffwhistle",
            "Race":"Halfling",
            "Occupation":"Cleric",
            "Skills":[
              "Cure Wounds",
              "Detect Magic"
            ]
        },
        {
            "Name":"Felix Bombershmidt",
```

```
                "Race":"Gnome",
                "Occupation":"Rogue",
                "Skills":[
                  "Sneak Attack",
                  "Cunning Action"
                ]
            },
            {
                "Name":"Phineas Rushfyr",
                "Race":"Half-Elf",
                "Occupation":"Ranger",
                "Skills":[
                  "Charm Person",
                  "hunter's Mark"
                ]
            }
        ]
}
```

Code Sample 14.7 MyNewCharacters.json File Output

World Map

Technical artists use JSON regularly to pass information between platforms. Most of technical artists' time dealing with them is not focused so much on the reading and writing of the content, nor converting the data from long strings to Python objects, but from parsing and digesting the data. The following example demonstrates how a technical artist may interact with arbitrary JSON data. The script was created when an art director, having no idea of the data contents, requested a technical artist to figure out what data contain. The example works with a *GeoJSON* file: a *JSON* format devoted for map making.

The data required for this example is downloaded from https://datahub.io/core/geo-countries. The needed file is 'countries.geojson'. This file generates an map image similar to Figure 14.6. Make sure to download this file from the website and store it in the same default folder you stored the 'MyCharacters.json' file. The data originates from Natural Earth, a community effort to making visually pleasing, well-crafted maps with cartography or GIS software at small scale. Credit is also due to Lexman and Open knowledge Foundation for making this information available.

Visualizing a *geoJSON* file inside Houdini is a bit challenging in that Houdini Python is prevented from generating new geometry except within a geometry *Python Node*. A *Python Node* is a customizable geometry node that enables artists to inject specific Python code at precise locations along a geometry's data process flow.

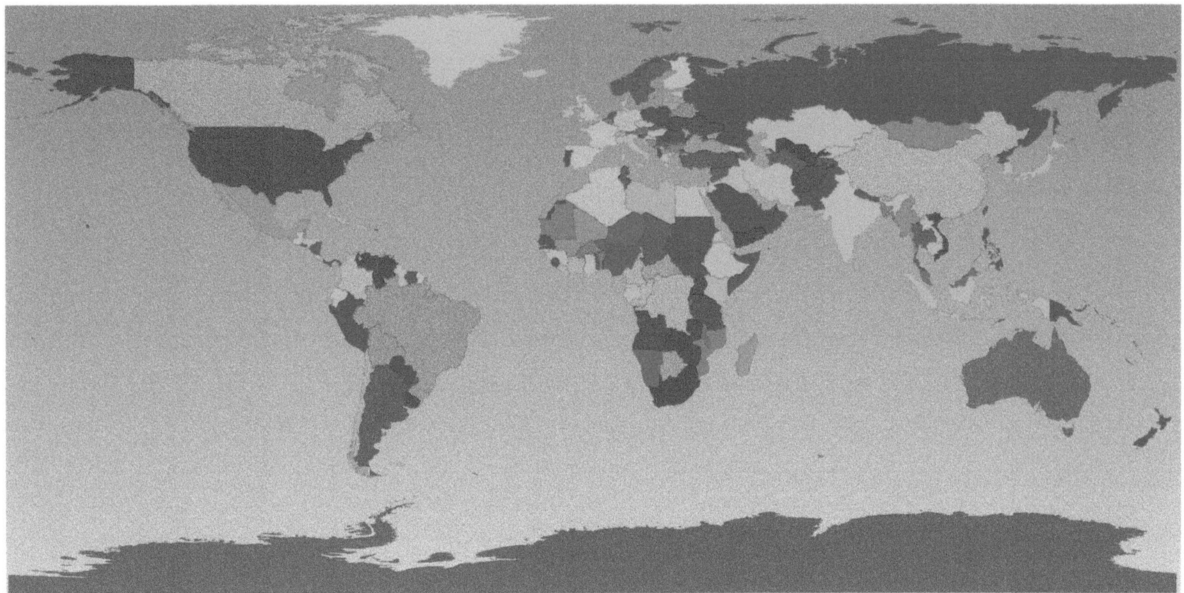

FIGURE 14.6 Countries.geojson data (Natural Earth, MIT license).

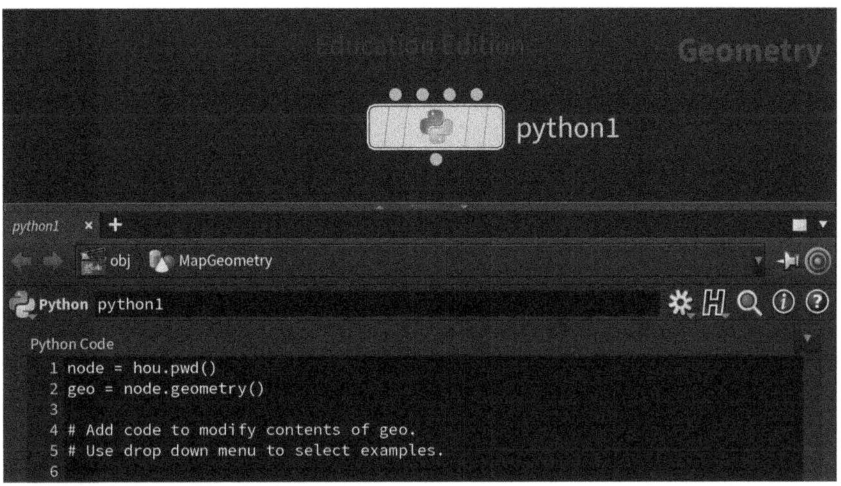

FIGURE 14.7 Houdini geometry Python Node.

All examples, up until this point in the text, operate holistically, in the world space perspective, using scripts stored on Python shelves. This example code applies only to local space geometry editing within *Python Nodes*.

Create a geometry node on the object level. Label the geometry node, *MapGeometry*. Double left-mouse click the *MapGeometry* node to descend into its local, geometry editing space. Drop down a *Python Node*, as shown in Figure 14.7. A *Python Node's* interface is a simple Python text editor. The code within this node can be used to create, destroy, or edit any geometry component.

To create a Python script to read a *geoJSON* and convert the data into visible geometry, replace the default code with Code Sample 14.8.

```
import json

node = hou.pwd()
Geo = node.geometry()

''' All-purpose function to create abstract polygons,
   whatever the data or color given a sequence of
   point positions and a color, this function creates
   a brand-new polygon with the provided color '''
def createPoly(myPts, myColor):
    ''' Take a sequence of points, make a polygon
        and assign point color'''
    #Create a brand-new Polygon
    newPoly = Geo.createPolygon()

    # Iterate over all the input point coordinates
    for spoint in myPts:
        # Create a new point
        point = Geo.createPoint()

        # Set the new point's position and color
        point.setPosition((spoint[0], spoint[1], 0.0))
        point.setAttribValue("Cd", myColor.rgb())

        # Append the new point as a vertex to the polygon
        newPoly.addVertex(point)

''' Go through the input data, extract the individual
    countries and create same-colored polygons for
    individual countries '''
def parseGeoJSON(dataObject):
    ''' Parse the object data and send to the
       polygon creator '''
```

```
# Grab the feature data set
features = dataObject["features"]
# Count the number of features =
# Number of countries
numCountries = len(features)

# Create the country color attribute
Geo.addAttrib(hou.attribType.Point, "Cd", (0.0, 0.0, 0.0))

# Count the countries as we iterate
countryCount = 0


# Iterate through each of the countries
for feature in features:
    # Grab the country's geometry
    geometry = feature["geometry"]
    # Get the country's geometry type
    geoType = geometry["type"]

    # Create a unique color for the country
    cColor = hou.Color((0.0, 0.0, 0.0))
    hVal = float(countryCount) /
          float(numCountries) * 360.0
    cColor.setHSV((hVal, 1.0, 1.0))

    # If the type is a polygon it is only one polygon
    if geoType == "Polygon":
        # Get the individual coordinates
        coords = geometry["coordinates"]
        # The points are always the first elements
        # In the list
        pts = coords[0]
```

```
            # Create a new polygon for the country
            createPoly(pts, cColor)

        # If the country is MultiPolygon then it may have
        # many polygons
        elif geoType == "MultiPolygon":
            # Get all of the polygons composing the country
            polys = geometry["coordinates"]

            # Create a new polygon for each new country segment
            for poly in polys:
                # Get the point coordinates
                pts = poly[0]
                # Create the new polygon
                createPoly(pts, cColor)

        # Increment the country counter
        countryCount += 1



fileName = r'countries.geojson'
# Open input file using with context manager
with open(fileName, "r") as infile:
    # Read file data
    inputJSONString = infile.read()

# Convert, parse and display the data
# Convert the JSON string into a python object
countriesObject = json.loads(inputJSONString)
# Parse and display the geometry data
parseGeoJSON(countriesObject)
```

Code Sample 14.8 Houdini GeoJSON File Reader

The supplied code imports the *json* module; required for converting the input file string to a Python object. Two global variables, *node* and *Geo*, provide global access to the node's geometry content. Two primary functions are defined: createPoly() **and** parseGeoJSON(). Code execution resumes near the bottom of the script where the *filename* string variable is assigned the name of the geoJSON input file. Note the 'r' preceding the file name. This notation is required to read the data as *raw* and be able to handle *backslash paths*. The *with* context manager protocol is used to import the file data into a single data string, *inputJSONString*. Using *json.loads()*, the string is converted to a Python object, *countriesObject*. The Python object is parsed, digested, and displayed using the *parseGeoJSON()* function.

The *parseGeoJSON()* function extracts each of the countries from the data object and creates new polygons for each. It grabs the *'features'* from the data set. *'Features'* is a single key/value dictionary containing a list of *feature* objects. Before generating any geometry, the script creates a point color attribute, *'Cd'*, which is given to every newly created point. A numerical country counter, *countryCount*, is created and initialized. It is used as a seed to help calculate the country's random color. Each of the *feature/country* objects is processed.

The *'geometry'* component from each *feature/country* is accessed. The *'geometry'* object is a dictionary containing two key/value pairs: *type* and *coordinates*. The *feature/country's 'geometry'* and *'type'* information are obtained and a unique country color is created. The *'coordinates'* from the *feature/country* are obtained and, depending on the *'type'* value, they are sent to the *createPoly()* function with its data points and country color as input attributes. When the *'type'* is 'Polygon' only one polygon is created. When the *'type'* is 'MultiPolygon' multiple polygons are created.

The *createPoly()* function receives a sequence of points, *myPts*, and a color, *myColor*. A new, empty polygon for the Houdini geometry is generated using the *createPolygon()* Houdini function. One by one, all of the points in the point sequence are generated. A new Houdini point geometry is created using the Houdini *createPoint()* function. The new point's position is set with the coordinates from the country data. The new point's color attribute is assigned the input color. The point is then added to the new polygon as a new vertex using the Houdini *addVertex()* function. Exiting the *createPoly()* function finishes the new country polygon and displays it to the screen.

XML Data

Sometimes, the data imported and exported from Python scripts flows more logically when organized into data structures other than dictionaries. The *XML* structure is visualized in Figure 14.8. A popular format, particularly

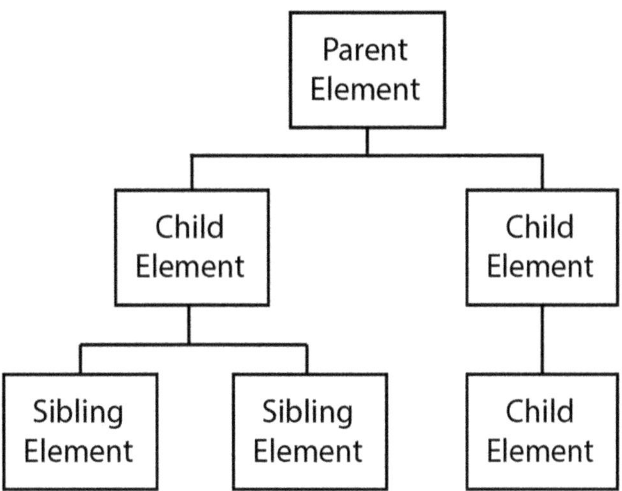

FIGURE 14.8 XML hierarchical structure.

effective when dealing with hierarchical data, is *XML*, or *Extensible Markup Language*. For example, from a technical artist's perspective, character mesh data are better formatted in a dictionary JSON file while a character's skeleton structure is better situated in XML.

Structure

XML files are composed of *XML elements* and each, as defined by Language Template 14.11, is made of tags and text. Elements are bookended by tags. The tags provide structure to the text data. There are three types of tags: an *opening tag*, '<tagName>', denoting the start of an XML element, a *close tag*, '</tagName>', denoting the end, and an *empty-element tag, '<tagName />'*, containing no element information. Tags may contain attribute identity information. Tag attributes are a name, followed with an equal sign, =, followed by a double-quoted string. There are no white spaces allowed in each attribute definition. White spaces are only used for delimiting multiple attributes. Tag attributes are case sensitive and their format must be conformed to otherwise errors occur. Between an *opening* and a *close* tag are zero or one text string and zero or many XML elements.

```
<tagName attributeNameA="foo" attributeNameB="bar">
  0 or 1 Text String
  0 or Many XML Elements
</tagName>
<EmptyTagName attributeName="Snafu"/>
```

Language Template 14.11 XML Data Element Structure

Every XML element requires an opening tag, '<tagName>', and a closing tag '</tagname>'. Every element tag may have zero or many attributes. *Empty-Element* tags are good for containing enumerable attribute information. An example XML data file is shown in Code Sample 14.9.

```
<?xml version="1.0"?>
<data>
    <character name="Stu">
      <race>Human</race>
      <level>2</level>
      <magic>
        <cantrips>
          <number>3</number>
          <known>
            <cantrip name="Fire Bolt">
              <range>120</range>
              <damage>1d10</damage>
```

```
                </cantrip>
                <cantrip name="Light">
                    <range>20</range>
                    <duration>1 hour</duration>
                </cantrip>
                <cantrip name="Mage Hand">
                    <range>30</range>
                    <duration>1 Minute</duration>
                </cantrip>
            </known>
        </cantrips>
        <spells>
            <number>3</number>
            <known>
                <spell name="Magic Missle">
                    <range>120</range>
                    <damage>1d4+1</damage>
                </spell>
                <spell name="Mage Armor">
                    <range>Touch</range>
                    <duration>8 Hours</duration>
                </spell>
                <spell name="Thunderwave">
                    <range>Self(15 ft)</range>
                    <damage>2d8+10feet/1d8+0feet</damage>
                </spell>
            </known>
        </spells>
    </magic>
  </character>
</data>
```

Code Sample 14.9 MyCharacters.xml

The first line of the above example is an *XML Declaration* which specifies the version of XML being used and any encodings employed in the document. XML is *well-formed* which means it follows strict syntactical rules. The declaration conforms to well-formed standards.

The primary element in this file is the *data* element. Its first child element, *character*, has one attribute: *name*. The *character* element has three child elements: *race, level,* and *magic*. The *race* and *level* child elements are simple, one text data elements. The *magic* element is composed of two other child elements: *cantrips* and *spells*. These two elements both have *number* and *known* elements. The *known* elements subsequently have lists of either *cantrip* or *spell* elements.

Implementation

Unlike *JSON* data files which are ultimately structured as Python dictionaries, *XML* data structures have no inherent Python structure. They must be implemented as their own, custom data classes.

XML Input and Node Structure

The *xml package* handles Python *XML* parsing; an otherwise challenging task for any technical artist to implement. Of all the submodules in the package, technical artists should be familiar with *ElementTree*. The *ElementTree API*: a simple and lightweight XML processor. It is found in the *etree* submodule. It is imported most easily using Language Template 14.12.

```
# ET is easier to work with than the full submodule name
import xml.etree.ElementTree as ET
```

Language Template 14.12 Importing the ElementTree XML Submodule

Code Sample 14.10 demonstrates how *ElementTree* is access and used to read in an XML file. *ElementTree* parses *XML* files using the simple *ET.parse()* method. Exception handling is not required. As demonstrated in the above example, xml datasets are parented by a single element node. This node is obtained with the *getroot()* method. Node objects are Python lists of other XML child element nodes. An element's tag is accessed from the *.tag* attribute. XML tag attributes are assigned as key/value dictionaries to the object's *.attrib* attribute. An object element's text data are accessed through the node's *.text* attribute. All of these functions are listed in Table 14.2. Once the top node element is obtained, the rest of the tree data are accessible.

TABLE 14.2 ElementTree Element Node Components

Element Node Component	*Component Type*	*Component Notes*
ElementNode[]	Element Node List	A list of zero to many child node elements
ElementNode.tag	String	Element Node tag name
ElementNode.attrib	Dictionary (string:string)	Zero to many Element Node key/value pair attributes. Key/value pairs are strings
ElementNode.text	String	Zero or one string of text data

```
# Import the ElementTree submodule as ET
import xml.etree.ElementTree as ET

# Tree is the parsed file data
tree = ET.parse('myCharacters.xml')
# Root is the top node of the XML data tree
root = tree.getroot()

# Recursive display function which displays a node's contents
# before exploring each child
def exploreXMLNode(parent, indent=0):
    ''' Display the contents of an xml node then explore all
       of its children. Indent variable keeps track hierarchy level '''
    print(f"{indent*'    '}Tag={parent.tag}, Attributes={parent.attrib}, \
            Text={parent.text}")

    # Parent is a list. Recursively explore parent's children
    for child in parent:
        exploreXMLNode(child, indent+1)


# With root node, explore it and its children
exploreXMLNode(root)


>>> Tag=data, Attributes={}, Text=

    Tag=character, Attributes={'name': 'Stu'}, Text=

        Tag=race, Attributes={}, Text=Human
        Tag=level, Attributes={}, Text=2
        Tag=magic, Attributes={}, Text=
```

```
Tag=cantrips, Attributes={}, Text=

    Tag=number, Attributes={}, Text=3
    Tag=cantrip, Attributes={'name': 'Fire Bolt'}, Text=

        Tag=range, Attributes={}, Text=120
        Tag=damage, Attributes={}, Text=1d10
    Tag=cantrip, Attributes={'name': 'Light'}, Text=

        Tag=range, Attributes={}, Text=20
        Tag=duration, Attributes={}, Text=1 hour
    Tag=cantrip, Attributes={'name': 'Mage Hand'}, Text=

        Tag=range, Attributes={}, Text=30
        Tag=duration, Attributes={}, Text=1 Minute
Tag=spells, Attributes={}, Text=

    Tag=number, Attributes={}, Text=3
    Tag=spell, Attributes={'name': 'Magic Missle'}, Text=

        Tag=range, Attributes={}, Text=120
        Tag=damage, Attributes={}, Text=1d4+1
    Tag=spell, Attributes={'name': 'Mage Armor'}, Text=

        Tag=range, Attributes={}, Text=Touch
        Tag=duration, Attributes={}, Text=8 Hours
    Tag=spell, Attributes={'name': 'Thunderwave'}, Text=

        Tag=range, Attributes={}, Text=Self(15 ft)
        Tag=damage, Attributes={}, Text=2d8+10feet/1d8+0feet
```

Code Sample 14.10 Simple XML Exploration

The above example is a simple demonstration of the recursive, hierarchical *XML* data structure. Each line of output represents one element node. The first line of code imports the *ElementTree* submodule. The module reads and parses the entire file contents with the *parse()* method. The root element node, *root,* is obtained with the *getroot()* method. The *exploreXMLNode()* function displays the input element node's contents before recursively calling itself for each of the node's children. The *indent* variable keeps track of the hierarchy level. The script's execution starts with the call to *exploreXMLNode()* on the input file's first element node, *root.*

XML Construction and Export

While not as common as reading from XML files, it is possible to write to XML files. Usually, data bases or other data-oriented applications are used to generate XML files. Python scripts use the *ElementTree* submodule.

Language Template 14.13 defines how new node trees are generated using the *ET.Element()* method (Language Template 14.13).

```
newXMLTree  = ET.Element('FirstNodeName')
```

Language Template 14.13 Generating New XML Tree Using ET.Element()

All child nodes are constructed using the *ET.SubElement()* method. XML child nodes can only be created using this method, explained in Language Template 14.14.

```
newChildNode  = ET.SubElement(ParentNode, 'ChildNodeName'))
```

Language Template 14.14 Generating XML Tree Subnode Using ET.SubElement()

Language Template 14.15 displays how node attributes are created by assigning a dictionary to the node's . *attrib* attribute.

```
attributeDictionary = {'AttributeKeyName':'AttributeValue'}
node.attrib = attributeDictionary
```

Language Template 14.15 Creating Node Attribute

Language Template 14.16 outlines how nodes' *text* components are generated by assigning a string object to the node's *.text* attribute.

```
node.text = 'NodeStringTextValue'
```

Language Template 14.16 Creating Node Text Component

The *ET.tostring()* method is used for converting XML node trees into writable strings. Unfortunately, the resulting string has no line returns or indention. XML trees written like this are difficult to read. The *XMLPython* module contains another submodule, *minidom,* to resolve this issue. The *minidom.parseString()* method parses a string exported from *ET.tostring()*. The *minidom.toprettyXML()* method is used to add line returns and proper indenting to the parsed string.

Code Sample 14.11 takes advantage of the *minidom* submodule to create a *prettyXMLString()* function to generate readable and writable text strings. The *ElementTree* root node is input to the function where the *ET. tostring()* method is used to convert it to a new string, *rawstr.* The *rawstr* string is parsed using the *minidom. parseString()* method. Line returns and indenting is injected using the *minidom.toprettyxml()* method and returned.

The first two lines of Code Sample 14.11 are devoted to importing the *ElementTree* and *minidom* xml submodules. A new XML tree, *data*, is generated using the ET.Element() method. A new node, *character*, is parented to the root node using the *ET.SubElement()* method. The *character* node parents three child sub-nodes: *race, level,* and *occupation.* The *occupation* node contains a *text* component, *Barbarian*, and a new subnode, *skills*. The *skills* node contains two additional sub-nodes: *rage* and *unarmoredDefense*.

After the XML tree is generated, it is converted to a writable string, *xmlStr*, using the *prettyXMLString()* function described above. Using the *with* context manager protocol, the string is written to an external file, *myNewCharacters.xml*.

```
# Import minidom for parseString and toprettyxml methods
from xml.dom import minidom

''' A function for pretty printing XML files generated in ElementTree'''
def prettyXMLString(element):
    # Convert Element Tree to a string
    raw = ET.tostring(element)
    # Parse the string using the minidom module
    miniParse = minidom.parseString(raw)
    # Reformat the string with line breaks and indentions
    xmlStr = miniParse.toprettyxml(indent="    ")
    return xmlStr


# Create the xml tree root
data  = ET.Element('data')
# Create a root child called 'Character' with name attribute of 'Steve'
steve = ET.SubElement(data, 'character')
steve.attrib = {'name':'Steve'}
# Create Child node for race
race = ET.SubElement(steve, 'race')
race.text = 'Dwarf'
# Create a sibling for race called 'level'
level = ET.SubElement(steve, 'level')
level.text = '1'
```

```
# Create 'occupation' Character child
occupation = ET.SubElement(steve, 'occupation')
occupation.text = 'Barbarian'
# Create a occupation child called 'skills'
skills = ET.SubElement(occupation, 'skills')
# Rage is the first skills child
rage = ET.SubElement(skills, 'rage')
# Rage has number and damage children
rageNumber = ET.SubElement(rage, 'number')
rageNumber.text='2'
rageDamage = ET.SubElement(rage, 'damage')
rageDamage.text='+2'
# Unarmored Defense is another Skill child
unarmored = ET.SubElement(skills, 'unarmoredDefense')
unarmored.text='10 + Dex + Const'

# Convert the ElementTree XML structure a printable string
xmlStr = prettyXMLString(data)
# Open output file using with context manager
with open('myNewCharacters.xml', 'w') as file:
    # Write file contents
    file.write(xmlStr)
```

Code Sample 14.11 Generating and Exporting New XML Tree Data

The results of the myNewCharacters.xml file are found in Code Sample 14.12.

```
<?xml version="1.0" ?>
<data>
    <character name="Steve">
      <race>Dwarf</race>
      <level>1</level>
      <occupation>
        Barbarian
```

```
            <skills>
                <rage>
                  <number>2</number>
                  <damage>+2</damage>
                </rage>
                <unarmoredDefense>10 + Dex + Const</unarmoredDefense>
            </skills>
        </occupation>
    </character>
</data>
```

Code Sample 14.12 MyNewCHaracters.xml Results

Bone Finder

In Chapter 9, we traversed through a very complicated character and quickly identifying all of the character's bones using a recursion technique. This same core concept can be extended to generating an XML file exposing the same data. The hierarchical nature of characters lends themselves to natural XML cataloging. XML provides an ideal data format to store hierarchical character information.

Code Sample 14.13 is an extension of the recursive *BoneFinder* script, Code Sample 9.33. Code Sample 14.13 is supplemented with XML and file overhead functionality introduced in the prior examples. Other than these additions, only subtle changes are made to the *boneFinder* function. The *level* parameter is no longer needed as character hierarchy is monitored by intrinsic XML structure. The *xParent* parameter stores the XML tree parent node upon which all bones are attached. The *node* parameter is essential for traversing the Houdini character network. Not all nodes in the Houdini character are bones and thus the *node* and *xParent* parameters are not necessarily the same. When the current *node* is a bone, a new *xParent* subelement is generated and appended under the old *xParent* element. All of the *node's* children are iterated on by recursively calling the *boneFinder()* function for each of the children.

The remainder of Code Sample 14.13 is devoted to creating a *root* node for the XML *ElementTree* and traversing the entire character with the initial call to *boneFinder()*. After character traversal, the *root* tree contains the XML bone hierarchy. Using the *prettyXMLString()*function, created in the prior example, the XML tree is converted to a string and the string is written to an external file using the *with* context manager protocol.

```
# Import the ElementTree submodule as ET
import xml.etree.ElementTree as ET
# Import minidom for parseString and toprettyxml methods
from xml.dom import minidom
```

```
''' A function for pretty printing XML files generated in ElementTree'''
def prettyXMLString(element):
    # Convert Element Tree to a string
    rawstr = ET.tostring(element)
    # Parse the string using the minidom module
    miniParse = minidom.parseString(rawstr)
    # Reformat the string with line breaks and indentions
    xmlStr = miniParse.toprettyxml(indent="    ")
    return xmlStr

    ''' Core function to flesh out XML stree with bone nodes '''
def boneFinder(node, xParent):
    ''' When node is a bone, the new subElement becomes
       the new xParent '''
    # Base Case
    if node.type().name() == 'bone':
        # Create a new Bone subElement
        xParent = ET.SubElement(xParent, node.name())

    # Get all node's children
    children = node.outputs()
    # Explore each of node's children
    for child in children:
        # Recurse to each child
        boneFinder(child, xParent)

# Script initialization and execution
# Create the XML Tree root
root = ET.Element('BoneList')
# Initial call to boneFinder
boneFinder(hou.node('/obj/simplefemale1/ctrl_cog'), root)
```

```
# Convert the Element Tree into a string
boneStr = prettyXMLString(root)
# Open external file using with context manager
with open('myBones.xml', 'w') as file:
    # Write file contents
    file.write(boneStr)
```

Code Sample 14.13 Bone Finder XML Tree Generator

Figure 14.9 displays what a portion of *myBones.xml* should look like.

```
<?xml version="1.0" ?>
<BoneList>
    <ctrl_rig_bone_hand_right>
        <rig_bone_little_1_right>
            <rig_bone_little_2_right>
                <rig_bone_little_3_right/>
            </rig_bone_little_2_right>
        </rig_bone_little_1_right>
        <rig_bone_ring_1_right>
            <rig_bone_ring_2_right>
                <rig_bone_ring_3_right/>
            </rig_bone_ring_2_right>
        </rig_bone_ring_1_right>
        <rig_bone_index_1_right>
            <rig_bone_index_2_right>
                <rig_bone_index_3_right/>
            </rig_bone_index_2_right>
        </rig_bone_index_1_right>
        <rig_bone_middle_1_right>
            <rig_bone_middle_2_right>
                <rig_bone_middle_3_right/>
            </rig_bone_middle_2_right>
        </rig_bone_middle_1_right>
        <rig_bone_thumb_1_right>
            <rig_bone_thumb_2_right>
                <rig_bone_thumb_3_right/>
            </rig_bone_thumb_2_right>
        </rig_bone_thumb_1_right>
    </ctrl_rig_bone_hand_right>
    <rig_bone_thigh_right>
        <rig_bone_calf_right>
            <rig_bone_foot_right>
                <rig_bone_toe_right/>
            </rig_bone_foot_right>
        </rig_bone_calf_right>
    </rig_bone_thigh_right>
    <rig_bone_thigh_left>
        <rig_bone_calf_left>
            <rig_bone_foot_left>
                <rig_bone_toe_left/>
            </rig_bone_foot_left>
```

FIGURE 14.9 MyBones.xml results.

When looking over the *myBones.xml* file, certain artists may be unsettled to observe that the pelvis bone is not the first node in the tree. There is a *pelvis* bone at the top of the hierarchy but it is also shared with other core level bone siblings such as *hand_right*, *spine_1*, etc. The rigger for this character simply created a flat, top-level hierarchy, parented under the single *BoneList* node. This flat hierarchy structure is challenging to observe when viewed outside of XML representation.

Pickling

Occasionally, technical artists are expected to read and write serialized, or *pickled*, files. *Pickling*, a form of *serialization*, is a process of converting Python objects to *byte streams* to be stored in external files or transported over the network. *Byte Streams* are binary representations of Python objects or classes and may be transferred as external files or as strings.

Pickle data are convenient in that any Python object or class can be converted to a byte stream. JSON requires the data to be converted to a dictionary-like format. XML requires data to be stored in its tree format. All Python objects are pickleable. Like the prior two formats, understanding of the structure of the pickle data is required for interpretation.

Pickle data are binary and are smaller and faster than JSON and XML. A risk of this freedom is that there is no way to verify the integrity of the pickle data. It is possible to inject malicious shell code into byte streams that execute arbitrary code. In other words, pickle data are susceptible to hacking.

Like JSON, pickle data are *dumped* when exported and *loaded* when imported. The data may be read and written directly to an external data file or to a string-based byte stream. After pickling, the data are in binary format and are no longer human-readable.

Pickle Dump

Python data are pickled to an external file or to a string. The *pickle.dump()* and *pickle.dumps()* methods are used to transport the data, respectively.

Pickle data are binary and are not human-readable. Language Template 14.17 displays how external files must be opened in binary mode, *'wb'*, to be writable.

```
# External file must be binary writable
with open('externalFile' , 'wb') as file:
# Python Object is written to file
pickle.dump(PythonObject, file)

# Python object is converted to a byte stream string
pickleString = pickle.dumps(PythonObject)
```

Language Template 14.17 pickle.dump() and pickle.dumps()

Code Sample 14.14 generates a Roberto character, accesses its geometry data, and dumps the point coordinates to an external file. The first line imports the *pickle* module. A Roberto character is created and assigned to the *roberto* variable. The *roberto* geometry is accessed using the Houdini *geometry()* method. The points are extracted and assigned to the *robertoPoints* list via the Houdini *points()* method.

While all of the points are stored in *robertoPoints*, they are not yet pickleable. A Houdini point is a compiled C++ class, exposed to Python, and cannot be pickled. All of the coordinate data from Houdini points must be extracted and assembled into true Python objects. A new, empty list, *pointList*, is initialized. Each of the points in *robertoPoints* is then processed. A new tuple, *pos*, is composed of the X, Y, and Z coordinates copied from the Houdini point object and appended to the *pointList* object. Once finished, *pointList* contains all of the point coordinate tuples and may now be pickled.

An external file, *RobertoPoints.cjr*, is opened for writing in binary mode using the *'wb'* mode argument. (The *.cjr* extension was invented by the author.) Using the *pickle.dump()* method, the *pointList* object is written to the file. The file is then closed.

```
# Import the pickle module
import pickle

# Create Roberto
roberto = hou.node('/obj').createNode('geo', 'Roberto').
                createNode(
                'testgeometry_rubbertoy')

# Grab only the geometry points
robertoPoints = roberto.geometry().points()
# Create an empty list
pointList =[]
# Append each point position as a tuple to the list
for point in robertoPoints:
    # Create an X, Y, Z Tuple
    pos =(point.position()[0], point.position()[1], point.position()[2])
    # Append the tuple to the list
    pointList.append(pos)

# Open output file using using with context manager
with open('RobertoPoints.cjr', 'wb') as file:
    # Pickle dump the pointlist to the file
    pickle.dump(pointList, file)
```

Code Sample 14.14 Pickle Roberto's Points

Pickle Load

Python data are read from a pickled file or a byte stream string using *pickle.load()* and *pickle.loads()* methods, respectively. As a reminder, the pickle data are binary and are not human-readable; thus, the external pickle file must be opened with binary read mode, 'rb'. Language Template 14.18 demonstrates this implementation.

```
# Open Pickle file for binary reading
with open('PickleFile', 'rb') as file:
# Load the pickled data from file
PythonObject = pickle.load(file)

# Load the pickled data from the byte stream string
PythonObject = pickle.loads(ByteStreamString)
```

Language Template 14.18 pickle.load() and pickle.loads()

Code Sample 14.15 reads pickled point data, created in Code Sample 14.14, and generates the points in the Houdini display window. Because geometry cannot be created using shelf Python scripts, a *Python Node*, like the one in Figure 14.10, is required in the object level to read the pickle data. To generate a *Python Node,* create a default *Geometry Node* in the Houdini *Object level*. Double left-mouse click the new geometry node to descend into it. Drop down a *Python Node.*

Insert Code Sample 14.15 inside the *Python Node.*

```
# Import the pickle Module
import pickle

# Create a pointer to the RobertoPoints object
node = hou.pwd()
# Create a pointer to the object's Geometry
geo = node.geometry()

# Open external file to read binary data
with open('RobertoPoints.cjr', 'rb') as file:
    # Pickle load file contents to robertoPoints
    robertoPoints = pickle.load(file)
```

```
# For every point-tuple in the data
for point in robertoPoints:
    # Create a new point
    newPoint = geo.createPoint()
    # Assign the new point's position with the point data
    newPoint.setPosition(point)
```

Code Sample 14.15 Python Node Pickled Point Reader

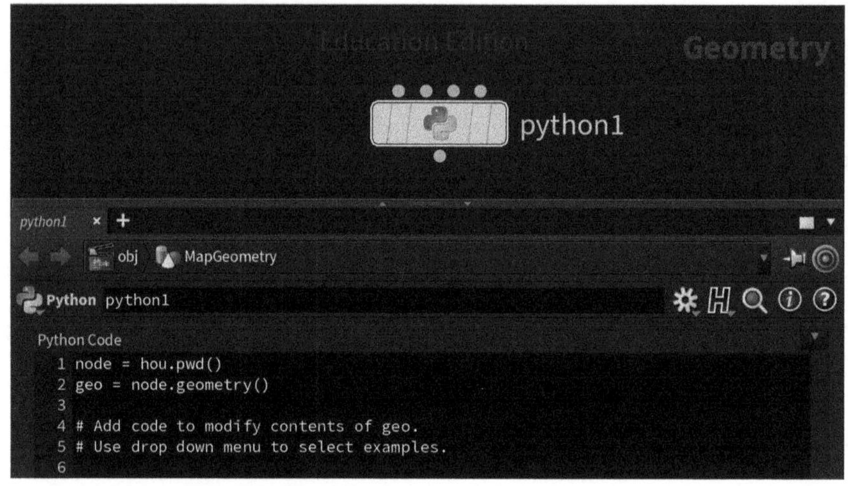

FIGURE 14.10 Houdini geometry and Python Node.

The first line of the script imports the *pickle* module. Pointer variables to the top node, *node,* and its geometry, *geo,* are assigned. The script utilizes the with context manager protocol to open the *RobertoPoints.cjr* points file and load its contents. Remember, because the file is written in binary, the open mode must be "*rb*". The pickled data are loaded from the file to the *robertoPoints* list using the pickle.*load()* method. The file is closed to finish the protocol.

Once the data are loaded, a simple loop is all that is required to plot the points. For each *point* in the *robertoPoints* list, a new point, *newPoint,* is generated using Houdini method *geo.createPoint()*. By default, all newly generated points are positioned at the origin. Since each of the components in *robertoPoints* is a tuple containing X, Y, and Z coordinates, the position of the new point is set directly with the *point* tuple, using the Houdini *setPosition()* method. The plotted points should look like Figure 14.11.

CONCLUSION

Reading and writing data to external files are one of the most important responsibilities Python programmers perform. The Python sequence for reading or writing to external files is a simple four-step process:

1. Open an external file.
2. Read and or …
3. … Write data strings to that file.
4. Close the external file.

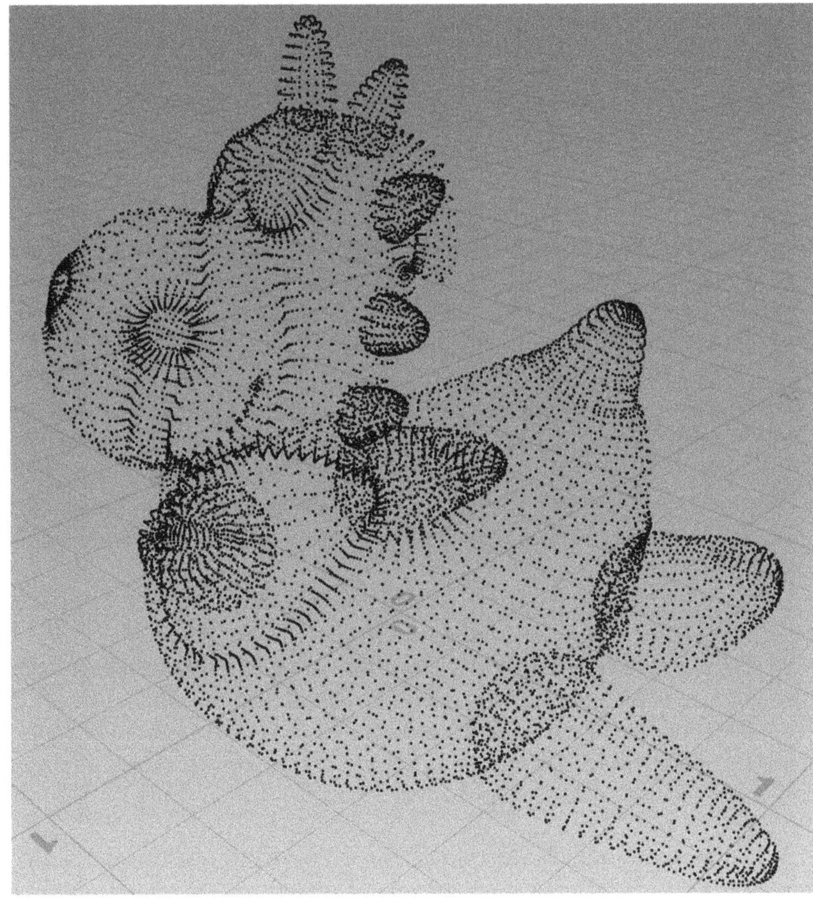

FIGURE 14.11 RobertoPoints.cjr plotted results.

There are more sophisticated variations to this sequence but the core elements remain consistent.

Opening an external file is performed using the Python *open()* command. It receives two input parameters: the external file path and the mode parameter informing if the file is to be opened for reading, writing, or both. Entire file contents are duplicated to single Python objects using the *read()* command. After data transfer, the external files should be released using the *close()* command. Releasing file resources is an important obligation all file access must achieve. Without releasing, opened files may become inaccessible to other applications and may require session log-out or even computer reboot to access.

To ensure responsible handling of external file data, programmers are encouraged to use the *with* context manager protocol to catch and handle all exceptions which occur when accessing and reading external data. The more verbose *try-finally* protocol provides the same safeguards.

Reading and writing to external files are simple and direct. Formatting and interpreting the data are challenging. Data formats such as *JSON* and *XML* standardize external information. Python provides modules for reading and writing with these formats. *JSON* is particularly effective representing long lists of structured data that fit within Python dictionaries. *XML* is effective for representing hierarchical data. Occasionally, technical artists are required to handle serialized, or *pickled* data. Being composed of binary Python objects, *pickle* data are light and fast. Any Python object or class may be *pickled* as it is not required to conform to established *JSON* and *XML* structures.

INTRODUCTION

It is hard to believe, but working with Python only within the context of Houdini may not always be practical. Technical artists have infinite opportunity outside digital content creation packages, (DCCs), to take advantage of scripting languages such as Python. Pipeline TAs often build custom tools which condition assets, move and rename files, and otherwise manipulate information that does not require graphical user interfaces (GUIs) of DCCs such as Houdini. These custom tools are accessed through the command line.

Many artists may not be familiar with the command line but all computer operating systems have some sort of simplistic interface allowing users to interact directly with the operating system. Command line interfaces are used to execute any application, perform any file related operation, (such as rename or delete a file), or reconfigure the operating system with lighting speed and accuracy. Custom scripts amplify user effectiveness more powerfully than any window interface. The command line affords all the cosmic power of the computer in an itty-bitty living space.

Technical artists need to be aware of their intended users when creating custom tools. Tools created for artists must have easy to read GUIs with intuitive flow. However, creating user-friendly interfaces can be time consuming. Tools created for technical artists by technical artists must be fast and lean and don't necessarily require GUIs. They tend to be minimalistic and perform primitive functions. These scripts are configured with arguments submitted in the command line during script invocation. Writing command line driven scripts provides a powerful technique for inputting variability without having to rewrite.

Creating Python scripts to be invoked from the command line are the focus of this chapter. This text assumes that if readers are accessing this chapter they already have another version of Python installed on their computers outside of Houdini. However, if another installation is unavailable, the Houdini Python installation should be adequate.

The first section of this chapter covers how to call Python from the command line. The second portion of this chapter introduces interaction with the command line: how to invoke Python scripts from the command line, and how to write custom scripts to receive and digest externally generated arguments.

COMMAND LINE ACCESS

Every operating system has a command line interface. However, if the reader has never heard the concept of "command line", this chapter is here to help. Technical artists have access to Houdini Python and possibly another installed version of Python. This text does not cover Python installation. Please consult with https://www.python.org/downloads for further instructions downloading and installing Python depending on your available operating system. This chapter covers command line access for basic Houdini, Windows, macOS, and Linux/UNIX.

Windows

Windows users have access to multiple command line interfaces including *cmd.exe* and *Powershell*. For simplicity, only access to *cmd.exe* is covered.

- Click the Windows "Start" icon
- In "Search programs and files" type: *cmd*

DOI: 10.1201/9781003016427-15

- A "Command Prompt App" icon should appear
- Hit "Enter"

A *Command Prompt* window should appear.

When Python has been successfully installed, typing the word *"python"* followed by the *Enter* button, like Command Line 15.1, initiates the Python command line interpreter.

```
Microsoft Windows [Version 10.0.19043.2006]
(c) Microsoft Corporation. All rights reserved.

C:\Users\croda>python
Python 3.8.8 (default, Apr 13 2021, 15:08:03) [MSC v.1916 64 bit (AMD64)]
:: Anaconda, Inc. on win32
Type "help", "copyright", "credits" or "license" for more information.
>>> quit()
```

Command Line 15.1 Windows Python Display

The output display varies on the type of Python installation. Within the context of the Python interpreter, python commands are given and executed. The *quit()* command exits the interpreter.

macOS

In macOS, the command line interface is called a *terminal*. To open a macOS terminal, perform the following steps:

- Depress the apple command key and hit the spacebar
- When the "search bar" pops up, type in the word *terminal*
- Button click on the *Terminal* application. It looks like a black rectangle with a ">_"
- The terminal application should now be open
- Dock the terminal, CTRL-click to pull up the menu, and select *Options->Keep*

The terminal application should now be open and it should be in your dock.

When Python has been successfully installed, typing the *python –version* command followed by *Enter* in the terminal should return the currently installed Python version, like the one displayed in Command Line 15.2.

```
$ python -version
Python 3.8.8 # Success!
```

Command Line 15.2 macOS Python Display

The output display varies on the type of Python installation. Within the context of the Python interpreter, python commands are given and executed. The *quit()* command exits the interpreter.

Linux/UNIX

There are many different flavors of Linux and UNIX. Since each may have its own window manager, they will have different methods for bringing up a command line interface. Look through the menu on the window manager and search for anything named *Shell, Terminal,* or *Prompt.*

Once the command line interface has been found and executed, the Python installation is verified by typing *python* and hitting *Enter.* When Python has been installed correctly, the display results should look something like Command Line 15.3. To exit the Python interpreter, type in the *quit()* command.

```
$ python
Type "help", "copyright", "credits" or "license" for more information.
>>> quit()
```

Command Line 15.3 Linux Python Display

Houdini Python

When alternative installations of Python are unavailable, Houdini Python must be used. By default, the path to Houdini Python is not appended to a computer's system path. Users comfortable or familiar with this concept are free to append to this path at their own discretion. Others must use the full Houdini Python pathname.

The full Houdini Python pathname is found in different places on different operating systems. Table 15.1 contains the default file locations for Linux/Unix, macOS, and Windows.

TABLE 15.1 Houdini Default Paths

Operating System	*Default Houdini Pathnames*	*Example*
Linux/Unix	/opt/hfs<Houdini Version>	/opt/hfs19.5.303
macOS	/Applications/Houdini/Houdini<Version>	/Applications/Houdini/Houdini19.5.303
Windows	C:\Program Files\Side Effects Software \ Houdini<Build Number>	C:\Program Files\Side Effects Software\ Houdini 19.5.493

Command Line 15.4 executes Houdini Python by typing in the default pathname followed by */python<version>/python*, (Forward slashes on macOS and Linux. Backward slashes on Windows). The Linux/Python strategy is shown in Command Line 15.5.

```
Microsoft Windows [Version 10.0.19045.2965]
(c) Microsoft Corporation. All rights reserved.

C:\Users\croda>"C:\Program Files\Side Effects Software\Houdini 19.5.493\
python39\python"
Python 3.9.10 (1 file(s) copied., Sep 15 2022, 19:40:17) [MSC v.1929 64
bit (AMD64)] on win32
Type "help", "copyright", "credits" or "license" for more information.
>>> quit()
```

Command Line 15.4 Windows Houdini Python

```
$ /opt/hfs19.5.368/python39/python
Python 3.9.10 (1 file(s) copied., Mar 29 2022, 10:47:25) [MSC v.1929 64
bit (AMD64)] on win32
Type "help", "copyright", "credits" or "license" for more information.
>>> quit()
```

Command Line 15.5 Linux/Unix Houdini Python

COMMAND LINE PYTHON

Python scripts launched from the command line do not require GUI assistance. They receive user input during invocation with command line arguments.

Script Execution

Any Python script is launchable from the command line. Using your favorite text editor, (Notepad, Atom, Vi, etc.), create Code Sample 15.1 as an external script.

```
# Import math module
import math

# Number of wedges
wedges = 10
fullAngle = 360.0
```

```
# Angle degrees for each wedge
angleSize = fullAngle/wedges
# Count from 0 to number of wedges
for count in range(wedges):
    # Calculate the angle amount
    angle = count * angleSize
    # Calculate sine for each angle
    sineValue = math.sin(math.radians(angle))
    # Display the results
    print(f'{angle} degrees -> {sineValue} radians')
```

Code Sample 15.1 angle2Rad.py

Save this script as "angle2Rad.py" in your default folder location, (the same folder where your command line opens).

Invoke the script using Language Template 15.1, with the *python* command followed by the name of the script.

```
python scriptname.py
```

Language Template 15.1 Python Script Invocation

When executed, the script should produce similar results as Command Line 15.6.

```
C:\Users\croda>python angle2rad.py
0.0 degrees -> 0.0 radians
36.0 degrees -> 0.5877852522924731 radians
72.0 degrees -> 0.9510565162951535 radians
108.0 degrees -> 0.9510565162951536 radians
144.0 degrees -> 0.5877852522924732 radians
180.0 degrees -> 1.2246467991473532e-16 radians
216.0 degrees -> -0.587785252292473 radians
252.0 degrees -> -0.9510565162951535 radians
288.0 degrees -> -0.9510565162951536 radians
324.0 degrees -> -0.5877852522924734 radians

C:\Users\croda>
```

Command Line 15.6 angle2rad.py Script Results

When non-Houdini Python installations are unavailable, the pathname to the Houdini Python installation can be used: Command Line 15.7.

```
C:\Users\croda>"C:\Program Files\Side Effects Software\Houdini 19.5.493\
python39\python" angle2rad.py
0.0 degrees -> 0.0 radians
36.0 degrees -> 0.5877852522924731 radians
72.0 degrees -> 0.9510565162951535 radians
108.0 degrees -> 0.9510565162951536 radians
144.0 degrees -> 0.5877852522924732 radians
180.0 degrees -> 1.2246467991473532e-16 radians
216.0 degrees -> -0.587785252292473 radians
252.0 degrees -> -0.9510565162951535 radians
288.0 degrees -> -0.9510565162951536 radians
324.0 degrees -> -0.5877852522924734 radians

C:\Users\croda>
```

Command Line 15.7 angle2rad.py Invoked with Houdini Python

Language Template 15.2 demonstrates scripts may be called from anywhere within the system as long as their pathnames are provided (Language Template 15.2).

```
python pathname/scriptname.py
```

Language Template 15.2 Python Path Script Invocation

In Command Line 15.8, the *angle2rad.py*script is copied to the folder *C:\Temp\EPTA*. The script is invoked directly using the *python* command or Houdini Python pathname.

```
C:\Users\croda>"C:\Program Files\Side Effects Software\Houdini 19.5.493\
python39\python" C:\Temp\EPTA\angle2rad.py
0.0 degrees -> 0.0 radians
36.0 degrees -> 0.5877852522924731 radians
72.0 degrees -> 0.9510565162951535 radians
108.0 degrees -> 0.9510565162951536 radians
144.0 degrees -> 0.5877852522924732 radians
```

```
180.0 degrees -> 1.2246467991473532e-16 radians
216.0 degrees -> -0.587785252292473 radians
252.0 degrees -> -0.9510565162951535 radians
288.0 degrees -> -0.9510565162951536 radians
324.0 degrees -> -0.5877852522924734 radians

C:\Users\croda>
```

Command Line 15.8 Full Script Path

Command Line Arguments

Information is passable to Python scripts through command line arguments. Language Template 15.3 illustrates how unlimited arguments can be inputted to user scripts through the command line.

```
python path.scriptname.py argument1 argument2 argument3 …
```

Language Template 15.3 Python Script Call with Arguments

The *sys* module is required for Python scripts to read in command line arguments. As explained in Language Template 15.4, arguments are stored in the *sys.argv* list.

```
import sys
sriptInputArguments = sys.argv
```

Language Template 15.4 Obtaining Argument List

The first list component, *sys.argv[0]*, contains the name of the script. The list remainder contains input arguments. Because input is imported into scripts from the command line, they arrive as strings. In other words, input strings must be must be converted to their correct non-string contexts such as *floats* and *ints*.

Language Template 15.5 outlines how the number of arguments is obtainable by calculating the length of the *sys.argv* list.

```
import sys
numberArguments = len(sys.argv)
```

Language Template 15.5 Obtaining Number of Arguments

In *Code Sample 15.1*, there are two constants: *wedges* and *fullAngle*. In Code Sample 15.2, *wedges* and *fullAngle* are inputted as arguments instead of hard-coded values. The number of arguments is assigned to the *numArgs* variable using the *len()* function on *sys.argv*. *Wedges* is used as an integer to drive the *for* loop and must be converted to an integer using the *int()* command. The *fullAngle* variable is required to be a float to calculate the correction division and must be converted using the *float()* command. The remainder of the script dissects the full angle amount by the number of wedges and displays the *sine* value of each wedge angle. The script is saved to *C:\Temp\EPTA\angle2radCL.py.*

```
# Import math module
import math
import sys

numArgs = len(sys.argv)
# Number of wedges
wedges = int(sys.argv[1])
# Full angle range
fullAngle = float(sys.argv[2])

# Display all input arguments
print('\nInput:')
print(f'{sys.argv[0]} inputs {numArgs} arguments:')
for count in range(numArgs):
  print(f'\t{count}: {sys.argv[count]}')

print('Output:')
# Angle degrees for each wedge
angleSize = fullAngle/wedges
# Count from 0 to number of wedges
for count in range(wedges):
  # calculate the angle amount
  angle = count * angleSize
  # Calculate sine for each angle
  sineValue = math.sin(math.radians(angle))
  # Display the results
  print(f'{angle} degrees -> {sineValue} radians')
```

Code Sample 15.2 angle2radCL.py Script with Arguments

As command line arguments, the number of *wedges* and size of *fullAngle* are arbitrary and are set only at the time of script execution. In Command Line 15.9, their values are 20 and 70, respectively.

```
C:\Users\croda>"C:\Program Files\Side Effects Software\Houdini 19.5.493\
python39\python" C:\Temp\EPTA\angle2radCL.py 20 270


Input:
C:\Temp\EPTA\angle2radCL.py inputs 3 arguments:
      0: C:\Temp\EPTA\angle2radCL.py
      1: 20
      2: 270
Output:
0.0 degrees -> 0.0 radians
13.5 degrees -> 0.2334453638559054 radians
27.0 degrees -> 0.45399049973954675 radians
40.5 degrees -> 0.6494480483301837 radians
54.0 degrees -> 0.8090169943749475 radians
67.5 degrees -> 0.9238795325112867 radians
81.0 degrees -> 0.9876883405951378 radians
94.5 degrees -> 0.996917333733128 radians
108.0 degrees -> 0.9510565162951536 radians
121.5 degrees -> 0.8526401643540923 radians
135.0 degrees -> 0.7071067811865476 radians
148.5 degrees -> 0.5224985647159489 radians
162.0 degrees -> 0.3090169943749475 radians
175.5 degrees -> 0.07845909572784507 radians
189.0 degrees -> -0.15643446504023073 radians
202.5 degrees -> -0.38268343236508967 radians
216.0 degrees -> -0.587785252292473 radians
229.5 degrees -> -0.7604059656000312 radians
243.0 degrees -> -0.8910065241883678 radians
256.5 degrees -> -0.9723699203976767 radians


C:\Users\croda>
```

Command Line 15.9 Command Line Execution of angle2RadCL.py

Working with scripts in the command line provides a powerful technique for inputting variability into scripts without having to rewrite them.

CONCLUSION

When writing tools for artists, technical artists create interesting graphical user interfaces with intuitive logic flow. However, they may create command line scripts providing efficient and powerful interfaces for themselves and other users. The command line provides a fast, powerful alternative for executing scripted functionality, with custom input, outside of scripting editors and DCCs.

All operating systems have access to interfaces enabling users to enter commands directly to the operating system called *command line interfaces*. They may also be called *terminals*, *consoles*, *shells*, and *prompt windows*. This chapter provides instructions for accessing macOS, Linux/UNIX, and Windows command line interfaces.

When Python is installed outside of Houdini, interpreters are executed from the command line with the *python* command. When Houdini Python is required, it is called with the operating system's default Houdini pathname followed by */python<version>/python*. To be command line executable, Python scripts must be unique files. They are invoked by including the script name after the *python* command.

Data and script configuration are inputted to scripts using arguments. Arguments are included after the *python* command and the script name, in the command line. The *sys* module must be imported into the script to receive command line arguments. The arguments are stored in the *sys.argv* list. The first component of the list is always the script name. The remaining list values are the arguments. All arguments are inputted as string objects and must be converted to their appropriate script contexts.

INTRODUCTION

Technical artists build tools for themselves and they build tools for others. Primitive, single-use tools are commonly invoked from the command line. Regretfully, most artists are not aware of the command line. They require accessible, intuitive, and visually pleasing workflows. Artist tools need graphic user interfaces (GUIs). Technical artists appreciate GUIs as well. They don't always have time to reverse engineer tools. Self-explanatory GUIs should tell them everything they need to know. GUIs may also remind tool creators themselves how their tools work. GUIs help improve tool usability.

This chapter explains how GUIs are implemented in Python and introduces their core integrations. There are multiple Python GUI packages, each with their benefits and limitations. This chapter is devoted to explaining how the core components of *PySide2*, a popular GUI package, are generated within the Houdini environment.

Graphical User Interface implementation is an enormous topic. This chapter does not attempt to provide justice for this vast discipline. Each GUI package is a unique language and requires time and dedication to master. Books are devoted to explaining the subtleties and nuances of each. Beyond implementation, the art of interface design is best explained through books like *Don't Make me Think* by Steve Krug and *The Design of Everyday Things* by Don Norman.

The GUI examples in this chapter are created using *PySide2* in Houdini. The author does not believe this is the best package for all users in all situations. When interested, readers should try other packages and decide which best satisfies the essential requirements for their tasks. *PySide2* is included with all Houdini installations and works well within the Houdini environment. Certainly not a thorough reference, readers are also encouraged to seek supplemental documentation found in https://doc.qt.io/qtforpython-5/contents.html.

INTERFACE MODULES

Multiple Python GUI packages are available. Some require licensing, such as *PyQt5*. Others, such as *Tkinter*, do not. While all have their advantages and disadvantages, some are more ideal for certain situations than others.

Tkinter

The *Tkinter* package installs with every standard version of Python. It is the standard Python interface to the *TCL/Tk* GUI toolkit. Since *TCL/Tk* has been available since the early 1990s, it is rock solid and predictable across most platforms. It has a very simple and brief syntax and is ideal for beginning programmers without a strong understanding of classes. This simplicity, however, becomes unwieldly with complex interfaces. As a wrapper for a *TCL* interpreter, the package may slow down translating every command to *TCL*. Debugging can be challenging. One of the biggest drawbacks against *Tkinter* when used for artists' tools is its appearance. See Figure 16.1. It has a 1990s presentation and may put off artists as not conforming to native operating systems' look-and-feel. Native simplicity is lost when the default style is altered.

PyQt5

PyQt5, supported by Riverbank Computing Limited, is an elaborate set of bindings for the Qt libraries. Written in C++, *Qt* provides GUIs for multiple platforms for a wide variety of desktop and mobile applications. *Houdini*, *Maya*, and *Nuke* are examples of popular interfaces generated with *Qt*.

DOI: 10.1201/9781003016427-16

FIGURE 16.1 Tkinter GUI window.

PyQt5 supports flexible coding in multiple platforms. It promotes communication between interface objects and smoothly handles interface events through the concept of *signals* and *slots* (introduced later in the chapter). It provides a plethora of widgets, including buttons and menus that complement the look and feel of their supported platforms (see Figure 16.2). Integrated support for networking, database, multimedia, and browser development is provided. Because *PyQt5* wraps the *Qt* libraries, its usage is user-friendly and straight forward. A GUI creation

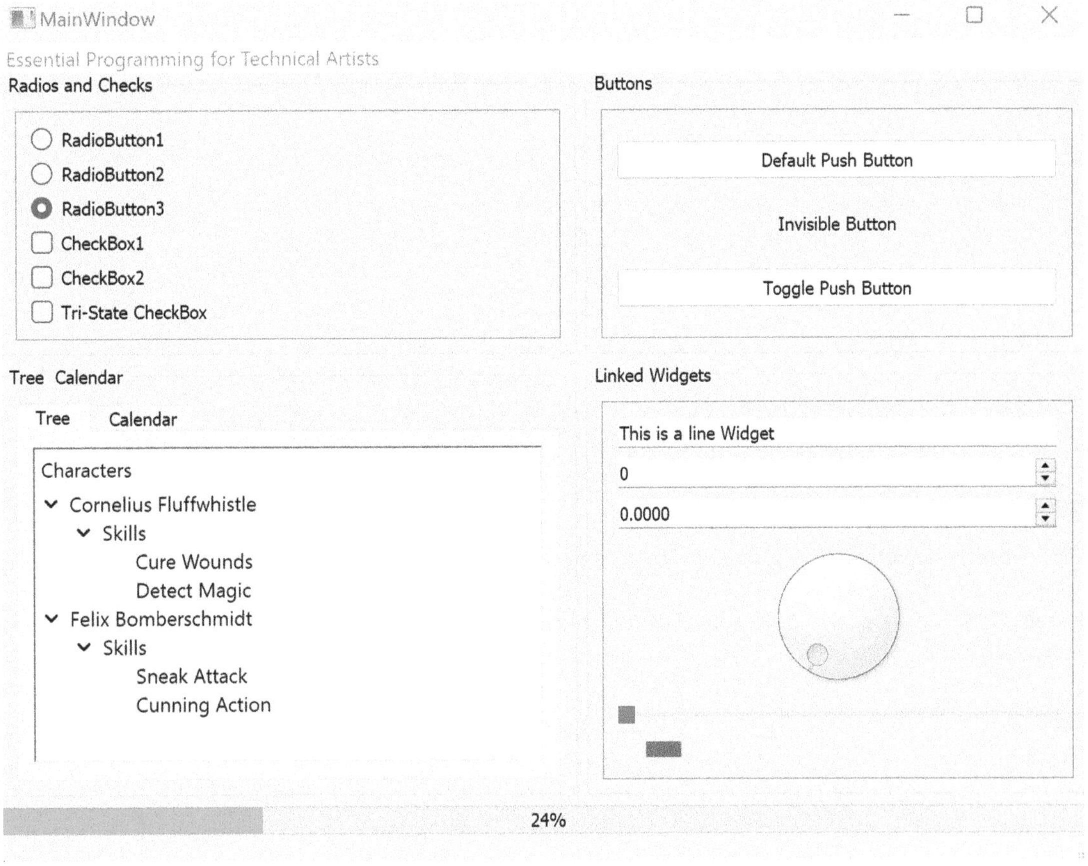

FIGURE 16.2 PyQt5 GUI window.

interface, *QtDesigner*, is provided to facilitate fast GUI creation. Interface code may be integrated within core Python code or be imported as external modules.

Mastering *PyQt5* requires a steep learning curve because the library is vast and there may not be adequate Python-specific documentation for the C++ classes. Learning and developing with *PyQt5* are free. *PyQt5*, however, is restricted by *GPL* licensing. This does not limit commercial sales of applications created with *PyQt5*. It means that the source code must be released with applications. When this is not a possibility, *Riverbank Commercial Licenses* must be purchased.

PySide2

To circumnavigate *PyQt5* licensing issues, there is *PySide2*. *PySide2* is the official module from *Qt for Python Project*, which provides access to the complete Qt framework. *PySide2* duplicates the syntax and functionality of *PyQt5* with very few differences. From the beginner's perspective, there is virtually no difference between the two software packages. *PySide2* installs with every version of Houdini and Maya and is easily accessible through Python scripting. When desired, *Pyside2* is easily installed into any Python installation outside of Houdini or Maya.

PySide is governed by *LGPL* licenses which means that the source code is only required to be released when the source for *PySide2* has been altered. Because of the licensing and ease of access, *Pyside2* is demonstrated in this chapter instead of *Pyqt5*.

When technical artists need their interfaces to be portable, *Qt.py* could be considered. It is available at https://github.com/mottosso/Qt.py. *Qt.py* is a wrapper that supports any of the supported bindings: *Pyside2*, *PyQt5*, *PySide*, and *PyQt4*. While the library requires installation, it is easy to use as it is written in the *PySide2* syntax but supports all of the mentioned bindings.

Other Packages

There are multiple other GUI packages available for Python including *Kivy*, *wxPython*, *Libavg*, and *PySimpleGUI*. They are good packages and have excellent application for their designed applications.

Kivy

Kivy is an excellent GUI package for creating mobile applications. It is an open source, multi-platform, GUI development Python library runnable on *iOS*, *Android*, *Windows*, *OS X*, and *GNU/Linux*. It can be a bit difficult to learn, especially when dealing with its *Size* and *Pos* (position) properties. However, once mastered Kivy can be used to create good looking applications with very few lines of code.

wxPython

wxPython is another open source, cross-platform Python GUI toolkit. Due to its simplicity and ease of use, it is considered as an alternative to *Tkinter*. It has a large variety of feature rich widgets and supports a modern look and design. There has not been a tremendous amount of recent support for the packages. However, a major version was released at the time of this book's writing.

libAvg

libAvg is another powerful Python GUI toolkit focusing on media-centric applications. It is a Python wrapper around a C++ core and uses *OpenGL* for output display. It is very effective for developing *Touch UI* applications (applications taking advantage of touch devices). It supports all the major touch drivers such as Windows Touch, Linux XInput, and TUIO.

PySimpleGUI

As the name implies, *PySimpleGUI* was created to empower Python programmers to create fast and simple interfaces that could require significantly more code than in other packages. The package itself wraps around *Tkinter, Qt5, wxPython*, and *Remi* (a web-based interface). The package has only been around since 2018 and may not be as robust as the prior mentioned interface packages. It, however, has very liberal licensing and encourages others to expand the library.

PYSIDE2 FUNDAMENTALS

The *PyQt5/PySide2* library is direct, forward, and easy to learn despite its extensiveness. This section of the chapter starts by introducing the very basics. Object-oriented structure is introduced to make organizational code flow more smoothly and give GUI code autonomy from the rest of the applications. The concepts of signals and slots are explained and demonstrated, and are essential for understanding widget library behavior.

First Window

The first window example is simple but there are subtle differences between the Houdini and non-Houdini PySide2 installations. The Houdini interface approach is explained first and then the non-Houdini, command line version.

Houdini Version

The first *PySide2* Houdini example is just a handful of lines long but requires thorough explanation. Create Code Sample 16.1 in a Houdini shelf Python tool.

```
# Import the QtWidgets module
from PySide2.QtWidgets import QWidget


# Instantiate the first widget object
window = QWidget()
# Display the widget
window.show()
```

Code Sample 16.1 PySideSimplest Widget

The first line of code imports the *QWidget* class from *PySide2*'s *QtWidgets* module. The next line instances the first *QWidget* object. This object is a simple, non-descript window. The final statement instructs the widgets to display itself in the viewport.

When the script is launched from the toolbar, a window pops onto the display for a moment and immediately disappears, or never appears at all.

Understanding of core level interfaces is required to explain this disappearance or lack of appearance. An interface window needs to exist on its own thread, almost like a baby program. When interfaces are part of original application threads, they freeze the applications while waiting for user interaction. The *Qt* widget library creates new threads to prevent interruption. However, Python is always cleaning memory and processes it thinks disposable. Our window's disappearance is the results of Python's garbage collection. To get around this pruning, we need to inform Python that our baby window is part of the larger Houdini application.

Houdini is built upon the core *Qt* library. Regretfully, it is so deep in code, and therefore, extra tools are needed to extract original thread information preventing removal during garbage collection. Code Sample 16.2 provides a few extra lines of code to display new widget windows without being 'cleaned' or freezing the interface.

To retrieve Houdini's core Qt thread information, the *QtCore* class from the *hutil.Qt* module must be imported after the *PySide2* QtWidgets. The *hou.qt.mainWindow()* method retrieves Houdini's main window thread and assigns it to the *parentWindow* object. The *setParent()* method from the *QWidget* object uses the window information to attach itself to Houdini's core window thread so that the new window is not cleaned during Python's garbage collection. When displayed, the new window will not be thrown out with the trash and appear like Figure 16.3.

```
# Import the QtWidgets module
from PySide2.QtWidgets import QWidget
# Import Houdini's Qt Tool
from hutil.Qt import QtCore

# Instantiate the first widget object
window = QWidget()
# Get Houdini's window thread
parentWindow = hou.qt.mainWindow()
# Attach to parent thread
window.setParent(parentWindow, QtCore.Qt.Window)
# Display the widget
window.show()
```

Code Sample 16.2 PySideSimple.py Code

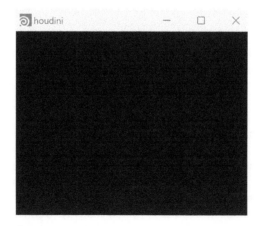

FIGURE 16.3 PySideSimple.py result window.

Command Line Version

The non-Houdini, command line example, Code Sample 16.3, does not require new widget windows to attach themselves to executing window processes. Instead, they use the *QtWidgets* module to create wrapper applications which shield new windows from Python garbage collection.

```
# Import the system tool module
import sys
# Import the QtWidgets module
from PySide6.QtWidgets import QWidget,QApplication

# Create a QApplication wrapper
app = QApplication(sys.argv)
# Create the first widget object
window = QWidget()
# Display the widget
window.show()

# Launch the wrapper application
app.exec()
```

Code Sample 16.3 CLPySideSimple.py

Code Sample 16.3 is called using the *python* command with the full path of the script. The result should look like Figure 16.4. (Note: Code Sample 16.3 imports its widgets from the *PySide6* library and the author assumes readers to have already installed the *PySide6* library to their Python environment.)

The first line of the script imports the *sys* module. This is used to provide any command line arguments for the application wrapper. The application wrapper is created using the *QApplication()* method. The *window* variable object is created using the *QWidget()* method and then displayed with the *show()* command. To prevent Python Garbage collection from cleaning the new window, application wrappers must be executed using the *exec_()* command. Once the wrapper is executed, the window is displayed and will persist until closed by the user. The only difference between interfaces launched in Houdini and launched from the command line is the inclusion of this wrapper function. In the earlier example, Houdini is the application the window is parented. In the prior example, the application must be created using the wrapper function.

FIGURE 16.4 Command line call and result of QtSimple.py.

Widget Classes

In the previous example, the interface code was written intermixed with core logic flow. (Technically, there was no core logic, just interface calls.) While there is technically nothing wrong with this approach, it does not promote smooth coding as the interface and core logic increase in size and complexity. A better strategy is to structure interfaces into their own object-oriented classes. Working in this way provides two benefits. First it separates interface creation and event handling from the functional purpose of the script. Second, because they are their own classes, they can be saved as separate Python modules and imported by multiple scripts.

Class Declaration

Declaring classes as children of existing widget classes defines new interface widget classes. In Code Sample 16.4, thearent classes'__init__() methods, launched via *super()* command, implement initialization. Once defined, new custom classes are ready to be instantiated and displayed.

```
# Import the QtWidgets module
from PySide2.QtWidgets import QWidget

# Declare class as a child class
class MyWidget(QWidget):
    def __init__(self):
        # Use inherited __init()__ method
        super().__init__()

# Instantiate Class
window = MyWidget()
# Display Widget
window.show()
```

Code Sample 16.4 MyWidget Class

When new child widget classes are used within the Houdini context, new interface threads require no attachment to Houdini windows to avoid garbage collection. Through instantiation of new child classes, they inherit relative parent window threads by default.

External Modules

Defining custom widget classes as external modules provides their utility to multiple scripts. External modules are created by saving class declarations to external files. Note that importing parent class modules is still required as custom child classes reference their methods.

When creating external modules in Houdini scripts, remember to store them to the *<User Default Path>**<Houdini version>**<Python Version>libs* folder.

When utilizing external modules for command line scripts, they must be stored in a folder covered by the *PYTHONPATH* system variable. Directory folders covered by *PYTHONPATH* are identified by printing the *sys.path* variable value within the Python interpreter. The custom module may be stored in any of the folders covered by the *PYTHONPATH* system variable. Code Sample 16.5 is written to be an external module.

```
# Import the QtWidgets module
from PySide2.QtWidgets import QWidget

# Declare class as a child class
class MyWidget(QWidget):
    def __init__(self):
        # Use inherited __init()__ method
        super().__init__()
```

Code Sample 16.5 External Module Saved as "CustomWidget.py"

The prior example module is stored in appropriate location as *"CustomWidget.py"*.

Houdini Usage

When integrated into Houdini scripts, custom modules are imported. Instantiations of the class are assigned and displayed. This is demonstrated in Code Sample 16.6.

```
# Import external module
from CustomWidget import MyWidget
# Import Houdini's Qt Tool
from hutil.Qt import QtCore

# Instantiate Class
widgetObject = MyWidget()
# Attach to parent thread
widgetObject.setParent(hou.qt.mainWindow(), QtCore.Qt.Window)
# Display Widget
widgetObject.show()
```

Code Sample 16.6 Houdini Script Using the External Custom Class Module

Regretfully, because *PySide2* modules are external files, new object classes must attach themselves to parent Houdini window threads before displaying.

Command Line Usage

Like the Houdini, command line scripts must import custom modules. They must also import the *sys* module and *QApplication* class from the *PySide2.QtWidgets* module. These are required to create a wrapper application, as shown in Code Sample 16.7, around the new widget instantiations to avoid Python garbage collection. (Code Sample 16.7 assumes that reader has already installed the PySide6 library to their Python environment.)

```
# Import the QtWidgets module
from PySide6.QtWidgets import QWidget

# Declare class as a child class
class MyWidget(QWidget):
    def __init__(self):
        # Use inherited __init()__ method
        super(MyWidget, self).__init__()
```

Code Sample 16.7 External Module Saved for Command Line Usage as "CustomWidget.py"

```
# Import external module
from CustomWidget import MyWidget
from PySide6.QtWidgets import QApplication
import sys

# Create the wrapper application
app = QApplication(sys.argv)
# Instantiate Class
widgetObject = MyWidget()
# Display Widget
widgetObject.show()

# Execute wrapper application
app.exec()
```

Code Sample 16.8 Command Line Script Using the External Custom Class Module

Code Sample 16.8 demonstrates the structure necessary for executing command line *PySide6* scripts: importing custom, sys and *QApplication* modules, creating wrapper applications, and executing them.

Layouts

Layouts provide the structure and order to Qt applications. Instantiations of *QLayout* widgets generate containers of symmetric, easy to read interface arrangements by procedurally manipulating the sizes and positions of contained child widgets. Their size constraints, alignments, margins, and spacings are configurable. Technical artists utilize *QBoxLayout* and *QGridLayout* subclasses most often. (Actually, *QBoxLayout is* further subdivided into *QHBoxLayout and QVBoxLayout* subclasses). Advanced users also employ *QStackedLayouts* (a subclass for creating "tab-stacked" widgets displaying only one tab at a given moment), and *QFormLayouts* (a convenience subclass for laying out widgets in two-column format).

FIGURE 16.5 QHBoxLayout.

Child widgets are appended into *QLayout* instantiations using the *addWidget()* command. Child widget instantiations are identified to their parent widget's layout using their *setLayout()* command.

QHBoxLayout

A *QHBoxLayout* organizes its child widgets in a horizontal structure, as displayed in Figure 16.5.

In Code Sample 16.9, a *QHBoxLayout* is instantiated to the *hbox* object. Simple buttons are created by instantiating *QPushButton* classes. The first argument for the *QPushButton* is the button's text display; the second is a reference to the parent *QWidget* class. Each button is appended to *hbox* using the *addWidget()* command. The *hbox* layout object is then identified as its *QWidget* parent class' layout using the *setLayout()* command.

```
# Import required widgets
from PySide2.QtWidgets import QWidget, QHBoxLayout, QPushButton


class HBoxDemo(QWidget):
    def __init__(self):
        # Initiate the parent's constructor
        super().__init__()

        # Instantiate QHBoxLayout
        hbox = QHBoxLayout()

        # Create a QPushButton Instantiation
        button1 = QPushButton('#1', self)
        # Append button instantiation to layout
        hbox.addWidget(button1)
        # Create a QPushButton Instantiation
        button2 = QPushButton('#2', self)
        # Append button instantiation to layout
        hbox.addWidget(button2)
```

```
        # Create a QPushButton Instantiation
        button3 = QPushButton('#3', self)
        # Append button instantiation to layout
        hbox.addWidget(button3)

        # set Widget's Layout
        self.setLayout(hbox)

# Create an instantiation of HBoxDemo class
demo = HBoxDemo()
# Display the instantiation
demo.show()
```

Code Sample 16.9 QHBoxLayout Instantiation

QVBoxLayout

A *QVBoxLayout* organizes its child widgets in a vertical structure, as displayed in Figure 16.6.

In Code Sample 16.10, a *QVBoxLayout* is instantiated to the *vbox* variable. Simple buttons are created by instantiating *QPushButton* classes. The first argument for the *QPushButton* is the button's text display; the second is a reference to the parent *QWidget* class. Each button is appended to *vbox* using the *addWidget()* command. The *vbox* layout object is then identified as its *QWidget* parent class' layout using the *setLayout()* command.

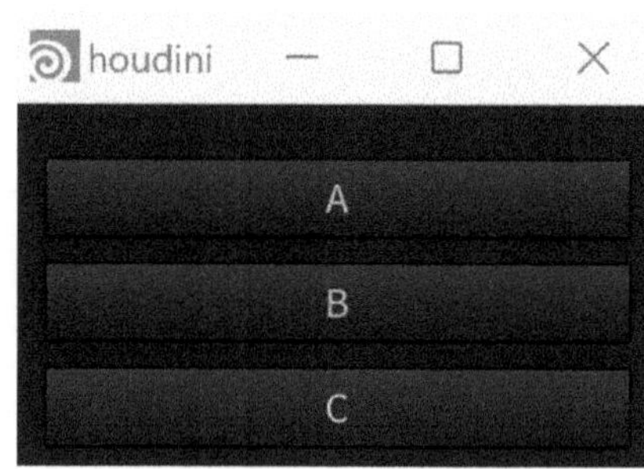

FIGURE 16.6 QVBoxLayout instantiation.

```
# Import required widgets
from PySide2.QtWidgets import QWidget, QVBoxLayout, QPushButton

class VBoxDemo(QWidget):
    def __init__(self):
        # Initiate the parent's constructor
        super().__init__()

        # Instantiate QVBoxLayout
        vbox = QVBoxLayout()

        # Create a QPushButton Instantiation
        button1 = QPushButton('#1', self)
        # Append button instantiation to layout
        vbox.addWidget(button1)
        # Create a QPushButton Instantiation
        button2 = QPushButton('#2', self)
        # Append button instantiation to layout
        vbox.addWidget(button2)
        # Create a QPushButton Instantiation
        button3 = QPushButton('#3', self)
        # Append button instantiation to layout
        vbox.addWidget(button3)

        # set Widget's Layout
        self.setLayout(vbox)

# Create an instantiation of VBoxDemo class
demo = VBoxDemo()
# Display the instantiation
demo.show()
```

Code Sample 16.10 QVBoxLayout Instantiation

QGridLayout

A *QGridLayout* organizes its child widgets in a grid-like structure. The big difference between *QBoxLayouts* and *QGridLayouts* is the *addWidget()* command. The *QGridLayout addWidget()* command not only requires a reference for the to-be-appended widget but also its row and column position, as explained in Language Template 16.1.

```
gridLayoutObject.addWidget(widgetObject, rowPosition, columnPosition)
```

Language Template 16.1 QGridLayout addWidget() Command

In Code Sample 16.11, a *QGridLayout* is instantiated to the *grid* object. The number of buttons and columns is defined respectively as: *numButtons* and *numColumns*. A simple *for* loop iterates variable *i* through the range of `[0→(numbuttons - 1)]`, to create a *numButtons* button grid; *numColumns* wide and **`numButtons/numColumns`** rows deep. For each iteration, a button is created using the iteration number as the button name. Each button is appended to the layout and includes its row and column positions, using the *addWIdget()* method. The row number is set using the floor division of the iteration number and the number of columns; **`i//numColumns`**. (Floor division returns the integer portion of the result and discards everything after the decimal.) The column number is set using the *modulus* of the iteration number and the number of columns; **`i%numColumns`**. The *grid* layout object is then identified as its *QWidget* parent class' layout using the *setLayout()* command. The two-dimensional button grid is displayed in Figure 16.7.

```
# Import required widgets
from PySide2.QtWidgets import QWidget, QGridLayout, QPushButton


class GridDemo(QWidget):
    def __init__(self):
        # Initiate the parent's constructor
        super().__init__()

        numButtons = 10
        numColumns = 5

        # Create QGridLayout Instantiation
        grid = QGridLayout()

        # For loop to create 10 buttons
        for i in range(numButtons):
            # Instantiate a button
            button = QPushButton(f'button {i}', self)
```

```
            # Append to grid layout with positions
            grid.addWidget(button, i//numColumns, i%numColumns)

        # set Widget's Layout
        self.setLayout(grid)

# Create an instantiation of GridDemo class
demo = GridDemo()
# Display the instantiation
demo.show()
```

Code Sample 16.11 QGridLayout Instantiation

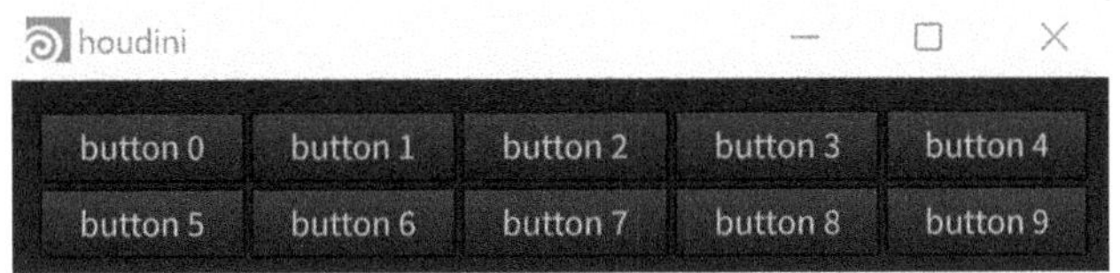

FIGURE 16.7 QGridLayout instantiation.

Signals and Slots

All user interactions are called *events*. Pressing a button, pulling a slider, moving the curser into a window, selecting a file, checking a box, etc., are all events. Events can be handled by one of two strategies: class functions, called *callbacks*, designated to handle those specific events and *signals and* slots, a Qt system for connecting multiple events with multiple functions.

Callbacks, introduced in Language Template 16.2, are subclass functions created to handle inherited events.

```
class CustomButton(QPushButon):
    def keyPressEvent(self, eventInfo):
        super(CustomButton, self).keyPressEvent(eventInfo)
```

Language Template 16.2 Abstract Custom Callback

A more dynamic strategy is required to handle literally hundreds of interactive gizmos and display devices interconnected to each other. Instead of requiring programmers to create callbacks to intercept all possible events, Qt supports a system of *signals and slots*. Whenever an interface object's internal state changes, it emits a *signal*. Signals propagate to all *slot* functions connected to them. *Slots* execute upon receiving connected signals. All functions are considered as potential *slots*. Multiple slots may be connected to single signals and multiple signals may be connected to single slots. For example, a single button press may generate multiple objects and bring up a new interface to edit these objects. Conversely, the "X" button on the upper window corner and the "Close" menu option may call the same shutdown process. Signals and slots provide a powerful component communication mechanism without requiring specific function calls for every callback possibility.

All possible Qt widget events emit signals. *Signals* are connected to *slots* by identifying the signal name followed by the *connect()* command with the *slot* name parameter. Their implementation is demonstrated in Language Template 16.3.

```
self.<Signal Name>.connect(<Slot Function Name>)
```

Language Template 16.3 Connecting a Slot Function to a Subclass Signal

Code Sample 16.12 demonstrates two concepts: how any function is connected to a widget signal, and how a widget can be enclosed around other widget. The *button.clicked.connect(self.printHello)* command connects the *printHello()* function to the *clicked* button signal. The *hbox* object is an instantiated *QHBoxLayout* widget. Layout widgets, such as *QHBoxLayout()*, organize its child widgets into specified layouts (a horizontal layout in this case). Once all widgets are instantiated and modified, they must be enclosed around other widgets to be displayed. The *hbox.addWidget(button)* command adds the *button* widget to *hbox* object. The *self.setLayout(hbox)* command identifies the *hbox* object as the primary layout enclosure for the parent *QWidget*. The *printHello()* function may do anything. It's only purpose in this context is to receive signals from the *button* widget and display a message.

```
# Import required widgets
from PySide2.QtWidgets import QWidget, QHBoxLayout, QPushButton


# Demo class is a subclass of QWidget
class SignalSlotDemo(QWidget):
    def __init__(self):
        # Initiate the parent's constructor
        super().__init__()

        # Create a Horizontal Layout box to contain our widgets
        hbox = QHBoxLayout()
        # Create a push Button Widget
        button = QPushButton('Hello', self)
        # Connect printHello function with button clicked signal
        button.clicked.connect(self.printHello)
        # Add the button to the Horizontal Layout Widget
        hbox.addWidget(button)
```

```
        # Add the Horizontal Layout widget to the QWidget
        self.setLayout(hbox)

    # Declare the connected slots for the button clicked signal
    def printHello(self):
        print("Essential Programming for Technical Artists")


# Create an instantiation of SIgnalSlotDemo class
demo = SignalSlotDemo()
# Display the instantiation
demo.show()
```

Code Sample 16.12 SignalSlotDemo Code

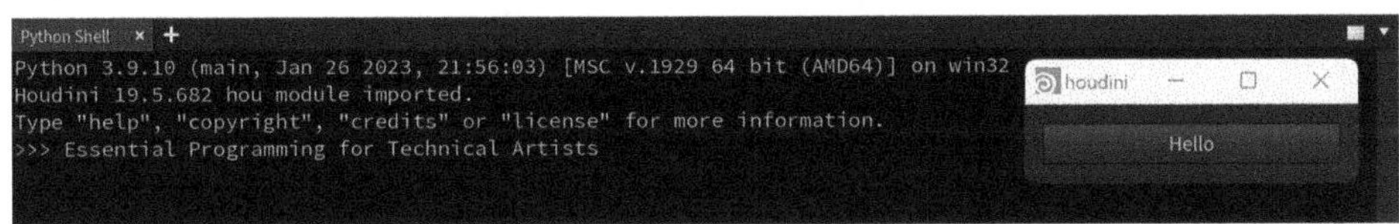

FIGURE 16.8 SignalSlotDemo widget and text output.

Code Sample 16.12 produces a widget like Figure 16.8 and outputs text message, "Essential Programming for Technical Artists", when the button is pressed.

The order upon which signals and slots are identified is important. Slots connected to signals after specific events have occurred cannot be expected to handle those prior events. However, they can handle future occurrences. As an example, consider Code Sample 16.13.

```
# Import required widgets
from PySide2.QtWidgets import QWidget, QHBoxLayout, QPushButton


# Demo class is a subclass of QWidget
class OrderDemo(QWidget):
    def __init__(self):
```

```
        # Initiate the parent's constructor
        super().__init__()

        self.setWindowTitle('Initial Order')
        # Connect slot to signal
          self.windowTitleChanged.connect(self.onWindowTitleChange)

        # Create a Horizontal Layout box to contain our widgets
        hbox = QHBoxLayout()
        # Create a push Button Widget
        button = QPushButton('Hello', self)
        # Connect the printHello function to clicked signal
        button.clicked.connect(self.printHello)

        # Add the button to the Horizontal Layout Widget
        hbox.addWidget(button)
        # Add the Horizontal Layout widget to the QWidget
        self.setLayout(hbox)

    # Declare the connected slots for the button clicked signal
    def printHello(self):
        print("Essential Programming for Technical Artists")

    # Define the onWindowTitleChanged slot
    def onWindowTitleChange(self, s):
        print(f'The output of the window change is "{s}"')



# Create an instantiation of OrderDemo class
demo = OrderDemo()
# Display the instantiation
demo.show()
```

Code Sample 16.13 WindowTitleChanged Event

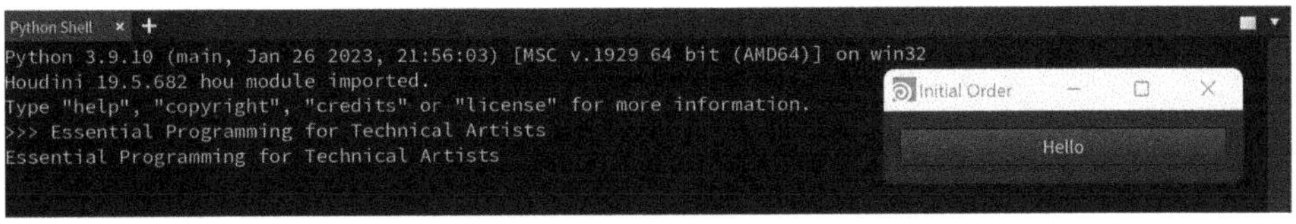

FIGURE 16.9 WindowTitleChanged order example.

The self.windowTitleChanged.connect(self.onWindowTitleChange) command connects the onWindowTitleChange() method to the windowTitleChanged signal. During execution, the onWindowTitleChange() method is never invoked since the setWindowTitle event happens prior to the *windowTitleChanged* signal connection. The output is displayed in Figure 16.9.

Code Sample 16.14 is almost a duplicate except there is a second *self.setWindowTitle()* command after the *onWindowTitleChange* slot has been connected to the *windowTitleChanged* signal. The second self.setWindowTitle() command changes the *MainWindow's* state, emitting a *windowTitleChanged* signal and handled by the *onWindowTitleChanged()* slot function.

```
# Import required widgets
from PySide2.QtWidgets import QWidget, QHBoxLayout, QPushButton


# Demo class is a subclass of QWidget
class OrderDemo(QWidget):
    def __init__(self):
        # Initiate the parent's constructor
        super().__init__()

        self.setWindowTitle('Initial Order')
        # Connect slot to signal
        self.windowTitleChanged.connect(self.onWindowTitleChange)

        # Title Changed after slot connected to signal
        self.setWindowTitle('Final Order')

        # Create a Horizontal Layout box to contain our widgets
        hbox = QHBoxLayout()
        # Create a push Button Widget
        button = QPushButton('Hello', self)
```

```
        # Connect the printHello function to clicked signal
        button.clicked.connect(self.printHello)

        # Add the button to the Horizontal Layout Widget
        hbox.addWidget(button)
        # Add the Horizontal Layout widget to the QWidget
        self.setLayout(hbox)

    # Declare the connected slot for the button clicked signal
    def printHello(self):
        print("Essential Programming for Technical Artists")

    # Define the onWindowTitleChange slot
    def onWindowTitleChange(self, s):
        print(f'The output of the window change is "{s}"')



# Create an instantiation of OrderDemo class
demo = OrderDemo()
# Display the instantiation
demo.show()
```

Code Sample 16.14 WindowTitleChanged Order Example 2

Note that while there were only subtle changes to the *QWidget* class, changing the title the second time elicits the onWindowTitleChange() function slot to display it's message shown in Figure 16.10.

Slots with Arguments

When connecting slots to widget signals using the *connect()* command, users may only provide one string identifying the name of the intended slot function. There are no provisions for adding arguments to the function calls. There are two techniques for providing signal slot argument customization: *lambda*, and *functools.partial()*..

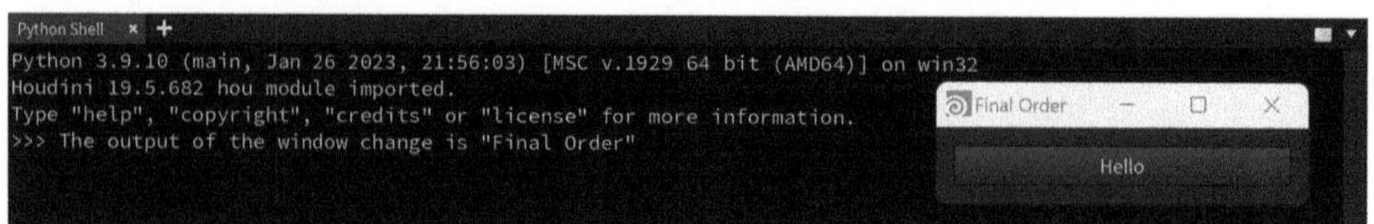

FIGURE 16.10 WindowTitleChanged order 2.

Lambda functions are covered in Chapter 9. As a review, lambda functions are simple, anonymous functions that have no name but can be assigned to variable objects. They may have any number of arguments but only return the results of one expression: Language Template 16.4.

```
variable = lambda argument(s): expression
```

Language Template 16.4 Python Lambda Function

The *lambda* function replaces the function name string with a full expression slot function call with arguments. Regretfully, *lambda* functions exhibit a peculiar side effect. For reasons beyond the scope of this text, when used within a loop, only the arguments of the last *lambda* call are utilized. Multiple *connect* calls using *lambda* require sequential coding. To get around this phenomenon, the *functools.partial()* method is encouraged.

Using *functools.partial()* is the preferred method for connecting slot functions with arguments. In a nutshell, the *functools* module creates higher order functions that interact with other functions. The *partial()* method "freezes" arguments of passed functions. In other words, the *functools.partial()*method allows successive *connect()* calls to be performed in loops without side effects.

Language Template 16.5 demonstrates the inputs to the *partial()* method are the function name, its arguments, followed by its keywords, when required.

```
functools.partial(functionName, /, *arguments, **keywords)
```

Language Template 16.5 functools.partial() Method

(Used within this context, the "/," and "**keywords" can be ignored.)

Code Sample 16.15 demonstrates both strategies. It creates four different *QtPushButtons* widgets. The first two widget clicked events are connected using lambda slot functions. The second two are performed in a loop using the *functools.partial()* strategy. Each lambda function has no arguments of its own and returns the results of the *self.printButton()* function with the button object argument. The *partial()* method "freezes" the argument states upon invocation and submits the results to the *connect()*command. The *self.printButton()* function receives the button parameter, acquires the text information from the button, and displays it in a text message. Only one slot function is required to handle all of the *clicked* signals.

```
# Import required widgets
from PySide2.QtWidgets import QWidget, QHBoxLayout, QPushButton
# Import functools.partial() to connect slots in loop
from functools import partial


# Demo class is a subclass of QWidget class lambdaDemo(QWidget):
    def __init__(self):
```

```
        # Initiate the parent's constructor
        super().__init__()
        self.setWindowTitle('Ramones')

        # Create a Horizontal Layout box to conotain our widgets
        hbox = QHBoxLayout()

        # Create a push Button Widget
        buttonA = QPushButton('Johnny', self)
        # Connect signal to the printButtonName Slot
        buttonA.clicked.connect(lambda:self.printButtonName(buttonA))
        # Add the button to the Horizontal Layout Widget
        hbox.addWidget(buttonA)

        # Create a push Button Widget
        buttonB = QPushButton('Joey', self)
        buttonB.clicked.connect(lambda:self.printButtonName(buttonB))
        hbox.addWidget(buttonB)

        # Loops should use functools.partial()
        for name in ('Marky', 'Dee Dee'):
            bx = QPushButton(name, self)
            # Only last prints last button!
            #bx.clicked.connect(lambda:self.printButtonName(bx))
            # functool.partial() avoids lambda loop problem
            bx.clicked.connect(partial(self.printButtonName, bx))
            hbox.addWidget(bx)

        # Add the Horizontal Layout widget to the QWidget
        self.setLayout(hbox)

    # Receive the Button object
    def printButtonName(self, button=None):
```

```
        # Insert the Button text information
        print(f'The {button.text()} button was pressed')


demo = lambdaDemo
demo.show()
```

Code Sample 16.15 Python Lambda as Signal Slot

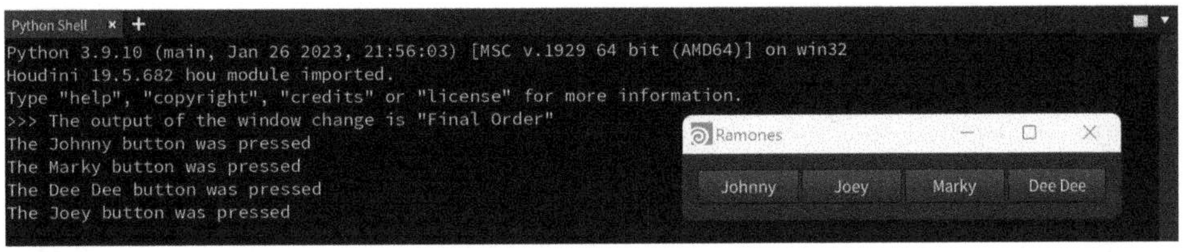

FIGURE 16.11 Slot argument demo results.

Figure 16.11 demonstrates the results of the interface and the displayed results after each of the buttons has been pressed.

Customizing with Icons and Pixmaps

Adding custom two-dimensional images to widgets is achieved with *QPixmaps* and *QIcons*. *QPixmaps* and *QIcons* are customizable, image processing mini-engines. They complement other interactive widgets. For example, *QLabels* receive *QPixmaps* and *QPushButtons* receive *QIcons*. *QPixmaps* display two-dimensional images from a wide variety of sources, such as "PNG" and "JPG". The objects provide reading, writing, and transformational functionality. *QPixMaps* display basic texture images. More sophisticated *QIcons* display larger, smaller, active, and disabled variations from provided pixmap sets. These displayable states make them ideal for complementing variable state action widgets.

Code Sample 16.16 takes advantage of *QPixmaps* and *QIcons* which must be imported from the *PySide2.QtGui* libray. A *QPixmap* object, *myPixmap*, is created from an external *.png* file. It is scaled using its inherited *scaledToWidth()* method. The *myPixmap* object is assigned to a *QLabel* object using its *setPixmap()* method. The example also has four *QtPushButtons*. Each button is complemented with a *QIcon*. Each *QIcon* loads an external two-dimensional image during its creation and is associated with its respective *QtPushButton* object using its *setIcon()* method. The results are displayed in Figure 16.12.

```
# Import required widgets
from PySide2.QtWidgets import QWidget, QHBoxLayout, QPushButton, QLabel
from PySide2.QtGui import QIcon, QPixmap
# Import functools.partial for the widget loop
from functools import partial
```

```
# Demo class is a subclass of QWidget
class imageDemo(QWidget):
    def __init__(self):
        # Initiate the parent's constructor
        super().__init__()
        self.setWindowTitle('Tech Art Goodies')

        # Create a Horizontal Layout box to contain our widgets
        hbox = QHBoxLayout()

        logo = QLabel(self)
        # Create and scale Pixmap
        myPixmap = QPixmap("C:\Temp\EPTA\pixmaps\logo.png").scaledToWidth(100)
        # Provide Pixmap to label
        logo.setPixmap(myPixmap)
        hbox.addWidget(logo)

        # Create list of goody names
        goodies = ('cake', 'cookies', 'candy-cane', 'hamburger')
        # Loop through all of the goodies
        for goody in goodies:
            # Create a push Button Widget
            bx = QPushButton(goody, self)
            # Connect signal to the printButtonName Slot
            bx.clicked.connect(partial(self.printButtonName, bx))
            # Set the button Icon
            bx.setIcon(QIcon(f"C:\Temp\EPTA\icons\{goody}.png"))
            # Add the button to the Horizontal Layout Widget
            hbox.addWidget(bx)

        # Add the Horizontal Layout widget to the QWidget
        self.setLayout(hbox)
```

```
    # Recieve the Button object
    def printButtonName(self, button=None):
        # Insert the Button text information
        print(f'The {button.text()} button was pressed')


demo = imageDemo()
demo.show()
```

Code Sample 16.16 QPixmaps and QIcons

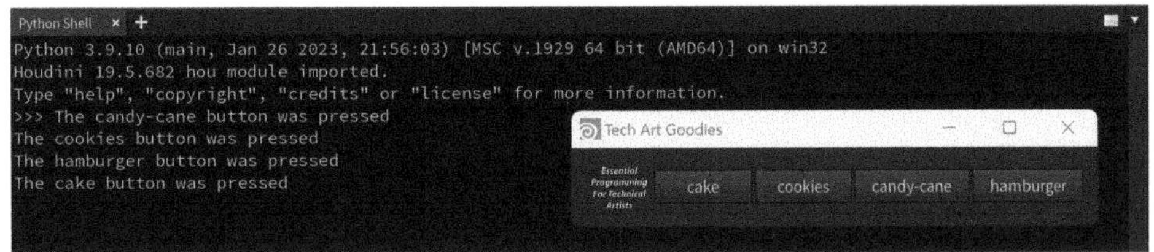

FIGURE 16.12 QPixmaps and qIcons.

Virtually any image may be used for an icon or a pixmap. Special consideration must be given to these images to maintain their integrity after being resized and re-oriented to fit within interfaces. An outstanding resource for small (16×16 pixels) and effective icons is the *Fugue Icons* set created by Yusuke Kamiyamane, https://p.yusukekamiyamane.com/. The set contains 3922 icons available under the *Creative Commons Attribution 3.0 License.* When not able to provide attribution for these icons, a royalty -free license may be purchased. The icons used in this text were taken from the *Fugue Icons* library.

QMainWindow

One of the anchor widgets in the *PyQt* library is *QMainWindow*. This widget is a fantastic foundation for creating general purpose applications. By default, the widget is equipped with a plethora of functional constructs: *tool bars, status bars*, and *menu bars*.

QMainWindows are created by declaring new classes as subclasses of the *QMainWindow* class. When defining class constructors in this context, it is always best practice to include *args* and *kwargs* arguments. Language Template 16.6 explains that inclusion of these arguments is essential when creating more robust, command line driven applications.

```
# Declare MyMainWindow as a QMainwindow Widget
class MyMainWindow(QMainWindow):
    def __init__(self, *args, **kwargs):
        super().__init__(*args, **kwargs)
```

Language Template 16.6 QMainWindow Subclass Constructor

In the Code Sample 16.17, *MyMainWindow* is declared as a subclass of the *QMainWindow* class. The *QMainWindow* and *QLabel* widgets are imported from the *QtWidgets* library. *Qt enums* are imported from the *QtCore* library. The class' main constructor includes **args and* ***kwargs* arguments to allow for future command line usage. Consistent with all *QWidgets*, all *QMainWindows* have window titles. Inside the main window is just a *QLabel* widget. *QLabels* are useful widgets to display text or image-base messages. The *AlignCenter* enum from the *Qt* library is required to set the label widget's alignment. After the label has been designated as the central widget for the class, it is ready for display, as in Figure 16.13.

```
# Import the essential QtWidgets
from PySide2.QtWidgets import QMainWindow, QLabel
# Import the Qt enum  from QtCore
from PySide2.QtCore import Qt

# Declare MyMainWindow as a QMainwindow Widget
class MyMainWindow(QMainWindow):
    def __init__(self, *args, **kwargs):
        super().__init__(*args, **kwargs)

        # Set the Window's title
        self.setWindowTitle('Essential Programming for the \
                   Technical Artist')

        # Create a QLabel Widget with initial text
        label = QLabel('This is a PySide2 QMainWindow')
        # Configure label widget's alignment
        label.setAlignment(Qt.AlignCenter)
        # Identify label as the MyMainWindow's central widget
        self.setCentralWidget(label)


mainWindow = MyMainWindow()
mainWindow.show()
```

Code Sample 16.17 QMainWindow Widget

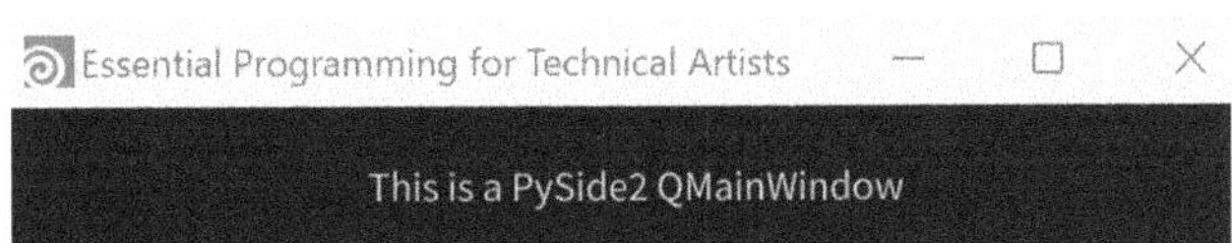

FIGURE 16.13 QMainWindow widget.

Toolbars

Surrounding *QMainWindows* are *QToolbars*. QToolBars are movable frameworks of buttons and controls which perform an unlimited variety of functions. Most applications' core functionalities are accessible through toolbars. *QToolbars* are added to *QMainWindows* by instantiating new toolbar objects and adding them as *QMainWindow* toolbars using the *addToolBar()* method. Code Sample 16.18 produced the toolbar shown in Figure 16.14.

```
# Import essential QtWidgets
from PySide2.QtWidgets import QMainWindow, QLabel, QToolBar
# Import the Qt enum  from QtCore
from PySide2.QtCore import Qt

# Declare MyMainWindow as a QMainwindow Widget
class MyMainWindow(QMainWindow):
    def __init__(self, *args, **kwargs):
        super().__init__(*args, **kwargs)

        # Set the Window's title
        self.setWindowTitle('Essential Programming for the \
                            Technical Artist')

        # Create a QLabel Widget with initial text
        label = QLabel('This is a PySide2 QMainWindow')
        # Configure label widget's alignment
        label.setAlignment(Qt.AlignCenter)
        # Identify label as the MainWindow's central widget
        self.setCentralWidget(label)

        # Instantiate a QToolBar
        toolbar = QToolBar('My Main Toolbar')
```

```
        # Add the QToolBar to the QMainWindow
        self.addToolBar(toolbar)


mainWindow = MyMainWindow()
mainWindow.show()
```

Code Sample 16.18 QToolBar

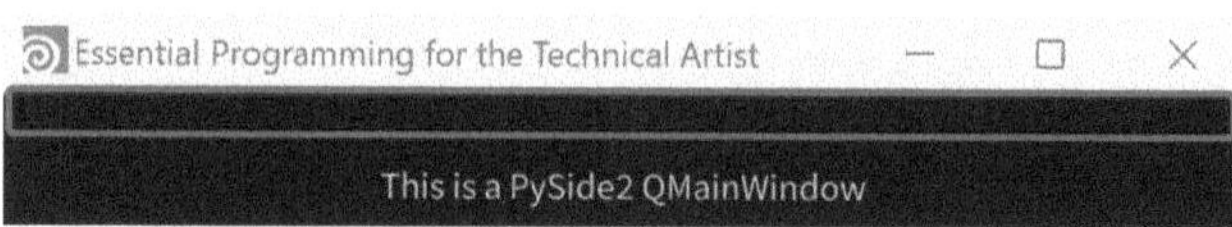

FIGURE 16.14 QToolBar in QMainWindow.

In the above example, a new *QToolBar* is instantiated to the *toolbar* object which is appended to the *QMainWindow* using the *self.addToolBar(toolbar)* command.

Simple to add, *QToolBars* by themselves are not much to look at. Grabbing the icon in the left corner of the *QToolBar* allows the user to move it along any of the surrounding edges of the window. To be more practical and functional, *QToolBars* need to be loaded with *QActions*, described in the next section.

QActions

QActions are the workhorses for *QToolBars* and *QMenus*. They are abstract user interface objects and typically manifest as buttons. They may contain icons, menu texts, shortcuts, "What's This?" texts, and tooltips. Equipped with a large variety of functions, slots and signals, they provide a plethora of functionality for menus and toolbars.

QActions are created by instantiating *QAction* classes to objects and then appending them to *QToolBars* or *QMenus* using the *addAction()* method. Order matters when configuring *QActions*. To ensure proper functionality, it is best to configure them before appending them to *QToolBars* or *QMenus*. Code Sample 16.19 demonstrates QAction creation.

```
# Import the essential QtWidgets
from PySide2.QtWidgets import QMainWindow, QLabel, QToolBar, QAction
# Import the Qt enum  from QtCore

from PySide2.QtCore import Qt


# Declare MyMainWindow as a QMainwindow Widget
class MyMainWindow(QMainWindow):
```

```
    def __init__(self, *args, **kwargs):
        super().__init__(*args, **kwargs)

        # Set the Window's title
        self.setWindowTitle('Essential Programming for the \
                            Technical Artist')

        # Create a QLabel Widget with initial text
        label = QLabel('This is a PySide2 QMainWindow')
        # Configure label widget's alignment
        label.setAlignment(Qt.AlignCenter)
        # Identify label as the MainWindow's central widget
        self.setCentralWidget(label)

        # Instantiate a QToolBar toolbar = QToolBar('My Main Toolbar')
        # Add the QToolBar to the QMainWindow
        self.addToolBar(toolbar)

        # Instantiate the QButton
        buttonAction = QAction('My Button', self)
        # Add a status tip to the QAction
        buttonAction.setStatusTip('This is my QAction Buttton')
        # Connect a slot to the triggered signal
        buttonAction.triggered.connect(self.onMyQActionClick)
        toolbar.addAction(buttonAction)

    # Define the buttonAction Slot
    def onMyQActionClick(self):
        print(f'My buttonAction clicked!')

mainWindow = MyMainWindow()
mainWindow.show()
```

Code Sample 16.19 QAction

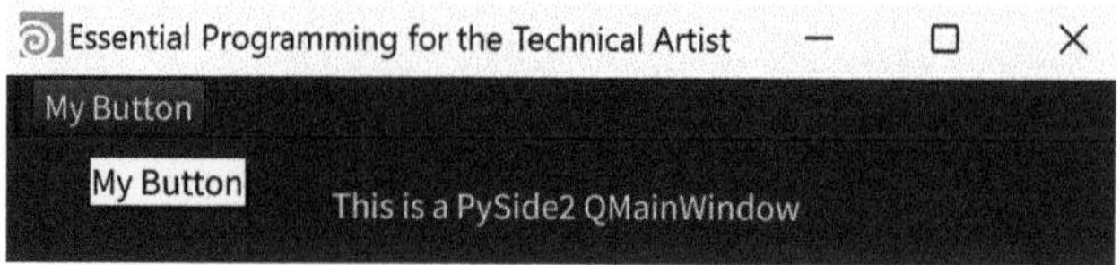

FIGURE 16.15 QAction button in QToolBar.

In the above example, a *QAction* is instantiated to the *buttonAction* object. A *status tip* is appended using the *setStatusTip()* method. The status tip is not viewable until there is a *status bar* attached to the same *QMainWindow*. The *triggered* signal is connected to the *onMyQActionClick()* function. This function simply echoes a report the *QAction* button has been clicked. Once configured, the *buttonAction* object is appended to the *toolbar* object using the *addAction()* method, and looks like Figure 16.15.

QActions may be embellished with icons and broadcast *changed, hovered, toggled, and triggered* signals. As displayed in the above figure, the name of the *QAction* object is displayed when hovered and its status tip is displayed within the presence of a *QStatusBar*.

QActions are checkable, which means that they may be toggled between *off/on* states. To make a *QAction* checkable, the *setCheckable()* method is used with either a *True* or *False* attribute state, depending on the desired result. Programmers may manually set or query *QAction* states using the *setChecked()* and *isChecked()* methods.

Code Sample 16.20 declares the *QAction* as checkable. When the toolbar is right mouse clicked, the check-ability toggle button appears. When toggled, the toolbar disappears. Please be aware that once a QAction has been *checked off* there is no way, by default, to bring it back. The application will need to be re-executed or the programmer needs to implement functionality to *uncheck* the *QAction* and turn it back on. The checkable QAction is shown in Figure 16.16. The toolbar is toggled off in Figure 16.17.

```
# Import the essential QtWidgets
from PySide2.QtWidgets import QMainWindow, QLabel, QToolBar, QAction
# Import the Qt enum  from QtCore
from PySide2.QtCore import Qt


# Declare MyMainWindow as a QMainwindow Widget
class MyMainWindow(QMainWindow):
    def __init__(self, *args, **kwargs):
        super().__init__(*args, **kwargs)

        # Set the Window's title
        self.setWindowTitle('Essential Programming for the \
                                Technical Artist')
```

```
        # Create a QLabel Widget with initial text
        label = QLabel('This is a PySide2 QMainWindow')
        # Configure label widget's alignment
        label.setAlignment(Qt.AlignCenter)
        # Identify label as the MainWindow's central widget
        self.setCentralWidget(label)

        # Instantiate a QToolBar
        toolbar = QToolBar('My Main Toolbar')
        # Add the QToolBar to the QMainWindow
        self.addToolBar(toolbar)

        # Instantiate the QButton
        buttonAction = QAction('My Button', self)
        # Add a status tip to the QAction
        buttonAction.setStatusTip('This is my QAction Buttton')
        # Connect a slot to the triggered signal
        buttonAction.triggered.connect(self.onMyQActionClick)
        # Identify buttonAction as checkable
        buttonAction.setCheckable(True)
        toolbar.addAction(buttonAction)

    # Define the buttonAction Slot
    def onMyQActionClick(self):
        print(f'My buttonAction clicked!')

mainWindow = MyMainWindow()
mainWindow.show()
```

Code Sample 16.20 Checkable QAction

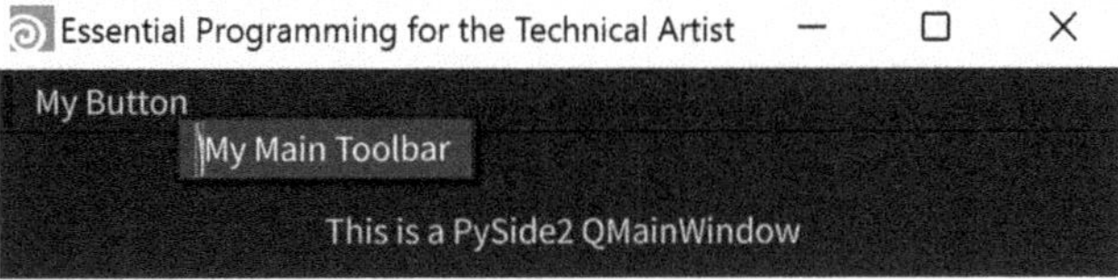

FIGURE 16.16 Checkable QAction.

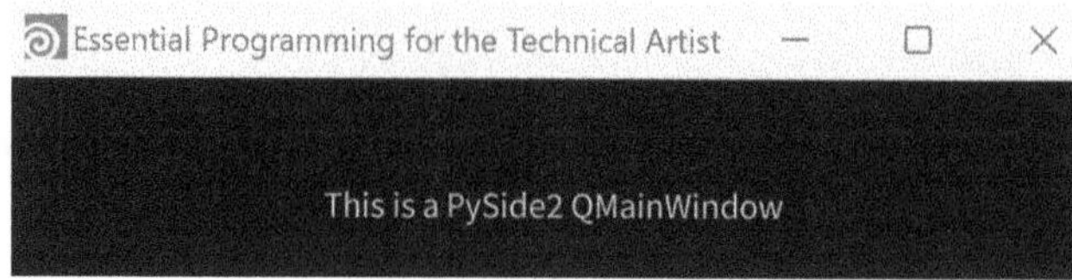

FIGURE 16.17 Toolbar toggled off.

Status Bar

A *QStatusBar* provides a horizontal bar for displaying *QMainWindow* status or any other text information. They are created by instantiating a *QStatusBar* object and adding that object to a *QMainWindow* using the *setStatusBar()* method.

There are three types of messages a *QStatusBar* may display: *Temporary, Normal*, and *Permanent*. Temporary messages are displayed using the *showMessage()* method. Displayed strings are input as string parameters. Temporary messages are replaced with either a new message or being timed out. The time out duration is added as an optional parameter to the *showMessage()* function. Normal messages are displayed when widgets declare their status with the *setStatusTip()* signal function or when added to *QStatusBar* objects using the *addwidget()* function. Permanent messages always display on *QStatusBars* when their associated widgets are added with the *addPermanentWidget()* method.

QStatusBars also provide *QSizeGrip* objects in their lower-right corners. A *QSizeGrip* is a small icon the user may grab when resizing windows. They may be disabled using the *setSizeGripEnabled()* function. Code Sample 16.21 creates a QStatus bar with timeout message.

```
from PySide2.QtWidgets import QMainWindow, QLabel, QToolBar
from PySide2.QtWidgets import QAction, QStatusBar
# Import the QtEnum  from QtCore
from PySide2.QtCore import Qt

# Declare MyMainWindow as a QMainwindow Widget
class MyMainWindow(QMainWindow):
    def __init__(self, *args, **kwargs):
        super().__init__(*args, **kwargs)

        # Set the Window's title
        self.setWindowTitle('Essential Programming for the \
                            Technical Artist')

        # Create a QLabel Widget with initial text
        label = QLabel('This is a PySide2 QMainWindow')
```

```
        # Configure label widget's alignment
        label.setAlignment(Qt.AlignCenter)
        # Identify label as the MainWindow's central widget
        self.setCentralWidget(label)

        # Instantiate a QToolBar
        toolbar = QToolBar('My Main Toolbar')
        # Add the QToolBar to the QMainWindow
        self.addToolBar(toolbar)

        # Instantiate the QButton
        buttonAction = QAction('My Button', self)
        # Add a status tip to the QAction
        buttonAction.setStatusTip('This is my QAction Buttton')
        # Connect a slot to the triggered signal
        buttonAction.triggered.connect(self.onMyQActionClick)
        toolbar.addAction(buttonAction)

        # Instantiate a QStatusBar
        statusBar = QStatusBar(self)
        # Add status bar to QMainWindow
        self.setStatusBar(statusBar)
        # Display a timed out, temporary message
        statusBar.showMessage('Welcome TAs', 2000)

    # Define the button Action Slot
    def onMyQActionClick(self):
        print(f'My buttonAction clicked!')

mainWindow = MyMainWindow()
mainWindow.show()
```

Code Sample 16.21 QStatusBar with Timed Out Message

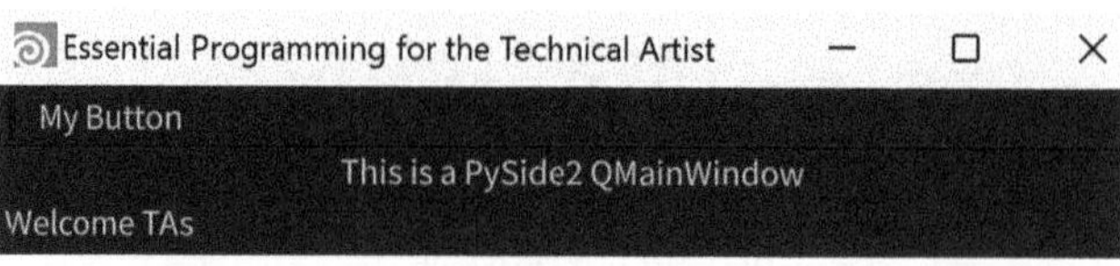

FIGURE 16.18 QToolBar with temporary Message.

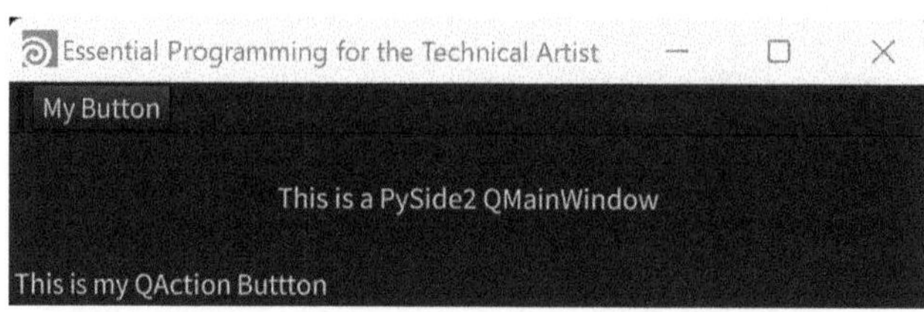

FIGURE 16.19 QStatusBar with tool tip message.

In Code Sample 16.21, a *QStatusBar* is instantiated to *statusBar*. It is then appended to the *QMainWindow* using the *setStatusBar()* command. The status bar also displays a temporary message using the *showMessage()* command. Figure 16.18 displays the toolbar message.

Normal messages are displayed when their associated widgets emit message signals with the *setStatusTip()* function. Figure 16.19 displays the tool tip message.

QMenuBar

QMenuBars empower interface creators to generate cascading layers of thematically relevant buttons. It is important to remember that *QMenuBars* are contributing components to *QMainWindows* and are composed of *QMenus*. *QMenus* can be thought as individual, hierarchal layers of interface objects. In other words, each *QMenu* is a linear strip of *QActions*, and other *QMenus*.

Language Template 16.7 demonstrates how a *QMenuBar* is created by assigning an instantiation of a *QMenuBar* and assigning that object to a *QMainWindow* using the *setMenuBar()* command.

```
# Instantiate QMenuBar to object
menuBarObject = QMenuBar(self)


# Assign object to QMainWindow
self.setMenuBar(menuBarObject)
```

Language Template 16.7 QMenuBar Creation and Assigning

Language Template 16.8 explains how *QMenus* are created by assigning instantiations of *QMenu* and assigning them to *QMenuBars* using the *setMenu()* command. More frequently, they are created using the *QMenuBar's* *addMenu()*command.

```
menuObject = QMenu(self)
menuBarObject.addMenu(menuObject)
or
menuObject = menuBarObject.addMenu(Title)
```

Language Template 16.8 QMenu Creation

QMenu objects are composed of *QActions* and other *QMenus*. *QMenus* are also populated with *sections* and *separators*, special *QActions* that establish visual regions within *QMenus*. *QMenus* may contain unlimited child *QMenus*. Code Sample 16.22 generates a *QMenu*.

```
from PySide2.QtWidgets import QMainWindow, QLabel, QToolBar
from PySide2.QtWidgets import QAction, QStatusBar, QMenuBar, QMenu
from PySide2.QtCore import Qt
from functools import partial


# Declare MyMainWindow as a QMainwindow Widget
class MyMainWindow(QMainWindow):
    def __init__(self, *args, **kwargs):
        super().__init__(*args, **kwargs)

        self.setWindowTitle('Essential Programming for the \
                            Technical Artist')

        # Create a QLabel Widget with initial text
        label = QLabel('This is a PySide2 QMainWindow')
        label.setAlignment(Qt.AlignCenter)
        self.setCentralWidget(label)

        # Instantiate a QToolBar to the QMainWindow
        toolbar = QToolBar('My Main Toolbar')
        self.addToolBar(toolbar)
```

```
# Instantiate the QButton, Connect a slot to the triggered signal
buttonAction = QAction('My Button', self)
buttonAction.setStatusTip('This is my QAction Buttton')
buttonAction.triggered.connect(self.onMyQActionClick)
toolbar.addAction(buttonAction)

# Instantiate a QStatusBar
statusBar = QStatusBar(self)
self.setStatusBar(statusBar)
statusBar.showMessage('Welcome TAs', 10000)

# Instantiate QMenuBar to object
menuBar = QMenuBar(self)
self.setMenuBar(menuBar)
fileMenu = menuBar.addMenu('File')

# Create a new QAction
nw = QAction('New', self)
nw.triggered.connect(partial(self.onMenuAction, nw))
fileMenu.addAction(nw)
fileMenu.addSeparator()

# Create and Assign a new Menu
characterMenu = fileMenu.addMenu('Characters')
# Create two new QActions
corny = QAction('Cornelius', self)
corny.triggered.connect(partial(self.onMenuAction, corny))
stu = QAction('Stu', self)
stu.triggered.connect(partial(self.onMenuAction, stu))
characterMenu.addAction(corny)
characterMenu.addAction(stu)
```

```
    # Define the buttonAction Slot
    def onMyQActionClick(self):
        print(f'My buttonAction clicked!')

    # Handle QAction signal and receive QAction parameter
    def onMenuAction(self, action):
        print(f'{action.text()} selected')


mainWindow = MyMainWindow()
mainWindow.show()
```

Code Sample 16.22 QMenuBar Creation

FIGURE 16.20 QMenu.

In Code Sample 16.22, a *QMenuBar* object is created, assigned to *menuBar* and identified as the *QMainWindow's* menu bar. Two *QMenus* are created: *fileMenu* as a child menu to *QMenuBar*, and *characterMenu* as a child menu to *fileMenu*. Three new *QActions* are created: *nw* is assigned to *fileMenu*, and *corny* and *stu* are assigned to *characterMenu*. All three *QAction* trigger signals are connected to the *onMenuAction()* function using the *functools.partial()* method. Figure 16.20 displays the results.

Interactive Widgets

One of the big advantages of working with the Qt library is the wide array of built-in, interactive widgets. The example below introduces some of the most common widgets technical artists use on a regular basis. All of the included widgets, except for *QComboBox*, are simple widgets which can be added quickly to any interface to provide primitive selection, activation, input, and display operations. These widgets are invoked in Code Sample 16.23 and displayed in Figure 6.21.

```
# Import all of the QWidgets
from PySide2.QtWidgets import *


# Declare MyMainWindow as a QMainwindow Widget
class MyMainWindow(QMainWindow):
```

```
def __init__(self, *args, **kwargs):
    super().__init__(*args, **kwargs)

    self.setWindowTitle("Widget Parade")

    layout = QVBoxLayout()
    # Define a list for all widget types
    widgets = [
        # Option button to be switched on or off
        QCheckBox('QCheckBox'),
        # All-purpose push button widget
        QPushButton('QPushButton'),
        # Groupable toggle switches, only one may be on
        QRadioButton('QRadioButton'),
        # Composite widget of a button and a popup list
        QComboBox(),
        # Widget for editing dates
        QDateEdit(),
        # Widget for editing time values
        QTimeEdit(),
        # Interactive widget to edit float values
        QSpinBox(),
        # Interactive widget to edit integer values
        QDoubleSpinBox(),
        # All-purpose text message display widget
        QLabel('QLabel'),
        # Interactive text editor
        QLineEdit('QLineEdit'),
        # Display widget for LCD numbers
        QLCDNumber(),
        # Graphical progress display widget
        QProgressBar(),
        # Interactive widgets for slider editing
        QSlider(),
```

```
            # Interactive dial widget
            QDial()]


        # For loop to adding al widgets from list
        for widget in widgets:
            layout.addWidget(widget)

        # Instantiate a generic widget
        centralWidget = QWidget()
        centralWidget.setLayout(layout)
        self.setCentralWidget(centralWidget)

mainWindow = MyMainWindow()
mainWindow.show()
```

Code Sample 16.23 Primitive Interactive Widget Parade

Composite widgets, such as *QComboBox*, are made from smaller, primitive operation widgets.

QDialog

Dialog windows, *QDialogs*, are top-level windows used primarily for short-term tasks and brief communications. These windows appear in two modes: *Modal* and *Modeless*. Modal dialogs block all user input to other application windows. Modeless dialogs appear independently from all other windows of the same application.

QDialogs are new windows populatable with other widgets to satisfy application needs. There are several *QDialog* subclasses, composed of multiple primitive widgets, which provide convenient, task-driven, pop-up windows. Of these subclasses, technical artists use *QMessageBox, QDialogButtonBox, QFileDialog*, and *QColorDialog* subclasses.

Modal Dialogs

Modal Dialogs are *QDialogs* that block user input to other visible windows in the same application until the dialog is released. Modal dialogs are used most often to illicit user confirmation, such as understanding choice consequences. For example, modal dialog may query users if they desire to exit with unsaved changes. They may also require specific user input, such as a file name.

Modal QDialogs are instantiations of the *QDialog class*. As introduced in Language Template 16.9, they are displayed using the *exec_()* command, block interactions with all other applications windows, and return *Accepted* or *Rejected* states depending on user context.

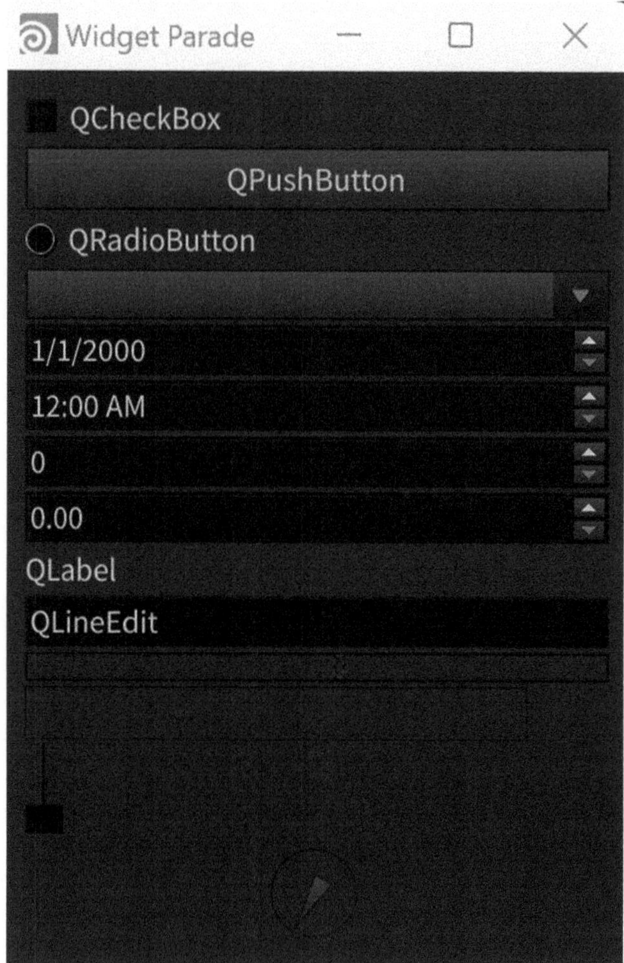

FIGURE 16.21 Primitive widget parade.

```
# Create a QDialog
dialog = QDialog(self)

# Make the Dialog 'Modal' and display it
dialog.exec_()
```

Language Template 16.9 Modal Dialog Creation

In Code Sample 16.24, a modal dialog is created as a callback for a button press. Extra widgets, *lcd* and *dial*, are provided to demonstrate the modal dialog's exclusivity. The results of a modal dialogue window are shown in Figure 16.22.

```
# Import all of the QWidgets
from PySide2.QtWidgets import *

# Declare MyDialogs as a QMainwindow Widget
class MyDialogs(QMainWindow):
    def __init__(self, *args, **kwargs):
        super().__init__(*args, **kwargs)

        self.setWindowTitle("Dialogs")

        layout = QVBoxLayout()

        # Create Modal Pushbutton
        modalButton = QPushButton('Modal Dialog')
        modalButton.clicked.connect(self.onModalButtonClick)
        layout.addWidget(modalButton)

        # Define a simple LCD display
        lcd = QLCDNumber()
        layout.addWidget(lcd)
        # Define a simple interactive dial
        dial = QDial()
        layout.addWidget(dial)
        # Connect valueChanged signal to lcd's display slot
        dial.valueChanged.connect(lcd.display)

        # Define a central widget
        centralWidget = QWidget()
        centralWidget.setLayout(layout)
        self.setCentralWidget(centralWidget)

    # Define slot for the modal button click signal
    def onModalButtonClick(self, s):
```

```
        # Create a QDialog
        dialog = QDialog(self)
        dialog.setWindowTitle('Modal Dialog')

        layout = QVBoxLayout()
        # Create a query message
        message = QLabel("Are you sure you want to QUIT?")
        layout.addWidget(message)
        QButtons = QDialogButtonBox.Ok | QDialogButtonBox.Cancel
        # Create a QDialogButtonBox
        buttonBox = QDialogButtonBox(QButtons)
        buttonBox.accepted.connect(dialog.accept)
        buttonBox.rejected.connect(dialog.reject)
        layout.addWidget(buttonBox)
        dialog.setLayout(layout)

        # Display the Dialog as 'Modal'
        dialog.exec_()


mainWindow = MyDialogs()
mainWindow.show()
```

Code Sample 16.24 Modal Dialog Creation

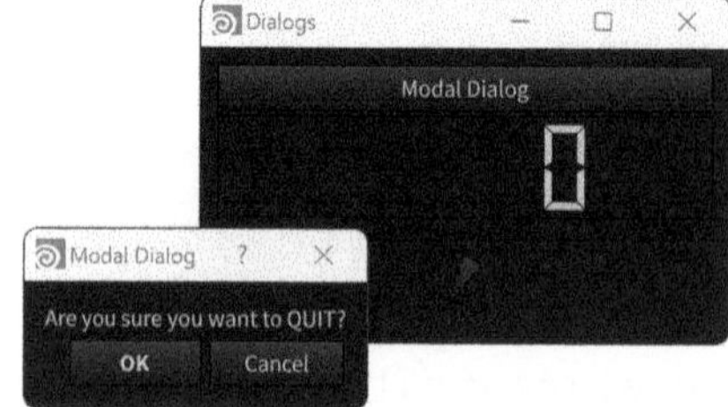

FIGURE 16.22 Modal dialog window.

All relevant *QDialog* code is present in the *onModalButtonClick* slot function. The *QDialog* is created with the *QDialog()* command and is displayed as a modal dialog with the *exec_()* command. When the *Modal Dialog* button is pressed, the *Modal Dialog* window appears. A QVBoxLayout is instantiated to contain the *QDialog* internal widgets. A *QDialogButtonBox* is instantiated to manage interactivity and appended to the layout object. A section on *QDialogButtonBox* objects is provided below. No interactivity with the application is allowed until the *QDialogButtonBox* is answered or the *Modal Dialog* window is closed.

Modeless Dialogs

Modeless Dialogs are *QDialogs* that operate independently and do not block other windows of the same application. They are useful for pop-up interface windows that interact with main windows such as animation character pickers.

Like *Modal Dialogs*, they are instantiations of the *QDialog* class. Language Template 16.10 demonstrates how they are displayed using the *show()* command instead of *exec_()*.

```
# Create a QDialog
dialog = QDialog(self)


# Make the Dialog 'Modeless' and display
dialog.show()
```

Language Template 16.10 Modeless Dialog Creation

Code Sample 16.25 appends to Code Sample 16.24 with with a second button, "*Modeless Dialog*". The *Modeless Dialog* is implemented in the button's *onModelessButtonClicked()* slot function. A *dialog* is instantiated from the *QDialog* class and displayed using the *show()* command. A *QVBoxLayout* is instantiated to contain the *QDialog* internal widgets. A *QDialogButtonBox* is instantiated to manage interactivity and appended to the layout object. A section on *QDialogButtonBox* objects is provided in Code Sample 16.25. Figure 16.23 displays a *modeless* dialogue window.

```
# Import all of the QWidgets
from PySide2.QtWidgets import *


# Declare MyDialogs as a QMainwindow Widget
class MyDialogs(QMainWindow):
    def __init__(self, *args, **kwargs):
        super().__init__(*args, **kwargs)


        self.setWindowTitle("Dialogs")


        layout = QVBoxLayout()

```

```
        # Create Modal Pushbutton
        modalButton = QPushButton('Modal Dialog')
        modalButton.clicked.connect(self.onModalButtonClick)
        layout.addWidget(modalButton)

        # Create Modeless Pushbutton
        modelessButton = QPushButton('Modeless Dialog')
        modelessButton.clicked.connect(self.onModelessButtonClick)
        layout.addWidget(modelessButton)

        # Define a simple LCD display
        lcd = QLCDNumber()
        layout.addWidget(lcd)
        # Define a simple interactive dial
        dial = QDial()
        layout.addWidget(dial)
        # Connect valueChanged signal to lcd's display slot
        dial.valueChanged.connect(lcd.display)

        # Define a central widget
        centralWidget = QWidget()
        centralWidget.setLayout(layout)
        self.setCentralWidget(centralWidget)

    # Define slot for the modal button click signal
    def onModalButtonClick(self, s):
        # Create a QDialog
        dialog = QDialog(self)
        dialog.setWindowTitle('Modal Dialog')
        # Modal interface left out for brevity
        # Make the Dialog 'Modal'
        dialog.exec_()
```

```
    # Define slot for the modeless button click signal
    def onModelessButtonClick(self, s):
        # Create a QDialog
        dialog = QDialog(self)

        layout = QVBoxLayout()
        message = QLabel("Select Facial Expression:")
        layout.addWidget(message)
        # Create a Combo Box
        comboBox = QComboBox()
        comboBox.addItems(("Smile", "Frown", "Confused",
                           "Afraid", "Excited"))
        layout.addWidget(comboBox)
        # Create a QDialogButtonBox
        buttonBox = QDialogButtonBox(QDialogButtonBox.Ok)
        buttonBox.accepted.connect(dialog.accept)
        layout.addWidget(buttonBox)
        dialog.setLayout(layout)

        dialog.setWindowTitle('Modeless Dialog')



        # Make the Dialog 'Modeless'
        dialog.show()

mainWindow = MyDialogs()
mainWindow.show()
```

Code Sample 16.25 Modeless Dialog Creation

When the *Modeless Dialog* is instantiated and displayed, none of the functionality of the original window is prohibited.

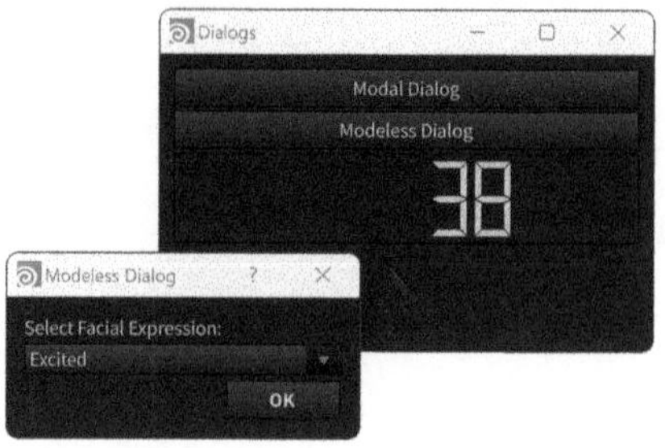

FIGURE 16.23 Modeless dialog window.

Custom Dialog Classes

The instantiating of *QDialog* classes creates new populatable windows, independent from their original spawning windows. Maintaining *new* window autonomy is conveniently achieved by creating custom, *QDialog* subclasses. Custom dialog classes ensure independence from their invoking applications and enable predictable re-use.

Custom dialog classes are created by declaring them as *QDialog* subclasses. As subclasses, these new custom classes inherit all of the *Qdialog* functionality. Custom classes are displayed as modal or modeless dialogs via the *exec_()* and *show()* functions, respectively. The *exec_()* function always returns either *Accepted* or *Rejected* states. When parent applications need this information, the function should be executed in the parent class and not within the subclass. The *show()* behaves similarly regardless of invocation inside or outside of the subclass.

In Code Sample 16.26, the *CustomDialog* class is defined as a *QDialog* subclass. It contains a horizontal box layout with two push buttons displaying "Yes" and "No". Both push buttons share the same signal slot, *onButton-Click*. The *CustomDialog* class is instantiated from within the MyDialog's onCallDialogButtonClick signal slot function. *CustomDialog* is displayed using the *exec_()* command. Because this display strategy makes the custom class *modal*, the results of the *onButtonClick* print statements are not displayed until the *CustomDialog* object is terminated.

```
# Import all of the QWidgets
from PySide2.QtWidgets import *


# Declare CustomDialog as a QDialog subclass
class CustomDialog(QDialog):
    def __init__(self, *args, **kwargs):
        super().__init__(*args, **kwargs)

        self.setWindowTitle('Custom Dialog')

        layout = QHBoxLayout()
```

```
        # Instantiate a 'Yes' Pushbutton
        yes = QPushButton('Yes')
      yes.clicked.connect(lambda:self.onButtonClick(yes))
        layout.addWidget(yes)

        # Instantiate a 'No' Pushbutton
        no = QPushButton('No')
      no.clicked.connect(lambda:self.onButtonClick(no))
        layout.addWidget(no)

        # Identify Custom Dialog's layout
        self.setLayout(layout)

    # Define the onButtonClick slot function
    def onButtonClick(self, button):
        print(button.text())


# Declare MyDialogs as a QMainwindow Widget
class MyDialogs(QMainWindow):
    def __init__(self, *args, **kwargs):
        super().__init__(*args, **kwargs)

        self.setWindowTitle("Dialogs")

        layout = QVBoxLayout()

        # Create Modal Pushbutton
        callDialogButton = QPushButton('Call Dialog Class')
        callDialogButton.clicked.connect(self.onCallDialogButtonClick)
        layout.addWidget(callDialogButton)
```

```
        # Define a central widget
        centralWidget = QWidget()
        centralWidget.setLayout(layout)
        self.setCentralWidget(centralWidget)

    # Define slot for the modal button click signal
    def onCallDialogButtonClick(self, s):
        dialog = CustomDialog(self)
        dialog.exec_()


mainWindow = MyDialogs()
mainWindow.show()
```

Code Sample 16.26 Custom Dialog Class

When the results from the custom class need to be displayed while still present, the class must be displayed using the *show()* command. The results are displayed in Figure 16.24.

QDialogButtonBox

Many dialog buttons play roles such as accepting or rejecting dialogs, requesting more information, or requesting interface actions (such as applying changes). Their intended behaviors trigger default class signals. *QDialogButtonBoxes* delegate the task of organizing dialog buttons.

Standard buttons are added to *QDialogButtonBox* instantiates by pre-creating *QPushButton* instantiations and adding them using the *addButton()* command. Language Template 16.11 introduces button objects and their *ActionRoles* are included as function parameters.

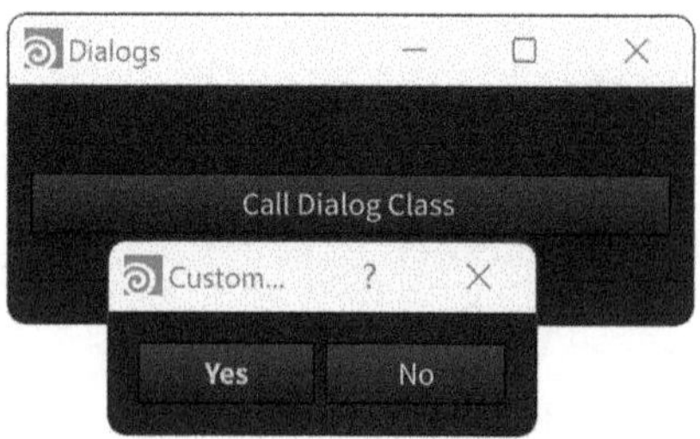

FIGURE 16.24 Custom dialog window.

```
myPushButton = QPushButton('Push Button')
myButtonBox = QDialogButtonBox()
myButtonBox.addButton(myPushButton, QDialogButtonBox.ActionRole)
```

Language Template 16.11 Adding Buttons as Action Roles to a QDialogButtonBox

Table 16.1 contains available button action roles.

An alternative method is concatenating *standard buttons* using the *or*, (|), operator. Language Template 16.12 introduces how standard buttons are connected with the following signals: *accepted, clicked, helpRequested,* and *rejected.*

```
qButtons = QDialogButtonBox.Ok | QDialogButtonBox.Abort
buttonBox = QDialogButtonBox(qButtons)
buttonBox.accepted.connect(self.acceptFunction)
buttonBox.rejected.connect(self.rejectFunction)
```

Language Template 16.12 Adding Buttons as Standard Buttons to a QDialogButtonBox

Table 16.2 contains available *standard buttons.*

The following example utilizes a *QDialogButtonBox* with the *CustomDialog* class. It implements the concatenating button technique for appending buttons to the widget. Note that there is a *QLabel* widget. An extra set of enums, *PySide2.QtCore.Qt,* needs to be imported in order to effectively set the *QLabel's* alignment.

TABLE 16.1 QDialogButtonBox Action Roles

Button Action Role	*Description*
QDialogButtonBox.InvalidRole	Button is invalid
QDialogButtonBox.AcceptRole	Causes dialog to be accepted (e.g. OK)
QDialogButtonBox.RejectRole	Causes dialog to be rejected (e.g. Cancel)
QDialogButtonBox.DestructiveRole	Causes destructive change (e.g. Discard) and closes dialog
QDialogButtonBox.ActionRole	Causes changes to elements within dialog
QDialogButtonBox.HelpRole	Request help
QDialogButtonBox.YesRole	Button is a "Yes"-like response
QDialogButtonBox.NoRole	Button is a "No"-like response
QDialogButtonBox.ApplyRole	Apply Current changes
QDialogButtonBox.ResetRole	Reset dialog fields to default

TABLE 16.2 QDialogButtonBox Standard Buttons

Standard Button	*Description*
QDialogButtonBox.Ok	Button defined with the AcceptRole
QDialogButtonBox.Open	Button defined with the AcceptRole
QDialogButtonBox.Save	Button defined with the AcceptRole
QDialogButtonBox.Cancel	Button defined with the RejectRole
QDialogButtonBox.Close	Button defined with the RejectRole
QDialogButtonBox.Discard	Button defined with the DestructiveRole
QDialogButtonBox.Apply	Button defined with the ApplyRole
QDialogButtonBox.Reset	Button defined with the ResetRole
QDialogButtonBox.RestoreDefaults	Button defined with the ResetRole
QDialogButtonBox.Help	Button defined with the HelpRole
QDialogButtonBox.SaveAll	Button defined with the AcceptRole
QDialogButtonBox.Yes	Button defined with the YesRole
QDialogButtonBox.YesToAll	Button defined with the YesRole
QDialogButtonBox.No	Button defined with the NoRole
QDialogButtonBox.NoToAll	Button defined with the NoRole
QDialogButtonBox.Abort	Button defined with the RejectRole
QDialogButtonBox.Retry	Button defined with the AcceptRole
QDialogButtonBox.Ignore	Button defined with the AcceptRole
QDialogButtonBox.NoButton	An invalid button

The *CustomDialog* class is displayed using an *exec_()* command embedded within an *if* statement in the button *onCallDialogButtonClick* signal slot. The *exec_()* returns either an *accepted or rejected* state. Positive or negative responses reflect the *QDialogButtonBox* results. Code Sample 16.27 demonstrates a *custom* dialog. Its results are shown in Figure 16.25.

```
# Import all of the QWidgets
from PySide2.QtWidgets import
from PySide2.QtCore import Qt


# Declare CustomDialog as a QDialog subclass
class CustomDialog(QDialog):
    def __init__(self, *args, **kwargs):
        super().__init__(*args, **kwargs)
```

```
        self.setWindowTitle('Custom Dialog')

        # Create QDialogButtonBox buttons
        qButtons = QDialogButtonBox.Ok | QDialogButtonBox.Abort
        buttonBox = QDialogButtonBox(qButtons)
        buttonBox.accepted.connect(self.accept)
        buttonBox.rejected.connect(self.reject)

        # Define a horizontal box layout
        layout = QVBoxLayout()
        message = QLabel('Make a choice')
        message.setAlignment(Qt.AlignCenter)
        layout.addWidget(message)
        layout.addWidget(buttonBox)

        self.setLayout(layout)


# Declare MyDialogs as a QMainwindow Widget
class MyDialogs(QMainWindow):
    def __init__(self, *args, **kwargs):
        super().__init__(*args, **kwargs)

        self.setWindowTitle("Dialogs")

        layout = QVBoxLayout()

        # Create Modal Pushbutton
        callDialogButton = QPushButton('Call Dialog Class')
        callDialogButton.clicked.connect(self.onCallDialogButtonClick)
        layout.addWidget(callDialogButton)
```

```
        # Define a central widget
        centralWidget = QWidget()
        centralWidget.setLayout(layout)
        self.setCentralWidget(centralWidget)

    # Define slot for the modal button click signal
    def onCallDialogButtonClick(self, s):
        # Create an instantiation of the customDialog class
        dialog = CustomDialog(self)
        # Display Custom Dialog and test if accepted or rejected
        if dialog.exec_():
            print('Everything OK')
        else:
            print('Abandon Ship')
            # Terminate the QMainWindow
            self.close()


mainWindow = MyDialogs()
mainWindow.show()
```

Code Sample 16.27 Custom Dialog with QDialogButtonBox

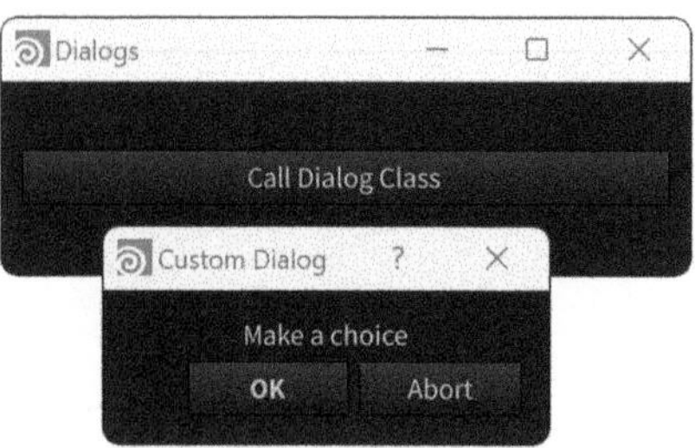

FIGURE 16.25 Custom dialog with QDialogButtonBox.

Within the *QDialogButtonBox*, pressing the *OK* button triggers an *Accepted* response while the *Abort* triggers a *Rejected* response. Note that upon a negative result, the *self.close()*command terminates the *QMainWindow* widget.

QMessageBox

Programmers do not need to create new classes for every pop-up dialog. Often, simple windows can ensure necessary user understanding. In these situations, *QMessageBox* instantiations work very well. A *QMessageBox* can be as simple or as complex as required to satisfy dialog needs.

Minimally, once instantiated and displayed, a *QMessageBox* displays a simple dialog window with a default push button that dismisses the window when depressed. The addition of a text message explains the purpose of the dialog.

In Code Sample 16.28, a *QMessageBox* is instantiated and displayed (using the *exec()* command) within the application's *onCallDialogButtonClick* slot function. The *setText()* function declares the box's intention. Upon employment, the *QmessageBox* is displayed and halts application interactivity until the default "*OK*" button is pressed. The results of Code Sample 16.28 are displayed in Figure 16.26.

```
# Import all of the QWidgets
from PySide2.QtWidgets import *

# Declare MyDialogs as a QMainwindow Widget
class MyDialogs(QMainWindow):
    def __init__(self, *args, **kwargs):
        super().__init__(*args, **kwargs)

        self.setWindowTitle("Dialogs")

        layout = QVBoxLayout()

        # Create Modal Pushbutton
        callDialogButton = QPushButton('Call MessageBox')
        callDialogButton.clicked.connect(self.onCallDialogButtonClick)
        layout.addWidget(callDialogButton)

        # Define a central widget
        centralWidget = QWidget()
        centralWidget.setLayout(layout)
        self.setCentralWidget(centralWidget)
```

```
    # Define slot for the modal button click signal
    def onCallDialogButtonClick(self, s):
        # Define a QMessageBox
        messageBox = QMessageBox()
        messageBox.setText('The Time to Decide Is Here!')
        messageBox.exec()


mainWindow = MyDialogs()
mainWindow.show()
```

Code Sample 16.28 Simple QMessageBox

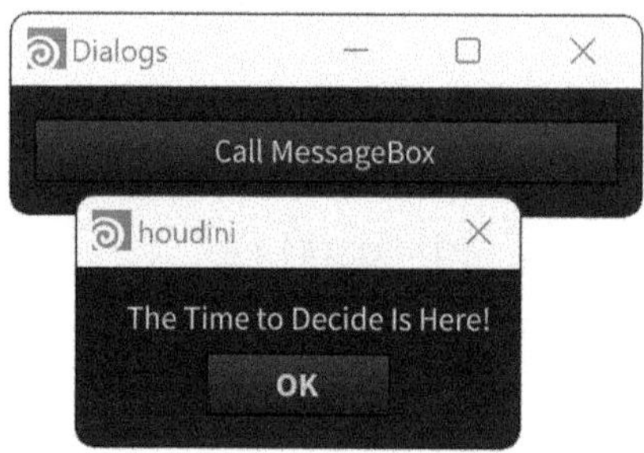

FIGURE 16.26 Simple QMessageBox.

QMessageBox instantiations are easily expanded by appending informative text, standard buttons, default buttons, check boxes, and icons. The *setStandardButtons()* command creates a series of buttons using the *or* operator ,(|), and *QMessage Box Standard Button*. The *exec()* command returns the identity of the depressed button. This short-cut eliminates the need to utilize the *signal/slot* paradigm to handle a button press event. Table 16.3 lists the standard *QMessageBox* buttons.

Code Sample 16.29 expands on Code Sample 16.27. It appends fuller text information to the user via the *setInformativeText()* command. Three standard buttons are appended with the *setStandardButtons()* command and *or* operators: *QMessageBox.Save, QMessageBox.Discard*, and *QMessageBox.Cancel*. The *save* button is highlighted using the *setDefaultButton()* command. The *exec()* command reports which button was pressed. Upon *Save* button press, the application is closed. The results for Code Sample 16.29 are displayed in Figure 16.27.

TABLE 16.3 QMessageBox Standard Buttons

Standard Button	*Description*
QMessageBox.Ok	Button defined with the AcceptRole
QMessageBox.Open	Button defined with the AcceptRole
QMessageBox.Save	Button defined with the AcceptRole
QMessageBox.Cancel	Button defined with the RejectRole
QMessageBox.Close	Button defined with the RejectRole
QMessageBox.Discard	Button defined with the DestructiveRole
QMessageBox.Apply	Button defined with the ApplyRole
QMessageBox.Reset	Button defined with the ResetRole
QMessageBox.RestoreDefaults	Button defined with the ResetRole
QMessageBox.Help	Button defined with the HelpRole
QMessageBox.SaveAll	Button defined with the AcceptRole
QMessageBox.Yes	Button defined with the YesRole
QMessageBox.YesToAll	Button defined with the YesRole
QMessageBox.No	Button defined with the NoRole
QMessageBox.NoToAll	Button defined with the NoRole
QMessageBox.Abort	Button defined with the RejectRole
QMessageBox.Retry	Button defined with the AcceptRole
QMessageBox.Ignore	Button defined with the AcceptRole
QMessageBox.NoButton	An invalid button

```
# Import all of the QWidgets
from PySide2.QtWidgets import *

# Declare MyDialogs as a QMainwindow Widget
class MyDialogs(QMainWindow):
    def __init__(self, *args, **kwargs):
        super().__init__(*args, **kwargs)

        self.setWindowTitle("Dialogs")

        layout = QVBoxLayout()
```

```
        # Create Modal Pushbutton
        callDialogButton = QPushButton('Call MessageBox')
        callDialogButton.clicked.connect(self.onCallDialogButtonClick)
        layout.addWidget(callDialogButton)

        # Define a central widget
        centralWidget = QWidget()
        centralWidget.setLayout(layout)
        self.setCentralWidget(centralWidget)

    # Define slot for the modal button click signal
    def onCallDialogButtonClick(self, s):
        # Define a QMessageBox
        messageBox = QMessageBox()
        messageBox.setWindowTitle('QMessageBox Example')
        messageBox.setText('The Time To Decide Is Here!')
        messageBox.setInformativeText(
                   'Do you want to commit your changes?')

        # Declare all of the buttons
        messageBox.setStandardButtons(QMessageBox.Save |
                                      QMessageBox.Discard |
                                      QMessageBox.Cancel)
        messageBox.setDefaultButton(QMessageBox.Save)

        # Display the button and collect the response
        answer = messageBox.exec()
        if answer == QMessageBox.Save:
            # When Save is selected, close the interface
            self.close()
        elif answer == QMessageBox.Discard:
            # Display the Discard message
            print('The Discard button was pressed!')
```

```
        else:
            # Display the Cancel message
            print('The Cancel Button was pressed!')


mainWindow = MyDialogs()
mainWindow.show()
```

Code Sample 16.29 Enhanced QMessageBox

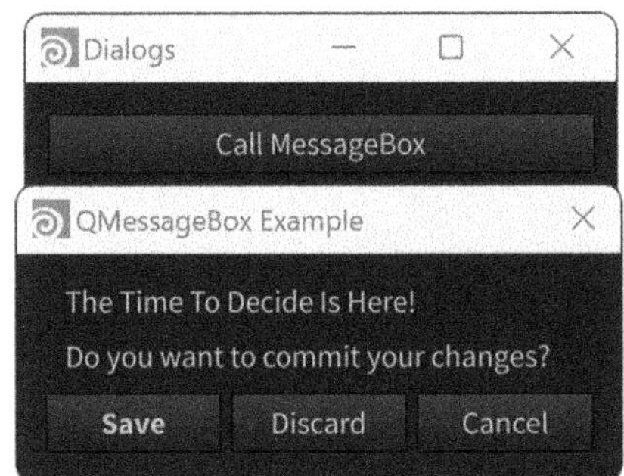

FIGURE 16.27 Enhanced QMessageBox.

QFileDialog

Accessing the user's choice of input files or output folders is an essential component in technical artist applications. Typing in correct, case-sensitive paths and filenames is too demanding. Providing file dialogs to navigate and select intended destinations significantly increases script success and reduces end-user frustration. The *QFileDialog* class is a robust *QDialog* subclass for creating and configuring custom file dialog windows.

Once a *QFileDialog* instantiation has been assigned, the *exec()* command displays the window and halts the application progression until a selection is made or the user cancels the dialog. When a correct selection is made, the decision is accessed via the *selectedFiles()* command. The *selectedFiles()*method returns a list of all selected files. A loop iterates through and displays all paths of selected files Code Sample 16.30 displays a QFileDialog as displayed in Figure 16.28.

```
# Import all of the QWidgets
from PySide2.QtWidgets import *


# Declare MyDialogs as a QMainwindow Widget
class MyDialogs(QMainWindow):
    def __init__(self, *args, **kwargs):
```

```
        super().__init__(*args, **kwargs)

        self.setWindowTitle("Dialogs")

        layout = QVBoxLayout()

        # Create Modal Pushbutton
        callDialogButton = QPushButton('Call File Dialog')
        callDialogButton.clicked.connect(self.onCallDialogButtonClick)
        layout.addWidget(callDialogButton)

        # Define a central widget
        centralWidget = QWidget()
        centralWidget.setLayout(layout)
        self.setCentralWidget(centralWidget)

    # Define slot for the modal button click signal
    def onCallDialogButtonClick(self, s):
        # Create QFileDialog instance
        fileDialog = QFileDialog()
        fileDialog.setWindowTitle('My Custom File Dialog Window')
        # Display the dialog is 'modal'
        if fileDialog.exec():
            # Grab all of the files selected in the dialog
            selectedFiles = fileDialog.selectedFiles()
            for filename in selectedFiles:
                # Display search selection
                print(f'The selected file is {filename}')


mainWindow = MyDialogs()
mainWindow.show()
```

Code Sample 16.30 QFileDialog Instantiation

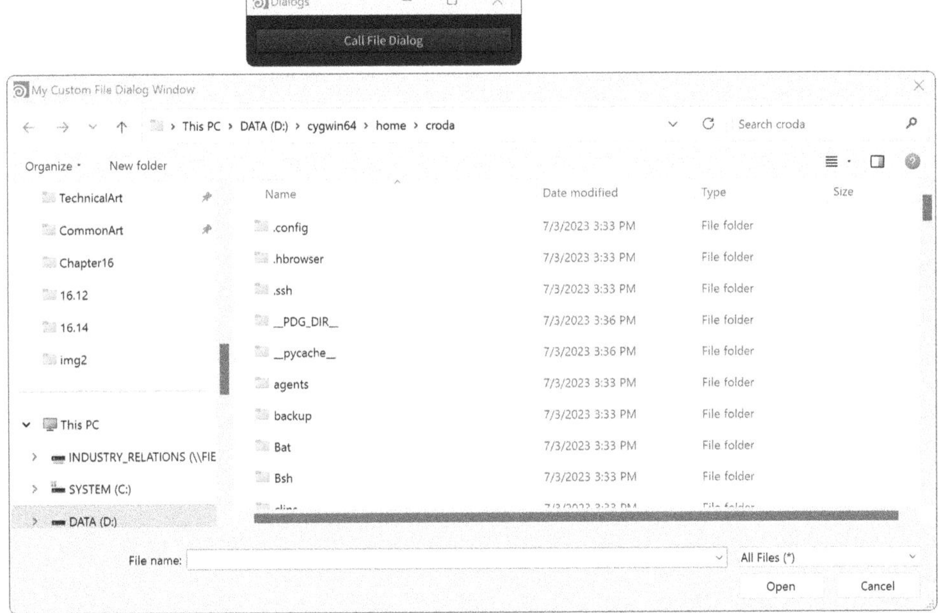

FIGURE 16.28 QFileDialog instantiation.

When brevity is required, the *QFileDialog* query can be reduced to one line. Code Sample 16.31 displays that the *getOpenFileName()* function is all that is required to bring up a file dialog and return a file selection.

```
# Define slot for the modal button click signal
def onCallDialogButtonClick(self, s):
    selectedFile = QFileDialog(self).getOpenFileName()
    print(f'The selected file is {selectedFile[0]}')
```

Code Sample 16.31 One-line QFileDialog Statement

Index *[0]* is required to access the filename found in a *QFileDialog* tuple.

QColorDialog

Technical artists often require color input from their users. The *QColorDialog* is a *QDialog* subclasses for quickly accessing color information. Once a *QColorDialog* instantiation has been assigned, the exec() command displays the window and halts application progression until a selection is made or the user cancels the dialog. When correct selection is made, the decision is accessed via the *selectedColor()* command. The *QColorDialog* returns *QColor* objects. The *QColor* class is a robust *Qt* object ideal for working with colors in *RGB*, *HSV*, and *CMYK* color spaces. The *toTuple()* command converts *QColor* objects to *RGB* mode and returns the components as tuples.

```
# Import all of the QWidgets
from PySide2.QtWidgets import *
from PySide2.QtGui import QColor

# Declare MyDialogs as a QMainwindow Widget
class MyDialogs(QMainWindow):
    def __init__(self, *args, **kwargs):
        super().__init__(*args, **kwargs)

        self.setWindowTitle("Dialogs")

        layout = QVBoxLayout()

        # Create Modal Pushbutton
        callDialogButton = QPushButton('Call Color Dialog')
        callDialogButton.clicked.connect(self.onCallDialogButtonClick)
        layout.addWidget(callDialogButton)

        # Define a central widget
        centralWidget = QWidget()
        centralWidget.setLayout(layout)
        self.setCentralWidget(centralWidget)

    # Define slot for the modal button click signal
    def onCallDialogButtonClick(self, s):
        # Create QColorDialog instantiation
        colorDialog = QColorDialog()
        # Display QColor object when selected
        if colorDialog.exec():
            print(f'The selected color is \
                {colorDialog.selectedColor().toTuple()}')
```

```
mainWindow = MyDialogs()
mainWindow.show()
```

Code Sample 16.32 QColorDialog Instantiation

When brevity is required, the *QColorDialog* query can be reduced to one line. In Code Sample 16.33, *QColorDialog(self).getColor()* is all that is required to bring up a file dialog and return a file selection (see Figure 16.29)

```
    # Define slot for the modal button click signal
    def onCallDialogButtonClick(self, s):
        # Get color information from a QColorDialog Class function
        selectedColor = QColorDialog(self).getColor()
        print(f'The selected color is {selectedColor.toTuple()}')
```

Code Sample 16.33 One-line QColorDialog

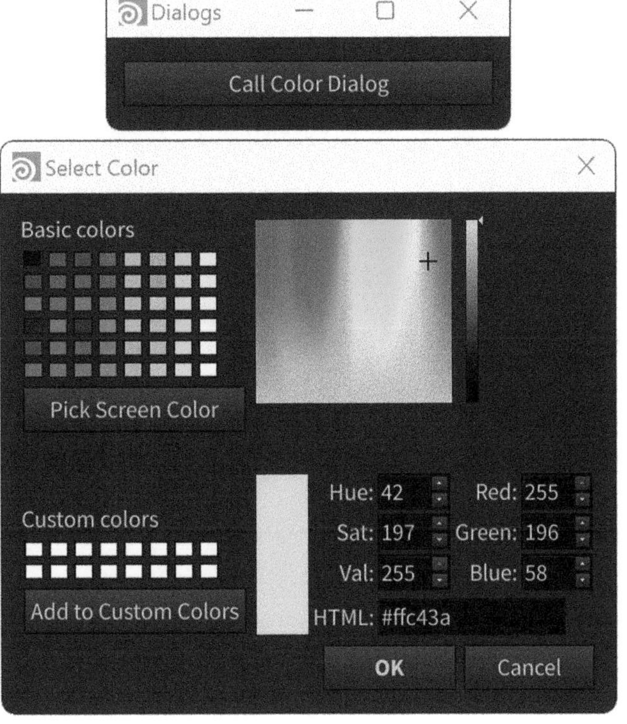

FIGURE 16.29 QColorDialog instantiation.

CONCLUSION

In the earliest days of Python, the language had no "official" interface package. Now, *Tkinter* is supported as the official graphical user interface module. Tkinter is simple and easy to use, and requires no additional package installation. A more stylistic and robust alternative is the *PyQt5* library. *PyQt5* is an industry standard interface package driving countless commercial applications. A license free alternative is *PySide2*. *PySide2* is the demonstrational library used in this text as it supports virtually all *PyQt5* functionality and accompanies each Houdini installation.

The very basics of the *PySide2* library are introduced displaying primitive windows in both Houdini and the command-line. Further details demonstrate effective procedures for translating *PySide2* interfaces into class objects. Working with instantiations of *PySide2* classes makes interface development easy to analyze and debug.

One of the most important *PySide2* classes is *QLayout*. *QLayouts* are interface containers manipulating the size and position of all enclosed widgets.

PySide2 supports an effective communication methodology called *Signals and Slots*. When interface events occur, the associated widget objects broadcast *signals* to all other connected widgets. Widgets opt to receive those signals by connecting *Slot* functions to the signals. One interface event may signal an unlimited number of function slots to handle broadcast signals. *Functools.partial()* and *lambda* are effective Python commands for creating customized signals for connected slots.

QMainWindow classes are robust, all-purpose widget containers. Structured to be complemented with toolbars, status bars, and menu bars, *QMainWindows* are the central widget class most interfaces are built around. *PySide2* supports a plethora of interface widget objects such as buttons, sliders, text boxes, dials, and other display devices. *QDialogs* are effective for generating top-level windows handling short-term tasks and brief communications. Dialog windows may be *modal* or *modeless*. When *modal*, the window interrupts all other application interaction until the window is terminated. *Modeless* windows operate concurrently with interfaces and block no other interactivity. Technical artists most frequently employ *QDialogButtonBoxes*, *QMessageBoxes*, *QFileDialogs*, and *QColorDialogs*.

INTRODUCTION

Learning interface APIs, such as PyQt and PySide, can be intimidating tasks especially for fledgling programmers. New interface developers do not need to feel intimidated as there are many tools available to assist designers to quickly assemble interfaces without having to worry about the widget logistics. (They are interfaces for designing interfaces.) The most popular tool for designing PyQt and PySide interfaces is QtDesigner.

QtDesigner is a thorough interface empowering users to quickly assemble and edit interfaces without dealing with code. Just as PyQt and PySide are non-trivial packages, QtDesigner requires some acclimation period. However, once understood, users will be able to implement fast and effective interfaces and integrate them within their Python code (or any other language) with relative ease.

Technical artists need to consider tools which help them build their own Python-tools as efficiently as possible. As artists, they also benefit from tools allowing them to visually drag, drop, and manipulate shapes instead of wrangling code. QtDesigner assists with both responsibilities. While coding by hand provides the ultimate amount of creative freedom, QtDesigner empowers rapid interface formulation.

To provide Qt and PySide coverage, QtDesigner is robust. This chapter does not attempt to replace more thorough texts explaining the tool's ins and outs. Instructions are provided to download and install a version of QtDesigner which works well with the Houdini environment. A roadmap explaining the tool's landscape is provided as well as instructions for creating first interfaces and integrating them with Houdini Python code. Quick explanations of QtDesigner's features are included as well as descriptions of widgets' integrations. Practice helps new programmers gain efficiency with QtDesigner. This chapter assists with their journey.

INSTALLATION

Installations of PyQt and PySide may include QtDesigner. However, for novice users unfamiliar with Python environments and folder hierarchies, finding and executing the tool may be challenging. For convenience, a link and installation instructions for an external version are provided, independent of PyQt or PySide.

Default Installations

For those comfortable with configuring Python environments, QtDesigner is available after installing *qttools5-dev-tools*, *qttools5-dev*, and *QtCreator* packages. While the locations will probably change with future versions of Qt, QtDesigner for Qt5 is found in the Python installation's *site-packages* folder: *PythonInstallation\site-packages\qt5_applications\Qt\bin*. QtDesigner is also included with each installed version of Houdini: *\Houdini<version>\python<version>\lib\site-packages-forced\PySide2*.

External Tool Installation

To assist with the complexity of accessing and executing QtDesigner, there exists a *stand-alone* version of the software. The stand-alone version can be placed wherever is convenient and is not dependent on current installations of Qt. It can be downloaded from *https://build-system.fman.io/qt-designer-download*. Special thanks go to Michael Herrmann and his *Fman Build System* (*https://build-system.fman.io/#features*) for providing this convenient stand-alone.

DOI: 10.1201/9781003016427-17

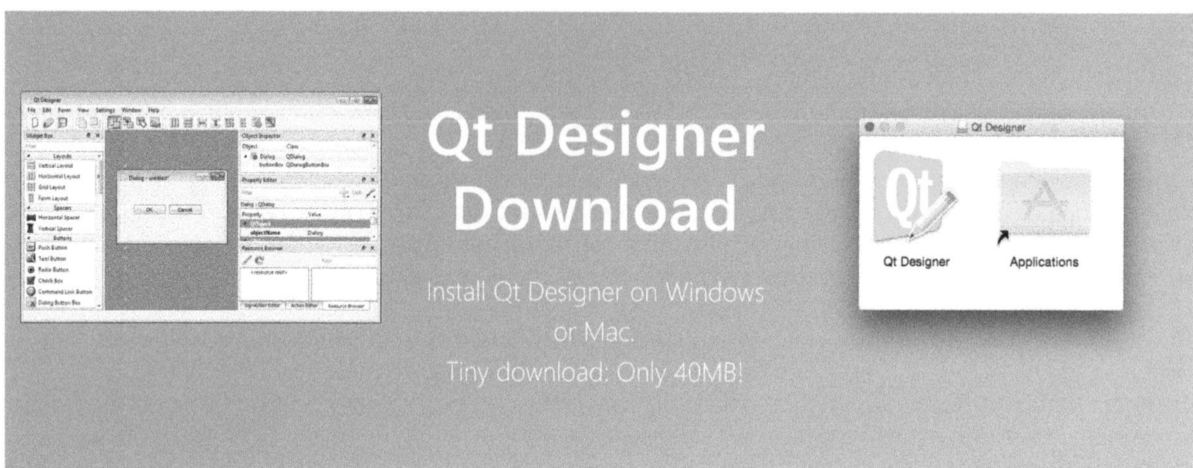
fman build system
Features Documentation Book Pro
Qt Designer
Download
Install Qt Designer on Windows
or Mac.
Tiny download: Only 40MB!
Qt Designer
Qt Designer
Applications
Many people want to use Qt Designer without having to download gigabytes of other software. Here are small, standalone installers of Qt Designer for Windows and Mac:

Windows (31 MB)

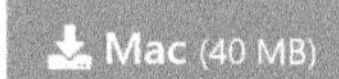
Mac (40 MB)

FIGURE 17.1 https://build-system.fman.io/qt-designer-download.

On the download page, as shown in Figure 17.1, select either the Windows or Mac installation. (Sorry Linux ☹)

After selection, a *QtDesigner Setup* application is downloaded. Execute the application to initiate the installation. The user is presented with an introduction screen: Figure 17.2. Press the *Next* button.

The application wizard prompts for the installation location. Enter the desired destination and press the *Install* button, shown in Figure 17.3.

After the application finishes installation, press the *Next* button: Figure 17.4.

Press the *Start QtDesigner* and *Finish* to start QtDesigner: Figure 17.5.

When launched correctly, the QtDesigner window should look like Figure 17.6.

A *New Form* pop-up window queries users if they would like to *Create* a new interface, *Open* an existing interface, open a *Recent* interface, or simply *Close* the selection interface. Unless users are very familiar with Qt or know exactly what they want, the *Main Window* template should be selected, followed by the *Create* button, shown in Figure 17.7.

QtDesigner will generate a new, Qt Main Window canvas available for users to populate: Figure 17.8.

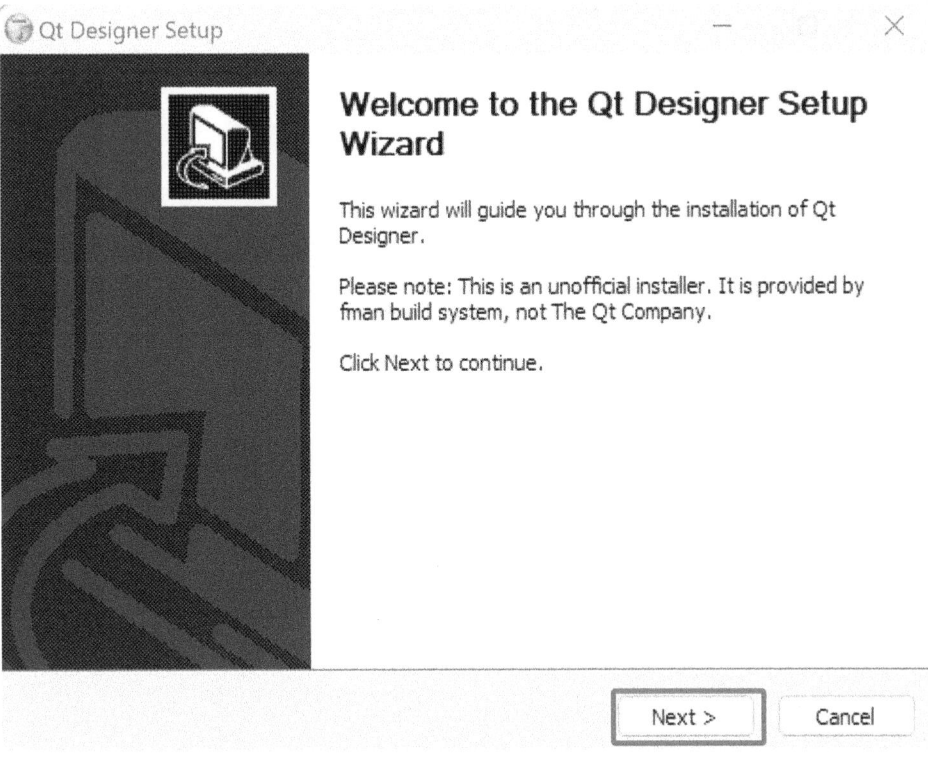

FIGURE 17.2 QtDesigner setup application.

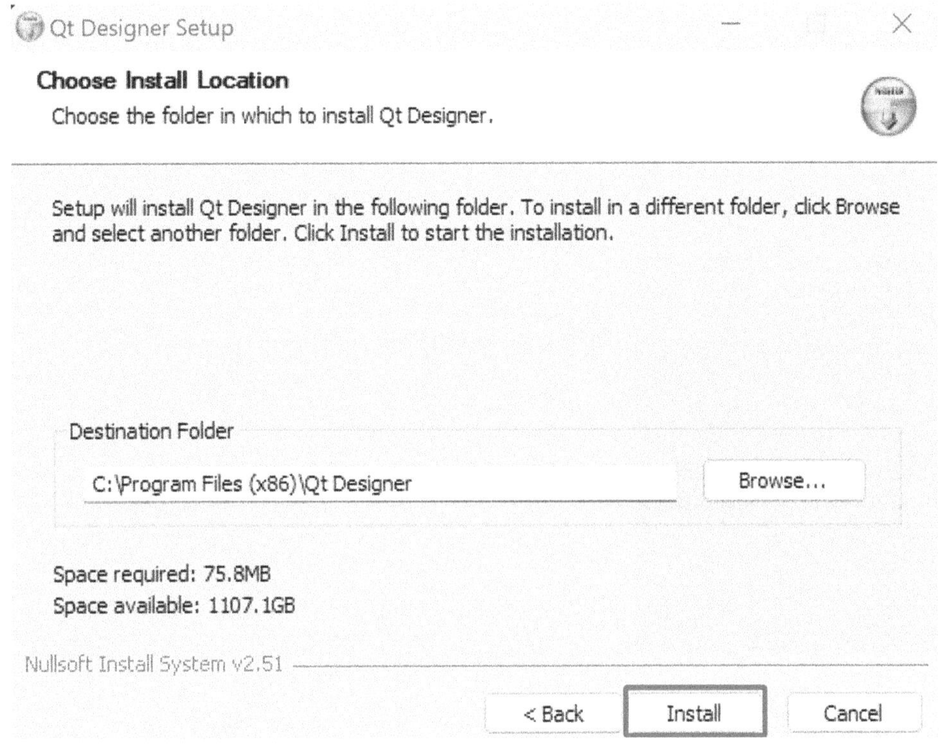

FIGURE 17.3 Installation location.

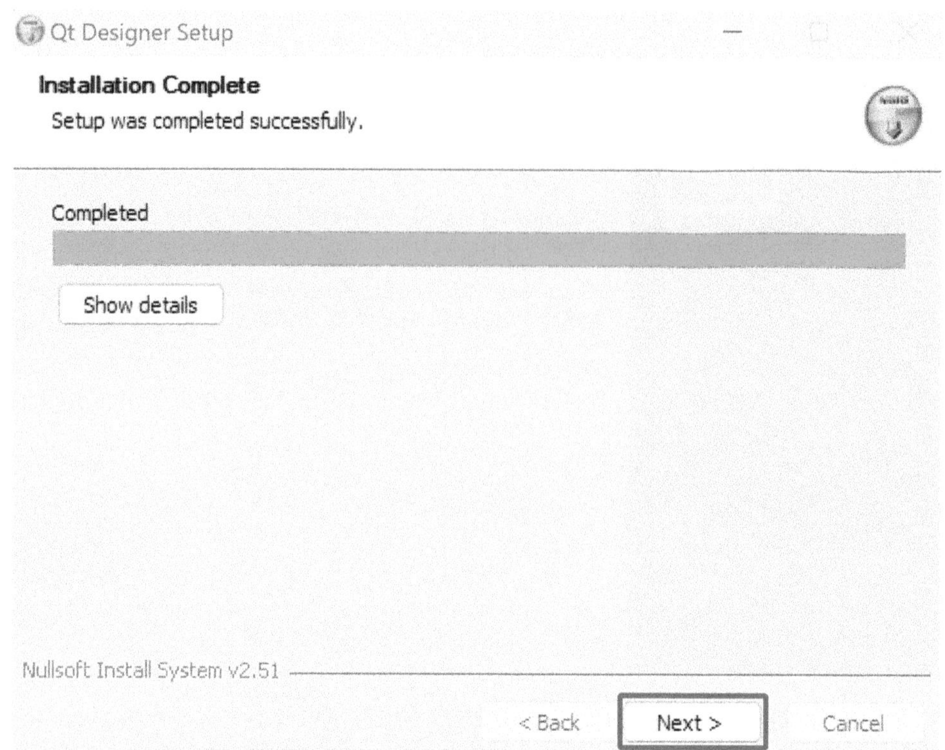

FIGURE 17.4 Complete installation.

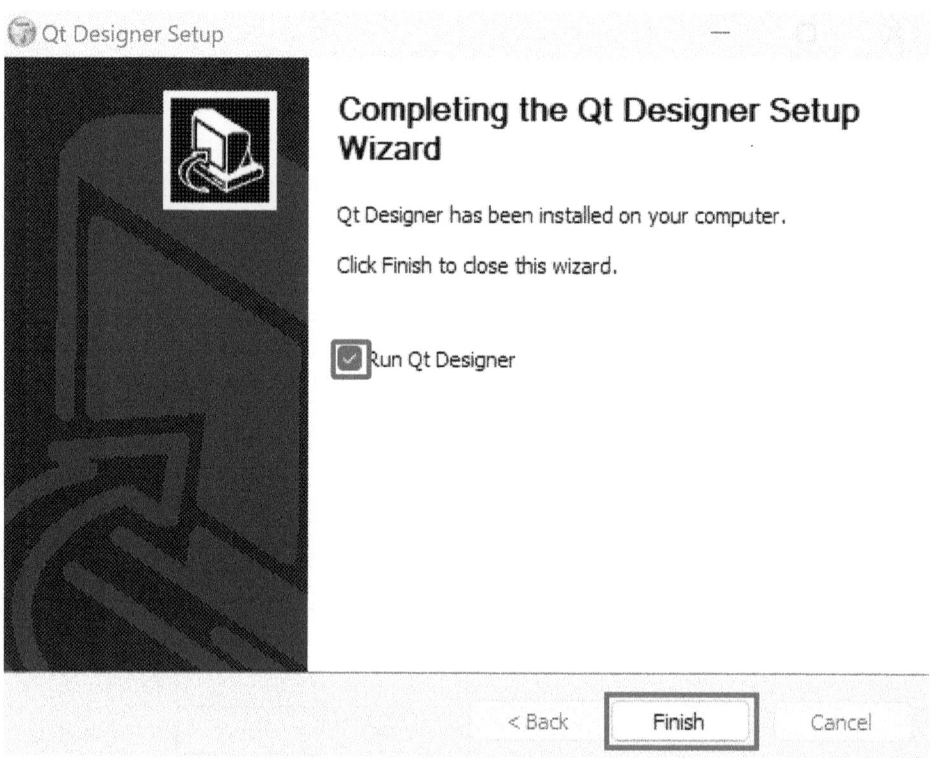

FIGURE 17.5 Finish and run QtDesigner.

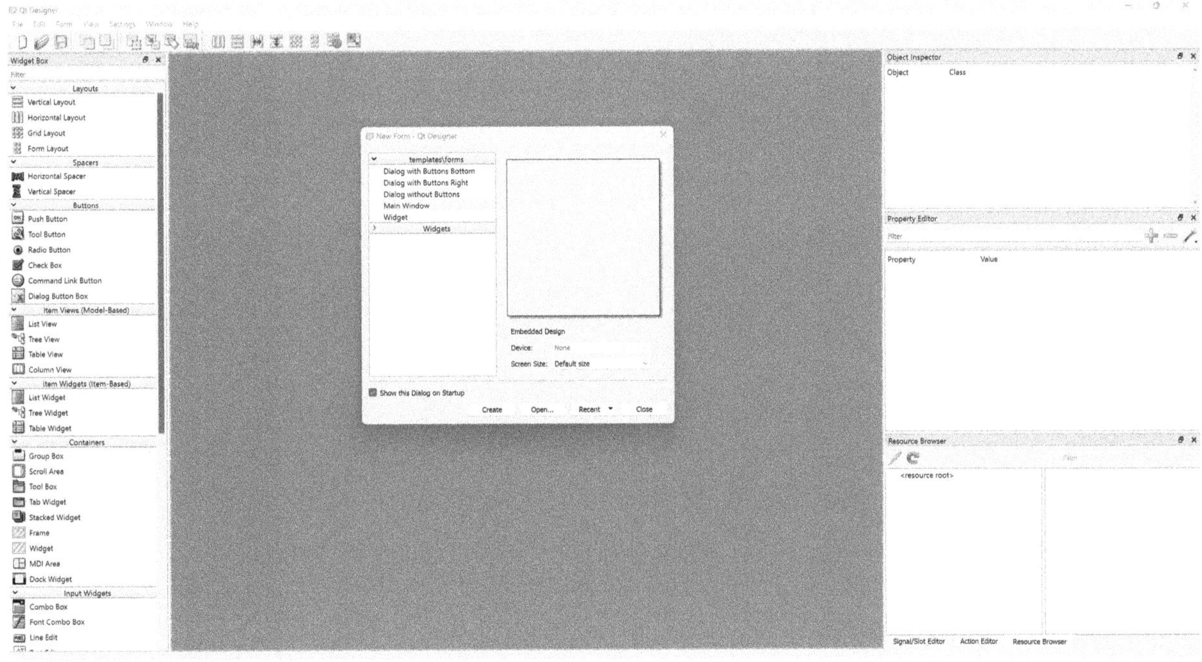

FIGURE 17.6 QtDesigner window.

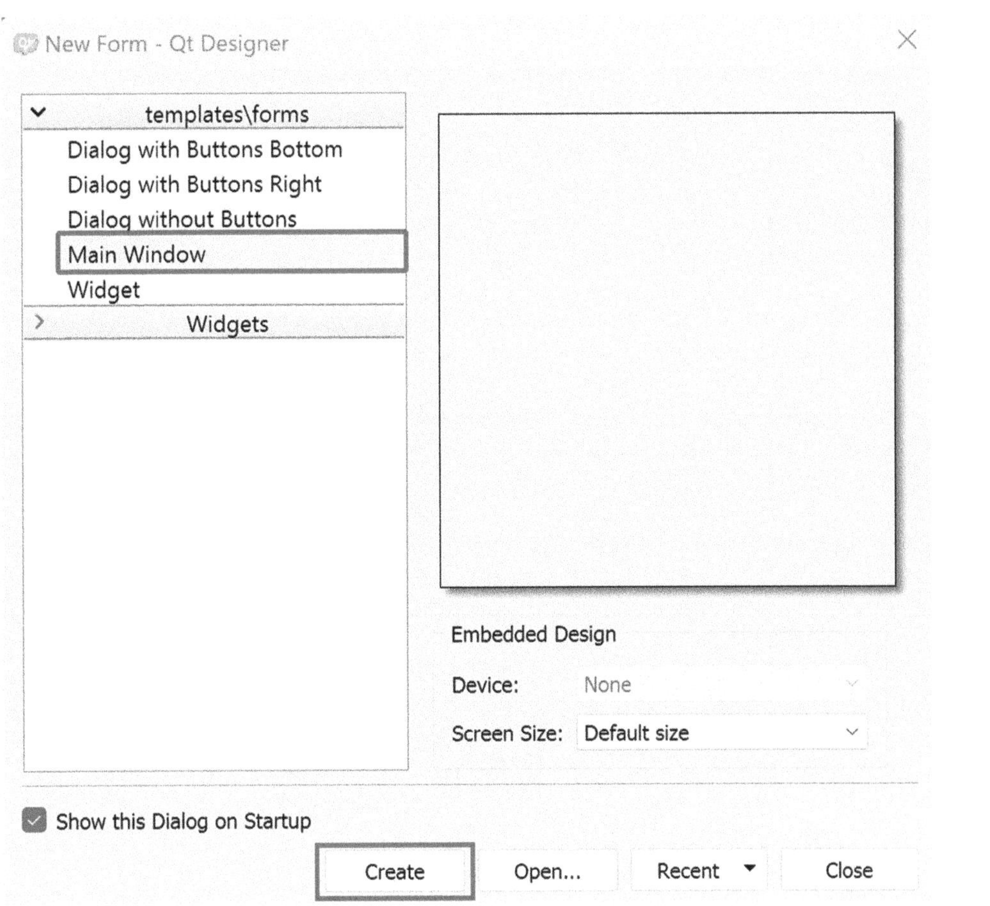

FIGURE 17.7 Create template pop-up.

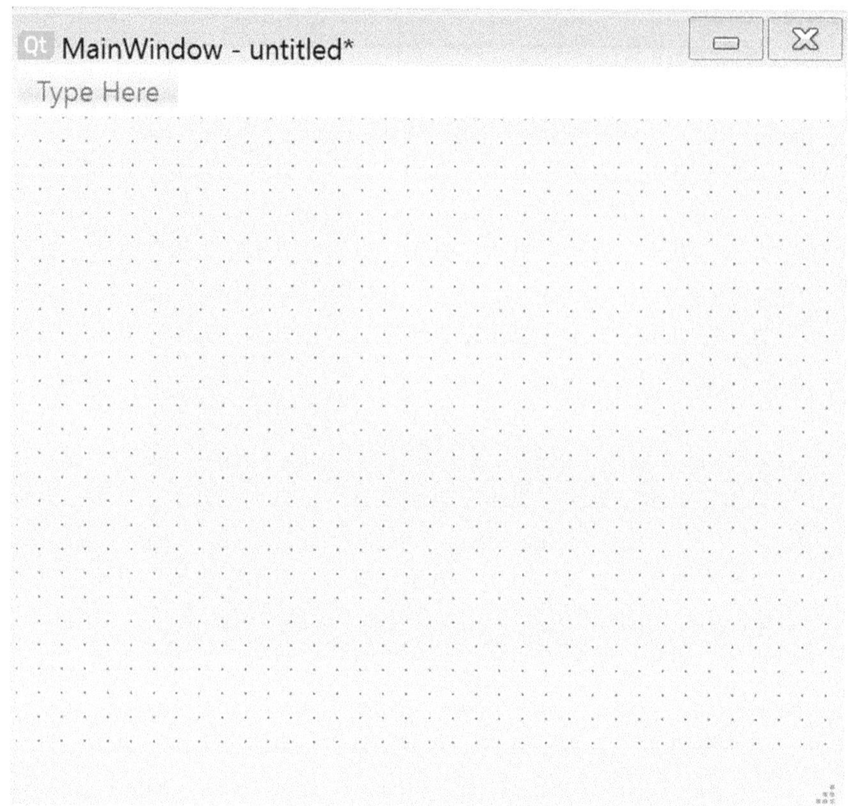

FIGURE 17.8 Empty Qt main window canvas.

TOOL LAYOUT

Figure 17.9 displays QtDesigner laid out into three main regions: the center canvas display, the left *Widget Box*, and the right attribute editor.

The central canvas contains the first *MainWindow* widget. Users construct their interfaces by laying out widgets and arranging them within the MainWindow's canvas. All added widgets are children of the MainWindow widget.

The left Widget Box is where primitive widgets are displayed. Users select desired widget icons from the box then drag and drop them into their desired location on the central MainWindow canvas. Most of the available box widgets are described in Chapter 16.

The right column is composed of five different tools allowing users to manipulate widgets attributes and parameters: Object Inspector, Property Editor, Signal/Slot Editor, Action Editor, and Resource Browser. The Object Inspector displays and allows users to select from a hierarchical list of tool objects laid onto the interface. The object's name, which is editable, is displayed along with its object class. The Property Editor displays editable attributes of currently selected objects in the Object Inspector. The attributes conform to the object's class type. The Signal/Slot Editor allows users to add, remove, and reconfigure signal/slot connections. Through double clicking the left mouse button, users may alter the source object and signal type as well as the receiver object and slot type. The Action Editor allows users to add, remove, and alter the behavior of QtActions. QtActions are the interactive widgets use by toolbars and menus. The Resource Bowser allows users to select, edit, and re-load resources to be specified together with the forms they are designed.

Window Preview

The QtDesigner experience is not entirely "What-You-See-Is-What-You-Get". To observe and interact with interfaces as they will behave when integrated within code, previews are required. Previews are generated from the

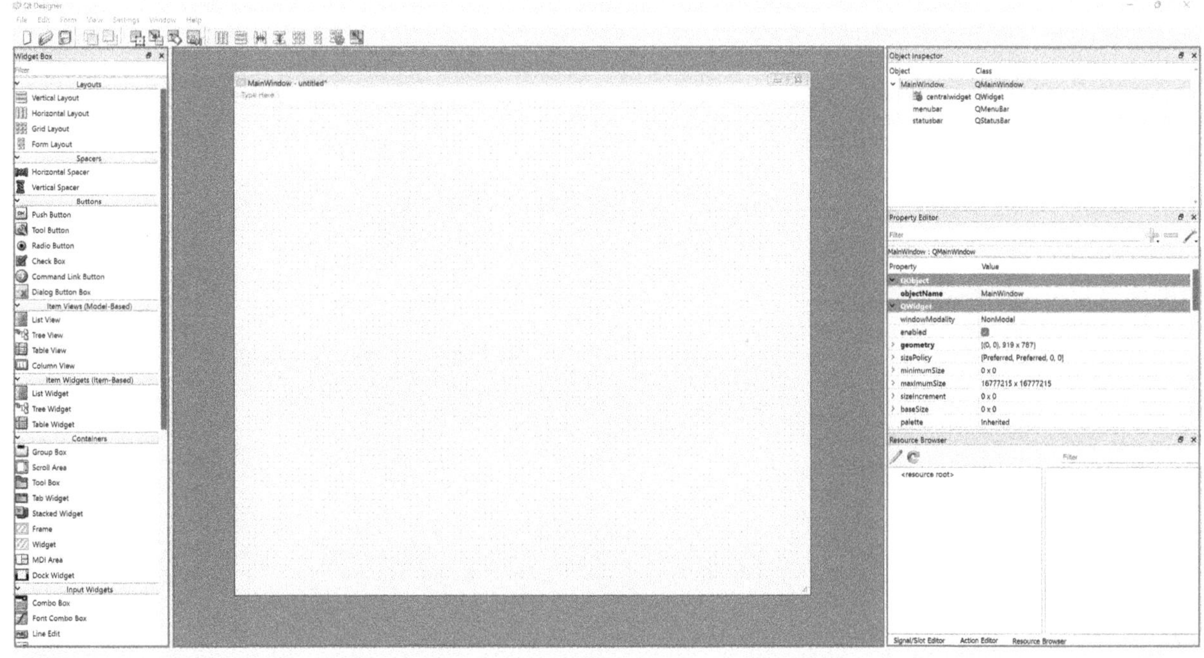

FIGURE 17.9 QtDesigner layout.

main window toolbar *Form->Preview*, or from the *ctrl+R hotkey*. The preview interface provides an indication how the interface will look and behave when fully integrated. All previews are terminable by pressing the "X" in the upper right interface corner.

DESIGN PHILOSOPHY

Much is required to explain tool creation than dropping a few widgets onto blank canvases. Widgets need to remain relative to each other and maintain intended proportion and position when the window is resized or its shape is altered. Qt library's primary tools for handling this are *layouts*.

Window Mobility

To demonstrate the importance of maintaining relative widget position and proportion, the reader is encouraged to try the following exercise. From the *Buttons* section on the left side Widget Box, randomly drag and drop button widgets and place them on a blank Main Window canvas, similarly to Figure 17.10. The buttons may have been placed irregularly without alignment but it has the start of a decent interface.

To preview the interface and observe how it behaves, press *ctrl+R*. This creates a preview, Figure 17.11, of how the tool will look and behave when integrated within a Python script.

A strange phenomenon happens when the preview window is resized. The buttons remain in their set position, even when being clipped. This phenomenon is captured in Figure 17.12.

Unless intended, this behavior is not desirable for most tool interfaces.

Layouts

Layouts are Qt strategies for organizing widgets and managing their relative size and position when the window is resized. Once widgets have been inserted into a layout, the layout explicitly controls their geometry; they must maintain their relative position and scale within the layout. Layouts may be created in any one of two ways: as a *Top-Level Layout* or as a Layout Widget.

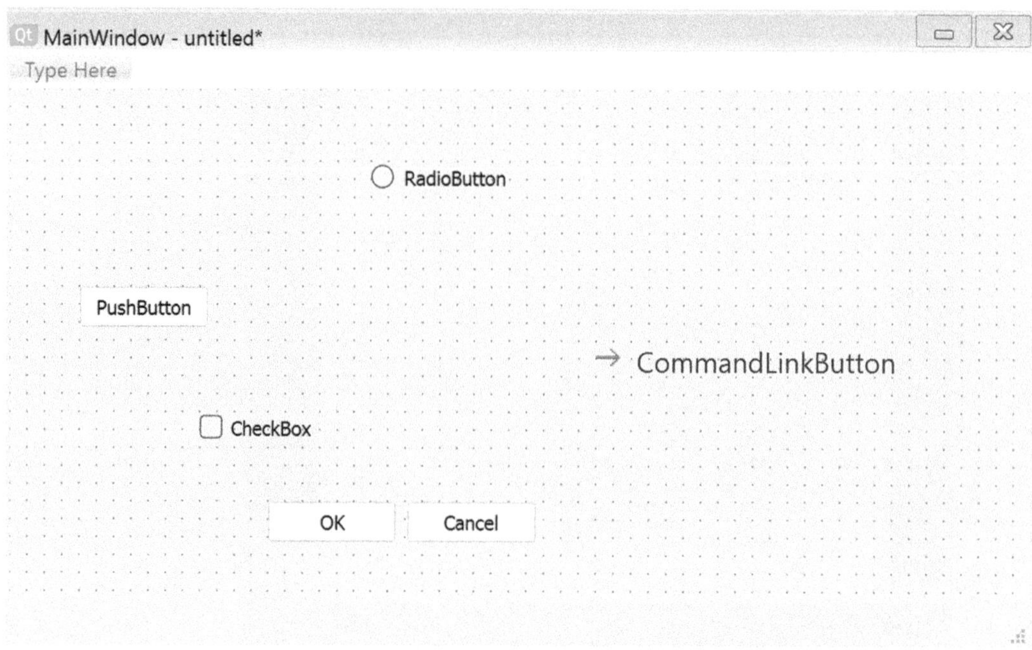

FIGURE 17.10 Randomly placed buttons.

FIGURE 17.11 Tool preview window.

Top-Level Layout

Any open space within an interface canvas can be declared as a layout. Widgets are first placed within the canvas, like in Figure 17.13.

The desired layout strategy is selected from the top row of buttons in the QtDesigner interface: Figure 17.14.

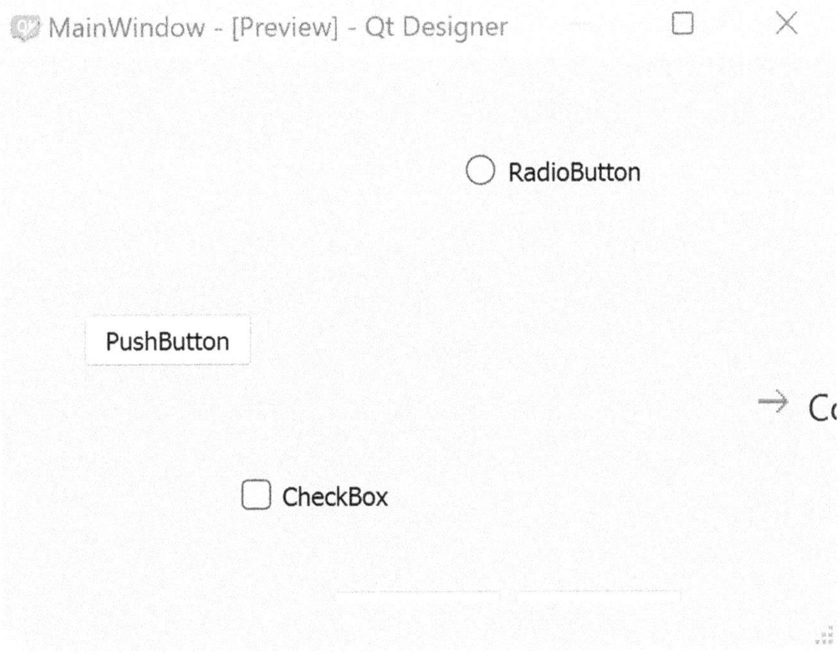

FIGURE 17.12 Clipped preview window.

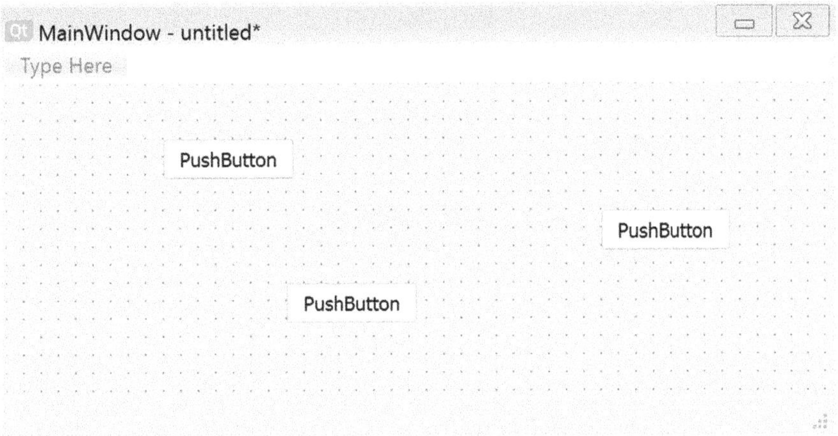

FIGURE 17.13 Arbitrary widgets.

FIGURE 17.14 Top-level layout options.

Selecting the desired layout strategy reorganizes and scales widget geometries to conform to the canvas: Figure 17.15.

When the interface is previewed (ctrl+R), the objects within the layout maintain their relative position and scale even when the window is resized, similar to Figure 17.16.

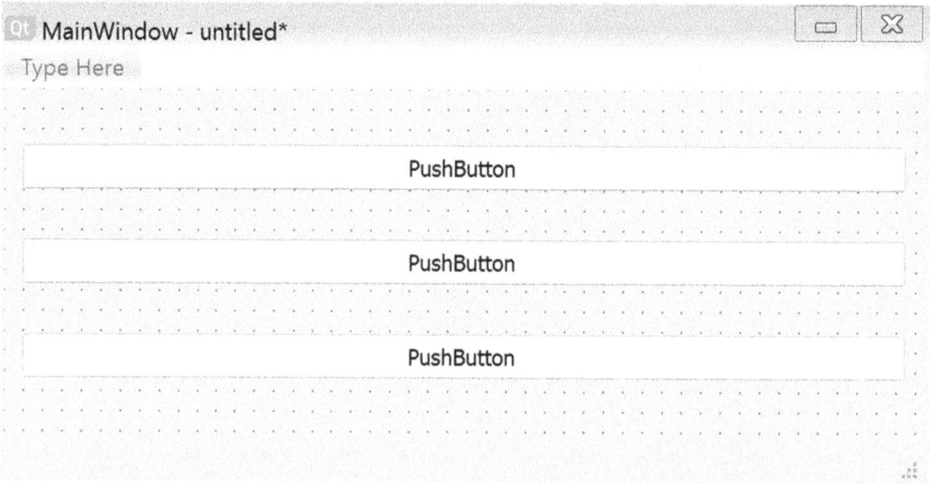

FIGURE 17.15 Vertical top-level layout.

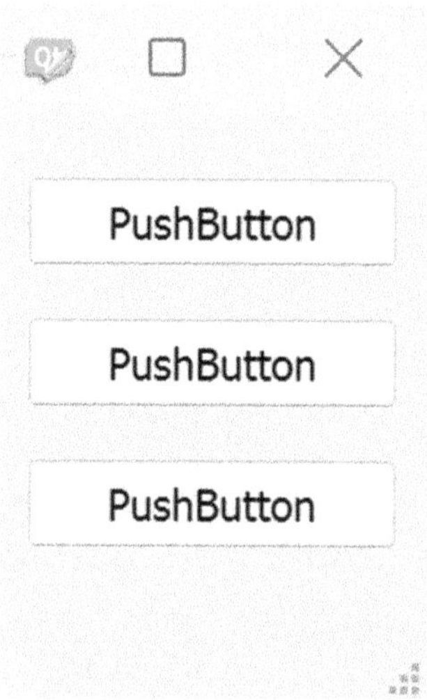

FIGURE 17.16 Resized preview top-level layout.

All future widgets conform to structure when dropped into layouts, as demonstrated in Figure 17.17.

Layout Widgets

Layouts can also be treated as widget objects. Just as any widget object must conform with its top-level layout, so too do layout widgets. Layout widgets are identified in window canvases as narrow, red-line boxes. Figure 17.18 contains a vertical layout widget in a horizontal top-level layout.

Layout widgets are crucial components for generating hierarchies of layouts. Users are encouraged to organize the desired layout structures into hierarchies before fleshing-in widget attributes, like Figure 17.19.

Layout Types

There are four layout types: vertical, horizontal, form, and grid.

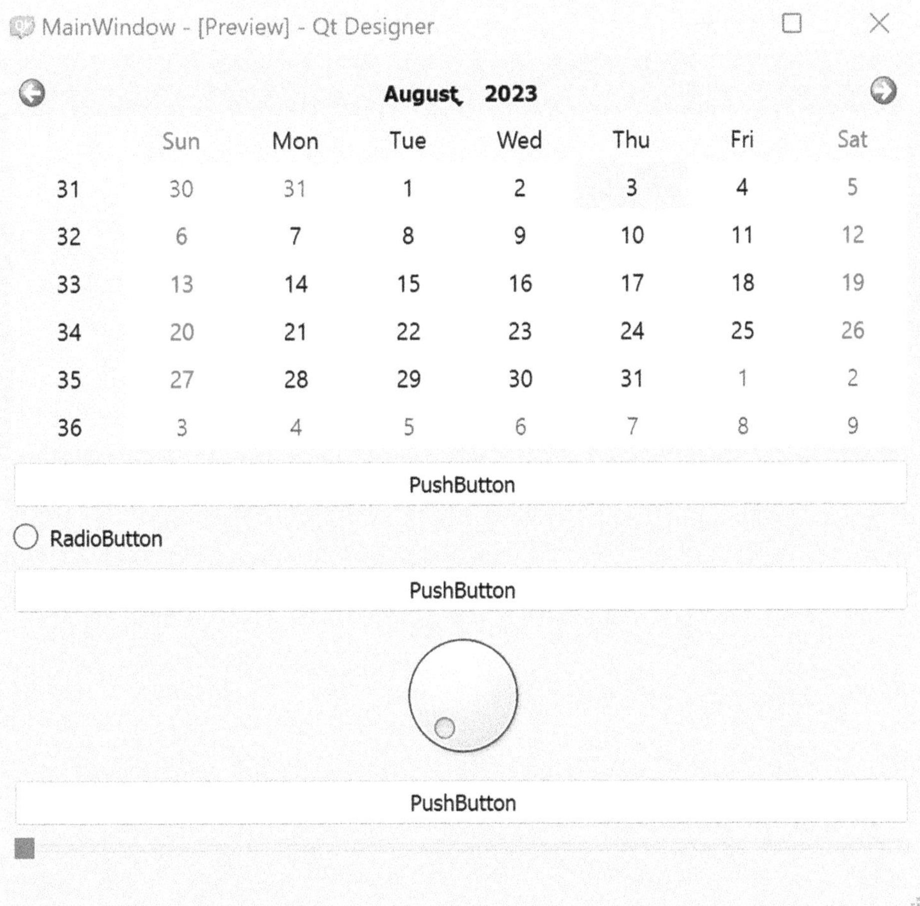

FIGURE 17.17 Additional widgets in vertical layout.

FIGURE 17.18 Vertical layout widget in horizontal top-level layout.

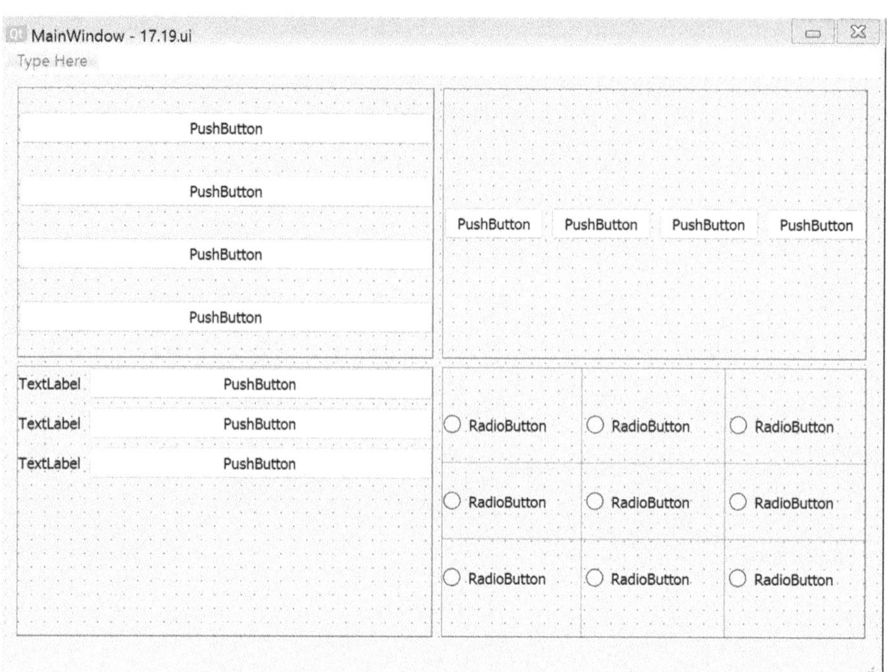

FIGURE 17.19 Hierarchy of layout widgets within a top-level grid layout.

Vertical Layout

Vertical layouts organize multiple widgets in a vertical direction. Users append new widgets to the layout by dropping them above, below, or in-between existing widgets, as in Figure 17.20.

Horizontal Layout

Horizontal layouts organize multiple widgets in a horizontal direction. Users append new widgets to the layout by dropping them to the left, right, or in-between existing widgets, similarly to Figure 17.21.

Form Layout

Form layouts organize pairs of widgets into two columns. New pairs of widgets are added to the layout above, below, or in-between existing widget pairs, as shown in Figure 17.22.

Grid Layout

Grid layouts organize widgets into **M** × **N** arrangements. When creating new rows or columns, new widgets are appended left, right, above, below, or in-between existing widgets. When the number of column widgets does not match the number of row widgets, red boxes identify potential new widget positions, as shown in Figure 17.23.

FIRST INTERFACE

Inventing interfaces in QtDesigner is fast and rapid. Their visual correctness may be previewed by pressing *ctrl+R*. However, programmers still need to integrate their interfaces with their Python code. QtDesigner only exports interface definitions as *'.ui'*, XML files. There are two strategies for incorporating these *'.ui'* XML files. The first strategy employs external tools (*pyside2-uic, pyuic, etc.*) to convert *'.ui'* XML files into Python classes, stored in external modules. These modules are importable to all Python code. The second strategy reads *'.ui'* XML files directly into Python code and converts them to Python objects. They may be converted into function objects or class objects. For simplicity, the later strategy is explained.

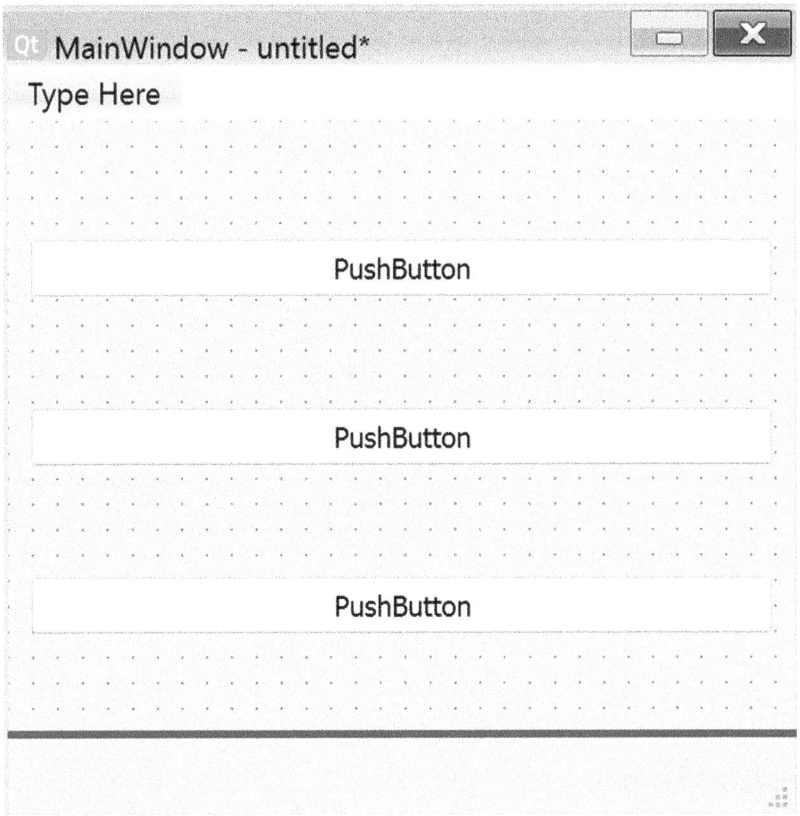

FIGURE 17.20 Vertical layout.

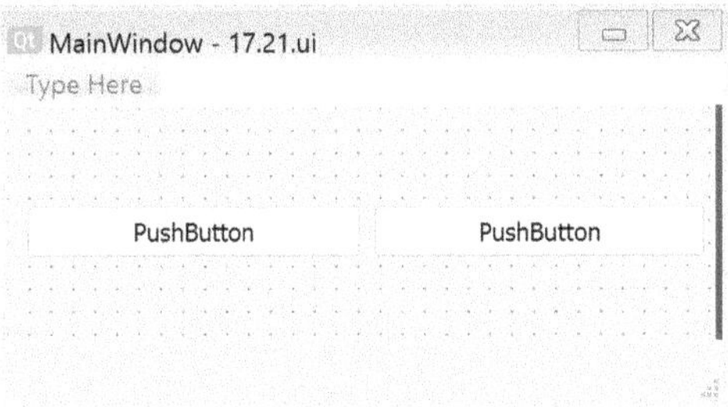

FIGURE 17.21 Horizontal layout.

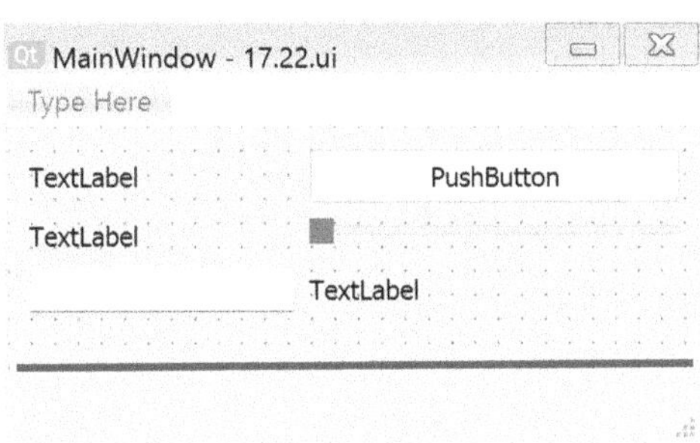

FIGURE 17.22 Form layout.

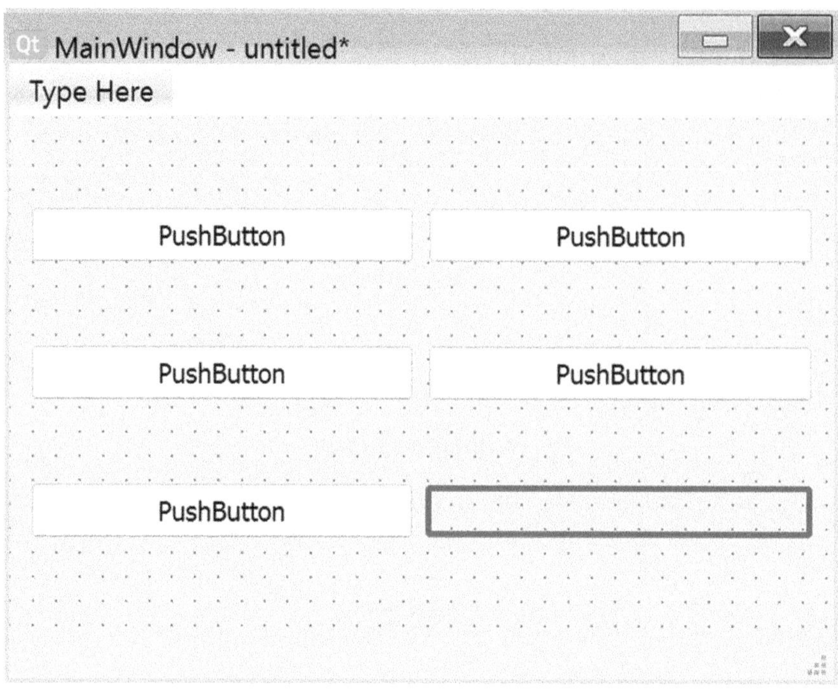

FIGURE 17.23 Grid layout.

Adding and Verifying Widgets

Create a new *Main Window* canvas. Drop in a push button widget. Select either vertical or horizontal layouts. Test the interfaces' stability by previewing it, *ctrl+R*. Verify the interface adjusts properly when the window is resized: Figure 17.24.

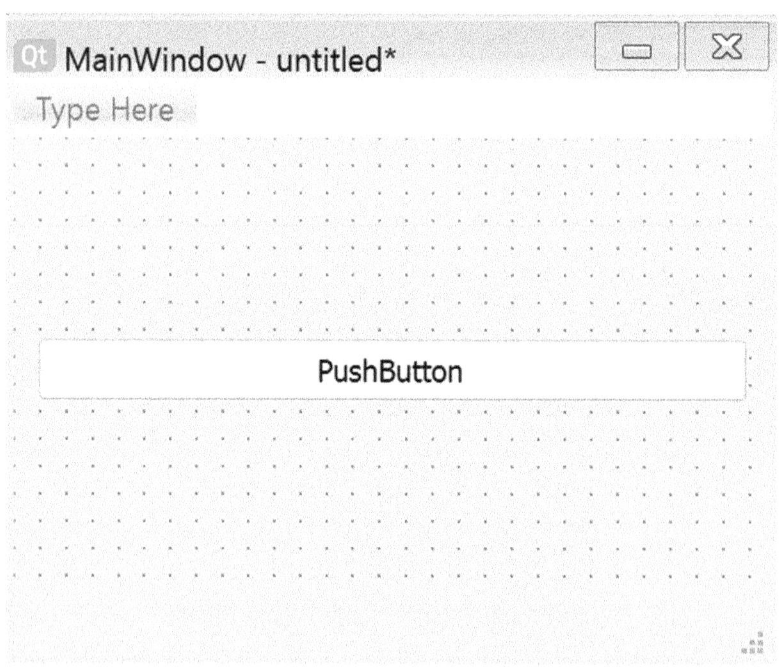

FIGURE 17.24 Widget in layout.

Widget Attributes

In the *Property Editor*, change the window's *objectName* attribute to "FirstInterface", as shown in Figure 17.25.

Notice the window label does not change. The object's name and its label are two different attributes. Identify the *windowTitle* attribute in the *Property Editor* and change the label to, "First Interface". The window title label changes to reflect the new value, like Figure 17.26.

The push button's object name and label need to change also. Select the push button object. Change the *objectName* attribute to "FirstPushButton". Change the push button *QAbstractButton's text* attributed to "First Push Button", as shown in Figure 17.27.

Preview the interface's integrity with *ctrl+R*.

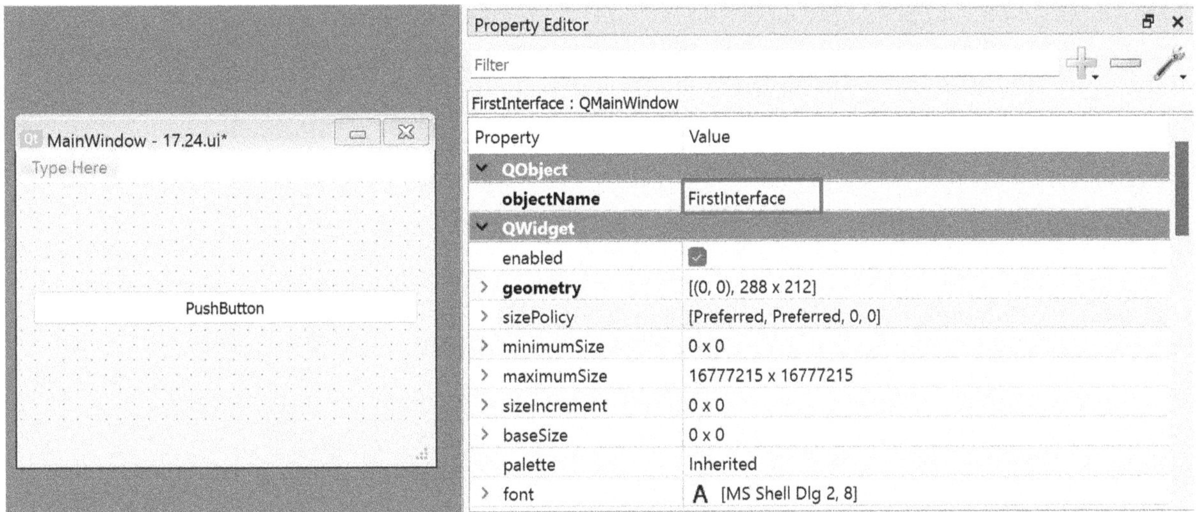

FIGURE 17.25 FirstInterface objectName.

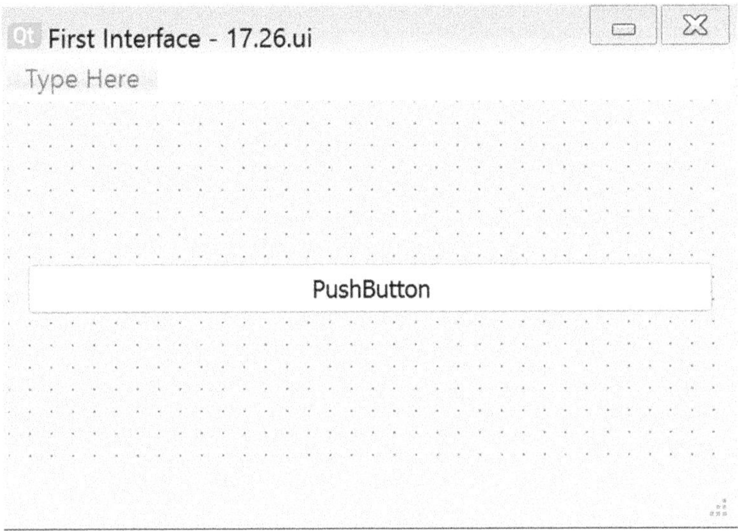

FIGURE 17.26 WindowTitle label changed.

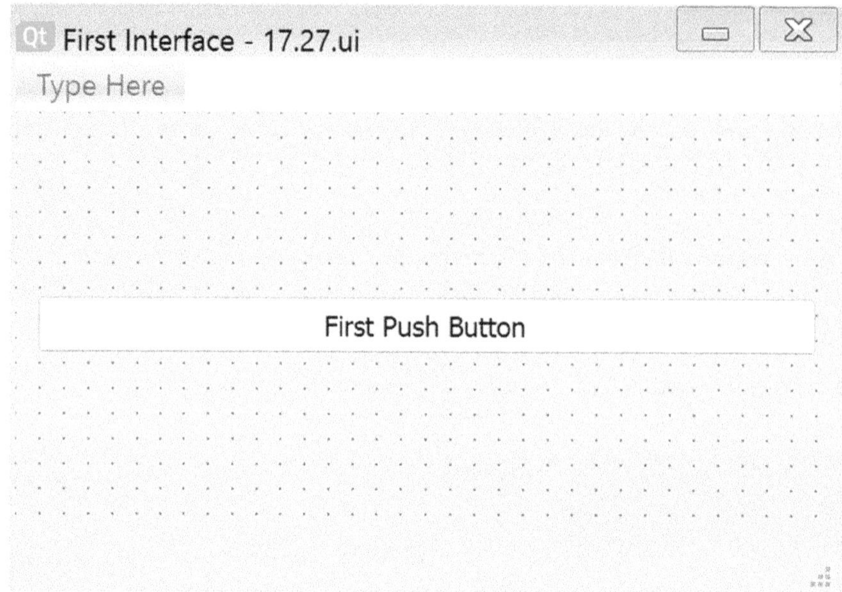

FIGURE 17.27 FirstPushButton object and text.

Interface File

Once satisfied with the interface, save it as "FirstQtDesigner.ui"; preferably in the same Python script folder. A '.ui' file is an XML document containing the interface's object hierarchy and attributes. The file's contents are shown in Code Sample 17.1. Everything needed to re-create the interface is stored in this file.

```
<?xml version="1.0" encoding="UTF-8"?>
<ui version="4.0">
 <class>FirstInterface</class>
 <widget class="QMainWindow" name="FirstInterface">
  <property name="geometry">
   <rect>
    <x>0</x>
    <y>0</y>
    <width>319</width>
    <height>196</height>
   </rect>
  </property>
  <property name="windowTitle">
   <string>First Interface</string>
  </property>
```

```
    <widget class="QWidget" name="centralwidget">
     <layout class="QVBoxLayout" name="verticalLayout">
      <item>
       <widget class="QPushButton" name="FirstPushButton">
        <property name="text">
         <string>First Push Button</string>
        </property>
       </widget>
      </item>
     </layout>
    </widget>
    <widget class="QMenuBar" name="menubar">
     <property name="geometry">
      <rect>
       <x>0</x>
       <y>0</y>
       <width>319</width>
       <height>21</height>
      </rect>
     </property>
    </widget>
    <widget class="QStatusBar" name="statusbar"/>
   </widget>
   <resources/>
   <connections/>
  </ui>
```

Code Sample 17.1 FirstQtDesigner.ui

Function Script

PySide is equipped with intrinsic tools for reading and integrating external *'.ui'* files. Regretfully their implementation is not as simple as opening an external file for reading or writing. They are best organized within functions. Code Sample 17.2 demonstrates a simple function structure incorporating these external files. The resulting window should look like Figure 17.28.

```
# Import os library to organize .ui file path name
import os
# Import core Pyside2 library
from PySide2 import QtCore
# Import PySide2 user interface toolset
from PySide2.QtUiTools import QUiLoader

# Declare function with UI file name parameter
def loadDesignerUIFile(file_path):
    # Create QUILoader instance
    qui_loader = QUiLoader()
    # Tell loader where to find file
qui_loader.setWorkingDirectory(os.path.dirname(file_path))
    # Define UI file as a Q object
    ui_file = QtCore.QFile(file_path)
    # Open object file contents
    ui_file.open(QtCore.QFile.ReadOnly)
    # Convert UI file to a new widget object
    widgetObject = qui_loader.load(ui_file)
    # Configure the new widget for display
widgetObject.setWindowFlags(QtCore.Qt.Widget)

    # Return the new top-level widget
    return widgetObject

# Call loader function with UI file path argument
myInterface = loadDesignerUIFile("C:\Temp\code\FirstQTDesigner.ui")

# Display top-level widget
myInterface.show()
```

Code Sample 17.2 ui File Loader Function

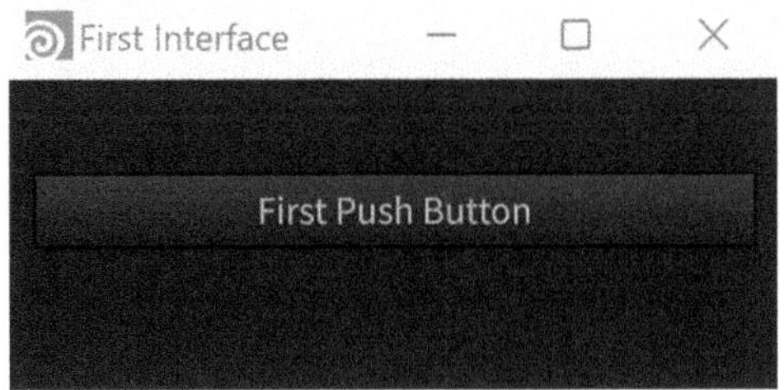

FIGURE 17.28 First QTDesigner results.

The *os* library is needed to extract the file path of the *'.ui'* file. The *QtCore* library is need to utilize *QFile* objects. The *QUiLoader* object method is loaded from the *PySide2.QtUiTools* module to transform the *'.ui'* file to a Qt object.

The *loadDesignerUIFile()* function takes a file path parameter, *file_path*, converts the contents of the external file to a Qt widget object, and returns it. For this to happen, a new *QUiLoader object is* instanced as *qui_loader*. The file path folder is loaded into the loader object using the *setWorkingDirectory()* method, employing the os.*path.dirname()* method. A *QFile* object is instanced to *ui_file*, and opened. The *qui_loader* loader object employs its *load()* method to read the *ui_file* contents and convert them to a Qt widget object variable, *WidgetObject*. The display flags for the widget object are configured with the *setWindowFlags()* method. The function finishes by returning the resulting *widgetObject*.

The first line of script code calls the *loadDesignerUIFile()* with the external file path argument and assigns the resulting widget object to variable *myInterface*. The *myInterface* widget object is displayed using its *show()* method.

Function Class

As with all Qt interfaces, they are easier to work with when bound within classes. The same principle applies when reading QtDesigner interfaces. Code Sample 17.3 integrates the interface loading function, *loadDesignerUIFile()*, into a class upon which the interface is created and reconfigured. Figure 17.29 displays the expected results.

```
# Import os library to organize .ui file path name
import os
# Import core Pyside2 library
from PySide2 import QtCore, QtGui, QtWidgets
# Import PySide2 user interface toolset
from PySide2.QtUiTools import QUiLoader


class MyDesignerClass():
    # Declare class constructor
    def __init__(self, *args, **kwargs):
        designerPath = "C:\Temp\code\FirstQTDesigner.ui"
        # Import QMainWindow widget from external UI FIle
        self.ui= self.loadDesignerUIFile(designerPath)
        # Configure Interface
        self.configUI()
```

```
    # Expose QMainWindow's show() method
    def show(self):
        self.ui.show()

    # Configure interface
    def configUI(self):

    self.ui.FirstPushButton.setText("New Button Label")

    # Class loader function
    # Declare function with UI file name parameter
    def loadDesignerUIFile(self,file_path):
        # Create QUILoader instance
        qui_loader = QUiLoader()
        # Tell loader where to find file
        qui_loader.setWorkingDirectory(os.path.dirname(file_path))
        # Define UI file as a Q object
        ui_file = QtCore.QFile(file_path)
        # Open object file contents
        ui_file.open(QtCore.QFile.ReadOnly)
        # Convert UI file to new widget object
        widgetObject = qui_loader.load(ui_file)
        # Configure new widget for display
        widgetObject.setWindowFlags(QtCore.Qt.Widget)

        # Return new top-level widget
        return widgetObject


# Instance MyDesignerClass
window = MyDesignerClass()
# Use class' exposed show() method
window.show()
```

Code Sample 17.3 QtDesigner Qt Interface Class

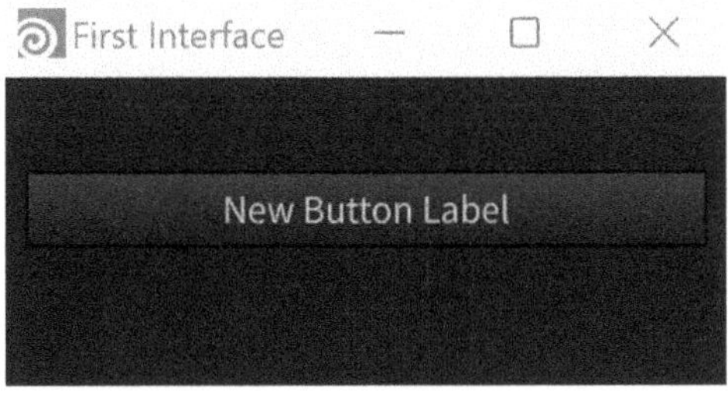

FIGURE 17.29 QtDesigner Qt interface class.

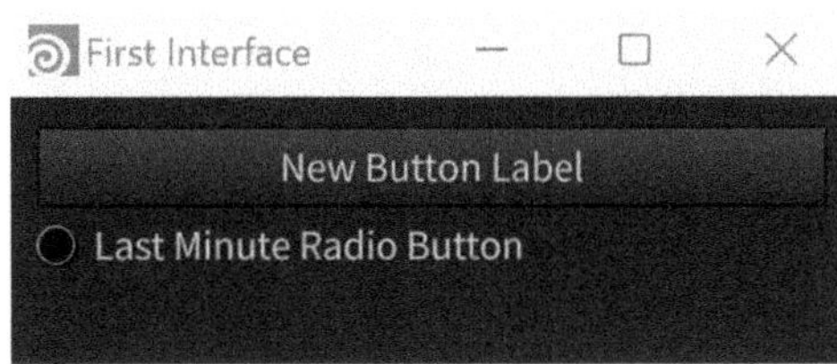

FIGURE 17.30 Result after QtDesigner file alteration.

This example imports the same *os*, *QtCore*, *QtGui*, *QtWidgets*, and *QUiLoader* libraries as code sample *17.2*. A new class, *MyDesignerClass()*, is declared. The constructor performs two functions: it loads the external *QtDesigner* file, and reconfigures the interface. The same function from the prior example, loadDesignerUIFile(), is integrated as a class method and assigns its returned widget object to class variable, *self.ui*. The class method, *configUI()* method, is used to make modifications to the imported interface and create essential class bindings. The *show()* method exposes the widgetObject's *show()* method. This is a convenient method and limits *self.ui* external exposure.

Convenient Feature

Strategies, such as using the *pyside2-uic* application for converting *'.ui'* XML files into importable custom classes, require re-converting QtDesigner files every time changes are made. The strategy from code sample *17.3* only requires saving over existing QtDesigner *.ui* files to incorporate last-minute changes without altering code.
The update is displayed in Figure 17.30.

Until interfaces are locked and frozen, this strategy promotes fast interface iteration and rapid development.

OBJECT SIGNAL BINDING

As described in Chapter 16, all Qt widget object events generate *signals*. *Slots* are object functions assigned to listen for those signals. When particular object events occur, they broadcast signals to all their connected slots. Intrinsic widget functions can be assigned to object signals using the *QtDesigner Signal/Slot* editor. All other signal/slot connections must be established in code. *Signal functions*, as defined in Language Template 17.1, are assigned to object *slots* by identifying the signal name followed by the *connect()* command with the *slot* name parameter.

```
object.<Signal Name>.connect(<Slot Function Name>)
```

Language Template 17.1 Connecting Slot Function to Object Signal

Code Sample 17.4 expands on Code Sample 17.3 demonstrating the *configUI()* function is an ideal location to create signal/slot connections. In the following example, a new class method, displayTitle(), is introduced to print a simple message. The *displayTitle()* slot function is connected to the *FirstPushButton.clicked* event in the *configUI()* method.

```
import os
# Import core Pyside2 library and interface toolset
from PySide2 import QtCore, QtGui, QtWidgets
from PySide2.QtUiTools import QUiLoader


class MyDesignerClass():
    # Declare class constructor
    def __init__(self, *args, **kwargs):

        designerPath = " C:\Temp\code\FirstQTDesigner.ui"
        # Import QMainWindow widget from external UI FIle
        self.ui= self.loadDesignerUIFile(designerPath)
        # Configure Interface
        self.configUI()

    # Abtract QMainWindow's show() method
    def show(self):
        self.ui.show()

    # Configure interface
    def configUI(self):
        self.ui.FirstPushButton.setText("New Button Label")
        self.ui.FirstPushButton.clicked.connect(self.displayTitle)

    # Class loader function
    # Declare function with UI file name parameter
    def loadDesignerUIFile(self,file_path):
        qui_loader = QUiLoader()
        qui_loader.setWorkingDirectory(os.path.dirname(file_path))
        ui_file = QtCore.QFile(file_path)
        ui_file.open(QtCore.QFile.ReadOnly)
        widgetObject = qui_loader.load(ui_file)
```

```
        widgetObject.setWindowFlags(QtCore.Qt.Widget)

        # Return new top-level widget
        return widgetObject

    # Simple slot to display title information
    def displayTitle(self):
        print('Essential Programming for the Technical Artist')


# Instance MyDesignerClass
window = MyDesignerClass()
# Use class' exposed show() method
window.show()
```

Code Sample 17.4 DisplayTile() Slot Method Connected to FirstPushButton.clicked Event

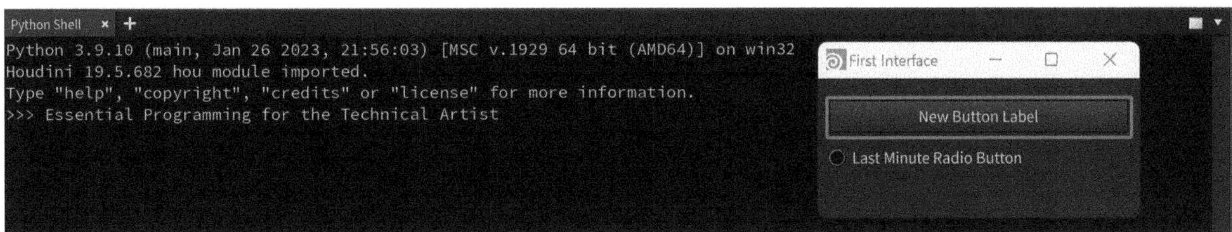

FIGURE 17.31 Python shell results when clicking FirstPushButton.

Once the signal/slot connection is made, whenever the *FirstPushButton* is pressed, "Essential Programming for the Technical Artist" is displayed to the Python shell, as shown in Figure 17.31.

SPACERS

Spacers push other objects until the minimal space required for the other object layouts is achieved. Spacers may be placed anywhere allowed by their respective layout. There are two types of spacers: horizontal and vertical.

Vertical Spacers

In vertical layouts, *Vertical Spacers* push other objects up and down until their minimal space requirements are achieved: Figure 17.32.

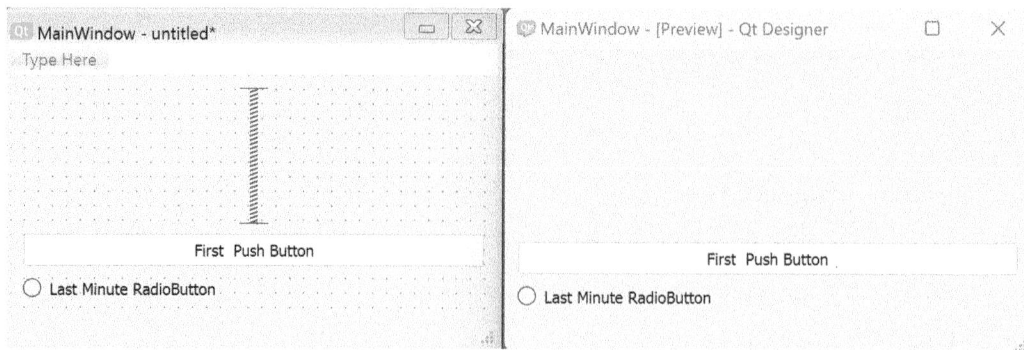

FIGURE 17.32 Vertical spacer.

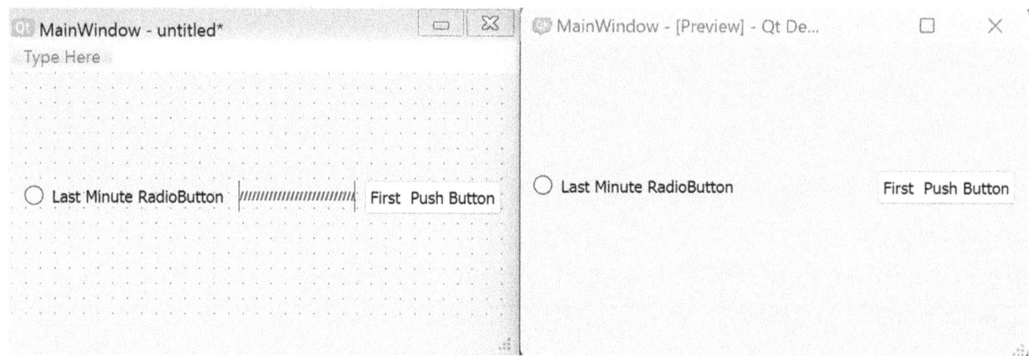

FIGURE 17.33 Horizontal spacer.

Horizontal Spacers

In horizontal layouts, *Horizontal Spacers* push other objects left and right until their minimal space requirements are achieved: Figure 17.33.

CONTAINERS

Container widgets allow users to organize multiple widgets within a defined region. They can manage input widgets, provide overlapping mini-canvases (called *Frames*) or behave as decorative fences for other objects. Containers may be Widgets, Frames, Group Boxes, Scroll Areas, Tool Boxes, Tab Widgets, Stacked Widgets, Dock Widgets, and MDI Areas.

Widgets

Widgets are base-level primitive canvases where Qt objects are placed and organized. They function as top-level layouts. When *Main Windows* are created, each has three child components: a Qwidget, a QMenuBar, and a QStatusBar. All interface input and output objects are placed within the QWidget, as displayed in Figure 17.34. They are parent for most visual interface hierarchy.

Frames

Frames are Widgets with stylized borders. By default, the borders may be simple boxes, panels, vertical or horizontal lines, or invisible. Their shadows may be raised, sunken, or invisible. Their widths are also configurable: Figure 17.35.

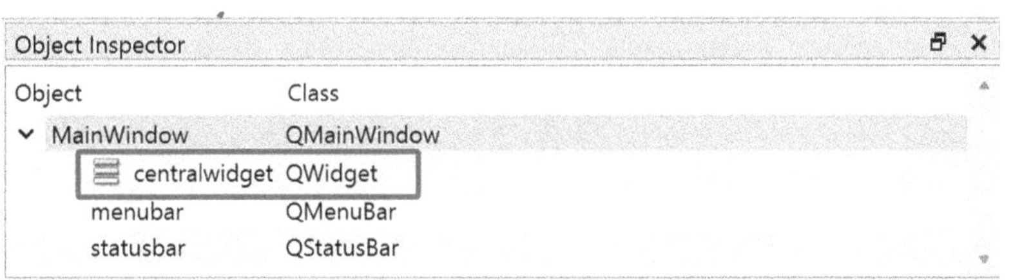

FIGURE 17.34 Primitive widget in main window hierarchy.

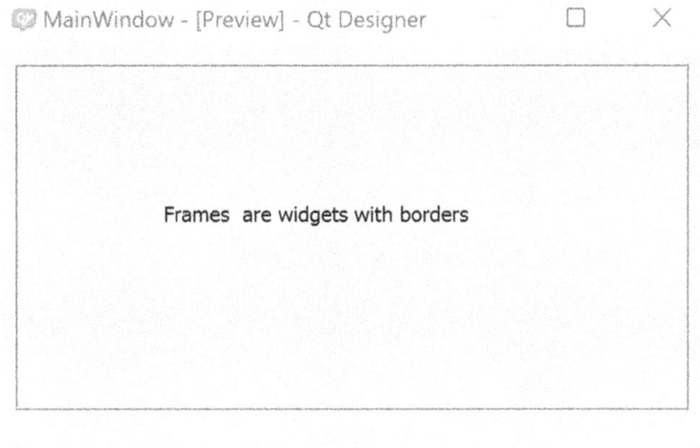

FIGURE 17.35 Frame container.

Group Boxes

Group boxes are simple Frames with visible titles. Their borders may be visible or a single horizontal line: Figure 17.36.

Scroll Areas

Scroll Areas are resizable Frames. When window sizes force default area dimensions to be smaller than original, vertical and horizontal scroll bars control area focus, as shown in Figure 17.37.

Tool Boxes

Tool Boxes are stacks of Frames. Selected Frames expand to display object contents, as shown in Figure 17.38. Tool Boxes provide scroll bars by default.

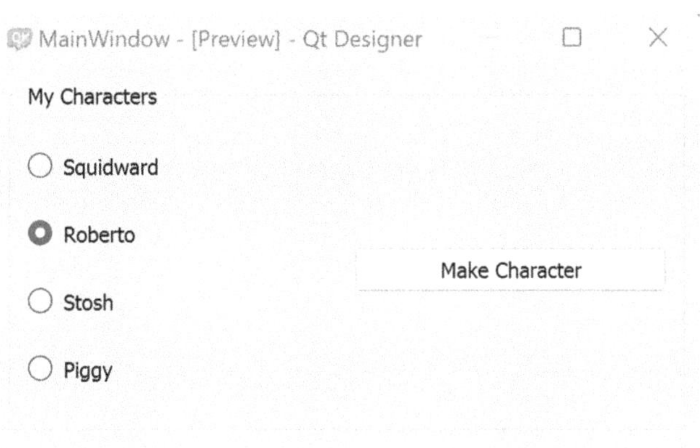

FIGURE 17.36 Group box container.

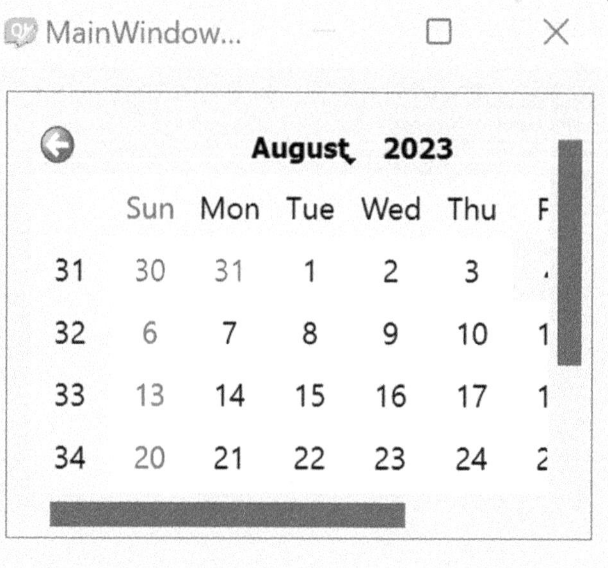

FIGURE 17.37 Scroll area container.

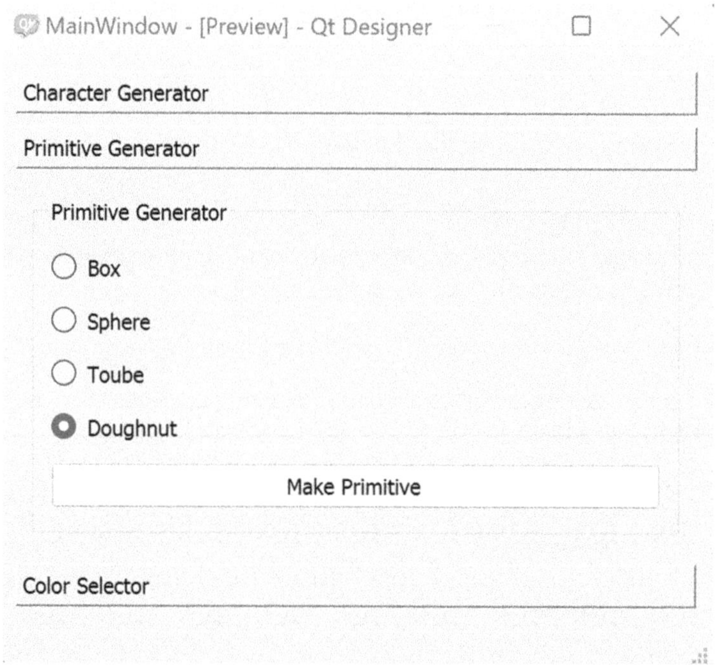

FIGURE 17.38 Tool box container.

Tab Widgets

Tab Widgets are overlapping frames identified by lists of tabs. Tabs are placed on the north, south, east, or west widget edges. Selected tabs expose Frame contents, as demonstrated in Figure 17.39. Tab Widgets provide scroll bars by default.

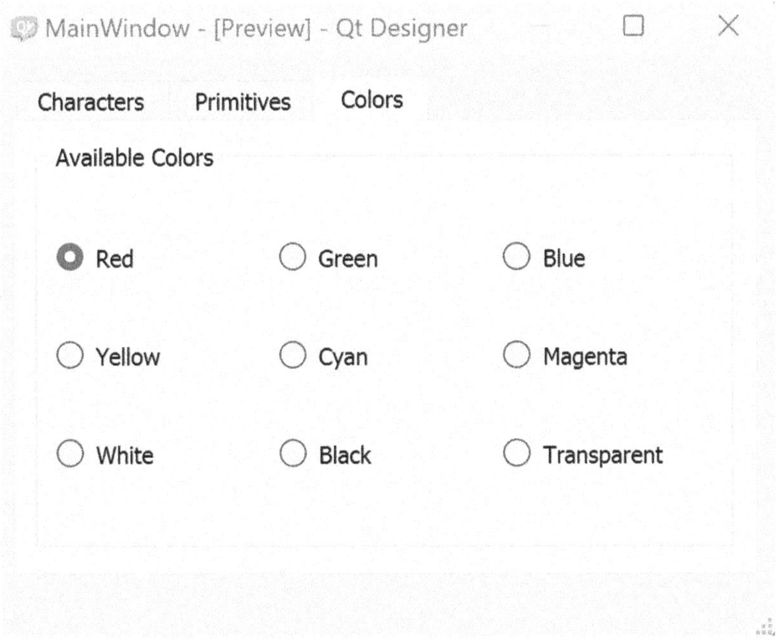

FIGURE 17.39 Tab widget container.

Stacked Widgets

Stacked Widgets are overlapping Frames selected via left and right arrows. Selected Frames expose frame contents. Stacked Widgets do not scroll when windows are resized, as demonstrated in Figure 17.40.

Dock Widgets

Dock Widgets are subwindow Widgets that may be detached from the interface's main window and reattached later. Docking locations as well as initial states are configurable: Figure 17.41.

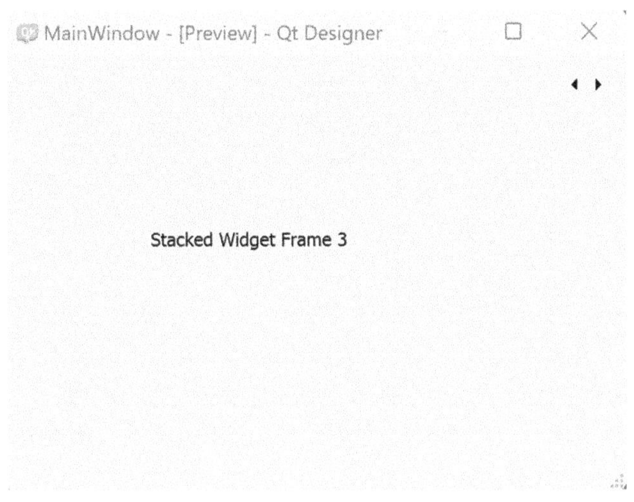

FIGURE 17.40 Stacked widget container.

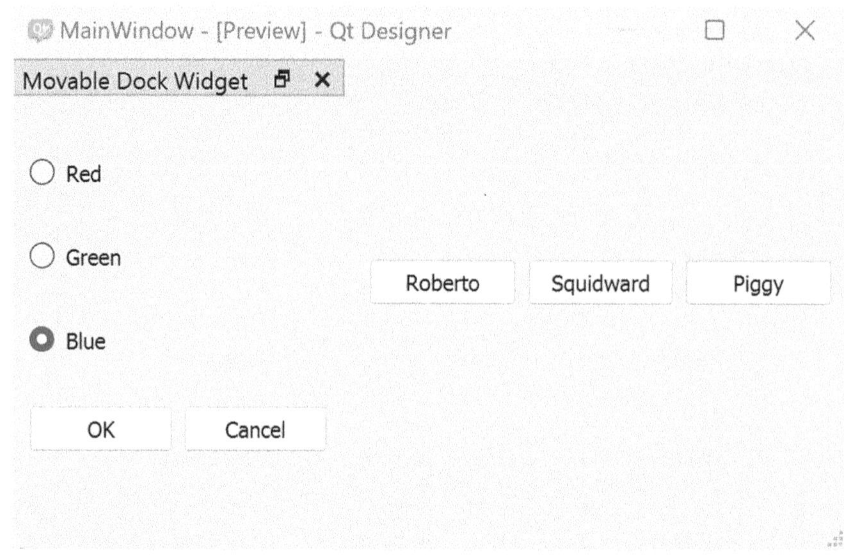

FIGURE 17.41 Dock widget container.

MDI Area

MDI Areas are an abbreviation for *Multiple Document Interface Areas*. These areas are window managers for MDI *sub-windows*. Within QtDesigner, Sub-windows are created by right mouse clicking within MDI areas and selecting *Add Subwindow*. Each subwindow contains a Frame and is scalable and movable within the MDI area, as demonstrated in Figure 17.42.

ITEM WIDGETS VERSUS ITEM VIEWS

There are two types of data item objects available in PySide2: *Item Views* and *Item Widgets*. Both are useful for displaying organized and hierarchical data in list, tree, table, and sometimes column formats. *Item Widgets* are simpler and data can be accessed using the index model. *Item Views* are useful when the source data are from databases or the data need to be presented in different ways. Item Views allow customizable model subclasses and can be more flexible than Widgets. Regretfully, full explanation of the *Model/View* programming model is

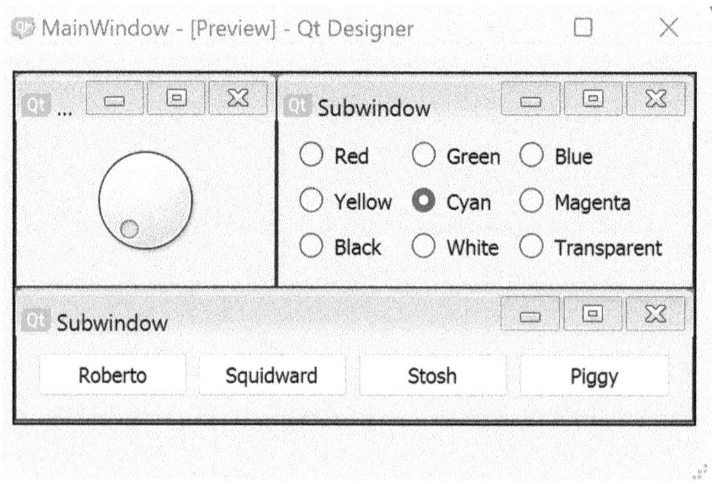

FIGURE 17.42 MDI area container.

out of scope of this text. More thorough explanation of the Qt Model/View Programming framework can be found in https://doc.qt.io/qtforpython-5/overviews/model-view-programming.html#model-view-programming.

BUTTONS

All button classes are child classes of the *QAbstractButton* class and share the same core functionality. Common attributes they share are *text, icon*, and *checkable*. They all emit *clicked(), pressed(), released()*, and *toggled()* signals. All receive *click(), toggle()*, and *setChecked()* slots. The available QtDesigner buttons, as shown in Figure 17.43, are *Push Buttons, Tool Buttons, Radio Buttons, Check Boxes, Command Link Buttons*, and *Dialog Button Boxes.*

Push Buttons

Push Buttons are the most commonly used widgets. They are depressed to broadcast *clicked()* or *pressed()* signals. They may display a text string and/or an icon.

Tool Buttons

Tool Buttons are typically associated with *QActions* (covered in Chapter 16), when creating toolbars and menus. They display icons by default but may also display text strings. Beyond initiating menu actions, they are often used for selecting tools from toolbars.

Radio Buttons

Radio buttons may be switched on (checked) or off (unchecked). Typically representing a "one of many" choice, only one radio button in a group is selectable (checkable) at any given time. When a radio button is selected, all other buttons in the group are unselected.

Check Boxes

Check boxes may be checked "on" or "off". They may have an optional "third state", which is neither on or off. Unlike Radio Buttons, Check Boxes are not exclusive. Many may be checked at the same time.

Command Line Buttons

Command Link Buttons were created to support Microsoft Windows Vista. While the operating system did not last, the buttons did. They are simply flat (no border) push buttons with an icon, and text.

Dialog Button Boxes

Dialog Button Boxes are covered in Chapter 16. They are useful for providing pre-defined answers to specific queries.

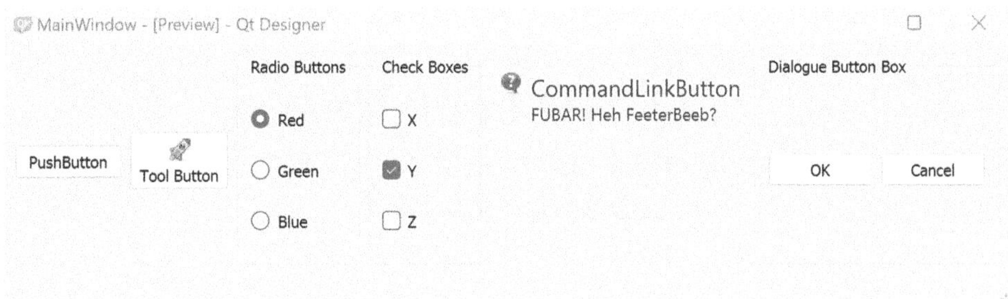

FIGURE 17.43 Push buttons, tool buttons, radio buttons, check boxes, command link buttons, and dialog button boxes.

INPUT WIDGETS

Input Widgets are Qt objects enabling interface interactivity. Available input widgets are: *Combo Boxes, Text Editors, Number Inputs, Time Inputs, Sliders,* and *KeySequence Editors.*

Combo Boxes

Combo Boxes enable users to select options provided by pull-down lists of available choices Figure 17.44 displays Character and *Font Combo Boxes. Font Combo Boxes* enable users to select from available fonts.

Text Editors

Text editors enable users to read or edit text information. *Line Edit* widgets allow users to interact with a single line of plain text. *Plain Text Editors* allow users to interact with multiple lines of plain text. *Text Editors* allow users to interact with multiple lines of rich text using HTML-style tags or Markdown format. Figure 17.45 demonstrates *single line, plain text* and *text edit* input widgets.

Number Inputs

Spin Boxes allow users to enter integer values. *Double Spin Boxes* handle floating point values. The up and down arrows increase or decrease the selected value amounts. Figure 17.46 displays *spin* and *double spin* input boxes.

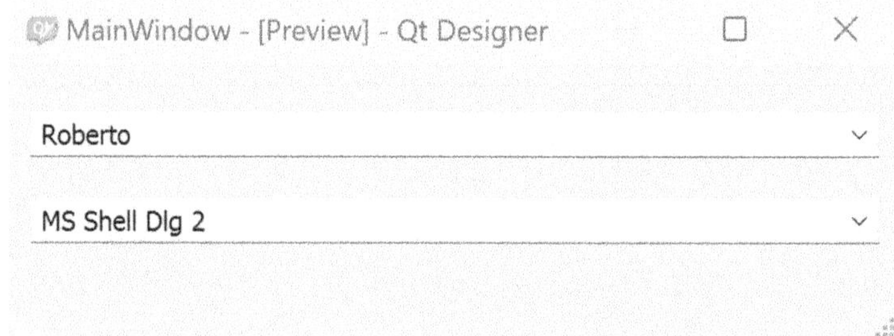

FIGURE 17.44 Combo and font combo input widgets.

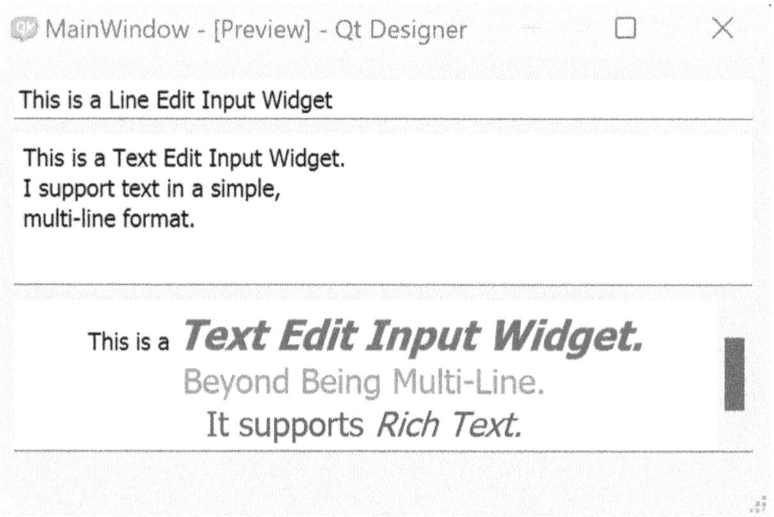

FIGURE 17.45 Single line, plain text, and text edit input widgets.

Time Inputs

Time Editors allow users to enter specific times. *Date Editors* allow users to enter specific dates. *Date/Time Editors* allow users to enter both time and date values. The up and down arrows increase or decrease the selected value amounts. Figure 17.47 demonstrates *time, date* and *date/time edit input* widgets.

Sliders

Sliders allow users to select between minimum and maximum values by positioning movable objects between two extreme states. *Vertical and Horizontal Scroll Bars* allow users to move sliders vertically or horizontally between two extreme values to adjust window focus. Arrows increase or decrease slider positions by incremental amounts. *Vertical and Horizontal Sliders* allow users to slide pucks vertically or horizontally between two extreme values. Optional tick marks are displayable. *Dials* are circular sliders allowing users to wheel between two extreme values. Tick marks are optional. Figure 17.48 shows *scroll bar, slider* and *dial input* widgets.

FIGURE 17.46 Spin and double spin box input widgets.

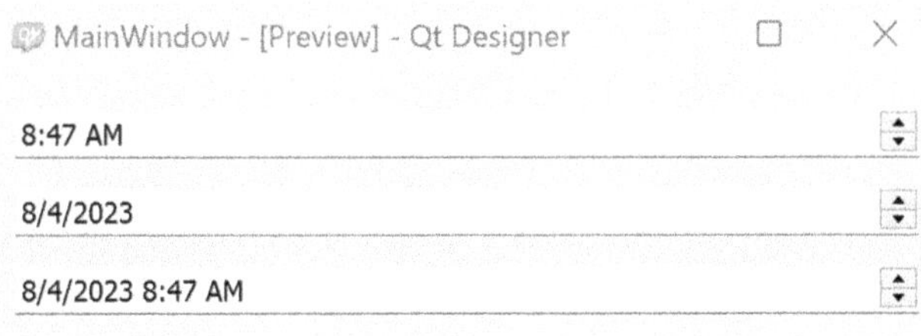

FIGURE 17.47 Time, date and date/time edit input widgets.

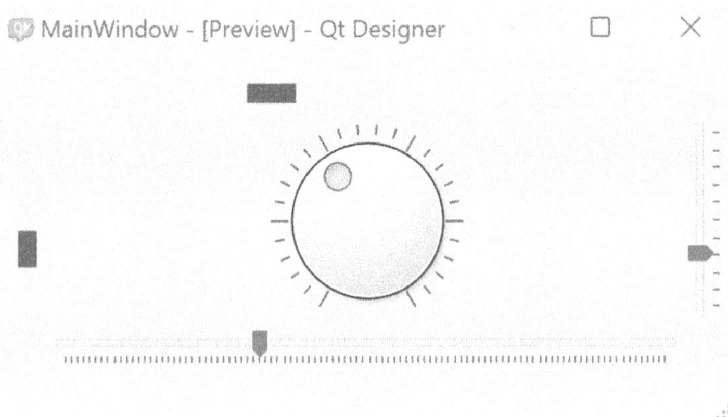

FIGURE 17.48 Scroll bar, slider and dial input widgets.

Key Sequence Editors

Key Sequence Editors allow users to choose shortcut *Key Sequences*. Figure 17.49 demonstrates a *key sequence input* widget.

DISPLAY WIDGETS

Display Widgets provide interface user feedback. Unlike Input Widgets, users may only read or observe widget contents. They may not interact with them. Available QtDesigner display widgets include: *Labels, Text Browsers, Calendar Widgets, LCD Numbers, Progress Bars, Lines, Graphics Views*, and *OpenGL Widgets*.

Labels

Labels are versatile display tools that display rich text or image-based messages. Technically, they are Frames and may display borders. Figure 17.50 shows a typical *label display* widget.

Text Browsers

Text Browsers are extensions of Text Editor input widgets. To prevent editing, their *setReadOnly()* flags set to *True* by default. Beyond they provide navigation functionality allowing users to follow links in hypertext documents.

Calendar Widgets

Calendar Widgets display calendars covering current month and day. Current month and day are selectable. Figure 17.51 displays a typical *calendar display* widgets.

LCD Numbers

LCD Numbers display numbers in just about any size. The displayed number may be in Decimal, Hexadecimal, Octal, or Binary. Figure 17.52 shows off an *LCD display* widget. Decimal points may be displayed but must consume one-digit position.

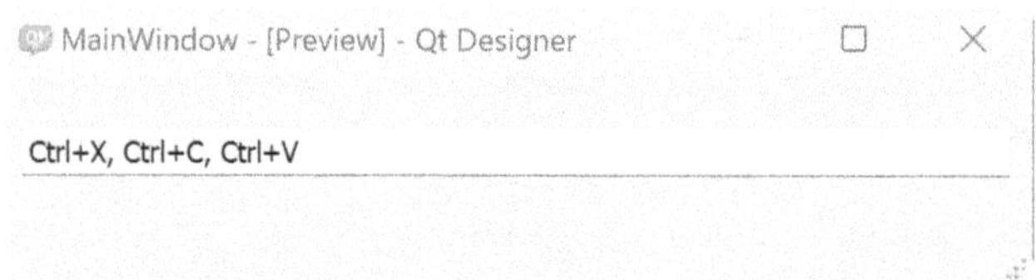

FIGURE 17.49 Key sequence edit input widget.

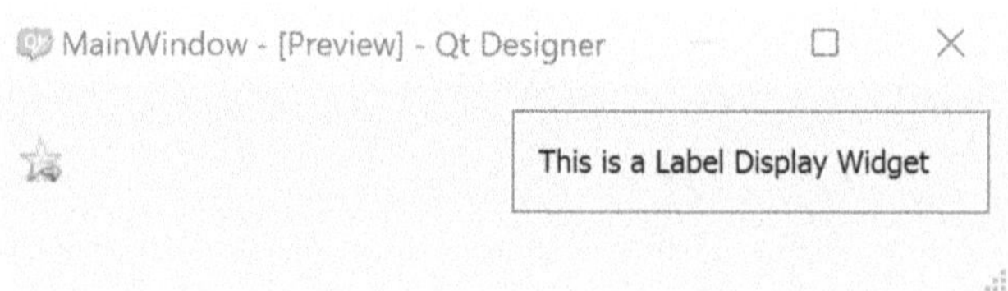

FIGURE 17.50 Label display widget.

MainWindow - [Preview] - Qt Designer

August 2023

	Sun	Mon	Tue	Wed	Thu	Fri	Sat
31	30	31	1	2	3	4	5
32	6	7	8	9	10	11	12
33	13	14	15	16	17	18	19
34	20	21	22	23	24	25	26
35	27	28	29	30	31	1	2
36	3	4	5	6	7	8	9

FIGURE 17.51 Calendar display widget.

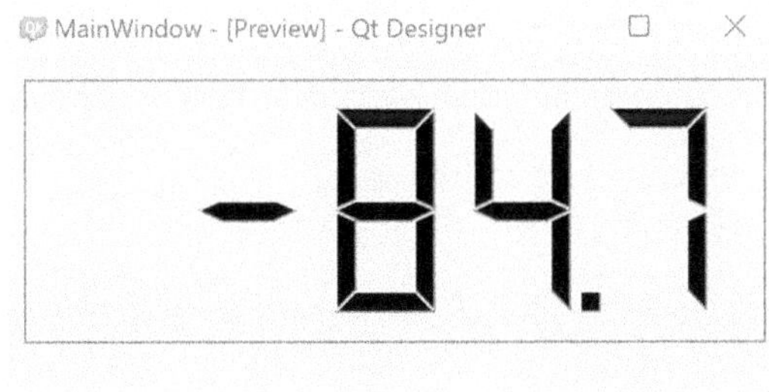

FIGURE 17.52 LCD number display widget.

Progress Bars

Progress Bars display any value between two extreme states. They are used to indicate operation progress, and reassuring users' applications are still running. The bars may be vertical or horizontal. Figure 17.53 demonstrates vertical and horizontal *progress bar* displays.

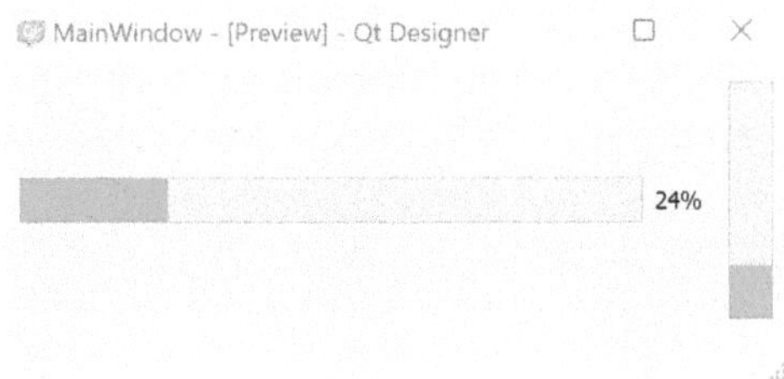

FIGURE 17.53 Progress bar display widget.

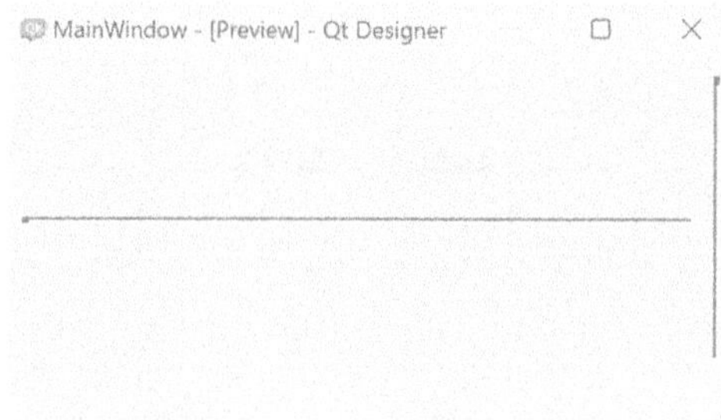

FIGURE 17.54 Vertical and horizontal line display widgets.

Lines

Line Widgets may be vertical or horizontal and are used to create visual separation between groups of widgets. Figure 17.54 displays vertical and horizontal *line display* widgets.

Graphics Views

Graphics Views provide view areas for *QGraphicsScenes*. Additional programming outside QtDesigner is required to populate these widgets. *QGraphicsScenes* and *Qt Graphics View Frameworks* are beyond the scope of this text. Documentation may be found at https://doc.qt.io/qtforpython-5/overviews/graphicsview.html#graphics-view-framework.

OpenGL Widgets

OpenGL Widgets provide view areas for OpenGL Graphics integrated with Qt interfaces. Additional programming outside QtDesigner is required to populate these widgets. OpenGL is beyond the scope of this text. Documentation with the QtGUI module may be found in https://doc.qt.io/qt-5/qtgui-index.html.

CONCLUSION

Mastering interface libraries such as Qt and PySide2 can require considerable amounts of time. New programmers are often intimidated by the large amount of understanding required to bring up just a simple button. Even with library familiarity, creating sophisticated interfaces requires an enormous amount of coding. Luckily, there are interface design tools that are as simple as dragging widgets from menus and dropping them onto interface canvases. One such tool is QtDesigner.

Depending on the Python and PySide2 (Pyqt) installations, the QtDesigner executables may not only be very difficult to find, but they may not have also been included with the installation. There is a copy of QtDesigner included with all Houdini Python installations. However, accessing the tool is challenging. Instead, users are encouraged to download a stand-alone version of the tool from Michael Herrmann and his *Fman Build System, https://build-system.fman.io/qt-designer-download*. Instructions for downloading and installing this tool are provided in this chapter.

Once the tool is installed and users are familiar with the QtDesigner layout, they can immediately start designing interfaces. QtDesigner outputs *'.ui'* XML files requiring conversion to Python code. Instructions are supplied for integrating interface files into Python scripts as Qt objects. A more useful strategy for integrating external files as Python classes is provided.

Layout familiarity is essential for creating sophisticated interfaces without code. Once layouts are understood, users may complete their interfaces with a wide variety of spacers, containers, data items, buttons, input, and display widgets.

INTRODUCTION

Python was created to be an easy-to-use language. Because code is read more often than it is written, readability significantly contributes to code comprehension. Python creators felt so strongly about this and they integrated it into the language. When *import this* is typed into the Python command line, an interesting reminder appears, as in Shell Example 18.1.

```
>>> import this
The Zen of Python, by Tim Peters


Beautiful is better than ugly.
Explicit is better than implicit.
Simple is better than complex.
Complex is better than complicated.
Flat is better than nested.
Sparse is better than dense.
Readability counts.
Special cases aren't special enough to break the rules.
Although practicality beats purity.
Errors should never pass silently.
Unless explicitly silenced.
In the face of ambiguity, refuse the temptation to guess.
There should be one-- and preferably only one --obvious way to do it.
Although that way may not be obvious at first unless you're Dutch.
Now is better than never.
Although never is often better than *right* now.
If the implementation is hard to explain, it's a bad idea.
If the implementation is easy to explain, it may be a good idea.
Namespaces are one honking great idea -- let's do more of those!
```

Shell Example 18.1 Import This

The *PEP 8* (Python Enhancement Proposal) *Standards* is a collection of best practices encouraging readable Python code. The language does not throw errors when these guidelines are not followed. They are understood by the Python community as the best strategies for keeping Python readable and easy to use.

DOI: 10.1201/9781003016427-18

Technical artists come from wide varieties of backgrounds including traditional art where straying from rules is often encouraged. However, "creative" code, contributed from many different individuals with different coding experiences, does not promote straight-forward, readable code. The PEP 8 Standards are a universal strategy for encouraging homogenous programming.

Many technical artists become members of tools teams where code readability is essential for managing code. They occasionally contribute to teams of seasoned programmers forged by years of consistent code-reviews. The *PEP 8 Standards* may not be strict Python coding rules. They do, however, promote team happiness.

CONSISTENCY

PEP 8 was intended to make code "readable". Code needs to be "readable" for it to be "maintainable". When *PEP 8* gets in the way of coherent coding, it should not be thrown away. It should, however, be considered as an option.

Consistent adherence to *PEP 8 Standards* is good. Consistency spread over a project is better. Consistency across modules is best. However, understanding when to break style is essential when generating readable code. The following are situations where readability is more important than standard adherence:

- Never breaking backward compatibility
- Maintaining older versions of Python that may conflict with the guide
- Staying consistent with surrounding code that also breaks style, especially when the code is older than the standard

CODE LAYOUT

The following suggestions apply to the most visible aspects of how Python code should be presented.

Indentation

Use four spaces per indentation. Each block of code should be indented in increments of four spaces, as in the Code Sample 18.1 example.

```
# No Indentation print('Zero Indentation')
if True:
    # 4 Spaces Indentation
    print('4 spaces indentation')
    for i in range(5):
        # 8 Spaces Indentation
        print('8 spaces indentation')
```

Code Sample 18.1 Four Spaces Indentation Increments

Line continuation is optional. While fours spaces of a line continuation are legal, care should be made to maintain consistent (vertically aligned when possible) visual separation from blocks of code, especially when dealing with long functional arguments and compound expressions, demonstrated in Code Sample 18.2.

```
# Correct:
# Aligned with opening argument delimiter
variableObject = long_function_name(argument1, argument2,
                                    argument3, argument4,
                                    argument5)

# Not aligned with code block indentation
for i in range(10):
    variableObject = long_function_name(argument1,
                argument2, argument3, argument4,
                argument5)
    print(variableObject)

if(long_expression_component
        and another_long_expression_component):
    print('Clear expression separation from code block')

# Wrong:
# Line continuations indistinguishable from code blocks
variableObject = long_function_name(argument1, argument2,
argument3, argument4, argument5)

for i in range(10):
    variableObject = long_function_name(argument1,
    argument2, argument3, argument4, argument5)
    print(variableObject)
if(long_expression_component
    and another_long_expression_component):
    print('Unclear expression separation from code block')
```

Code Sample 18.2 Clear Code Block Separation

The same code block separation applies to pairs of braces, brackets, and parenthesis. The terminating character should be vertically aligned with its components or on the first column of the code block, as introduced in Code Sample 18.3.

```
# Verticle alignment
my_long_sequence = [
        'a', 'b', 'c',
        'd', 'e', 'f'
        ]
# First code block column
variableObject = long_function_name(argument1,
        argument2, argument3, argument4, argument5
)
```

Code Sample 18.3 Pairs of Braces, Brackets, and Parenthesis

Tabs or Spaces

Python 3 allows tab or space indentations but not both. Mixing indentation types triggers errors. Configure your editor to replace tabs with fours spaces to ensure consistency.

Line Length

A line of code should be no longer than 79 characters. Document strings and comments should be limited to 72 characters.

When possible, braces, brackets, and parenthesis should be used to take advantage of implicit line continuation. When logically or syntactically unavailable (such as complicated lambda expressions) backslash characters, \, are usable. Code Sample 18.4 demonstrates an essential backslash.

```
# Un-continuable lambda expression
# Note: When wrapped in parenthesis, backslash is not required
objectFunction = lambda argument1, argument2, argument3,\
                    argument4, argument5: long_function_name(
                    argement1, argument2, argument3, argument4,
                    argument5
        )
```

Code Sample 18.4 Essential Backslash

Line Beaks

Line breaks should occur before binary operators, not after. Doing so minimizes eye fatigue and maintains mathematics tradition. Code Sample 18.5 demonstrates correct and incorrect line breaks.

```
# Incorrect:
variableObject = (argument1 + argument2 +
                  argument3 + argument4 +
                  argument5)


# Correct:
variableObject = (argument1 + argument2
                  + argument3 + argument4
                  + argument5)
```

Code Sample 18.5 Line Breaks Before and After Binary Operators

Blank Lines

Two blank lines should surround top-level functions and classes, while single blank lines should surround class method definitions.

Single blank lines may be used to separate groups of related functions and identify logical sections. Code Sample 18.6 utilizes blank lines with groups and logical sections.

```
import math


object = hou.node('/obj').createNode('geo')


# Blanks to separate groups of related function
object.parm('tx').set(0.2)
object.parm('ty').set(-0.4)
object.parm('tz').set(0.6)


# Blanks to separate logic sections
for angle in range(0, 370, 10):
    rads = math.radians(angle)


object.parm('ry').set(math.degrees(math.sin(rads)))
print(f"object Ry={object.parm('ry').eval()}")
```

Code Sample 18.6 Blanks Around Groups and Logical Sections

Imports

Module imports should be called on unique lines while sub-modules and objects may be imported on the same line accompanying a *from* statement. Code Sample 18.7 uses both import lines and same line sub-modules and objects.

```
# Modules on unique lines
import math
import os
# Sub-modules and objects on same line
from json import loads, dumps
```

Code Sample 18.7 Unique Import Lines and Same-line Sub-modules and Objects

Imports should be placed at file top, below comments, and documentation strings, *docstrings*, and above globals and constants. They should be grouped in the following order:

- Standard library imports
- Related third party imports
- Local application/library specific imports

Wildcard imports should be avoided, as in Code Sample 18.8.

```
# Wildcards discouraged
from PySide2.QtWidgets import *
```

Code Sample 18.8 Avoid Wildcard Imports

Dunder Names

Module level dunder names should be defined after module docstrings. Code Sample 18.9 demonstrates proper dunder placement.

```
'''
    This is a module docstring,
    Defining all the cool module functionality
'''
__officiallist__ = ['a', 'b', 'c', 'd']
__objectnum__ = 42
__name__ = 'Essential Programming for Technical Artists'
```

Code Sample 18.9 Module Dunder Placement

STRING QUOTES

Single-quote strings, ', and double-quote strings, ", mean the same thing. Choose one and stick with it.

WHITESPACE

Whitespace in expressions and statements should encourage readability and avoid ambiguity.

Extraneous

Extra whitespaces should be avoided in the following situations: Code Sample 18.10 displays correct and incorrect white space usage.

```
# Immediately before and after parenthesis, brackets and braces
# Correct:
character('Reggie', weapon[3], {spells: 2})
# Incorrect:
character( 'Reggie', weapon[ 3 ], { spells: 2 } )

# Between trailing commas and close parenthesis
# Correct:
objects = (3,)
# Incorrect:
objects = (3, )

# Immediately before colons, semicolons and colons
# Correct
if cause and answer: print(cause, answer); cause, answer = answer, cause
# Incorrect
if cause and answer : print(cause , answer) ; cause , answer = answer ,
cause

# Index slice colons should have equal space on either side
# Correct:
characters[2:10:2]
characters[start+inc : end-inc+1]
# Incorrect
characters[2: 10 :2]
characters[start+inc: end-inc+1]
```

```
# Immediately before open parenthesis starting functional arguments
# or indexing or slicing
# Correct
myfunction(84)
newDictionary['key'] = oldlist[pos]
# Incorrect
myfunction (84)
newDictionary ['key'] = oldlist [pos]

# Aligning assignment operators
# Correct:
characterA = 'Tom'
characterB = 'Dick'
newStrangerCharacter = 'Bubba'
# Incorrrect:
characterA           = 'Tom'
characterB           = 'Dick'
newStrangerCharacter = 'Bubba'
```

Code Sample 18.10 Incorrect Extra Whitespaces

Trailing Whitespaces

Avoid trailing whitespaces on any line. They may create confusion with interpreters and editors.

Operators

Surround binary assignment, comparison, and Boolean operators with single-spaces. Code Sample 18.11 demonstrates correct single-space usage.

```
spell = 'Magic Missle'
if character == MagicUser and level >= 2:
    pass
```

Code Sample 18.11 Binary Assignments, Comparisons, and Booleans

Arguments

When indicating keyword arguments, do not use spaces around equality,(=), operators. Code Sample 18.12 displays correct spacing around keyword arguments.

```
# Correct
def character(name='Player', occupation='Fighter'):
    return initCharacter(name=name, occupation=occupation, level=1)

# Incorrect
def character(name= 'Player', occupation = 'Fighter'):
    return initCharacter(name= name, occupation =occupation, level = 1)
```

Code Sample 18.12 No Spaces around Keyword Arguments

Compound Statements

Avoid stringing together multiple statements on the same line, including *if/for/while* commands. Correct, bad and worse examples are given in Code Sample 18.13.

```
# Correct
critter = hou.node('/obj').createNode('geo').createNode(objectType)
if objectType == 'box':
    critter.parm('scale').set(2)
critter.parm('tx').set(1)
critter.parm('ty').set(2)
critter.parm('tz').set(3)

# Discouraged
critter = hou.node('/obj').createNode('geo').createNode(objectType)
if objectType == 'box': critter.parm('scale').set(2)
critter.parm('tx').set(1); critter.parm('ty').set(2); critter.parm('tz').
set(3)
for ry in range(360): critter.parm('ry').set(ry)
while ry > 0: ry -= 1
```

```
# Bad!
if objectType == 'box': critter.parm('scale').set(2)
else: critter.parmTuple('s').set((1.0, 1.0, 1.0))
try: createCharacter()
finally: cleanup()
```

Code Sample 18.13 Avoid Compound Statements

TRAILING COMMAS

When creating singleton tuples, enclose values in parenthesis. While not illegal, Code Sample 18.14 demonstrates accepted usage.

```
# Correct
returnTuple = (76,)

# Incorrect
returnTuple = 76,
```

Code Sample 18.14 Singleton Tuples

Code Sample 18.15 demonstrates how trailing commas are also acceptable in multi-line assignments or arguments.

```
# Correct
characters = [
        'Crag',
        'Piggy',
        'Squidward',
        ]
critter = hou.node('/obj').createNode('geo').createNode(
        'testgeometry_rubbertoy',
        'Roberto',
        )
# Incorrect
characters = ['Crag', 'Piggy', 'Squidward',]
hou.node('/obj').createNode('geo').createNode
('testgeometry_rubbertoy','Roberto',)
```

Code Sample 18.15 Multi-line Assignments and Arguments

COMMENTS

Comments should be complete sentences; complete with capital first characters and terminating periods. There should be two spaces after a sentence-ending period. Please comment in English and when doing do, follow Strunk and White.

Block

Block comments apply to the code they precede. They should be indented at the same level. Each line should start with a hashtag and a space, "# ". Paragraphs should be separated by lines containing a single hashtag.

Inline

Inline comments should be separated with at least two spaces from the statement they are documenting. This is demonstrated in Code Sample 18.16. They should start with a hashtag, followed by a space, "# ". Inline comments should be used sparingly and describe the non-obvious.

```
# Correct
vertex += 1          # Shift to the next vertex object


# Incorrect
vertex += 1# Increment vertex
```

Code Sample 18.16 Inline Comments

Document Strings

Documentation strings (*docstrings*) should describe the functionality for all modules, functions, classes, and methods. They should appear after *class* and *def* statements. When creating multi-line docstrings, the terminating triple-quotes, ''', should appear on a new line, as shown in Code Sample 18.17. They should appear on the same line for single line strings. Studios may follow their own standards and may even have tooling to generate *html/pdf* documents from code. When no standards are present, chose one and stick with it.

```
def generateCharacter():
    ''' This function generates a new character,
        Make sure to have all of the vertices in place!
    '''
    pass


def killCharacter()
    ''' Return the character vertices to the bit-bucket '''
    pass
```

Code Sample 18.17 Document Strings

NAMING CONVENTIONS

Overriding Principle

Variable names should reflect usage instead of implementation.

Descriptive Naming Styles

There is a plethora of naming styles (i.e. camel case, snake case, kebab case, etc.). Pick one of the styles and stick with it. Consistency is the key factor.

Prescriptive Naming Conventions

Avoid

Never use the following single character variable names: lowercase letter 'el', (*l*), uppercase letter "oh", (*O*), or uppercase letter "eye", (*I*).

Modules and Packages

Modules and packages should be short, all-lowercase names. Modules may employ underscores to improve readability. Packages may not.

Class Names

Class names should follow *CapWords* convention; camelCase with a leading capital letter: Code Sample 18.18.

```
class EssentialProgramming:
    pass
```

Code Sample 18.18 Class CapWords Convention

Type Variable Names

Type variable should use short, CapWords convention: Code Sample 18.19.

```
from custom_module import CustomType
```

Code Sample 18.19 Type Variable Names

Exception Names

Exceptions are classes and should follow class naming convention. The "*error*" suffix should be used on all error exceptions.

Functions

Append function names which clash with reserved keywords with single, trailing underscores, "_": Code Sample 18.20.

```
def assert_():
    pass
```

Code Sample 18.20 Clashing Function Name

Use *self* as the first argument for all instance methods. Use *cls* as the first argument for all class methods.

Method and Instance Variables Names

Method and instance variable names should be lowercase with single underscores separating words. Non-public names should be led with single underscores, as demonstrated in Code Sample 18.21.

```
class Character:
    def __init__(self, name='Bart'):
        # Method and Instance variable
        self.known_spells = ['Magic Missle', 'Identify Magic']
        # Non-public variable
        self._true_character_name = 'Asser'
```

Code Sample 18.21 Method and Instance Variable Names

Globals

Global variable names should follow function naming convention.

Constants

Constants should be written in all capital letters with underscores separating words.

Inheritance

Public attributes should have no leading underscores. Attributes clashing with reserved keywords should append with single trailing underscores. When classes are intended to be *subclassed*, attributes which are not desired to be used by sublasses should be led with double-underscores, __. Please note that leading with double-underscores generates a *dunder* and names will be altered with code mangling.

PROGRAMMING

Other Languages

Certain implementations of Python employ special considerations (such as *CPython* in-place string concatenation). Do not employ these special features when there is a remote possibility; the code will be used with different implementation interpreters.

Singletons

Equality operators should not be used when making comparisons with singletons, such as *None*: Code Sample 18.22.

```
# Correct
if x is None:
    pass

# Incorrect
if x == None:
    pass
```

Code Sample 18.22 Singleton Comparisons

Is Not

Use *is not* operator instead of *not … is*: Code Sample 18.23.

```
# Correct
if x is not None:
    pass

# Incorrect
if not x is None:
    pass
```

Code Sample 18.23 Is Not Operator

Lambda

Use a function statement instead of directly binding an identifier with a lambda expression: Code Sample 18.24.

```
# Correct
def sqr(x):
    return x*x

# Incorrect
sqr = lambda x: x*x
```

Code Sample 18.24 Lambda Binding

Exception Derivation

Derive exceptions from *Exception* class instead of *BaseException*.

Bare Except

Always catch specific exceptions instead of catching bare *except:* clauses. Use *except Exception:* when catching all other exceptions. These exceptions are demonstrated in Code Sample 18.25.

```
try:
    file = open('characterData.json', 'r')
except IOError:
    print('Could not find file!')
except Exception:
    print('Error opening file!')
```

Code Sample 18.25 No Bare excepts

Try Statements

Try statements should be simple to avoid source confusion. Code Sample 18.26 introduce simple and complicated *try* statements.

```
# Correct
try:
    inFile = open('character.json', 'r')
except IOError:
    print('Error inputting character data')
else:
    print('Input data correctly read')


# Incorrect
try:
    # Too broad!
    character = buildCharacter('character.json')
except IOError:
    # Will also catch IOError when in buildCharacter()
    print('Error inputting character data')
else:
    print('Input data correctly read')
```

Code Sample 18.26 Simple Try Statements

Return Statements

Be consistent with all return statements. When functions have at least one code path returning a value, all paths should as well. When returning values, do not return nothing when *None* is the desired return value. Code Sample 18.27 demonstrates correct *return* implementation.

```
# Correct
def myDiv(a, b):
    if b == 0:
        return None
    else:
        return a/b

# Incorrect
def myDiv(a, b):
    if b != 0:
        return a/b

def myDiv2(a, b):
    if b == 0:
        return
    else:
        return a/b
```

Code Sample 18.27 Consistent Return Statements

Slicing Strings

Use *.startswith()* and *.endswith()* when slicing strings for prefixes and suffixes: Code Sample 18.28.

```
# Correct
if inputAsset.endswith('.fbx'):
    pass

# Incorrect
if inputAsser[-4:] == '.fbx':
    pass
```

Code Sample 18.28 Using .endswith()

Isinstance

Use *isinstance()* when comparing object types: Code Sample 18.29.

```
# Correct
if isinstance(object, int):
    pass

# Incorrect
if type(object) == type(84):
    pass
```

Code Sample 18.29 Type Comparisons with isinstance()

Empty Sequences

Take advantage of empty sequences having *False* Boolean value, as demonstrated in Code Sample 18.30.

```
# Correct
if mySquence:
    pass
if not mySequence:
    pass

# Incorrect
if len(mysequence):
    pass
if not len(mysequence):
    pass
```

Code Sample 18.30 Empty Sequences Have False Value

Boolean Comparisons

Do not use == or *is* when comparing Boolean values: Code Sample 18.31.

```
# Correct
if boolVal:
    pass

# Incorrect
if boolVal == True:
    pass
if boolVal is True:
    pass
```

Code Sample 18.31 Comparing Boolean Values

Flow Control

When using *try … finally*, use flow control statements (*return/break/continue*) to prevent flow from jumping out of the *finally* block. Code Sample 18.32 demonstrates improper usage.

```
# Incorrect
def myDiv(a, b):
    try:
        result = a/b
    finally:
        return 0
```

Code Sample 18.32 Use Flow Control to Avoid Jumping out of Finally

FORMATTERS

Adhering to *PEP 8 Standards* is an intimating task especially for novice programmers. Luckily, there are a plethora of auto-formatters available in all sorts of shapes and sizes to cater to various team needs and specifications. All require installation into current Python environments.

Some formatters rewrite script contents to leave only cleanly formatted code while some address only specific issues. Some fix transgressions while others merely identify them. Some are invoked from the command line while others collaborate with code editors. All follow *PEP 8* Standards and are typically configurable to ignore or occlude particular issues.

Popular formatters are *autopep8*, *black*, and *yapf*. These are command line driven tools that replace existing code with cleanly formatted code. Not all teams employ these tools. Consult with your teams before employing the usage of these formatters.

CONCLUSION

The Python *PEP 8 Standards* is a collection of best practices encouraging readable Python code. They are not hard rules but guidelines for writing mutually understood, cleanly written code. Technical artists come from wide varieties of backgrounds with unlimited variations of coding habits and practices. Adhering to *PEP 8 Standards* not only promotes clean Python authoring and is understandable by all team members, but also simplifies future maintenance when original authors are unavailable.

INTRODUCTION

A regular expression, also known as a *regex*, is a formalized, textual pattern recognition string. In other words, regexes are search pattern strings defined by sequences of characters. They are used for parsing strings, identifying certain patterns within strings, and performing operations on those patterns, such as searching, replacing, validating, coordinating, and reformatting.

Found Everywhere

Regex strings can be found in most text editors. They provide more robust functionality than default *Search and Replace*. They are integrated with almost all programming languages including all *C* flavors and Python. All engines and packages which support these languages inherently support regex strings. The drawback to their diverse implementation is that there is no one single implementation style or *flavor*. The core ideology supporting each regex flavor, however, remains constant.

Concerning Technical Artists

Regular expressions are one of the most beneficial tools in technical artists' toolkits. They are available in virtually any environment, and once core fundamentals are understood, they are useful in almost any situation involving text strings.

Time is technical artists' most valuable resource. Project and job integrity depend on it. The success of their company may also be dependent on their time allocation. Regular expressions are under-used tools which often provide time saving and elegant strategies to what would otherwise call for brute-force solutions.

As useful as regexes are, they are not suitable for all text related problems. File formats such as *HTML* may present regex issues. Other tools, such as *PyParsing*, may provide more convenient results. Technical artists should become familiar with regex behavior and understand their limitations to avoid killing themselves using regular expressions for all text string situations.

Python Integration

The regex library is imported into Python using the *re* module, as defined in Language Template 19.1.

```
# Import Regular Expression module
import re
```

Language Template 19.1 Import Regular Expression Module

Some technical artists may be reluctant to employ the Python regex library for fear of poor performance. Regex performance varies radically across various languages. Without support of proper benchmarking, technical artist should have no concern integrating the Python regex library into their code.

DOI: 10.1201/9781003016427-19

TABLE 19.1 Traditional Literal Characters

A	B	C	D	E	F	G	H	I	J
K	L	M	N	O	P	Q	R	S	T
U	V	W	X	Y	Z				
a	b	c	d	e	f	g	h	i	j
k	l	m	n	o	p	q	r	s	t
u	v	w	x	y	z				
0	1	2	3	4	5	6	7	8	9
`	~	!	@	#	%	&	-	_	=
;	:	'	"	,	<	>	/		

REGULAR EXPRESSION STRINGS

Regex strings are composed of any sequence of *literal characters*, *metacharacters*, and *metasymbols*. These characters may be any ASCII digit, letter, punctuation mark, symbol, or even Unicode character.

Literal Characters

Literal characters are constant characters within regex strings which do not take on any special meaning. Table 19.1 provides all traditional literal characters.

The literal value of these characters may be altered when preceded by a backslash, \, or within the immediate proximity of metacharacters.

Metacharacters

Metacharacters are punctuation marks and other symbols that take on special meaning when in context of regex strings. Table 19.2 provides the basic regular expression metacharacters.

The most important metacharacter is the backslash, \. When preceding another metacharacter, the backslash escapes, (converts), them to their literal value. When preceding traditionally literal characters, backslashes may convert them to *metasymbols*. Table 19.3 provides the standard *metasymbols*.

TABLE 19.2 Basic Regex Metacharacters

Metacharacter	*Name*	*Meaning*
****	Backslash (Escape)	Converts metacharacter to literal or literal to metasymbol
^	Caret	Start of a string or class negation
$	Dollar Sign	End of a string
.	Period	***ANY*** character except a *newline*
?	Question Mark	Zero or one repetition
*	Asterisk	Zero or multiple repetitions
+	Plus Sign	At least one repetition
{}	Curly Braces	Specified number of repetitions
()	Parenthesis (Group)	A specified regex string, (to be used after a match)
[]	Square Brackets	A set of individual characters
|	Pipe	Matches either, (or), regex on sides of pipe

TABLE 19.3 Standard Metasymbols

Metasymbol	*Meaning*	*Metasymbol*	*Meaning*
\d	Any decimal digit 0-9	**\a**	Alarm
\D	Any character other than a decimal digit	**\e**	Escape
\w	Any word character A-Z, a-z, 0-9	**\f**	Form feed
\W	Any non-word character	**\n**	Newline
\s	Any white-space character	**\r**	Return
\S	Any non-white-space character	**\t**	Tab
\0	Null Character		

Metasymbols

Metasymbols are combinations of backslashes preceding traditionally literal characters which cause them to take on special meanings, depending on regex flavor.

MATCHING

Matching is the most fundamental regex operation. The *match function, re.match()*, compares regex strings against beginnings of input strings. When regex strings successfully match input string beginnings, regex *match objects* are returned. Otherwise, *None* is returned. Regex match objects contain information about successful matches including start and end positions of the regex strings, any identified *groups* found in the matches, and the strings passed into the function. Code Sample 19.1 demonstrates simple regular expression matching.

```
# Import Regex Library
import re

# Assign input String
title = 'Essential Programming'
# Assign regex string
regexString = 'Prog'
# Perform match and assign to matchObject
matchObject = re.match(regexString, title)
print(f'{matchObject}')

# Reassign regex string
regexString = 'Ess'
# Perform match and assign to matchObject
matchObject = re.match(regexString, title)
if matchObject:
    print(f'{regexString} in {matchObject.string} -> span={matchObject.
span()}')
```

```
>>> None
Ess in Essential Programming -> span=(0, 3)
```

Code Sample 19.1 Simple Regex Match

In the previous example, the successful regex string is composed of three literal characters: "E", "s", and "s". When working with constant input strings, literal characters are fine. However, more abstract matches require more abstract regex strings. Metasymbols and metacharacters provide that abstractness.

\w and \W

The *\w* and *\W* metasymbols match any word and any non-word characters, respectively. Word characters are any upper or lower-case alphabetical characters, *(A–Z, or a–z)*, or any numeric characters, *(0–9)*, as demonstrated in Code Sample 19.2.

```
import re

# Match three word characters
regexString = '\w\w\w'
inputString = 'Essential Programming'
print(re.match(regexString, inputString))

# Match three non-word characters
regexString = '\W\W\W'
inputString = '!$ TechnialArtists'
print(re.match(regexString, inputString))

>>> <re.Match object; span=(0, 3), match='Ess'>
<re.Match object; span=(0, 3), match='!$ '>
```

Code Sample 19.2 \W and \w in Regex Strings

\d and \D

The *\d* and *\D* metasymbols match any decimal and any non-decimal characters, respectively. Decimal characters are any numeric characters, *(0–9)*, demonstrated in Code Sample 19.3.

```
import re

# Match four decimal characters
regexString = '\d\d\d\d'
inputString = '2023 Essential Programming'
print(re.match(regexString, inputString))

# Match three non-decimal characters
regexString = '\D\D\D'
inputString = 'TechnialArtists'
print(re.match(regexString, inputString))

>>> <re.Match object; span=(0, 4), match='2023'>
<re.Match object; span=(0, 3), match='Tec'>
```

Code Sample 19.3 \D and \d in Regex Strings

\s and \S

The *\s* and *\S* metasymbols match any white-space and any non-white-space characters, respectively. Typesetting characters such as form feed, "*\f*", newline, "*\n*", return, "*\r*", and tab, "*\t*", are considered white-space characters, as demonstrated in Code Sample 19.4.

```
import re

regexString = '\w\w\w\s'
# Match one white-space after three word characters
inputString = 'Ian Bristlebrush'
print(re.match(regexString, inputString))

regexString = '\S\S'
# Match two non-white-space characters
inputString = 'TechnialArtists'
print(re.match(regexString, inputString))
```

```
regexString = '\s\s'
# Match two white-space(tabs) characters
inputString = '      Essential Programming'
print(re.match(regexString, inputString))

>>> <re.Match object; span=(0, 4), match='Ian '>
<re.Match object; span=(0, 2), match='Te'>
<re.Match object; span=(0, 2), match='    '>
```

Code Sample 19.4 \S and \s in Regex Strings

Period

A *period*, '.',, matches any character except for a newline, "\n". The period is considered as a wildcard character since it catches all characters except for a newline character. Code Sample 19.5 demonstrates period usage.

```
import re

# Match one white-space after three word characters
regexString = '\w\w\w\s'
inputString = 'Ian Bristlebrush'
print(re.match(regexString, inputString))

# Match two non-white-space characters
regexString = '\S\S'
inputString = 'TechnialArtists'
print(re.match(regexString, inputString))

# Match two white-space(tabs) characters
regexString = '\s\s'
inputString = '      Essential Programming'
print(re.match(regexString, inputString))

>>> <re.Match object; span=(0, 4), match='Ian '>
<re.Match object; span=(0, 2), match='Te'>
<re.Match object; span=(0, 2), match='    '>
```

Code Sample 19.5 Periods in Regex Strings

Question Mark

A *question mark*, '?', catches only zero or one repetitions of the regex object preceding it. Code Sample 19.6 demonstrates question mark usage.

```
import re

# Match a dollar sign, a decimal and one or no zeroes
regexString = '\$\d0?'
inputString = '$1000'
print(re.match(regexString, inputString))

>>> <re.Match object; span=(0, 3), match='$10'>
```

Code Sample 19.6 Question Marks in Regex Strings

Asterisk

An *asterisk*, '*', catches zero or multiple repetitions of the regex object preceding it. Code Sample 19.7 demonstrates asterisk usage.

```
import re

# Match a dollar sign, a number and unlimited zeroes
regexString = '\$\d0*'
inputString = '$1000'
print(re.match(regexString, inputString))

>>> <re.Match object; span=(0, 6), match='$1000'>
```

Code Sample 19.7 Asterisks in Regex Strings

Plus Sign

A *plus sign*, '+', catches at least one repetition of the regex object preceding it. Code Sample 19.8 demonstrates plus sign usage.

```
import re

# Match a dollar sign, a number and at least one zero
regexString = '\$\d0+'
inputString = '$1000'
print(re.match(regexString, inputString))
```

```
inputString = '$1'
print(re.match(regexString, inputString))

>>> <re.Match object; span=(0, 5), match='$1000'>
None
```

Code Sample 19.8 Plus Signs in Regular Expressions

Square Brackets

Regular expressions attempt to match any single character surrounded by square brackets, '[]'. No delimiters separate characters or character ranges within the square brackets. Code Sample 19.9 demonstrates square bracket usage.

```
import re

inputString = 'Essential Programming'
# Match 'E', 't', or 'p'
regexString = '[EtP]'
searchObject = re.match(regexString, inputString)
print(searchObject)

>>> <re.Match object; span=(0, 1), match='E'>
```

Code Sample 19.9 Simple Class Matching E, t, or P

Ranges of characters are connected with dashes, -, between the first and final characters, inclusive, as demonstrated in Code Sample 19.10.

```
import re

inputString = 'Essential Programming'
# Match any capital letter between A and L
regexString = '[A-L]'
searchObject = re.match(regexString, inputString)
print(searchObject)

>>> <re.Match object; span=(0, 1), match='E'>
```

Code Sample 19.10 Class Searching for Capital Letters between A and L Literal Characters

A preceding caret, ^, negates identified characters. The regex tries to match anything but the identified characters. Code Sample 19.11 demonstrates caret usage.

```
import re


inputString = 'Essential Programming'
# Match any characters but letters between L and Z
regexString = '[^L-Z]'
searchObject = re.match(regexString, inputString)
print(searchObject)

>>> <re.Match object; span=(0, 1), match='E'>
```

Code Sample 19.11 Carets Negate Class Contents

Multiple characters and character ranges are stacked into square brackets without delimiters, as shown in Code Sample 19.12.

```
import re


inputString = 'Essential Programming'
# Match any decimal, A through L, or any white-space
regexString = '[0-9A-L\s]'
searchObject = re.match(regexString, inputString)
print(searchObject)

>>> <re.Match object; span=(0, 1), match='E'>
```

Code Sample 19.12 Complex Class

Curly Braces

Curly braces , '{}', surrounding an integer attempt to match exactly the integer number of repetitions of the preceding regular expression. Code Sample 19.13 demonstrates curly brace usage.

```
import re


inputString = '6060-842'
# Match exactly 4 repetitions of 0 or 6
regexString = '[06]{4}'
```

Code Sample 19.13 Curly Braces

Curly braces surrounding two integers, (a minimum and a maximum), attempt to match as many of the minimum to maximum number of repetitions, as demonstrated in Code Sample 19.14.

```
import re


inputString = '6060-842'
# Match exactly 4 repetitions of 0 or 6
regexString = '[06]{1,4}'
searchObject = re.match(regexString, inputString)
print(searchObject)


>>> <re.Match object; span=(0, 4), match='6060'>
```

Code Sample 19.14 Matching as Many as the Minimum to Maximum Repetitions

Omitting the minimum integer establishes a lower bound of zero repetitions, while omitting the maximum removes any upper bound of repetitions.

Pipe

The *pipe* sign, '|', generates a composite regular expression matching either the preceding or following regular expressions surrounding the pipe. Code Sample 19.15 introduces pipe usage. When the preceding regular expression registers a match, the following is not evaluated.

```
import re


inputString = '867-5309'
# Match three numbers preceding four OR
# four numbers preceding three
regexString = '\d{3}-\d{4}|\d{4}-{\d3}'
searchObject = re.match(regexString, inputString)
print(searchObject)


>>> <re.Match object; span=(0, 8), match='867-5309'>
```

Code Sample 19.15 Pipe Generated Composite Regular Expression

SEARCHING

The *match()* operation always attempts to match the beginning of the search string. The *re.search()* operation behaves the same except it scans the entire input string and identifies the first location where the regex string produces a match. A *match object* is returned upon discovery and *None* when no match is found.
Code Sample 19.16 demonstrates the match() function.

```
import re

inputString = 'Essential Programming for the Technical Artist'
# Simple Regex string
regexString = 'Prog'

# Print the regex search results
print(re.search(regexString, inputString))

>>> <re.Match object; span=(10, 14), match='Prog'>
```

Code Sample 19.16 Regex re.search() Operation

The *caret*, ^, and dollar sign, $, characters anchor the regex string to the search string in Code Sample 19.16.

Caret

A *caret*, '^', anchors the regex string to the start of the input string: Code Sample 19.17.

```
import re

# Match the input string start, word characters,
# a whitespace and 'Prog'
regexString = '^\w+\sProg'
inputString = 'Essential Programming'
print(re.search(regexString, inputString))

>>> <re.Match object; span=(0, 14), match='Essential Prog'>
```

Code Sample 19.17 Caret in Regular Expressions

Dollar Sign

A dollar sign, '$', anchors the regex string to the end of the input string: Code Sample 19.18.

```
import re

# Match 'ing' to the end of the string
regexString = 'ing$'
inputString = 'Essential Programming'
```

```
print(re.search(regexString, inputString))

>>> <re.Match object; span=(18, 21), match='ing'>
```

Code Sample 19.18 Dollar Sign in Regular Expressions

REGULAR EXPRESSION OBJECTS

When specific regex strings are to be used multiple times within the same script, it is often more efficient to convert them into *regular expression objects*. Regex objects are created using the *re.compile()*function, as introduced by Language Template 19.2.

```
import re

regexObject = re.compile(regexString)
```

Language Template 19.2 Regular Expression Object Compile

Once compiled, regex objects perform the same operations as those found in the *re* module, as demonstrated in Code Sample 19.19.

```
import re

# Compiled regular expression objects perform the same
# Operations as the re module
inputString = 'Essential Programming for the Technical Artist'
# Compiled regular expression object
regexCompiled = re.compile('\s\w+\s')
regexResult = regexCompiled.search(inputString)
print(f'Regex Object -> {regexResult}')

# re module regex expression
matchResult = re.search('\s\w+\s', inputString)
print(f're Module -> {matchResult}')

>>> Regex Object -> <re.Match object; span=(9, 22), match=' Programming '>
re Module -> <re.Match object; span=(9, 22), match=' Programming '>
```

Code Sample 19.19 Regular Expression Object Versus re Module

GROUPS

Any regex expression bound by *parenthesis, ()*, establishes a matched *group*. Regex expressions may contain more than one group. Specific groups are retrieved after successful matches using the match object *group()* function. The *group()* function arguments identify which parenthesized groups are returned. When more than one argument is provided, the matched groups are retuned in a tuple. Note that group counting begins at *1* instead of zero. Group index zero, *group(0)*, returns the entire matched string. Grouping is demonstrated in Code Sample 19.20.

```
import re

inputString = 'Essential Programming for the Technical Artist'
# Match input string into six groups
regexCompiled  = re.compile('
       (\w+)\s(\w+)\s(\w+)\s(\w+)\s(\w+)\s(\w+)')
searchResult = regexCompiled.search(inputString)
# Display the first matched group
print(searchResult.group(1))
# Display a tuple of group numbers 2, 4 and 6
print(searchResult.group(2, 4, 6))
# Display the entire matched string
print(searchResult.group(0))

>>> Essential
('Programming', 'the', 'Artist')
Essential Programming for the Technical Artist
```

Code Sample 19.20 Identifying Matched Groups

The *groups()* function returns tuples containing all of the parenthesized match groups. Code Sample 19.21 displays all of the matched groups.

```
import re

inputString = 'Essential Programming for the Technical Artist'
# Match input string into six groups
regexCompiled = re.compile(
       '(\w+)\s(\w+)\s(\w+)\s(\w+)\s(\w+)\s(\w+)')
searchResult = regexCompiled.search(inputString)
# Return a tuple of parenthesized groups
for gp in searchResult.groups():
    print(gp)
```

```
>>> Essential
Programming
for
the
Technical
Artist
```

Code Sample 19.21 Display All Parenthesized Groups

Individual groups may be tagged with unique identities in order to utilize those identities in the future. Initiating "?P<name>" within parenthesized groups provides them with unique identities. Identified groups may be referenced by their provided names in the *group()*, *start()*, *end()*, and *span()* functions. The unique names and matched groups constitute key-value dictionaries stored in the match objects. Dictionary contents are accessed using the *groupdict()* function. Implementation of identifying groups with names is demonstrated in Code Sample 19.22.

```
import re

inputString = 'Essential Programming for the Technical Artist'
# Identify the first two groups
regexCompiled = re.compile('(?P<foo>\w+)\s(?P<bar>\w+).*')
searchResult = regexCompiled.search(inputString)

# Display the 'foo' group
print(f'"foo" Group ={searchResult.group("foo")}')
# Display the 'bar' group span
print(f'"bar" Group Span={searchResult.span("bar")}')
# Display the match object group dictionary
print(f'Group Dictionary = {searchResult.groupdict()}')

>>> "foo" Group =Essential
"bar" Group Span=(10, 21)
Group Dictionary = {'foo': 'Essential', 'bar': 'Programming'}
```

Code Sample 19.22 Parenthesized Group Identified with Names

SPLIT

Given a regex string and an input string, the *re.split()* function returns a list containing the components of the input string, separated by the regex string. The *split()* function usage is demonstrated in Language Template 19.3.

```
splitList = re.split(regexString, 'inputString', maxsplit=0)
```

Language Template 19.3 Regex split() Function

The *split()* function works the same for compiled regex objects, as demonstrated in Code Sample 19.23.

```
import re

inputString = 'Johnny, Joey, Dee Dee, Marky'
# Split on commas
splitList = re.split(',', inputString)
print(splitList)

# Compiled Regex object
splitRegex = re.compile(',')
print(splitRegex.split(inputString))

>>> ['Johnny', ' Joey', ' Dee Dee', ' Marky']
['Johnny', ' Joey', ' Dee Dee', ' Marky']
```

Code Sample 19.23 Regex split() Function

In the previous example, the *re.split()* function breaks the input string into list components and excludes the regex string. When the regex string is desired to be part of the output solution, any portion of the regex string enclosed in parenthesis, *()*, is included, as demonstrated in Code Sample 19.24.

```
import re

inputString = 'Johnny, Joey, Dee Dee, Marky'
# Split and return commas but no white spaces
splitList = re.split('(,)\s', inputString)
print(splitList)

>>> ['Johnny', ',', 'Joey', ',', 'Dee Dee', ',', 'Marky']
```

Code Sample 19.24 Include Split Regex with Output

When regex strings match the beginning or end of the input string, null strings are returned in the output list. When this happens, the regex components are found in the same relative indices of the output list, demonstrated in Code Sample 19.25.

```
import re

inputString = '...Johnny, Joey, Dee Dee, Marky...'
# Split on sequences of non-word characters
splitList = re.split('(\W+)', inputString)

# Returns beginning and end null strings
print(splitList)

>>> ['', '...', 'Johnny', ', ', 'Joey', ', ', 'Dee', ' ', 'Dee', ', ',
'Marky', '...', '']
```

Code Sample 19.25 Null Strings Are Returned at Beginning and End Matches

When the *maxsplit* argument of the *split() function* is non-zero, the regex only splits the indicated number of matches and returns the rest of the input string as the last output component, as demonstrated in Code Sample 19.26.

```
import re

inputString = 'Johnny, Joey, Dee Dee, Marky'
# Split only first two matches
splitList = re.split('\W+', inputString, maxsplit=2)

# Return the rest as the last component
print(splitList)

>>> ['Johnny', 'Joey', 'Dee Dee, Marky']
```

Code Sample 19.26 Split Only the First Two Matches and Return the Rest

SUBSTITUTION

The re function, *re.sub()*, as introduced in Language Template 19.4, is used for replacing an input regex string with a replacement based on an input string. The replacement may be a regex string or a function.

```
substitue = re.sub(regexString, replacement, intputString, count=0)
```

Language Template 19.4 Regex re.sub() Function

The *re.sub()* function works the same for compiled regex objects, demonstrated in Code Sample 19.27.

```
import re

inputString = 'Johnny, Joey, Dee Dee, Marky'
# Replace Comma and white space with an ampersand
result = re.sub(',\s', ' & ', inputString)
print(result)

# Compiled Regex Object
regexCompiled = re.compile(',\s')

print(regexCompiled.sub(' & ', inputString))

>>> Johnny & Joey & Dee Dee & Marky
Johnny & Joey & Dee Dee & Marky
```

Code Sample 19.27 Regex sub() Function and Compiled Object

When parenthesized groups are implemented in the regex, they may be referenced in the replacement as *backreferences*. Depending on the regex flavor, backreferences may be represented as:

1. Backslashes followed by the group number, ex. \1
2. Backslash "g" followed by the group number in equivalency brackets, ex. \g<1>
3. Backslash "g" followed by the group name when using the '*?P<name>*' format, ex. \g<name>

```
import re

inputString = 'Lee Ving, Philo Cramer, Spit Stix, Derf Scratch'
# Replace first and second groups with a hyphen
result = re.sub('(\w+)\s(\w+)', '\g<1>-\g<2>', inputString)
print(result)

regexCompiled = re.compile('(?P<first>\w+)\s(?P<second>\w+)')
# Replace using group names
result = regexCompiled.sub('\g<first>-\g<second>', inputString)
print(result)
```

```
>>> Lee-Ving, Philo-Cramer, Spit-Stix, Derf-Scratch
Lee-Ving, Philo-Cramer, Spit-Stix, Derf-Scratch
```

Code Sample 19.28 Substitute Using Backreferenced Groups

Backreferenced group substitution is demonstrated in Code Sample 19.28.

The re.sub() function replacement argument may be a function, called for every non-overlapping occurrence of the regex string or object. Language Template 19.5 defines *res.sub()* implementation. The function receives a single match object and returns the replacement string. Code Sample 19.29 provides an *re.sub()* usage example.

```
substitue = re.sub(regexString, functionName, inputString)
```

Language Template 19.5 re.sub() with Function Name

```
import re

# Replacement function receives a match object and
# Returns replacement string
def hyphenate(matchObj):
    return f'{matchObj.group(1)}-{matchObj.group(2)}'

inputString = 'Lee Ving, Philo Cramer, Spit Stix, Derf Scratch'
# Replace using replacement function
result = re.sub('(\w+)\s(\w+)', hyphenate, inputString)
print(result)

>>> Lee-Ving, Philo-Cramer, Spit-Stix, Derf-Scratch
```

Code Sample 19.29 sub() Using Replacement Function

When the *sub()* function *count* argument is a non-zero integer number, only the number of occurrences will be replaced. Code Sample 19.30 demonstrates substituting a specific number of instances.

```
import re

inputString = 'Lee Ving, Philo Cramer, Spit Stix, Derf Scratch'
```

```
# Replace only first 2 occurrences
result = re.sub('(\w+)\s(\w+)', '\g<1>-\g<2>', inputString, count=2)
print(result)

>>> Lee-Ving, Philo-Cramer, Spit Stix, Derf Scratch
```

Code Sample 19.30 Replace Only First 2 Occurrences

PRACTICAL EXAMPLES

Code Sample 19.31 addresses the age-old dilemma of converting an arbitrary numbered file name to the same file name but zero-padded to a desired number of digits. The function *paddFrame()* accepts two input parameters: the original name string and the desire number of padded digits. The regular expression searches for three groups: the filename before the number, the number itself, and the file type. When the search is successful, the reformatted name is returned. String function *zfill()* is used to zero-padd the number to the desired number of digits.

```
# Input regular expressions
import re


def paddFrame(inputName, paddNum):
    # Search input string for three groups
    groups = re.search('(\w+)-(\d+).(\w+)', inputName)

    # If search is successful, return reformatted name
    if groups:
        # Start output buffer with first group
        newName = f'{input.group(1)}.'
        # Append second group padded with zeros to desired place
        newName += f'{input.group(2).zfill(paddNum)}.'
        # Append Third Group as file type
        newName += f'{input.group(3)}'
        return(newName)
    # Report when search unsuccessful
    else:
        return("Unrecognized File")


print(paddFrame("starburst-1.jpg",4))
print(paddFrame("liquidSim-84.json",5))
```

Code Sample 19.31 PaddFrame() Function

Sometimes, objects are identified by their hierarchical descriptions. There may also be multiple variants of the same hierarchy. The next example function, in Code Sample 19.32, *namePath()*, receives a single geometry object name identified by an underscore delimited hierarchical description and a variant number. Two regular expressions follow. The first splits the name based on its underscores. The second expression searches the last split element for two groups: the variant number and the file type. When the variant number group is successfully found, a new path name is generated with a subfolder named for each hierarchical element. The variant number is padded to two digits and is appended to the new path name along with the original filename.

```
# Import regular expressions
import re

def namePath(objectName):
    ''' Return the full path based on object name.
        Two regex passes: First pass splits the name on underscores,
        Second pass parses last split element to obtain variant number.
    '''
    # Split name on underscores
    first = re.split("_", objectName)
    # Break apart last split element
    second = re.search("(\d+)\.(\w+)", first[-1])

    # When the variant number is found, generate the new path
    if second:
        # Initialize an empty output string
        path = ""
        # Concatenate all but the last split element
        for i in range(len(first)-1):
            path += f"/{first[i]}"
        # Append the number and object to path
        path += f"/variants/{second.group(1).zfill(2)}/{objectName}"
        return(path) # Return new path
    else:
        return("Variant Number not found!")

print(namePath("Armor_Helmet_Human_Male_01.fbx"))

>>>/Armor/Helmet/Human/Male/variants/01/Armor_Helmet_Human_Male_01.fbx
```

Code Sample 19.32 namePath() Function

Texture maps have a wide variety of applications and compositions. They are not treated equivalently in-engine. To help account for this wide variability, texture types are often appended to their texture names. For example, a texture with a "**N**" suffix will be treated as a normal map and loaded into engine in linear color space. In this final example, Code Sample 19.33, the *textureType()* function receives a single name string as input and returns the texture type based on its suffix. The function begins by declaring a dictionary, *textureTypes*, containing all of the texture types index by their respective suffixes. A regular expression searches the name string, *textureName*, for the suffix. Note that the suffix group is anchored with a dollar sign, *$*, which means that the group must be at the end of the name string. Within the group, a subset of capital letters is bound by square brackets, *[]*. The square brackets effectually treat each individual letter as their own *if* case. The square brackets are prefixed by the letters, "*SM*", and a vertical bar. The vertical bar is treated as a Boolean *Or* statement. Because the square brackets only consider individual letters, the *Or* statement considers "*SM*", (multiple letters), first. If an appropriate suffix if found, it indexes the dictionary to retrieve its respective texture type, and the type is returned. When the search fails to identify a known texture type, an error message is returned.

```
import re # Import regular expressions


def textureType(textureName):
    # Define all texture types into one dictionary
    textureTypes = { "D":"Diffuse", "N":"Normal", "R":"Roughness",
                          "A":"Alpha", "O":"Ambient Occlusion",
                          "B":"Bump", "E":"Emissive", "S":"Specular",
                          "M":"Metallic", "MK":"Mask"
                   }

    # Search for "MK" or any of the single letter texture types
    typeSearch = re.search("\w+_(MK|[ABDEMNORS]$)", textureName)

    # If found return type as dictionary index
    if typeSearch:
        return(textureTypes[typeSearch.group(1)])
    # Report when not found
    else:
        return("Unrecognized Type")

print(textureType("T_Cannon_D"))
print(textureType("T_Helmet_MK"))
print(textureType("T_Sword_O"))
print(textureType("T_Saber_T"))
```

```
>>> Diffuse
Mask
Ambient Occlusion
Unrecognized Type
```

Code Sample 19.33 textureType() Function

CONCLUSION

Technical artists' careers and their companies are dependent on speed. One of the most prevalent and dynamic tools at technical artists' disposal is *regular expressions*. A regular expression, *regex*, is a formalized, textual pattern recognition string used for finding patterns within input strings. Matched patterns are useful for parsing information, splitting input, and replacing with new patterns.

Regex patterns are defined by formally structured strings. Regex strings are composed of literal characters, metacharacters, and metasymbols. Literal characters are constant characters that do not take on any additional meaning. Most commonly, they are upper- and lower-case alphabetical letters or numerical digits, 0 to 9. When certain literal characters are prefixed with backslashes, \, they become metasymbols and take on new, abstract meaning. For example, *d* represents a single digit character and \s represents a single white-space character. Metacharacters are punctuation characters providing context to associated characters. The most important of these is the backslash, \, which converts other metacharacters to their literal equivalents and literal characters to metasymbols. Other examples are the plus sign, +, representing at least one or more repetitions of preceding objects and the caret, ^, representing beginnings of input strings.

Matching, *re.match()*, is the most fundamental regex operation. When regex strings are found at the beginning of input strings, *match objects* are returned. Otherwise, *None* is returned. Regex match objects contain information about the match including regex string start and end positions, and any identified groups found in the match. The *re.search()* function behaves the same except match objects are returned when regex strings are found anywhere within input strings. The *re.compile()* function transforms a regex string into a compiled *regex object*. Regex objects have the same matching and searching functionality and are conveniently mobile when repeated multiple times.

When portions of regex strings are surrounded by parenthesis, they become matched *groups*. Match groups are *match object* components and are retrieved using the *group()* function. The function argument identifies referenced group object indices. Counting of group objects begins at 1. when regex parenthesis includes "*?P<name>*", the unique names identify their groups. Unique names and their matched values are stored as match object, key-value pair dictionaries. Matched groups may be referenced through match object dictionaries or via unique names.

Two more frequently used regex operations are *split()* and *sub()*. The *split()* function uses regex strings to subdivide input strings into sub-string lists. Depending on the structure of the regex string and functional arguments, the number of list sub-strings may be regulated. Regex *sub()* functions identify portions of input strings and replace them with replacement regex strings. Matched regex string groups may be backreferenced in replacement regex strings. Depending on regex flavor, backreferences are represented by a backslash followed by the matched group index, or a backslash-g followed by the index or group name in equivalency brackets, *g<index/name>*. Like *split()*, the number of substitutions may be limited.

EARLY DAYS

Programming is a phenomenal artists' tool. In the earliest days of computer graphics, before real-time rendering engines, almost all digital artists knew how to program. Because of the scarcity of resources and interest, the qualification of entry into the realm of 3D computer graphics required master's degrees in animation or fine art and in computer science. Early digital artists were collaborative pioneers inventing a new and magical industry.

The ability to program opened unlimited opportunity to create tools only artists could dream of. Since there were very few commercially available packages, they were not bound by interface limitations. Instead of anxiously awaiting the announcements for the next releases for their favorite software, they created the tools necessary at that time. Evolution of commercially available tools accelerated the creative process. However, no single tool performed all functionality required by the hands of an experienced artist.

Coding can be a laborious process. Even when assisted by the experience of a master's degree in computer science, the required time and effort coding specific tools can be greater than the creative enthusiasm that invented the tool in the first place. As tools grow in complexity, so do the amounts of skill and understanding required to operate them.

LIMITED RESOURCES

Modern real-time production environments now employ technical artists to navigate other artists around technical barriers inhibiting the creative process. Typically understaffed, teams of technical artists must creatively leverage available resources.

Most companies rarely have enough money to purchase all of the tools required by their staff. They traditionally allocate enough funds providing for only what is absolutely necessary. (The decision of "what is absolutely necessary", is a political battle-field all production companies must wrangle.) Rarely are there enough funds left over to provide for the "should have" or "would be nice" tools. Technical artists must be able to program at least "short-term" solutions for artists' day-to-day situations.

No technical artist has enough time to create all of her code from scratch. They play the role of a modern Dr. Frankenstein cobbling together chunks of code from various sources to create programming monstrosities. They are granted only adequate time to address single, or simple, emergencies. Technical art coding often demands creation of tools performing simple operations thousands of times.

Modern real-time engines may be substantial and impressive but very rarely do they possess all artist desired functionality. Abstract interfaces simply cannot be extensive enough to address all artists' needs. Technical artists bridge those gaps and code the necessary patches required to, at least temporarily, fill those needs.

SCRIPTING: THE GREAT COMPROMISE

Most artists do not typically possess technical artist coding skills. Luckily, most tasks do not require creation of entire systems nor do they require the time and dedication for building tools from the ground-up. Subtle tweaks, adjustments, and extrapolations are often all that are necessary for addressing most technical art situations.

Coding and compiling tools from the ground-up are often over-kill for tool creation. Scripting is the great technical artist compromise. Scripting languages, such as Python, are built on interpreted environments facilitating creation

DOI: 10.1201/9781003016427-20

of fast, efficient, and portable tools. Many larger programs are equipped with node-based scripting environments facilitating even faster and easier functionality. While not able to handle all core-based programming needs, scripting breaches the boundaries imposed by interface and is able to address most artists' immediate needs.

FUTURE PYTHON

The demand for technical artist contribution in real-time production continues to increase. While the rigors of coding, compiling, and linking, are not always required, the demands for scripting are present every day. All modern real-time rendering engines have some sort of implemented scripting capability. Python is one of the major modern scripting languages found in almost all real-time rendering engines and digital content creation programs. Created to be easy to read and fun to use, Python is an ideal language to enter into the world of real-time graphics programming. Beyond graphics scripting, Python is also used heavily in data visualization, artificial intelligence, machine learning, and web development. Regardless of the readers' involvement with real-time graphics production, Python is a readily available and commonly used language that will take readers to their desired destinations.

Index

Milton Keynes UK
Ingram Content Group UK Ltd.
UKHW050441111024
449327UK00050B/442